The International Handbook of Shipping Finance

Manolis G. Kavussanos • Ilias D. Visvikis
Editors

The International Handbook of Shipping Finance

Theory and Practice

palgrave
macmillan

Editors
Manolis G. Kavussanos
Athens University of Economics and Business
Athens, Greece
e-mail: mkavus@aueb.gr

Ilias D. Visvikis
World Maritime University
Malmö, Sweden
e-mail: iv@wmu.se

ISBN 978-1-137-46545-0   ISBN 978-1-137-46546-7   (eBook)
DOI 10.1057/978-1-137-46546-7

Library of Congress Control Number: 2016957773

© The Editor(s) (if applicable) and The Author(s) 2016
The author(s) has/have asserted their right(s) to be identified as the author(s) of this work in accordance with the Copyright, Design and Patents Act 1988.
This work is subject to copyright. All rights are solely and exclusively licensed by the Publisher, whether the whole or part of the material is concerned, specifically the rights of translation, reprinting, reuse of illustrations, recitation, broadcasting, reproduction on microfilms or in any other physical way, and transmission or information storage and retrieval, electronic adaptation, computer software, or by similar or dissimilar methodology now known or hereafter developed.
The use of general descriptive names, registered names, , trademarks, service marks, etc. in this publication does not imply, even in the absence of a specific statement, that such names are exempt from the relevant protective laws and regulations and therefore free for general use
The publisher, the authors and the editors are safe to assume that the advice and information in this book are believed to be true and accurate at the date of publication. Neither the publisher nor the authors or the editors give a warranty, express or implied, with respect to the material contained herein or for any errors or omissions that may have been made.

Printed on acid-free paper

This Palgrave Macmillan imprint is published by Springer Nature
The registered company is Macmillan Publishers Ltd. London
The registered company address is: The Campus, 4 Crinan Street, London, N1 9XW, United Kingdom

About the Editors

Manolis G. Kavussanos is Professor at the Athens University of Economics and Business (AUEB), Greece. He is the director of the MSc program in International Shipping, Finance and Management and of the Laboratory for Finance since their inception. He is also a member of the steering committees of the MSc program in Accounting and Finance, of the Athens MBA program, and was for five years the director of the MSc and PhD programs in Accounting and Finance at AUEB. He holds a BSc and an MSc (Economics) from the University of London and a PhD (Applied Economics) from City University Cass Business School (Cass), London. He launched and directed, until he joined AUEB, the MSc in Trade, Logistics and Finance at Cass. He has held various posts as professor of finance and shipping in universities in more than eight countries around the globe, such as the UK, France, The Netherlands, Belgium, Italy, Singapore, China, Greece and Cyprus. He has provided consultancy and executive training services in finance and shipping to private companies and public sector national and international organizations, has been a member of international committees for the evaluation of academic programs in tertiary academic institutions and for the award of prestigious prizes and research funding. Professor Kavussanos has written extensively in the areas of finance, shipping and applied economics, and is the author of numerous academic papers published in top international refereed journals, in conference proceedings and in books. He is a member of the editorial board on a number of international scientific journals. His work has been presented in international conferences and professional meetings around the world, gaining awards for its quality, financed by both public (e.g. European Community) and private sector organizations, companies and foundations (e.g. the Propontis Foundation) and cited extensively by other researchers in the area. Since 1992 he has worked in developing the area of risk analysis and management in shipping and is the co-author of three books in this area.

Ilias D. Visvikis is Professor of Shipping Finance and Risk Management, and Director of Executive Education and Professional Development at the World Maritime University (WMU) in Malmö (Sweden), founded by the International Maritime Organization, a specialized agency of the United Nations. He is Co-Director of the Postgraduate Diploma in Executive Maritime Management, jointly delivered by WMU and the DNV GL Maritime Academy. He is a Visiting Professor at the ICMA Centre—Henley Business School of the University of Reading (UK). He has previously held academic appointments at the ALBA Graduate Business School at the American College of Greece, having the position of Associate Professor and Academic Director of its shipping programmes. He has taught (either at BSc, MSc and MBA levels) in several universities around the world, including Sweden, the United Kingdom, the Netherlands, Belgium, China, Germany, Greece and Cyprus, while he has extensive international experience in consultancy and executive education. He has trained managerial-level maritime professionals in the areas of shipping finance and shipping freight derivatives from numerous companies around the world. At the same time, he has designed and directed postgraduate academic programmes (MSc and MBA) and also directed and coordinated professional development courses delivered in Asia, Europe and Africa. His research work has been published in international refereed scientific journals, books and magazines. He has extensively presented his work in international academic and business conferences held in the USA, Europe and Asia. He serves as an editorial board member of several scientific journals, and has served as a member of conference steering committees and as a reviewer for several scientific journals. He holds a degree in Business Administration from the University of the Aegean (Greece), an MSc in International Financial Markets from the University of Southampton, an MSc in International Shipping from the University of Plymouth, and a PhD in Finance from the Cass Business School of City University in London.

Book Chapter Reviewers

The editors would like to thank sincerely the following chapter reviewers for their commitment and support in providing constructive comments and feedback to the book contributors.

Basil Karatzas	Karatzas Marine Advisors & Co.
Cecilie Lind	Jefferies LLC
George Theocharidis	World Maritime University
Simon Norton	Cardiff Business School
Fotis Giannakoulis	Morgan Stanley
Henriette Brent-Petersen	DVB Bank SE
Ioannis Alexopoulos	Eurofin Group
Lars Patterson	Pacomarine Ltd.
Wolfgang Drobetz	University of Hamburg
Marc Huybrechts	University of Antwerp
Photis Panayides	Cyprus University of Technology
Siri Strandenes	NHH—Norwegian School of Economics
Ron Crean	IHS Maritime & Trade
Ted Petropoulos	Petrofin
Tony Foster	Marine Capital Ltd.

Special thanks are due to Stella Moysiadou for her diligent reading and feedback on all chapters, which helped improve the presentation and explanation of the concepts.

Preface

Following the financial collapse of 2008, the financing of shipping activities and the financial management of maritime enterprises have become extremely important for the performance and ultimately the survival of shipping companies around the world.

The current handbook provides a balanced blend between the theory and practice of shipping finance. It comprises a series of chapters, written by leading expert practitioners and academics in the field, discussing the best practices in the area. Chapter contributors represent different market segments involved in shipping finance. These include shipping companies, charterers, banks, consultants, traders, financiers, maritime lawyers and academics, among others. Thus, individual chapters in the book cover the different aspects of shipping finance, offering to the reader a spherical view of the relevant issues in this area.

This comprehensive handbook is of great value to both shipping practitioners and the academic community, as it contributes to the training and education of market participants, academics and students and, as such, is a must-read for everyone already involved or likely to be involved in the maritime industry. It offers to its readers a rigorous understanding of the different aspects of modern shipping finance, financial management and investment, the various characteristics of the available products, the capital needs and requirements, and a clear view on the different financial management strategies through a series of practical examples and applications. It can be used as the main reference point for companies and organizations involved in shipping finance, and as a teaching and reference textbook in both undergraduate and postgraduate maritime programs in universities worldwide.

The handbook comprises 16 chapters. **Chapter 1**, "Shipping Markets and their Economic Drivers", is written by Jan-Henrik Hübner of DNV GL, and serves as an introduction to the shipping industry and its various markets. He considers current developments and trends in shipping sub-markets, and analyses the economic factors that influence them. More specifically, the chapter starts by presenting the various "players" in the ship transportation value chain; that is, shipowners, shipyards, charterers, cargo owners, freight forwarders, ship managers and shipbrokers. It presents the various markets involved in the shipping industry; that is, newbuilding, sale and purchase (S&P), demolition, and time charter and spot freight markets. The cost structures of different types of vessels are also discussed and there is analysis of the various demand and supply factors that drive developments in shipping markets and their performance. It then presents in detail the shipping markets for various vessel types, which involves their supply–demand factors and current developments, including the dry-bulk market, tankers, the market for containers and the offshore shipping markets.

Chapter 2, "Asset Risk Assessment, Analysis and Forecasting in Asset Backed Finance", is by Henriette Brent-Petersen of DVB Bank SE. She discusses the overall cyclicality of the shipping and offshore industries with primary focus on the supply side—shipyard capacity and future asset prices. She also outlines the methodology of forecasting the markets for dry bulk and container vessels, as well as the importance of evaluating the quality of the individual asset and the mitigation of the risks involved. Global demand and the role of China is examined in the effort to understand cyclicality and super cycles, sectoral cycles and counter-cycles, while the variables that affect cyclicality are discussed in detail. She applies the above notions in providing a market outlook of container and dry bulk markets, and finishes with the evaluation of the individual competitive advantages of the assets in relation to peers and the prior-mentioned analysis, as well as the quality of the asset (vessel) and the risks associated with the assets in asset-backed finance.

Chapter 3, "Overview of Ship Finance", is by Fotis Giannakoulis of Morgan Stanley. He presents the available sources of finance for the maritime industry, arguing that "the ability of a shipping company to navigate the ebbs and flows of the market is primarily dependent on the timing of its investments and its chartering policy, with the selection among funding alternatives being of equal importance". He discusses in detail: financing from banks, including mortgage-backed loans, newbuilding financing, mezzanine, unsecured/corporate loans and leasing finance; high yield bonds; convertible notes; initial public offerings (IPOs); follow-on offerings; master limited partnerships (MLPs); special purpose acquisition companies (SPAC); and private equity offerings.

Chapter 4, "Shipbuilding Finance", by Charles R. Cushing of C. R. Cushing & Co. Inc., discusses vessel acquisitions. The first part of the chapter outlines: the reasons for undertaking and alternatives to a new construction; project financing; issues that can go wrong in ship acquisition projects; project management issues; strategic planning and sub-plans, such as business, financing, operations, marketing, technology, competitor, human resources and organization plans; mission statements; and vessel design. The second part of the chapter discusses the choice of sources of funds for ship construction, such as: debt financing; loan syndication; mezzanine financing; high yield bonds; leasing; export credit agencies (ECAs); hybrid financing schemes, such as Kommanditgesellschaft—K/G, Kommandittselskap—K/S, DIFKO, blocked currency and barter trades; Islamic bank financing; government grants; public equity financing; private placements; and MLPs. The chapter concludes with financial aspects of shipbuilding contracts and progress payments.

Chapter 5, "Debt Financing in Shipping", is contributed by George Paleokrassas of Watson Farley & Williams. He discusses the various types of debt financing, including the standard loan facility; that is, the lender, the borrower, syndications, the financing vessel, the facility amount, the conditions precedent, the currency, the tenor and repayment of the loan facility, the interest, the representations and warranties, the covenants, the governing law and jurisdiction, the events of default, and the bank fees; forms of leasing; bond financing; mezzanine financing; and ECAs. Then, the security package that the lender can receive from the borrower and its group is discussed, as this is critical in terms of assessing the risk in any particular transaction. The ship mortgage is then presented, followed by the assignment of earnings, charter hire, insurances, requisition compensation, charge or pledge over accounts, shares charge or pledge, and pre-delivery security assignment.

Chapter 6, "Public Debt Markets for Shipping", by Basil M. Karatzas of Karatzas Marine Advisors & Co., discusses shipping bond financing and its details. This includes an example of a shipping bond issue, its pricing in the secondary market, the process of filing the relevant prospectus, of obtaining a credit rating, selecting an underwriter, the timing of the issue and the interest rate cost. The differences between shipping bonds and shipping loans are also outlined. The classification of shipping bonds based on collateral, and the covenants and special conditions, are discussed in detail. Finally, the chapter provides the main taxonomy of bonds, with special emphasis on those that are more suitable for shipping companies.

Chapter 7, "Public and Private Equity Markets", is by Jeffrey Pribor and Cecilie Skajem Lind of Jefferies LLC. It focuses on the most relevant equity products available to private shipping companies. The discussion includes: the pros and cons of being a public versus a private company; IPO structures and processes; and the role of private equity in the maritime industry. The chapter starts with an overview of public equity capital, such as C-corporations, limited partnerships, MLPs and SPACs, and continues by outlining the advantages and disadvantages of being a public company. It proceeds with the evolution of the shipping equity landscape since 2000, and continues with stock exchanges where there is shipping capital market activity. The four-phase process of an IPO is then analysed; that is, company preparation; drafting, diligence and initial Securities and Exchange Commission (SEC) filing; SEC review and response; and marketing, pricing and aftermarket. Also dealt with are what makes a good IPO and the pitfalls to avoid in the process. Equity valuation metrics are proposed, such as those of net asset value (NAV), forward earnings—earnings before interest, taxes, depreciation and amortization (EBITDA)—and dividend yield metrics. The chapter concludes with an overview of private equity (PE) in shipping and the relationship between PE firms and company management.

Chapter 8, "Structured Finance in Shipping" is by Ioannis Alexopoulos of Eurofin Group and Nikos Stratis of Augustea Group. They present structured finance instruments, as sets of complex financial transactions, and in particular ECA-backed shipping finance, leasing and mezzanine shipping finance. They start by explaining what ECAs are, their role in shipping finance, the various ECA shipping financing structures, the ECA requirements and OECD guidelines, and the pros and cons of ECA finance for shipping. Ship leasing, the types of leases, their benefits and drawbacks and the providers are then discussed prior to a detailed overview of mezzanine finance for shipping, the forms that it takes, the important issues to consider, the applications of it, and its pros and cons.

Chapter 9, "Key Clauses of a Shipping Loan Agreement" is by Kyriakos Spoullos of Norton Rose Fulbright. It provides a general overview of certain key clauses (commercial terms), commonly found in shipping loan agreements. Besides the financial terms of the relevant loan (e.g. the loan amount, the margin, the repayment profile, the interest periods, the last availability date), the chapter presents the operative clauses which constitute the "heart" of most financing documents. These clauses include the: representations and warranties; conditions precedent; covenants (e.g. minimum value clause, financial ratios); events of default; mandatory prepayment events; and assignment and transfer provisions.

Chapter 10, "Legal Aspects of Ship Mortgages", is written by Simon D. Norton of Cardiff Business School, Cardiff University and Claudio Chistè of Investec Bank plc. They put forward the legal definition of mortgages, the limitations of ship mortgages as a form of security, the registration and priority of mortgages, the powers of mortgagees (power of sale, power to take possession and the appointment of a receiver) and the rights of the mortgagor (right/obligation to insure the vessel, right to sell the vessel, application for sale by court order, the right to redeem the mortgage and foreclosure). The chapter closes with the authors' views of the likely future directions in ship mortgages as a form of financing, through the process of securitization.

Chapter 11, "Reasons and Mechanics of Handling Defaulted Shipping Loans and Methods of Recovery", is written by Dimitris Anagnostopoulos and Philippos E. Tsamanis of the Aegean Baltic Bank. They present the standard actions and procedures applied when handling problematic bank loans, the early detection of signs and, once the problem is detected, how to handle it. They proceed by explaining the preparation for remedial action when a loan approaches default and the determinants of the bank's course of action. This includes several considerations, including financial, ship management and market outlook, collateral and bank related. They conclude with a discussion of the loan recovery process that takes place through the auction of the collateral vessel and the possible situations the bank may face during the arrest of vessels.

Chapter 12, "Marine Insurance", is written by Marc A. Huybrechts of the University of Antwerp and Theodora Nikaki of Swansea University. They focus on insurance coverage needs taken out by the shipyard, the vessel's financiers and the shipowners as operators of the vessel. They discuss the specifics of marine insurance, which an insured should always keep in mind. These are: the "risks" that a shipowner wants to be covered for, including property, liability, legal issues, lost time, compulsory risks and the associated insurances; the need to purchase insurance cover for the successful and safe operation of the vessel; by whom these risks could be insured against; and who the providers of the insurance cover are. Finally, the cost of each type of insurance and other specific aspects of marine insurance are presented.

Chapter 13, "Maritime Investment Appraisal and Budgeting", is contributed by Wolfgang Drobetz of the University of Hamburg, Stefan Albertijn of HAMANT Beratungs- und Investitions GmbH and Max Johns from the German Shipowners' Association. They present the basic principles of vessel valuation, by illustrating the "mark-to-market" approach, and the long term asset value (LTAV) method as an example of the discounted cash flow (DCF) approach ("mark-to-model"). They also discuss the necessary conditions for the equivalence of market prices and the fundamental values of vessels. The valuation of listed shipping companies using the above methods and other commonly used financial ratios is compared with a matched sample of manufacturing firms, where it is found that: ratios generally tend to be less cyclical in the manufacturing sector; shipping companies have a much higher leverage than comparable manufacturing companies; and, as shipping companies are portfolios of vessels, asset tangibility is notably high in the shipping sample.

Chapter 14, "Financial Analysis and the Modeling of Ship Investment" is contributed by Lars Patterson of Pacomarine Limited. He presents several practical examples of financial models for the evaluation of shipping investments, their assumptions, the key ratios and indicators, and the theory behind investment criteria and value drivers. The value of flexibility (optionality) for the shipowner is also discussed in terms of the timing of the purchase of a ship, its sale, the type of charter chosen and the amount of debt financing utilized. Key practical issues in maritime financial analysis are also discussed, including: purchasing the ship and the timing of the exit; going for a newbuilding versus a second-hand purchase; scrapping; the selection of operating expenses; the type of employment in terms of charter parties; and the financing methods. The chapter concludes by considering ships as investments, with important features determining their valuation that include the market price of the vessel, its cash flow, its charter, market expectations, the secondary markets for trading vessels, the age of the vessels, as well as market risk and credit risk.

Chapter 15, "Maritime Business Freight Risk Management" is written by Manolis G. Kavussanos of the Athens University of Economics and Business and Ilias D. Visvikis of the World Maritime University. They cover the freight derivatives market and the latest developments and trends in this area, including: freight rate indices and routes that are used as the underlying assets of freight derivatives; the available freight derivative products, that is, freight futures, forward freight agreements (FFAs) and freight options; the freight markets established around the word; and the various usages of freight derivatives for risk management—hedging—purposes. The various trading screens for freight risk management, as well as the latest regulations in derivatives markets, are included in this chapter.

Chapter 16, "Mergers and Acquisitions in Shipping" is contributed by George Alexandridis of Henley Business School at the University of Reading and Manish Singh of V.Group Ltd. The chapter provides a detailed overview of M&As in shipping and the motives behind them, including their role in attaining operating synergies operating synergies in the form of cost reduction and revenue enhancement opportunities; financial synergies; market share enhancement and reduction of competition; and diversification of the asset base. The discussion on the M&A process also covers: strategy formulation; identification and analysis of M&A targets; cultivation of the targets; due diligence; and the post-acquisition integration process. The chapter provides a road map of M&A valuation in shipping and in particular cash flow, asset based and relative valuation methods. The financing of shipping M&As is also discussed. The chapter concludes by presenting new empirical research on whether shipping M&As create value for shareholders.

Manolis G. Kavussanos
Athens University of Economics and Business
Athens, Greece
e-mail: mkavus@aueb.gr

Ilias D. Visvikis
World Maritime University
Malmö, Sweden
e-mail: iv@wmu.se

September 2016

Contents

1 **Shipping Markets and Their Economic Drivers**   1
   Jan-Henrik Hübner
   1.1 An Introduction to Shipping   1
   1.2 The Drivers of Shipping Markets   9
   1.3 Shipping Market Performance   13
   1.4 The Bulk Shipping Market   15
   1.5 The Tanker Shipping Market   20
   1.6 The Container Shipping Market   26
   1.7 The Offshore Market   31
   1.8 Summary   37
   Bibliography   38

2 **Asset Risk Assessment, Analysis and Forecasting in Asset Backed Finance**   41
   Henriette Brent-Petersen
   2.1 Introduction   41
   2.2 Global Demand and China: Cyclicality, Super Cycles, Sector Cycles and Counter-Cyclicality   43
   2.3 The Shipping Sector Market Outlook   53
   2.4 The Asset: Importance of Asset Specifications   63
   2.5 Mitigation of Risks   65
   2.6 Conclusion   66

3 Overview of Shipping Finance — 71
Fotis Giannakoulis
- 3.1 Introduction — 71
- 3.2 Sources of Ship Financing — 72
- 3.3 Conclusion — 93
- Bibliography — 94

4 Shipbuilding Finance — 95
Charles R. Cushing
- 4.1 Introduction — 95
- 4.2 Conclusion — 123
- Bibliography — 124

5 Debt Financing in Shipping — 125
George Paleokrassas
- 5.1 Introduction — 125
- 5.2 Types of Debt Financing — 126
- 5.3 Security Package — 141
- 5.4 Conclusion — 144
- Bibliography — 145

6 Public Debt Markets for Shipping — 147
Basil M. Karatzas
- 6.1 Introduction — 147
- 6.2 Basic Concepts of Bonds — 147
- 6.3 Bond Issuing Example — 149
- 6.4 Bond Pricing in the Secondary Market Example — 149
- 6.5 Issuing of a Shipping Bond — 150
- 6.6 Filing a Prospectus — 150
- 6.7 Obtaining a Credit Rating — 151
- 6.8 Selecting an Underwriter — 152
- 6.9 Timing of Issuing Shipping Bonds — 154
- 6.10 Shipping Bonds and Interest Rate Cost — 155
- 6.11 Considerations for the Cost of Shipping Bonds — 156
- 6.12 Difference from Shipping Loans — 157
- 6.13 Classification of Shipping Bonds Based on Collateral — 160
- 6.14 Covenants and Special Conditions — 163
- 6.15 Types of Shipping Bonds — 164
- 6.16 Conclusion — 167

7 Public and Private Equity Markets — 169
Jeffrey Pribor and Cecilie Skajem Lind
- 7.1 Introduction — 169
- 7.2 Public Equity — 170
- 7.3 Private Equity — 184
- 7.4 Conclusion — 188
- References — 189

8 Structured Finance in Shipping — 191
Ioannis Alexopoulos and Nikos Stratis
- 8.1 The Changing Landscape of the Ship Financing Market — 191
- 8.2 ECAs — 193
- 8.3 Leasing Ship Finance — 199
- 8.4 Mezzanine Ship Finance — 206
- 8.5 Conclusion — 209
- Bibliography — 211

9 Key Clauses of a Shipping Loan Agreement — 213
Kyriakos Spoullos
- 9.1 Introduction — 213
- 9.2 Operative Clauses — 214
- 9.3 Representations and Warranties — 216
- 9.4 Conditions Precedent — 217
- 9.5 Covenants — 218
- 9.6 Events of Default — 224
- 9.7 Mandatory Prepayments — 225
- 9.8 Assignment and Transfer — 226
- 9.9 Conclusion — 228
- Bibliography — 229

10 Legal Aspects of Ship Mortgages — 231
Simon D. Norton and Claudio Chiste
- 10.1 Mortgages: A Definition — 231
- 10.2 Limitations of Ship Mortgages as a Form of Security — 234
- 10.3 Registration and the Priority of Mortgages — 236
- 10.4 Powers of Mortgagees — 238
- 10.5 Rights of the Mortgagor — 245
- 10.6 Future Directions in Ship Mortgages as a Form of Financing: Securitization — 249

10.7 Conclusion	250
Bibliography	251

11 Mechanics of Handling Defaulted Shipping Loans and the Methods of Recovery — 253
Dimitris C. Anagnostopoulos and Philippos E. Tsamanis

11.1 Introduction	253
11.2 The 1981–86 Shipping Crisis vs the Post-2008 Period	254
11.3 The Mechanics of Handling Problematic Bank Loans	255
11.4 Early Detection of Signs	255
11.5 Once the Problem Is Detected	256
11.6 Preparation for Remedial Action	258
11.7 Determinants of the Bank's Course of Action	260
11.8 Loan Recovery Through Auction of the Collateral Vessel	263
11.9 Situations a Bank May Face During a Vessel's Arrest	265
11.10 Conclusion: The Other Side of the Coin	266
References	266

12 Marine Insurance — 267
Marc A. Huybrechts and Theodora Nikaki

12.1 Overview	267
12.2 Builders' Risk Insurance	268
12.3 Financiers' Insurance	269
12.4 Owners' Insurance	271
12.5 Conclusion	279
References	282

13 Maritime Investment Appraisal and Budgeting — 285
Stefan Albertijn, Wolfgang Drobetz, and Max Johns

13.1 Introduction	285
13.2 Market Approach	287
13.3 Discounted Cash-Flow Approach	295
13.4 Comparing Value and Price	302
13.5 Financial Analysis of Shipping Companies	304
13.6 Conclusion	307
References	312

14 Financial Analysis and the Modeling of Ship Investment — 315
Lars Patterson
   14.1 Introduction — 315
   14.2 An Example of a Financial Model — 316
   14.3 Theory Behind the Ship Investment Criteria and Value Drivers — 320
   14.4 A Few Comments on Ship Investment Practice — 324
   14.5 Ships as an Investment — 332
   14.6 Conclusion — 334
   References and Links — 334
   Bibliography — 335

15 Maritime Business Freight Risk Management — 337
Manolis G. Kavussanos and Ilias D. Visvikis
   15.1 Introduction — 337
   15.2 Freight Derivatives Market — 338
   15.3 Freight Rate Indices: The Underlying Assets of Freight Derivatives — 340
   15.4 Freight Derivatives Markets and Products — 349
   15.5 The Baltic Forward Assessments — 358
   15.6 Trading Screens — 360
   15.7 Regulations in Derivatives Markets — 362
   15.8 Conclusion — 365
   Bibliography and References — 367

16 Mergers and Acquisitions in Shipping — 371
George Alexandridis and Manish Singh
   16.1 Introduction — 371
   16.2 The Shipping M&A Market — 372
   16.3 Motives for M&As in Shipping — 377
   16.4 M&A Process — 381
   16.5 Shipping M&A Valuation — 385
   16.6 Financing of Shipping M&As — 394
   16.7 Value Creation in Shipping M&As — 398
   16.8 Conclusion — 407
   References — 411

Index — 415

About the Contributors

Stefan Albertijn joined the Baltic Exchange Board as Shareholders Director in 2012 and became Chairman of Baltic Exchange Information Services Ltd, which produces the Baltic shipping benchmarks and indices, in 2014. He started his career in 1999 when he joined Deutsche Bank AG, holding various corporate and investment banking positions in Germany and Belgium before joining the shipping department at ADM Alfred C. Toepfer International GmbH in 2005 and becoming its Global Head of Risk Management in 2010. In 2015 he joined Ocean Finance & Consultancy BVBA (Oficon) and Hamant Beratungs- und Investitionsgesellschaft mbH, niche consultants specializing in risk management for the shipping and agri-industries, as Managing Director. He has been a Guest Lecturer in shipping finance at Hamburg University since 2009 where he was also a founding member of the Hamburg Financial Research Centre. Furthermore he is a member of various shipping, financial and grain trading associations in Belgium and Germany and is actively engaged in the alumni groups Alechia and VEUK. He studied economics at the Universities of Antwerp and Konstanz and has authored various publications on shipping finance and financial derivatives.

George Alexandridis is an Associate Professor of finance at the ICMA Centre of Henley Business School, University of Reading, UK. He is also the program area director for all finance masters at the ICMA Centre and is the co-founder and director of the MSc in International Shipping and Finance. He is renowned for his work on mergers and acquisitions and shipping finance. His research is published in leading international journals and presented at major global conferences. As part of his role as Director of Shipping Programmes at Henley, he has established international collaborations with universities and business schools as well as relationships with financial institutions, shipping companies and other organizations. He also frequently appears as a commentator on financial and political issues on national television. He is an affiliate member of the Chartered Institute for Securities & Investment and is a fellow of the Higher Education Academy.

Ioannis Alexopoulos has more than 15 years of professional experience in the shipping, banking and the maritime finance industries. He is a Director at the Athens office of Eurofin Group; a ship-financing, investment boutique established in 1984 with offices in London, Athens and Singapore. Mr. Alexopoulos gained experience in shipping through short-term employments with Golden Union Shipping Co. (which included time at sea), Carriers Chartering S.A. in Piraeus and Angus Graham & Partners in London. He then joined Laiki Private Banking in Cyprus, an HSBC Group associate in 1999 where he held positions in both portfolio management and client advice, servicing expatriate as well as offshore High Net Worth Individuals. He joined the Athens office of Eurofin Group in 2002 and is responsible for the Group's ship financing operations in Greece. In addition, he is a key part of the Eurofin team, which acts as a Consultant to KfW IPEX-Bank for its Greek debt shipping portfolio. He has delivered a number of speeches on ship finance, at several Shipping and Shipfinance Conferences around the world. He is a visiting lecturer on Shipping Finance, at the ALBA Graduate Business School in Athens, Greece and on Maritime Economics, at the Henley Business School of the University of Reading in the UK. He holds a BSc in Economics and Business Economics from Southampton University and an MSc in Shipping, Trade and Finance from Cass Business School, City University in London.

Dimitris Anagnostopoulos has over 40 years of experience in shipping, shipping finance and bank management. He obtained his BSc at the Athens University of Economics and Business. His career began in the 1970s as Assistant Lecturer at the same university followed by four years with the Onassis Shipping Group in Monaco. He has also held various posts at the National Investment Bank of Industrial Development, the Continental Illinois National Bank of Chicago, the Greyhound Corporation and ABN AMRO Bank, where he has spent nearly two decades, holding the positions of Senior Vice President and Head of Shipping. Since 2010 he has been an advisor and board member of the Aegean Baltic Bank. He has been a speaker and panelist at various shipping conferences in Europe, and is a regular guest lecturer at the City University Cass Business School in London and the Erasmus University in Rotterdam. He is a member (and ex-vice chairman) of the Association of Banking and Financial Executives of Greek Shipping and an Associate Member of the Institute of Energy of South East Europe. He was in 2008 named by the Lloyd's Organization as Shipping Financier of the Year.

Henriette Brent-Petersen is Managing Director of the Shipping and Offshore Research department with DVB Bank, which provides fundamental shipping and offshore research in all sectors and is an integrated part of the bank's business model. Externally she represents DVB by presenting shipping and offshore market outlooks to customers and rating agencies and is a frequent speaker at conferences such as Marine Money, Capital Link, Informa, Euromoney and ibc. She is also a voting member of the bank's investment fund SIIM. Before joining DVB Bank, she had headed for almost a decade the Maersk Broker Research Department, which provided research on all sectors of the maritime shipping industry for international companies, banks and other stakeholders. She also has a strong financial background from Citibank where she started as a management associate before working for several years as a relationship manager, joining Maersk Broker in 2003. She started her working life as a country and bank analyst, covering Eastern Europe and CIS with the Danish ECA, Eksport Kredit Fonden. She holds a master's degree in economic science from Copenhagen University and has worked as an external teacher, lecturer and examiner for almost a decade at the Copenhagen Business School—initially in the field of financial statement analysis and marketing, but today in relation to the blue MBA.

Claudio Chistè works at Investec Bank plc in the Shipping and Marine Finance Team. His career began as an officer in the South African Navy, graduating from the Military Academy (Faculty of Military Science of the University of Stellenbosch) with a degree in mathematics and nautical science. Four years at sea followed, when he served as both gunnery and diving officer, culminating in being appointed for a period in command of a vessel within the Mine Countermeasures Flotilla. He also completed a B.Comm (Hons) through the University of Cape Town whilst serving. After leaving the Navy, he qualified as a yacht skipper and scuba diving instructor, going on to manage a 28-meter luxury motor yacht in the Mediterranean. Subsequently, he chose a land-based career and read for a master's degree in shipping, trade and finance at London's Cass Business School as a means to bridge the gap between practical skills and the commercial world. He was ranked in the "Next Generation" of Lloyd's List in their "On our Radar" (for the most influential people in shipping). He is the chairman of the Shipping Professional Network in London, a networking forum for young shipping professionals, having a strong following of over 1,000 members and associates with industry backing from the UK Chamber of Shipping.

Charles R. Cushing is a naval architect and marine engineer. His firm C.R. Cushing & Co. was founded in 1968 and has designed and/or supervised the construction or conversion of over 250 vessels of all types in most major shipyards worldwide. Because of his pioneering work at Sea-Land in the early 1960s and ongoing expertise in this field, he was inducted into the National Academy of Engineering. He has received numerous awards and is a member of several maritime professional societies. He is a licensed deck officer and a graduate of USMMA (BS), MIT (BS, NA & ME), SUNY Maritime (MS, OT) and Cardiff University (PhD, maritime studies). He has been an adjunct professor at the World Maritime University, both in Malmo, from 1988 (where he received a DSc (Hon) degree), and in Dalian, China, from 2005.

Wolfgang Drobetz is Professor of Corporate Finance and Shipping Finance at the University of Hamburg. He holds a PhD in economics from the University of St. Gallen and completed his habilitation at the University of Basel. He taught financial theory at the Bucerius Law School and the WHU Otto Beisheim Graduate School. His research interests include corporate finance, corporate governance, asset management and shipping finance. His research has been published in leading academic and practitioner journals. He is a member of the editorial board of several academic journals and served as Co-President of the European Financial Management Association.

Fotis Giannakoulis is the Lead US Maritime Analyst at Morgan Stanley, covering tankers, dry bulk, containership, gas carriers and offshore supply vessels, which he joined 2010. Since then he has worked on a number of public offerings, raising over USD10 billion. He is the no. 1 winner of the 2015 Thomson Reuters StarMine Analyst Award for the marine sector. Prior to joining Morgan Stanley, he was a banker at Fortis Bank (currently ABN AMRO) and Poten Capital Services, putting together a number of debt and equity financings and working on several advisory mandates. He holds a bachelor's degree in economics from the University of Piraeus and earned his MBA with honors from Loyola University Chicago, where he was the Walter F. Mullady scholar.

Jan-Henrik Hübner is the global head of DNV GL's Shipping Advisory. Together with his team he is supporting shipping companies, ship financing banks and funds, yards, terminals and governmental organizations across a wide range of strategic and operational challenges, including energy management and operational improvement programs for ship operators as well as portfolio analyses and decision support for ship financing banks. Before joining DNV GL in 2010 he worked for nine years for the global management consulting firm McKinsey & Company. He advised clients in various process industries on strategic and operational challenges. Key aspects were operational improvement programs and various aspects of energy efficiency. He graduated in wood science and technology at the University of Hamburg and received his PhD on the effects of emission trading and other aspects of environmental economics.

Marc A. Huybrechts received a Doctor of Laws from the Catholic University of Leuven in 1964, and an LLM from Berkeley, Boalt Hall (California) in 1966. He is a member of the Antwerp Bar and is Emeritus Professor of Law at the Catholic University of Leuven and at Antwerp University (Belgium). He is also Visiting Professor at the Dalian Maritime University in the People's Republic of China, and at ALBA in Athens. He is Emeritus Auxiliary Justice at the Antwerp Court of Appeal and a former board member of the Antwerp Bar; Arbitrator in the International Maritime Conciliation and Mediation Panel (London); Editor for Transport Law of the Encyclopedia of International Law; and member of the editorial board of *Tijdschrift voor Vervoer en Recht*. He is a titular member of the Comité Maritime International (CMI) and a member of the Law Commission to revise the Belgian Maritime Law.

Max Johns is Managing Director at VDR German Shipowners' Association in Hamburg. He has taught shipping finance at the Maritime Business School of the Hamburg School of Business Administration (HSBA) since 2008 and has become a professor at HSBA in 2016. He holds BA and MA degrees from the Université Paul Valéry Montpellier III in France, an MBA from KU Leuven in Belgium and was awarded a doctoral degree from the University of Tübingen in Germany. He publishes frequently on maritime issues.

Basil M. Karatzas is the CEO of Karatzas Marine Advisors & Co based in New York, a shipping finance advisory and ship brokerage firm, advising and representing shipowners and institutional investors on shipping and financial matters. He has an extensive and successful record on representing, upon exclusive mandate, financial owners of vessels seeking asset management optimization through remarketing, disposition, restructuring, co-investments and private placements, and has worked with the biggest players in the industry. He is a member of numerous industry bodies and organizations and a frequent speaker at industry conferences and a contributor to business publications. He holds an MBA from Rice University in Houston, Texas.

Cecilie Skajem Lind is an associate in the Global Industrials Investment Banking Group at Jefferies LLC, which she joined in August 2014. Previously she had worked in operations and risk management at A. M. Nomikos & Son, a Greek dry bulk shipowner and operator, and was an investment advisor at Beacon Shipping Investments. She received an MBA from Harvard Business School and a BA (Hons) from University College London.

Theodora Nikaki joined Swansea University in 2005 as a lecturer and was promoted to Associate Professor in 2013. She is currently Deputy Head of the Department of Postgraduate Legal Studies, College of Law. She is a graduate of the Aristotle University of Thessalonica (LLB and LLM in commercial and economic law, with distinction). Having worked in private practice for several years, she also obtained an LLM degree in admiralty and maritime law from Tulane Law School (New Orleans, USA) in 2001 with distinction. She then went to work in a maritime law firm in the United States before undertaking her PhD degree in the carriage of goods by sea and transport law in the UK. Her principal research interest is in the field of carriage of goods by sea, but her interests extend to private international law and multimodal transport. During the 2011–12 academic year she was awarded a visiting fellowship at the Institute of Advanced Legal Studies (University of London) and a visiting researcher position at the Scandinavian Institute of Maritime Law in Oslo. She is an active researcher and has published in several significant journals such as *The Journal of Business Law*, the *Journal of Maritime Law and Commerce*, the *Berkeley Journal of International Law* and the *Tulane Maritime Law Journal*.

Simon D. Norton lectures at Cardiff Business School in the field of banking law and regulation and financial crime, principally money laundering. He holds a doctorate in shipping finance and is the course director for this subject with the Institute of Chartered Shipbrokers, for which he has written the standard textbook. He also lectures in shipping finance and maritime law at an international business school in the West Indies. He has previously worked in the capital markets in London with a 'Top 10' Japanese finance house where he specialized in interest rate and currency swaps, and new issues. It was here that he developed his interest in complex financial structures and their applicability to ship financing. He also has a current interest in the application of Islamic finance principles and instruments to ship purchase. He maintains his interests and contacts in the practical (as opposed to academic) maritime world through attendance at workshops and social engagements with bankers, lawyers and brokers. He recently wrote a practitioner-oriented course on the commercial aspects of setting up and running, from scratch, a ship-owning business.

George Paleokrassas is a partner in the asset finance group of Watson Farley & Williams and is head of the firm's Greek office. For more than 20 years he has worked on a broad range of transactions in the maritime sector, acting for major shipping lenders and shipowners in the structuring and restructuring of loan transactions, the acquisition, sale and transfer of shipping loan portfolios, transactions involving distressed assets as well as for owners, operators and investors in shipbuilding projects, long-term charter arrangements, leasing transactions, joint ventures and other general corporate matters involving shipowning groups. Watson Farley & Williams is a leading international law firm dedicated to client care, industry focus and investment in its people, delivering valued advice on a wide range of corporate and finance transactions and disputes from 14 offices in major financial centres in Europe, the Middle East, Asia and the USA.

Lars Patterson is a graduate of the Norwegian School of Economics. He started his working career in shipping and finance with the merchant bank Samuel Montagu & Co and the shipbroking firm Galbraith's (Galbraith Montagu). During his time working for Torstein Hagen and Marine Investments S.A. he learnt to appreciate the value of financial modeling and how the process can improve the quality of analysis and create value for shareholders. Over the last 25 years he has been a non-executive director, advisor and consultant to a large number of shipping companies. From 2003 to 2015 he worked as a shipping investment analyst with London-based investment manager Marine Capital Limited. Together with Marcus Martinsson he is a founder and shareholder of Pacomarine Limited which provides software applications for the analysis of shipping investments.

Jeffrey Pribor is a managing director and Global Head of Maritime Investment Banking at Jefferies LLC. He has more than 30 years of corporate finance and maritime shipping experience. Prior to joining Jefferies, he was the Chief financial officer (CFO) of General Maritime, a leading international tanker company, which he helped guide through a pre-arranged Chapter 11 bankruptcy proceeding, and where he helped to conduct a successful hostile takeover defense and a leveraged recapitalization with a USD500 million special dividend to shareholders. Prior to joining General Maritime, he was Managing Director and President of DnB NOR Markets, Inc. and a senior banker at Merrill Lynch. He received a JD and an MBA from Columbia University and a BA from Yale University.

Manish Singh, as a third-generation seafarer, he started his maritime career with seagoing experience on tankers, dry cargo and self-unloaders. With over 20 years of industry experience, Manish has held diverse roles in ship management, marine conversions and infrastructure projects, offshore, marine financial and commercial services. As Group Commercial Director, Manish is responsible for the formulation and implementation of V.Group's commercial and corporate strategies and leads on acquisition projects and the Group's legal function. Since 2007, Manish has held senior management roles in V.Group's corporate team, with responsibilities including Offshore, Asset Management and Business Development for Asia region. Manish is a Master Mariner and an MBA from Cranfield University – School of Management. When not pursuing all things marine, Manish loves to travel, is a voracious reader, follows folk music and plays traditional Indian percussion. Manish writes extensively as a columnist on various industry, management journals and on his blogs.

Kyriakos Spoullos studied law in Greece and obtained his degree from the Kapodistrian University of Athens. He obtained his master's degree in shipping, trade and finance from the Sir John Cass Business School of the City University in London. He joined Norton Rose Fulbright in June 2006 from a Greek leading law firm (V&P). He is a member of the Athens Bar and is a UK solicitor. He represents a number of major Greek and international banks that do business in shipping as well as numerous large shipping groups based or doing business in Greece; he specializes in various finance sectors and industries, including shipping and asset finance, project finance and structured and complex banking products. He has vast experience in big syndicated and bilateral loans, secured and unsecured facilities, bond loans, restructuring and work out arrangements, monitoring "problem" loans as well as contract negotiations (i.e. charterparties, Memorandum Of Agreements (MOAs) and shipbuilding contracts). Additionally, he has significant experience in international capital markets, M&As, Initial Public Offerings (IPOs), joint ventures schemes and sale and purchase of shares agreements in shipping. Norton Rose Fulbright is a top 10 global legal practice with more than 3800 lawyers and other legal staff based in more than 50 cities across Europe, the United States, Canada, Latin America, Asia, Australia, Africa, the Middle East and Central Asia.

Nikos Stratis currently serves as a managing director with Chief financial officer (CFO) responsibilities for Augustea Group dry bulk business unit, which collectively controls a fleet of 35 vessels. Prior to that he co-founded Northern Shipping Funds where from 2008 to 2014 he held positions in the fund's investment committee and board of portfolio companies and operated as a senior investment manager responsible primarily for European and Middle East markets. His role included sourcing, structuring and the execution of shipping investments as well as investor relations. From 2001 to 2008 he was employed by DVB Bank, seconded to the bank's shipping investment fund as a senior investment manager. He was instrumental in the launching of a series of shipping funds, including the then largest Islamic Shipping Fund. He holds a BEng and an MSc in marine engineering from the University of Newcastle-upon-Tyne and an MSc in shipping, trade and finance from the City University Business School, London. Prior to joining DVB Bank, he gained experience in various shipping firms such as Lloyd's Register of Shipping, Aeolos Maritime and Ionian Tugboats, where he also served as an officer on ocean-going vessels.

Philippos E. Tsamanis has been with Aegean Baltic Bank, a Greek bank specializing in shipping finance, since its establishment in 2002. From 2006, he has headed the Bank's Business Development Department and since 2008 has been the Head of Shipping. He is a member of the Bank's Credit Committee and its Assets & Liabilities Committee. Previously, he worked for Euro Finance Services SA (1995–2002), a shipping finance and advisory firm specializing in the arrangement and management of syndicated shipping loans, the handling of problematic loans/third party accounts, and the providing of consultancy to shipping companies and banks on shipping debt and equity capital raising. Following his graduation from Athens College, he obtained a BA in government and economics from the University of Essex. He also holds a master's degree in shipping, trade and finance from Cass Business School of the City University of London.

List of Abbreviations

AHTs	Anchor handling tugs
ANPL	Arrears and non-performing loans
APV	Adjusted present value
ASEAN	Association of Southeast Asia Nations
BALMO	Balance-of-month
Baltex	Baltic Exchange trading screen
BCI	Baltic Capesize Index
BCTI	Baltic Clean Tanker Index
BDI	Baltic Dry Index
BDTI	Baltic Dirty Tanker Index
BEDT	Baltic Exchange Derivatives Trading
BEP Asia	Baltic Exchange Panamax Asia
BES 58 Asia	Baltic Exchange Supramax 58 Asia
BES Asia	Baltic Exchange Supramax Asia
BFAs	Baltic Forward Assessments
BHAR	Buy-and-hold abnormal return
BHSI	Baltic Handysize Index
BIS	Bank of International Settlements
BITR	Baltic International Tanker Route
BOA	Baltic Options' Assessments
bp	Basis points
BPI	Baltic Panamax Index
BSI	Baltic Supramax Index
BSI 58	Supramax Index
BSPA	Baltic Sale and Purchase Assessments
BUNKER	Civil liability for bunker oil pollution damage
CAGR	Compound annual growth rate
CAPEX	Capital expenses

CAPM	Capital asset pricing model
CAR	Cumulative abnormal return
CCFI	China Containerized Freight Index
CCP	Central counterparty clearing house
CEXIM	Chinese Export Import Bank
CFDs	Contracts-for-difference
CFSAs	Container forward swap agreements
CFTC	Commodity Futures Trading Commission
CGT	Compensated gross tonnage
CIRR	Commercial interest reference rate
CLC	Civil liability for oil pollution damage
CLO	Collateralized loan obligations
CLTX	Cleartrade Exchange
CME Group	Chicago Mercantile Exchange Group
COA	Contract of affreightment
ConTex	Container Ship Time Charter Assessment Index
CPT	Capesize 2014 time-charter basket
CTARs	Calendar time abnormal returns
CTC	Capesize time-charter basket
CTR	Calendar-time approach
DCF	Discounted cash flow
DCM	Designated contract market
DCO	Derivatives clearing organization
DD	Dry docking
DFA	Dodd-Frank Wall Street Reform and Consumer Protection Act
dwt	Deadweight tonnage
E&P	Exploration and production
EBIAT	Earnings before interest and after taxes
EBITDA	Earnings before interest, taxes, depreciation and amortization
ECA	Export credit agency
ECGD	Export Credit Guarantee Department (UK)
EEDI	Energy Efficiency Design Index
EGC	Emerging growth company
EIBC	Export-Import Bank of China
EMIR	European Markets Infrastructure Regulation
ERSB	European Systemic Risk Board
ESMA	European Securities and Markets Authority
EU	European Union
Euribor	Euro Interbank Offered Rate
EV	Enterprise value
EXIM	Export-Import Bank of U.S.
FATCA	Foreign Account Tax Compliance Act
FCA	Financial Conduct Authorities

FCF	Free cash flows
FDI	Foreign direct investment
FEU	Forty-foot equivalent unit
FFA	Forward freight agreements
FFABA	FFA Brokers Association
FMV	Fair market value
FPSO	Floating production storage and offloading
FR	Financial ratio
FSRU	Floating storage and regasification unit
GAAP	Generally accepted accounting principles
GCM	General clearing member
GDP	Gross domestic product
GT	Gross tonnage
H&M	Hull and machinery
HFO	Heavy fuel oil
HTC	Handysize time-charter basket
Hx	Handymax
ICBR	Institute Clauses for Builders' Risks
ICE	Intercontinental Exchange
ICS	International Chamber of Shipping
IDR	Incentive distribution rights
IGA P&I	International Group of P&I Clubs
IM	Information memorandum
IMAREX	International Maritime Exchange
IMF	International Monetary Fund
IMIC	Institute Mortgagees' Interest Clauses
IOSCO	International Organization of Securities Commissions
IPO	Initial public offering
IRR	Internal rate of return
ISM	International safety management
ISPS	International ship and port facility code
JOBS	Jumpstart Our Business Startups
JBIC	Japan Bank for International Cooperation
JV	Joint ventures
KEXIM	Export-Import Bank of Korea
LBO	Leveraged buyout
LCH	London Clearing House
LCH.Clearnet	London Clearing House Clearnet
LDT	Light displacement ton
LIBOR	London Interbank Offered Rate
LLMC	Limitation of Liability for Maritime Claims
LNG	Liquefied natural gas
LP	Limited partnership

LPG	Liquefied petroleum gas
LR	Long range
LSE	London Stock Exchange
LTAV	Long term asset value
LTV	Loan to value
LWT	Lightweight tonnage
M&A	Mergers and acquisitions
MAC	Material adverse change
MAPP	Mortgagee's Additional Perils (Pollution) Insurance
MarCAR	Marine Construction All Risks
MAS	Monetary Authority of Singapore
Mbpd	Million barrels per day
MIA	Marine Insurance Act
MiFID	Markets in Financial Instruments Directive
MiFIR	Markets in Financial Instruments Regulation
MII	Mortgagees interest insurance
MLP	Master limited partnership
MOU	Mobile offshore unit
MQD	Minimum quarterly distribution
MR	Medium range
MRP	Market risk premium
MSA	Merchant Shipping Act
MSP	Major swap participants
MTF	Multilateral trading facility
MV	Market value
MVC	Minimum-value clause
NAFTA	North America Free Trade Agreement
NAV	Net asset value
NBSE	Ningbo Shipping Exchange
NCFI	Ningbo Containerized Freight Index
NDA	Non-disclosure agreements
NOS	Norwegian Options and Futures
NOTC	Norwegian OTC
NPV	Net present value
NYMEX	New York Mercantile Exchange
NYSE	New York Stock Exchange
OB	Oslo Børs
OECD	Organisation for Economic Co-operation and Development
OLS	Ordinary least squares
OPEC	Organization of Petroleum Exporting Countries
OPEX	Operating expenses
OSV	Offshore support vessel
OTC	Over-the-counter

OTF	Organized trading facility
P&I	Protection and indemnity
PAL	Carriage of passengers and their luggage by sea
PE	Private equity
PIK	Pay in kind
PIPE	Private investment in public equity
PSV	Platform supply vessel
PTC	Panamax time-charter basket
RM	Regulated market
RMO	Recognized market operator
ROA	Real options analysis
ROA	Return-on-assets
ROE	Return on equity
RV	Residual value
S&N	Stay-in and negotiate
S&P	Sale and purchase
SCAR	Standardized cumulative abnormal return
SCFI	Shanghai Containerized Freight Index
SD	Swap dealers
SDR	Swap data repository
SEC	Securities and Exchange Commission
SEF	Swap execution facility
SEHK	Stock Exchange of Hong Kong
SGX	Singapore Exchange Limited
SGX AsiaClear	Singapore Exchange AsiaClear
SHCH	Shanghai Clearing House
SIN	Clarkson Shipping Intelligence Network
SPAC	Special purpose acquisition company
SPC	Special purpose company
SPPx	Super Post Panamax vessel
SPV	Special purpose vehicle
SPx	Sub-Panamax
SS	Special survey
SSE	Shanghai Shipping Exchange
SSEFC	Shanghai Shipping Freight Exchange Co.
STC	Supramax time-charter basket
STC	Straight-through processing to clearing
STP	Straight-through processing
TC	Time charter
TCE	Time-charter equivalent
TEU	Twenty-foot equivalent unit
TR	Trade repository
TSE	Tokyo Stock Exchange

List of Abbreviations

ULCC	Ultra large crude carrier
ULCV	Ultra large container vessel
UNCTAD	United Nations Conference on Trade and Development
VDD	Vendor due diligence
VLBC	Very large bulk carrier
VLCC	Very large crude carrier
VLCS	Very large container ship
VLOC	Very large ore carrier
VMC	Value maintenance clause
WACC	Weighted average cost of capital
WCI	World Container Index
WS	Worldscale rate
WTO	World Trade Organization
YTM	Yield-to-maturity
ΔNWC	Change in net working capital

List of Figures

Fig. 1.1	The maritime value chain	2
Fig. 1.2	Overview of the global merchant fleet	5
Fig. 1.3	Cost structure of a panamax container vessel	8
Fig. 1.4	Cost structure of a VLCC	9
Fig. 1.5	Earnings in merchant shipping since 1965 (ClarkSea Index)	14
Fig. 1.6	Dry bulk demand development (seaborne trade)	17
Fig. 1.7	Dry bulk fleet development	18
Fig. 1.8	Dry bulk (expected) contracting	18
Fig. 1.9	Dry bulk (expected) deliveries and removals	18
Fig. 1.10	Dry bulk, one-year, time charter rates	19
Fig. 1.11	Dry bulk newbuilding and secondhand prices	20
Fig. 1.12	Tanker demand development	23
Fig. 1.13	Tanker fleet development	23
Fig. 1.14	Tanker (expected) contracting	24
Fig. 1.15	Tanker order book vs existing fleet	24
Fig. 1.16	Tanker (expected) deliveries and removals	25
Fig. 1.17	Crude oil tanker earnings	25
Fig. 1.18	Tanker newbuilding and secondhand prices	26
Fig. 1.19	Container vessel demand development (containerized trade)	28
Fig. 1.20	Container vessel fleet development	29
Fig. 1.21	Container vessel (expected) contracting	29
Fig. 1.22	Container vessel (expected) deliveries and removals	29
Fig. 1.23	Container vessel idle fleet	30
Fig. 1.24	Container freight rate development (CCFI China—Europe)	30
Fig. 1.25	Container vessel, one-year, time charter rates	31
Fig. 1.26	Container vessel newbuilding and secondhand prices	32

List of Figures

Fig. 1.27	Offshore exploration and production CAPEX	33
Fig. 1.28	Offshore vessel fleet development (MOU)	34
Fig. 1.29	Offshore vessel fleet development (offshore support vessels)	35
Fig. 1.30	Offshore vessel (expected) contracting	35
Fig. 1.31	Offshore vessel (expected) deliveries and removals	36
Fig. 1.32	Offshore vessel, one-year, time charter rates	36
Fig. 1.33	Offshore vessel newbuilding prices	37
Fig. 2.1	Timeline of shipbuilding related policy in China	44
Fig. 2.2	Shipping market cycle	45
Fig. 2.3	Shipbuilding countries market share and shipyard start-ups by major shipbuilding country	46
Fig. 2.4	Shipbuilding capacity	47
Fig. 2.5	Flooding effect across segments	49
Fig. 2.6	China gaining market share with more lucrative orders	50
Fig. 2.7	Average time to delivery at contracting time	51
Fig. 2.8	Chinese shipyard capacity utilization rate and estimated capacity	51
Fig. 2.9	Forecasted structure of the Chinese shipbuilding industry	52
Fig. 2.10	Manufacturing-Sourcing Cost Index: total landed costs	55
Fig. 2.11	Cascading of larger capacity vessels (December 2013–December 2014)	57
Fig. 2.12	Cascading of smaller capacity vessels (December 2013–December 2014)	58
Fig. 2.13	Container market outlook: trend indicator	59
Fig. 2.14	Dry-bulk market outlook: trend indicator, demand–supply modeling	62
Fig. 2.15	Vessel developments over the years	64
Fig. 3.1	Clarkson's ClarkSea index	72
Fig. 3.2	Clarkson's ClarkSea index volatility	73
Fig. 3.3	World vessel contracting	73
Fig. 3.4	Second-hand vessel transactions	74
Fig. 3.5	New capital to the shipping industry	74
Fig. 3.6	Aggregate bank shipping portfolios	76
Fig. 3.7	Bank lending activity	76
Fig. 3.8	Top 20 shipping bank loan portfolios by bank	77
Fig. 3.9	Shipping loans interest cost: spread over LIBOR (basis points)	80
Fig. 3.10	Example of a leasing transaction	84
Fig. 3.11	Indicative shipping corporate bond issuances	86
Fig. 3.12	Global shipping public offerings of common equity	88
Fig. 3.13	Global shipping public offerings of common equity by country	88
Fig. 3.14	US-listed shipping public offerings of common equity	89
Fig. 3.15	Non-US shipping public offerings of common equity	89
Fig. 3.16	Typical MLP structure	90

List of Figures   xxxix

Fig. 3.17	US-listed shipping public offerings of common equity by payout strategy	92
Fig. 3.18	Blank check IPOs in the shipping industry	93
Fig. 3.19	Private equity investments in the shipping industry	93
Fig. 6.1	Credit rating of bonds and typical distribution of shipping bonds	153
Fig. 7.1	Equity options available to public and private companies	170
Fig. 7.2	US C-corporation structure vs MLP structure	172
Fig. 7.3	Advantages and disadvantages of going public	173
Fig. 7.4	IPO process on a senior exchange in the USA	177
Fig. 7.5	Aftermarket trading: shipping IPOs 2008–14	180
Fig. 7.6	Net asset calculation	183
Fig. 7.7	VLCC and Capesize ~ 180,000 dwt dry-bulk second-hand prices	185
Fig. 7.8	Monetizing investments	186
Fig. 8.1	Export Credit Agency guaranteed financing structure	196
Fig. 8.2	Export Credit Agency direct loan to buyer/importer	196
Fig. 8.3	Ship leasing structure	202
Fig. 8.4	Capital structure with mezzanine finance	206
Fig. 10.1	Enforcement flow chart	246
Fig. 14.1	Ship investment risk and returns	321
Fig. 14.2	Historical ship prices and one-year TC rates	324
Fig. 14.3	Historical ship prices for five-year-old and ten-year-old dry-bulk Panamax	325
Fig. 14.4	Dry-bulk Panamax scrap value and ship price	327
Fig. 14.5	Comparison of six-month, one-year and three-year TC rates	329
Fig. 15.1	Weekly average of total trade FFA dry-bulk volumes (in lots)	339
Fig. 15.2	Baltic Capesize, Panamax, Supramax and Handysize Indices (January 2000–December 2015)	345
Fig. 15.3	Baltic Dirty and Clean Tanker Index (January 2000–December 2015)	347
Fig. 15.4	Weekly average trade volumes cleared vs OTC by sector (in lots)	349
Fig. 16.1	Shipping M&A key participants and flows	373
Fig. 16.2	Breakdown of shipping M&As, 1990–2014	375
Fig. 16.3	Shipping M&A activity vs freight rates	376
Fig. 16.4	Main motives in shipping M&As	378
Fig. 16.5	Consolidation in liner shipping	379
Fig. 16.6	The M&A process	381
Fig. 16.7	M&A pricing framework	386
Fig. 16.8	Overview of DCF valuation approach	388
Fig. 16.9	Forward valuation multiples for selected container/liner companies	391
Fig. 16.10	Selected M&A transaction multiples	392
Fig. 16.11	Shipping M&A financing methods	395
Fig. 16.12	Shipping M&A financing: 1990–2014	397

Fig. 16.13	Financing terms of a shipping mega-deal	399
Fig. 16.14	Measuring M&A value creation	403
Fig. 16.15	Recent research of value creation through shipping M&As	404
Fig. 16.16	Some key ingredients of shipping M&A success	406

List of Tables

Table 4.1	Islamic financing terms	117
Table 6.1		162
Table 8.1	The most important export credit agencies for the maritime, cruise and offshore shipping sectors	194
Table 8.2	Examples of publicly reported export credit agency transactions concluded in the maritime, cruise and the offshore shipping sectors	195
Table 8.3	OECD guidelines: export credits for ships	198
Table 11.1	Market characteristics in relation to the impact on shipowning and banking institutions	258
Table 13.1	Sales of Capesize ships	289
Table 13.2	LTAV sample computation	300
Table 13.3	Financial analysis of listed shipping companies	305
Table 14.1	Example of a financial model of ship investment for a five-year-old Panamax (USD millions)	316
Table 14.2	Assumptions for simple financial model	317
Table 14.3	Sensitivity table I: sensitivity of equity IRR to changes in assumptions	318
Table 14.4	Sensitivity table II: sensitivity of equity IRR to changes in ship residual value and average TC rate	318
Table 14.5	Key ratios and indicators	319
Table 14.6	Individual bank lending criteria (illustrative assumptions)	331
Table 14.7	Calculation of loan trade out rate	331
Table 15.1	The Baltic Exchange Dry-Bulk Freight Indices, January 2016	341
Table 15.2	The Baltic Tanker Freight Indices, January 2016	346
Table 15.3	Shanghai Containerized Freight Index (SCFI), January 2016	348
Table 15.4	World Container Index (WCI), January 2016	348
Table 15.5	CME group freight futures, January 2016	350

Table 15.6	ICE futures Europe, January 2016	352
Table 15.7	NASDAQ OMX futures, January 2016	353
Table 15.8	Freight derivatives cleared at LCH.Clearnet, January 2016	354
Table 15.9	Freight derivatives cleared at SGX AsiaClear, January 2016	355
Table 15.10	Freight derivatives cleared at CME Clearing Europe, January 2016	356
Table 15.11	CME group tanker freight options, January 2016	357
Table 15.12	NASDAQ OMX options, January 2016	358
Table 15.13	LCH.Clearnet dry-bulk freight options, January 2016	358
Table 15.14	ICE Futures Europe freight options, January 2016	359
Table 15.15	Baltex trading screen products, January 2016	361
Table 15.16	CLTX trading screen products, January 2016	362
Table 15.17	SSEFC trading screen products, January 2016	362

1

Shipping Markets and Their Economic Drivers

Jan-Henrik Hübner

1.1 An Introduction to Shipping

Before diving into the drivers of shipping markets and looking at their performance, a short introduction will be given into the maritime value chain, the various shipping segments and the types of shipping markets. An overview of the cost structures will also help to provide an understanding of the conduct of shipping markets.

1.1.1 The Maritime Value Chain

Numerous types of economic participants with specific functions constitute the maritime value chain. From a shipping finance perspective, the yard, the owner, the charterer and of course the capital are obviously the most important ones. A broader view of shipping markets, however, requires attention also be given to ship managers, freight forwarders, cargo owners, brokers and all types of other market participants. Depending on the shipping segment, these functions are typically combined (integrated) to a different degree. In general, everything between a single purpose company and a fully integrated shipping division or a larger corporate structure is feasible. For an overview see Fig. 1.1.

J.-H. Hübner (✉)
DNV GL Maritime, Brooktorkai 18, 20457 Hamburg, Germany

© The Author(s) 2016
M.G. Kavussanos, I.D. Visvikis (eds.), *The International Handbook of Shipping Finance*, DOI 10.1057/978-1-137-46546-7_1

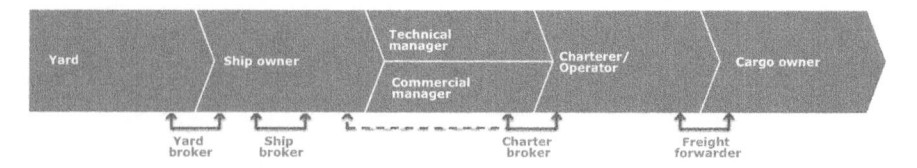

Fig. 1.1 The maritime value chain (*Source*: Own graph)

1.1.1.1 Ship Owner

The ship owner is a person, a company or an investment fund which acquires a vessel from a yard or from the second-hand market to hire it out to a charterer. The owner's earnings are the difference between the charter rate and the sum of the costs incurred by owning the vessel (interest and repayments, potentially subject to exchange rate fluctuations, are the capital expenses—CAPEX) and making it available (maintenance and repair, including docking, stores and lubricants, crewing, insurance as well as management and administration are the operating expenses—OPEX). The owner mandates a ship manager to run the vessel with crew, maintenance and so on (technical ship management) and to market the vessel to charterers (commercial ship management). The latter can be facilitated via a ship broker. On the income side, the owner's risks lie in the charter rate, employment and the lifetime of the vessel with regard to the second-hand value (for ongoing employment or scrapping). On the cost side, both OPEX and CAPEX bear risks for the earnings. The risk with regard to the earnings potential of other voyage related costs (which are primarily fuel and costs of port and passage (canal fees)) can lie with the owner or with the charterer/operator (for more details see Figs. 1.3 and 1.4).

1.1.1.2 Shipyards

Vessels are built, maintained, repaired and eventually scrapped (recycled) in shipyards. Traditionally, yards offered all three services (newbuilding, maintenance and repair) but further specialization has taken place during recent decades. Scrapping in yards, as opposed to beaching vessels (dismantling of vessels purposely run aground), develops with increasing environmental regulations. With respect to shipping finance, yards mainly interact with shipowners during the newbuilding stage, and with ship managers who take care of maintenance and repair of the vessel during docking on behalf of the owner.

1.1.1.3 Charterers

The charterer's business is to hire a vessel from the shipowner and sell transport services to a cargo owner or freight forwarder. In some segments, the charterer may also be called the operator. He or she may provide this transport service on fixed routes and schedules doing "liner" business, as is typical in container shipping, or employ the vessel based on a single (or trip-by-trip varying) cargo owner's requirements, as is typical in bulk shipping for example. The charterer's business risk lies in the spread between the existing charter contract and the freight rate development, and in his or her ability to utilize (fill) the vessel efficiently. The charterer may use brokers to charter the vessel and sell transport services.

1.1.1.4 Cargo Owners

Cargo owners want their raw materials or goods to be supplied to an intended destination. Depending on their annual transport needs and volumes, they either buy transport services directly from the owner, acting as a charterer themselves (common e.g. in the iron ore and crude oil business), from the charterer/operator (common e.g. for large consumer goods customers or in project cargo) or from a freight forwarding company (common e.g. for smaller volumes of containerized cargo). The cargo owner's commercial risk lies in the development of freight rates.

1.1.1.5 Freight Forwarders

Freight forwarders provide transport and related services to cargo owners, whose limited regular demand for transport does not justify a logistics department of their own with all the required functions and expertise. Rather, they buy transport services from the vessel's charterer/operator and sell it on to cargo owners. In container shipping, freight forwarders are among the biggest customers of container liners. As freight forwarders typically pass on the actual costs of the transport service and gain their earnings from a fairly stable mark-up for their services, their exposure to freight market rate volatility is rather moderate. Their risk lies rather in the variability of demand for their services.

1.1.1.6 Ship Managers

A ship manager is mandated by the shipowner to run and maintain the vessel (technical management, crewing) and market it to charterers (commercial management). All the operating expenses of the vessel are borne by the owner, based on pre-agreed crewing and the OPEX budget. The ship manager typically receives a fixed annual fee to administer the vessel. Hence, he or she is not directly exposed to charter rate volatility. Only a limited share of ship management contracts is related to the charter rate earned or to performance indicators.

1.1.1.7 Brokers

Brokers with various specializations act as intermediaries in shipping markets. Yard brokers facilitate contracts between yards and shipowners, especially in newbuilding, but also for repair and regular docking. Shipbrokers support the S&P of second-hand tonnage as well as the chartering of vessels (linked to commercial management). Freight brokers can facilitate larger freight contracts, for example in bulk and project cargo.

1.1.2 The Shipping Segments

According to Clarkson Research Services Limited (2014), the global merchant fleet comprised about 88,000 vessels above 100 GT (gross tons, a measure for a ship's volume), worth about USD900 billion in spring 2014. The main segments are bulkers (36% of GT at 10,046 vessels), crude and product tankers (23% of GT at 9,243 vessels) and container vessels (17% of GT at 5,087 vessels). Significant by number but small in terms of gross tonnage are also tugs (<1% of GT at 16,297 vessels), general cargo ("other dry", 6% of GT at 15,837 vessels), offshore vessels (4% of GT at 10,199 vessels). For more details, see Fig. 1.2. Looking at the distribution from vessel value or value of goods shipped, container vessels gain share compared with tankers and especially bulk carriers.

1.1.3 The Various Shipping Markets

A single vessel is subject to various shipping markets. The newbuilding market, the S&P market and the demolition market look at the ownership of the vessel, while the freight market (time charter and voyage charter, amongst other forms of charterparties) looks at the transport service of the vessel. Another differentiation of shipping markets has also been provided by Stopford (2009). The key markets will be introduced briefly in the following, while a more detailed explanation of the market drivers can be found in Chap. 2.

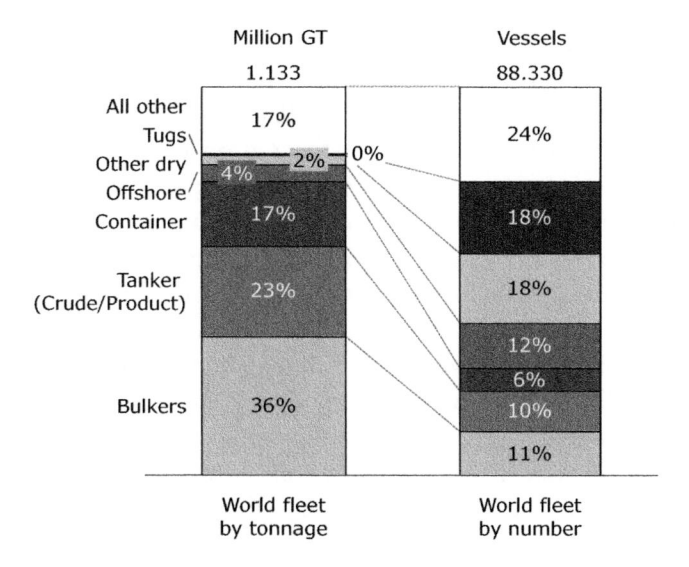

Fig. 1.2 Overview of the global merchant fleet (*Source*: Clarksons)

1.1.3.1 The Newbuilding Market

Usually buyers of vessels enter the newbuilding market as they either want to employ the vessel on their own, assuming future employment on the freight market, or plan to charter it out either based on a long term contract they have already agreed or on speculation of a good spot (voyage) market. They will accept about two years of waiting time for a newbuild, as opposed to purchasing existing tonnage, if no suitable vessels (size, efficiency, etc.) are available on the second-hand market. When shipping markets are booming and yard slots are scarce, yards show a limited willingness to change specifications relative to their standard designs. When markets are low, buyers can tender their newbuilding order amongst several qualified yards, especially if they are looking at a series of vessels. Typically, newbuilding prices of different segments of vessels develop largely in parallel (see Sects. 1.4, 1.5 and 1.6 and Figs. 1.11, 1.18 and 1.26), as many yards are flexible.

1.1.3.2 The S&P Market

The S&P market structure and conduct depend on the phase of the shipping cycle. At advanced recovery and peak times, the S&P of vessels is typically a very simple private transaction between seller and buyer, facilitated by one or two shipbrokers. The banks of the seller and buyer are involved but don't play a major role in the transaction. Second-hand prices are based on recently reported transactions of "similar" vessels and the indices built on them. During heydays, buyers are focused on the availability of vessels judged on their condition solely on the records provided by the seller, and pay hardly any attention to energy efficiency. Second-hand prices can even exceed newbuilding prices due to their immediate (or prompt) availability. Conduct changes when markets fluctuate. Banks become more active and may initiate an auction if the owner isn't able to service the loan or put the vessel up for sale on their own initiative. Vessel condition and energy efficiency are looked at more carefully, though the reported prices seem to reflect differences in efficiency to a limited degree only. Overall, about 1,000–1,200 merchant vessels are traded per year. In relative terms, bulkers and tankers are traded about twice as often (*c.*6% per year when comparing reported transactions with the existing fleet) as container vessels (*c.*3% per year).

1.1.3.3 The Demolition Market

The final stage of a vessel's economic life cycle is the demolition market. Vessels are bought based on their scrap value, which is determined by their lightweight tonnage (LWT). Buyers pay a certain price in USD per LWT. The owner either sells the vessel directly to a scrap yard or uses a cash buyer for the vessel's last journey. The price differs depending on the environmental care that will be required during scrapping. Qualified scrapyards typically pay lower prices than cash buyers who beach the vessel. With upcoming regulation at the EU and global level (the Hong Kong Convention), more environmental care will be enforced.

1.1.3.4 The Charter Market

Charter markets for ships subdivide into voyage charter (also referred to as spot charter) and time charter. Both are differentiated by the duration of the contract and some related obligations. A voyage charter contracts a vessel to transport a certain cargo between two specified ports. This is common in dry-bulk and tanker shipping. A variation is the contract of affreightment (COA), where a shipowner agrees to ship a certain amount of cargo between two specified ports in a series of shipments within a certain period of time. If time allows, he or she can perform other voyage charters in between. Pools of vessels, which could be seen as another variant of voyage charter, are groups of comparable bulkers or tankers which are marketed jointly and share income according to a specific agreement. A time charter fixes the vessels for a certain period of time (between two months and ten years). While time charter is basically the only charter contract relevant in container shipping and in all segments with vessels built to purpose (e.g. ferries, cruise, offshore), other merchant segments like dry bulk and tanker use both time and voyage charter. The charterer can dispose of the vessel during the charter period, potentially even performing voyage charter trips for other cargo owners. A bareboat charter is a variant of a time charter in which the charterer takes care of the crewing and maintenance. Bareboat charter is common if the owner is a financial investor who is not involved in shipping operations.

1.1.3.5 The Freight Spot Market

While the charter market refers to the transport capacity of the entire vessel, the freight market just looks at parcels smaller than a total vessel. Today, as tramp shipping with part-loads of mixed cargo does not play a major role anymore, freight markets with small parcel sizes are most relevant in container shipping. Besides the regular rate announcements of the leading container lines, the Shanghai Containerized Freight Index (SCFI) is the typical reference for freight rates of container shipments, for example from Shanghai to Northern Europe. Alliances, in turn, must not align freight rates, but share the cargo capacity of vessels to increase their utilization. In dry-bulk and tanker shipping, freight spot markets correspond to voyage charter fixtures, as the traded parcels typically match vessel capacities.

1.1.3.6 Forward Freight Agreements

Forward freight agreements (FFAs) are derivatives instruments used to hedge freight rates against future market developments, based on a specified single freight route, a basket of freight routes or a freight index (such as the Baltic Dry Index—BDI). FFAs are principal-to-principal contracts between actual buyers and sellers of transport services in an over-the-counter (OTC) market typically facilitated by a freight broker, or they are exchange-based on regulated derivatives exchanges. FFAs are common in the dry bulk and tanker market. More details about the freight derivatives market and their instruments can be found in Chap. 15.

1.1.4 Cost Structures in Shipping

The last aspect to be mentioned before looking into the drivers of shipping markets are the cost structures and the "Who bears what cost?" category. As the cost structures differ significantly between vessel segment, speed, bunker price and other factors, two examples will suffice at this point to illustrate what the different shipping markets cover.

Figure 1.3 shows the cost structure of a midsize container vessel at today's speed pattern and a bunker price of 600 USD/t heavy fuel oil (HFO). The owner bears the capital costs (CAPEX) as well as the fixed and some voyage related operating costs (OPEX) of the vessel, and charters it out in a time charter contract to an operator who additionally bears the bunker costs and terminal charges. From the owner's perspective, about two-thirds of his or her costs are capital costs (interest and repayment) while about one-third are operating expenses. All these operating expenses are handled typically via a ship manager who crews, runs and maintains the vessel on behalf of the owner. From the operator's perspective, charter is about one-third of total costs; bunker and terminal charges each about one-fourth; and other costs of passage and port (canal, tugs, etc.) make up the rest.

Figure 1.4 shows the cost structure of a very large crude carrier (VLCC) at today's speed pattern and a bunker price of 600 USD/t HFO. The owner charters out the vessel in a voyage charter contract to a cargo owner (e.g. an oil major). In this case, the owner bears all costs (CAPEX, OPEX as well as bunker) and receives the voyage charter rate from the cargo owner. In his or her

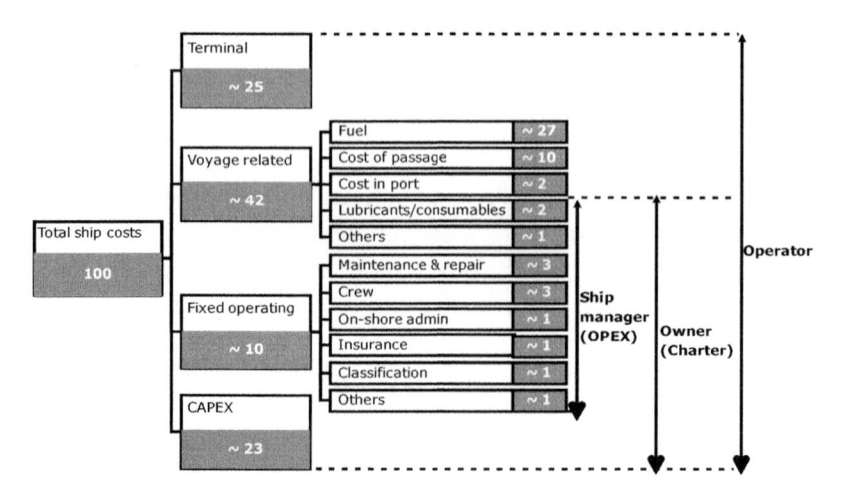

Fig. 1.3 Cost structure of a panamax container vessel (*Source*: Own model)

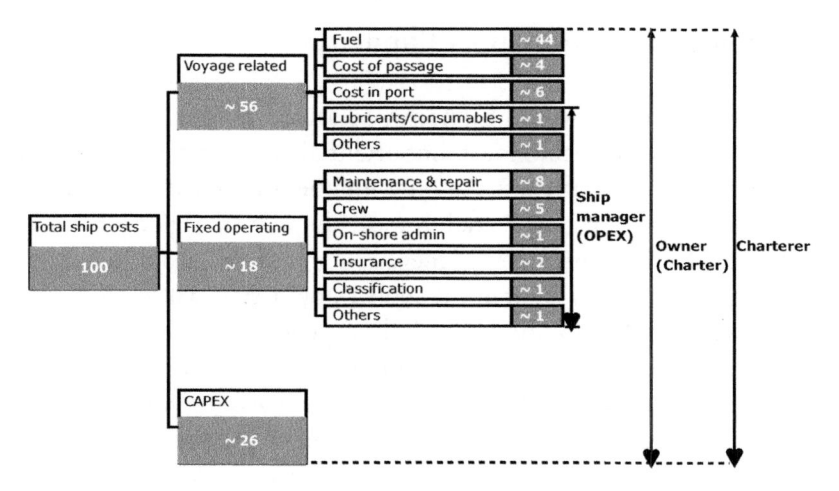

Fig. 1.4 Cost structure of a VLCC (*Source*: Own model)

cost structure, bunker accounts for 40–50% of total costs, CAPEX for about one-fourth, OPEX for about one-fifth, and the rest consists of costs of passage and port. The higher cost shares of fuel and some OPEX items for a VLCC, compared with a container ship, might be surprising at first sight. However, the cost shares in container shipping are significantly diluted by the high terminal costs, with each container move accounting for about USD250.

1.2 The Drivers of Shipping Markets

Markets are the simple mechanism that determine optimal volumes and prices, based on demand and supply. External influences and boundaries, behavior-related imponderabilities, timing effects and other "disturbances" complicate real markets, as opposed to simplified market models. This also applies to shipping markets, the newbuilding and S&P market as well as charter and freight markets. This section provides an overview of the drivers of demand and supply for tonnage and transport services and also for shipping market performance and cyclicality. The specifics for the dry-bulk, tanker and containership shipping markets will constitute subsequent sections; together these sub-segments represent 27% of all merchant vessels, but make up 76% of gross tonnage and, presumably, a similarly high share of the total fleet value. In many of the smaller segments, the vessels are designed and built for a specific charterer (e.g. ferries and cruise ships as well as offshore) rather than for a general market, which results in less liquidity and markets with many characteristics. Hence, a detailed discussion of these segments would exceed the scope of this book.

1.2.1 Demand for Transport Capacity

The development of the world economy, measured in gross domestic product (GDP), is the first and most important driver for shipping markets. Nevertheless, it is obviously less the pure number of "global GDP" which is driving the need for transport work but more the way the regions interact and generate global GDP. Some global megatrends underlie economic development. Fang et al. (2013) assume the global population will grow from 6.9 billion people in 2010 to about 8.0 billion people in 2030, with 96% of population growths coming from developing countries. The population in developed countries will decline, in turn, and increase significantly in age. Urbanization will continue, with more and more megacities being located by the sea and having direct access to international trade.

Political decisions co-determine how the global megatrends translate into trade and shipping. Are capitalism, free trade and Western lifestyle the aim of sociocultural evolution? What would these mean in terms of resource requirement and production? How will we react to climate change and global debt? Is inequality needed to fuel economies? Different answers and political pathways to these questions are conceivable and will affect shipping. Regional trade blocks in Europe (the EU), North America (NAFTA), Southeast Asia (ASEAN), among others, may continue to stimulate trade within their own areas. The World Trade Organization (WTO) may come to further global free trade agreements, reducing the relevance of regional trade blocks. A backwards trend with more economic sanctions, isolation and nationalization of economies is also possible.

Under the more likely political pathways, some economists estimate global GDP will more than double or nearly triple between 2010 and 2030, with China as one of the main drivers, potentially resulting in a 20% share of global GDP in 2030, and India and Brazil as new entrants into the global Top 5 besides the USA and Japan (Fang et al. 2013). These economists assume the purchasing power in Asia will increase by a factor of 8 by 2030, while granting a factor of 3 only to the OECD countries.

However, looking ahead, many uncertainties have the potential to affect trade flows and shipping. Geopolitical and social conflicts, such as the tense situation between Ukraine and Russia or the Arab Spring and radicalization in some Islamic countries in the Middle East, limit economic development and trade in these regions. Environmental regulation impacts upon trade flows (e.g. an accelerated nuclear phase that drives out the trade in liquefied natural gas (LNG)). Economic challenges lie in the high debts of countries and private households, and an excess of liquidity due to cheap central bank money (stimulus packages) along with a deflation risk and devaluation of certain currencies, leading to drastic effects on exchange rates (currency war). Kim (2014) argues that an "end of normal" scenario (high debt, no or negative growth) is 40% probable, that a "new normal" (high debt, slow growth) is 50% probable, while attaching just a 10% probability to the "back to normal" scenario (high debt, strong growth). The nearly "traditionally" good prospects for China also seem to have become cloudy lately. A cooling down of the real estate boom bears some risk for the hard landing of the shadow banking sector. Despite growth rates of still about 7%, China's decelerating GDP growth seems to have begun to follow the earlier trends of more mature economies such as Taiwan, South Korea and Japan (De la Rubia 2014).

The question now is how global GDP—or rather the way the regions collaborate and generate global GDP—can translate into seaborne trade. The basic economic principles of the "division of labour" (Adam Smith, 1776, in *The Welfare of Nations*), the "comparative advantages" of nations and their effects on foreign trade (David Ricardo, 1817, in *On the Principles of Political Economy and Taxation*), and globalization with continued relocation of production and processing from developed to emerging countries are well understood. According to Stopford (2009) the "west line" in the development of sea trade started in 3000 BC in Mesopotamia. While these classical theories apply evidently to trades between countries with differing factor endowments (e.g. raw materials), they seem to lack reasoning regarding intra-industry trade, which means export and import of the same type of goods by one country (e.g. cars from Germany to Korea and back). However, as the "same type of good" does not mean the "same product", intra-industry trade can be understood via economies of scale by limiting the variety of production in one country while exchanging with another (the "new trade theory" attributed to Paul Krugman).

It is difficult to forecast seaborne trade based on the development of global economic indicators. Looking at seaborne trade in total—not yet at specific segments—economists are not very successful in their attempts to correlate GDP growth with trade growth. Even the International Monetary Fund (IMF) and leading banks don't have a conclusive explanation as to why 3.4% GDP growth in 2012 resulted in just 2.8% trade growth, while 3.9% GDP growth resulted in 5–6% trade growth in 2015 (Kounis 2014). Also, the indicator "seaborne trade per capita"—with 2.5–5.5 tons in OECD countries, about 1.5 tons in China and below 1.0 tons in most of South America, India and Africa—is just an indication that the latter countries will catch up in trade volumes (Clarkson Research Services Limited 2014). Obviously, a segment specific perspective is needed to forecast shipping markets, rather than a bottom-up approach, segment by segment.

1.2.2 The Supply of Transport Capacity

The supply side of shipping markets is determined by the existing fleet, newbuildings and scrapping. The laying-up of vessels and the variation of vessel speed offer some flexibility to react to supply–demand imbalances. A high level overview of the existing fleet was given in the previous section 1.1.2. According to Clarkson Research Services Limited (2014), historical newbuilding orders had an average of about 2,200 merchant vessels and about 65 million GT per year in the time frame 2000–2013. With less than 20 million GT, average annual scrapping was by far lower, resulting in an annual fleet growth of 4.9% (in GT) during 1996–2013, with a peak of 6.5–8.0% in each year between 2005 and 2011. This compares to a growth in tonnage requirement (trade) of 3.9% in the time frame 1996–2013.

Newbuilding and scrapping activities are increasingly pushed by changes in regulatory boundaries, infrastructural limitations and factor costs. On the regulatory side especially, environmental requirements (double hulls for tankers in the 1990s, sulfur emission limitations in emission control areas in the 2000s and upcoming ballast water treatment) have put pressure on existing vessels and accelerate their economic aging. Increasing bunker prices and upcoming ECO designs with 30% better energy efficiency at today's operating profiles force less efficient vessels to leave the market. The "cascading effect" of using the largest possible design on a given route acts in the same way. Also, the extension of the Panama Canal and the Suez Canal, the newbuilding of the Nicaragua Canal and the potential opening of the Arctic route will shake up the existing fleet and open up opportunities for larger vessels with lower specific transport costs.

The slowing down of vessels during the current shipping crisis in order to benefit from lower bunker costs per 1,000 cargo miles had a positive side effect for shipowners. In the container segment about 2.0 of 17.0 million TEU (12%) are absorbed compared to pre-crisis speed patterns (Alphaliner 2015). The laying-up of vessels has a similar effect: capacity is temporarily removed from the market. Visibility is best in the container sector, as vessels are typically on time charter contracts. As late as 2014/early 2015, 110–120 vessels with a total capacity of 230,000 TEU have been laid up, equaling 1.3% of the total container fleet. During the trough of the crisis, lay-ups peaked at nearly 600 vessels, five times as many as today (Alphaliner 2015).

1.3   Shipping Market Performance

Although shipping enjoys a fairly stable increase in transport demand of about 4% per annum in the long run, it regularly suffers from strong cyclicality. Stopford (2009) differentiates three cycle lengths in shipping: seasonality, mid-term cycles of about seven years and long-term cycles of 30 years and more. Seasonality originates from fluctuations on the demand side. While transport capacity is largely fix within a 12-month time period, transport demand—for example, from consumer goods being shipped from China to Europe in the fall for the Christmas business, or not being shipped during the Chinese New Year in February—varies and, as such, impacts on the utilization of container vessels and the respective freight rates. This effect can be easily traced in the development of the SCFI.

The actual challenges for shipping investments are the mid-term cycles. In contrast to seasonality, they are largely supply driven, with a few exceptions from external shocks to the demand side (for example, the financial crisis that followed the collapse of Lehman Brothers Bank in 2008). Against the background of a fairly stable increase of 4% per year of the global transport demand, the regular oversupply in shipping is "home made". This originates from timing effects and mass psychology on very fragmented markets with low entry barriers for vessel ownership. Two to three years lead time from order to delivery of a vessel regularly leads to significant over-ordering when charter rates are good. A well-known actor typically starts the order rally, potentially backed with long-term charter contracts. Many others follow, trusting his or her market judgment (e.g. favorability of ECO ships, the need for LNG carriers) and hoping to find employment for their additional vessels, even if they have not backed the orders with charter contracts yet. The availability of yard capacity and financing may be limiting factors for these followers at times, but usually there are no real entry barriers (e.g. private equity firms and export credit agencies step in when regular ship financing gets scarce). As soon as the vessel is delivered, it supplies capacity for the next 25 years. With a typical split of 60% CAPEX and 40% OPEX from the owner's perspective, shipowners may accept the temporary employment of their vessels at cash costs (OPEX plus interest share of CAPEX) or marginal costs (OPEX or even just the OPEX of the vessel in operation minus the OPEX of the vessel laid up), which puts pressure on the charter rates on the market. A market collapse results in reduced orders, but, due to time lags, it may take years for the excess capacity to be absorbed by the global trade growth. Stopford (2009) analyzed that cycle lengths came to an average of seven to even ten years peak-to-peak, but discovered a quite high volatility of the cycle length.

The long-term cycles of 30 and more years are less relevant for shipping investments, as their length exceeds a vessel's economic life cycle and especially their amortization schedule. More research would be needed to bridge them to the long waves of about 50 years identified by Kondratieff and Schumpeter, who link them to major technical innovations. Yet, Kondratieff cycles and long-term shipping cycles don't seem to match fully.

Given the cyclicality of shipping markets, many shipowners do their business with the ambition of earning at least cash costs during the bad times and to survive and earn high margins during the few good years. Operators of vessels typically own a certain number of the vessels they run, while chartering the other ones. They typically keep vessels throughout their lifetimes (as their business model is the provision of a transport service rather than asset play), while riding the cycle with the chartered ones.

Looking at the earnings of merchant vessels in total, a few composite indices can be used. Best known is the ClarkSea Index, a weighted average of the charter income (before deduction of OPEX and CAPEX) from tankers, bulkers, container vessels and gas carriers (see Fig. 1.5). To determine the ability to service CAPEX and potentially get a return on investment as an owner, OPEX (the costs of maintenance and repair, including docking, stores and lubricants, crewing, insurance as well as management and administration)

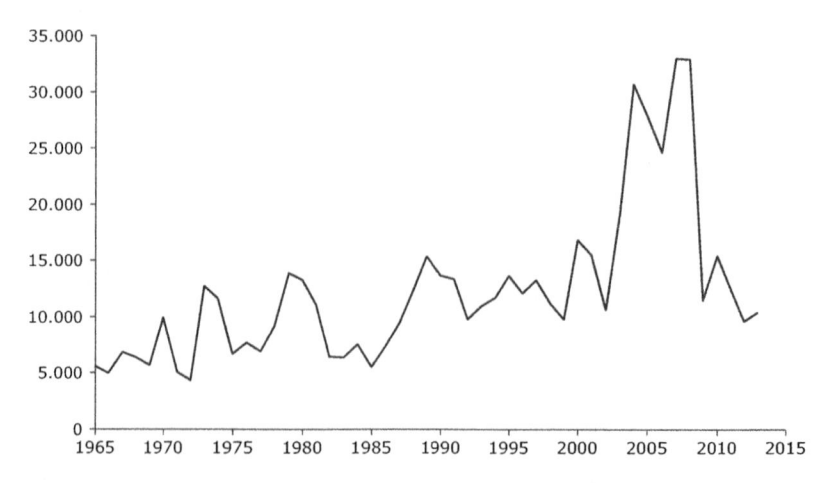

Fig. 1.5 Earnings in merchant shipping since 1965 (ClarkSea Index) (*Source*: Clarksons)

of currently about USD500 per day on average over the four vessel segments need to be deducted. It needs to be noted that the index is quoted in nominal terms. An average annual increase of the ClarkSea Index of 3.1% (the slope of the linear regression from 1965 to 2013) may be compared to an average USD inflation rate of 4.2% in the same time frame. This development has increasingly put pressure on the profitability of shipping, even if the 4.2% refers to the USA and not necessarily to global shipping factor costs.

1.4 The Bulk Shipping Market

1.4.1 The Structure of the Bulk Shipping Market

The bulk shipping market comprises about 10,000 vessels with a total tonnage of about 400 million GT (a 36% share of the total merchant fleet). The main sub-segments with their cargo capacity are listed in the table below. Size ranges per sub-segment may vary slightly depending on the source.

Very large ore/bulk carrier (VLOC/VLBC)	200,000–400,000 dwt
Capesize	100,000–200,000 dwt
Panamax	65,000–100,000 dwt
Handymax	40,000–65,000 dwt
Handysize	10,000–40,000 dwt

In addition, there are further sub-segments named according to infrastructural limitations (e.g. Kamsarmax with length up to 229 meters, Newcastlemax with beam up to 47 meters) and cargo owners (e.g. Valemax with 400,000 dwt). Further differentiation comes with the vessel's equipment (e.g. geared vs gearless). As outlined before, both voyage charters and time charters are commonly used for chartering contracts in dry-bulk shipping.

1.4.2 The Drivers of the Bulk Shipping Market

The main products in bulk shipping are coal, iron ore, grain and various minor bulks such as rice, sugar, wood chips, fertilizers and cement. According to Torp (2014), global dry-bulk shipping amounted to 4.3 billion tons in 2013 with a 29% share of coal, 27% iron ore, 14% grain/oilseeds/sugar and 30% minor bulks. Since 2004, dry-bulk shipment grew with a compounded annual growth rate (CAGR) of 5.6%, showing a good correlation of development with global GDP. In 2013, 40% of global dry-bulk shipments were imports to China, of which 67% was iron ore and 27% coal.

In 2013, 75% of global ore shipments were going to China. Since 2008, China has been importing more ore than all other countries together (De la Rubia 2014). From 2013 to 2014, its iron ore imports were projected to grow from about 800 million tons to 900 million tons. China imported about 1.3 times as much as the big four iron ore producers Vale, Rio Tinto, BHP Billiton and FMG jointly produce (Zhang 2014). The main production and shipments originate from Australia and Brazil (each with about 20% of global reserves). This strong increase of Chinese ore imports has been driven by a similar increase in the output of the country's steel mills. The domestic supply of iron ore couldn't keep up with the demand and is continuously losing its share against imports. With China's GDP growth slowing down from above 10% during recent years to the roughly 7% that economists expect, and especially with construction activity shrinking for the first time in a decade, crude steel production and ore imports are likely to slow down over the coming years, though increasing steel exports may compensate for a slowing domestic demand to some degree (Zhang 2014). At the same time the big mining companies are undergoing a heavy expansion scheme, which is expected to increase the global iron ore supply substantially for the years to come. Just Vale's plans to double iron ore exports until 2020 could potentially create demand for 230 additional Capesize bulk carriers. Other significant recent developments in the dry-bulk markets have been two agreements between Vale and two Chinese state companies to coordinate the shipment of iron ore. The cooperation between Vale and Cosco involves the newbuilding of ten VLOCs of 400,000 dwt each. In addition, Cosco will take ownership of four of Vale's existing VLOCs. In the other agreement, Vale will cooperate with China Merchants Group in a newbuilding program for ten VLOCs (DNV GL 2014).

Even if most global coal production is used in domestic markets (e.g. inside China), coal lies ahead of iron ore with 29% of global dry-bulk shipments. India and China are the biggest importers; Australia and Indonesia the biggest exporters (Fang et al. 2013). While China's domestic coal production is flattening, imports cover the gap, resulting in fast growth in coal imports (Torp 2014). However, environmental challenges are forcing tighter regulation: China announced that it would restrict the production, consumption and import of coal with high impurity levels in a bid to fight smog, much of which is caused by using coal for heating and electricity. However, the possible effects on seaborne coal imports are difficult to predict. Firstly, it remains to be seen to whom the restrictions will apply, since there is some confusion as to which industries will be affected. Secondly, if domestic coal production cost starts to rise, the cleaner coal from sources far away from China could be more cost competitive, potentially increasing long-distance tonne-miles (DNV GL 2014).

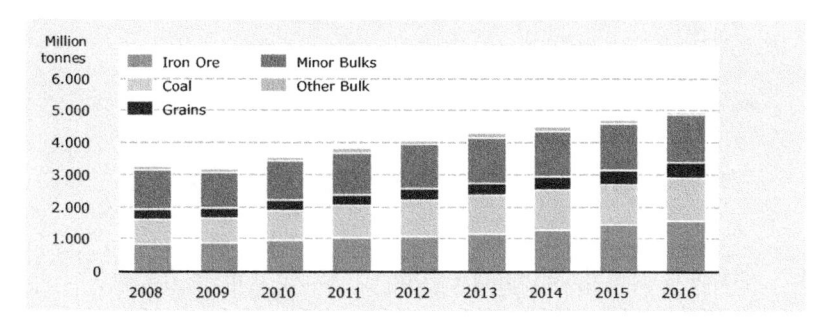

Fig. 1.6 Dry bulk demand development (seaborne trade) (*Source*: Clarksons (2008–14, actuals), DNV GL (2015/16 projections))

The markets for grain, oil seed and sugar are also assumed to grow. Some forecasts have a 50% growth from 2010 to 2030 with the USA and Russia remaining as the main exporters, and Africa, Latin America, the Middle East and Southeast Asia being the main importers (Fang et al. 2013).

1.4.3 Bulk Shipping Market Development

1.4.3.1 The Demand Side

As indicated above, the dry-bulk seaborne trade grew steadily over the past ten years with an exception in 2009 only. From 2008 to 2013, the CAGR amounted to 5.6% (Clarkson Research Services Limited 2015b) and the journey is expected to continue for the next couple of years with a CAGR of 4.7% for 2013 to 2016 (DNV GL 2015). Figure 1.6 shows the development by type of cargo since 2008.

1.4.3.2 The Supply Side

During recent years, the fleet has grown above transport demand. The CAGR from 2008 to 2013 was 11.2% and is expected to be 4.0% from 2013 to 2016 (IHS Maritime & Trade 2015). Figure 1.7 shows the development by sub-segment since 2008.

This fleet growth originated from a contracting boom in 2010, which resulted in strong deliveries in 2011 and 2012, when even high scrapping activity could not balance supply with demand (IHS Maritime & Trade 2015). Strong contracting in 2013 and 2014 will result in a further imbalance shortly. Figure 1.8 shows contracting by sub-segment since 2008, and Fig. 1.9 shows deliveries and removals.

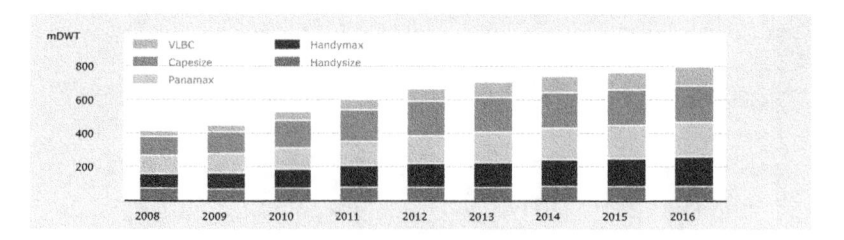

Fig. 1.7 Dry bulk fleet development (*Source*: IHS Maritime & Trade)

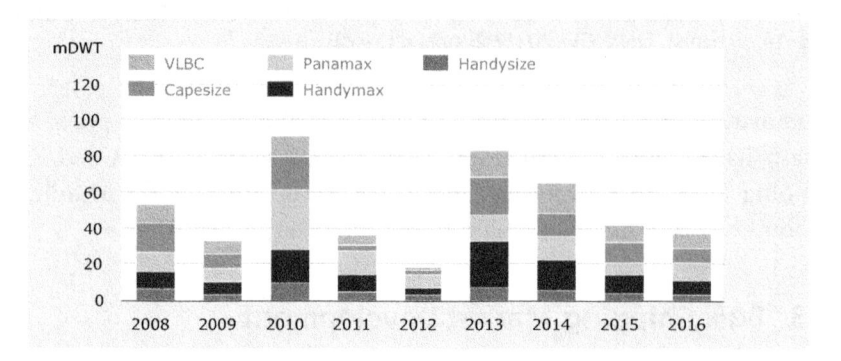

Fig. 1.8 Dry bulk (expected) contracting (*Source*: IHS Maritime & Trade)

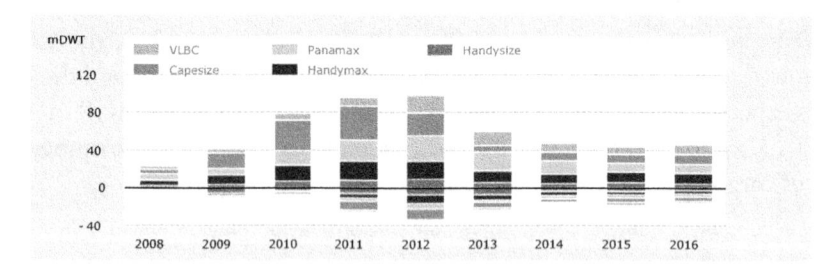

Fig. 1.9 Dry bulk (expected) deliveries and removals (*Source*: IHS Maritime & Trade)

1.4.3.3 Earnings

The earnings of bulkers can be expressed in one-year time charter rates (see Fig. 1.10 and Clarkson Research Services Limited 2015b) or on an aggregated level in the BDI. With the financial crisis of 2008 and its impact on the world economy, charter rates of Capesize bulk carriers dropped from about USD130,000 per day in 2008 to just slightly above USD20,000 per day

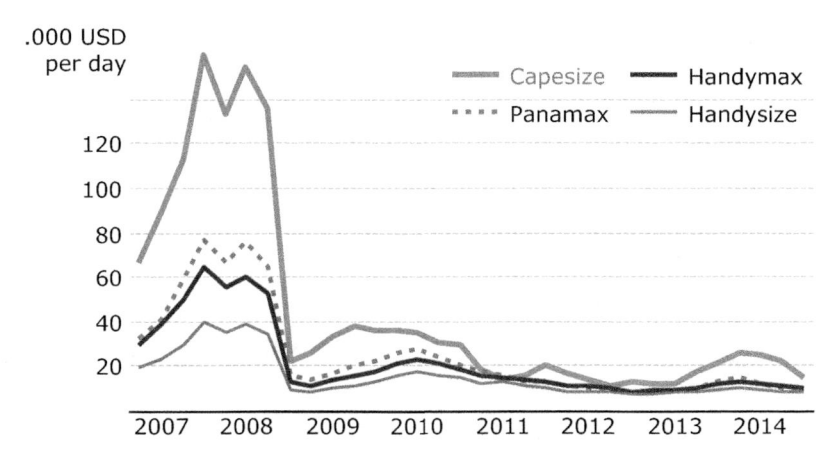

Fig. 1.10 Dry bulk, one-year, time charter rates (*Source*: Clarksons)

(a decrease of 85%). An increase to nearly USD40,000 per day in 2009 resulted in the order boom of 2010, which again put pressure on rates. In the smaller bulker segments the drop in 2008 was slightly lower. Since 2011, interestingly, the charter rates of Handysize, Handymax and Panamax bulk carriers hardly differ from each other. Looking ahead, the expected increase in transport demand for dry bulk should help earnings, but the strong contracting in 2013 and 2014 is likely to put continuous pressure on the rates.

1.4.3.4 Prices

Newbuilding and second-hand prices follow earnings. While the correlation between earnings and second-hand prices seems very high (they have dropped by about 60–70% since 2008), newbuilding prices follow earnings more moderately (they dropped by about 50% compared with 2008). The explanation lies in the shorter remaining lifetime (and thus investment horizon) of second-hand vessels compared with newbuildings. Figure 1.11 (Clarkson Research Services Limited 2015b) also shows that in the boom times the prices of second-hand vessels exceed those of newbuildings due to their immediate availability. The net present value of the second-hand vessels is mainly driven by the immediate high earnings during the current boom and only to a smaller degree by the cash flows of the mid and longer-term future. Due to the time lag between order and delivery, newbuildings may not benefit anymore from the current boom. Their net present value is rather driven by the mid and longer-term earning potential.

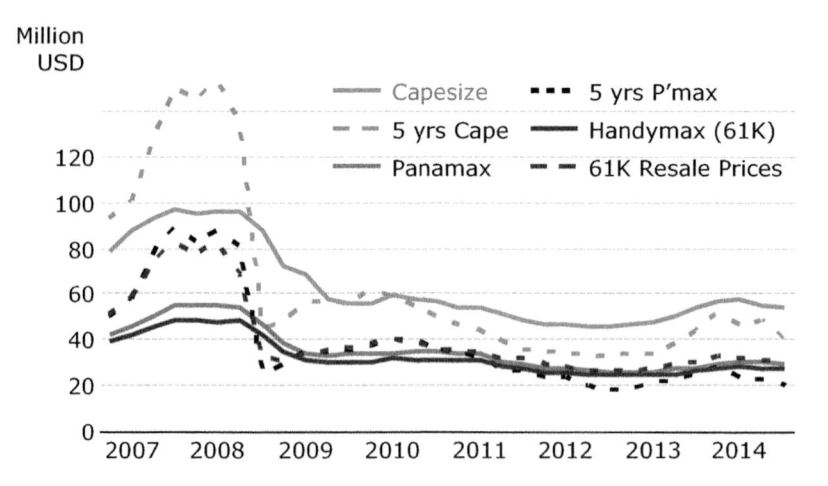

Fig. 1.11 Dry bulk newbuilding and secondhand prices (*Source*: Clarksons)

1.5 The Tanker Shipping Market

1.5.1 Structure of the Tanker Shipping Market

The tanker market comprises about 9,200 crude and product tankers with a total tonnage of about 265 million GT (a 23% share of the total merchant fleet) and about 1,600 liquefied petroleum gas (LPG) and LNG tankers of about 50 million GT (a 4% share of the total merchant fleet). The main sub-segments with their cargo capacity are listed in the table below. Size ranges per sub-segment may vary slightly depending on the source.

From a loading capacity (deadweight) perspective, the sub-segments appear to be overlapping. The difference, however, lies in the type of cargo; for example, that between crude oil (dirty tank cargo) and products and chemicals (clean tank cargo). As outlined earlier, both voyage charters and time charters are commonly used charter contracts in tanker shipping.

Crude	Ultra large crude carrier (ULCC)	>320,000 dwt
	VLCC	200,000–300,000 dwt
	Suezmax	115,000–200,000 dwt
	Aframax	70,000–115,000 dwt
	Panamax	50,000–70,000 dwt
	Handysize	10,000–50,000 dwt
Product	Long range 2 (LR2)	80,000–160,000 dwt
	Long range 1 (LR1)	55,000–80,000 dwt
	Medium range (MR)	25,000–55,000 dwt
Gas	LNG	Differentiated by volume and tank type
	LPG	Differentiated by volume and tank type
	Ethylene and other gas carriers	Differentiated by boiling point of the gas

1.5.2 Drivers of the Tanker Shipping Market

The main products in wet tanker shipping are crude oil and chemical products. "Dirty tankers" typically carry crude and heavy oil, while "clean tankers" carry refined petroleum products and chemicals. Seaborne crude trade is estimated at 37 mbpd (million barrels per day), while product trade is at about 22 mbpd (Clarkson Research Services Limited 2014).

In 2011, the main crude oil importers were Europe, North America, China and South Asia. Exports mainly came from the Middle East, Africa and the Commonwealth of Independent States (CIS), the regional organization whose participating countries are the former Soviet republics. Until 2030, economists are assuming strong import growth in China (even a tripling by 2030), South Asia and Southeast Asia, while exports are expected to grow from the Middle East and Africa. It is assumed that these trends will result in a massive increase in crude oil trade from the Middle East eastwards to China and other Asian countries (Fang et al. 2013). Russia and the USA are likely still to be the main producers in 2030, but uncoupling to some degree from seaborne crude trade. The USA is expected to develop from a crude importer to an increasing exporter of oil products and, potentially, even crude, due to the tight and shale oil "revolution" initiated by the wide use of hydraulic fracking in domestic oil and gas exploration. The new production technology has added 3 mbpd of production over the past two years and is now the highest since 1986. The drop in US crude imports, however, is likely to be (over-) compensated by the increase of Chinese crude imports (Sand 2014). Looking at the impact on crude oil tanker demand, the trend may even be positive, as relatively short voyages from West Africa to the USA are replaced by longer voyages to China/Asia. The longer hauls are said to lead to a 2.1% increase in tonnage demand (DNV GL 2014). Mid and longer-term development depends on the success of Saudi Arabia's attempt to force US tight and shale oil and gas producers out of business, with extremely low oil prices based on high production volumes. The continued low price environment obviously creates financial problems for costly US tight/shale oil producers but also for many other members of the Organization of Petroleum Exporting Countries (OPEC), who might try to influence Saudi Arabia to reduce production to sustainable price levels again. The use of VLCCs as floating storage is a temporary effect of a low oil price.

Trade with petroleum products and chemicals is less straightforward than crude oil trade. There are trends towards more local value add, with investments into refinery capacity in China, in the Middle East and in the USA, though build up in Latin America and Africa is limited; Europe is by comparison losing refining capacity. This indicates a need for more long-haul product trade through the Atlantic towards Europe which seems to have stimulated the heavy contracting of LR2 product tankers in 2013 (Hartland Shipping Services Ltd 2014). The demand increase for MR product tankers appears to be fueled by intra-Asia trades but may cool down again as soon as Chinese refinery capacity is up and running.

Looking at gas tankers, LNG needs to be differentiated from LPG and other gaseous products such as ethylene. LNG faces a boom as an energy source, especially since the Fukushima Daiichi accident in Japan in March 2011, with the increasing political intention to phase out nuclear power in many developed countries. Major investments into production and liquefaction capacity are currently being made in the Middle East, the USA, Australia, West Africa and Malaysia. Also, for the Arctic region there are plans for LNG floating production storage and offloading (FPSO) and floating storage and regasification units (FSRUs) (Roger et al. 2014). If these plans materialize, they will have a very significant impact on the need for VLGCs. For US exports alone, 80–130 LNG carriers could be needed by 2020. The pace and extent of this development, however, also depend on the development of the price of crude oil.

1.5.3 Tanker Shipping Market Development

1.5.3.1 The Demand Side

Overall, seaborne crude trade was steady in 2014 with about 37 mbpd. Due to longer hauls from West Africa to Asia, instead of shorter transatlantic routes to the USA, the deadweight demand increased by about 2.1%, which was mainly covered by the larger sub-segments (VLCC demand grew by about 4.2%). Also, floating storage has started to absorb capacity. Mid-sized crude tankers, as Aframaxes, suffered from lower European imports. Looking ahead, there is significant uncertainty, driven by the development of the oil price. Demand for product tanker capacity is increasing above 4%, mainly driven by MRs used in intra-Asian trades and by LR2s for the longer hauls (Fig. 1.12).

1.5.3.2 The Supply Side

The capacity of crude and product tankers has grown steadily over the past decade. The CAGR from 2008 to 2013 was 4.5% and is expected to be 2.7%

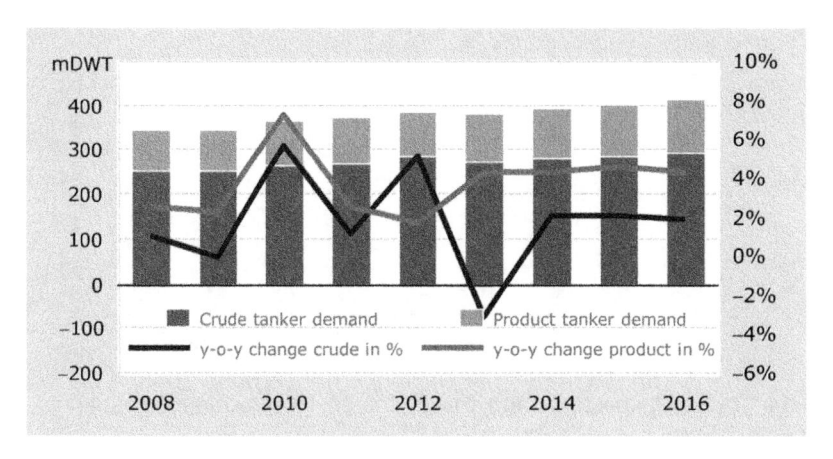

Fig. 1.12 Tanker demand development (*Source*: Clarksons (2008–14, actuals), DNV GL (2015/16 projections))

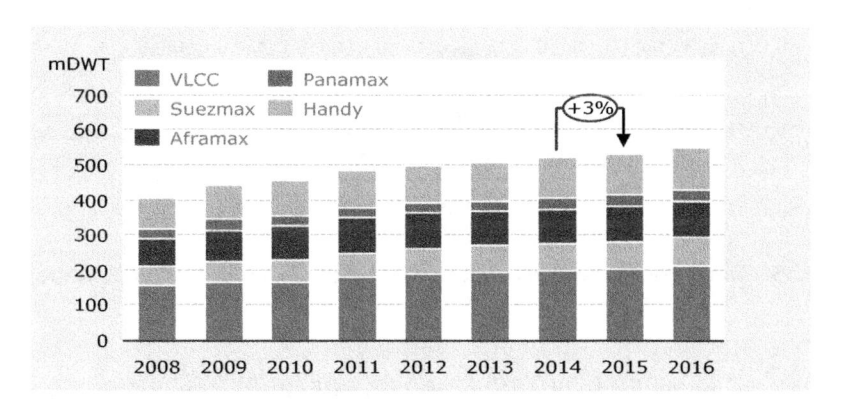

Fig. 1.13 Tanker fleet development (*Source*: IHS Maritime & Trade)

from 2013 to 2016 (IHS Maritime & Trade 2015). Figure 1.13 shows the development by sub-segment since 2008.

Contracting was low in 2011 and 2012 but strong in 2013 and 2014 (IHS Maritime & Trade 2015). Overall 12%, depending on the sub-segment between 7 and 18%, of the current tonnage is still in the order books (especially MR/Handysize and VLCCs). Figures 1.14 and 1.15 display recent and forecasted contracting and order books.

Scrapping activity was above average in 2010, 2012 and 2013, taking highest relative effect among Aframax vessels and VLCCs (see Fig. 1.16;

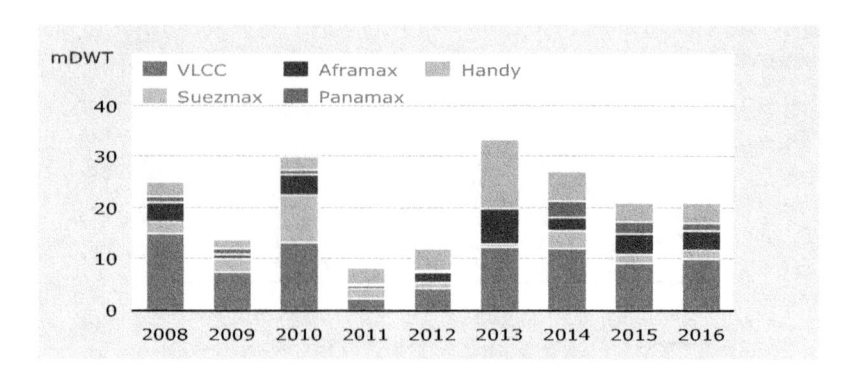

Fig. 1.14 Tanker (expected) contracting (*Source*: IHS Maritime & Trade)

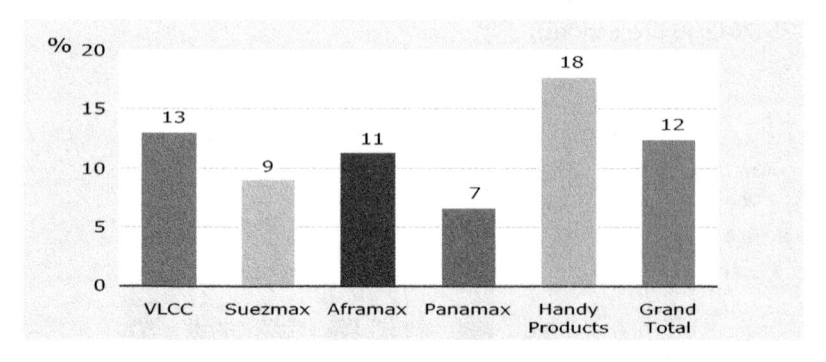

Fig. 1.15 Tanker order book vs existing fleet (*Source*: IHS Maritime & Trade)

IHS Maritime & Trade 2015). With currently high scrap values of about USD525 per ldt, this may remain an attractive option for semi-elderly vessels.

1.5.3.3 Earnings

Tanker earnings show a similar picture as displayed for bulk carriers. A sharp drop from 2008 to 2009 of about 80%, some recovery in 2010 and a largely horizontal development since then with some seasonality; that is, spikes towards the winter season in the crude segments. Interestingly, VLCCs, Suezmaxes and Aframaxes don't differ much in their freight rates, as seen in Fig. 1.17 (Clarkson Research Services Limited 2015b).

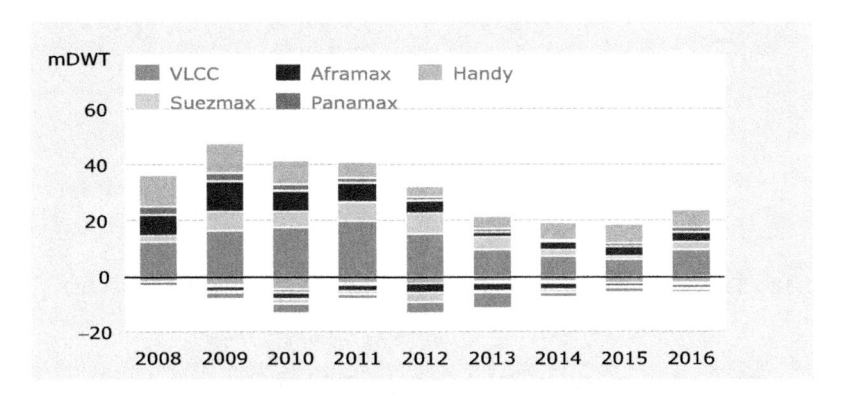

Fig. 1.16 Tanker (expected) deliveries and removals (*Source*: IHS Maritime & Trade)

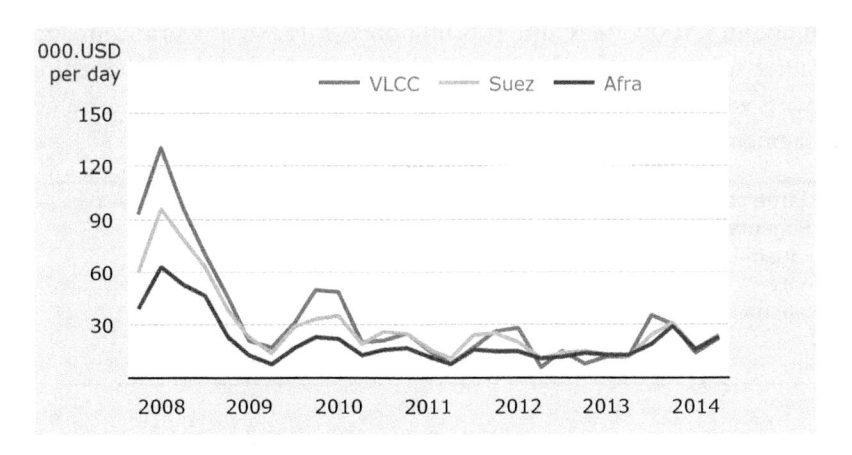

Fig. 1.17 Crude oil tanker earnings (*Source*: Clarksons)

1.5.3.4 Prices

Again second-hand prices largely follow current earnings, whereas five-year-old VLCCs can achieve prices about twice as high as those of Aframaxes and MR/Handysize, which were converging from 2008 to early 2014. As expected, newbuilding prices are more stable and showed largely horizontal development since 2009 (Clarkson Research Services Limited 2015b) (see Fig. 1.18).

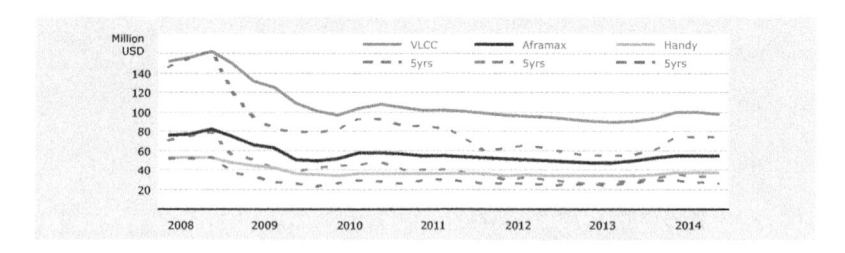

Fig. 1.18 Tanker newbuilding and secondhand prices (*Source*: Clarksons)

1.6 The Container Shipping Market

1.6.1 Structure of the Container Shipping Market

With about 5,100 vessels and 188 million GT (17% of world tonnage) the container segment is the third largest in merchant shipping. The main sub-segments with their cargo capacity are listed in the table below. Size ranges per sub-segment may vary slightly depending on the source.

Ultra large container vessels (ULCV)	>14,000 TEU
New Panamax	8,000–14,000 TEU
Post Panamax	5,000–8,000 TEU
Panamax	3,000–5,000 TEU
Sub Panamax	2,000–3,000 TEU
Handy	1,000–2,000 TEU
Feeder	<1,000 TEU

Further sub-segments are named according to infrastructural limitations (e.g. Bangkokmax with a draft of 27 feet), and differentiation is made based on the vessel's equipment, especially in the smaller segments (e.g. geared vs gearless). As outlined earlier, container vessels are typically chartered out in time charter contracts initially up to ten years, with subsequent short-term contracts down to two months.

1.6.2 The Drivers of the Container Shipping Market

Containerships transport all types of cargo in small parcel sizes; at first these were in 20 foot containers, but today 40 or even 45 feet are the norm. As containerized transport costs are higher compared to bulk shipment, goods in small parcel sizes or with a high specific value are shipped in containers. These are typically consumer goods. In 2005, the OECD published statistics with specific freight values ranging from USD20,000 per 40-foott container (retail prices) for assembled furniture to USD3.6 million for mid-range clothing. Consumer electronics ranged from USD70,000 to 430,000 (retail value). Even assuming a 100% trade margin and 20% VAT, this amounts to a cargo value from USD4,200 per TEU up to USD750,000 per TEU. At the upper end of cargo value, container shipping competes with air freight based on voyage duration and the resulting capital employment for the cargo.

Looking at trade routes in 2013, Asia to Europe (head haul westbound) made up 35% of global TEU miles, transpacific (head haul eastbound) 29%, intra-Asia 12%, intra-Europe 3%, transatlantic (head haul westbound) 3%, and 18% for other trades (Lunde 2014). Analysts anticipate container trade growth, especially intra-Asia, the Far East to the Middle East (head haul westbound), the Far East to Europe (head haul westbound), the Far East to Latin America east coast (head haul eastbound through the Panama Canal) and North America to Latin America (Fang et al. 2013). A major trend in recent years has been the increase in trans-shipments: 10% in the 1980s to about 30% today. More than 50% of these trans-shipments happen in China, Southeast Asia and other Asian countries (Frew 2014). Neglecting the current shipping crisis with overcapacity in container lines, this trend towards trans-shipments does not seem to have ended, especially with more ULCVs being delivered, which cannot access many ports. Another trend, accelerated by the shipping crisis, is the cascading effect. With overcapacity and high bunker prices (at least until mid-2014), economies of scale have gained more importance. Hence, the liners employ the largest possible vessels in their services to minimize slot costs. This cascading effect puts severe pressure on mid-sized and smaller container vessels (Frew 2014).

The growth in global GDP is typically used as an approximation for container trade development. Prior to 2003, there was a long term multiple of 3, between 3% GDP growth and 9% growth in containerized freight; 3% of the 9% originated from GDP, 3% from increasing globalization and 3% from the increasing containerization of cargo from bulker or reefer vessels to container vessels. Since 2003, this multiple of 3 does not hold true anymore. For 2014–2016, Howe Robinson expects a ratio of about 1.2 for global trade growth vs global GDP growth, and of 1.6 for containerized trade growth vs global GDP growth. In 2012 and 2013, both ratios have been about 1.0, and each of the figures grew by a good 3%. Hoehlinger (2012) evaluates further macro-variables to predict container ship trade, but not all of the correlations shown seem to be plausible explanations.

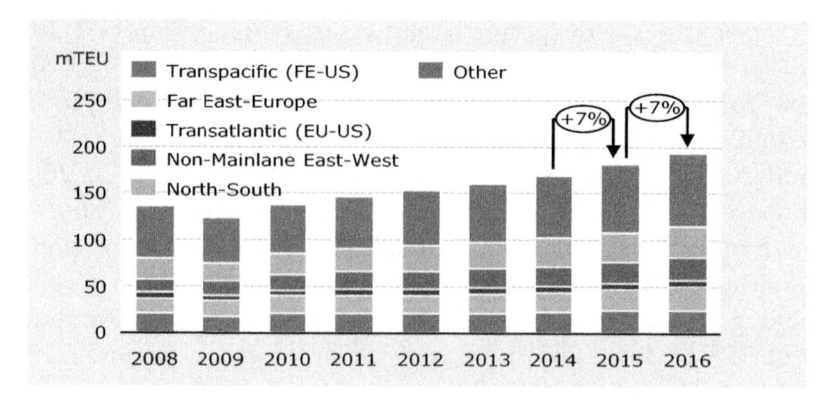

Fig. 1.19 Container vessel demand development (containerized trade) (*Source*: Clarksons (2008–14, actuals), DNV GL (2015/16 projections))

1.6.3 Container Shipping Market Development

1.6.3.1 The Demand Side

Between 2008 and 2013, the demand for containerized trade grew with a CAGR of 3.4%. Considering the drop in 2009 the CAGR was as high as 6.6% up until 2013 (Clarkson Research Services Limited 2015b). Analysts predict a CAGR of 6.3% for 2013–2016 (Hartland Shipping Services Ltd 2014), as also seen in Fig. 1.19.

1.6.3.2 The Supply Side

The supply of container tonnage grew even above demand with a CAGR of 7.3% from 2008 to 2013, and is predicted to increase further with a CAGR of 5.3% from 2013 to 2016, based on today's order book (IHS Maritime & Trade 2015). This growth will mainly come from new Panamax and ULCVs, as seen in Fig. 1.20.

After a limited market recovery in 2010, massive contracting was seen in 2011 and again in 2013 and 2014, based on the race between lines for bigger and more energy efficient capacity (IHS Maritime & Trade 2015). Of the new orders, 80–90% relate to vessels above 8,000 TEU, as seen in Fig. 1.21.

Based on 2013 and 2014 contracting, massive deliveries arrived on the market in 2014 and will continue to arrive in 2015 and 2016 (IHS Maritime & Trade 2015). Even if scrapping activities, especially in the Panamax segment, took some capacity out of the market, capacity growth above demand

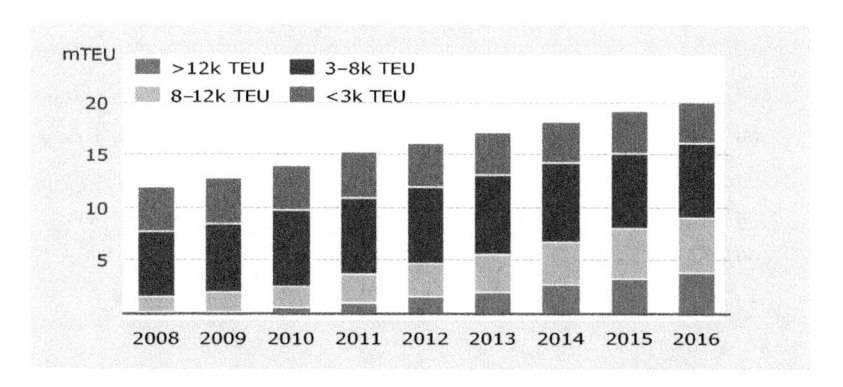

Fig. 1.20 Container vessel fleet development (*Source*: IHS Maritime & Trade)

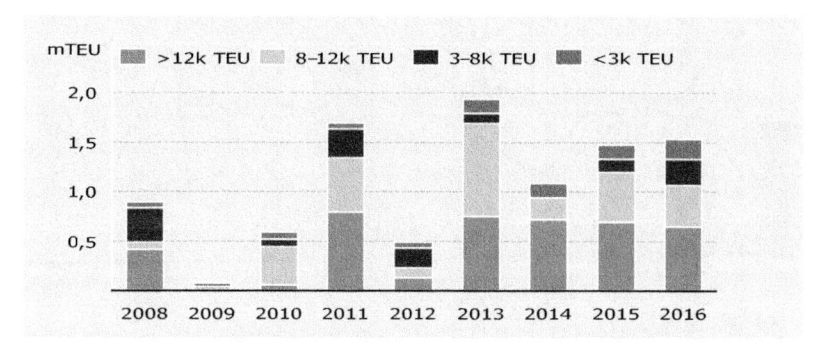

Fig. 1.21 Container vessel (expected) contracting (*Source*: IHS Maritime & Trade)

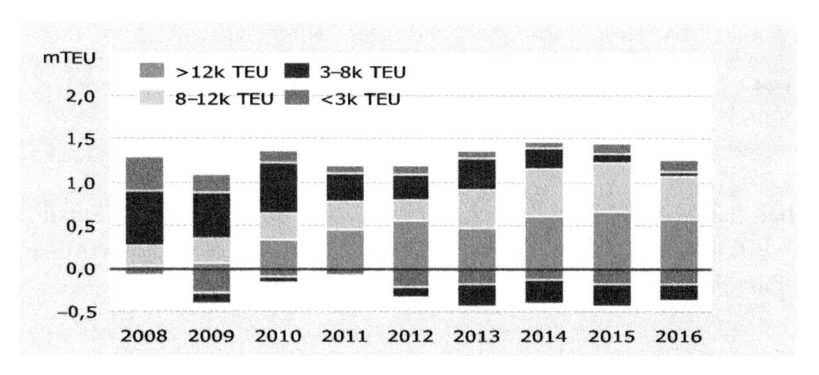

Fig. 1.22 Container vessel (expected) deliveries and removals (*Source*: IHS Maritime & Trade)

growth cannot be hindered, as seen in Fig. 1.22. The average scrapping age has decreased from 30 years in 2007 to 21 years in 2014 (Hartland 2014).

Between 2012 and 2014, we saw an idle (laid-up) container fleet of up to 300 vessels or 0.8 million TEU or 5% of the total. At the end of 2014, the idle

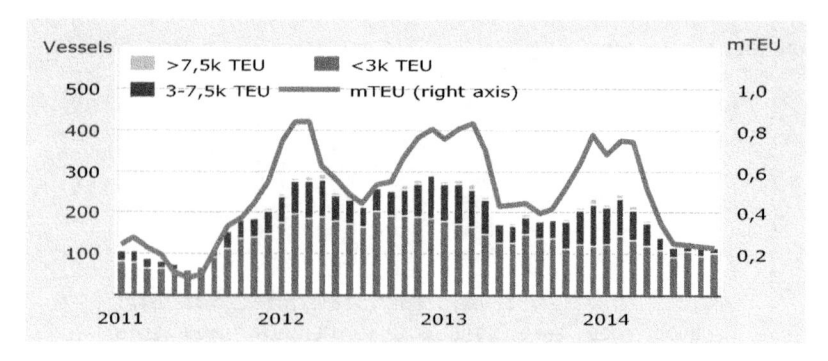

Fig. 1.23 Container vessel idle fleet (*Source*: Alphaliner)

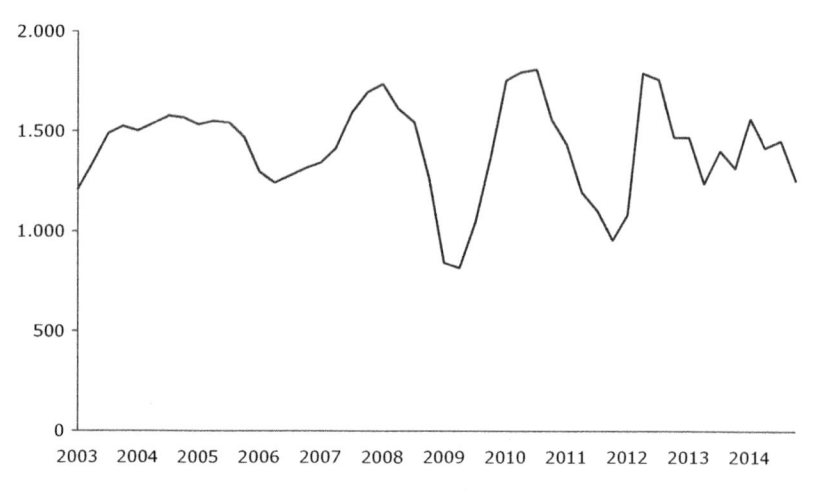

Fig. 1.24 Container freight rate development (CCFI China—Europe) (*Source*: Clarksons)

fleet had reduced to 1.3%, as seen in Fig. 1.23 (Alphaliner 2015). In addition, about 2.0 million TEU are currently absorbed by slow steaming, compared to pre-crisis speed patterns.

1.6.3.3 Earnings

As container shipping is determined by container lines, a first look at earnings needs to form a view on the development of freight rates. The SCFI and the China Containerized Freight Index (CCFI) are the most commonly used indicators of freight rate development, as seen in Fig. 1.24 (Clarkson Research Services Limited 2015b).

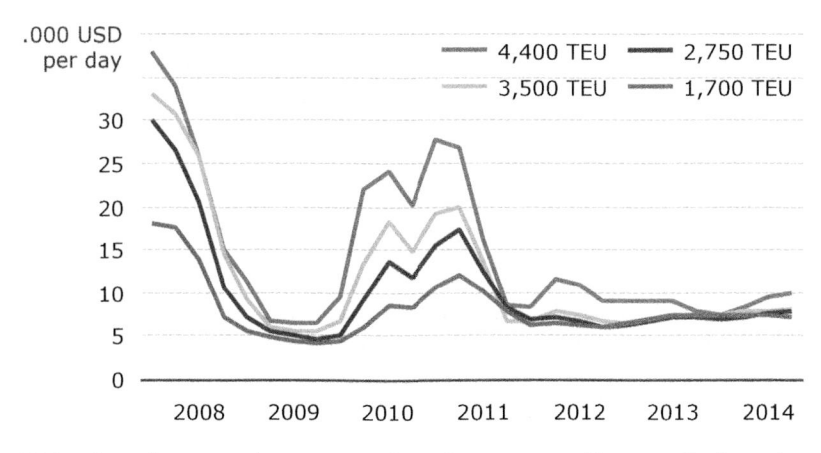

Fig. 1.25 Container vessel, one-year, time charter rates (*Source*: Clarksons)

Looking at the charter rates, various indices can be used: the Howe Robinson Container Index (see Howe Robinson 2014), Harper Petersen's HARPEX, the Container Ship Time Charter Assessment Index (ConTex) and others of lower importance; see Fig. 1.25 (Clarkson Research Services Limited 2015b). Comparing freight and charter rate development, charter rates are much more stable, as they look at longer time horizons and neglect seasonal effects.

1.6.3.4 Prices

As we have seen when looking at dry-bulk and tanker shipping, second-hand as well as newbuilding prices follow charter rates to some degree, with newbuilding prices obviously more stable than the second-hand prices. The price differences between the sub-segments remain fairly stable. Overall, newbuilding prices are about 40% below the 2008 level, a difference significantly smaller than in the other vessel segments. Also, the drop in second-hand prices was a bit more moderate, whereas the number of deals is very limited (76 in the first half year 2014). Many owners (or their banks) didn't seem to be willing to sell at low market prices, as seen in Fig. 1.26 (Clarkson Research Services Limited 2015b).

1.7 The Offshore Market

1.7.1 Structure of the Offshore Market

The offshore market comprises about 10,200 vessels (a 12% share of the total merchant fleet) with a total tonnage of just 50 million GT (a 4% share of the

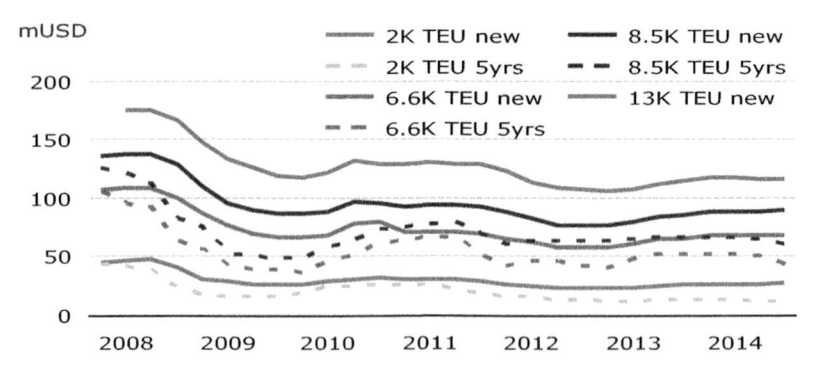

Fig. 1.26 Container vessel newbuilding and secondhand prices (*Source*: Clarksons)

total merchant fleet; Clarkson Research Services Limited 2014). The segment comprises numerous groups of offshore support vessels (OSV) as platform supply vessels (PSV), anchor handling, salvage and transportation tugs, cranes and erection vessels (including semi-submersibles), cable and pipe laying vessels, and all kinds of rigs and other mobile offshore units (MOUs). Overall, the sector is dominated by vessels serving the oil and gas industry. Compared to merchant ships, these vessels are largely fit for their specific purpose, and the liquidity on their markets is usually limited. A very detailed overview on the market is provided, for example, by the *Offshore Intelligence Monthly* report of Clarkson Research Services (Clarkson Research Services Limited 2015a).

1.7.2 Drivers of the Offshore Market

As the segment is dominated by vessels serving the oil and gas industry, the oil price is the single key driver for market development. While in the long run the oil price equals the marginal costs of exploration and production (E&P), it, in turn, determines which oil and gas fields can be explored and brought into production. In times of high oil prices, activities in challenging regions (deep sea, arctic) increase. In times of low oil prices, investments into these projects are reduced or stopped. This is what we currently observe.

The offshore market has been under pressure and is expected to remain oversupplied for at least the next two years. The current overproduction of oil (around 2 mbpd) has its impact on the oil price and hence the whole offshore industry. In addition more drilling vessels will enter this falling market in 2015 and 2016. The drilling contractors have taken the worst hit. Three of the five worst performers in the Standard and Poor's 500 index in 2014 were in fact drilling contractors (DNV GL 2015). As oil companies keep reducing their spending, more field developments are being postponed or cancelled. Due to the current situation, the ordering volumes for offshore units were reduced substantially in 2014; 2015 and 2016 are expected to be even worse. In the light of diminishing profits, rig owners are trying to cut their costs, and scrapping activity has started to increase. As many as 20 units have already been announced to be removed from the market, and we can expect this number to continue to grow (DNV GL 2015). In addition, the cold-stacking of old units has increased in order to remove the excess capacity. The rig utilization rate continues to go down as the gap between supply and demand widens. Many units compete for the same projects, which lead to falling day rates. As the day rates are moving towards break-even levels, fixing activity is also low.

1.7.3 Offshore Market Development

1.7.3.1 The Demand Side

As outlined above, the demand for the majority of offshore vessels is driven by oil and gas exploration and production. Sharp oil price increases from 2006 to 2008, and again from 2010 to 2013, have led to increased offshore activities reflected in E&P CAPEX, as seen in Fig. 1.27. According to Rystad Energy (2015), offshore CAPEX for 2014 have grown by only 4.9%. This year's forecast shows a negative development of 3.5%. Several oil companies have announced significant cuts in their E&P spending in the region of 20–30%. Nevertheless, Rystad expects that the prolonged level of low upstream spending will eventually lead to a lower oil supply and hence higher prices and also increased investments from 2017 to 2018.

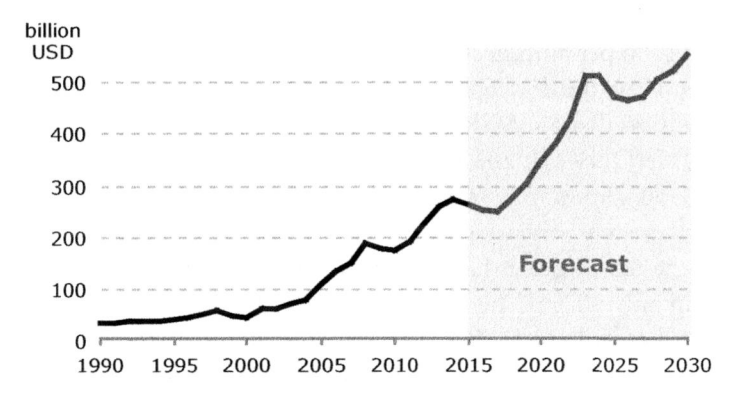

Fig. 1.27 Offshore exploration and production CAPEX (*Source*: Rystad Energy)

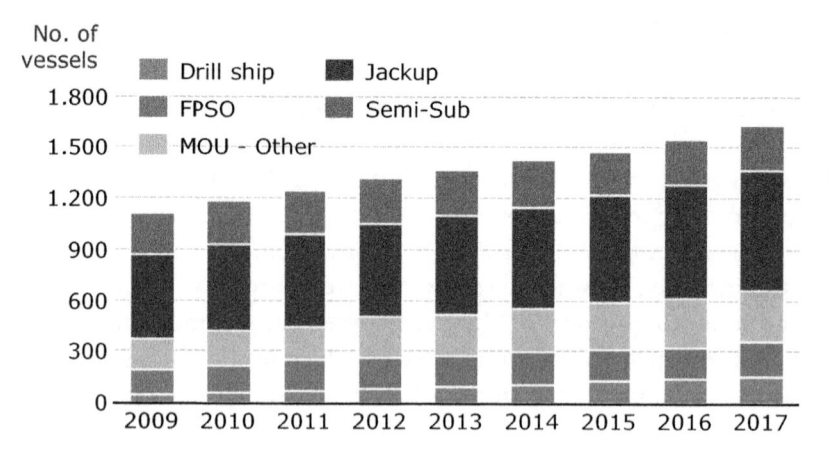

Fig. 1.28 Offshore vessel fleet development (MOU) (*Source*: Clarksons (2008–14, actuals), DNV GL (2015/16 projections))

Utilization rates have been steadily falling for the past year, with jack-up units being less affected compared to the floaters. The current utilization rate hovers around 90%, which is regarded as low.

1.7.3.2 The Supply Side

During recent years, the offshore fleet has grown steadily in number. For MOUs, the CAGR from 2009 to 2014 was 5.2%, with more than 20% annual growth in drill ships (Clarkson Research Services Limited 2015a, b). Assuming that contracted vessels will actually be delivered, this trend is going to continue until 2016/17 (DNV GL 2015); see Fig. 1.28.

Offshore support vessels have shown a similar development recently, with an overall CAGR of 6.2% from 2009 to 2013, with construction vessels growing at 12% per annum (Clarkson Research Services Limited 2015a, b). Figure 1.29 shows the development by vessel type. Known orders have already slowed down, so that a CAGR of about 2% is expected for fleet growth from 2014 to 2017 (DNV GL 2015).

Figure 1.30 shows the (expected) contracting for MOUs and OSVs (Clarkson Research Services Limited 2015a). In 2014, there were only 370 vessels contracted, which is far behind the number registered in recent years, representing only 40% of the volume contracted in 2007, which was a record year in terms of ordering. MOU contracting will probably also be lower in the next year (especially for drilling units). The uncertainty in the market has held back OSV owners from contracting new vessels. They seem to have taken

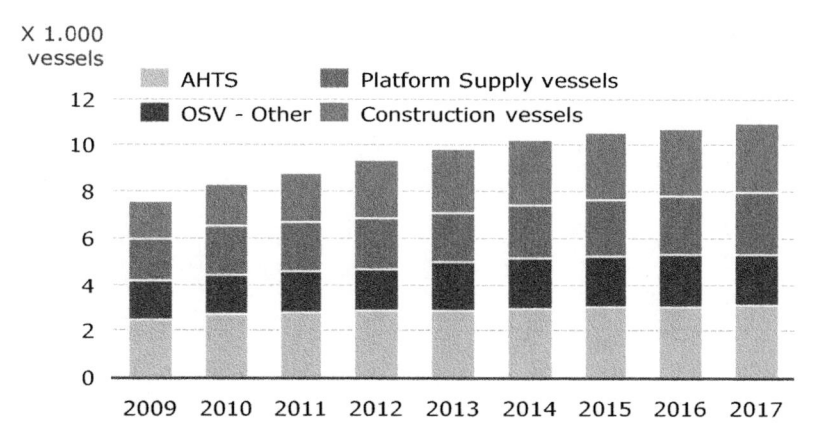

Fig. 1.29 Offshore vessel fleet development (offshore support vessels) (*Source*: Clarksons (2008–14, actuals), DNV GL (2015/16 projections))

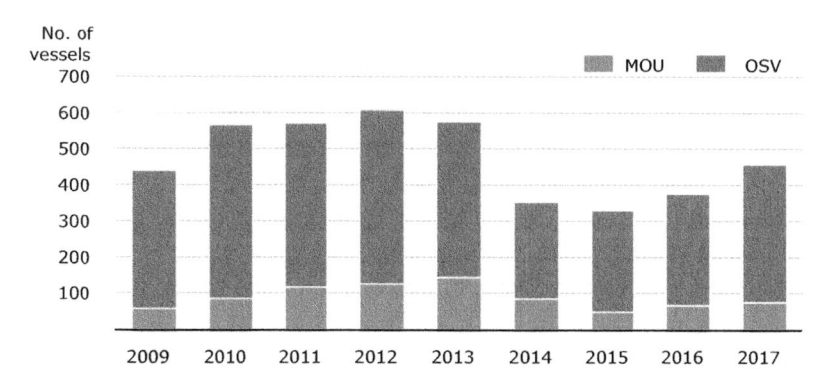

Fig. 1.30 Offshore vessel (expected) contracting (*Source*: Clarksons (2008–14, actuals), DNV GL (2015/16 projections))

a "wait and see" approach. DNV GL expects limited ordering, particularly in the PSV sector as the oversupply increases (DNV GL 2015).

Figure 1.31 displays expected deliveries and removals of OSVs and MOUs. With 550 vessels entering the market in 2014, newbuilding deliveries have been high (Clarkson Research Services Limited 2015a). Another 480 vessels are expected to be delivered in 2015. There will be fewer OSVs, but still a considerable amount of MOUs. As many as 200 drilling units are scheduled for delivery in the coming years, though several are being built on speculation and are likely not to be delivered on time, or even cancelled. Stacking and scrapping continues, as owners have to reduce their cost base.

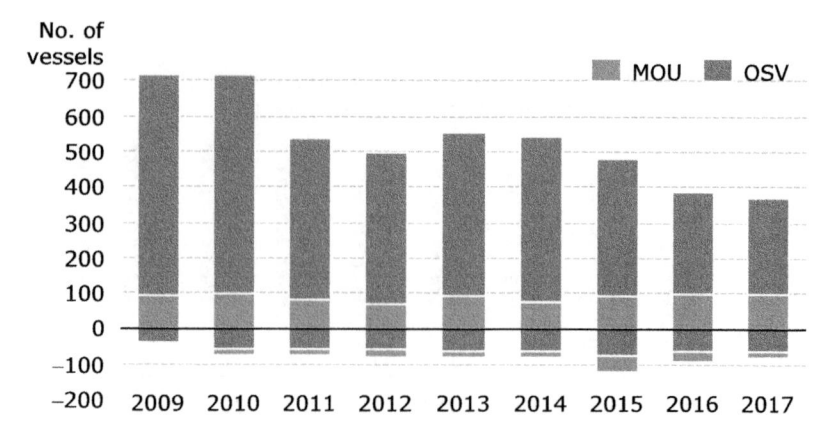

Fig. 1.31 Offshore vessel (expected) deliveries and removals (*Source*: Clarksons (2008–14, actuals), DNV GL (2015/16 projections))

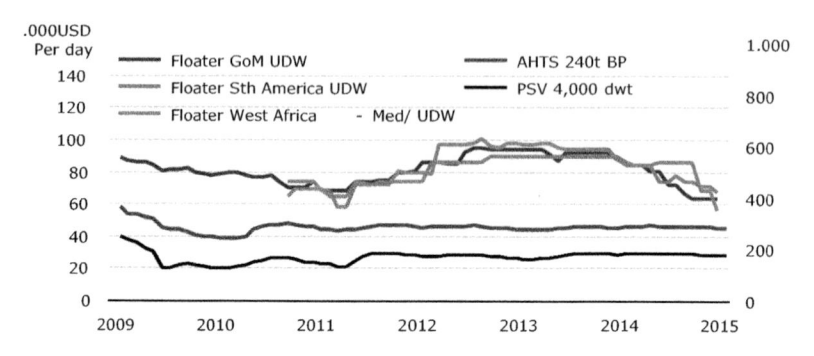

Fig. 1.32 Offshore vessel, one-year, time charter rates (*Source*: Clarksons)

A total of 33 old, uncompetitive and capital intensive floaters have been announced to be scrapped since January 2015. Most of them were semi-sub-drilling units, built in the 1970s. More removals are expected to be announced (DNV GL 2015).

1.7.3.3 Earnings

The earnings in the offshore segment can be expressed in one-year time charter rates (see Fig. 1.32). While OSV (for example anchor handling tugs (AHTs) and PSVs) earnings have been fairly flat since 2011/12, MOUs entirely lost in 2015 the 35% earnings increase they made between 2011 and 2013 (Clarkson Research Services Limited 2015a). Despite high rig availability, fixing activity has remained low, and oil companies have started to renegotiate existing contracts.

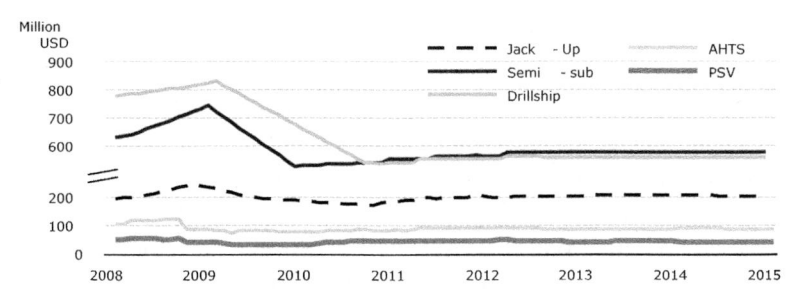

Fig. 1.33 Offshore vessel newbuilding prices (*Source*: Clarksons)

1.7.3.4 Prices

Newbuilding prices of MOUs, especially of drill ships, fell sharply after the financial crisis of 2008 and towards 2010, but have moderately recovered in 2012 and remain fairly stable. Prices of OSVs have been less affected and have remained fairly constant since 2011; see Fig. 1.33 (Clarkson Research Services Limited 2015a, b).

1.8 Summary

In the maritime value chain, shipowners, yards, charterers, cargo owners, freight forwarders, ship managers and brokers constitute various "shipping markets" regarding the vessel itself (newbuilding market, S&P market and demolition market) and the transport service which comes with it. Whereas the development of the world economy is the first driver of demand for shipping, the development of "global GDP" does not provide a valuable approximation for the demand side of shipping markets. Rather the ways regions interact and generate global GDP need to be looked at, resulting in shipping sector specific perspectives. The supply of transport capacity is determined by the existing fleet, newbuildings and scrapping. The laying-up of vessels and the variation of vessel speed offer some flexibility for reacting to supply–demand imbalances. Although shipping enjoys a fairly stable increase of transport demand of about 4% per annum, it regularly suffers from strong cyclicality. The actual challenge lies in the mid-term cycles of about seven years. Low entry barriers (sufficient yard capacity and availability of capital), fragmented markets with well-known leaders and many followers, timing effects (two to three years lead time until delivery, 25 years vessel lifetime) and a cost structure which allows temporary pricing at cash or marginal costs regularly result in shipping crises. The dry-bulk market is driven by coal

(29%, dominated by imports to China and India), iron ore (27%, of which 75% of imports go to China), grain and other agricultural goods (14%) and other minor bulks (30%). The wet-tanker market constitutes crude oil shipments (62%) and chemical product shipments (38%). Gas tankers primarily transport natural gas in the form of LNG and LPG but also numerous specialty gases. The third biggest segment is container shipping which covers all types of goods in small parcel sizes or with high specific value. The majority of them are consumer goods. The Asia to Europe trade route made up 35% of global container miles in 2013, followed by transpacific (29%) and intra-Asia (12%). The offshore segment is driven by oil and gas exploration and production. Ordering, delivery and scrapping follow the crude oil price. Rates are fairly stable for OSVs but have dropped for MOUs since the oil price decline in the first half of 2014.

Bibliography

Alphaliner. (2015). *Alphaliner Monthly Monitor January 2015*. London: Alphaliner.
Clarkson Research Services Limited. (2014). *Shipping Market Overview*. London: Clarkson Research Services Limited.
Clarkson Research Services Limited. (2015a). *Offshore Intelligence Monthly*. London: Clarkson Research Services Limited.
Clarkson Research Services Limited. (2015b, February 7). *Shipping Intelligence Network*. London: Clarkson Research Services Limited.
De la Rubia, C. (2014). Outlook for the world economy. *German Shipping & Ship Finance Conference* (pp. 1–21). Hamburg: Informa.
DNV GL. (2014). *Trend Report 3rd Quarter 2014*. Hamburg: DNV GL SE.
DNV GL. (2015). *Trend Report 4th Quarter 2014*. Hamburg: DNV GL SE.
Fang, I., Cheng, F., Incecik, A., & Carnie, P. (2013). *Global Marine Trends 2030*. London: Lloyd's Register Group Limited.
Frew, J. (2014). The small containership market. *German Ship Finance Conference* (pp. 1–21). Hamburg: Informa.
Hartland Shipping Services Ltd. (2014). Shipping markets outlook. *11th Annual Istanbul Ship Finance Forum* (pp. 1–24). Istanbul: Marine Money.
Hoehlinger, P. (2012). Global and regional flows to 2015. *Global Liner Conference* (pp. 1–12). London: Informa.
Howe Robinson. (2014). *The Containership Market*. London: Howe Robinson.
IHS Maritime & Trade. (2015, February 7). *Maritime World Register of Ships*. Coulsdon, United Kingdom: IHS Global Ltd.
Kim, D. D. (2014). 2015 Global Economy—From the new normal to the end of normal? *KMI's 33rd Annual International Seminar of World Shipping Market Outlook* (pp. 3–39). Seoul: Korea Maritime Institute.

Kounis, N. (2014). 2015 Economic outlook. *Marine Money Greek Ship Finance Forum* (pp. 1–22). Athens: Marine Money.

Lunde, A. (2014). Container charter market 2014–2017. *German Shipping & Ship Finance Conference* (pp. 1–10). Hamburg: Informa.

OECD. (2005). *DSTI/DOT/MTC(2005)5/REV1*. Retrieved from http://people.hofstra.edu/geotrans/eng/ch3en/conc3en/table_containershippingcosts.html

Roger, S., Dufour, G., & Kawachi, N. (2014). Investments and capital in LNG shipping. In L. Paul, *Ship Finance Review 2014/15* (pp. 10–15). Colchester: Euromoney Trading Ltd.

Rystad Energy AS. (2015). *DCUBE (Demand Database)*. Oslo: Rystad Energy AS.

Sand, P. (2014). What can we expect from tankers? *German Ship Finance Conference* (pp. 1–12). Hamburg: Informa.

Stopford, M. (2009). *Maritime Economics*. London: Routledge.

Torp, H. (2014). Shipping and China—Impact on global freight dynamics. *12th Coaltrans China* (pp. 1–15). Shanghai: Euromoney Institutional Investor PLC.

Zhang, Y. (2014). The development trend of Chinese iron ore and steel industry. *KMI's 33rd Annual International Seminar of World Shipping Market Outlook* (pp. 69–79). Seoul: Korea Maritime Institute.

2

Asset Risk Assessment, Analysis and Forecasting in Asset Backed Finance

Henriette Brent-Petersen

2.1 Introduction

In asset backed financing structures, security for repayment of the loan is primarily based on the asset as collateral. The structuring of the financing is therefore heavily dependent on the assessment of the current and future value and liquidity of the asset. This differs from corporate backed funding, where security primarily depends on the credit worthiness of the corporate and, thereby, on the corporate credit evaluation. In asset backed financing, the evaluation and risk assessment of the asset necessarily becomes critical for each financing transaction as well as from a portfolio risk perspective. The value and the liquidity of the asset today and in the future is the central element of the credit evaluation process.

Historically, asset backed financing is mostly known in the public sphere within real estate financing, where investors are spread across the world geographically. They range from small private investors to institutional investors, financial institutions and pension funds, and are not only limited to players within the industry. In a number of other industries, like the shipping industry, financing has historically concentrated within the industry itself—except for the German KG scheme in the 1990s and 2000s, which was dominated

---

H. Brent-Petersen (✉)
DVB Bank SE, WTC Schiphol Tower F 6th Floor, Schiphol Boulevard 255, 1118 BH Schiphol, The Netherlands

© The Author(s) 2016
M.G. Kavussanos, I.D. Visvikis (eds.), *The International Handbook of Shipping Finance*, DOI 10.1057/978-1-137-46546-7_2

by the "German dentists" tax driven investments in German owned container vessels. With this kind of niche sector financing, combined with relatively limited access to funding within the transportation sector, as well as limited speculative investments, there has historically been relatively limited interest from "outside" money to the industry. However, with the international financial crisis in 2008 and with the sudden global excess supply of liquidity looking for a home with a decent return, the cyclicality of the shipping sector suddenly became the center of focus and attention for investors outside the traditional transportation sector, such as private equity (PE) funds and hedge funds. At the time, there was no doubt that the strategy of the PEs and the hedge funds was to make investments in the shipping sector at a historical low point of the cycle, in order to make an exit two to five years down the road, hopefully at the top of the cycle—a strategy representing a significant yield of return in a relatively short period of time. The planned exit was expected either as an initial public offering (IPO), when the market sentiment would price the investment according to the expected improved market sentiment (as a result of the next stage in the cycle of the sector), or as a simple sale/asset sale, when second-hand values would have increased sufficiently. This "IPO strategy"/"asset flip" has not materialized due to the fact that the cyclicality of the shipping and offshore industries has not rebounded to the expected extent.

Some have argued that this extra access to funding for the shipping and offshore industry has led to over-ordering and thereby excess supply of vessels—leading to institutional investors like the PEs and hedge funds being considered as the main reason for the disappearance of the cyclical nature of the shipping industry in itself. But is that really true, or are the institutional investors just using a self-inflicted (by the industry) opportunity in the sector? If it is indeed self-inflicted, why is that so, and why is it important to understand the cyclical nature of the industry when doing asset backed financing and when assessing the asset risk? What is the situation regarding PEs and hedge funds and access to funding within the shipping industry today? Do they really all have the same strategy or have we "landed" with a global map of institutional investors with a broad range of well thought through short as well as long-term strategies? Why is asset backed financing more flexible and perhaps less risky than corporate backed funding in the future global shipping and offshore corporate picture? These are central questions to answer in order to understand and eventually be able to forecast markets and risks within the shipping industry.

Some of the areas of key importance to analyze and address when assessing shipping asset risks today are: the recent cyclical behavior or lack of the same in the shipping industry and the path towards restoration of its typical cyclical nature; the forecasting cyclicality and subsector cyclicality; and the potential changes in the structure of funding within the shipping industry. In this chapter I discuss the overall cyclicality of the shipping and offshore industry with a primary focus on the supply side—the shipyard capacity and future asset prices. Furthermore, I discuss the methodology of forecasting market outlook for the dry-bulk and the container markets, as well as the importance of evaluating the quality of the individual asset and how to mitigate risks.

2.2 Global Demand and China: Cyclicality, Super Cycles, Sector Cycles and Counter-Cyclicality

2.2.1 Global Economic Development and China as the Key Driver of Shipping Sectors

Understanding global economic growth and its drivers (see Chap. 1) is crucial to understand the future landscape of shipping and the demand for tonnage in the respective sectors. However, the global economic growth impact is not always the same on the various sectors. As will be seen later on, the impact of the 2008 financial crisis was immediate on the container shipping sector, due to reduced consumption of goods. However, the impact of the crisis was the complete opposite for the dry-bulk sector, with the crisis leading, amongst other factors, to a stimulation package in China which targeted infrastructure projects that led to strong growth in steel production and imports of iron ore. When studying economic growth in China, it is also important to relate economic policies to the shipping industry and to understand and translate the economic policy as outlined in the five-year plan, and to focus on all the policies targeting the shipping industry, and translate the same into the future trends and drivers of the shipping industry; see Fig. 2.1. It is also central to translate all economic growth ingredients impacting on the commodities traded in the various shipping sectors.

Understanding global energy developments and translating economic and geopolitical developments into global energy related developments, such as US energy independence and global shale resources and developments as well as new refining capacity projects and changes in the oil price, is critical to understand the key drivers of future trade patterns and their changes for the respective tanker and offshore sectors. However, this will not be discussed in this chapter.

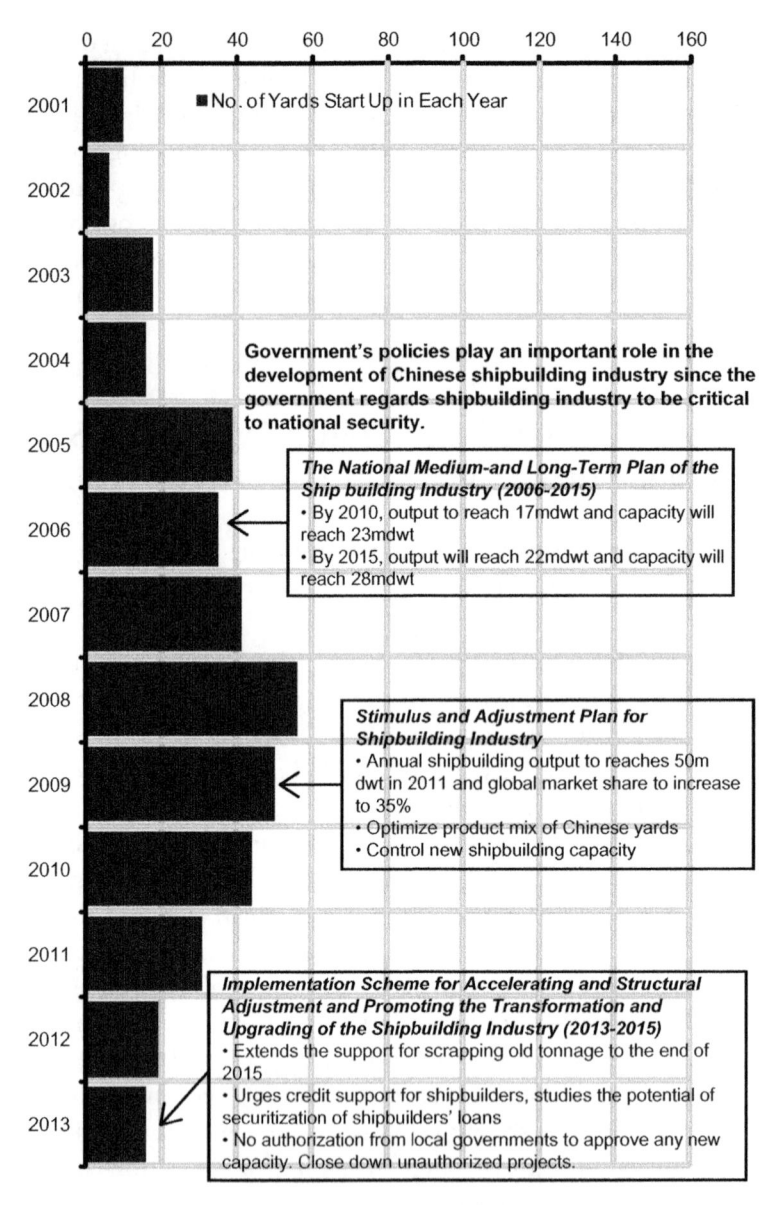

Fig. 2.1 Timeline of shipbuilding related policy in China (*Source*: DVB Shipping Research, Clarksons)

2.2.2 Cyclicality and Variables Affecting Cyclicality: A Political Variable in a Commercial Industry

In cyclical markets, such as the shipping and offshore industries, understanding the overall cyclicality, the respective sector and subsector cyclicality, and

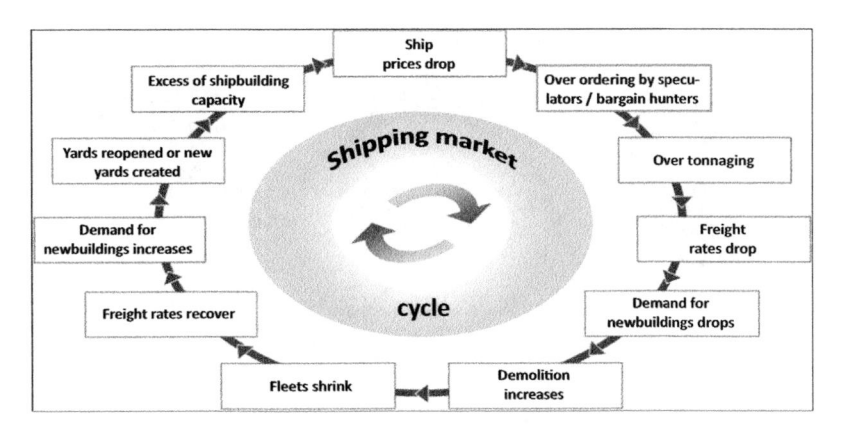

Fig. 2.2 Shipping market cycle (*Source*: DVB Shipping and Offshore Research)

the associated risks and implementation of these in forecasting scenarios is critical. Understanding the history and identifying changes and shocks (expected and non-expected, on a scenario basis) in the industry, as well as in the respective sectors and subsectors, is what enables a good analyst to prepare reliable forecasts for both earnings and asset values, as well as to identify risks in the respective sectors and subsectors.

As can be seen in Fig. 2.2, a "normal" shipping cycle is characterized by developments across the cycle, starting from a low level of newbuilding prices causing massive ordering of new tonnage which eventually, upon delivery, results in excess vessel capacity. With a demand–supply imbalance, with supply growing faster than demand, this leads to a downward pressure on freight rates, which again results in a slowdown in newbuilding orders and an increase in scrapping of old tonnage. This, in turn, brings about an improved demand–supply balance, driven by a slowdown in supply growth. As a consequence, a recovery in freight rates occurs, which again induces increases in demand for newbuildings, subsequently increasing investment in shipyard capacity, thus putting downward pressure on newbuilding prices. When orders resume, an upward pressure on newbuilding prices follows. In this way, the cyclicality is commercially held in check. However, due to the fact that shipyard capacity has always been a politically dominated variable in the equation, which has been true for all major shipbuilding countries including Japan, Korea and China, this has led to a market that has not stabilized newbuilding prices according to a commercial demand–supply balance.

So why, for commercial shipyards, has a capacity-demand equilibrium not materialized over time? Why are we further from an equilibrium than ever before, and what are the consequences? During the last decade, global shipbuilding output has experienced a super cycle with total output increas-

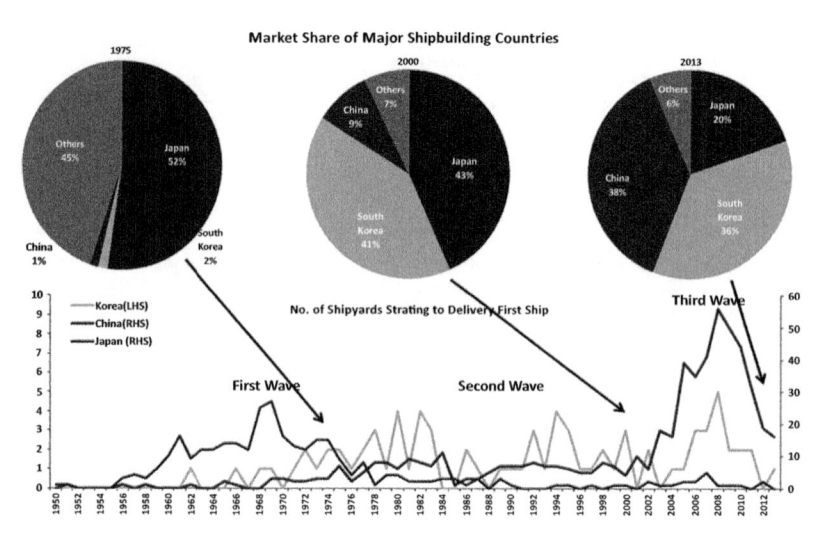

Fig. 2.3 Shipbuilding countries market share and shipyard start-ups by major shipbuilding country (*Source*: DVB Shipping and Offshore Research)

ing from only 18.3 million compensated gross tonnage (CGT) in 2001 to the historical peak of 52.6 million CGT in 2010, representing a compound annual growth rate (CAGR) of 12.5% over this period.[1] When going back even further in the history of global shipbuilding capacity, a significant build-up of shipyard capacity is evident, which has been driven by the development of three major shipbuilding countries from the 1970s until today, following the "flying geese paradigm" that was part of the economic development of East Asian countries, as described by Kaname Akamatsu.[2]

With the surge of the Japanese economy in the 1970s, the center of the global shipbuilding industry started to move east to Japan, where in 1975 it accounted for 52% of total global shipbuilding production (Fig. 2.3). As one of the "Four Asian Tigers", South Korea started to emerge as a fast growing economy in the 1980s and, following the path of the Japanese shipbuilding industry, South Korean yards continued increasing their market share which accounted for almost 30% of the global shipbuilding output by the beginning of 2000. Since then, the center of the global shipbuilding industry shifted again and continued to move westbound to China, which followed up the growth model of the East Asian economies, with its market share of the global shipbuilding industry increasing from only 7% in 2000 to approximately 38% in 2013, thereby reaching its political ambition as per its then five-year plan of becoming the world's largest shipbuilding nation.

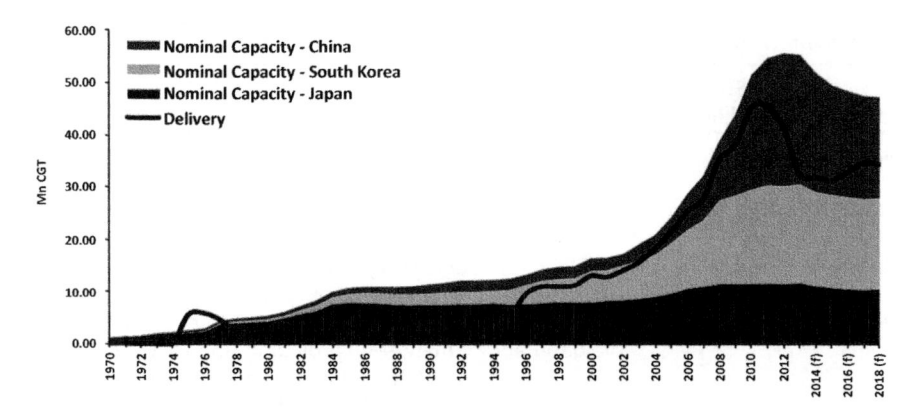

2 Asset Risk Assessment, Analysis and Forecasting in Asset Backed...

Fig. 2.4 Shipbuilding capacity (*Source*: DVB Shipping and Offshore Research)

As can be seen in Fig. 2.4, Chinese shipbuilding capacity has experienced the strongest growth over the last decade—during the peak in 2008, more than 50 Chinese yards started to deliver their first vessel. The trend after 2008 has been a decline in the opening of new shipyards and, in 2013, less than 20 delivered their first vessel.

However, market conditions in 2015 put significant and increasing pressure on Chinese yards, especially small, privately owned ones. The initiated decrease in Chinese shipbuilding capacity is expected to continue, although at a modest pace and not sufficiently to lead to a commercially viable supply–demand balance in global shipbuilding capacity. This is due to the government's policies playing an important role in the development of its shipbuilding industry, since the government considers the industry to be critical to national security. First of all, the booming shipping market before 2008 was the main driver for the industry. Policies from the central government also boosted the surge. In the meantime, local governments were motivated to encourage new shipbuilding capacity (some even contrary to guidance from the central government) in order to take advantage of the tax-sharing system. Besides overcapacity concerns, and as a result of overcapacity and, consequently, the lack of a sufficient order book coverage, the industry is experiencing serious liquidity constraints. This is due to the lack of down payments for new orders placed and a lack of shipyard utilization, amongst other things. In order to protect its strong ambition to maintain and protect China's long-term market share within the global shipbuilding and offshore industry, the government is channeling new orders toward its state owned shipyards and encouraging consolidation. In the meantime, CEXIM (Chinese Export Import Bank) also supports orders at domestic shipyards by providing loans to foreign owners.

Policy Bank Supports Shipowners Ordering in State Owned Shipyards

Date	USD (millions)	Shipyard/group	Comments
May 2013	146	CSSC	CEXIM provides Angelicoussis Group with secured loan facility for three VLCCs
May 2013	30	CSSC	CEXIM provides Diana Shipping with loan for two bulkers
May 2013			CEXIM signed strategic cooperation with Dynagas to build LNG carriers in China
Aug 2013	312	Shanghai Waigaoqiao/ CSSC	CEXIM supports CSSC to move into VLCS market by providing finance to three 16,000 TEU containers, to be chartered out to CMA CGM

Note: *CSSC* China State Shipbuilding Corporation, *CMA CGM* Compagnie Maritime d'Affrètement Compagnie Générale Maritime

The government has published a "white list" of 51 shipyards which "qualify" for further policy support, such as export tax rebates and bank credit.[3] The shipyards benefiting the most from the government's visible supportive hand are the state owned ones; this is to fulfill the government's ambition to secure their survival and to support consolidation in the industry. It is also important to note that these 51 yards account for the majority of the Chinese shipbuilding capacity, which is expected to continue as it is.

Korea's "Big Three" (i.e. Hyundai Heavy Industries, Samsung Heavy Industries and Daewoo) historically have grown to today's leading positions with strong support from the Korean government, and are now considered guarded from closure in the short to medium term. This is because their respective order books are dominated by high value offshore units, containerships and gas carriers. However, other medium-sized Korean yards also face deleveraging pressure, mainly due to their order book focus on conventional merchant ships, such as bulkers and tankers.

Japan's shipbuilding capacity is not expected to see significant reduction due to its relatively good capacity management. Japanese yards are also benefiting from "Abenomics"[4] (i.e. the yen's depreciation and a wave of new orders from non-domestic owners).[5] Except for bulk carriers, which are mainly from domestic orders, the product mix of Japanese yards focuses on LNG carriers, chemical tankers and LPG carriers, which require technical "know-how" to build.

All in all, this big, global, idle, "hidden" shipyard capacity is not expected to disappear completely, will continuously put pressure on newbuilding prices and may have a "flooding" risk to the shipping markets (i.e. it is important to consider the substitution risk amongst shipping and offshore sectors).

This flooding effect is not expected to have the same impact on all shipping sectors. In Fig. 2.5, the historical variation in lead time by ship types

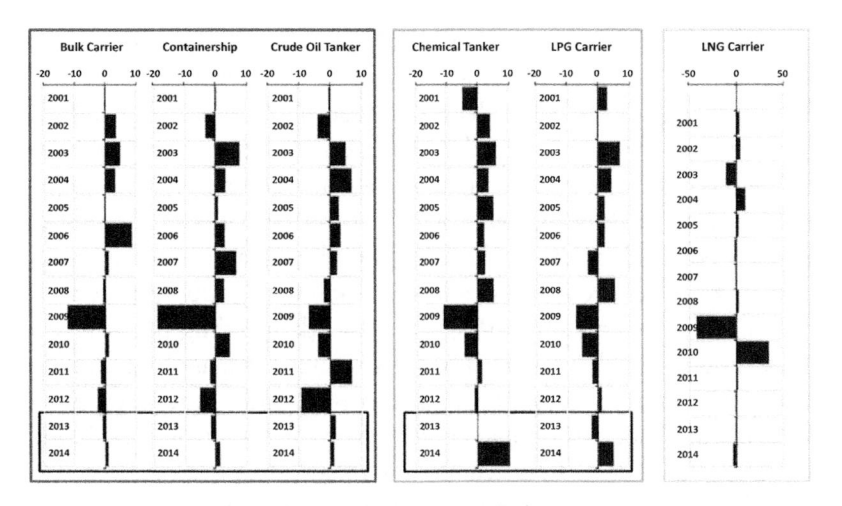

2 Asset Risk Assessment, Analysis and Forecasting in Asset Backed... 49

Fig. 2.5 Flooding effect across segments (*Source*: DVB Bank Shipping and Offshore Research)

is illustrated. The figure shows the difference in lead time from year to year, with "lead time" defined as the time between the contracting date and the delivery date (i.e. the order book period coverage). With small annual changes in lead time, the shipbuilding market is supply driven (i.e. there is plenty of shipbuilding capacity to satisfy the demand when it picks up). With big changes in lead time, shipbuilding capacity for a specific segment is scarcer. Bulk carriers, containerships and crude oil tankers are vulnerable to this flooding effect, as Fig. 2.5 shows, as lead time responds less to contracting. This is due to the supply of these slots, which is overwhelmingly larger than demand. Chemical tankers and LPG carriers remain relatively immune to the limited number of slots available; as the graph shows, lead time responds more to contracting activities, because building these types of vessels requires specific experience, which is only available to certain shipyards. Hence, the supply is a constraint. The building capacity of LNG carriers is ample (dominant by Korean yards), which means that the supply side can easily be adjusted according to demand. However, we still expect a cap in available LNG carrier slots as yards will need to balance between other high value added ship types. This means that chemical tankers and LPG carriers are relatively better protected by excess yard capacity. However, under the current situation with excess liquidity and excess shipyard capacity, no sector is safe forever. Once a certain sector becomes a "buzzword" for the market, it is inevitable that an over-ordering in this sector will be seen—as shipyards move up the value chain, the flooding effect will make a stronger impact, including on the more lucrative segments.

So, what about offshore? Has offshore been relatively safe from this flooding effect? The answer here does not seem to be very optimistic either. China has been moving up the value chain by securing an increasing market share of the more lucrative orders in the offshore industry during high markets, up to the second half of 2014, thereby allowing some relief of the pressure to secure orders in shipping sectors. As can be seen in Fig. 2.6, China has already started to enter the offshore shipbuilding market, initially from the lower end of the value chain (i.e. anchor handling tug supply vessels (AHTs) and platform supply vessels (PSVs)). With yards speeding up their learning curves, Chinese yards have also started to take market shares in building jack-ups and semi-subs from Singaporean and Korean yards—they have moved up the value chain. Also, part of their current five-year plan includes shipbuilding as one of nine core industries, which now targets quality, as discussed above. The drillship market is still dominated by the Korean yards, though Chinese yards have also started entering the construction market, as shown in Fig. 2.6.

As can be seen in Fig. 2.7, global excess shipyard capacity is putting significant pressure on lead time. The average time to delivery at the time when the order was contracted has decreased across segments from the good times up to 2008, when shipowners had to wait up to 50 months to get their vessels delivered. Today, delivery in most segments can take place within 24 months.

During the boom period (2004–08), the utilization rate of Chinese shipyards had increased from about 75% in 2004 to 85% in 2010 with the strongest growth in the period 2004–2008, as illustrated in Fig. 2.8. This shows that Chinese shipyards were trying their best to deliver the ship as soon as possible and, due to the tight production arrangements, lead time inevitably increased. However, the utilization rate has significantly reduced: to 75% in 2013. This shows that yards have (intentionally or unintentionally, which usually comes from the request of shipowners to postpone delivery) slowed down their production processes. On one hand, it is good for shipyards to keep their production line running, since, once it stops, it is very difficult

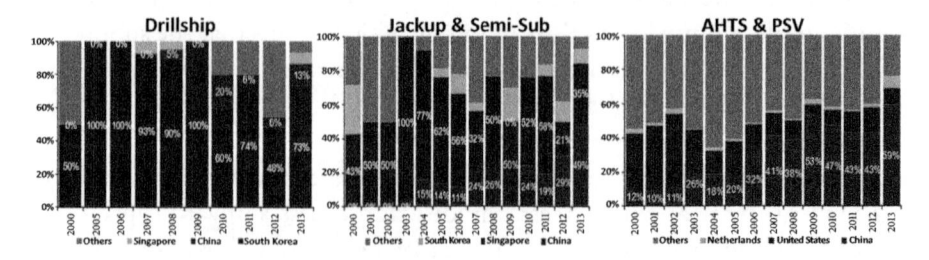

Fig. 2.6 China gaining market share with more lucrative orders (*Source*: DVB Bank Shipping and Offshore Research)

2 Asset Risk Assessment, Analysis and Forecasting in Asset Backed... 51

to restart. On the other hand, this causes a vicious cycle of overcapacity and further dampens the yards' cash flow.

During this process, small privately owned Chinese shipyards are expected to suffer the most, with almost 75% of their capacity likely to disappear. Together with other types of Chinese yards, it can be argued that approximately 25% of the total nominal Chinese shipbuilding capacity is expected to disappear from 2014 to 2016. Another 10% of total nominal capacity is expected to face tremendous pressure, and its survival will depend on market conditions and the government's policies. As a result, total nominal Chinese shipbuilding capacity is expected to reduce to close to the level seen in 2010

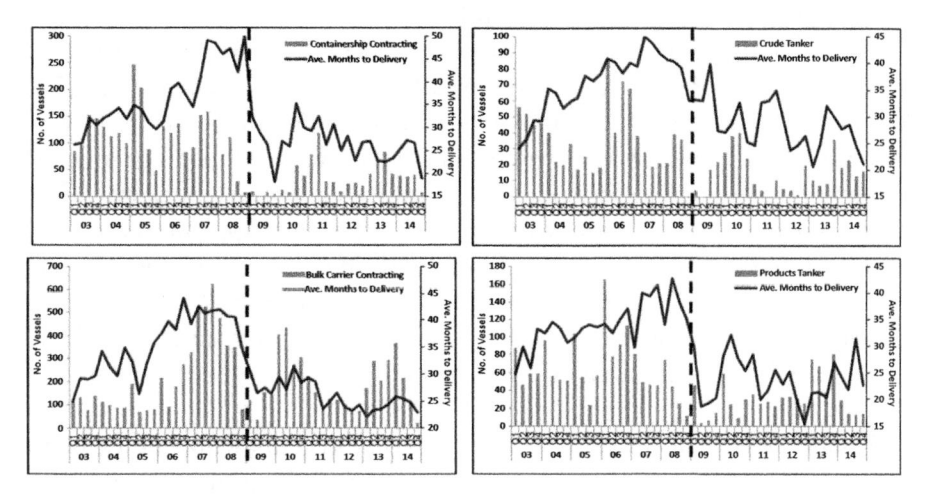

Fig. 2.7 Average time to delivery at contracting time (*Source*: DVB Bank Shipping and Offshore Research)

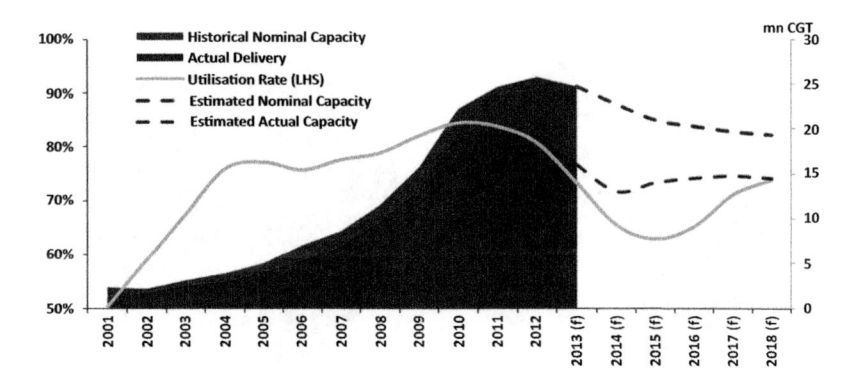

Fig. 2.8 Chinese shipyard capacity utilization rate and estimated capacity (*Source*: DVB Bank Shipping and Offshore Research)

(in terms of CGT). Another important factor is the utilization rate of shipyard capacity, which, if it is factored in and remains at its current level (75%), actual Chinese shipyard capacity might reduce to almost half of its peak by 2018 (see Fig. 2.8).

Together with the "deleveraging" process, the market structure of the Chinese shipbuilding industry is also expected to change with the rise of state owned shipyards—it is expected that this capacity share will increase from 40% in 2013 to 50% in 2018 (see Fig. 2.9). During the same period, it is expected that for small privately owned shipyards the capacity share will decrease from 20% in 2013 to 10% in 2018. This is in line with the government's intention to consolidate the industry.

Newbuilding prices for major ship types are expected to remain subdued for some years more, due to excess shipyard capacity. The "hidden" shipbuilding capacity may flood the market when newbuilding prices start to face an upward pressure, thereby keeping prices in check. Not until the shipyard deleveraging process reaches its end, can a sustainable recovery of newbuilding prices be expected. In the meantime, this inelasticity of supply in certain sectors might provide a sufficient condition for seeing some sustainable recovery in them. With the demand side of these sectors eventually showing positive developments, asset values, including newbuilding prices and secondhand prices, are slowly bottoming out, which could potentially lead to the start of a new cycle.

Under the current situation with excess liquidity and excess yard capacity, the supply side can easily be changed and may work against any potential recovery. Thus, owners tend to choose good shipyards, which can deliver good quality assets, so as to compete with the threat of increasing ordering activity.

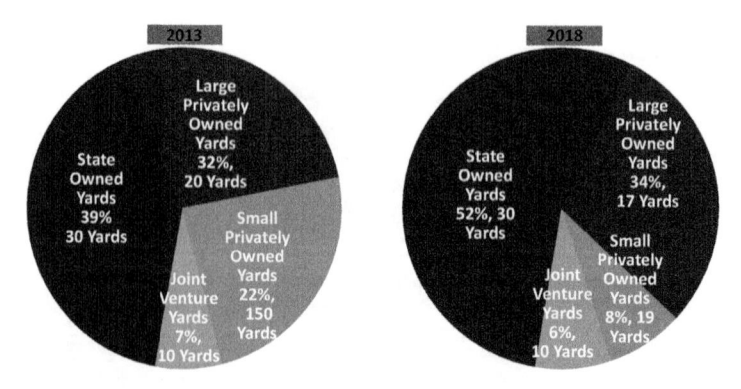

Fig. 2.9 Forecasted structure of the Chinese shipbuilding industry (*Source*: DVB Bank Shipping and Offshore Research)

As a result, a two-tier market in the shipbuilding industry is expected to continue, where owners prefer top tier yards, and second tier yards offer lower prices to attract new business.

2.3 The Shipping Sector Market Outlook

It is imperative to understand the overall cyclicality of the shipping and offshore industry, as discussed later in this chapter. Having mapped out the bird's-eye view of the overall shipping and offshore supply-side cyclicality, it is equally important to understand the cyclicalities of the respective sectors as well as the short-term volatility and seasonality. In this part of the chapter, a review and different methodologies as well as key challenges for some of the shipping sectors are discussed.

2.3.1 The Container Shipping Sector

When looking at the current overall demand and supply growths of the container market, the numbers seem very similar to the dry-bulk market (i.e. supply growing slightly more than demand in both 2015 and 2016). So, why is the container market and its forecasts so different from the dry-bulk market, which has been facing significant and growing challenges for at least two more years, in contrast to the container market, which has been in a slow stable recovery mode? In the container industry, there has historically been a rule of thumb that global growth in tonnage demand is equal to global GDP growth, multiplied by a factor of around 2.5, and that this can be translated further down to a country's containerized imports, equal to 2.5 times the GDP growth of the country. This may have been the case many years ago, but this has definitely not been the case for at least the last 15 years.[6, 7] The container market is liner traffic, so increases in trade in one direction, the strong trade leg, which is not matched by the same increase in the reverse direction, will automatically lead to growing imbalanced trade. This ultimately leads to a stronger tonnage demand growth than the growth in actual transported TEU. This was increasingly the case in the years up to 2008 when China was perceived as the factory of the Western world, where the annual US and eurozone foreign direct investments (FDI) in China stood at double-digit growth rates.[8] These strong FDIs in manufacturing plants in China eventually led to increasing exports with goods destined for the USA and eurozone markets. Eventually, this FDI driven increase in exports led to an increase in trade requiring containerized transport of the final goods and thereby representing one of the strongest growth drivers of containerized trade in the years 2000–2008. In this period, China was experiencing annual GDP growth rates between 8.3 and 14.2%, but was "only" experiencing average annual growth in imports of containerized trade/transported TEU of 9%. Thus, the rule of thumb of GDP growth multiplied by a factor of 2.5, that should lead to the import growth in transported TEU, may, to some extent, have been correct for the USA and the eurozone but not for China in the years 2000–2008, and so it no longer holds for the total global containerized trade.

After 2008, the increases in imbalanced containerized trade came to a halt with the financial crisis, leading to a sharp decrease in US and eurozone consumption of containerized imports. Various fiscal stimulus packages targeting US and eurozone economic growth and consumption only had temporary and limited/short-lived effect; the eurozone in particular is still struggling on the path to economic recovery (see Chap. 1).[9] At the same time, China put further emphasis on its, at the time, 11th five-year plan, targeting a stronger transformation of the economy from an export driven one towards a more domestic consumption driven one. This was implemented through various monetary measures, including its CNY4 trillion fiscal stimulus package of September 2008, as well as through the implementation of structural reforms. All in all, developments are leading to increasing growth in regional trade, especially intra-Asia, and decreasing trade growth in the previous long haul driver routes of Asia to the USA and Asia to the eurozone. With an increasing US and eurozone unemployment rate from 2008 onwards, the flexibility of the labor market, together with increasing production costs in China and a renminbi which has appreciated 30% against the US dollar since 2005, has led to a developing trend of production moving closer to the end consumer in the USA and the eurozone. While the USA turns increasingly competitive, the story is not simply one of manufacturing returning back to the home country. Mexico's strong manufacturing base and its proximity to the USA make it highly attractive, though in some segments of the supply chain, China will remain competitive. The AlixPartners Manufacturing-Sourcing Cost Index analyzes a variety of manufactured products and compares the cost of producing them in various low-cost countries and transporting them to the USA. It can be seen in Fig. 2.10 that it is increasingly costly to source goods from China for the end-consumer in the USA.

When looking at the longer-term mega-trends and game changers for the industry it is also important to understand global innovation cycles and which innovations can potentially impact on the transport of goods and especially the transport of container goods. Technological innovations like 3D and 4D

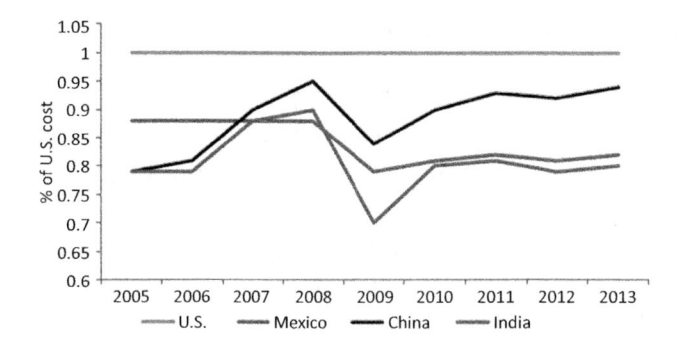

Fig. 2.10 Manufacturing-Sourcing Cost Index: total landed costs (*Source*: AlixPartners, DVB Shipping and Offshore Research)
Note: The AlixPartners Manufacturing-Sourcing Cost Index analyzes a variety of manufactured products and compares the cost of building them in various low-cost countries and transporting them to the USA. It includes labor costs, transportation costs, raw-materials costs, inventory costs, capital-equipment costs, overhead costs, duties and exchange rates

printing is expected to have a significant impact on the longer-term future container trade. One could argue that the world is getting bigger again.

However, one could also counter-argue that new trade agreements and expansions of existing ones continuously come to the drawing board, such as the expanding trade agreement/relations between the eurozone and the USA, which eventually will lead to increases in trade distances. Furthermore, when studying future mega-trends, demographic developments, improving workers skills and labor shortages leading to migration, will eventually develop into a more dynamic economic and open trade environment and put pressure on reversing the trend of regionalism.[10]

So, one could also argue that the world is getting smaller. When forecasting future containerized trade, it is essential to understand the mega-trends, the history and the changing global trade patterns and to implement these changes (the increasing imbalances, driven by Asia to US and Asia to eurozone trade up until 2008, then an increasingly balanced trade thereafter). It is important to be able to implement all trends on the future map of global containerized trade. Furthermore, in order to capture the shorter term dynamics and ongoing change in trends, it is essential to understand and model the relation between the development of growth in transported TEU in relation to GDP growth, on a country-by-country basis and over time, in order to translate this development into a reliable forecast and most importantly to capture the changing trends over time.

Having mapped the history and modeled the future expected containerized trade from a country-by-country perspective, with a dynamic multiplier taking into consideration historical developments in transported TEU in relation to GDP and shocks, it is possible to aggregate this into a global total of an expected CAGR of 8.1% in transported TEU for 2015–19.[11] Thereafter, distances and changes in imbalanced trade and increase/decrease in empty container traffic can be taken into account toward the goal of estimating total demand for container tonnage. Before reaching a final conclusion, the average speed of the floating container fleet and its expected changes need to be applied, as well as estimations of expected congestion and changes of these variables—such as the estimated impact of the low oil price and its future changes on the future average speed of the fleet. The bunker price is typically hedged for some time but, with a consistent change of the oil price, will it eventually lead to a change in the speed of vessels? Finally, and perhaps most importantly, with the over-ordering of ULCCs and following an increase in the average size of vessels at a pace not seen before (during 2010–18), the cascading pressure and low utilization of VLCSs will have a significant cascading pressure on the container subsectors. Having taken into account all these variables, an expected CAGR of 8.9% in total demand for 2015–19 for container tonnage can be concluded.[12]

Having mapped and forecasted the demand side of the equation to such a detailed level that allows for building future scenarios as well as determining the specific need for various container-vessel sizes, it is time to investigate the supply side, which, by nature, is far simpler. In the first part of this chapter we studied the cyclicality of shipyards and argued that, due to excess shipyard capacity, the lead time is historically relatively short, with less than 20 months in 2015. That is, ordering a container vessel in the conditions prevailing in 2015—irrespective of size—resulted in a vessel delivery time of no longer than two years. When forecasting container supply growth, it is not only important to look at the existing order book, but also to forecast the expected future contracting activity and its deliveries (i.e. implementing the cyclicality of new orders placed in the forecasting of future deliveries). Furthermore, it is important to study the age profile of the total fleet and its specific subsectors in order to forecast the future scrapping activity. The container fleet in 2015 has an average age of 10.7 years, but there are no vessels larger than 10,000 TEU and which are less than five years old. In the handy segment of 1,000–1,999 TEU, 43.6% of the vessels are more than 15 years old, and in the Sub-Panamax segment of 2,000–2,999 TEU, 25.9% of the vessels are more than 15 years old, while the order books in the respective segments are respectively 7.7% and 11.7% of the fleet.[13] This in turn means that scrapping activity will materialize in the segments with the least orders for delivery. When applying a future contracting scenario with a forecasted delivery schedule as well as a future scrapping scenario, we can calculate the

2 Asset Risk Assessment, Analysis and Forecasting in Asset Backed...

future expected fleet growth of CAGR to be 5.8% for 2015–19, with the fleet growing by 8.1% in 2015.[14]

When studying the order book, most of the orders are concentrated in the very large segments of Super Post Panamax (SPPx) and very large container ship (VLCS) subsectors, which has resulted in a rapid increase in average sizes for newbuilding deliveries. Larger capacity vessels are a double-edged sword. They offer better economies of scale to owners on an individual basis but, if the majority of shipowners are able to own such vessels, the industry will suffer from chronic overcapacity. However, due to the economies of scale, the larger vessels can operate at a lower utilization rate and therefore "hide" capacity in the overall container market capacity. Such a situation would not put pressure on the overall container market to the extent that it would if the total amount of TEU in the order book had been evenly spread out across segments.

Forecasting in today's container market is therefore more complicated than just comparing the demand with supply growth, because there is a strong mismatch between the size of the vessels being delivered and where the current demand growth is concentrated. Furthermore, one could also argue that a large share of the VLCSs are ordered more for competitive reasons and are not justified by the actual demand. These vessels will therefore not put pressure on the current market because they can operate at lower utilization levels during their first years of employment. However, these larger vessels, already delivered and those that will be delivered, are putting significant pressure on the smaller vessels—the cascading process.

As can be seen from Figs. 2.11 and 2.12, newbuilt VLCSs which were delivered between December 2013 and December 2014 are being deployed

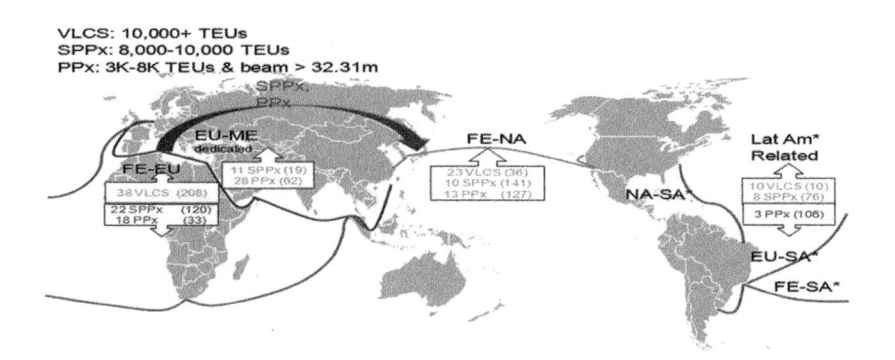

Fig. 2.11 Cascading of larger capacity vessels (December 2013–December 2014) (*Source*: DVB Shipping and Offshore Research)
Note: The number of vessels entering are in green and exiting are in red for each route; the total number of vessels deployed on the route are in parentheses

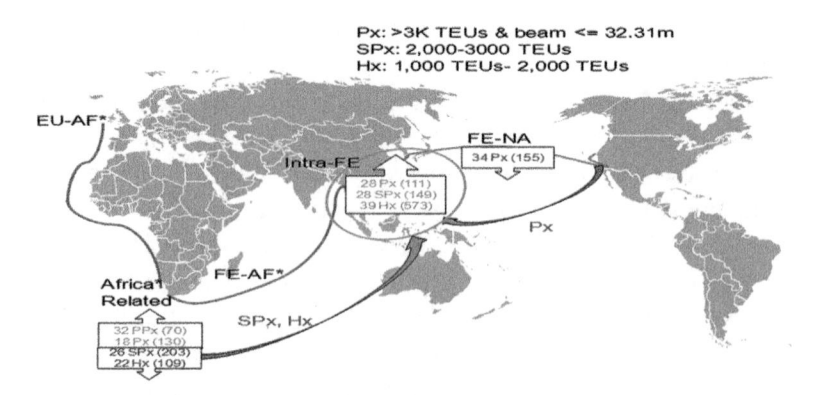

Fig. 2.12 Cascading of smaller capacity vessels (December 2013–December 2014) (*Source*: DVB Shipping and Offshore Research)
Note: The number of vessels entering are in green and exiting are in red for each route; the total number of vessels deployed on the route are in parentheses

on all possible long haul routes including the Far East to South America. SPPxs, once the primary workhorse in the Asia to Europe route, are now being employed in relatively short haul trades, such as the eurozone to the Middle East and the Far East to the Middle East. Similarly, the presence of Post Panamax (PPx) vessels in long haul routes is decreasing at a steady rate. The destinations for displaced Panamax (Px) include Intra-Asia and Africa related trades. Sub-Panamax (SPx) and Handymax (Hx) are still in heavy use in Intra-Asia. In order to understand the demand for the various subsectors, it is thus important to understand the cascading and the pace at which it is happening with the massive influx of new VLCSs. In addition, it is important to understand and study the fast development/expansion of ports, which enables them to cater for larger and larger vessels at an increasing pace, thereby putting pressure on the smaller container sectors. The need for replacement of tonnage when vessels are scrapped is not one-to-one because of decreasing demand. That is, a lot of scrapping potential in a segment with a small order book does not necessarily mean a market opportunity.

Comparing the development in overall container tonnage demand growth with the development in the overall container tonnage supply growth, we get the utilization rate development[15] index (for 1996), which has a strong correlation to the container time-charter market, as can be seen in Fig. 2.13.

When evaluating the drivers and trends in the container market, it is important to determine the variables in this sector that affect demand and supply. On the demand side, the changing global trade patterns and their drivers need to be considered, as well as the short, medium and long-term trends and speed, cascading and congestion. On the supply side, the overall

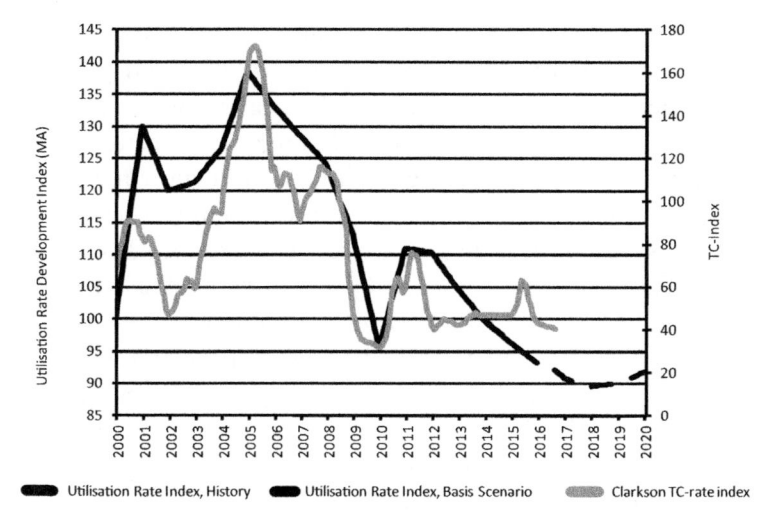

Fig. 2.13 Container market outlook: trend indicator (*Source*: Own modeling (moving average of the development in the utilization rate indexed with 1996 = 100))

structure of the container market is leading to ordering that is driven by economies of scale. This again has been leading to an imbalanced order book in relation to the demand growth, which is ultimately leading to significant cascading pressure across the industry. During the cascading process, some of the smaller subsectors will experience significant volatility of what seems to be a temporary rebound, but which is ultimately the cascading process on the path towards the "end game", where some of the smaller subsectors will change from being a key container segment to a niche player segment.

2.3.2 The Dry–Bulk Shipping Sector

When studying the dry-bulk market and comparing this sector to the container sector, the challenges are very different, as seen from a commercial perspective, but yet relatively similar from a methodological forecasting analysis perspective. When analyzing the demand side of the dry-bulk sector, there are four major commodities to understand. First, iron ore and coal are the two most important cargos for the dry-bulk market. For steel production, iron ore and coking coal are the most important ingredients, and steel is used in construction as well as in manufacturing processes across the world. Second, thermal coal is used in power generation. Third, grain cargo is highly dependent on population growth, finding use as a feedstock and for human consumption, though traded more regionally due to its perishable nature. Therefore, it cannot be considered either as a driver of total dry-bulk tonnage demand or a determinant of changes in trade distances, which are rather constant over time. Finally, part of the dry-bulk cargo also constitutes the minor bulk commodities,[16] which are correlated to industrial growth via their use in construction, the automobile industry and infrastructure development.

During 2014, seaborne trade of iron ore accounted for 31.5% of the total dry-bulk trade, coal accounted for 28.7%, grains for 10.1% and minor bulks for 29.7%.[17] However, the key growth driver amongst the dry-bulk commodities, for the last decade, has been iron ore imports into China for steel production. The continuous focus on developing the Chinese infrastructure and urbanization during the last decade has led to a strong increase in the demand for steel products and ingredients, which, for the dry-bulk trade, can be translated into a particularly strong demand for iron ore imports. China's domestic iron ore is of lower quality and therefore not preferable for steel production. Imports, especially from Brazil, Australia and Canada, where the quality of the iron ore is higher, have therefore been preferred and are increasing. This is also generating longer trade distances and therefore stronger growth in the total demand for dry-bulk tonnage, when adding the ton-mile effect. During the financial crisis from 2008 onwards, a number of countries implemented financial packages, including China's CNY4 trillion stimulus package. A number of these packages targeted infrastructure development projects, leading to a boost in demand for steel ingredients, such as iron ore and coal, leading thus to a stronger growth of demand for iron ore imports. One could therefore argue that the financial crisis has been beneficial for the overall dry-bulk tonnage demand. One could definitely argue that the dry-bulk sector has been spoiled with strong tonnage demand growth during the decade 2004–14, with annual growth rates between 4 and 14%, showing a decline not before 2009 to a growth rate of 2.4%.[18]

Iron ore consumption has been on a general uptrend since the turn of this century and, even more importantly for dry-bulk tonnage demand, the share, which is seaborne traded, has continued to increase. Even in 2009, when global iron ore consumption fell, mainly due to reduced steel production in the Western world, Chinese iron ore imports helped maintain the momentum in seaborne trade. This was primarily driven by the stimulus package targeting infrastructure-development projects requiring steel; for instance, the expansion of the railway network. In 2012, global seaborne imports of iron ore accounted for slightly more than half of the global iron ore consumption (56.1% in 2013), and it can be expected that this trend will continue to increase in the coming years, with seaborne trade estimated to reach close to 65% of global iron ore consumption by the end of 2015. This growth is primarily driven by China sourcing iron ore imports from further distances, especially Australia and Brazil. When studying iron ore trade, Brazil and Australia are expected to remain the dominant suppliers of iron ore to China. Currently, China imports about 50% of its requirements from Australia while another 25% is sourced from Brazil. In the coming years, the share of Chinese imports from Australia is expected to grow and reach about 55% while imports from Brazil are estimated to decline to about 20%. With almost 70% of globally seaborne traded iron ore imported by China, the expected slowdown in steel production in China will have a huge impact on the iron ore trade and therefore on the total dry-bulk tonnage demand growth.[19, 20]

Similar to iron ore, coal consumption has been on an uptrend, driven by the increasing demand for electricity and steel, though the growth in seaborne trade has been complex and characterized by its not being a one-way street. This is primarily because China has the world's third largest coal reserves, and only in 2009 turned into a net coal importer.[21] Furthermore, Chinese imports are mainly driven by price-arbitrage opportunities between the domestic and international market and therefore are relatively difficult to forecast. On the other hand, India will continue to import coal to meet the demands of its energy sector, and the use of alternative, more eco-friendly energy sources is not expected either in the short or in the medium term. Overall, seaborne coal trade accounted for about 38% of global coal consumption in 2012, and this is expected to increase to about 40% by the end of 2015. Australia and Indonesia are the biggest coal exporters, followed by South Africa and Colombia. With its shale gas boom, the USA has also become a key exporter. The major change in the coal trade that could be expected from 2015 is the Colombian coal exports to be directed toward Asian markets instead of the USA. This trade will be further aided by the expanded Panama Canal, which will boost the ton-mile and therefore total tonnage demand.

When studying the demand side of the dry-bulk sector, it is essential to understand the key commodities and the various demand drivers for these. For instance, it is important to study the current Chinese five-year plan and translate it into infrastructure projects, thence forecasting future demand for steel and related demand for imports of iron ore. It is also important to analyze where it is sourced from and whether to expect changes in future trade patterns and the sourcing countries' share of the iron ore exports. Furthermore, it is important to consider whether one of the key drivers for coal—India—will continue to show strong growth rates in demand for coal imports for the energy sector, not only in the short and medium term, but also in the longer term, or whether the move toward alternative energy sources could accelerate.

There is no doubt that, when studying the historical development of the dry-bulk tonnage-demand growth, one cannot blame the world economy for the current low dry-bulk market. The dry-bulk demand side has shown stable strong growth for tonnage since the turn of the century. However, the problem has come from the strong growth in supply exceeding the growth in demand for tonnage leading to the mismatch in the demand supply balance. This has led to the current situation of excess supply that needs to be absorbed into the fleet before a fundamentally supported rebound occurs. When taking into account the massive order book for delivery in the full year 2015 and especially 2016, with fleet growth of, respectively, 6.7 and 7.2%, compared with an expected dry-bulk tonnage demand of around 4% in both 2015 and 2016, the depressed markets with excess supply are expected to continue for at least two more years, as illustrated in Fig. 2.14. The dry-bulk market is also characterized by seasonality, which is sometimes confused with cyclicality, and accordingly market players have been placing orders for new vessels on expectations of a change in market conditions. When delivered, these orders then put further pressure on the already excessively supplied market and counter a rebound in itself. Such a situation occurred in autumn 2013 when the seasonal upswing triggered a massive ordering activity, which resulted in the massive order book for delivery in 2015 and 2016.

In Fig. 2.14, the utilization rate development index for the dry-bulk market is illustrated. It is calculated as the development in the difference (or the ratio) between the forecast capacity of the fleet and the forecast total demand

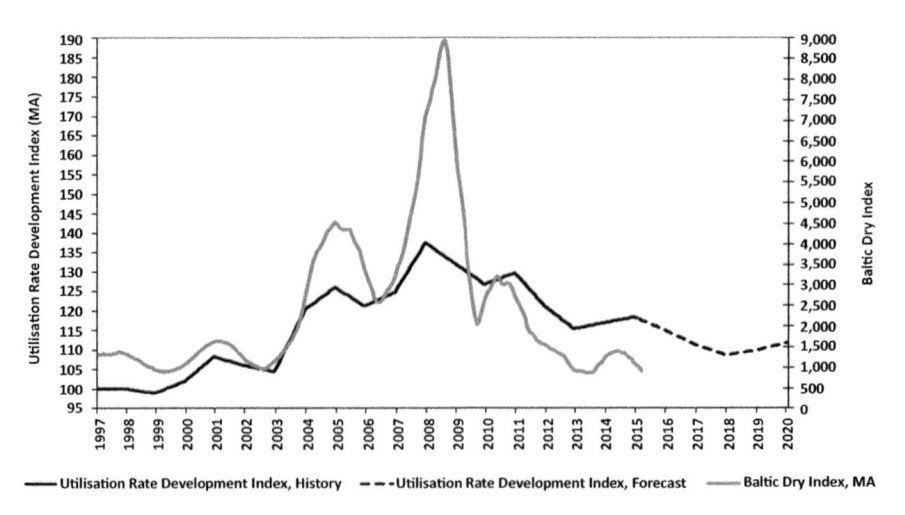

Fig. 2.14 Dry-bulk market outlook: trend indicator, demand–supply modeling (*Source*: Own modeling (moving average of the development in the utilization rate, indexed with 1996 = 100))

for seaborne dry-bulk tonnage. Total demand for seaborne dry-bulk tonnage, including a slowdown in the expected future growth of imports of iron ore into China as well as continued strong growth of coal imports into India, is implemented in the global bilateral country-by-country trade and aggregated to a global demand for tonnage, including expected changes in trade distances and changes in the annual average speed and congestion. Furthermore, future expected scrapping activity and shipbuilding contracting activity (including the forecasting of the delivery profile calculated on the basis of shipyard capacity and shipyard utilization) is translated into a fleet growth and compared with the total tonnage demand, leading to the above trend indicator. Thus, expectations are for the dry-bulk market to remain suppressed for at least another two years before a fundamentally supported rebound can occur. Seasonality and volatility throughout the years is expected, however.

2.4 The Asset: Importance of Asset Specifications

We have now reviewed and discussed how to analyze the overall cyclicality of the shipping and offshore industry, and the respective cyclicality for some selected shipping sectors and subsectors. We have also seen how to determine a general utilization forecast and translate this into asset value forecasts, as well as earnings' forecasts and employment risks. It is of course likewise important to evaluate the individual competitive advantages of the assets in relation to peers and the prior-mentioned analysis, as well as the quality of the asset. A technical inspection of the vessel is of utmost significance, in order to evaluate the state of the asset, the risks associated with the technical condition and the likely future needs for its maintenance. Likewise, it is important to evaluate whether any legal requirements will be put in place in the industry, which will make changes necessary or lead to the vessel becoming less or more attractive in the future. Examples include the double hull requirement for tankers, which made single hull tankers less attractive over the phase out period; and the Energy Efficiency Design Index (EEDI)[22] requirements for the dry-bulk vessels. Furthermore, it is important to evaluate whether the margin paid for an eco-vessel is justified—both in terms of the future second-hand value-forecast premium, compared with non-eco vessels, but also in terms of bunker savings in the future cash flow generation of the asset. With potential downward/upward fluctuations in oil prices, eco-vessels could suddenly become less/more attractive due to the focus on fuel consumption becoming less interesting from a cost perspective, which could eventually lead to old, cheap, non-eco vessels being preferred over expensive eco-vessels. With the oil-price drop in late 2014, it happened that some time-charter parties of expensive eco-vessels were canceled and, instead of eco-tonnage, the operator chartered old tonnage, as fuel consumption became less important. The paradox in itself was that it was often seen that the time-charter party was canceled due to fuel-consumption not being low enough. Actually, this was used as the exit excuse—the easiest way to exit the charter and the only legally valid way to exit the time-charter party.

When discussing eco-vessels, it is also important to evaluate the risk of technological improvements of the vessels over time, the pace at which they have happened and, more importantly, the pace at which they are expected to happen in the future. This is essential when evaluating the future attractiveness of the vessel in question and its future second-hand value. In Fig. 2.15, the developments of the dry-bulk Supramax to Ultramax are shown, and it is important to note the speed at which the development and increase of size have taken place. More modern, larger and more efficient Ultramax vessels have taken significant orders in 2012 and 2013 and will cannibalize on the Supramaxes, which were the most advanced vessels when they were introduced, in 2004. At the time, everyone expected the Supramaxes to be the most preferred vessels for several years; however, one always needs to remember that a vessel's expected life-time is around 20 years and one should not get carried away by the advanced vessels of today when evaluating future attractiveness.

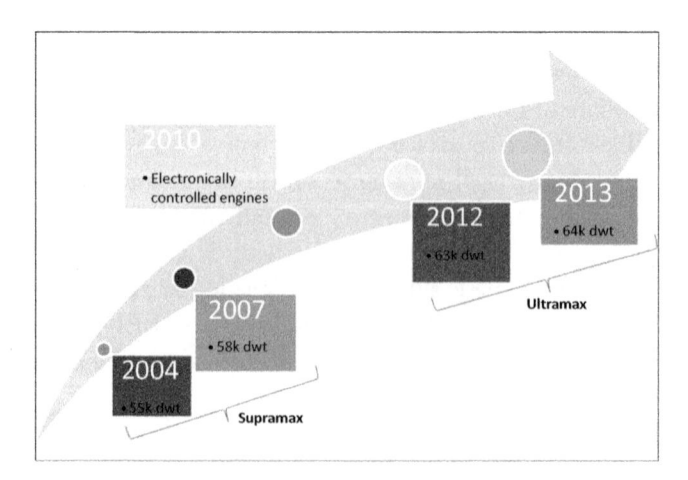

Fig. 2.15 Vessel developments over the years (*Source*: DVB Shipping and Offshore Research)

In addition to the vessel design, when evaluating the asset attractiveness, the shipyard where the vessel is to be built is crucial. In fact, the fair market value (FMV) of a vessel built in a Tier I shipyard[23] will have a premium of 5–20% above a similar unit built in a Tier II shipyard, depending on the sector and the subsector. Furthermore, when a large number of vessels are available for selection, charterers have preference for vessels built in Tier I shipyards, which could lead to a premium in charter rates for those vessels, as well as less risk of unemployment. Vessels built in Tier I shipyards are also expected to have a longer economic life, compared with units built in Tier II yards, *ceteris paribus*. The combination of a longer economic life and a premium in charter rates could justify their FMV premium being above similar units built in Tier II shipyards.

2.5 Mitigation of Risks

In this chapter we have so far discussed how to evaluate the risks associated with the assets in asset-backed finance. This part of the chapter discusses how to mitigate these risks. When mitigating the asset value risk, it is important to understand the cyclicality of the business, where we are on the cycle at a given time and then structure the transaction accordingly—i.e. on the high of a cycle with high asset values, it is important to consider carefully the loan to value (LTV) ratio since the FMV is high due to the sector being on the high of the cycle. The future second-hand value can therefore decline significantly when approaching the low point of the cycle.

When mitigating the performance risk, it is important to consider that, in a depressed market, at the bottom of the sector cycle, the risk for the vessel not obtaining employment is relatively high—and even more significant if the vessel is in a segment where the norm is spot employment.[24] In this case, it is important to consider several annual off-hire days in the cash flow modeling. For instance, in a depressed crude market and with a conservative view, employment can be evaluated at 310 days per year, which can rise up to 355 days per year in a crude market where demand is growing by more than supply—that is, in a market with no excess supply. Furthermore, the quality of the asset is also important when evaluating the employment risk, as an old low quality asset will have more off-hire days for repairs and maintenance, compared with a new, modern vessel. Likewise, the earnings forecast is a central element of cash-flow modeling and should reflect the market outlook as concluded in the market outlook/utilization rate outlook performed for the specific sector and subsector.

2.6 Conclusion

In this chapter we have discussed methodologies on how to assess the current and future value and the liquidity of the asset. We have discussed the importance and the overall cyclicality of the shipping and offshore industry, with a primary focus on the supply side—the shipyard capacity and future newbuilding prices. In the current situation, in 2015, with excess liquidity and excess yard capacity, supply can easily change and may work against any potential recovery. Newbuilding prices for major ship types are expected to remain subdued for some years more, due to the excess shipyard capacity. Hidden shipbuilding capacity may flood the market when newbuilding prices start increasing, thereby keeping prices in check. Not until the shipyard deleveraging process reaches its end, can a sustainable recovery of newbuilding prices be expected. However, owners tend to choose good shipyards, which can deliver quality assets, so as to compete with the threat of increasing ordering activity. As a result, a two-tier market in the shipbuilding industry is expected to continue, where owners prefer top tier yards, while second tier yards need to lower their prices to attract new business.

We have also discussed the methodology for forecasting the market outlook for the dry-bulk and the container markets, as well as the importance of evaluating the quality of individual assets and how to mitigate risks. While comparing the result of a basic demand/supply analysis of the container market and the dry-bulk market, we have argued that it is always important to dig as deep as possible into the details, which often reveal the differences and key drivers for the respective segments, which may ultimately lead to completely different market outlooks, despite appearing similar at first glance. When evaluating the drivers and trends in the container market, it is essential to distinguish and evaluate the variables in this sector and implement these variables in the overall demand/supply analysis. On the demand side, all the variables that change global trade patterns, as well as technological innovations like 3D and 4D printing which will probably diminish containerized trade in the long-term future, are to be considered short, medium and long-term, and be translated into future demand for containerized trade. Furthermore, speed and congestion, and various other variables discussed, need to be taken into account. On the supply side, the overall structure of the container market is leading to ordering, driven by economies of scale. This in turn is leading to an imbalanced order book in relation to demand growth, which is ultimately leading to significant cascading pressure across the industry. Ultimately the need for some subsectors will change from being a key container segment to a niche player segment, which is a short-term opportunity. Container vessels are getting bigger at an accelerating pace not seen before in any other segment.

We can thus conclude that important issues to analyze, when assessing and evaluating asset risks today are whether the recent cyclical behavior in the shipping industry has changed and what it takes to restore its typical patterns; and the importance of subsector market analysis, trends, technical specifications as well as subsector cyclicality.

On a final note, one could also argue that, as long as there is excess shipyard capacity in the shipping and offshore industry, in conjunction with easy access to funding globally, then cyclicality will only exist when speculators stop acting on the expectation of using the cyclicality for quick yield. There is ample shipyard capacity to deliver required capacity soon enough to kill the rebound in any sector before it actually occurs.

Notes

1. DVB Shipping and Offshore Research.
2. Ref: United Nations, Discussion Papers, "The Asian developmental state and the flying geese paradigm", Discussion Papers No 213, November 2013.
3. http://www.miit.gov.cn/n11293472/n11293832/n12845605/n13916898/n16151565.files/n16151494.pdf.
4. http://www.cfr.org/japan/abenomics-japanese-economy/p30383; Krugman, P. "Currency Regimes, Capital Flows, and Crises", IMF Economic Review, Vol. 62, No. 4, 2014 International Monetary Fund.
5. Liu, L. "What's the matter with Japan? The Japanese Economy From a Historical Perspective", Penn Asian Review, 12/18/2012.
6. EUDA, Hiroshi, MIYAKE, Koichi, KADO, Hiromi and NAGANO, Hiromichi, "An Analysis of marine container transportation in the asian region", Proceedings of the Eastern Asia Society for Transportation Studies, Vol. 5, pp. 617–630, 2005.
7. Corbett, J. and Winebrake, J. "The Impacts of Globalisation of International Maritime Transport Activity—Past trends and future perspectives", Energy and Environmental Research Associates, the United States, as a contribution to the OECD/ITF Global Forum on Transport and Environment in a Globalising World, 10–12 November 2008.
8. With FDIs into China of USD38,399,300,000 in 2000, USD186,797,550,544 in 2008 and USD167,070,808,699 in 2009; see http://data.worldbank.org/indicator/BX.KLT.DINV.CD.WD?page=2.

9. Coenen, G., Straub, R. and Trabandt, M., "Gauging the Effects of Fiscal Stimulus Packages in the Euro Area", ECB, Working Paper Series, No 1483, October 2012.
10. Fontagne, L., Foure, J. and Keck, A. "Simulating world trade in the decades ahead: driving forces and policy implications", WTO Working Paper ERSC-2014-05.
11. DVB Shipping and Offshore Research.
12. DVB Shipping and Offshore Research.
13. DVB Shipping and Offshore Research.
14. DVB Shipping and Offshore Research.
15. The term "utilization of the fleet" can be measured by the development in the difference (or the ratio) between the capacity of the fleet and the demand.
16. Examples of minor bulks are agribulks and softs (raw sugar and white sugar), soymeal, oilseed, rice, phosphates, potash, sulfur, urea, coke, petroleum coke, pig iron, direct reduced iron/hot briquetted iron (DRI/HBI), scrap, manganese ore, anthracite, cement, salt, nickel ore and copper concentrates.
17. Source: MSI.
18. Own modeling, UN statistics and IHS/GTN.
19. Ref.: http://www.wsj.com/articles/chinas-steel-demand-falls-1422526887.
20. Ref.: http://www.reuters.com/article/2014/09/25/us-china-steel-id USKCN0HK0Z320140925.
21. Ref.: http://www.eia.gov/todayinenergy/detail.cfm?id=16271.
22. The EEDI for new ships is the single most important technical measure aimed at promoting the use of more energy efficient equipment and engines. The EEDI requires a minimum energy efficiency level per capacity mile (e.g. tonne-mile) for different ship type and size segments. It is expected to stimulate continued innovation and technical development of all the components influencing the fuel efficiency of a ship from its design phase. As long as the required energy efficiency level is attained, ship designers and builders are free to use the most cost-efficient solutions for the ship to comply with the regulations. The EEDI provides a specific figure for an individual ship design, expressed in grams of carbon dioxide per ship's capacity-mile (the smaller the EEDI the more energy efficient is the ship design), and is calculated by a formula based on the technical design parameters for a given ship (source: https://www.dnvgl.com/maritime/energy-efficiency/eedi-and-eeoi.html). EEDI calculator: https://www.bimco.org/Products/EEDI.aspx.

23. Shipyards can be classified according to the quality and experience of their shipbuilding capacity. Tier 1 shipyards are considered the best for the specific vessels in question.
24. Kavussanos, M., "Business risk measurement and management in the cargo carrying sector of the shipping industry", The handbook of the maritime economics and business, Chapter 30, Grammenos, C. 2002, LLP.

3

Overview of Shipping Finance

Fotis Giannakoulis

3.1 Introduction

The international shipping industry is both large and highly important to the global economy as it carries over 90% of global trade. According to UNCTAD, there are over 45,000 ships in the world. The International Chamber of Shipping (ICS) estimates the number of seafarers at around 1.2 million. According to ISH Global Insight, liner shipping alone contributes over USD430 billion to world GDP and 13.5 million jobs. The shipping industry is inherently capital intensive and requires significant amounts of capital to be invested every year in newbuilding vessels, with the cost of building a ship often exceeding USD200 million. During the last ten years, orders of newbuilding vessels have averaged more than USD130 billion per annum, reaching USD266 billion in the peak of 2007. Furthermore, ships are liquid assets that change hands with high frequency and, as a result, the financing requirement is likely to be even higher as shipowners seek to fund second-hand acquisitions. According to Clarksons, over 1,000 vessels have changed hands on average every year in the last decade and the aggregate annual transaction value between 2004 and 2014 has exceeded USD25 billion, reaching a peak of USD47 billion in 2007.

F. Giannakoulis (✉)
Morgan Stanley, 1585 Broadway, 38th Floor, New York, NY 10036, USA

© The Author(s) 2016
M.G. Kavussanos, I.D. Visvikis (eds.), *The International Handbook of Shipping Finance*, DOI 10.1057/978-1-137-46546-7_3

Earnings and vessel prices are highly volatile, characterized by sudden and violent moves alongside the shipping cycle. During the last 20 years, the annualized volatility of quarterly earnings of the four major shipping sectors, as measured by the Clarksea Index, has averaged 37%. The earnings volatility of dry-bulk and tanker vessels, which comprise the two largest components of the global shipping fleet, averages even higher, at 47 and 66%, respectively. Containerships and gas carriers are relatively more stable. Market data show that the volatility has significantly increased during the last ten years across all shipping segments, as Chinese trade growth has dominated the market. In such an extreme market environment, one would expect that the financing of shipping assets would be primarily the domain of equity funding. Nevertheless, due to the capital intensive nature of the shipping industry and the fact that shipping assets are relatively homogeneous assets of considerable value, providing for the most part a highly liquid collateral, debt financing has been a key source of funding capital requirements (Figs. 3.1, 3.2, 3.3, 3.4 and 3.5).

3.2   Sources of Ship Financing

The extensive capital requirements to finance newbuilding programs and second-hand acquisitions have led shipowners to seek financing beyond their own private funds. European merchant banks have a long history in financing shipping assets, which can be traced back to the United Kingdom in the 1850s, with the expansion of the steamship fleet. Bank

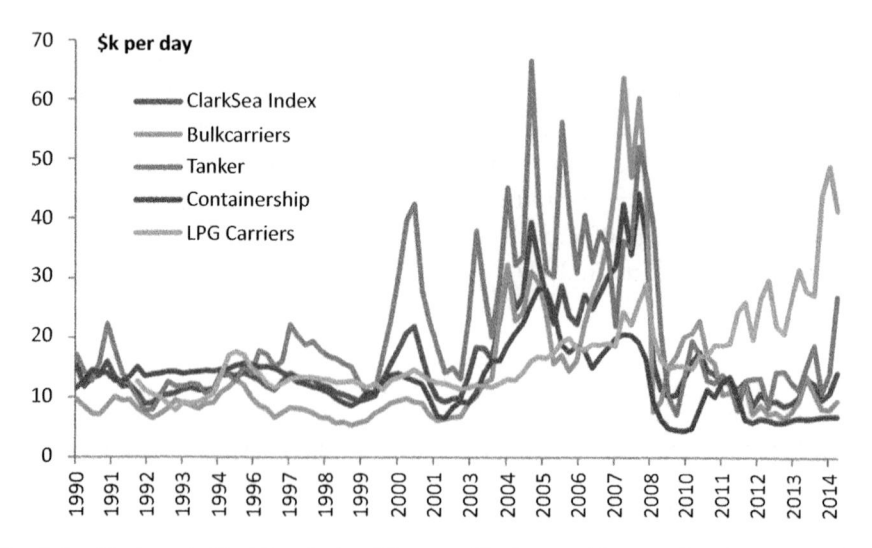

Fig. 3.1 Clarkson's ClarkSea index (*Source*: Clarksons, Morgan Stanley Research

debt financing remains the most important source of capital for the shipping industry today. The capital market's embracing of the shipping industry, especially during the last decade, has opened the doors to a much wider range of capital beyond bank debt. Shipping companies today have an array of financing alternatives that range from traditional mortgage-backed loans to more complex financing structures that may include: high yield debt; sale and leasebacks; mezzanine financing and other forms of equity-linked debt; private equity or funding through the formation of publicly listed spin-offs, such as master limited partnerships (MLPs) and special purpose

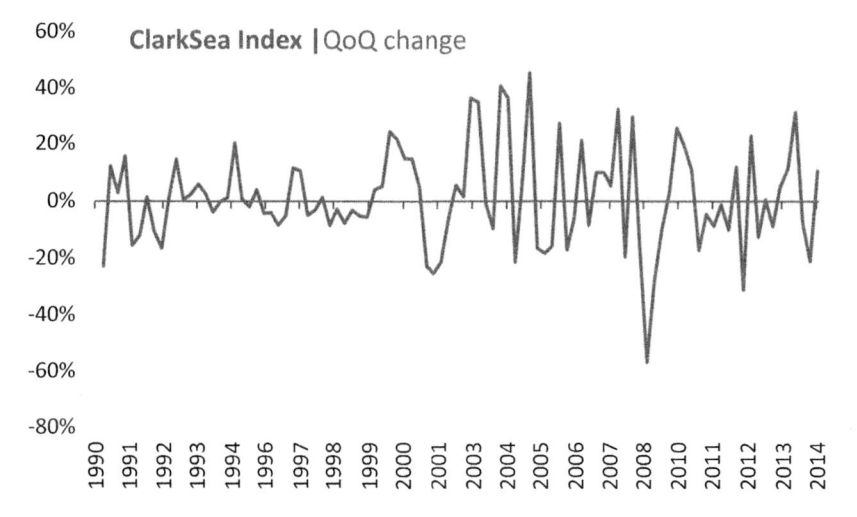

Fig. 3.2 Clarkson's ClarkSea index volatility (*Source*: Clarksons, Morgan Stanley Research)

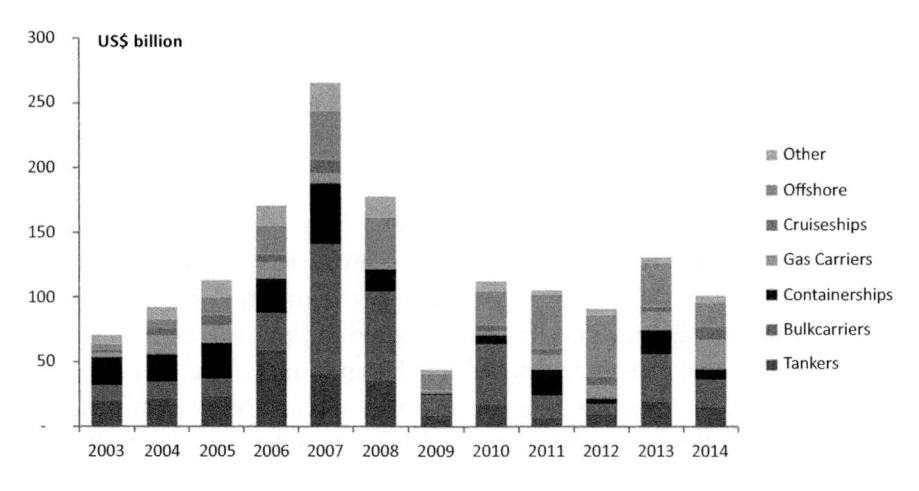

Fig. 3.3 World vessel contracting (*Source*: Clarksons, Morgan Stanley Research)

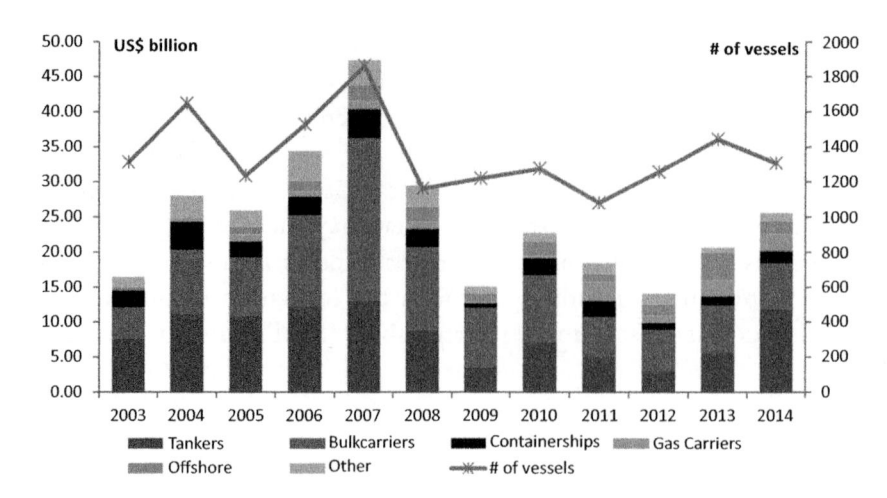

Fig. 3.4 Second-hand vessel transactions (*Source*: Clarksons, Morgan Stanley Research)

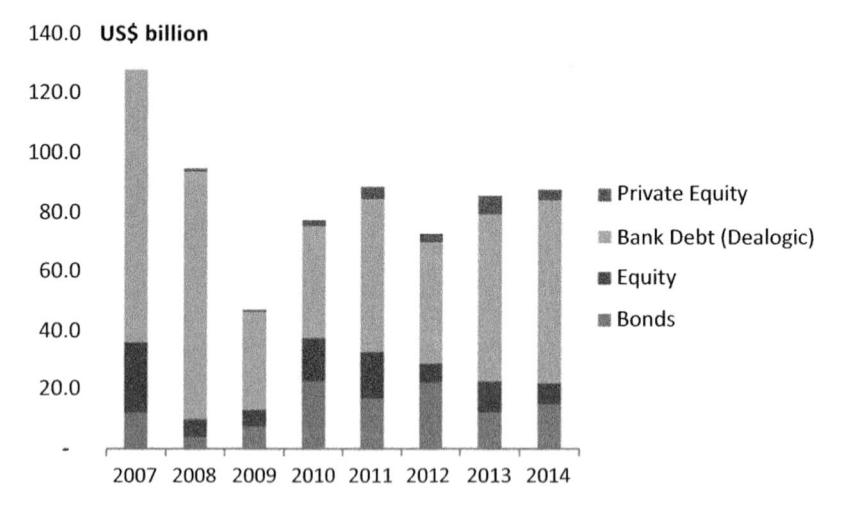

Fig. 3.5 New capital to the shipping industry (*Note*: Excludes bilateral bank loans. *Source*: Marine Money International)

acquisition companies (SPACs). While the ability of a shipping company to navigate the ebbs and flows of the market is primarily dependent on the timing of its investments and its chartering policy, the selection among all these funding alternatives can be of equal importance. Together with the market conditions, these factors also dictate the availability of the financing alternatives that each company has in its arsenal at any given time, as seen below:

Bank financing	Capital markets	Other
Mortgage-backed loans	High yield bonds	Seller's credit
Newbuilding financing	Convertible notes	Finance lease
Unsecured/corporate loans	IPOs	Operating lease
Mezzanine	Follow-on offerings	Private equity
	At-the-market offerings	Securitization
	MLPs	Export agency finance
	SPACs	

3.2.1 Financing from Banks

Bank financing is the main source of capital to the shipping industry, providing a flexible and low cost of capital to the shipping companies. Banks are the most reliable and long-term oriented capital providers to the industry, accounting for the greatest majority of the shipping capital every year. Based on data from Dealogic, over USD60 billion of bank debt was issued in 2014 and this number does not include bilateral loans. According to 2014 estimates of *Marine Money International*, the global shipping loan portfolio is around USD380 billion. European merchant banks have been traditionally the most reliable and consistent lenders to the shipping industry, accounting for over 65% of the global lending portfolio. Germany's HSH Nordbank and Commerzbank, and Norway's DnB, are the largest lenders to the shipping industry, although the ranking is expected to change significantly in the near future as a number of banks made the decision after 2008 to reduce their shipping exposure or even fully exit the sector. For the shipping companies, bank debt is considered the most attractive form of financing at an interest cost of 200–300 basis points (bp) above LIBOR. Even after the 2008 financial crisis and the decision of a number of banks to reduce their shipping exposure, the cost of bank financing remains highly competitive for shipowners as compared with any other source of capital. From the banks' perspective, the shipping industry remains a favorable sector to do business with, despite the volatility and the relatively low margins. Banks manage to increase their returns on low margin financings as vessels change hands on a regular basis causing loans to be refinanced before their maturity. Furthermore, the liquidity and homogeneous nature of the shipping assets allow banks to deploy large amounts of capital with relatively low overheads. Many banks have specialized departments that provide a wide range of banking products to the shipping companies and their principals, ranging from traditional mortgaged-backed loans to interest rate derivatives (i.e. swaps), exchange rate derivatives, freight derivatives, liquidity management, advisory services and investment products through their private wealth divisions (Figs. 3.6, 3.7 and 3.8).

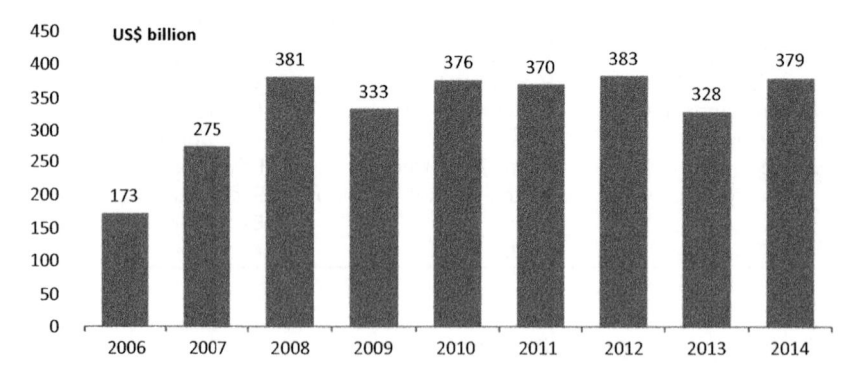

Fig. 3.6 Aggregate bank shipping portfolios (*Source*: Marine Money International)

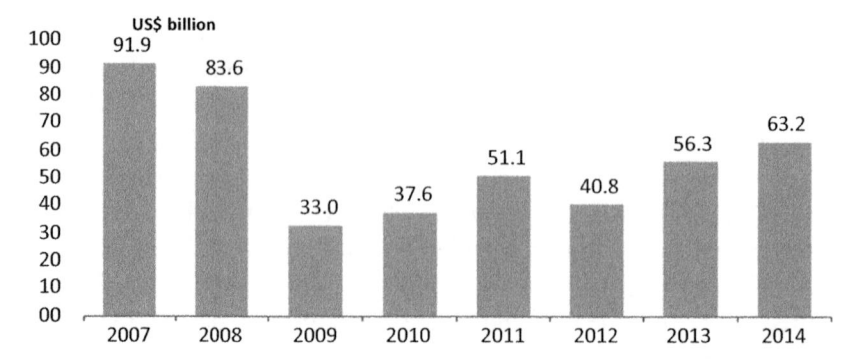

Fig. 3.7 Bank lending activity (*Notes*: Syndicated and "club deal" loans only; excludes bilateral loans. *Source*: Marine Money International; Dealogic data)

3.2.1.1 Mortgaged-Backed Bank Loans

Mortgaged-backed bank financing has been the single most important source of capital for the international shipping industry. With the exception of equity invested by the shipowner, mortgage-backed loans are often the only type of capital in the capital structure of shipping companies. Mortgaged-backed bank debt has been historically around 70–75% of the total capital invested. The weak shipping markets after 2008 and the difficulty in obtaining bank debt financing, coupled with the greater availability of capital from private equity firms and the capital market, has reduced the availability of bank debt to around 50–60%. A mortgage-backed loan uses the ship as collateral to secure the lender's exposure. This means that the vessel has to be delivered from the shipyard in order for the borrower to be in a position to write a mortgage to a lender, a process that takes place simultaneously with the issuance of the loan. The borrower is typically a single-purpose company that

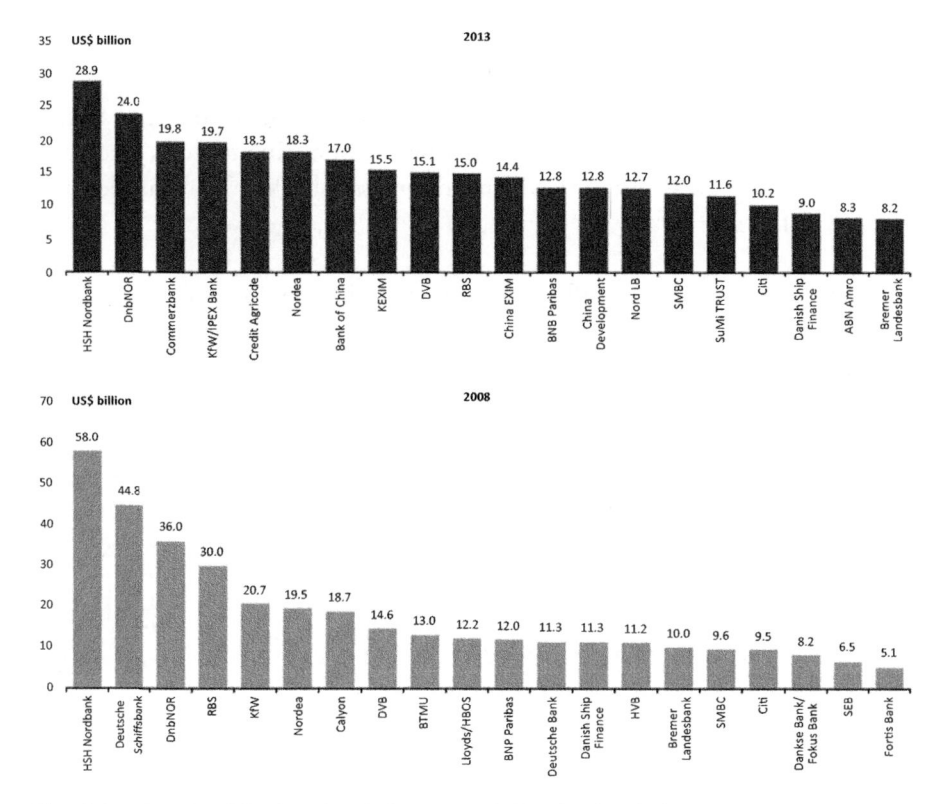

Fig. 3.8 Top 20 shipping bank loan portfolios by bank (*Source*: Marine Money International)

owns the collateral vessel and is registered in a legally acceptable jurisdiction, most likely in Liberia, the Marshall Islands or Panama. This offers the lender direct access to the collateral and isolates the vessel from any claims or liabilities unrelated to the financed asset. In many cases, the holding company that owns the shares of the single-purpose company acts as a guarantor of the obligations of the borrower. A mortgage-backed loan may finance multiple vessels that are cross-collateralized and, when this happens, the loan is usually split in different tranches, which facilitates the repayment in the event of the sale of any of the vessels. This usually happens when the shipping company is acquiring a fleet of multiple vessels that are financed by the same bank or when the lender is asked to enhance the collateral package adding debt-free vessels in order to reduce the leverage of a credit facility.

The amount and terms of the financing determines the cost of capital for the shipowner, and also the ability of the borrower to meet its obligations and navigate through the volatility of the market. As shipping rates and vessel values fluctuate widely throughout the cycle, the terms of the debt must be structured in such a way that the earnings of the vessel can serve the debt covering the cash break-even and the vessels provide enough collateral against the loan outstanding. Therefore, negotiating the financing terms is a key part of the lending process. The main terms of an asset-backed loan can be summarized as follows:

1. **Financing amount.** Usually ranges between 50 and 80% of the collateral vessel depending on the age of the vessel, the freight outlook of the respective subsector and the available securities, including any existing time-charter contracts and other corporate guarantees. In certain situations where there is a long-term contract with a very high creditworthy counterparty, the financing amount can be even higher as the lender's exposure is secured by the charterparty. Lenders require the equity from the owner to be paid first before the loan is available to be drawn, although these two transactions in reality happen simultaneously.
2. **Tenor.** The duration during which the loan has to be repaid usually ranges between five and ten years and depends on the bank's ability to secure funding as well as the age of the vessel.
3. **Repayment.** The loans are usually repaid in semi-annual or quarterly installments, usually of equal amount, with a balloon at the maturity of the loan. The repayment profile of the loan depends mainly on the age of the vessel. The loan amortization is usually faster than the depreciation of the vessel to assure reduced exposure for the lender. A typical financing for a newly built vessel with a 25-years useful life has a repayment profile of around 15 years, suggesting that the loan is repaid at a pace of 1/15 every year during the loan tenor, with the outstanding amount payable in one balloon payment at maturity. However, the repayment profile may vary significantly depending on the leverage and the collateral vessel. The older the vessel is, the shorter is the repayment profile, in order to assure that the loan can be safely repaid during its useful life. One of the key factors that lenders use to determine the repayment schedule of the loan is the cash break-even rate that the collateral vessel will have earned in order to pay its operating expenses and serve both the interest cost and principal repayments. In certain cases, the loan repayment may be front-loaded as banks prefer to reduce their exposure quickly and attain lower leverage, and therefore refinancing risk, as the vessel ages. Therefore, when there is a charter contract, the repayments during the charter period may be higher. Banks usually avoid financing older vessels, which means that they target the maturity of a loan to take place at least five years prior to the end of the vessel's useful life.

4. **Interest rate.** Asset-backed debt loans are usually priced as a spread (margin) over LIBOR, which ranges between 100 and 400bp depending on the creditworthiness of the shipowner, the quality and liquidity of the collateral and the competition in the ship financing market. During the frothy 2006–08 market peak, the margins for high-quality owners had shrunk in some cases below 100bp, but in the current market top-tier borrowers have to pay between 250 and 300bp.
5. **Fees.** In addition to the interest rate, the arranger of the loan is entitled to fees for arranging and administering the loan. A 1% arranging fee is typical for mortgage-backed loans, while additional annual fees are paid to the agent of the loan. There is also a commitment fee that usually covers the lenders costs of tying up capital that has not been drawn down, and is usually around 40% of the margin.
6. **Securities.** A mortgage on the vessel is the main security that the lender has in the event of a default. However, other securities are also common, such as corporate guarantees from the holding company that owns the collateral vessel, charges on the earnings accounts of the vessel, assignments on any charter contracts associated with the collateral vessel, assignments of the borrower's insurance proceeds and pledges over the shares of the borrower.
7. **Financial covenants.** The most typical covenant on mortgage-backed loans is the value maintenance clause that requires the market value of the collateral vessel to exceed the outstanding loan amount usually by at least 140%. In the event that the market value of the vessel falls below this threshold, the borrower must either provide additional security by way of cash or additional security acceptable to the lender, or prepay the loan to restore the covenant. Other financial covenants may include a minimum liquidity of the borrower or a cap on the total indebtedness of the guarantor.
8. **Non-financial covenants.** Mortgaged-backed shipping loans usually have a number of non-financial covenants that administer the flag and jurisdiction of the borrower, the required insurance coverage, the manager of the vessel, the regular provision of financial accounts to the lender and the completion of satisfactory technical surveys.

Similar to the financing of real estate assets, vessels can be financed with more than one mortgaged-backed loan provided by separate groups of lenders. The loan that has the seniority is called the "senior" loan and its lenders enjoy a first mortgage, while the second loan is called the "junior" or "subordinated" loan, with the lenders receiving a second mortgage which provides security access to the collateral after the first mortgagees have been served. That allows the company to increase the leverage on the vessel and improve its

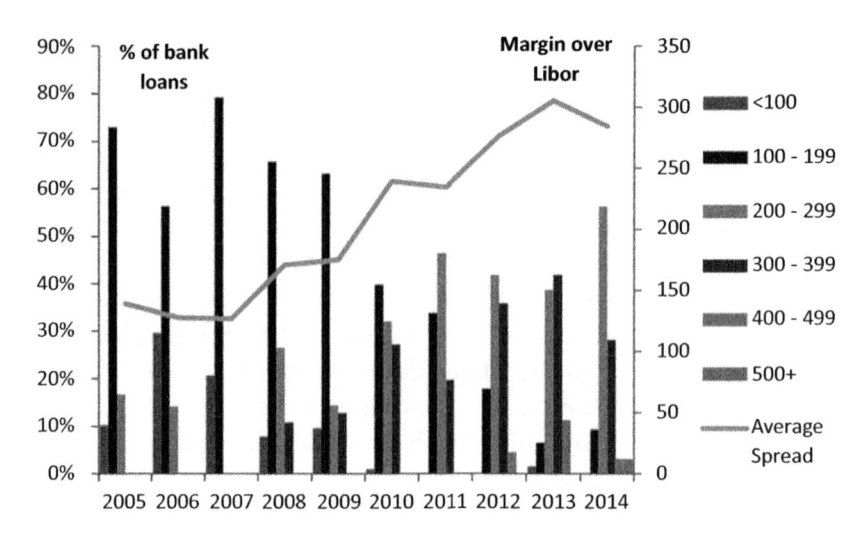

Fig. 3.9 Shipping loans interest cost: spread over LIBOR (basis points) (*Source*: Marine Money International)

equity return. When there is more than one mortgage on a vessel, the lenders of both facilities enter into a subordination agreement, which determines the order in which the liens will be paid if the vessel is sold.

The majority of these mortgaged-backed loans are "bilateral", loans between one single lender and the borrowing entity, or "club deal" syndicates, loans between a small group of lenders and the borrower, where one bank acts as an agent of the lending consortium and all lenders share equal, or nearly equal, parts of the fees earned from the loan facility. Over the last ten years and as the industry has expanded, an increasing number of mortgaged shipping loans have been issued by larger syndicates, often in underwritten deals or best-effort syndications. Loan syndication offers shipping companies the advantage of financing large acquisitions that are usually not possible to be financed by a single bank. The expanded syndicated loan market that was growing rapidly until the 2008 financial crisis has recently slowed down as most European banks have limited lending capacity and most new loans are either bilateral or club deals Fig. 3.9.

3.2.1.2 Newbuilding Financing

Financing of newbuilding vessels follows the same principles as mortgaged-backed loans. However, while the financing of a newbuilding vessel that has been delivered is a straightforward mortgage loan, the pre-delivery financing of a vessel under construction is more complicated. In the case of the financing of an existing vessel, the bank has a mortgage on a collateral asset that earns revenue and offers security against its loan exposure. In the case of a pre-delivery loan, the vessel is not available to be mortgaged and there are no earnings that can be used to repay the loan. That means that the loan can be repaid only after the vessel has been delivered from the shipyard, which can be two to three years after the loan is initially arranged. Instead of a mortgage, the borrower assigns the newbuilding contract to the shipyard, which, in the event of default, is transferred to the lender. However, as the contract payments are staggered during the construction period, if the lender defaults, the bank becomes responsible to the shipyard for the completion of the construction. As a result, the risk for the lender is significantly higher than the original loan amount of the pre-delivery financing. Therefore, the pre-delivery financing is structured as a separate loan that will be repaid upon vessel delivery, typically from the proceeds of the post-delivery loan. Most often, the lender that provides the pre-delivery loan is also willing to finance the vessel following its delivery from the shipyard.

Another risk that the bank has to deal with is the event that the shipyard does not complete the construction of the vessel, for example due to a bankruptcy or the vessel having technical problems. Therefore, when the construction takes place in an unproven shipyard or in countries with political uncertainty, the lender may require additional guarantees, which may be provided by the shipowner in the form of additional collateral or corporate guarantees, or from the shipyard, which could involve bank or government guarantees. The shipyard's payments of a newbuilding vessel usually take place in stages with the largest portion paid upon vessel delivery. The timing of these payments, as well as the drawdown of the pre-delivery financing, are negotiable and often coincide with specific milestones of the vessel's construction process (e.g. 10% upon signing of the newbuilding contract, 10% at steel cutting, 10% on keel laying, 10% on launching and the rest upon delivery). Almost always, the shipyard is required to provide the shipowner with refund guarantees from a respectable bank that secures the installment paid throughout the construction process and which is assigned to the lender that provides the pre-delivery financing. Similar to post-delivery loans, pre-delivery financings fund only a portion of the shipbuilding installments, usually around 50–60%. The drawdown of the pre-delivery loan could take place on a *pari passu* basis with the equity financing, although the lenders may require the full, or at least a large part, of the equity to be paid up front.

3.2.1.3 Mezzanine Financing

In the situation where a company is trying to maximize its returns without investing more equity and has exhausted its ability to add traditional secured debt, mezzanine is often a favorable middle-ground solution. Mezzanine financing can be structured either as debt or equity, and represents a claim on the vessel that is senior only to the common equity. As a result, the cost of the mezzanine is higher than that of traditional secured debt, but less expensive than the cost of equity. Traditional shipping banks are the main providers of mezzanine financing, although during the last few years private equity firms or hedge funds have also proved willing to enter into this type of transaction, covering the void caused by the gradual exit of a number of traditional lenders. One of the most common structures of mezzanine financing is a subordinated debt with an equity kicker. In this case, the lender provides a subordinated debt that has a second or third mortgage on the vessel, coupled with a higher interest rate and lighter (or often no) repayments than the traditional mortgaged-backed loan(s). At its maturity, the mezzanine lender receives a certain percentage of the equity in the vessel, which increases its return as the market rises and the vessel's value appreciates. The equity upside of the mezzanine investors can be linked to either the value of the vessel or the cash flows, and can kick in after certain negotiable thresholds.

3.2.1.4 Corporate Loans

In addition to the loans that finance specific vessels, either existing vessels or vessels under construction, banks may also provide loans to large established companies, based on their balance sheet. These loans can be unsecured and are typically available to publicly listed companies with access to the capital markets. Corporate loans provide financial flexibility to the shipping companies and allow them to manage their liquidity. Some of these loans are revolving credit lines that offer the company the flexibility to draw the loan when the funds are needed. The loans may vary in terms of duration, covenants or repayment terms, as they depend on the balance sheet of the lender, the stability of the company's cash flow and its ability to serve the other liabilities on its assets. From the lender's perspective, the main consideration is the balance sheet of the company, and therefore the most typical covenants are the corporate leverage ratio and the interest coverage ratio.

3.2.2 Leasing Financing

One of the tools that companies have to finance their operations is to enter into leasing agreements of some of the assets they operate. Such agreements allow the company to operate assets without having ownership of them, thus without investing any capital. In other words the company ("lessee") leases the vessel from its owner ("lessor") for a period that might extend to multiple years. Companies often enter into sale and leaseback agreements, selling a vessel to the lessor and leasing it back usually at a fixed daily bareboat rate where they remain responsible for the vessel's operation. The lease agreement may come with an option or an obligation to buy back the vessel at the end or during the leasing period, at a pre-agreed price. When the company has a purchase option or purchase obligation, or when the vessel is leased for a period that extends beyond 75% of its useful life or when the present value of the lease payments are over 90% of the vessel's market value, the transaction is accounted as a capital lease and the company has to include the vessel on its balance sheet. In this case, a portion of the lease is expensed as interest and the remainder flows through the company's cash flow statement against the repayment of the capital lease obligation. Otherwise, the lease is considered as operating and the payments are expensed in the company's income statement. Companies may also time charter in a vessel from another shipping company, paying a fixed time-charter rate to the vessel's owner, who remains responsible for its operation. In this case, the company usually charters in the vessel for a period at a discounted rate to the spot market, and tries to achieve a spread on the higher spot rates. On the other side, the owner has secured a fixed employment for the vessel, which allows him or her to lever it and repay the debt obligations without having to deal with the volatility of the spot market. Charter-in agreements provide companies with additional leverage, without the use of traditional debt. However, in the event of a falling freight market, lease agreements may add a disproportional burden to the company's balance sheet as spot rates may drop below the level that is required to cover the lease payments and the cost of operating the vessel.

During the late 1980s and up until 2008, a large number of sale and leaseback transactions were executed in Norway and in Germany through the formation of private entities whose investors would acquire assets that would be leased back to their original owner. The Norwegian K/S were limited partnerships formed as standard companies that offered investors tax benefits as they allowed them to depreciate the capital at an accelerated rate. The German KG funds played a similar role, being structured as limited liability companies. The shares of these entities could be sold through brokers, although the liquidity and regulation of these transactions were fairly limited. While Norwegian K/S and German KG funds would also acquire assets and separately find long-term time charters, in most cases they were involved in leasing transactions. The importance of the German KG market, particularly for the containership industry, strengthened through the late 1990s and mid-2000s as the liner operators increased the chartered-in fleet to fund their expansion and those vehicles provided a tax efficient investment for wealthy private individuals, given Germany's high marginal tax rates. According to Stopford (2009), between 1991 and 2004 the portion of the container fleet chartered in by the liners increased from 15% to over 50% (Fig. 3.10).

3.2.3 Financing from Capital Markets

The capital markets have become an essential source of financing for the shipping industry. The expansion of the global fleet and the increasing need for funding has led shipping companies to seek funds from the capital markets. At the same time, the growth of global trade, especially after China's entry into the WTO in 2002, and the anticipation of high returns associated with this growth, increased the visibility of the shipping industry to a wider universe of participants beyond the traditional market participants such as shipowners and European banks. Today, hedge funds, pension funds and every type of institutional and individual investor have the opportunity to invest in the shipping industry through debt or equity securities. New York, Oslo, Honk Kong and Singapore are today the most important financial centers for shipping companies that seek to raise capital outside traditional bank debt financing. Corporate bonds, convertibles, preferred equity, common equity, private placements, master limited partnerships and private equity are some of the products that are available to shipping companies. In the aftermath of the 2008 financial collapse, capital markets have managed to close the funding

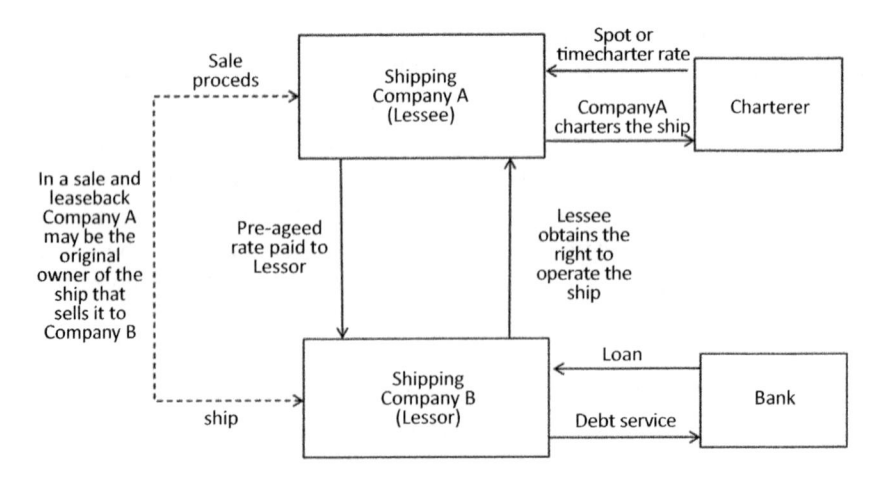

Fig. 3.10 Example of a leasing transaction

gap created by the withdrawal of many European banks from the shipping market and the gradual shrinkage of their portfolios.

3.2.3.1 Corporate Bonds

Corporate bonds offer larger and more established shipping companies an alternative to the bank loan market. While they are almost always more expensive compared to bank debt, they can enhance the company's liquidity, providing greater financial flexibility as bonds tend to be non-amortized with the entire amount paid upon maturity. Given the volatility of the shipping industry and the relatively small size of the companies, all shipping bonds are characterized as high yield rather than investment grade, and the coupon they have to pay is usually in the high single digits. Typically, bonds are issued with a fixed coupon, although some have floating interest terms (i.e. a spread over LIBOR). Shipping bonds may be secured or unsecured by a company's vessels, and can be issued as either senior or subordinated debentures depending on their hierarchy in the company's capital structure. The low interest rate environment has increased the attractiveness of the bond market as an alternative source of financing and can be taken on in addition to the traditional bank debt with its strict covenants and heavy repayment schedules. Many of these bond issuances are unsecured with light covenants and no repayments, allowing the companies to enhance their equity returns and buy assets, without issuing equity, thus avoiding shareholder ownership dilution. Corporate bonds may also be convertible into equity, offering the issuer the advantage of a lower coupon in exchange for providing the holders with the option to convert them into the company's shares at a certain price.

Despite the advantages, bonds can add significant risk to a shipping company in a weak market, as bond terms are very difficult to alter in the event of a default. Altering bank debt in the event of default is much simpler as the lender can waive certain covenants or change the repayment profile. Furthermore, as vessels depreciate and the company's fleet ages, the non-amortizing nature of the bonds may increase the leverage above sustainable levels. While bonds might work as a medium-term boost to a company's liquidity and purchasing power, they do not provide a permanent substitute for equity. The lessons from the shipping bond issuances of the 1990s when many companies defaulted on their coupon payments, as well as the cases of companies like OSG and General Maritime that were forced into a Chap. 11 restructuring during the tanker collapse in 2012 after they failed to refinance their maturing bonds, illustrate the risks that bonds might entail for shipping companies. Similar was the fortune of dry-bulk owner Excel Maritime that defaulted on its convertible notes in 2013 (Fig. 3.11).

3.2.3.2 Public Equity Offerings

Capital markets offer an efficient and quick way for shipping companies to raise the equity that they seek in order to grow their fleet and deal with the increasing capital requirements of the industry. New York, Oslo, Hong Kong and Singapore are the main financial centers that have attracted the majority of the publicly listed shipping companies and that offer access to investors and ample availability of capital. According to Morgan Stanley Research data, between 2004 and 2014, shipping companies raised over USD60 billion of common equity in 363 public offerings of which 118 were IPOs. Half of this activity was in the

Company	Issued	Amount	Currency	Coupon	Maturity
Star Bulk Carriers Corp.	7-Nov-14	50,000,000	USD	8.00%	1-Jan-2019
Scorpio Tankers Inc.	28-Oct-14	45,000,000	USD	7.50%	1-Jan-2017
A. P. Moller-Maersk A/s	16-Sep-14	750,000,000	USD	2.55%	1-Sep-2019
A. P. Moller-Maersk A/s	16-Sep-14	500,000,000	USD	3.75%	1-Sep-2024
Dynagas LNG Partners	8-Sep-14	250,000,000	USD	6.25%	1-Jan-2019
Scorpio Tankers Inc.	25-Jun-14	300,000,000	USD	2.375%	1-Jan-2019
Teekay Offshore Partners LP	30-May-14	275,000,000	USD	6.00%	1-Jan-2019
Paragon Shipping Inc.	9-May-14	25,000,000	USD	8.375%	9-May-2021
Scorpio Tankers Inc.	7-May-14	50,000,000	USD	6.75%	1-Jan-2020
Seaspan Corporation	2-Apr-14	345,000,000	USD	6.375%	30-Apr-2019
Navios Maritime Acquisition	31-Mar-14	60,000,000	USD	8.125%	1-Jan-2021
Global Ship Lease Inc.	19-Mar-14	420,000,000	USD	10.00%	1-Jan-2019
Ridgebury Tankers	14-Mar-14	210,000,000	USD	7.625%	14-Mar-2017
Matson Navigation Co.	28-Jan-14	100,000,000	USD	4.35%	28-Jan-2044
Navios Maritime Holdings Inc	29-Nov-13	650,000,000	USD	7.375%	1-Jan-2022
Navios Maritime Acquisition	14-Nov-13	610,000,000	USD	8.125%	1-Nov-2021
Navigator Gas	1-Dec-12	125,000,000	USD	9.00%	1-Dec-2017
Viking Cruises	12-Oct-12	250,000,000	USD	8.50%	15-Oct-2022
Navios Maritime Holdings Inc	10-Jul-12	88,000,000	USD	8.875%	1-Jan-2017
General Maritime Corporation	30-Jul-11	300,000,000	USD	12%	30-Jul-2017
Navios Maritime Acquisition	26-May-11	105,000,000	USD	8.83%	26-May-2017
Dryships Inc.	28-Apr-11	500,000,000	USD	9.50%	28-Apr-2016
CMA CGM (CMACG)	21-Apr-11	475,000,000	USD	8.50%	21-Apr-2017
Navios Maritime Holdings Inc	28-Jan-11	350,000,000	USD	8.13%	28-Jan-2019
Navios Maritime Acquisition	21-Oct-10	400,000,000	USD	8.63%	21-Oct-2017
Hapag-Lloyd AG	8-Oct-10	250,000,000	USD	9.75%	15-Oct-2017
American Petroleum Tankers	17-May-10	275,000,000	USD	10.25%	15-May-2015
Overseas Shipholding Group Ltd.	30-Mar-10	300,000,000	USD	8.13%	30-Mar-2018
SK Shipping	19-Mar-10	100,000,000	USD	Float	9-Mar-2013
Overseas Shipholding Group Ltd.	1-Mar-10	300,000,000	USD	8.13%	1-Mar-2018
Berlian Laju Tanker	10-Feb-10	125,000,000	USD	12.00%	10-Feb-2015
Teekay Corp	1-Jan-10	450,000,000	USD	8.50%	1-Jan-2020

Fig. 3.11 Indicative shipping corporate bond issuances (*Source*: Clarksons, Morgan Stanley Research)

USA with the Oslo market being the distant second-most-important market for raising capital. Most of the activity outside of the USA and Oslo came from a small number of container liner operators. Apart from its depth and availability of capital, the US market has usually offered the highest valuation, making it the most attractive destination for international shipping companies who look to go public. There are currently around 50 publicly listed shipping companies on the NYSE or NASDAQ, most of which became public after 2004. In 2005 alone, 15 companies went public in these two markets, signaling the dynamic entry of the shipping industry into the US capital markets. Since then, US-listed shipping companies have raised more than USD30 billion in 228 public offerings. These numbers do not include the offshore sector, which is more closely tied to the oil and gas industry, or public offerings of preferred equity, which have also become attractive as yields are low and companies look to raise equity without diluting common shareholders. Since 2012, companies like Costamare, Diana Shipping, Safe Bulkers, Navios and Tsakos Energy Navigation have successfully issued preferred equity to fund acquisitions.

In the USA, IPOs are regulated by the Securities and Exchange Committee (SEC) under the Act of 1933. The company planning to go public files a prospectus—a financial document that provides the potential investors with information about the company's business, financial information and risk factors—with the SEC. After the prospectus has been approved by the SEC, the company and its underwriters market the offering to the investors during a roadshow that usually lasts around two weeks. During the roadshow, the underwriters collect the investors' orders ("book building") and arrive at the pricing of the company's shares based upon the new equity that is raised. In the USA, the whole IPO process, from initial preparation of the prospectus until final pricing, usually takes between four and six months. As soon as the company is public and the stock is trading, the company has a public currency that allows it to return to the market for additional capital by issuing more shares to investors through follow-on offerings. While the vast majority of the global shipping fleet still remains in the hands of private companies, an increasingly larger number of vessels are owned by public companies as more of them go public and the existing public companies expand with the assistance of newly raised capital (Figs. 3.12, 3.13, 3.14 and 3.15).

3.2.3.3 High Payout Structures and Master Limited Partnerships

The structures of the shipping companies that access the public markets have varied significantly according to market valuations and investors' appetites. The decline in interest rates during the last ten years and the increasing appetite for yield, particularly in the USA, has created a demand for companies

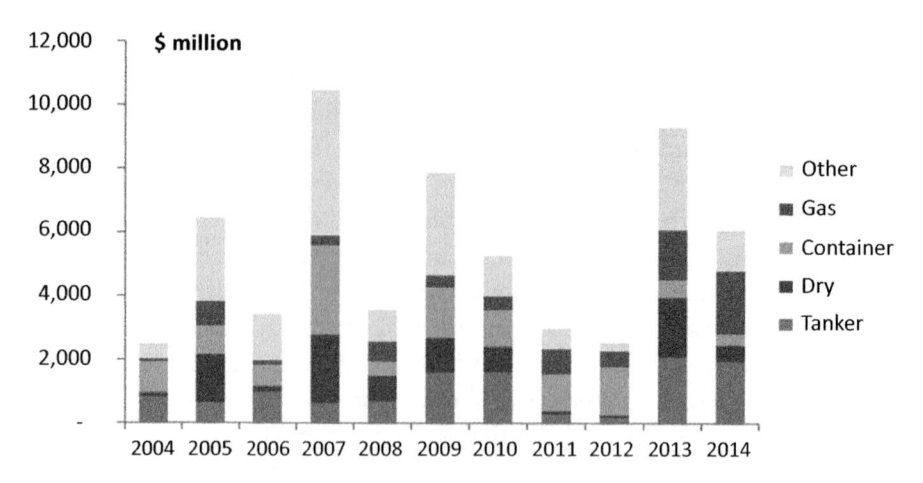

Fig. 3.12 Global shipping public offerings of common equity
(*Note*: Excludes underwriters' over-allotment option and listings in the offshore sector
Source: Morgan Stanley Research)

	US			Oslo			Hong Kong			Other			Total	
	# of Offerings	Amount ($m)	Mkt share	# of Offerings	Amount ($m)	Mkt share	# of Offerings	Amount ($m)	Mkt share	# of Offerings	Amount ($m)	Mkt share	# of Offerings	Amount ($m)
2004	11	1,204	48%	2	60	2%	2	1,065	43%	2	161	6%	17	2,490
2005	20	3,608	56%	2	335	5%	2	1,428	22%	8	1,078	17%	32	6,448
2006	13	1,713	50%	3	404	12%	-	-	0%	9	1,311	38%	25	3,427
2007	23	3,488	33%	4	313	3%	1	1,470	14%	10	5,196	50%	38	10,467
2008	15	2,372	66%	1	350	10%	1	35	1%	2	810	23%	19	3,567
2009	22	2,639	34%	3	276	4%	1	98	1%	9	4,855	62%	35	7,868
2010	27	3,297	63%	3	357	7%	2	429	8%	9	1,176	22%	41	5,259
2011	13	1,478	50%	2	359	12%	-	-	0%	4	1,141	38%	19	2,978
2012	10	1,055	42%	-	-	0%	-	-	0%	5	1,485	58%	15	2,540
2013	40	4,871	52%	17	3,232	35%	-	-	0%	9	1,192	13%	66	9,296
2014	34	3,888	64%	11	1,344	22%	-	-	0%	11	832	14%	56	6,063
Total	228	29,614	49%	48	7,030	12%	9	4,525	7%	78	19,236	32%	363	60,405

Fig. 3.13 Global shipping public offerings of common equity by country
(*Note*: Excludes underwriters' over-allotment option and listings in the offshore sector
Source: Morgan Stanley Research)

that pay dividends. A large number of companies adopted a high or full-payout dividend strategy due to the market's willingness to pay significant valuation premiums relative to the market value of the fleet for companies with high dividends. More than half of the equity raised in the USA during 2004–14 was by companies that had a high or full-payout strategy, including companies structured as master limited partnerships (MLPs).

MLPs are publicly listed entities that combine stable revenue and tax benefits under US federal law when the majority of their income is generated from qualifying resources, mostly related to energy or other natural resources, such as petroleum and natural gas extraction and transportation. Most MLPs are

	IPOs		Additional		Total	
	# of Offerings	Amount ($m)	# of Offerings	Amount ($m)	# of Offerings	Amount ($m)
2004	3	510	8	694	11	1,204
2005	15	3,041	5	567	20	3,608
2006	5	898	8	815	13	1,713
2007	6	1,276	17	2,213	23	3,488
2008	4	554	11	1,818	15	2,372
2009	-	-	22	2,639	22	2,639
2010	5	878	22	2,419	27	3,297
2011	3	453	10	1,026	13	1,478
2012	1	329	9	726	10	1,055
2013	5	1,379	35	3,492	40	4,871
2014	3	490	31	3,398	34	3,888
Total	50	9,807	178	19,807	228	29,614

Fig. 3.14 US-listed shipping public offerings of common equity
(*Note*: Excludes underwriters' over-allotment option and listings in the offshore sector
Source: Morgan Stanley Research)

	IPOs		Additional		Total	
	# of Offerings	Amount ($m)	# of Offerings	Amount ($m)	# of Offerings	Amount ($m)
2004	4	1,195	2	91	6	1,286
2005	9	2,729	3	111	12	2,840
2006	7	1,191	5	524	12	1,715
2007	11	6,666	4	313	15	6,979
2008	2	810	2	385	4	1,195
2009	2	134	11	5,095	13	5,229
2010	8	1,061	6	901	14	1,962
2011	4	549	2	951	6	1,500
2012	4	285	1	1,200	5	1,485
2013	8	1,402	18	3,023	26	4,425
2014	9	855	13	1,320	22	2,175
Total	68	16,876	67	13,914	135	30,791

Fig. 3.15 Non-US shipping public offerings of common equity
(*Note*: Excludes underwriters' over-allotment option and listings in the offshore sector
Source: Morgan Stanley Research)

limited partnerships, but they can also be limited liability companies or business trusts that are managed and operated by a general partner who is owned by the sponsor. Because MLPs are classified as partnerships, they are treated as "pass through" for tax purposes and avoid corporate income tax at both state and federal levels, reducing therefore their cost of funding which allows them to pay higher distributions. MLPs typically distribute all their available cash flow after taking into consideration the necessary retained reserves for maintenance, operating and growth expenditures. The lack of corporate taxes for shipping companies has eliminated the requirement of shipping MLPs to be structured as partnerships that issue complicated Schedule K-1s; instead, they are structured as regular corporations that issue their unit holders a simple Form 1099.

In a typical MLP structure, there are three classes of shares or units, with the public investors or limited partners holding the common units that are publicly traded and the general partner holding the subordinated units and the general partner units which usually correspond to 2% of the holding company, that is the owner of the vessels. The general partner may also own common units in the MLP. The common units are entitled to a minimum quarterly distribution (MQD), which means that only after the common unit holders have received their dividends do the rest of the units qualify for any additional distribution. The general partner also receives incentive distribution rights (IDRs) entitling them to a higher proportion of distributions as certain distribution targets are reached. This mechanism gives the sponsor the incentive to pursue accretive transactions that will increase the distribution of the MLP (Fig. 3.16).

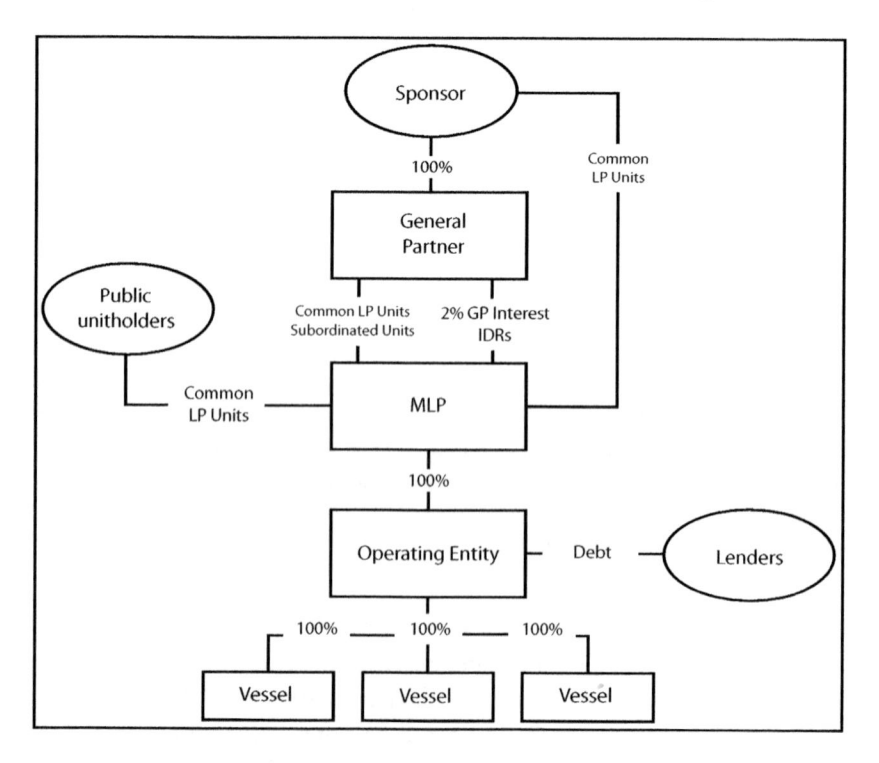

Fig. 3.16 Typical MLP structure

While international shipping companies receive income from worldwide activities and are registered in offshore jurisdictions (e.g. Liberia, the Marshall Islands, Panama or Malta) with favorable tax regimes that render corporate taxes meaningless, the MLP model has attracted significant attention after Teekay created the first shipping MLP in May 2005. Teekay LNG Partners raised USD132 million with an initial fleet of four LNG carriers and five Suezmax-class crude oil tankers with long-term charters ranging between 16 and 20 years. Since then, shipping MLPs have raised over USD7 billion of equity, nearly a quarter of the total equity raised in the US markets. As these entities are trading based on their yield, which usually ranges between 6 and 8%, the valuation premium versus the traditional publicly listed companies is significant, despite the lack of any tax advantages. This has also led non-energy related shipping companies that have vessels with long-term contracts, such as owners of containerships, to form MLP-type entities so as to take advantage of the arbitrage between the yield-based valuation and the market value of their assets.

The increasing appetite of investors for yield and the significant premium that yield-based valuation offers have also driven a number of shipping companies to adopt a high dividend payout strategy. Non-MLP structured high payout shipping companies listed in the USA raised around USD9 billion of common equity between 2004 and 2014, most of which was raised by dry bulk and tanker companies that tended to operate in a highly volatile market environment, and operate their ships under short or medium-term contracts. As many of these companies lacked long-term contracts and used back-loaded debt facilities to enhance their free cash flow, the collapse of the shipping markets after 2008 forced many of them to suspend dividend payments, resulting in an abrupt drop of their stock price. Since 2010, only a few companies that are not MLPs maintain a high payout strategy and the amount raised has shrunk to just a couple of hundred million USD every year from over USD2 billion at the peak of 2007 (Fig. 3.17).

3.2.3.4 Special Purpose Acquisition Companies

A special purpose acquisition company (SPAC) is a publicly traded buy-out company, also commonly called a "blank check" company, which raises money through an IPO in order to pursue a business combination or the acquisition of an existing company or group of assets that fall within the parameters described in the prospectus. SPACs raise a blind pool of money that is placed in a trust account until the consummation of the proposed

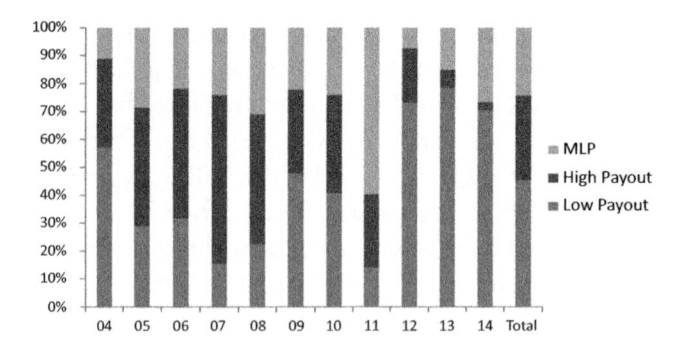

Fig. 3.17 US-listed shipping public offerings of common equity by payout strategy (*Source*: Company data, Morgan Stanley Research)

transaction that must first be approved by the shareholders, a process that must be completed within a predetermined period (usually 18–24 months) from the IPO. In the event that the shareholders reject the proposed transaction, the SPAC has to be dissolved and the funds returned to the investors after paying the fees and underwriting expenses that are usually funded by the sponsor of the IPO. In December 2004, International Shipping Enterprises was the first blank check company that raised USD171 million to invest in vessels or an operating business in the shipping industry. In the summer of 2005, the SPAC completed the acquisition of Navios Maritime Holdings, a dry bulk shipping company with a fleet of 27 vessels, for a total of USD594 million in cash, which was funded from the proceeds of the SPAC's IPO and bank debt. During 2004–07, five SPACs raised nearly USD1 billion to invest in the shipping industry, one of which had to be liquidated as the public shareholders rejected the proposed acquisition. The last IPO of a blank check company was completed in 2011, raising only USD48m that was used to acquire a fleet of offshore supply vessels (Fig. 3.18).

3.2.3.5 Private Equity

The dynamic entry of the shipping industry to the public markets has also attracted the attention of a large number of financial sponsors for private investments. Especially following the collapse of ship values after 2008, a number of private equity firms have shown interest in acquiring vessels, aiming to take advantage of the historical low asset prices and the anticipated subsequent recovery, either through an asset sale or through an IPO. Some of these investments have taken place in the form of joint ventures with a shipowner where both parties contribute capital such as Oaktree with Petros

Date	Company	Ticker	Offering size ($m)	Consumed
07/14/11	Nautilus Marine	NMARU	48	Yes
12/17/04	Int'l Shipping Enterpr.	ISHPU	171	Yes
12/15/05	Star Maritime	SEAU	189	Yes
07/18/06	EIAC	EII	203	No
02/28/07	Oceanaut	OKN-U	150	Yes
07/09/07	Seanergy	SRGU	220	Yes

Fig. 3.18 Blank check IPOs in the shipping industry (*Source*: Company data, Morgan Stanley Research)

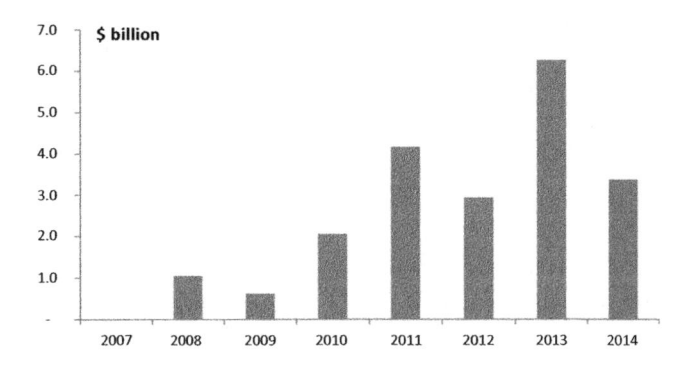

Fig. 3.19 Private equity investments in the shipping industry (*Source*: Marine Money International)

Pappas (Oceanbulk), and Kelso with George Youroukos (Technomar). In other cases the private equity put together a management team of experienced shipping executives, creating a new company with the purpose of eventually going public, such as Greenbriar investment in Ardmore Shipping. From the shipowners' perspective, the lack of bank financing and the opportunity to expand their operations during the market downturn has led them to seek capital through partnership with private equity investors. According to *Marine Money International*, over USD20 billion of capital has been invested in the industry since 2008 (Fig. 3.19).

3.3 Conclusion

Despite the ebbs and flows of the shipping cycles, the maritime industry will continue to expand, driven by the growth of the global economy and the need of developing countries to access resources that have to be shipped from distant parts of the world to support their growth. As the global trade expands, the need for significant investment in larger and more sophisticated assets will continue to grow, requiring greater amounts of capital. During this course, shipping companies and capital providers will have to face the risks of highly volatile operating cash flows and vessel prices, making risk management a central consideration of every investment decision. While bank debt financing is likely to remain the most important source of capital for the industry, a great array of alternatives is available today to shipping companies. The dynamic entry of the shipping industry to the capital markets has widely increased the number of products that shipping executives can choose from, adding at the same time complexity to their decision-making process. These decisions require these executives not only to be constantly informed about the availability of these products, but also to understand the risks that they entail as well as the impact on the value of their company.

Bibliography

Stopford, M. (2009), Maritime Economics.

Albertjn, S., Bessler, W. and Drobetz, W. (2011), Financing Shipping Companies and Shipping Operations: A Risk-Management Perspective, Journal of Applied Corporate Finance, 24(4), 70–82.

Campbell Houston. (2014), Overview of Ship Finance, Presentation at 2014 Marine Money

Clarksons Intelligence Network Database

4

Shipbuilding Finance

Charles R. Cushing

4.1 Introduction

Unquestionably, the acquisition of a vessel is a major undertaking. It is a project that involves the expenditure of a vast amount of money, manpower and other resources. Frequently, such an acquisition program calls for acquiring not just one vessel but several at the same time. This makes the project even more financially significant. Because of the amount of money involved, the long-term major commitment of the buyer and the risks involved, a vessel acquisition program requires a formal and disciplined approach to the project. This includes strategic planning, the development of a mission statement, the use of professional advice, the identification of risks, the development of a schedule and budget, and strict adherence to them—in short, disciplined project management.

4.1.1 Reasons for Vessel Acquisition

The acquisition of a vessel may be driven by a number of reasons. For a shipping company, it may be to create more shipping capacity in an expanding trade or to capture more market share. It may be to open new trade routes or to develop

---

C.R. Cushing (✉)
C. R. Cushing & Co., Inc., 30 Vesey Street, 7th Floor, New York, NY 10007, USA

© The Author(s) 2016
M.G. Kavussanos, I.D. Visvikis (eds.), *The International Handbook of Shipping Finance*, DOI 10.1057/978-1-137-46546-7_4

the capability to carry new or different cargoes. Another reason is to replace aging or technologically obsolete vessels, or to take advantage of new technology. Non-transportation users of vessels are driven by the same reasons, that is new services, expansion of project work, obsolescence and technology.

A second category of business interests that acquire ships is the "non-user" investor. Investors may purchase vessels as an investment opportunity, a method to put their capital to work. Lenders satisfy their investment objectives by aiding and financing end-users who are capital deficient. Financiers use a variety of techniques to charter or lease the vessels to the users.

4.1.2 Alternatives to New Construction

This chapter discusses the financing aspects of the construction of vessels, that is "new buildings". However, there are other routes to satisfying the needs described above. Instead of building new vessels, the buyer or investor may consider:

1. Second-hand vessel purchase;
2. Ship conversion;
3. Chartering (voyage, time, bareboat);
4. Leasing;
5. Contracts of affreightment;
6. Mergers;
7. Pooling and slot chartering.

Many of the issues discussed in this chapter could apply to the above alternatives, but we will focus mainly on new vessel acquisition.

4.1.3 Reasons for an Orderly Approach to Vessel Acquisition and Project Financing

The commercial ship acquisition process is not well documented in the literature. While much is written on the subject of naval vessel acquisition, this is not so with merchant vessels. Some techniques such as design-built or construction-management may be flawed or contain serious risks to the commercial vessel buyer or investor. The careers of some managers are often transient and a vessel acquisition project may be a once-in-a-lifetime experience. Yet many managers with little experience and lack of regard for the risks will control the acquisition process. The acquisition of a vessel is a major capital undertaking and requires disciplined and proven project management techniques.

There is much money at stake in the building of a vessel, and the buyer's company's very survival may be at risk. In the case of non-users, such as financial institutions, buyers may lack vessel-owning, operation or acquisition experience. In a buyer's market, the buyers are often subjected to aggressive shipbuilder marketing efforts. Therefore, the buyer's staff must use every technique and disciplined effort to stay on proper course.

4.1.4 What Can Go Wrong in Ship Acquisition Projects?

Current methods may omit some or many good or best practices. Planning is the most ignored step. Many buyers will omit competitive bidding, believing that their negotiation skills are sufficient to reach a best price. The concepts of formulation and mission statement are almost always omitted. Frequently, important factors in economic analyses are ignored, omitted or misapplied. These include objectives-of-the-firm, depreciation, taxation, life of the asset, residual value and the effects of inflation. Other poor practices include reliance on letters of intent, heads-of-agreements, non-definitive contract plans and specifications, inexperienced construction project managers (such as operating personnel without project management or shipyard experience), learners-on-the-job and class surveyors.

A major deficiency in vessel acquisition projects is to underestimate seriously the daunting tasks ahead. Participants may undertake many of the tasks themselves and fail to engage experienced professionals in such areas as legal, technical, finance, ship brokering and project management. This false economy is often done to save consulting fees or commissions, which are in many cases only 1% or less of the entire project cost. This is especially important because of the many pitfalls mentioned above.

4.1.5 What Is Project Management?

Project management is the process of planning, organizing and controlling project activities so as to meet specific goals and objectives. Projects are temporary rather than continuous processes. They have definite starting and completion dates. The process includes:

1. Planning and defining the project, developing plans, mission statement, defining goals, developing work and work-breakdown plans.
2. Establishing and controlling the schedule, defining interrelationships between tasks, sequencing tasks and establishing milestones, timing and deadlines.

3. Preparing and controlling the budget, including identifying and estimating all costs, providing margins for contingencies and adopting financial controls.
4. Controlling the entire project, including proper staffing, good communications, identifying critical paths and bottlenecks, taking corrective action and quality control.
5. Financial and contingency planning.

4.1.6 Strategic Planning

Examples of strategic planning date back thousands of years: Sun Tzu's *The Art of War* (2,400 years ago), Miyamoto Musashi's *Book of Five Rings* and Napoleon's campaigns. These evolved over time into a formal process. Simply, strategic planning involves:

1. Setting goals and a mission;
2. assessing the environment;
3. appraising the organization's capabilities;
4. developing a strategy;
5. implementing the strategy;
6. monitoring and controlling the strategy.

Good financial planning and financial analysis are integral parts of a strategic plan. The ability to assess adequately international markets as well as the impact of inflation and taxation and their trends during the environmental analysis phase are important. During the development of strategies phase of the plan, pro forma projections need to be developed and compared so that an optimum strategy can be selected. During the strategic planning phase, the buyer must be able to articulate the corporate objectives. Profitability, return on investment and financial resources are some of the important areas of concern. Finance policies and accounting practices are controllable strategic objectives and should also be reviewed and defined.

4.1.7 Forecasting

In planning, the determination of historical and current shipping pricing levels is a relatively straightforward task; but the forecasting of transportation pricing even over a short period is much more difficult. Current and past price levels are available through conferences, stock analysts, brokers, agents, published rates, trade publications and other research sources. The practice of rebating, while very prevalent in the past, but now illegal in many places, is also difficult to quantify since both shippers and carriers are reluctant to discuss details. The availability of bulk transport pricing data is even more readily available, especially when the trading is on a worldwide basis. Such pricing is reported in absolute terms, as charter fixtures, or keyed to freight indices. When bulk transportation is carried out under contracts of affreightment, the pricing is usually private and confidential information, and even more difficult to obtain.

An important element in price forecasting is the cost analysis. The elements of the cost analysis, particularly the operating costs, are closely linked to national and international economic indices. Appropriate elements of these indices, such as labor and energy components, can be applied to the cost patterns of one's own and one's competitor's operations. The forecasting of prices is carried out by charting, fundamental and statistical analyses, or a mixture of these methods. The simplest form of charting is the extrapolation of historical data. Difficulties arise, however, as rates fluctuate. Zannetos (1966) and other chartists have made a lifetime study of charting and predicting tanker rates, and attempting, with limited success, to determine the periodicity of such fluctuations. On the other hand, the fundamentalists attempt to predict the future environment and the impact of events on the pricing of transportation, according to supply and demand fluctuations.

Price forecasting is easier in stable trades, which occur where there are high entry barriers, closed conferences, pooling agreements and consortia. Conversely, there is more volatility in trades with such characteristics as low barriers to entry, weak conferences, low levels of profitability, the presence of marginal operators and when vessels engage in other light back-haul or triangular trades looking for cargoes of opportunity. Supply and particularly severe over-capacity or over-tonnaging will have a dramatic impact on rates. Government aid to shipping and/or shipbuilding will also stimulate the supply side and depress rates. Conversely, prosperity and, perversely, international conflicts and calamities will have the effect of raising rates. These events are very difficult to predict. New entrants or the introduction of new technology or ships with added capacity (larger or faster vessels) usually will also depress rates. Competition, predatory pricing practices and price wars will artificially or temporarily depress prices.

All of these factors make the work of the pricing forecaster extremely difficult. Nevertheless, such forecasts must be carried out since revenue represents one half of the equation, which defines profitability. Rate projections must be combined with a realistic assessment of capacity utilization in order to arrive at planned income or revenue levels. It is important that the strategic planner understands the reliability of the assumptions, which must be made, limitations in such forecasts and the confidence limits in the projections. It is therefore necessary that sensitivity studies and risk analyses be carried out.

4.1.8 Plans

During the final phases of a strategic plan a number of sub-plans should be developed covering (1) business, (2) financing, (3) operations, (4) marketing, (5) technology, (6) competitors, (7) human resources and (8) the organization. The business, financing plans and financial model are of particular interest here. At the outset, lenders want to see and review the shipping company's business plan, which should consist of at the very least company ownership, its financial health, assets, indebtedness, a history of the company, a description of the company, its marketing strategy, its management team and organization, personnel, operations, funds required, their use and timing, other financial data, risks, entry and exit plans, contingency plans, sensitivity studies (worst case and best case), legal issues and insurance considerations. The financing plan must define the budget and budgetary controls to be used for the business plan, the cash flow and capital requirements and what the borrower is prepared to put forward as collateral and guarantees, both corporate and personal, as well as acceptable mortgage terms.

4.1.9 Mission Statement

It is essential that the shipping company's chief financial officer and finance team be aware of and have an opportunity to provide input and even participate in the strategic plan. They and other key departments need to understand the details of the acquisition plan. This can best be done by using a mission statement and communicating it to those in the vessel acquisition process. The complexity of researching, designing and building a vessel is apparent. The criteria to be used for the design and acquisition may involve hundreds of factors. For the sake of good order, and so as to communicate a common standard to the entire team, it is essential that the basic criteria be set down in a mission statement. The principal results of the technology plan should form a part of the mission statement. The objectives of the firm or owner and key elements of the company's strategic plan should also be embodied in the mission statement.

A second purpose of the mission statement is to prevent the unintentional or accidental deviation from the original objectives. It prevents deviation from the agreed upon strategic plan, which in turn results in changes and cost overruns. When and if the early objectives change, the mission statement records these modifications. The mission statement becomes a control document that aids management and the vessel acquisition team in staying on course.

4.1.10 Vessel Design

The design process should be of interest to all involved in ship finance. Traditionally, the design process is divided into four phases: concept, preliminary, contract and detailed design. The concept design is the starting phase where innovation can be introduced into the process. It involves very little in the way of drawing, calculating and design, but is the phase where the concepts and objectives from the strategic plan begin to take form and shape. Importantly, it is where there is an opportunity to add or develop innovative features and their economic implications to the vessel and even to anticipate future competition.

The preliminary design phase is where the principal features of the vessel are determined. From a financial perspective, the work during this phase should be monitored to ensure that the objectives of the strategic plan and mission statement are being adhered to, especially regarding costs, revenue and hence profitability. During this phase the volume and weight of the vessel and the required power will be determined. Therefore, a reasonable estimate of the cost of building the ship emerges for the first time in the process. It is also possible to estimate fuel and lubrication consumption, the single largest operating cost center, by far. During the phase, the carrying capacity of the vessel (i.e. the revenue generating capability of the vessel) is determined. Whether it is deadweight type cargo or volume cargo, the number of tons of liquid or dry bulk, the number of containers, cars or trucks, pallets or passengers, all must meet the objectives set out in the mission statement. Excessive cost and/or insufficient revenue generating capability will be apparent at this stage. If necessary the design and/or objectives can be changed at this early stage. The contract design phase develops a definitive specification and set of drawings with sufficient detail to permit shipyards to quote a fixed price to be used for a contract. The detailed design is developed by the builder after the contract.

4.1.11 Sources of Ship Finance

There are three main sources of funds available to a purchaser to support the acquisition of a vessel: debt financing, equity financing and grants. There are many variations within these three conceptual sources. These will be discussed in greater detail. Debt financing includes bank loans, bond issuers, shipyard credit, private and public offerings, loan syndications, high yield corporate debt (junk bonds), leasing and other debt instruments. Equity includes owner's equity, limited partnerships, sale of shares, sale of assets, cash flow and initial public offerings (IPOs). There are also combinations of debt and equity in hybrid schemes. These include convertible debt, debt with warrants, K/S and K/G partnerships, blocked currency schemes, tax supports, barter trade deals and other unusual methods. Grants and gifts include government aid and grants, government loan guarantees, cash grants, subsidies, favorable tax treatment, moratoria on debt repayment, subsidized interest rates and many other similar sources.

The decision on which method or combination of methods to use depends on a great number of factors. The Harvard Business School recommends that, before selecting a financing method, five important factors be analyzed. This approach is called flexibility, risk, income, control and timing (FRICT). Credit ratings are issued by credit rating agencies. Where the borrower does not have a credit rating, potential lenders will evaluate the credit worthiness of the borrower. The three largest credit rating agencies are Moody's Investor Services, Standard & Poor's Rating Services and Fitch Ratings, which together control about 95% of the business. The rating agencies rate financial institutions, insurance companies, issuers of securities and corporations. In ship finance, the latter is of most interest. Credit ratings are issued on the creditworthiness of the shipping company, that is will a loan be repaid or will the company default on its loans. The rating range is from AAA at the top to D at the bottom. Anything below Fitch's or S&P's BBB⁻ (Moody's Baa3) is considered below investment grade or speculative/risky. The significance to the shipping company seeking shipbuilding loans is that the rating will dictate what method of finance is likely to succeed. Factors that should be considered and the possible financing method include:

Condition	Financing method
Unused tax depreciation	Leasing
Excess debt	Equity
Potential business risk	Equity
Buyer's market	Shipyard credit
Strong earning power	Debt
Predictable earnings	Debt
Long-term, fixed rates	Bonds
Buyer's market	Export credits
Low stock prices	Hybrid
High risk	Junk bonds, mezzanine financing

4.1.12 Ship Finance

Ship finance provides sources of funds for the building of new vessels or major conversions. More typically, the buyer of vessels seeks finance from lenders or investors. But a buyer or investor in vessels may provide funds from his or her own assets, the liquidation of physical assets or investments, or from retained earnings. Non-owner/operators, and investors who see investment opportunities in shipping, almost always seek finance to share in the cost of new construction. Banks, insurance companies, pension funds and similar organizations seeking opportunities to put their deposits to work will engage in shipbuilding.

The purchaser of vessels sometimes will finance them in two stages, namely bridge financing for construction then long-term financing. They may be done by the same lenders. Bridge, interim or construction finance may come from one or more entities, such as shipyard financing, shipyards' banks or the central or government banks in the shipbuilder's country. This is done to stimulate or encourage production in the host country. Bridge financing covers the period of construction. It is customary in shipbuilding contracts for the buyer to provide progress payments during construction. These payments are keyed to contractually defined milestone events such as contract signing, keel laying, steel and machinery deliveries to the yard, commencement of construction, percentage of completion of steel work and other activities, and successful completion of trials and delivery. The owner's inspection staff at the yard or third parties sign off that the payment milestones have been met.

The title to the new vessel passes from the builder to the buyer at one of a number of different events depending on the defined contract terms and the laws of the jurisdiction of the contract and, in some cases, *lex situs* (the law of the place of construction). These events may be during construction, the completion of the work, the full payment of the contract price and extras, the registry of the vessel (flag rising) or during the formal delivery protocols. At this time, long-term or permanent ship financing should be in place.

4.1.13 Choosing a Source of Funds for Ship Construction

There are many sources of funds available to a shipowner planning new construction. For shipowners, commercial bank ship mortgage loans have been the most usual source. With the tightening of credit, more conservatism in bank loan reserves, and cyclical economic and market forces, shipowners have had to turn elsewhere. Lease financing has filled some of the gap. Shipping has turned to equity investors for funding and the public markets for large financings. The availability of funds from different entities will depend on many factors, such as international and domestic economic conditions, the health of the shipping industry and particularly the ship-type sector (for example tanker, bulk carrier, container vessel, cruise), oversupply or scarcity of the type of vessel, the history and economic health of the shipowner, the quality of his or her business plan, and business opportunities, risks and many other factors. These will determine which lending sectors are more likely to attract favorable sources of funding. These sources include: commercial banks, commercial credit companies, export credit agencies (ECAs), government or central banks, government subsidies, high risk investors, hybrid financing schemes, insurance companies, investment and merchant banks, Islamic banks, leasing companies, limited partnerships, master limited partnerships (MLPs), mezzanine financing, mortgage banks, international banks, owner's equity, partnerships, pension funds, private placement, public markets, shipyard credit, syndicated loans, underwriters and wealth management banks, and in some unusual cases blocked currency schemes and barter trading.

Commercial bank credit is available in the form of ship mortgage loans, which are structured for a fixed period of time with period repayments, at agreed upon interest rates, provisions for collateral and usually a mortgage. The collateral may include: first mortgage, second mortgage (for subordinated loans), assignment of charter hire (assuming the owner will charter the vessel), guarantees, corporate and/or personal, and assignment of insurance. A bank when considering whether to provide a loan, will consider: the history of the company, the character of the management, the use of funds and the nature of the project. The bank will also consider: the financial health of the borrower, by reviewing (1) the current ratio (current assets and liabilities), (2) the interest earned, (3) the debt to equity ratio, (4) the total debt coverage, (5) the operating ratio and any guaranteed cash-flow charter contracts.

4.1.14 Debt Financing

Any form of financing that requires repayment is, in reality, debt financing. This in general refers to secured and unsecured loans or bonds. Borrowed funds are usually the least expensive but most restrictive form of ship finance. The most usual source of debt financing is through commercial or government sources. Such loans are almost always collateralized with ship mortgages and other forms of security. Bank and similar loans never cover 100% of the funds required. As their availability becomes restrictive, such loans will only cover 60–80% of the value of the new vessel. There are two main reasons why banks no longer lend 100% of the value of the new vessel to be built. First, the banks want the owner to be seriously committed to the venture; second, in the event of liquidation, the bank is more likely to recover this loan fully.

Commercial bank loans are by far the most common method of ship finance. The traditional sources are from commercial banks and ship finance banks, investment banks, government or central banks, institutional investors, finance companies, pension funds, insurance companies, manufacturers of components of a new vessel, vendors and individual investors. Banks may group together to cover a project, that is syndicated loans. The owner may also issue bonds in the public market. Commercial bank loans, capital raised from insurance companies and pension funds, together with bonds, will be regarded as senior debt, meaning that in the event of default they are usually ahead of mezzanine or subordinated debt.

The advantages of debt financing for shipowners include:

1. Maintaining control of the shipping operation and ownership of the shipping company.
2. Tax benefits, wherein interest on business loans is deductible from taxes. This has the effect of lowering the real bank rate of interest.

The disadvantages include:

1. Higher interest rates if economic conditions impact on the shipowner's loan or his or her credit rating deteriorates.
2. Repayment obligations to the lender regardless of success or failure of the shipping venture. Repayment to lenders takes precedence over any equity investors.
3. Deterioration of credit rating (such as Moody's or Standard & Poor's) and resulting higher interest rates on the current or future loans.

4.1.15 Loans Syndication

With large shipbuilding loans, commercial banks prefer to spread the risks by assembling a group of banks to share in both the loan and the risk. This is called a "syndicate". A commercial or investment bank ("arranger") assembles and organizes the participating banks. The issuer pays a fee to the arranger.

One bank assumes the role of lead bank, which manages the loan process and interfaces with the shipping company and prepares the documentation. The lead bank also coordinates the needs of the borrower with the willingness of the participating bank to provide its portion of the funds. If the syndicate consists of a large number of smaller or inexperienced banks, the group becomes unwieldy and the process takes time. A more efficient syndicate has a few, say four or five, large, experienced banks. In either case, the lead bank earns its fees and commission for setting up the syndicate and for the ongoing management of the loan.

There are three types of syndications: (1) underwritten, (2) best-effort and (3) club deal. In the underwritten syndication, the arranger(s) guarantee the commitment and then syndicate the loan to the other participating banks. In the best-effort syndicate only a portion of the loan is guaranteed by the arrangers. The remainder may or may not materialize. If not, the deal may fail or have to be restructured. In the club syndicate, a smaller loan is divided among a few banks of similar size and type which share equally or nearly so in the arranger fees.

4.1.16 Mezzanine Financing

In an effort to raise a higher percentage than would otherwise be obtained by first-mortgage funding, and where the bank or other lenders are unwilling to provide sufficient funds to close the deal, the owner may resort to mezzanine financing, which is a form of debt finance lower in rank than senior debt but superior to ordinary equity. The secondary lender is prepared to take the risk that if the borrowing company defaults he or she will fully recover the loan after the senior debt has been paid. He or she is willing to take that risk because of a high rate of return, through higher interest rates, and possibly other benefits such as conversion rights. The debt may be in the form of second-mortgage loans, but may also be secured and unsecured loans, stock, junk bonds, subordinated loans or preferred shares. The advantages to the shipping company are several: (1) it provides a source of funds, which the senior lender is not prepared to provide; (2) it can provide a more flexible repayment term; (3) it may mitigate the covenants and financial tests that are demanded by the senior lender; and (4) it spreads the dependence on debt financing across more than one source. Such mezzanine financing is often provided to small shipping companies. Non-bank lenders tend to finance borrowers that traditional banks shun. Such borrowers include smaller vessels, smaller deals, financially inferior vessel owners or vessels of non-traditional registries. Such borrowers may need to provide other methods that reduce risks, such as corporate guarantees, personal guarantees or additional collateral. Hence, higher rates are charged for mezzanine financing. These mezzanine lenders tend to have less influence on the vessel construction process.

4.1.17 Bonds

A shipowner may raise capital by issuing bonds. These are debt instruments of longer term (i.e. maturity is longer than one year), but they mature at a given date. However, in some cases the bond may have a call option that allows the issuer to redeem the debt early. The borrower's shipbuilding bonds are certificates of indebtedness issued for a specific purpose and at specific rates.

4.1.18 High Yield ("Junk") Financing

For some shipping companies such as those rated at below investment grade, high yield (junk) bond financing provides access to capital and the ability to leverage that would not be available from commercial banks. While the borrower pays a higher interest rate, the advantage to the shipping company is that it does not dilute its ownership by resorting to equity financing. Junk bond financing provides higher interest rates to compensate the lender for the higher risks. In times of financial crisis, where bank financing is scarce and harder to obtain, shipowners have resorted to high yield (junk) bond financing. Concurrently, investors in search of higher yield lending opportunities have been willing to accept "covenant lite" terms that give lenders certain rights when the borrower has problems. High yield bonds typically have longer terms (ten years) than traditional bank loans (seven to ten years). High yield bonds also differ from commercial bank loans as they can be amortizing or non-amortizing. When they are non-amortizing, the borrower only pays interest throughout the terms of the bond and repays the principal at maturity (a so-called "bullet"). An exception to this is where the bond has an amortization feature where the borrower pays a portion of the principal during the terms of the loan.

4.1.19 Shipyard Credit

Another source of shipbuilding finance is shipyard credit, which is a way of competing for orders. Such financing may be (1) *buyer's credit* (the most usual form of shipbuilding credit), where the loan is made directly to the buyer to permit him or her to pay for the vessel before delivery; or (2) *builder's or supplier's credit*, where the loan is made to the shipyard which agrees to defer repayments or a portion of the payments by the buyer until some time after delivery of the vessel. The interest rate charged on yard credit is sometimes supported or subsidized by some governments as a method to attract orders to their yards. Governments also have provided shipbuilding credit to stimulate work in their country's yards. This kind of credit is in fact disguised subsidy, though the OECD and national credit agencies, such as Export-import Bank of South Korea (KEXIM), Export-import Bank of U.S. (EXIM), CEXIM (China), Export Credit Guarantee Department (UK) (ECGD), Hermes (Germany) and Export-import Bank of China (EIBC), should ensure fair competition. The OECD and the WTO also attempt to control fair trade principles.

4.1.20 Leasing

Leasing is a method of increasing assets without equity input from shareholders. It is also a method for a shipping company to obtain lower financing rates by giving up tax advantages that they may not be able to use. The lessor (owner) is able to deduct depreciation from taxes. In offshore companies that pay little or no corporate tax, the benefits may be nil. Lease financing has been a major source of ship financing for decades. Long-term charters may even be considered a form of lease finance. A finance lease (sometimes referred to as a "dry lease") is a full payout lease wherein the lessor structures the lease so as to provide the equity portion and recover the full cost of the vessel. The lessee is responsible for making the lease payments and to provide all operating costs of the vessel, including maintenance, repair, insurance, crew costs, stores and suppliers, and other operating costs. The lessor is the owner of the vessel and essentially "rents" the vessel to the shipping company. The lease is for a stated period of time, and payments are made at regular intervals such as monthly, quarterly or annually. The lessee may have an option to renew the lease at termination of the period and at a lower rate.

In a finance lease, the lessor owns the vessel and charters it to the shipping company. The lessor typically has other taxable income in other operations, and as owner takes tax deductions for depreciation, interest expenses and investment incentives such as investment tax credits. The lessor, in taking advantage of these tax benefits, is able to pass along some of these to a shipping company. The lessor also gains, unless otherwise agreed to, by owning the residual value of the vessel at the end of the lease. The lessor can then re-lease or sell the vessel. The operating lease is sometimes referred to as a "wet lease", where the lessor is responsible for providing the operating costs and maintaining, insuring and crewing the vessel.

Most vessel leases are "leveraged leases", where an investor provides a portion of the purchase price of the vessel, say 20–40%. The remainder of the vessel price is raised as debt and is secured by a mortgage and assignment of lease payments to the bank financier. In a finance lease, the banks always insist on "hell or high water" terms (i.e. the lease payments are always paid regardless of any difficulties encountered). The investor, as owner, enjoys benefits, such as depreciation, interest and investment, tax credits and residual value. The key issue in leasing is who retains the residual value and under what terms.

Off-balance sheet financing is a technique in which neither the asset nor the indebtedness appears on the books of the lessee, who is able to incur an increased amount of debt. For many years, in the USA, the major tanker fleets and the major oil companies engaged in chartering, particularly with the view that the charters would not appear on their balance sheet and encumber further borrowing. US laws and generally accepted accounting principles (GAAP) now prohibit this practice, although it is to be found in many parts of the world. Nevertheless, sophisticated lenders, in doing due diligence searches, always enquire for details of any existing charter obligations.

International accounting standard setters have been trying for years to change lease accounting. They want shipping companies to record lease obligations on their balance sheets. The shipping industry balks at these proposals, arguing that a time charter is not a lease and that, while it does involve an asset (the ship), it is also a contract for services. This leads to complexity in dividing the balance sheet obligations. Until these issues are resolved, the ship financier or investor should move cautiously and identify all the borrower's obligations and assure that there is sufficient equity in the transaction before lending.

In summary:

1. frequently, leasing provides a way of increasing assets without equity input from shareholders;
2. commitment often does not appear on the balance sheet;
3. as it is not always a long-term commitment, the company can increase debt;
4. the owner cannot take advantage of shifting asset values (i.e. buying and selling);
5. leasing provides tax benefits.

4.1.21 Interest Rates

When loans are made, the interest and repayment are paid to the lender. Islamic financing is an exception, as the concept of interest is contrary to Islamic law. The rate may be fixed or floating. The loan agreement establishes the type and amount of interest to be paid. In the USA and Britain, LIBOR is commonly used for floating rates. In Europe, the Euro Interbank Offered Rate (Euribor) is sometimes used as an index. Floating rates are tied to an index, usually LIBOR, which is the average rate at which leading banks in London are willing to place deposits and charge other banks. The LIBOR rate is set daily by the Intercontinental Exchange. An interest rate cap allows shipowners to protect themselves against increasing debt funding costs as a result of rising interest rates, whilst also allowing them to retain the benefit of lower rates. The buyer of an interest rate cap is required to pay an upfront premium to the cap seller. An interest rate floor provides its holder with protection against downward movements in interest rates. An interest rate collar is a combination of a cap and a floor: an agreement by the borrower to pay the difference between the actual interest and an agreed floor level, when the latter is above the actual level. This enables the buyer of the collar to fix a maximum and minimum rate payable on his or her liabilities. For example, a borrower would buy a cap at one level (say 9%) and sell a floor at another level (say 6%). By buying the cap they will be protected against rates exceeding 9%, but by selling the floor they are committed to paying a minimum of 6% and will not benefit should rates fall below this level. Often the collar is constructed on a zero-cost basis with the premium payable on the cap being offset by the premium receivable on the floor. A method for reducing the extra cost for a cap is to arrange a collar. An interest rate swap, in its simplest form, involves an exchange of fixed interest payments for floating rate payments, usually linked to an index such as LIBOR. For shipowners with LIBOR-linked borrowings, a swap can be used to transform the floating rate facility into a fixed rate loan. The shipowner will receive a floating rate payment on the swap, which offsets the floating rate interest cost on the borrowings. The fixed rate paid by the shipowner on the swap becomes the effective cost of borrowing and provides protection against rising interest rates. The spread is the interest rate paid in addition to a risk free rate (i.e. LIBOR). An interest rate swap is a deal between banks and companies where borrowers switch floating-rate loans for fixed-rate loans. The advantage to this is that one company may have access to lower fixed rates and the other company may have access to lower floating rates—so they trade. The most common type of a swap is refereed to as a "plain vanilla swap". Here the companies typically exchange fixed rate payments against floating rate payments. The principal amounts are not exchanged, and are known as the notional principal. Where two counter-parties exchange a stream of interest payments (at a fixed rate) for (a floating rate), the two streams of payments are called "legs".

4.1.22 Ship Mortgages and Other Loan Security

The senior lender or lenders will require a first or preferred mortgage as part of the security they require. The purposes of the mortgage are to create a public record of the lien, and most importantly to establish the priority of the mortgage over any other liens or claims which may exist or arise against the vessel. In the event of default or bankruptcy, the holders of the first mortgage stand second in line to be paid out, after any outstanding crew wages (which stand in first priority). It is also the basis for an agreement between the lender and the owner concerning the issues of operation, maintenance, insurance and trading areas. The mortgage must be executed with the assistance of an experienced lawyer. Such ship mortgages are filed with authorities in the vessel's home port. The existence of the mortgage is noted on the ship's papers and must also be posted on the navigation bridge. A second mortgage is a subordinated mortgage and, in the event of default, is paid out only after the first mortgage is fully repaid.

Depending upon the loan agreement, very often the borrower will agree to the assignment of income to pay interest and loan repayments. If there is a mishap resulting in insurance claims, the loan agreement may call for the assignment of insurance proceeds, which could include hull, machinery, protection and indemnity (P&I), war risk and loss of earnings. The lending agreement may also contain matters relating to the operation of the vessel and a requirement for maintenance, and will record the types and value of the insurance. Trading limits may restrict the areas of the world where the vessel may operate.

The loan document will include such information as:

1. flag state endorsement of record;
2. date and time of recording;
3. applicable law;
4. enforceability of lien;
5. covenants, such as:
    (a) definitions;
    (b) description of vessel;
    (c) insurance type and amount;

(d) trading restrictions, if any;
(e) maintenance and repair standards;
(f) compliance with regulations;
(g) payment of expenses;
(h) payment of future liens;
(i) posting of mortgage in the vessel;
(j) payments in event of default;
(k) other lender remedies in event of default, including taking possession of vessel and owner's power of attorney;
(l) application of insurance proceeds;
(m) application of liquidation proceeds.

Liquidation proceeds are usually applied for in the following sequence:

1. expense advanced on behalf of owner;
2. senior debt;
3. junior debt;
4. creditors;
5. owners.

The shipowner has the obligation to notify the mortgagor if the vessel is seized, libeled or detained. The owner may not sell, abandon, long-term charter or remortgage the vessel without the permission of the mortgagor. The second mortgagor does not have priority over an earlier registered mortgage ship, repairer lien or any maritime liens. Other forms of security required by lenders may include:

1. assignment of income certainty;
2. assignment of insurances certainty, including hull, machinery, protection and indemnity, war risk and loss of earnings insurance;
3. corporate guarantees;
4. personal guarantees.

Security maintenance in the mortgage documents most of the time requires the owner to provide additional security if the value of the vessel falls below an agreed upon loan-to-value amount. These maximum loan to value covenants are the most important ones governing most ship financing. The problem with ship valuations in a declining market is that the traditional method for valuation is the potential price in the current market, but representative prices may be hard to find. Ship valuations are provided by approved valuation experts on a "willing seller, willing buyer" basis. This methodology allows for the circumstances described here—for example, in a weak market there may be no "willing seller" and therefore the perceived market price is not the same as the valued price. The loan agreement will contain a minimum value constraint that if the value of the vessel drops below a certain percentage of the remaining debt, say 120%, then the lender may require additional security and, absent that, foreclose.

Documents that the prospective shipowner should present to the potential lender include:

1. background memorandum:
    (a) company ownership;
    (b) corporate structure;
    (c) company history;
    (d) current and future strategy;
    (e) management team;
    (f) business or operating philosophy;
2. transaction details;
3. vessel details;
4. shipbroker valuations (if any);
5. borrower's financial statements;
6. corporate guarantor's financial statements;
7. personal guarantor's financial statements;
8. fleet list and employment details;
9. cash flow forecast;
10. proposed time charters (if any);
11. proposed ship construction contract;
12. references from bankers, brokers, charterers, suppliers and agents.

4.1.23 Export Credit Agencies (ECA)

A further source of funding to a shipowner or a shipbuilder seeking to assist the owner in financing his or her project is through an export credit agency, sometimes called an export-import bank (in the USA) or an investment insurance agency. Most developed, industrial countries have export credit agencies, mainly to stimulate manufacturing within their own country. Export credit agencies may be either private institutions or agencies of the government. Export credit agencies can provide direct lending to a project, provide intermediary loans to commercial banks, subsidize the loan interest rate or provide loan guarantees. In shipbuilding scenarios, the benefits provided by export credit agencies are usually tied to specific domestically manufactured vessels.

4.1.24 Hybrid Financing Schemes

There are and have been a number of hybrid ship finance schemes which did not fit under the simple debt or equity categories. The German K/G system and the Danish DIFKO systems, for example, take advantage of favorable tax treatment. Unique, government sponsored, hybrid, limited partnerships exist. These limited partnerships were a method for wealthy individuals to shelter their taxable income by investing in shipping. They first appeared in the 1980s in Norway (K/S), Denmark (DIFKO), Germany (K/G) and to some extent in the UK Business Expansion Scheme, countries which had high personal tax rates. The Norwegian K/S (*Kommandittselskap*) market collapsed in the 1990s due to the infusion of large corporate investors and changes in Norwegian tax laws.

The K/G System has been a German limited partnership system available to German tax payers for German flag vessels, which holds individuals liable only for the amount of their investment. The benefit to German taxpayers, especially those in the higher tax brackets, is that they can take tax deductions accruing from investment losses and depreciation. This accelerated depreciation, *Sonderabschreibung*, permitted an additional 40% on top of the 8.33% in the first year and 82% in the first five years. Characteristics of the K/G system include:

1. *Kommanditgesellschaft* is a limited partnership;
2. equity financing from "retail" high-net worth individuals (e.g. doctors and dentists 30–40%);
3. the remaining 60–70% is from bank sources;
4. 12–25-year investment periods;
5. strong tax incentives;
6. mostly smaller vessels.

With over-tonnaging and the economic recession starting in 2008, the K/G system lost viability as a financing scheme and has undergone severe stress. By 2010, it had fallen out of favor with investors.

The A/G is a public limited company, whereas a GmbH (*Gessellschaft mit beschränkter Haftung*) is a private limited company.

DIFKO is a limited partnership with tax benefits, sometimes called the Danish "Money Machine", and is a tax investment company which finances ships built in Denmark using a three-tiered arrangement, namely:

1. a K/S partnership;
2. ship finance credit;
3. a Danish bond scheme (where the owner places his or her capital on deposit and takes out a loan at a lower rate—the difference between the ship interest credit rate and the long term bond rate).

Blocked currency schemes are where multinational companies find themselves with profits in countries that prohibit the export of their currencies. In such cases, where the countries have shipbuilding industries, these companies are able to provide local funds to finance the building of vessels for export (such as in the Polish-Pepsico International construction of bulk carriers, and McDonnell-Douglas's financing assistance to Del Monte for their Spanish-built refrigerated cargo ships during the 1980s).

Barter trade deals are usually done on a government-to-government basis where fundamental commodities such as grain, oil and natural gas are traded for manufactured goods such as ships. In modern international trade, the system is rare, inefficient and archaic but is still to be found.

4.1.25 Islamic Bank Finance

Islamic bank financing is based on traditional Islamic principles. Islamic banking is a general term for the investment of money according to Islamic Law (sharia). There is a desire on the part of Muslim governments and businesses to use funds and revenues, particularly from the sale of petroleum and chemicals, to assist in the development of the infrastructure in Muslim countries and to aid Muslim owned businesses in a manner consistent with Islamic values. Islamic banks have a large, stable customer base in most Muslim countries, but particularly in Kuwait, Qatar, Malaysia, the UAE, Iran, Pakistan, Nigeria and Saudi Arabia.

A basic feature of Islamic bank financing is that receipt and payment of interest (*riba*) is prohibited and any return on funds employed by the bank be earned by way of profit derived from a commercial risk taken by the bank. This means that the bank shares in the risks and rewards of the venture undertaken by the customer. Therefore, the bank's return is based on the customer's success rather than an income stream based on the financial market's interest rates. *Gharar* (uncertainty) and *maisir* (direct speculation) are also banned by Islamic law. Financing cannot be made available to projects that contradict Islamic principles. Different forms of Islamic financing are suitable for different types of ship finance. For example, for new construction, *istisna* is used, where title to the vessel passes directly to the buyer upon delivery. For the purchase and sale of second-hand vessels, *ijara* is used; it is also used for leasing. There are differences of opinion as to whether *sukuk* (bonds) are strictly in line with Islamic principles. An alternative is leasing (bare boat charter) at fixed rates with the lessee buying the vessel at a pre-agreed price and date.

In theory, some Western banking practices are prohibited under Islamic banking principles (e.g. currency futures and forward trading), because they are considered speculative (i.e. gambling), and also because they treat currency (trading) as a commodity. Under Islamic banking principles, money is not regarded as a commodity such as wheat or oil: it must be put to use for productivity. Currency swaps are acceptable providing there is no interest-rate swap. Islamic banks have difficulty managing liquidity positions (especially short term ones).

The Islamic banking market in the Arabian Gulf is in the hundreds of billions of dollars. Depositors place their funds on deposit interest-free, and receive a share of the bank's profits. Islamic banks benefit greatly from the inherently low cost of funds available to them from depositors. Banks have boards of Islamic scholars (advisors) to review methods and operations and to act as advisors.

4.1.26 Government Grants

Financing assistance from government sources is done to aid and stimulate domestic shipbuilding or shipping. Such assistance takes many forms and these include but are not limited to:

1. government loans;
2. subsidizing interest rate;
3. cash grant to owner;
4. cash grant to shipbuilder;
5. cash or credit to allied industries;
6. operating subsidies tied to shipbuilding agreement;
7. favorable taxation incentives: lower or no taxes, deferrals, write-off of previous loans, accelerated depreciation, tax-free reserves;
8. guarantee of private loans, i.e. risk transfer;

Table 4.1 Islamic financing terms

Beial urbun	Acceptable only to Hanbali school of Islamic jurisprudence, an Islamic option. Islamic investor purchases goods on behalf of real purchaser and keeps 10% of real purchaser's deposit
Beibi salam/ beibisalif	Forward financing transactions to provide working capital to buy raw materials. *Salam* identifies the goods. *Salif* refers to goods in generic terms. The goods must exist at time of sale. Does not apply to shipbuilding
Gharar	Uncertainty: excessive uncertainty, risk or ambiguous outcome
Ijara	Equivalent to leasing. Bank purchases asset and rents to third party
Ijara irta	Lease purchase
Istisna	Islamic institution places order to build ships and sells at an agreed price at an agreed date
Joalah	Simply a fee for rendering a service
Mudaraba	A silent partnership fund that participants subscribe to; the bank manages the investment (i.e. trustee finance). A percentage of profits go to investor-customers. Bank charges fees. Shares in funds can be bought and sold
Muqarada	Bonds issued to finance projects
Murabaha	Cost-plus method for project financings, which includes an honest declaration of cost
Musharaka	A fuel partnership that provides venture capital by establishing a special purpose company. Bank and customer are shareholders and share profits and losses (i.e. equity financing)
Riba	"Increase, growth" (i.e. interest)

9. favorable loan terms: low interest rate, long grace period, little or no down payment, more than 100% financing, repayment out of profits only, long loan term, balloon payment at end of loan, little or no security or collateral required;
10. write-off of previous losses;
11. moratoria on debt repayment;
12. training funds;
13. custom duties waived on imported materials;
14. shipbuilding research and development funds;
15. vessel scrapping subsidies;
16. grace period before repayment;
17. restructuring aid;
18. insolvency and closure aid;
19. aid for regional or other investment;
20. R&D aid;
21. aid for environmental protection.

4.1.27 Equity Financing

An alternative source of ship finance is equity financing. Either the shipowner invests his or her own money or sells equity shares in the company. In other words, the owner gives up some portion of ownership in the company. Equity financing is another way of raising funds for the building of a new ship or ships, especially if the company is "all borrowed up" or is involved in a risky shipping venture. Equity here is in the sense of ownership in or shares in the profits or future value of the shipping company. The sources of equity funds may come from the shipping company's retained earnings, or out of cash. It may involve the sale of assets. It may also involve the sale of stocks (shares) in the company (common or preferred stock). Finally, it may involve forming limited partnerships.

The sale of shares may involve (1) common stock, (2) preferred stock or (3) convertible preferred stock. Common stock carries voting rights that can impact on the managing of the shipping company. Preferred stock does not have the privilege of voting, but has the advantage of being paid dividends before they are paid to other shareholders. Convertible preferred stock is preferred stock that can be converted to a defined number of shares of common stock, which is another option of the shareholder. The many shareholders in large publicly traded companies exercise their voting rights by electing members to the board of directors. The company managers and board members have a fiduciary obligation to the shareholders.

In the USA, the term "common stock" is frequently used. Elsewhere, it is called "voting share" or "ordinary share". Common stock may be of the voting or non-voting type. The dividends to holders of common stock are uncertain and depend on earnings, the need for capital (i.e. reinvestment) and the decisions of the board of directors, all of which will be covered, both legally and practically in the borrowing agreements. Preferred stock is characterized by a preference in dividends, in a liquidation a preference in assets, convertibility to common stock, callability, permitting the company to repurchase the shares, non-voting, usually has a fixed dividend (i.e. par value), but may have a floating interest rate keyed to an index, cumulative preferred stock permitting any unpaid dividends to accumulate for future payment. There are many variations on both common and preferred stocks relating to voting, convertibility, exchangeability, redemption dates or absence of such, put privileges (where the holder may require the company to redeem the shares) and other features. Each country, such as the UK, Germany, the USA, Brazil, Canada and other countries, has differing and specific limitations and requirements on the issuance of preferred stock.

4.1.28 Public Offerings

A privately owned shipping company may raise capital for fleet expansion or replacement by obtaining a public listing. It does this by offering shares in the company to institutional investors that in turn offer them to the public at stock exchanges. This process is called an IPO, stock launch or "going public". The advantage of an IPO is that huge amounts of money may be raised for new vessel construction for fleet expansion or replacement. The disadvantages are the underwriting, legal, auditing and other costs that can amount to 1–8% of the money raised. The process is expensive, time consuming, complex and may even fail to raise the required funds (i.e. be under-subscribed).

For a company to sell shares through a public offering, an investment bank or syndicate of investment banks will act as underwriters and agree to sell the shares to investors, for which they receive management and underwriting fees. A prospectus is prepared and a price for the initial offering is set. If the price is set too low, the company may potentially lose too much money. If set too high the issuer may be under-subscribed. The prospectus is submitted to government authorities for their approval. The US NYSE and NASDAQ have been the leading issuers of IPOs but the exchanges in Hong Kong, Shanghai and Shenzhen have overtaken the US exchanges. Exchanges in Tokyo, Oslo and Copenhagen are also important for shipping IPOs. The prospectus must reveal to the public detailed information about the company, its financial condition, the management and the intended use of funds. The release of this confidential information is one of the disadvantages of going public.

4.1.29 Private Placement

Another method for raising equity for ship investments is through the private placement market, using such institutions as property and casualty insurance companies, private and public sector pension funds, mutual funds and finance companies. Funds available in the private placement market are enormous, amounting to hundreds of billion of dollars. To access this market, an owner must find an investment bank or advisor with a strong record of success in this field. While governments have regulations controlling private placement, they are not as restrictive as public offerings. Private placements are also offered to select groups of investors, and may be for stocks, bonds, warrants or promissory notes.

With the financial crisis starting in 2008 and the drying up of ship finance sources, the industry in 2012 and 2013 turned to a merging of private equity investors and shipowners. In 2013 shipowners sought funds from private equity firms. However, difficulties arose due to a basic disconnect in their fundamental ways of doing business. Shipowners typically have complete control of operations, investment decision-making, chartering and reporting (or the lack of). Private equity firms, on the other hand, and notwithstanding that they need the shipowner's experience and expertise, want to control investment and divesture decisions and to participate in operating and chartering decisions. They prefer transparency and full reporting. Further, once they have achieved the targeted results they look to sell the assets, contrary to the traditional shipowner's mode of operation.

4.1.30 Venture Capital

Another source of funds for a shipowner for construction is from a venture capitalist. Venture capital is a form of private equity, sometimes referred to as "angel investing". Venture capital, initial investing, seed funding or Series A round of fundraising is important to new, small companies. They are too young to be able to enter the public markets or to obtain loans and debt financing. The venture capitalist initially provides the seed funding, and after start-up, growth and expansion exits the venture. The new shipowner must have a good business plan, a good experienced management team and solid business opportunities such as charters in place in order to attract venture capital.

4.1.31 Master Limited Partnership (MLP)

A non-traditional method for investors in shipping to enjoy certain tax benefits is to enter into an MLP. This type of limited partnership is one that can be traded on an exchange, giving it liquidity. IPOs may be in the form of MLPs. The advantage to the investor (partner) is that they avoid paying corporate tax and are able to depreciate in proportion to their holdings. The MLP is required to pay a fixed distribution quarterly to the limited partners. The distributions are, however, taxed. MLPs depend on a predictable and stable cash flow. Because of the volatile nature of shipping, especially in the tanker and bulk sectors, regular distributions are put at risk. MLPs should be approached with caution.

4.1.32 Financial Aspects of the Shipbuilding Contract

Shipbuilding contracts may be of a standard form, some of which are slanted towards the shipbuilder and hence are favored by them. Others favor the owners. When using the standard forms, it is common for there to be amendments and riders resulting from the negotiations between the parties.

Some of the most common standard forms include:

1. BIMCO's NEWBUILDCON: Baltic and International Maritime Council;
2. AWES Form: Association of West European Shipbuilders;
3. MARAD Form: US Maritime Administration;
4. SAJ Form: Shipowners Association of Japan;
5. CMAC Shanghai Form 2011;
6. Norwegian Form.

Alternatively, the shipbuilding contract may be drafted by either the owner's experienced lawyer or the builder's legal department. Whether it is a standard form or specifically drafted, the contract is usually the subject of much negotiation on specific terms. Regardless, there are certain basic elements common to all shipbuilding contracts that impact on ship finance. They include:

1. the price, for each vessel;
2. the currency in which the payments are to be made;
3. options: the price for any optional additional vessels, if any;
4. extra costs or credits for changes to the contract;
5. penalty clauses for late delivery, deficiencies in speed, fuel consumption, carrying capacity (DWT) and other features of the vessel;
6. schedule of progress payments;
7. dispute resolution: mediation, arbitration or courts;
8. escalation clauses, if any;
9. unit costs to be applied if additional work is required;
10. consequential yard expense in the event that changes disrupt the work schedules;
11. retaining at the end of the construction period to cover guaranteed work;
12. insurance: amounts, types, named and sharing in insurance proceeds;
13. performance bonds (selection of jurisdiction is important as enforceability is sometimes difficult);
14. refund guarantees issued by a bank which are acceptable to the buyer, and refunding of progress payments in the event of rescission of contract;
15. taxes, duties, fees, classification costs, registry and similar;
16. fuel and lubrication credits at delivery.

All of the above, and many other terms in the contract and specifications, will impact on the amount and timing of the flow of funds to the shipbuilder.

It is one of the duties of the owner's on-site representative to monitor the progress of construction and provide timely advice to the owner as precisely when milestones will be met and progress payments are due.

4.1.33 Progress Payments

An important component of the shipbuilding contract relates to the progress payments that the shipowner pays the shipbuilder during the construction of a vessel. The quantity and timing of these payments is often a matter of intense negotiation pre-contract. The owner may want to pay as little as possible up front and backload the schedule, whereas the builder wants to frontload the schedule and get as much as possible early. The fairest settlement of this issue is where the shipyard progress payment schedule is structured so that the yard receives about as much as they are spending.

The second issue is to select milestones to which progress payments can be definitively identified, such as contract signing, commencement of steel construction, delivery of main engine at the yard and successful completion of sea trials. Milestones such as 40% completion of steel work and 60% completion of electrical work are not definitive and should be avoided. The BIMCO NEWBUILDCON proposes that the first installment be due and payable "five (5) banking days after the refund guarantee has been provided". The final installment "shall be due and payable on delivery", and "the sums due or refundable as a result of modification … shall be added to or deducted from the original installment". The intermediate installment shall be as agreed upon between the shipowner and shipyard.

4.1.34 Performance or Surety Bond

There are occasions when a shipowner wants financial assurance that a shipyard will deliver the ship in a timely manner according to the plans and specifications, and meeting the approval of the regulatory authorities. To reduce the owner's risk, he or she may require the shipyard to provide a performance bond, sometimes referred to as a "surety bond" or a "performance bond", or if issued by a bank, they are called a "bank guarantee". The shipowner's concerns are that the yard may end up in bankruptcy, or fail to pay for labor or materials. Since 1932, all US Federal Government and many state and municipal construction projects must be backed by performance bonds.

The shipyard or contractor can obtain such a bond from a bank or insurance company. The cost of the performance bond to the shipyard will depend on the type of bond, the amount of the bond and, most importantly, the risk of the applicant. The surety bond underwriters will closely examine the project, the history of risks, claims and litigation with the yard. The underwriters will then assign the bond price. This can cost, usually between 1 and 15% of the project price. The price of the bond is then passed on to the shipowner. The "penal sum" is the maximum amount that will be paid under the bond. The shipowner is the obligee, the shipyard is the principal and the issuer of the bond is the surety. If the obligee makes a claim, and the surety determines the claim is valid, he or she will pay the agreed upon bond amount to the obligee. The surety will then attempt to recover the amount paid and his or her legal costs from the principal.

4.1.35 Refund Guarantees

A shipbuilding contract should contain a provision for a refund guarantee. After contract signing and during construction, the shipowner will have been making progress payments. If the shipyard becomes insolvent or is declared bankrupt or otherwise defaults on the contract, the owner will want his or her progress payments returned. The usual procedure is for the shipyard to arrange with his or her bank to provide a refund guarantee to the shipowner. It is important that the bank's guarantee be properly worded and signed by an authorized bank official. If the shipowner is financing the ships, the lending agreement will contain a clause requiring that the shipbuilding contract have a refund guarantee and that proceeds from it are paid to the lender.

4.2   Conclusion

Because the financing of ships involves massive investments it must be approached with care and caution. The world financial condition and the economics of the maritime industry are constantly changing and create risks. This is especially true because the term of the investment and the life of the asset are long and may be subject to one or more market cycles. The best financing strategy in one period may not be the right solution in another. The rewards may be great but the risks are real. Therefore, the shipowner-buyer should study all the financing options, weigh the risk and avail him or herself of the best professional assistance available, especially investment bankers and maritime lawyers.

Bibliography

A Guide to the European Loan Market, Standard & Poor's, New York, 2010.
Bartsch, G.; *Finance & Investment Briefing*, Watson, Farley & Williams, Hamburg, 2012.
Cleary, T.; *The Art of War*, translated, Shambhala Pocket Classics, Boston, MA, 1991.
Curtis, S.; *The Law of Shipbuilding Contracts*, Lloyd's of London Press, London, 1991.
Debt Finance Issue, Marine Money, Stamford, CT, 1996.
Duru, O.; *The Ship Mortgage Crisis*, The Maritime Executive, 2014.
El-Gamal, M. A.; *A Basic Guide to Contemporary Islamic Banking and Finance*, Rice University, Houston, TX, 2000.
Hunt, E. C. and Butman, B. S.; *Marine Engineering Economics and Cost Analysis*, Cornell Maritime Press, Centreville, MD 1994.
Hussain, M.; *Legal Aspects of Islamic Finance*, Stephenson Harwood, London, 2002.
Islamic Finance, Special Report, Financial Times, London, 2007.
Kokkinos, G. A.; *Handbook on Shipping Finance—Theory and Practice*, Athens, 2004.
Ma. S.; *Maritime Economics*, WMU, Malmo, Sweden, 2007.
McGroarty, R. D.; *Koranic Structures*, Lloyds Shipping Economists, 2008.
Orfanidis, A.; *Shipping Finance, Approach to the Hellenic Market*, Athens, 2004.
Paine, F.; *The Financing of Ship Acquisitions*, Fairplay, Survey 1989.
Proceedings of the 6th International Ship Finance Conference, Lloyd's of London Press Ltd., London, 1994.
Risk Management in the Marine Transportation System, Transportation Research Board, NRC, Washington, DC, 1999.
Shipbuilding Contracts and Related Ship Finance Issues, Maritime Business Forum, London Shipping Law Centre, Inc & Co., London, 2010.
Shipping Market Review 2014, Danish Ship Finance A/S, Copenhagen, 2014.
Sloggett, J. E.; *Shipping Finance*, Fairplay Publications, Survey 1998.
Stokes, P.; *Ship Finance; Credit Expansion and the Boom-Bust Cycle*, Lloyd's of London Press, London, 1992.
Stopford, M.; *Maritime Economics*, 2nd Edition, Routledge, London, 1997.
Sundararajan, V. and Errico, L.; *Islamic Financial Institutions and Products in the Global Financial System*, IMF Working Paper WP/02/192, 2002.
Tevis, R. L.; *The Functions of Lease Financing*, ASME, New York, 1968
The Credit Rating Controversy, Council on Foreign Relations, Washington, DC, 2015.
Utmark, G.; *Hedge Funds—Take Two*, Marine Money, Stamford, CT.
Where's the Money?, The Baltic, 2010.
Zannetos, Z. S.; *The Theory of Oil Tanker Ships Rates*, MIT Press, Cambridge, MA, 1966.

5

Debt Financing in Shipping

George Paleokrassas

5.1 Introduction

When a lender advances money to a shipowner, the lender needs to ensure that it is adequately protected and secured against the insolvency of the borrower, its failure to perform its obligations on a timely basis and the loss, or attachment by other creditors, of the ship. The owner, whose fundamental objective is to increase the return on his or her investment, is, by contrast, seeking to limit the lender's interference with its business and to maintain the greatest flexibility in the conduct of its business and the operation of its ship.

In the current environment where there is limited bank liquidity and with banks under greater scrutiny and pressure from regulators (as well as from their own internal risk, compliance and anti-money-laundering departments which are playing an increasingly prominent role within banks), debt financing in shipping, which has always been considered to be capital-intensive and risky, is becoming more difficult to obtain. This applies in particular to owners who—as a result of the size of their fleet or operations, the lack of corporate structure or the lack of transparency in the ultimate beneficial ownership of their group—do not meet the minimum criteria required by

---

G. Paleokrassas (✉)
Watson Farley & Williams, Building B, 348 Syngrou Avenue, Kallithea, Athens 17674, Greece

© The Author(s) 2016
M.G. Kavussanos, I.D. Visvikis (eds.), *The International Handbook of Shipping Finance*, DOI 10.1057/978-1-137-46546-7_5

many banks in order to become their customers. In an increasingly cautious climate, banks need to ensure that the loans they book do not contravene any international or local laws or regulations concerning sanctions, tax avoidance and share ownership, and also that they will comply with the capital adequacy requirements to which they are subject. The underlying principle of the debt financing of ships is that a lender advances a debt facility and that the ship and other such collateral as the borrower provides secures the repayment of the facility through the ship's earnings, backed by that security.

5.2 Types of Debt Financing

Shipping was traditionally financed by owners' private equity. It is the market's demand for more tonnage during recent decades, and the desire of owners to increase the return on their shipping investments combined with the development of the global financial system, that has led owners to turn to other sources of funding, including debt financing, the main types of which are discussed below.

5.2.1 Standard Loan Facility

Debt financing is the most common type of ship financing. The owner will borrow funds from a lender (in most cases a bank) and will undertake to repay them within a certain period of time. The terms of the transaction will be reflected in a loan agreement, which will include the following main characteristics.

5.2.1.1 The Lender

Despite the fact that shipowning is far from a low-risk investment (earnings and asset values are constantly fluctuating and ships are constantly traveling between different ports around the world), financial institutions and individual investors have historically been attracted to act as lenders in shipping loans, drawn by the potential returns to be made from what is still a form of secured lending. Ship financing facilities are found in the portfolios of many international banks, and especially in countries with a background in shipping. Many of those banks have developed specialized shipping departments focusing on financing shipping assets.

5.2.1.2 Syndication

Loan syndication is driven by the lenders' need to spread the risk of large projects among several participants. A syndicated loan facility is granted by a group of lenders and structured by one or more of them who acts as arranger(s) (usually the "house" bank of the borrowing group or the bank with which the borrowing group has the closest relationship). Administration of the facility is usually conducted by one of the lenders acting as facility agent, for which a fee is usually paid by the borrower. It is becoming more common to see banks outsourcing agency duties due to the perceived benefits in efficiency or for banks to set up separate departments to conduct the agency functions chiefly with liability considerations in mind (so that there are separate teams within the same bank, one of which undertakes the lending functions and the other the agency functions with strict "Chinese walls" between the two teams).

In order to regulate affairs between lenders, who may have different exposures under the facility, the loan agreement sets out those powers which can be exercised by the agent alone and those which require the authorization of all, or a stipulated majority, of the lenders. Unanimity is usually required for major decisions, including any change to the manner of repayment of the loan (or the tenor of the loan) or any decrease in the margin applicable to the loan or the release of security. The existence of certain "reserved" matters which require the unanimous decisions of all lenders means that any one lender may, by refusing to give its consent to such matters, acquire the power to hold the other banks to ransom over a particular decision—and this is a tactic often used by banks which want to find a way to exit a facility, usually in the hope that another bank or the borrower will buy out their participation in the facility. The securities are usually granted in favor of an appointed security trustee or agent, who then holds the security on trust and administers it for the lenders.

In syndicated facilities, the obligations of the lenders are separate. Each lender is committed to lend its part of the loan and is not liable if any of the other lenders do not contribute their participation. One of the advantages of syndication is that a syndicated loan agreement provides for relatively user-friendly procedures (involving limited documentary requirements) for the transfer of all or a part of any lender's participation to a new or existing lender, should a lender wish to transfer its participation (whether in whole or in part) in the facility. Understandably, an owner may wish to limit the lenders' freedom in this respect as it will want to have a say as regards the composition of its lending group. On the other hand, a greater number of lenders are insisting on having an unfettered right to transfer their participation in shipping loans which is particularly useful when a lender is seeking to sell or transfer the whole or a part of its shipping portfolio (there have been a number of examples of such portfolio transfers in the last few years) or to sell its participation in a non-performing loan or a loan with a customer with which the lender does not want to continue a lending relationship.

5.2.1.3 The Borrower

Depending on the structure of the shipowners' group, the borrower under the loan agreement will almost always be:

(a) a single purpose company (SPC), an entity whose sole asset is the financed ship; or
(b) a company which is the registered owner of a number of sister ships (e.g., ferry companies do not use SPCs); or
(c) a holding company, being the direct or beneficial owner of the SPC, which owns the financed ship.

In the case of (c), the holding company will on-lend the facility to the shipowning company which will usually participate as a collateral guarantor (i.e. the holding company will itself lend to the shipowning company the facility it receives from its lender, therefore passing on the facility to the shipowning company). The use of single purpose shipowning companies is very common in the shipping industry as a way in which owners attempt to limit their liability, and principally as a way to ensure the convenient organization of the business of each ship and, in the process, insulate other ships from liability as "sister ships". The use of such structures is permitted under English law, although the extent to which such structures can protect ships from sister ship arrest depends on the jurisdiction of arrest. So, for example, South Africa permits creditors to arrest ships in the same ultimate beneficial ownership as "associated" ships. Certain other jurisdictions, such as France, permit creditors to pierce the corporate veil of the SPC owner to make other owners in the group liable where the SPC owner has not properly respected its autonomous character, for example when the owning group has freely applied vessel earnings to meet the liabilities of other vessels.

5.2.1.4 The Financed Ship: Newbuildings and Second-hand Vessels

If the ship being financed is a newbuilding, a part of the facility may finance the pre-delivery or "milestone" payments to be made to the shipbuilder during the construction of the ship (this is commonly referred to as "pre-delivery" financing). In a pre-delivery financing the lender will want to satisfy itself regarding the reputation of the shipbuilder, in particular the ability of the latter to complete the construction of the newbuilding in accordance with the terms of the contract (including its ability to fund the construction), and to ensure that the construction will be properly supervised by the site team to be appointed by the borrower, either from personnel in its management company or other specialist managers. Further, the lender will scrutinize the credit of the bank which is to guarantee the refundment obligations of the shipbuilder under the contract as well as the guarantee to be provided by that bank (commonly referred to as a "refund guarantee"). As, in almost all cases, title to a newbuilding is only transferred to the borrower upon completion (when the same is delivered to the borrower by the shipbuilder), the lender will, in respect of a pre-delivery financing, require security from the borrower in the form of an assignment of the borrower's rights under the shipbuilding contract and the refund guarantee.

Until the credit crunch of 2008, pre- and post-delivery financing for newbuildings was widely available. (Post-delivery finance refers to a facility, which is advanced at the time of delivery of a newbuilding. In the past, this would refinance the pre-delivery facility for the same newbuilding and finance the final "milestone" payment payable upon the delivery of the newbuilding to its buyer). This has changed since 2008, with many banks not offering pre-delivery financing at all or significantly restricting its availability. In this period, the majority of shipowners have funded pre-delivery installments using their own funds and have obtained debt financing which may only be drawn at the time of delivery of the newbuilding to its owner/buyer. During this period, shipbuilders have accepted an increase in the percentage of the contract price payable on delivery of newbuildings thereby reducing the payments which owners are required to fund from their own resources during the pre-delivery stage of construction, which has, to a certain extent, mitigated the effect of the restricted availability of pre-delivery financing. A post-delivery financing will be secured by a mortgage over the newbuilding (upon delivery of the same to its buyer) together with the other security usually taken by a lender in a ship finance transaction (as described in greater detail below).

Apart from building new vessels, owners may choose to increase their tonnage through the acquisition of second-hand ships. In this case, the lender will seek to receive a survey report in respect of the ship's condition, ask to review the records of the applicable classification society and ask its lawyers to obtain evidence that, at the time of its acquisition by the borrower, the ship is registered in the ownership of the borrower under a flag acceptable to the lender and is free of liens and other encumbrances. In addition, the lender will require that its mortgage has been duly registered with the requisite priority at the ship's registry (as well as ensuring that all other security for the facility has been received by it). It will also want to be satisfied with regard to the income-generating capacity of the financed ship and will, if the ship is subject to a long-term charter (in most cases a charter having a duration of 12 months or more), seek to receive a specific assignment of the borrower's rights under that charter.

5.2.1.5 Facility Amount

The amount of finance which a borrower may obtain from a bank to assist it in acquiring a ship is usually determined by reference to the purchase price of the ship and also the market value of the ship (as calculated by an independent shipbroker or shipbrokers appointed or approved by the lender). In some cases, lenders only take into account the independently appraised market value of a ship (ignoring the purchase price, for purposes of determining the maximum amount of the loan to be made available by it). A lender may also take into account any employment to which the financed ship is, or will become, subject in determining the amount and term or tenor of the facility. The loan agreement sets out the mechanism as to how a ship's value will be determined, both so as to determine the initial amount of the loan (as referred to above) and to determine compliance with the minimum value/asset cover test stipulated in the loan agreement. This requires the borrower to ensure that the value of the lender's security (mostly comprised of the market value of the financed ship(s)) is maintained, at all times, above a specified percentage of the outstanding amount of the loan. Any shortfall that may arise will have to be rectified by a partial prepayment of the loan or the provision of additional security.

5.2.1.6 Conditions Precedent

The lender's commitment to advance a loan is always subject to the satisfaction of certain conditions precedents, including the absence of an event of default, the satisfaction of the minimum value/asset cover requirement, the "know your customer" requirements of the lender, the granting of the required securities, the provision of valid ship certificates and the receipt by the lender of legal opinions confirming, amongst other things, the due incorporation and valid existence of the borrower and any other party which is providing security to the lender and the validity and enforceability of the lender's security.

5.2.1.7 Currency

Since most of the income in the shipping industry is generated and payable in United States dollars, the borrower will wish to ensure that its loans are advanced in that currency to avoid exposure to currency fluctuations. However, depending on the borrower's needs, the facility may be granted or denominated in another currency (e.g., euros, pounds sterling or Japanese yen—as, in some cases, Japanese shipbuilders will require the contract or purchase price for a newbuilding to be constructed by them to be paid in yen). In the latter case, the loan agreement will include an option entitling the borrower to convert the loan into one other currency (dual currency option) or one of a number of currencies (multi-currency option). A dual or multi-currency option will allow the borrower to benefit from the low interest rates applicable to the, or one of the, optional currency/ies at the relevant time, but also to expose it to exchange rate fluctuations. Other derivatives instruments (which are offered by certain lenders in conjunction with loan facilities) may be used by a borrower to deal with any payment obligations it has to make in a currency other than United States dollars. As referred to above, one example is where an owner has ordered a newbuilding in Japan and is required to pay the purchase price in Japanese yen while the loan it has received from its European or US-based lender is denominated in United States dollars.

5.2.1.8 Tenor and Repayment of Loan Facility

Secured term loans are made available to the borrower in one or more tranches or advances, repayable over a fixed period of time in installments (usually quarterly or semi-annual). The amortization schedule is determined by taking into consideration the projected earnings (whether arising from any long-term employment or otherwise) and the age of the financed ship. It is also common that a final "balloon" installment (one linked to the expected market value, or sometimes the expected scrap value, of the ship when the loan matures) is payable on the final repayment date.

Revolving credit facilities are also appropriate for borrowers wishing to obtain finance for their working capital needs or for borrowers who want a "war chest" to finance the acquisition of ships to be identified by them in the future (sometimes referred to as a "hunting license"). As opposed to a term loan facility (under which any repaid amounts cannot be reborrowed), a revolving facility guarantees a maximum facility amount, which the borrower can draw, repay and redraw during the tenor of the facility. The borrower pays a commitment fee to maintain the availability of the facility and have the flexibility to decide the frequency and the amount of each drawdown depending on its cash flow needs or on the acquisition opportunities it identifies in the market. The whole facility will have to be repaid by a certain date or, in the case of a reducing revolving facility, the maximum amount which may be drawn or which is available to be drawn will be reduced at fixed dates during the tenor of the facility and will be fully repaid on the date on which the facility matures.

The loan agreement also contains provisions for extraordinary repayments. The borrower usually has the right to prepay a part or the whole of the facility at the end of an interest period, with prior notice to the lenders and without penalty. The lender is entitled to be indemnified by the borrower for any funding break costs it may incur if the prepayment is not made on an interest rollover date. A mandatory prepayment obligation will arise if the financed vessel is sold or becomes an insurance total loss and in situations when the minimum value/asset cover requirement (as described above) has been breached. Other significant events or circumstances (e.g. a change of control of the borrower or a corporate guarantor or, in the case of a facility providing pre-delivery financing for the construction of a newbuilding, the cancellation, termination or rescission of a shipbuilding contract) may additionally be included in the loan agreement as events which trigger a mandatory prepayment of the loan.

5.2.1.9 Interest

Interest in respect of the facility will be expressed to accrue at a percentage rate per annum and to be calculated either at a floating or fixed rate. Most facilities are subject to a floating rate of interest, dependent on the rates the lender will pay to obtain funds on each interest rollover date (which it will, in turn, lend to the borrower) in the interbank market or such other sources as are available to the lender. In a fixed rate loan facility, an agreed uniform rate applies throughout the life of the loan. It is not uncommon for banks to offer derivative instruments to a borrower (in conjunction with a loan facility) so as to allow the borrower to fix the interest rate applying to its loan facility.

The floating interest rate is expressed as the aggregate of the London Interbank Offered Rate (LIBOR) (or the Euro Interbank Offered Rate

(Euribor) if the facility is advanced in euros), the agreed margin and, in certain cases, mandatory costs (being the lender's cost of compliance with the requirements of the central bank to which it is subject and/or any other applicable regulatory authority such as the Financial Services Authority or the European Central Bank). If the borrower is in default of any of its payment obligations under a loan agreement, an increased interest rate will be payable (usually between 1 and 2% over the then applicable interest rate for the facility, calculated in the manner outlined above).

The loan agreement also sets out an agreed mechanism for the determination of an alternative interest rate in case LIBOR (or Euribor) is not available, the lender is unable to fund itself in the currency in which the facility was made available at the time, or if the lender's funding costs are higher than the applicable LIBOR (or Euribor) rate. If such an event occurs, which is known as a "market disruption event", the loan agreement provisions usually entitle the lender to cancel its commitment to grant the loan (or any part of it) if the loan has not yet been advanced and, if the loan has been advanced, the borrower to prepay the loan. The obligation to prepay the loan will arise if no agreement for an alternative interest rate is reached within a specified negotiation period (usually up to 30 days) when the lender and borrower seek to agree an alternative interest rate which will apply to the loan for the duration of the market disruption event.

The tenor of the facility is divided into successive interest periods (usually of one, two, three, six or, in some cases, nine or even twelve months' duration) and the applicable interest rate will be determined with reference to that period. Interest is payable on each rollover date and usually, in the case of an interest period of longer than three months, every three months during that interest period.

5.2.1.10 Representations and Warranties

As part of its due diligence process on the borrower, the lender requires that the borrower make certain declarations in relation to its legal, financial and regulatory affairs at the time of execution of the loan agreement. Standard representations and warranties will relate to:

(a) the borrower's corporate and tax good-standing;
(b) the borrower's corporate authority;
(c) the acquisition and maintenance of any necessary governmental consents (or consents from any other applicable regulatory body);

(d) absence of conflict (that the borrower's assumption of obligations under the transaction documentation does not conflict with any laws, regulations or the borrower's own constitutional documents);
(e) the validity and enforceability of the borrower's obligations under the loan documentation;
(f) the absence of any event of default;
(g) the absence of any litigation or insolvency proceedings against the borrower;
(h) the accuracy of all financial information provided to the lender.

The borrower will reaffirm these declarations at the time of drawdown of the facility (or each part of it). They will also be deemed to be repeated at the beginning of each interest period.

5.2.1.11 Covenants

The loan agreement covenants are essentially the promises that the borrower is required to make in order to satisfy the lender that it will be able to meet its payment and other obligations and that the securities granted in favor of the lender will not be jeopardized. The loan agreement includes general, corporate, financial and ship-related covenants, either positive or negative. The borrower undertakes to maintain its valid legal existence and any required consents, to remain in good standing, to comply with laws and its tax obligations, to deliver its financial statements and other required financial information to the lender, and to inform the lender of any default. It may also be required to comply with certain financial covenants (which are commonly imposed on borrowers or guarantors which are holding companies) or to retain a minimum amount of cash in its accounts with the lender (and/or with other banks or financial institutions) during the tenor of the facility.

As the ship is the primary security of the transaction, the loan agreement contains an extensive list of covenants in respect of the ship's ownership, flag, classification society, seaworthiness, employment and insurances. The borrower will further undertake to refrain from certain actions, such as the disposal of its assets, the payment of dividends or other distributions to its shareholders or the incurrence of any further financial indebtedness (although in certain cases, especially in cases where the borrower is a holding company, the payment of dividends and the incurrence of further financial indebtedness is permitted subject to the satisfaction of certain conditions). As tax, financial and trade regulations worldwide become more complicated and far-reaching, sophisticated clauses in relation to the borrower's compliance with environmental laws, imposed sanctions, money laundering legislation and requirements of the US Foreign Account Tax Compliance Act (FATCA) have been introduced into, and are now commonly found in, loan agreements.

5.2.1.12 Governing Law and Jurisdiction

In view of the multi-jurisdictional nature of ship lending and the primacy of English law in agreements and other contracts relating to shipping, most loan agreements are governed by English law, with disputes being subject to the jurisdiction of the English courts. There are notable exceptions to this, for example banks lending out of the USA will often require their loan agreements to be governed by New York law and be subject to the jurisdiction of the New York courts, while loan agreements entered into between Norwegian banks and Norwegian borrowers will invariably be governed by Norwegian law and be subject to the jurisdiction of the local courts.

5.2.1.13 Events of Default

The loan agreement sets out a list of events and circumstances, the occurrence of which will release the lender from its obligations and entitle it to pursue the remedies granted to it under the loan agreement or by law. A borrower's default will trigger the acceleration of the loan (usually upon service of a notice from the lender to the borrower) and allow the lender to declare the loan amount and all accrued interest and expenses immediately due and payable.

A standard event of default clause will include the following:

(a) breach of payment obligations;
(b) breach of representations and warranties;
(c) breach of covenants;
(d) cross-default (a default arising under any other agreements which may be entered into by the borrower, a guarantor or any other security party);
(e) insolvency/bankruptcy of the borrower, a guarantor or any other security party or other similar event such as the appointment of an administrator or the entry into any form of payment moratorium with creditors;
(f) depreciation in the value of the ship (resulting in the breach of the minimum asset cover requirement which is not rectified within the contractually agreed period);
(g) material adverse change;

(h) change of control;
(i) invalidity of governmental authorization or consent;
(j) invalidity of any of the loan documents;
(k) unlawfulness.

The events of default may be distinguished between those which will have an immediate effect and others which will entitle the lender to accelerate the loan only if they are not remedied within a certain grace period. Payment defaults always fall in the first category (even though certain borrowers who are considered by lenders to be particularly strong credits may be granted a short grace period for payment defaults).

5.2.1.14 Fees

The borrower undertakes to reimburse the lender for all administrative, legal, enforcement costs and expenses to be incurred by the lender in relation to the loan agreement. It is also required to pay certain fees to the lender, set out in the loan agreement or in a separate fee agreement, which will include:

(a) an arrangement fee in a fixed amount in respect of the structuring of the facility;
(b) a commitment fee, being a percentage per annum of the undrawn amount of the facility for the period during which the lender is committed to advance the facility to the borrower;
(c) in the case of a syndicated facility, an agency fee payable to the facility agent for conducting its agency tasks and certain other fees may be payable for the structuring, underwriting and syndication of the facility.

5.2.2 Leasing

An alternative method of financing the acquisition of a ship (by a shipping company) may be through a lease, usually in the form of a bareboat charter or a long-term time charter. In structures of this type, the financial institution involved acquires title to the ship and further enters into a lease agreement with the shipping company, pursuant to which the latter has the right to use and operate the ship. Instead of relying on security in the form of a mortgage to mitigate its risks, a financial institution acting as lessor becomes the owner of the ship, acquiring in this way the increased protection owners are afforded by law. The lessor's position may be further enhanced by way of the lessee assigning in its favor any rights the lessee has under the insurance policies regarding the ship and/or any contracts of employment to be entered into by the lessee. The lessor may in turn offer the ship and title to it as security to a lender in order to obtain financing itself. This will be the case if the lessor is a subsidiary or affiliate of a major lender formed for the purpose of acting as the leasing arm of such lender, and it is therefore dependent on its holding company or affiliate when it comes to the availability of funding.

To finance a leasing acquisition involving newbuildings, the contract for the construction of the ship is usually novated or transferred from the original buyer, which is usually the "true" shipping company, to the financial institution, which is acting through a subsidiary formed for this purpose. That subsidiary assumes the obligation to pay the contract price due under the shipbuilding contract and becomes entitled to register the ship in its ownership. In order for the shipping company to be able to make use of the ship, it and the lessor, simultaneously with the acquisition of the ship by the lessor, enter into a bareboat or time charter or other leasing agreement which usually contains the standard rights and obligations of owners and bareboat/time charterers (or lessor and lessees) and also contains provisions as to the payment of hire or lease payments on certain agreed dates. The aggregate amount of the installments of hire or the lease payments are often calculated so as to be equal to the cost initially paid by the SPC (as lessor) to the shipbuilder and the amount of interest to be charged by the lessor's lender to the lessor. The lessor will then use the hire to repay the debt financing it will have received to finance the acquisition of the ship.

In a leasing transaction the risks arising from the ownership and operation of the ship are undertaken by the lessee, which finds itself in a similar position to that of a borrower under a standard debt financing. Once all hire payments have been paid, the lessor is under an obligation to transfer title to the ship to the lessee, since the intention is for the operator of the ship to receive the benefit of the residual value of the ship. It is not uncommon for a lessee to have the option to purchase the ship for a fixed price at certain times during the currency of the lease. The amount of the purchase option usually equates to the aggregate amount of the hire or lease payments payable from the date of exercise of the option until the end of the term of the lease.

5.2.3 Bonds

The section above dealing with syndicated debt financing provided a summary of the manner in which more than one lender may participate in a debt financing. An alternative to arranging such a syndication is for a borrower to issue bonds, which usually incorporate only the key terms applicable to the bonds such as the principal amount, the applicable interest rate and their maturity, whilst the remaining detailed provisions in respect of the obligations undertaken by the issuer are set out in a master document, such as an indenture or (in Greece) a program. The master agreement does not require that it be entered into by each of the bondholders and therefore the structure ensures that the bonds and therefore the rights they carry are easily transferable. At the same time a variety of corporate information and financial and other covenants can be included in the indenture or the program.

Bonds share certain common characteristics with shares as they may both be traded on an organized exchange or market and are considered to be liquid instruments. One advantage of issuing bonds (as compared to issuing shares) is that certain limitations of corporate law, which sets out the basic characteristics of each instrument, do not apply to bonds to the same extent as they apply to shares, as a bond remains a debt instrument. The issuing company may however structure the bonds in many different ways depending on the particulars of the transaction and the characteristics of the investor or investors being targeted by the issuer.

One advantage, which bondholders hold over shareholders, is that, as a creditor of a company, a bondholder has, in an insolvency or dissolution of a company, priority over the shareholders when it comes to the assets of the company (or the proceeds from the disposition of those assets). Bonds may be subordinated to other forms of debt incurred by the issuer making the bonds akin in this respect to shares, where the shareholder only has a residual claim ranking after all creditors of the issuer. Such types of bonds are attractive to investors seeking to invest primarily in equity, but who are not content with the basic or "plain vanilla" nature of traditional shares. These instruments grant to their holders the right to share in the profits of the issuing company although they offer less certainty as to recovery given that they are unsecured and dependent upon the issuing company's assets exceeding its liabilities to creditors. Since holders of this type of structured bonds agree to be subordinated to other creditors of the company, such as lenders under loan facilities, they are usually able to negotiate a higher interest rate and a more favorable return on their investment than that applying to the senior loan facilities. In certain cases, bonds issued by shipping companies are secured, thus offering the bondholders significant priority over the shareholders or other unsecured creditors of the same company. The proceeds from the enforcement of the collateral asset(s) will first be applied against repayment of the secured creditors (being the secured bondholders) and only then will they be available to unsecured creditors.

There was a large number of shipping companies which issued bonds in the late 1990s in the US capital markets. Many of the issuers ended up buying back their bonds at a discount (in certain cases significant) either because they were unable to pay the coupon applicable to the bonds (being the agreed interest payments) or because they claimed they would be unable to meet future coupon payments. However, the issuance of these bonds resulted in the creation of a tracking market for analysts in the capital markets, particularly in the USA and Norway. This development, in turn, set the stage by 2003 for the return of shipping companies to the capital markets in the form of equity issuances.

Following the significant reduction in the availability of debt financing after 2008, shipping companies looked again to the capital markets for additional sources of capital. With the bond market offering low interest rates, the opportunity for bond issuances arose again and shipping companies issued bonds in the US and Norwegian capital markets. Bonds are attractive to investors where the issuer can show, through the long-term employment of its assets, that it has the required cash flow to meet all its coupon payments. This is why companies, which operate in those sectors of the shipping industry where it is customary for the assets to be subject to long-term employment arrangements, such as the offshore, LNG, oil and gas and container sectors, have looked closely at issuing bonds or have in fact done so.

5.2.4 Mezzanine Financing

Mezzanine finance represents a combination of the characteristics of debt and equity (in many cases it is viewed as representing "quasi-equity"). Financial institutions providing this type of financing agree with the borrower, its shareholders and its senior lenders that the financing provided by the latter will take priority in terms of repayment and security. Mezzanine lenders will enter into a junior or subordinated financing agreement which regulates the lender's ability to be repaid, usually only from the surplus income which may be generated by the borrower after the senior loan has been serviced and operating expenses have been paid. In the absence of such a surplus, there will be no payment to the mezzanine lenders under the subordinated financing agreement. Mezzanine lenders, who rank between the senior lenders and the shareholders, are rewarded for assuming a significantly greater level of risk—as compared to the senior lenders—with a higher return in the form of a higher interest margin, a fee or "promote" (an agreed percentage of the profits or income of the borrower, usually above a certain threshold) or even the right to convert their debt into shares of the borrower. Any such fee or promote will be payable on the condition that certain targets (set by reference to the internal rate of return, net positions, income, etc.) are achieved and will allow the mezzanine lender to share in the profits of the borrower or to receive shares in the borrower (or a right to buy shares at a pre-agreed price within a specified period, in the form of a warrant).

As explained above, the position of a mezzanine lender is similar to that of an equity holder, as the lender has the right to participate in the profits of the borrower even though, strictly speaking, the lender is a creditor who expects its debt to be repaid in full, subject to the usual risks of insolvency of the borrower. While the senior lenders are also exposed to the risk of insolvency of their borrower, their exposure is less because they will always rank ahead (both in terms of rights to the borrower's cash flow and security) of the mezzanine lenders. The safer position assumed by the senior lenders (who will almost always provide the large majority of the debt) is reflected in the amount of their return (usually significantly lower than that of the mezzanine lenders) and also by the fact they will not usually have a right to participate in any of the borrower's profits. While there are some specialist providers of mezzanine debt to shipping companies, in many cases the same syndicate of lenders will provide both the senior debt and the mezzanine debt, whilst the extent of the participation of each bank in the senior or the mezzanine debt will vary and depend on its risk appetite.

5.2.5 Export Credit Agencies

A number of countries with long traditions in shipbuilding, such as China, Japan, Korea, Norway and the Netherlands, seek to support their local shipbuilding industries, and increase demand for vessels or machinery built by shipbuilders operating in those countries, through export credit agencies (ECAs). ECAs are usually government-controlled organizations providing financing or insurance coverage to prospective investors. A shipping company considering whether it should place an order for a newbuilding will increasingly be influenced in its decision-making process by the availability of financing (or insurance or other cover for its financing) from ECAs in connection with the acquisition of newbuilding(s).

The significance of ECAs is underlined by the fact that almost all member countries of the OECD are also members of the OECD's Working Party on Export Credits and Credit Guarantees or Export Credit Group. Amongst its objectives is the review and evaluation of the relevant policies of ECAs and the development of common guiding principles. Accordingly, the OECD has updated its arrangement on officially supported export credits, which sets out guidance on various aspects of an ECA-backed financing, including the maximum repayment term and frequency of interest payments.

Either ECAs will finance part of the acquisition cost of a newbuilding by participating in a syndicate of lenders or the participation in the facility by the commercial banks will be covered by an insurance policy arranged by an ECA. Recently we have seen a number of examples of debt facilities in which one ECA participates in the facility by making available debt funding to the borrower while another ECA issues an insurance policy to the commercial lenders, in connection with their participation in the debt facility.

The participation by one or more ECAs in a debt facility will usually result in the borrower paying a lower interest rate for that part of the facility funded, or covered, by an ECA and also allow the borrower to receive a higher percentage of financing than that available, particularly in the current market, from commercial lenders (given that commercial lenders will view the participation of an ECA in a debt facility as transferring the default risk from the borrower to the ECA, which is considered to be equivalent to the risk of default by a sovereign). There are however significant costs payable (in the form of fees and insurance premia) in order for ECAs to participate in debt facilities, which do not arise in a syndicated debt facility made available by commercial banks.

The expertise of commercial lenders with a track record in financing shipping companies will be relied upon by ECAs which will participate in the financing as a member of a syndicate of lenders. One of the commercial lenders will arrange the facility and bring in the ECA(s). The arranger will usually also act as the facility agent and as the security trustee or agent. In recent years, we have seen certain ECAs, particularly in the Far East, entering into direct debt financing arrangements with certain owners (rather than doing so in conjunction with commercial lenders who have historically been lenders to the owners) but usually after having participated in previous debt financings with the same owners (arranged by commercial lenders).

5.3 Security Package

A critical consideration for the lender in terms of determining its assessment of the risk in any particular transaction is the security package that it can receive from the borrower and its group. A notable development in this area is the increase in corporate, rather than personal, guarantees, owing to the increase in shipping groups adopting a corporate structure, together with the increasing frequency of pledges of shares being demanded as part of a lender's security package. Lenders will always need to check with local counsel any perfection requirements in the relevant jurisdictions, as these will be critical in ensuring a lender's priority over unsecured creditors in an enforcement situation.

5.3.1 The Ship Mortgage

The ship mortgage is the cornerstone of a lender's security as, critically, it gives the lender rights against the vessel itself, rather than personal rights against the owner. These rights give the mortgagee the invaluable right to take possession of, and sell, the ship in a default situation, although the usefulness of these remedies may be complicated by the jurisdiction in which the mortgagee tries to enforce its security.

(i) **Types of Mortgage and Registration**

Ship mortgages are usually governed by the law of the ship's flag state and fall into two categories, statutory mortgages and "preferred" mortgages. Statutory mortgages are usually brief, summarizing the particulars of the ship and the basis of the secured debt. This is the English form of mortgage which has been adopted in most jurisdictions which have a legal system based on that of England, such as Cyprus, Malta, Hong Kong, the Bahamas, Malta and Singapore. Given the limited scope of adapting a statutory form mortgage to the transaction parties' needs, a practice has developed in those jurisdictions, which employ statutory mortgages of entering into separate "deeds of covenant". These contain the covenants and other provisions, which one finds in the form of mortgages that do not base their legal system on English law, notably mortgages over ships registered in Greece, Liberia, the Marshall Islands and Panama. As with all security, the perfection and registration requirements vary from one jurisdiction to another and lenders are advised to obtain, and follow, local law advice to ensure the mortgage security maintains its priority (in England, as with most jurisdictions, the priority of a ship mortgage is determined by reference to the date and time of registration) and the valuable rights conferred by the mortgage.

(ii) **The Principal Rights of a Mortgagee**

One of the principal remedies of a lender is the right to take possession of the mortgaged ship, which can be done either actually or constructively through the giving of notice to the owner and any charterer. However, this right is rarely exercised by lenders in practice as, whilst taking possession of the ship entitles a lender to receive the ship's earnings, a mortgagee-in-possession becomes responsible for its trade debts which often cannot be accurately determined by a lender. The lender can also usually choose to enforce its mortgage by arresting the mortgaged ship and selling it, usually at an auction or through a different court-approved procedure. The enforcement of a mortgage is however an option of last resort for a lender; and it is rare for the latter to take such a decision unless it has lost total confidence in the borrower and/or its ability to run its business and repay the loan. Both the publicity surrounding a hostile enforcement, the practical risks and difficulties of enforcement and the likely crystallization of significant book losses are important reasons to discourage a lender from taking such action. For every mortgage enforcement, there are dozens of other solutions involving a refinancing of the debt, a restructuring or other workout of the debt, the transfer of the ship(s) to a different customer (often referred to as a "white knight") of the lender and, in some cases, settlements involving debt forgiveness.

5.3.2 The Assignment of Earnings, Charter Hire, Insurances and Requisition Compensation

To ensure that, on default, a ship's charterer, and any others from whom earnings may be due, can be called on to pay any earnings to the lender (free of any claim from the borrower or its liquidator), a lender will usually demand an assignment of the earnings and the benefit of the insurances of a mortgaged ship. Such assignment will generally cover the following categories of income: earnings, charter hire (in the case of a long-term charter, this is documented by way of a separate specific assignment of the charter), insurances and requisition compensation. These must, in order to take effect as a legal rather than an equitable assignment under English law, meet the following requirements. The assignment must be:

(a) in writing;
(b) signed by the assignor;
(c) absolute;
(d) notified to the debtor (being, in the case of the earnings, the charterer, and in respect of the insurances, the insurer(s)).

The final requirement determines the date that the assignment takes effect and determines the priority of such assignment.

5.3.3 The Charge or Pledge Over Accounts

Another means by which the lender controls the ship's earnings is through a charge or pledge of sums standing to the credit of the account to which the earnings are paid, from which the lender may also request that the borrower make regular payments into a blocked retention account. Lenders may require that a minimum balance must be standing to the credit of an earnings account throughout the term of a facility.

5.3.4 The Shares Charge or Pledge

It is becoming increasingly common for lenders, as part of their security package for ship finance transactions, to receive a charge or pledge over the shares in single-purpose ship owning companies. Although rarely exercised, such charges or pledges enable the lender to sell the ship owning company on the borrower's default, and thereby permit a beneficial charter of the ship to remain in place (as such a charter may have to be terminated on the sale of a ship or following its arrest).

5.3.5 The Pre-delivery Security Assignment

As mentioned above (and although less frequent in the current climate), lenders who advance pre-delivery finance will seek to control and preserve the value of their security in an asset that is still under construction. This is usually done by way of an assignment of the shipbuilding contract, through which the lender aims to limit any amendments to the shipbuilding contract which could affect the value or specifications of the ship or the availability and effectiveness of the lender's security, and also the refund guarantee.

5.4 Conclusion

As described in this chapter, the developments in the banking and debt markets over the years have resulted in there being an increased number of options available to ship owning groups when determining how to structure transactions involving the debt financing of ships. An owning group will consider whether it will finance a ship or ships through a standard loan or credit facility (and whether or not this will be backed by an export agency), a leasing structure, a bond issue or, in addition to a standard loan or credit facility, a mezzanine facility. The option to be chosen in each case will depend on a number of factors such as the risk-appetite of a lender, the commercial requirements of a borrower, the relative bargaining strength of the parties and the market conditions prevailing at the relevant time.

Bibliography

Arrangement on Officially Supported Export Credits (10 January 2015) *Publication of the Trade and Agriculture Directorate of the Organisation for Economic Co-operation and Development*

Orestis Schinas, Carsten Grau and Max Johns Eds. (2015) *HSBA Handbook on Ship Finance,* Euromoney Books

Russel (2006) *Shipping Finance, 3rd Edition,* Stephenson Harwood, London

Loan Market Association, *Users Guide to Investment Grade Primary Documentation,* (last updated 12 December 2014)

Loan Market Association, *Summary Note on FATCA* (last updated 9 June 2014)

6

Public Debt Markets for Shipping

Basil M. Karatzas

6.1 Introduction

For shipowners, borrowing monies from shipping banks has been the most prominent way of financial leverage in the shipping industry. The capital markets have also been a source of borrowing for larger, more sophisticated shipowners for several decades now, and it is expected that access to these markets will become ever more crucial in the future. The present chapter provides an introductory discussion to the public debt markets in shipping, its primary differences, advantages and disadvantages against shipping loans, and the main considerations that shipowners will have to face in order to navigate successfully the public debt markets.

6.2 Basic Concepts of Bonds

Bonds are negotiable debt instruments where the borrower (debt issuer or debtor) borrows money from the investors (creditors or bondholders) by issuing securities (bonds or indentures) via the engagement of an underwriting or advisory firm. Bonds are similar in principle to loans, as in both cases there

---

B.M. Karatzas (✉)
Karatzas Marine Advisors & Co., One World Financial Center, 30F, New York, NY 10281, USA

© The Author(s) 2016
M.G. Kavussanos, I.D. Visvikis (eds.), *The International Handbook of Shipping Finance*, DOI 10.1057/978-1-137-46546-7_6

is a borrower, a lender and an amount of money exchanged (borrowed) in good faith, with the promise to be repaid under certain pre-agreed terms and at a cost of capital not directly related to market conditions. However, there are practical and logistical differences between bonds and loans, the cardinal difference being that, for bonds, there is a secondary public market for their trading (thus "negotiable") among the bond holders (investors) during the life of the bond. In practical terms, in the eyes of the borrower, it means that the lenders can change during the time of the indenture without the terms of the underlying loan agreement being affected; in the case of a loan, the lender typically remains the same throughout the maturity of the loan. Since bonds are tradable instruments, they are more liquid assets than loans and they appeal to a wider market of investors who can obtain greater lending capacity and a greater appetite for risk than traditional lenders through the banking system; however, being tradable instruments it is required that their terms, covenants and pertinent information (reflecting the certainty that the borrowed amount will be repaid) are publicly available during the time of the indebtedness. Also, since bonds are tradable instruments in the secondary market, they resemble public equities (shares) in effect, although bonds are debt instruments.

The amount of money borrowed when the bonds are originally issued is called the "principal amount" (or par value or face value, in reference to the denominations); the period of time within which the principal amount has to be paid back to the investors is called "maturity"; and the maturity date is that on which the last repayment of the principal is due. The "price", which the borrower pays for utilizing the principal amount for one calendar year, is called the "coupon" (comparable to "annual interest rate" for loans); payments of the interest take place typically annually or semi-annually and are called "coupon payments", which typically remain constant during the maturity of the bond. The original buyers of the bonds from the underwriter constitute the primary market, while the subsequent trading of them among investors constitutes the secondary market. Bonds typically are issued in denominations of USD1,000. Market conditions are normally expected to change during the maturity of a bond, and with them most likely the borrower's ability to perform in relation to the bonds. Since the coupon payment is constant and the investors may change their opinion about the "value" of the bonds, the latter will change in price by fluctuating on what investors would pay for the original USD1,000 investment in the secondary market—for the right to keep collecting the same coupon. When market conditions deteriorate or the ability of the borrower deteriorates, the value of the bonds drops (they are known to trade at a discount); in such a case, the yield increases (the coupon remains constant, thus the same coupon payment is received for a smaller investment), and thus the value and yield on the bonds move in an inverted relationship. Likewise, bonds trading above their face value are said to be trading at a premium, and their yield drops accordingly. The annual interest payment divided by the current market value of the bond is called the "current yield" or "running yield". Taking into consideration all future coupon payments for the life of the bond, and the principal amount to be repaid on the maturity date divided by the current market value of the bond, is called the "yield to maturity" or "redemption yield", which reflects the internal rate of return of the bond.

6.3 Bond Issuing Example

Shipowner Mr Big Ship borrows USD10,000,000 in the bond market with a six-year maturity. Let's assume that: the coupon is set at 8% annually at the time of issue, thus USD800,000 annually is due for interest payments (typically, payments take place in arrears, at the end of the period); the borrower will pay USD4,800,000 in total during the time of the indebtedness for the benefit of using USD10,000,000; the original amount borrowed is due on the maturity date at end of year six, for a fixed-coupon bond with a balloon repayment schedule. Since bonds are typically issued in USD1,000 denominations, in this case 10,000 bonds each of USD1,000 nominal or face value would be issued (the bond price is then quoted as 100.00 in the financial press), thus an original bond investor, Mr Early Bird, can buy as little as USD1,000 in bonds (or multiples of such denomination, if so desired). If the coupon is agreed to be payable semi-annually, then payments of USD400,000 each are due at the end of each six-month period from the date of issue; for an original investor of a USD1,000 bond, there will be two coupon payments due every year at USD40 each.

6.4 Bond Pricing in the Secondary Market Example

It is one year since Mr Big Ship has issued bonds, and let's presume that the market has improved, either because freight rates have improved and Mr Big Ship is now perceived as having greater ability to meet his future bond obligations, or the overall interest rate environment has benefited from expansionary monetary policy and interest rates in general have dropped. Thus, the 8% annual interest on Mr Big Ship's bonds now looks comparatively more attractive, and investors in the secondary market would now have a stronger appetite to buy these bonds. Let's say that they bid the price of the bonds to 125.00 (from 100.00 that was the face value), bringing the current yield down to 6.4 from 8% (USD40 coupon payments twice in one year over a USD1,250 investment yield 6.4%). Nothing otherwise has changed with the terms of the bonds themselves, and Mr Big Ship is still responsible for paying an 8% coupon on an annual basis, despite his improving fortunes. However, while the original investor, Mr Early Bird, was getting paid 8% to lend money to Mr Big Ship (bought at 100.00), now the new lender (Mr Late Sleeper) gets paid 6.4% (bought at 125.00). There is no material impact on Mr Big Ship's cash outflows, but now he has the pleasure of having a new "benchmark" and theoretically could issue new bonds now at more competitive terms (at 6.5%).

6.5   Issuing of a Shipping Bond

Mr Big Ship, having evaluated all the options in obtaining debt financing for the shipping business and having decided that bond issuing is the optimal venue, typically has to retain a registered underwriter (investment bank or advisor) to consult him or her on how best to proceed and actually access the investor community and raise the money on the shipowner's behalf. For publicly offered bonds, an investment case—running into several hundred pages—has to be prepared by the underwriter, which provides pertinent information to the investors about the bond and the business opportunity and which contains sections describing the borrower, the market, the purpose of the offering and use of proceeds, the terms of repayments, the underlying asset and the business. The investment case document, called the prospectus, is filed with the prospective authorities and regulators where the offering is to take place (such as the US Securities and Exchange Commission (SEC) in the USA, one of the most active debt markets worldwide). The investors buying the bonds directly via the underwriter when they were first issued are collectively called the primary market; in future they will be able to trade the bonds with other investors in the secondary market, with the transfer agent keeping track of bond ownership, coupon payments, etc.

6.6   Filing a Prospectus

In the event that the borrower is aiming at raising the bond privately from one or two qualified investors (creditors) through a private placement, most of the time no filing with the regulators is required, and this private bond placement can very much resemble a custom-offered loan, only that in this case the creditor is not a bank (a creditor holding a banking license) but an institutional investor, a family office or even a wealthy individual. A private placement may offer more flexibility on structuring the terms and covenants than a public bond offering or a shipping loan, but typically private debt placements are best suited for smaller amounts borrowed and are extremely limited when it comes to selling the loan in the secondary market. For private debt placements, the lenders have to be qualified or accredited investors (effectively high net worth individuals or professional investors), thus the placement cannot be offered to broad market retail investors; also, private debt placements may require special licensing in certain jurisdictions (such as in Germany) where lending activities are more tightly controlled by the regulators.

6.7 Obtaining a Credit Rating

For a public bond offering, a credit rating is usually strongly advised, but not obligatory. An independent credit rating bureau (agency) has to be engaged to delve into the details of the offering and assign a credit rating: the likelihood that the creditors will be compensated as per the terms outlined in the prospectus. Credit ratings can range from the highest, reflecting almost absolute certainty that bondholders will be repaid ("AAA" or similar at the top of the investment grade range), to speculative probability that bondholders will get repaid ("D" or other similar assignments in the "junk status" territory). Major credit rating agencies such as Standard & Poor's (S&P) or Moody's can be engaged to assign a credit rating, but it is often the case that several, lesser known rating agencies, whether local (e.g. CreditReform) or with specialization in the shipping industry, can also be acceptable. As one would expect, the higher the rating achieved, the lower the cost of the financing, as the degree of likelihood that bondholders will see the terms of the offering honored and their principal and coupons diligently paid is higher. However, keeping in mind that in assigning a rating on a bond, the "beta" (the market volatility) of the industry to which the bond pertains has to be incorporated in the credit rating model, and given the volatility of the shipping industry (the variance of freight rates, e.g. the variance of the Baltic Dry Index (BDI) over the last five years) is higher than most other industries, few bonds in the industry can practically attain investment grade (especially in the upper echelons of it). As one would expect, the rating of bonds of major shipping companies can attain higher grades (investment grade or thereabouts), reflecting characteristics of their business model that make performance of such bonds less susceptible to market volatility. Characteristics that typically and positively affect credit ratings are long-term contracts with end-user charterers (e.g. mining and major oil companies, steel mills), trading houses or importers and exporters with high credit standing; additional characteristics are bond issuers benefiting from strategic advantages such as access to ports and port facilities, and niche or protected markets, such as companies with vessels involved in coastal or cabotage trades or the liner business. The rating of bonds for shipping companies with their operations mostly in commodity shipping (notably in the volatile dry-bulk and crude oil tanker markets, especially when the vessels are involved in tramp trades and fully exposed to the spot market) is invariably of non-investment grade. Non-investment grade bonds are collectively known as "high yield bonds" reflecting the relatively high cost (coupon) for their borrowings; they are also pejoratively known as "junk bonds" reflecting the higher probability of default and loss of the principal (or part thereof) (Fig. 6.1).

6.8 Selecting an Underwriter

Raising bonds in the public market entails selecting and mandating an underwriter (investment bank) to advise the issuer and advertise the business prospect to the investors. For major shipping companies, investments banks that are household names may be engaged (e.g. Goldman Sachs, Citibank, Morgan Stanley). Shipping bonds issued by major shipping companies and underwritten by the main investment banks are typically distinguished by the fact that: (a) there is already plentiful public information about the issuer and that their track record in the capital markets is already well known (often their previously issued bonds are already trading in the secondary market); (b) typically large sums of money are sought to be raised (several hundred millions of dollars) at the issuing; (c) these bonds are of higher quality and can be securitized by cash flows from for example operations, and thus can be of interest to the large pool of institutional investors that a bulge bracket investment bank can access, that is investors with no special focus on the shipping markets. However, for shipping bonds issued by smaller shipowners, with shorter track records in business, with smaller amounts to be raised (less than USD100 million) or with bonds to be collateralized by assets (vessels) only, typically smaller and specialized underwriters are likely to be a better option for the shipowner. Shipping bonds offered by such smaller issuers are typically at borderline investment grade or lower (thus of higher risk) and require underwriters with shipping market expertise in order to access and convey to niche investors the industry-specific characteristics of the bonds. Such specialized underwriters can be investments banks that have built a reputation on issuing and trading shipping bonds over several business cycles or have access to specific groups of

CREDIT RATING	SHIPPING BONDS	CATEGORY DEFINITION
AAA	INVESTMENT GRADE	An obligation rated 'AAA' has the highest rating assigned by Standard and Poor's. The obliger's capacity to meet its financial commitment on the obligation is extremely strong.
AA		An obligation rated 'AA' differs from the highest-rated obligations only to a small degree. The obligor's capacity to meet its financial commitment on the obligation very strong.
A		An obligation rated 'A' is somewhat more susceptible to the adverse effects of changes in circumstances and economic An obligation rated 'A' is somewhat more susceptible to the adverse effects of changes in circumstances and economic conditions than obligations in higher-rated categories. However, the obligor's capacity to meet its financial commitment on the obligation is still strong.
BBB		An obligation rated 'BBB' exhibits adequate protection parameters. However, adverse economic conditions or changing circumstances are more likely to lead to a weakened capacity of the obligor to meet its financial commitment on the obligation.
BB; B; CCC; CC; C	NON-INVESTMENT GRADE (HIGH-YIELD OR JUNK)	ASSET BACKED SHIPPING BOND REALM / SHIPPING BOND S / PB POIN ND GS	Obligations rated 'BB', 'B', 'CCC', 'CC', and 'C' are regarded as having significant speculative characteristics. 'BB' indicates the least degree of speculation and 'C' may be outweighed by large uncertainties or major exposures to adverse conditions. highest. While such obligations will likely have some quality and protective characteristics, these
BB			An obligation rated 'BB' is less vulnerable to nonpayment than other speculative issues. However, it faces major ongoing uncertainties or exposure to adverse business, financial, or economic conditions which could lead to the obligor's inadequate capacity to meet its financial commitment on the obligation.
B			An obligation rated 'B' is more vulnerable to nonpayment than obligations rated 'BB', but the obligor currently has the capacity to meet its financial commitment on the obligation. Adverse business, financial, or economic conditions will likely impair the obligor's capacity or willingness to meet its financial commitment on the obligation.
CCC			An obligation rated 'CCC' is currently vulnerable to nonpayment, and is dependent upon favorable business, financial, and economic conditions for the obligors to meet its financial commitment on the obligation. I the event of adverse business, financial, or economic conditions, the obligor is not likely to have the capacity to meet its financial commitment on the obligation.
CC			CC an obligation rated 'CC' is currently highly vulnerable to nonpayment.
C			A 'C' rating is assigned to obligations that are currently highly vulnerable to nonpayment, obligations that have payment arrearages allowed by the terms of the documents, or obligations of an issuer that is the subject of a bankruptcy petition or similar action which have not experienced a payment default. Among others, the 'C' rating may be assigned to subordinated debt, preferred stock or other obligations on which cash payments have been suspended in accordance with the instrument's terms or when preferred stock is the subject of a distressed exchange offer, whereby some or all of the issue is either repurchased for an amount of cash or replaced by other instruments having a total value that is less than par.
D	OR JUNK)	BONDS	An obligation rate 'D' is in payment default, The 'D' rating category is used when payments on an obligation are not made on the date due, unless Standard & Poor's believes that such payments will be made within five business days, irrespective of any grace period. The 'D' rating also will be used upon the filing of a bankruptcy petition or the taking of similar action if payments on an obligation are jeopardized. An obligation's rating is lowered to 'D' upon completion of a distressed exchange offer, whereby some or all of the issue is either repurchased for an amount of cash or replaced by other instruments having a total value that is less than par.
NR			This indicates that no rating has been requested, that there is insufficient information on which to base a rating, or that Standard & Poor's does not rate a particular obligation as a matter of policy.

*The rating from 'AA' to 'CCC' may be modified by the addition of a plus (+) or minus (-) sign to show relative standing within the major

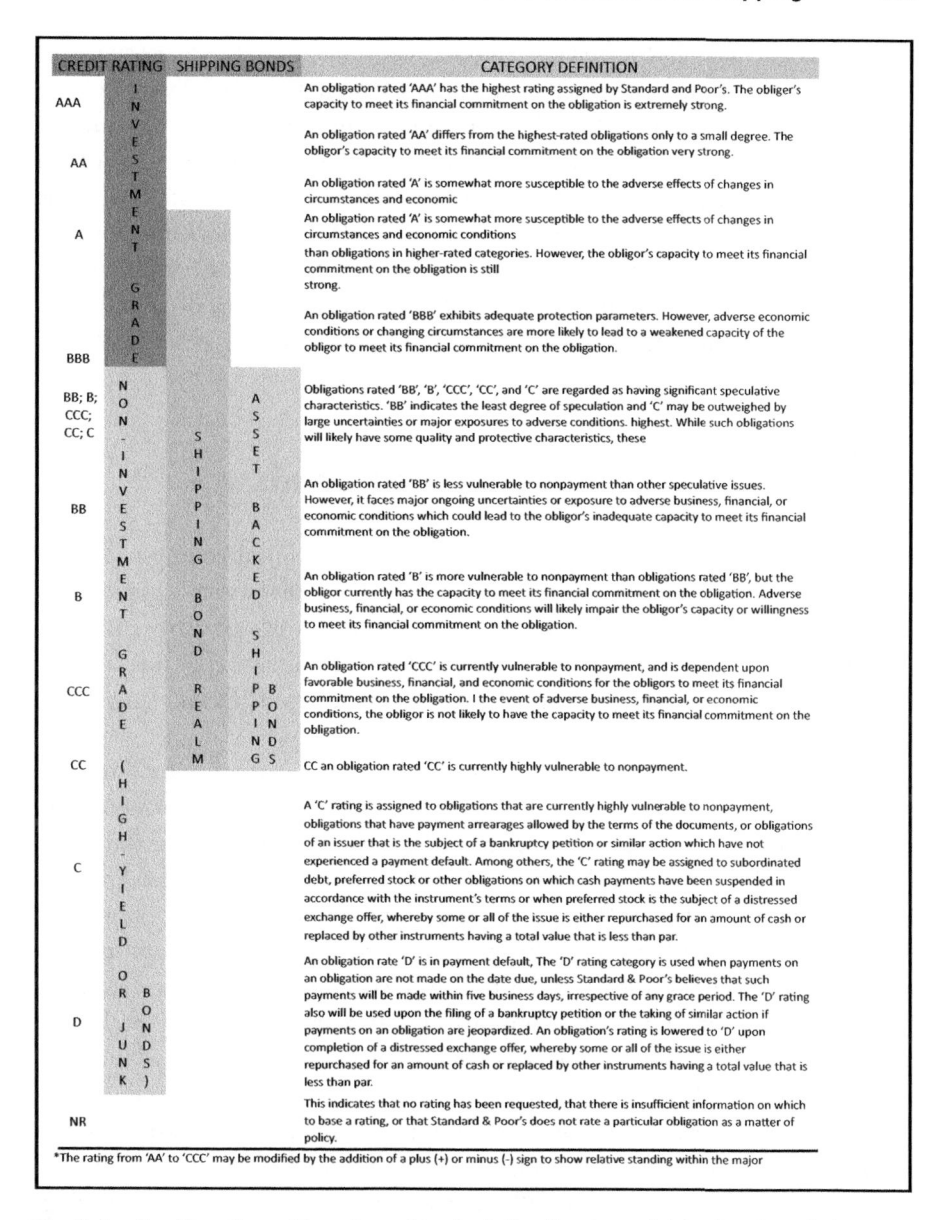

Fig. 6.1 Credit rating of bonds and typical distribution of shipping bonds (*Source*: The ratings from 'AA' to 'CCC' may be modified by the addition of a plus (+) or minus (–) sign to show relative standing within the major)

investors with an appetite for such riskier bonds; for instance, a group of investors whose mandate is for riskier investments or investors with deep knowledge of the shipping industry—such as Norwegian investors, who are already familiar with shipping investments in public (Oslo Børs) or private equity

(KS funds and sale and leaseback transactions)—offer a natural prospect for buying shipping bonds. Choosing the best underwriter is a decision to be considered diligently and by taking into consideration many parameters such as shipping market expertise, the ability to successfully access investors with the proper risk profile, a track record, dedication and professionalism. As a rule of thumb, smaller specialized underwriters may offer the best choice for relative newcomers to the public debt markets, and as the familiarity of the issuer with the public markets increases, along with their track records and need and capacity to raise more money, then a bigger lead underwriter may offer better prospects.

6.9 Timing of Issuing Shipping Bonds

As already mentioned, the preponderance of shipping bond issuings, whether asset-backed or cash-flow based, are rated below investment grade with the better tranche of them close to the borderline with investment grade. Characteristic of debts bearing a higher risk of default, such bonds have to have a coupon high enough to entice creditors to accept such risk (high yield bonds).

When then is issuing bonds a viable option for a borrower in shipping, given the usually high coupon? Clearly, when borrowing from banks is cheap, the issuing of (expensive) bonds cannot be justified on purely economic factors (but can be justified if the issuer is trying to establish a broader financial basis or establish a record for dealing with public capital markets). However, as the appetite for risk by the debt investors can vary and the premium they assign to risk declines, there can be an intersecting point where low coupons for such bonds (in the 6–8% coupon) are attractive enough or preferable alternative options exist for the borrower. As extreme examples, when shipping banks have plenty of liquidity and low cost of capital, shipping bonds do not make an ideal option for most shipping companies. Similarly, at times when investors are seeking the highest security on their lending, shipping bonds are not optimal choices. When economies worldwide are prospering, when the promise of new technologies and paradigm shifts bring euphoria to investors, and the new prevailing investment thesis is "risk on", then it's easy for the investors to have a more normalized view of the risks associated with shipping and shipping bonds. A glaring example of an increased appetite for shipping bonds was the high-yield era of the late 1990s. Those were the years with historically strong economic growth in the USA when stock indices were setting all time new highs and retail investors were day-trading as hobby on the promise of new technologies and the "dot.com" era boom; those were also the years when China ascended to the WTO and the early hope of a new huge market joining the world stage. Almost 15 years later, and with a profound financial crisis forcing governments and central banks worldwide to embark on never-seen-before expansionary policies and exceptionally low interest rates, the prospect of shipping bonds has become an appealing investment, on comparative terms, this time around.

For well-established shipping companies, such as AP Moeller Maersk, MOL, NYK and other companies of similar caliber, the bond markets are typically available throughout the phases of the cycle, though, of course, at prevailing market conditions as far as interest expense (coupon) is concerned. For smaller shipping companies and asset-backed shipping bonds, the windows of opportunity are occasional and relatively small, and have to coincide with when the appetite for risk allows investors to be satisfied with relatively low coupons for the relatively risky shipping business, but also for the coupon to be competitively low enough so as not to burden the company with unserviceable debt through the phases of the business cycle.

6.10 Shipping Bonds and Interest Rate Cost

Depending on overall market conditions, junk bonds in shipping usually have to yield several hundred basis points (bp) above the risk-free rate to compensate for the industry risk; that is, shipping high yield bonds have been yielding 6% at the very least, and more typically in the 7–9% range, while the same bonds bearing coupons of 12% or more are not unheard of. A few representative examples of terms and coupons obtained in shipping bond markets in the recent past are as follows. In 2009, during their restructuring process, tanker owner General Maritime based in New York issued USD300 million in senior unsecured bonds bearing a 12% coupon, reflecting the weak state of the tanker market and the particular circumstances of the issuer. In 2013, Teekay LNG issued USD150 million in senior unsecured bonds in the Norwegian bond market with a 6.43% coupon, reflecting the company's good reception in the markets and the relatively low risk exposure of the business toward energy and natural gas transportation. In 2013, Navios Maritime Acquisition issued approximately USD670 million in shipping bonds secured by a fleet of VLCC tankers and their employment with a coupon of 8.13%. In 2014, US-based and private equity (PE)-sponsored Ridgebury Tankers raised asset-backed bonds in the Norwegian market with a 65% leverage (meaning 65% of the then present value of the assigned vessels) on a 6.75% coupon, which was slightly better than prevailing ship lending conditions, though with two strong advantages attached to the bond issuing: (a) the principal was due on the maturity date (while any ship mortgage arrangement would have a meaningful amortization schedule) and (b) no employment restrictions or time-charter requirement capped the company's market exposure in the event of strong freight rates (a scenario that did develop actually).

6.11 Considerations for the Cost of Shipping Bonds

Even for low yielding shipping bonds at 6% at times when interest rates by central banks are historically extremely low (usually 0.50%) and the US Treasury Bill is at 0.25%, a meaningful risk premium of more than 5% is implied for the industry. The relatively high risk premium associated with the industry can partially be explained by its volatility and the notion that the BDI has moved between a maximum of 13,000 and a minimum of 600 index points within a few years of the shipping down-cycle. High yield bonds carry a high interest cost that makes survival in weak freight markets precarious when freight revenue may not be strong enough to cover operating expenses and the coupon payment. In the 1990s, there was a rush of high yield bonds for shipping with 35 issuings,[1] with most of them failing shortly after their issuance, given that the weakening freight market made it impossible to service the debt.

Besides the empirical observations for the pricing of shipping bonds, proper academic research on the subject has documented that the main determinants of global cargo-carrying companies' shipping bond spreads are found to be the liquidity of the bond issue, the stock market's volatility, the bond market's cyclicality, freight earnings and the credit rating of the bond issue.[2] In order to consider issuing shipping bonds at a relatively high cost, a shipowner must have been left with a limited set of financing options, and, economically, all of them will have to be comparably expensive. In most of the first decade of this century, when liquidity was plentiful as shipping banks were overly aggressive on their lending terms (high leverage, thin margins, loose covenants, etc.), there has been a dearth of shipping bonds issued by smaller shipowners. This was logical as a typical shipping loan was averaging 75% leverage, a 200bp spread (LIBOR + 2%) and large balloon payments on principal; shipping bonds for smaller shipowners are clearly much more expensive than this. However, post-Lehman Brother collapse when shipping banks stopped lending to second-tier owners and debt financing could be found from credit funds at much higher rates and stricter terms, shipping bonds have become again a viable option given the alternatives.

6.12 Difference from Shipping Loans

Shipping bonds are debt instruments and therefore very similar conceptually to shipping loans. In both cases, money is borrowed and eventually has to be repaid, and again, in both cases, the money can be accessed at a cost primarily tied to the borrower's creditworthiness and secondarily correlated to the performance of the investment or related to market conditions. However, there are crucial differences between shipping loans and shipping bonds, and based on the circumstances, the borrower may have a preference between obtaining a shipping loan or issuing a shipping bond.

When Mr Big Ship approaches his shipping bank to borrow money to finance the acquisition of a new vessel, the bank bases its decision on whether to extend a loan on factors that the bank's management itself has qualified. These can be objective, quantifiable criteria applicable to all the clients of the bank, such as the amount of leverage to be extended or the minimum spread over LIBOR. However, the bank's credit committee may also wish to consider "softer" subjective criteria for extending a shipping loan, such as the extent and length of the banking relationship with the borrower, complementary business opportunities (e.g. cross-selling of private wealth products) and the overall strategic value of the borrower to the bank. For a shipping bond issuing, since there will be several buyers in the primary market and several more investors afterwards in the secondary market, the criteria pertaining to the quality of the bond have to be objective and to the satisfaction of the plentiful investors. Therefore, a shipping loan is typically a bilateral contract where the "personal element" may be of certain gravity, while a shipping bond is a multi-party agreement based on quantitative decision-making.

Information that a shipping bank has collected on a borrower is typically proprietary and often privileged information, while pertinent information about the borrower and the bond are in the public domain and filed with the pertinent authorities. While a bank has its own credit committee to assess the creditworthiness of a borrower, a third-party rating agency is often engaged to evaluate the bonds and the probability that the borrower will perform on their obligations. In terms of expedience, although the time a shipping bank can authorize a loan depends on several factors, in general the issuing of bonds is much more time consuming in terms of preparing and filing documentation and mainly concerns communicating with investors, holding a roadshow and getting the fund commitments. Accordingly, the associated costs and fees are much higher for bonds than the origination and commitment fees that a typical shipping loan will cost. Therefore, shipping loans depend upon and assure privacy and discretion between the parties, and they are typically time and cost efficient as compared to shipping bonds where information is public, and time and costs required to access the public markets are of a higher order. As a rule of thumb, shipping bonds require approximately one month or more of effort and can cost twice as much in fees and expenses than a loan. However, for shipping bonds with principal amounts in the range of hundreds of million dollars, costs are very competitive and well justified (2–3% of the principal amount, which is slightly higher than origination fees charged by most shipping banks for smaller amounts).

Given that shipping loans (a) can be facilitated by personal relationships and ancillary considerations, (b) do not require public disclosure and (c) are both time and cost efficient, one may be tempted to say that shipping bonds should be a resource of last resort in the financial arsenal of Mr Big Ship. Indeed, traditional shipping loans (ship mortgages) dominate the shipping debt markets for independent, smaller shipowners. However, there are strong considerations in favor of shipping bonds as well. During the course of a full business cycle, the lending capacity of shipping banks can be limited and not extend credit to large shipowners, or be unable to provide sufficient liquidity to meet competently market demand, or be dissatisfied with the quality of the credit of potential buyers (state of the market). The issuing of bonds typically has the full benefit of the depth and breadth of the public capital markets where relatively large sums of money can be raised and where there are multiple investors with varying degrees of appetite for credit quality, asset class concentration and geographic focus.

Shipping loans can be in small amounts, as small as a few million dollars, depending on the shipping banks' criteria. Like any other type of publicly traded security, a shipping bond must have a sufficient amount offered in order to be appealing to institutional investors and to sustain continued trading activity in the secondary market (liquidity). Therefore, bond issuings have to be sizeable as a stand-alone offering (usually more than USD50 million based on market conditions) or be smaller amounts for a series of bonds from the same issuer. However, such issuings could take place for substantially smaller amounts, often reflecting the practical reason that shipping bonds are a small sub-set of the public bonds markets and that many bond issuers in the shipping industry are comparatively small; thus, smaller issuers have to be accommodated as well. It should be noted that substantial shipping companies or shipowners with relatively large fleets, businesses well established over the long term, proven track records and business models often get the most attention and the best pricing and terms of issuing, including smaller transaction fees.

An aspect associated with shipping bonds, which is usually highly appreciated by shipowners, is that the whole amount borrowed (principal amount) is typically due as a bullet payment on the maturity date (a typical ship mortgage requires at least partial repayment of the principal amount during the maturity period). In the bond issuing example above, the USD10,000,000 raised from the bond issuing is due at the end of year six, while for a similar amount of a shipping mortgage amortizing equally on the same period, there will be an additional principal payment of USD4,566 per diem; the timing of the principal repayment can free cash flows to invest elsewhere or lower the cost basis for operating the vessels. In a weak freight market that barely covers vessel operating expenses, a lower cost base can be an advantage of paramount importance.

Not that one wishes to see a borrower ever default on their debt obligations, but it has happened in the shipping markets from time to time. In the event of default on debt, who the creditors are can have a profound impact on the options the borrower has. In the event of a loan default when a shipping bank (or syndicate of banks) is the creditor, discussions on finding a solution after the default are typically private, bilateral and discreet as the two sides try to work out an optimal solution. The outcome of the negotiations can be subjective as personalities and relationships can drive discussions, and there is usually one creditor (shipping bank) to be satisfied (or a group of like-minded creditors in the event of a syndicated loan). As a rule of thumb, shipping banks are known to prefer resolution over confrontation, in which case they can allow for several options to be explored. In the event of a default on a bond, the standard route is that the rule of law in the jurisdiction the bond was issued (and stipulated in the prospectus) takes precedence over personalities and negotiations, with much less patience and proclivity for working out a solution. In the event of a bond default, the bondholders create a committee to represent their interests (different types of creditors may end up having their own representative committee) and retain both a legal counselor and a financial advisory in order to optimize their benefit.

Bondholders may be both retail investors (small lenders having invested in the bonds but none of them holding a meaningful stake) or institutional investors (where one or a handful of them can hold a predominant position and thus can control the creditors' committee). When the bondholders are institutional investors, they are professional money managers, driven mainly by returns on their investments and having in-house expertise and access to advisors and bankruptcy lawyers (most likely they have had to deal with a bond default before, if not in shipping then in other industries). In the past, mostly during the defaults in the 1990s, there have been cases where the majority of retail bondholders didn't manage to mount a spirited representation and stance or the investment bank holding a stake in the bonds preferred, for their own reasons, to take a meaningful loss. However, as a rule of thumb, in the case of defaulting on shipping bonds where the bondholders' committee is controlled by institutional investors, typically the borrowers can expect stronger negotiations and professional efforts to recover as much money as possible, exhausting all options and legal venues.

6.13 Classification of Shipping Bonds Based on Collateral

A bond, as a standard debt instrument, has to offer to creditors certain assurances that the borrower will be able to perform on the bond and make good on coupon payments and return of principal amounts. The higher the assurances that the bond issuer can offer, whether subjectively or objectively, the better the reception of the bonds, the higher the principal amount can be, and the lower the coupon. Subjective determinants can be the length of time the shipowner has been in business (a subjective criterion in shipping since, typically, there are no formal corporate structures and many vessels can be held by offshore entities), name recognition, industry reputation or business track record. However, objective criteria usually bear higher weighting on bond issuing, usually by accessing the overall creditworthiness of the issuing party or the form of collateral offered as a pledge for performing on the bonds.

For major shipowning companies with a long and active record of existence and access to the public capital markets, companies such as AP Moeller Maersk, MOL and NYK typically can easily and very competitively access the public debt markets for issuing bonds, can raise principal amounts in the billion dollar range, expect competitive pricing, low issuing fees (as a percentage of the issuing) and a rather active secondary market for the trading of their bonds. Large companies typically offer corporate bonds, meaning that the parent company is responsible for their payment, based on their credit rating and track record, but they do not have to pledge specific assets (vessels) for the bonds. Corporate bonds of course can have their own standing in the pecking order of other forms of debt, and can be senior or subordinate in reference to the priority of the creditors to be compensated in the event of default; but again, there is no recourse in the event of a default for creditors to have the right to arrest named vessels as security. As an example of a major shipping company accessing the bond market on a regular basis, AP Moeller Maersk issued USD6 billion in corporate bonds on 11 occasions in five different currencies between 2009 and 2014, with maturities ranging from five to ten years, and an average coupon of 3.68%. Please see adjacent table (Table 6.1, Selective Bond Issuings by A.P. Moeller Maersk).

The majority of shipping companies looking to access the public debt markets have a relatively short history of existence (predominantly much shorter than ten years in business) and often may also lack a proper corporate structure, solid corporate governance or even consolidated audited financial statements. For such shipowners, a corporate "promise" that they will perform diligently on new corporate bond issuings is not sufficient to have a successful bond raising; this disadvantage is even more pertinent for the commoditized and volatile sectors of dry-bulk and crude oil tankers, especially when vessels are operated in the spot rate market and thus fully exposed to the vicissitudes of market forces: bondholders are prepared to take a risk (almost by definition) but not a market risk that equity investors should be prepared to take. In such cases, when the "promise" or "faith" in repayment is not strong enough, creditors can provide tangible assurances for the bonds by offering them collateralized by hard physical assets (ships) and/or earnings associated with such vessels. Thus, in the event of default, the creditors (to the extent practicable) have the legal right to foreclose on the actual, named vessels stated in the prospectus. Under this scenario, certain vessels can be provided as collateral, in the same way that a vessel is provided as collateral in order to secure a ship mortgage from a bank. Additionally, if so desired or feasible, the borrower may offer, as additional collateral for the issuing of the bonds, the earnings—ideally earnings already attached to the vessels through time charter contracts. In such a scenario, the bondholders are offered both the ships and their earnings as collateral, for which they are expected to lower the interest rate and increase the amount of the bonds, since the likelihood of a default is now lower and the capital at risk in the event of a default is also lower. Such bonds are called covered or asset-backed bonds (as compared with corporate bonds mentioned earlier, which are secured by the cash flows of the parent company). Also, asset-backed bonds are directly comparable to typical shipping loans (first preferred ship mortgages, where the named vessel is pledged as security against the shipping loan).

As a variation on a theme, asset-backed bonds in shipping are not always issued solely by shipowners. Shipping banks may opt to issue bonds based on shipping mortgages they hold in order to raise their own capital from the public capital markets; in the go-go days of financial engineering prior to

Table 6.1

ISSUER NAME	ISSUE DATE	PRINCIPAL AMT	CURRENCY	USD EQUIVALENT	COUPON RATE	COUPON DESCRIPTION	MATURITY DATE
A. P. Moeller-Maersk A/S	16-Sep-14	75,00,00,000	USD	$75,00,00,000	2.55%	2.55%	1-Sep-19
A. P. Moeller-Maersk A/S	16-Sep-14	50,00,00,000	USD	$50,00,00,000	3.75%	3.75%	1-Sep-24
A. P. Moeller-Maersk A/S	26-Mar-13	30,00,00,000	GBP	$45,64,50,000	4.00%	4.00%	4-Apr-25
A. P. Moeller-Maersk A/S	26-Oct-12	1,40,00,00,000	SEK	$20,84,60,000	3.75%	3.75%	26-Feb-18
A. P. Moeller-Maersk A/S	26-Oct-12	1,10,00,00,000	SEK	$16,37,90,000	2.50%	STIBOR+2.10%	26-Feb-18
A. P. Moeller-Maersk A/S	28-Aug-12	75,00,00,000	EUR	$93,84,75,000	3.38%	3.38%	28-Aug-19
A. P. Moeller-Maersk A/S	22-Mar-12	3,00,00,00,000	NOK	$52,11,00,000	2.50%	NIBOR + 2.10%	22-Mar-17
A. P. Moeller-Maersk A/S	24-Nov-10	50,00,00,000	EUR	$67,63,00,000	4.38%	4.38%	24-Nov-17
A. P. Moeller-Maersk A/S	16-Dec-09	2,00,00,00,000	NOK	$34,44,00,000	2.50%	NIBOR+1.85%	16-Dec-14
A. P. Moeller-Maersk A/S	16-Dec-09	2,00,00,00,000	NOK	$34,44,00,000	6.25%	6.25%	16-Dec-16
A. P. Moeller-Maersk A/S	30-Oct-09	75,00,00,000	EUR	$1,10,68,50,000	4.88%	4.88%	30-Oct-14
			TOTAL	$6,01,02,25,000	3.68%	AVERAGE	

Source: Karatzas Marine Advisors & Co.

the Lehman Brothers collapse, such bonds were effectively collateralized loan obligations (CLOs), but the market for shipping loans offered as collateral had never taken off. As mentioned already, asset-backed shipping bonds are relatively expensive forms of debt; any bond issuing, in order to have economic value, should have achieved premium pricing (low interest rate)—an impossible feat when shipping banks were lending at LIBOR + 2%. A special case has been the *Schiffspfandbriefgesetz* (Pfandbrief Act or "ship covered bond act") in Germany with its special provisions to allow shipping banks to issue bonds collateralized by ship mortgages. Such practice was followed on limited basis prior to Lehman Brothers, and mostly by wholesale banks like DVB Bank SE[3] which has a higher cost of funding than most traditional retail/shipping banks. Post-Lehman Brothers, more German banks have opted to issue shipping bonds based on the Pfandbrief Act, such as Commerzbank AG[4] and HSH Nordbank AG.[5, 6]

6.14 Covenants and Special Conditions

Bonds, as debt instruments, are subject to the rule of the "Four Cs of Credit", where character, capacity, collateral and covenants determine whether debt will be available at all, and if so, at what terms. Character (or credit) stands for the track record of the borrower and past performance, such as having borrowed and repaid loans in the past, overall integrity, having performed to professional standards and enjoyed a good market reputation. Capacity stands for the ability to make good on debt obligations based on cash flows, assets, financial capacity to borrow and repay debt obligations. Collateral refers to the tangible assets that the borrower can put up as collateral for the debt obligations, collateral on which debtors can irrevocably access in case of a default; in the case of asset-backed bonds, the shipping assets themselves are offered as collateral for the bonds. Finally, covenants stand for the special terms, conditions and limitations in the debt agreement that the debtor is prepared to accept in order to provide additional assurances to the debtors. Covenants can be either affirmative or negative; that is, in the case of the former, the debtor has the obligation to take certain actions or is obliged by certain terms; typically, for shipping bonds, this could be to make coupon payments by certain dates or to maintain debt ratios within certain levels of earnings or cash flows. More interestingly, negative covenants pertain to certain actions that the debtor cannot undertake, such as selling assets (collateralized or not), declaring and paying dividends, or obtaining additional debt (within certain restrictions).

6.15 Types of Shipping Bonds

Bonds can be categorized on several matrices, and generally there is a market for each sub-category of bonds in the public debt markets. The main taxonomy of bonds is provided with special emphasis on those that are typically suitable for shipping companies.

6.15.1 Types of Bonds Based on Maturity

Debt securities with maturities up to one year are called bills; those with maturities of one to five years are called notes; and those with maturities longer than five years are called bonds. Nomenclature based on maturity is not absolute. In shipping, debt securities with maturities less than one year are rather rare, and most shipping bonds have maturities ranging from three to eight years. In this chapter, Ie opt to employ the term "bond" irrespective of the maturity period, fully recognizing that strict adherence to the terms would require otherwise. In June 2013, Rederi AB Transatlanic in Sweden issued the equivalent of USD22 million (maturing in six months at a cost of 10%) in a typical example of short-term bills issued for general corporate purposes and until the company can place long-term financing. In a more typical maturity, in November 2014, Star Bulk—publicly listed in the USA—issued USD200 million of senior unsecured bonds at an 8% coupon with a five-year maturity, while in September 2014, AP Moeller Maersk issued USD200 million of bonds in the USA at a 3.45% coupon with a ten-year maturity.

6.15.2 Origin of Issuer or Currency

The United States dollar is the predominant currency of the shipping industry, for collecting freight revenue and also paying expenses in a preponderance of transactions. However, there have been occasions when bonds have been issued in another currency because the issuer has most of their business denominated in that currency. Also, bond issuers may opt to issue bonds in other currencies than the US dollar if favorable interest rates, strong investor appetite and market conditions are prevalent. Typical alternate currencies for shipping bonds are: the Norwegian krona (in 2014, US-listed GasLog issued NOK500 million with a 5.99% coupon and a maturity in 2018); the Singaporean dollar (in 2012, Neptune Orient Lines issued SGD300 million at a 4.4% coupon with a maturity in 2019); the euro (German based Hapag Lloyd issued in 2014 EUR200 million of shipping bonds at a 7.5% coupon with a 2019 maturity); the Chinese Renminbi, but also the offshore Chinese Renminbi (dim sum bonds in Hong Kong, for example; COSCO issued RMB5 billion in 2010 with a 2020 maturity at 4.35%); the Japanese yen, which is often the currency of preference for bond issuings by the Japanese major liners Mitsui MOL, NYK and K-Line. For international shipowners issuing bonds in local currencies in an effort to exploit favorable interest rates or market conditions, special effort and currency hedging need to be considered as well, so as not to compound additional risk in the already volatile shipping market and the borrower not to end up obligated to make coupon payments and principal repayments in an appreciating currency.

6.15.3 Debt Repayment Schedule

Bonds can also be categorized based on the timing of the repayment of the principal amount, with fixed-coupon bonds paying a steady coupon over predetermined time intervals but with the principal amount taking place in one payment (balloon payment) on the maturity date of the bond. With zero-coupon bonds all interest payments during the term of the bond as well as the principal amount are all repaid together at once on the maturity date (in 2014, Mitsui OSK Lines, reflecting their strong standing, issued zero-coupon shipping bonds in the USA totaling USD500 million with 2018 and 2020 maturities); with annuities, the principal amount is repaid gradually over the term of the bond, while with step-up bonds there is an increasing interest payment and principal payment with the passing of time. An interesting type of bonds are perpetual bonds where the principal amount is never repaid and coupon payments are due in perpetuity, or at least as long the bond is outstanding.

The most common types of shipping bonds are fixed-coupon bonds, as zero-coupon bonds require a strong issuer, while annuities and step-up bonds cannot always secure timely cash flows in a volatile shipping market. Perpetual bonds[7]—effectively quasi-equity—require the strongest credit and presume that the issuer will be in business forever; such bonds are only rarely seen in the shipping industry and they are usually associated with shipowners with strong balance sheets or affiliated with government businesses and long-term bankable charters. Perpetual bonds may also be associated with capital restructurings when the borrower cannot support both interest and principal repayments, and a perpetual schedule of coupon payments is in the best interest for the time being for both lenders and borrower.[8] In 2013, Euronav, based in Belgium, issued USD150 million of perpetual convertible bonds[9] with a coupon of 6%. In 2012, Swiber Holdings and Ezion Holdings, both active in the offshore industry, issued SGD80 million at a 9.75% coupon and SGD125 million at a 7.8% perpetual note, respectively.

6.15.4 Interest Rate Commitment

Bonds can bear a fixed interest rate throughout their maturity or a variable interest rate, where the effective rate is related to a base rate, such as LIBOR, or to the inflation rate plus an agreed upon constant premium (spread) for floating-rate bonds or inflation-linked bonds, respectively. Fixed interest rate bonds are definitely preferable in a low interest rate environment as they lock in a low cost of financing and do not have any interest rate risk when rates move higher. In reality, in shipping, most bonds are floating-rate as bondholders typically do not wish to compound credit risk with interest rate risk in this volatile industry.

6.15.5 Option Characteristics

As defined earlier in this chapter, bonds are debt obligations that bear an interest rate and a pledge to repay the principal amount borrowed by the maturity date. However, there may be trigger mechanisms that can confer certain rights either on the issuer or the bondholders under well-defined parameters. The issuer may have the right to call (retire) the bonds earlier than the maturity date if they have found less expensive sources of capital or, otherwise, if the management has decided to pay off the principal. Callable bonds can be retired at fixed prices and on fixed dates, and usually require a higher coupon to other comparable bonds, all things being equal, given the optionality they confer to the borrower. Reversely, there are putable bonds where the bondholder has the right to put (force) the issuer to buy back the bonds at fixed prices and dates. As a matter of practice, shipping bonds are often callable and rarely putable.

Additionally, bonds may come attached with rights or warrants to convert to equity at predetermined rates (convertible bonds). The mechanism for bonds to convert to equity can be triggered when financial ratios move away from predetermined bands—usually when the financials of the issuer deteriorate, after the passing of a certain amount of time, or possibly when the share price of the issuer moves higher than a predetermined threshold. Convertible bonds are effectively "sweetened deals" for the lenders, as they offer the promise of a typical interest payment (on the bond) but also allow upside participation (now as equity) when the market or the borrower develops in a favorable way. Shipping bonds, being risky in nature, typically require "sweeteners" for buyers of bonds to be enticed. The convertible is the commonest way to allow a better return to the bondholders, which, at least initially, does not impair the issuer's cash flows.

6.15.6 Seniority

The bondholders, as lenders to the company, have preferred access to the company's assets in the event of default or bankruptcy, well before the owners (shareholders) can recover any of their investments in the business. However, not all the creditors or bondholders share the same order in the hierarchy of claimants or equal rights in the event that the company's outstanding assets are not sufficient to satisfy all creditors' claims. Bondholders ranking higher on the claimants list (seniority) are entitled to get repaid first, wholly or partially, before proceeds from the liquidation can cascade down to the creditors with lower ranking. As one would expect, the higher the seniority of the bonds, the more preferable they are, thus they are satisfied with a smaller coupon payment and/or a smaller discount or premium to the face value.

Senior secured bonds are the safest in the hierarchy of bonds and they are directly securitized by shipping assets (asset backed bonds) or cash flows from named assets or lines of business (long term charters and other contracts). Typically, these are the most common shipping bonds, often issued by relatively newly established shipowners, and such bonds are collateralized by a group of vessels.

Senior unsecured bonds are corporate shipping bonds that are not directly secured by named assets or cash flows from named assets or lines of business but they have the faith of the corporate borrower to make good on their obligations; in the event of liquidation, senior unsecured bonds enjoy the earliest priority to be repaid among all other unsecured bondholders. Senior unsecured shipping bonds are typically issued by better established shipping companies, or are issued at times when there is strong appetite among bond investors and thus higher willingness to take risk. Subordinated bonds are those with the lowest ranking on the claimant hierarchy. This type of bond is rarely seen in shipping, and if it is it is primarily for well-established shipping companies with an elaborate capital structure and substantial balance sheet.

6.16 Conclusion

Shipping bonds are just another tool in the financial toolbox of a shipowner for accessing financial gearing. Until the financial crisis of 2008, there had been sufficient capacity from shipping banks to provide shipping loans plentifully and cheaply so that shipping bonds were mostly utilized by major shipping companies that could issue corporate bonds with low coupons; in such an environment, shipping bonds, especially asset-backed bonds, were a novelty for most other shipping companies that were opportunistically at limited amounts. A lack of lending capacity from shipping banks, coupled with relatively large spreads, has opened the window for many shipping companies to explore the option of shipping bonds more actively and to bring a renaissance to the market. It is expected that traditional shipping banks will now have to focus on new and tighter regulations, creating a funding gap that will have to be filled with other forms of debt financing. Partly out of necessity and partly due to the fact that shipowners are getting ever more financially sophisticated, shipping bonds are expected to be a more active market and an active venue to be pursued by many shipowners, including those who are still at the early and growth stage of their business.

Notes

1. Research in Transportation Economics, Volume 21—Maritime Transport: The Greek Paradigm, Athanasios Pallis, Editor; JAI Press (Elsevier), 2007.
2. The determinants of credit spreads changes in global shipping bonds; Manolis G. Kavussanos, Dimitris A. Tsouknidis; Transportation Part E (Elsevier), 2014.
3. http://www.dvbbank.com/media/press-releases/pr2010/29-11-2010.aspx?sc_lang=en.
4. http://www.bloomberg.com/news/articles/2013-07-21/ex-commerzbank-banker-pitches-bonds-backed-by-german-ship-loans.
5. http://www.coveredbondnews.com/Article/3423760/HSH-Nordbank-shows-ships-are-in.html.
6. https://www.hsh-nordbank.com/en/presse/pressemitteilungen/2013/press_release_detail_3098112.jsp.
7. http://tradehaven.net/market/sgd-new-issue-review-ezion-7-perpetual/.
8. http://www.law360.com/articles/590133/french-shipper-raises-130m-in-perpetual-debt-issuance.
9. http://rmkmaritime.com/press/PressRelease_issuancePCP_ENG.pdf.

7

Public and Private Equity Markets

Jeffrey Pribor and Cecilie Skajem Lind

7.1 Introduction

The public and private equity markets constitute viable sources of ship financing alongside bank debt and other debt alternatives. Although a less traditional source of ship finance, the equity capital markets and private investors offer a plethora of opportunities as seen in Fig. 7.1, for both public and private shipping companies, albeit some solutions are more favored and applicable than others. As illustrated in Fig. 7.1, a private company may issue common stock in the public markets in a registered initial public offering (IPO), or they may choose to do an equity private placement. A public company may access additional capital in the public markets by pursuing a private investment in public equity (PIPE), a follow-on offering or through an equity-linked security such as convertible debt. Execution tactics are dictated by market conditions, investor appetite, structural considerations and trading dynamics. This chapter primarily focuses on the most relevant equity products available to private shipping companies with a particular emphasis on the benefits and drawbacks of being a public versus a private company, IPO structures and processes, as well as the role of private equity within the maritime sector.

J. Pribor (✉) • C.S. Lind
Jefferies LLC, 520 Madison Avenue, New York, NY 10022, USA

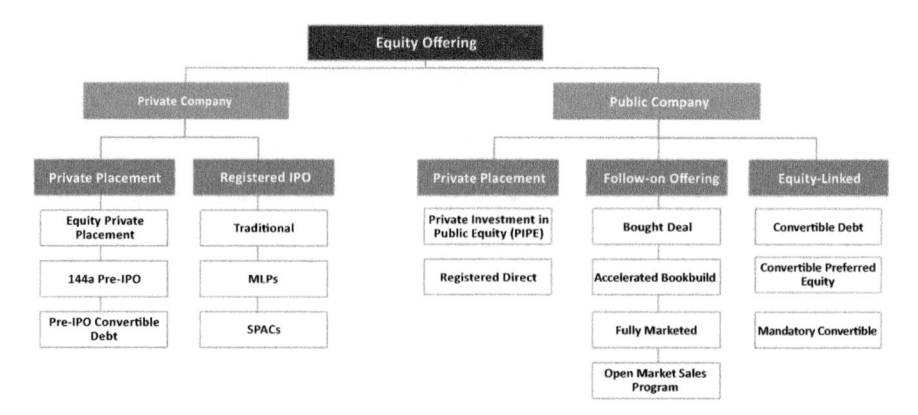

Fig. 7.1 Equity options available to public and private companies (*Source*: Jefferies)

7.2 Public Equity

7.2.1 Public Equity Overview

Public equity is an asset class of which institutional and/or individual investors can purchase ownership in shares of a company through unregulated and regulated public markets. Within the public equity asset class there are different types of equity, depending on the type of company that issued the equity as well as the seniority of the equity. In the shipping public equity landscape, the main types of equity available to investors are common and preferred equity (preferred equity is rated higher than common equity in liquidation) issued by C-corporations and units issued by master limited partnerships (MLPs).

C-corporations A C-corporation is a legal business entity that is taxed separately from its owners and is the most common structure for major companies. Shareholders of C-corporations own stock in a company which allows them to elect the board of directors, vote on certain strategic decisions and entitles them to a corporation's earnings, which are distributed through dividends unless reinvested back into the business for growth purposes.

Limited Partnerships (LPs) and MLPs An LP is another form of company structure, with an MLP being a type of limited partnership that is publicly traded. LPs are structured as pass-through entities and therefore avoid double taxation. The LP formation is often used by companies established to invest in industries linked to natural resources as well as real estate development. There are two categories of partners in LPs and MLPs: the limited partners and the general partner. The limited partner is an individual investor or a group of investors that provides the capital to the partnership; that is, the limited partner holds "units" and receives periodic income distributions from the partnership's cash flow. The general partner is responsible for managing the partnership's business and receives compensation that ideally is linked to the performance of the entity. To qualify, entities must satisfy the MLP qualifying income criteria requiring that the company must derive at least 90% of its gross income from real estate, mineral and natural resources (excluding renewable resources). Many MLPs are focused on the midstream sector of the supply chain as the qualifying income rule includes the storage and transportation of such resources but does not allow marketing these resources to the end users at the retail level. Pipelines and storage facilities are especially common MLP candidates as these companies' assets tend to have long-term contracts in place with stable cash flow outlook and visibility. However, MLPs are also common in shipping where vessels can be chartered out on long-term charter contracts. The advantage of the MLP corporate structure is that it combines the tax benefits and lower associated cost of capital of a limited partnership, as profit is only taxed when unit holders receive distributions, with the liquidity and flexibility of a publicly traded company. A comparison and overview of the MLP structure versus the C-corporation structure is laid out in Fig. 7.2. The tax benefits associated with MLPs are less important for shipping MLPs as shipping companies tend to be registered in jurisdictions with favorable tax regimes and therefore do not bear heavy tax burdens even if the entity is structured as a C-corporation or equivalent. This also gives shipping MLPs the advantage of only needing to file form 1099 for tax reporting purposes, as opposed to the more complicated schedule K-1 required for traditional MLPs. MLPs typically distribute a high percentage of their income through cash distribution policies or generous dividend payout policies compared to C-corporation entities, which causes the higher MLP dividend yield results. Strong investor appetite for yield, and the premium that is attached to yield-based valuation, have driven the wave of shipping MLP formations in the past few years.

Special Purpose Acquisition Vehicles (SPACs) A SPAC, often referred to as a "shell company" or a type of "blank check company", is a development stage company that has indicated that its business plan is to acquire another company with the proceeds of its public offering. SPACs typically have an 18–24 months deadline to complete an acquisition that must satisfy specified

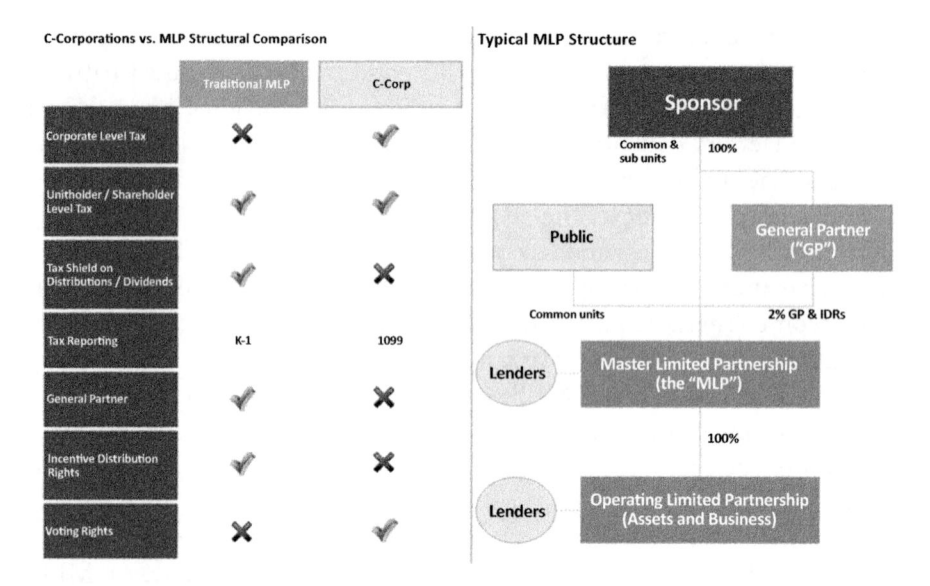

Fig. 7.2 US C-corporation structure vs MLP structure (*Source*: Jefferies)

requirements. If the SPAC is unsuccessful in making an acquisition, the proceeds—plus interest earned—must be returned to investors. SPACs are often used as vehicles in reverse mergers in order to facilitate the process of taking the private purchasing entity public. Reverse mergers allow private companies to become public without raising additional capital.

Advantages and Disadvantages of Being a Public Company Being a public company offers a range of advantages and disadvantages that shape the key decisions surrounding the corporate structure and various financing options (see Fig. 7.3).

Advantages:

Higher Company Valuation Public companies tend to have substantially higher market values than any of their private counterparts. The market liquidity of the company is a key factor in boosting a public company's valuation as investments in them can be easily bought, sold or traded, whereas trading investments in private companies usually go through a much more time consuming and costly process. Besides market liquidity, proper governance structures, easy access to audited financials, compliance with regulatory standards, transparency, preferential access to deal flow and market opportunities, and access to the capital markets are also factors that drive higher valuation premiums for publicly listed companies versus privately held ones, *ceteris paribus*.

Advantages	Disadvantages
■ Higher company valuation	■ Extensive listing requirements
■ Ability to fund growth	■ Business transparency
■ Increased liquidity, improved access to capital and reduced need for alternative financing options	■ Costly process
	■ Pressure from market to focus on short-term results and hit earnings estimates
■ Better economics for raising capital	■ Increased scrutiny of management
■ Ability to use stock as currency for acquisitions and assets	■ Risk of takeover and loss of control by founders and management
■ Human resources	
■ Exit and retirement strategy for founters, investors, and shareholders	
■ Public credibility	

Fig. 7.3 Advantages and disadvantages of going public (*Source*: Jefferies)

Ability to Fund Growth The process of going public can inject meaningful cash to fund various business initiatives and acquisitions, making it potentially easier for a company to execute on its growth strategy.

Increased Liquidity, Improved Access to Capital and Reduced Need for Alternative Financing Options Access to public equity creates another option for company financing. Private equity may at times be difficult to obtain and various debt structures unviable, but by being public a company is able to cast a broader net for financing providers. This gives the company greater flexibility with diverse options to finance growth, thereby increasing its bargaining position and strengthening its balance sheet.

Better Economics for Raising Capital On average, the cost of capital has historically been lower for publicly traded companies, especially with respect to equity. Investors are more willing to purchase smaller pieces of equity in a public company, which is liquid and easy to trade, than in the equity of a private company. This essentially lowers the cost of capital for public companies. Additionally, because public companies have higher valuations they would have to sell less stock to raise a certain amount of capital and thus realize less ownership dilution.

Ability to Use Stock as Currency for Acquisitions and Assets The ability to use stock as consideration in merger and acquisition deals once again provides a public company with greater flexibility than its private counterparts. This ability makes growth via acquisitions a less costly and easier process whilst preserving the company's cash position.

Human Resources A public company is able to use its public equity as a method of creating employee incentive packages that could attract talent and improve retention. Although a private company could provide employees with equity in the private business, it would be much more difficult for employees to potentially monetize that equity due to the limited liquidity.

Exit and Retirement Strategy for Founders, Investors and Shareholders The superior flexibility and liquidity of a public company is especially important when considering exit strategies for its founders and investors. Exit windows will be more readily available and more viable for public companies.

Public Credibility Going public is in many ways a "branding event" bringing added public awareness of the company as analysts begin covering the company and thereby improving its visibility. This sense of improved credibility can lead to better supplier and customer contracts and also potentially attract and retain talented senior management who seek prestige, credibility and professional growth in their employment opportunities.

Disadvantages:

Extensive Listing Requirements Public companies need to comply with the reporting requirements established by the regulating bodies governing the public exchange on which the public company is traded. These listing requirements may be extensive as well as expensive to adhere to.

Business Transparency The listing requirements may also necessitate sharing sensitive information with the public that may reveal trade secrets, as well as competitive and confidential information. More readily available information could potentially lessen a company's bargaining power by revealing to clients and suppliers its contracts and earning position.

Costly Process The process of going public is expensive and time-consuming with costly fees related to the necessary administrative, legal, accounting, filing, printing and underwriting aspects. Additionally, there is also the risk that an IPO offering may not be successful—meaning that all fees and expenses incurred during the roadshow will, for the most part, not be recoverable.

Pressure from Market to Focus on Short-Term Results and Hit Earnings Estimates Public companies may increase the focus on short-term results instead of long-term growth strategies, as a response to pressure from the market to meet or exceed current earnings estimates. Public investors often have short-term investment objectives, sometimes at the cost of curtailing long-term opportunities, thus putting pressure on the company's management for immediate positive results that will drive the stock price higher as opposed to valuing meaningful long-term strategic decisions that may have a negative impact on the immediate earnings. Private companies on the other hand are guarded from this public analysis as financial results are not publically distributed.

Increased Scrutiny of Management Along with evaluation of earning results, public companies are also subject to increased scrutiny of management. Increased transparency facilitates public scrutiny of management's role, actions and compensation. Additionally, there is a higher risk of exposure to civil liabilities for the public companies and the management and directors for any false or potentially misleading statements made. The elevated risk as well as the more focused market and media attention may also cause the management to spend less time dealing with the operational aspects of running a company that could positively impact on its financial results, and instead spend more time on public relations and responding to market pressure.

Risk of Takeover and Loss of Control by Founders/Management Public companies are exposed to hostile takeover attempts through tender offers and may suddenly find themselves sold against their will. A variety of preventive measures such as golden parachutes, supermajority rules, a staggered board of directors, dual class stock and poison pills may be instituted to guard against hostile takeovers, but are not always entirely effective and take time and effort to implement successfully.

7.2.2 Public Shipping Equity

Shipping Equity Landscape Evolution (2000–15) Traditional merchant bank loans continue to be the most popular source of funding for shipping companies; however, the last decade has seen the funding universe widen. Public equity played a minimal role in the shipping industry up until the early 2000s with IPOs few and far between. The booming freight rates and robust global trade fundamentals, especially the industrialization of the Chinese economy that drove strong demand for raw materials, supported high charter rates and boosted shipping asset values higher, which in turn drove favorable company valuations. The strong fundamentals provided shipping companies with the ability to promise investors high dividend yields and potential for capital appreciation. As the shipping industry's relationship with the public equity market has developed, the composition and characteristics of public shipping companies has evolved alongside it. In the early 2000s, shipping companies with small fleets, often with a vessel count below ten, found enough traction to go public. In the past couple of years, the shipping equity landscape has altered and mainstream shipping companies operating in dry-bulk, crude oil tankers or the container shipping segments find that the potential for extensive scale economics is viewed as essential. Therefore, a larger fleet of on-the-water vessels and/or contracted newbuildings is often critical to launch successfully in the public equity markets. Also, in the past couple of years, the only IPOs that have launched successfully without scale have been for specialized shipping companies operating in niche markets such as liquefied petroleum gas (LPG) and liquefied natural gas (LNG), which, for the most part, attracted strong initial investor interest, above-range pricing and robust after-market trading; such investor interest was not directly for the shipping companies per se but their "proxy" value in the energy markets (oil, shale, gas, etc.).

Shipping Markets/Exchanges Shipping capital market activity is found in both over-the-counter (OTC) markets as well as stock exchanges. The most active stock exchanges for shipping companies are the New York Stock Exchange (NYSE), the NASDAQ, Oslo Børs (OB), the London Stock Exchange (LSE), the Tokyo Stock Exchange (TSE) and the Stock Exchange of Hong Kong (SEHK). Each exchange tends to cater for their regional shipping companies; for example, most Scandinavian shipping-related public companies are listed on OB while Asian public shipping companies are listed on the TSE or the SEHK.

NYSE/NASDAQ The NYSE and NASDAQ cater for American shipping companies but also international companies that are looking to access the American extensive and well-developed capital market. The US Securities and Exchange Commission (SEC) governs the publicly traded companies listed on the NYSE and NASDAQ stock exchanges and requires that these companies comply with an extended list of standards. These requirements include comprehensive public reporting requirements, minimum financial standards, such as minimum share price or number of shares, as well as other transparency and maintenance standards. For shipping companies who have traditionally operated in a comparatively opaque cross-border business environment and kept the majority of any company information confidential, the SEC's transparency standards can be challenging to accept. It is often a key deterrence in keeping a company from pursuing an IPO on a regulated exchange.

OTC Exchanges Of the OTC markets, the Norwegian OTC market (NOTC) is the most active in the shipping sector. For most issuers, time is money, and with short windows available for a potential IPO/follow-on offering, the speed to market and ease of execution are very important factors. The NOTC provides an issuer with a few key advantages to a stock exchange like the NYSE or OB. Being an OTC exchange, the NOTC imposes fewer regulating requirements. For example, the NOTC does not require quarterly filings. Comparatively fewer regulatory barriers and maintenance requirements expedite the process substantially. An additional advantage of the NOTC is that the associated listing costs are lower than those of stock exchanges. OTC exchanges can also be considered as an attractive entry point into another market. For example, the NOTC would provide a company with access to the Norwegian investor base, which has historically been very focused on the maritime industry due to its key role in the Norwegian economy. However, if the OTC listing is a company's sole public listing location, the company's management often plans to shift to a regulated stock exchange with time. This is primarily due to the less liquid profile of OTC listed companies, which can pose significant limitations.

7.2.3 Initial Public Offerings (IPOs)

The process of taking a company public is demanding, time consuming and involves cooperation with several parties such as lawyers, accountants, investment bankers, company management and board of directors (see Fig. 7.4). The process can be divided into four main phases:

Company Preparation	Drafting, Diligence & Initial SEC Filing	SEC Review & Response	Marketing, Pricing & Aftermarket
Considerations / Focus • Corporate Structure • Financials / Accounting • Corporate Governance • Exchange selection	**Considerations / Focus** • Organizational Meetings • Due Diligence • S-1 (F-1) Drafting	**Considerations / Focus** • SEC "Quiet Period" • Roadshow Preparation • Investor Targeting	**Considerations / Focus** • Roadshow & Bookbuilding • Pricing • Aftermarket Trading

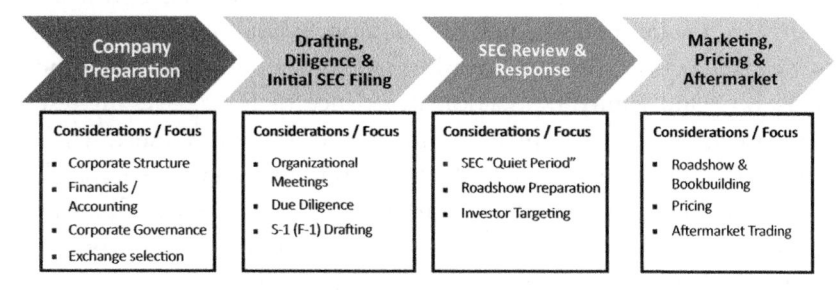

Fig. 7.4 IPO process on a senior exchange in the USA (*Source*: Jefferies)

1. company preparation;
2. drafting, diligence and initial SEC filing;
3. SEC review and response;
4. marketing, pricing and aftermarket.

Company Preparation A key component of the company preparation phase is to analyze the company to determine the most appropriate corporate and capital structure for it. It is not necessary, but most often recommended, that a company is structured as a C-corporation prior to beginning the IPO process. If the company therefore has to convert from another entity form, such as an S-corporation, adjustments need to be made and the resulting taxes covered (S-corporations do not pay corporate taxes but pass this burden onto shareholders instead). Authorized equity capital should be adjusted to reflect the required number of shares of common stock for the IPO. This first phase also includes preparatory accounting work, which means having historical audits prepared if not already assembled, and preparing specific presentations as required by regulations like Sarbanes-Oxley. The SEC requires that companies report specific segment data that are consistent with how management evaluates company performance both internally and externally. Pitfalls can occur when the company unintentionally presents itself as having different reporting segments. Auditors will often provide guidance on the best method to report their revenues and expenses before they file with the SEC, so as to minimize the requirement to report in segments. Employing an accounting firm that is familiar with the IPO process is often a helpful start to the process and can provide a company with meaningful guidance. Additional key decision points in this phase include selecting the most appropriate exchange for the company to be listed on, revisiting and refreshing key management contracts with incentive and compensation elements in place and a general corporate governance structure, and creating organizational documents which will be requested for legal and business diligence. The company must also select an investment bank to be the lead bookrunner and potential additional bookrunners and co-managers. Key factors that companies consider when selecting bookrunners include previous IPO and equity transaction experience of firms, relevant research analyst coverage, industry experience, investor relationships and distribution platforms, and how much capacity the firm has to focus on the company. The number of bookrunners is usually determined by the relative size of the offering to be distributed, and with the aim of achieving an optimal level of control and accountability whilst instilling some sense of competition in respect to performance. Co-managers on the other hand are primarily used for aftermarket support and can be helpful in providing incremental retail distribution.

Drafting, Diligence and Initial Filing The second phase centers on the working group reviewing due diligence materials, determining the final structure and timing of the deal, as well as preparing valuation and marketing materials. The working group typically includes the company, company counsel, underwriters and underwriters' counsel. The due diligence performed spans the business, legal and financial aspects of the company and is a critical element in the offering process as it helps to ensure that disclosure documents provide a complete and accurate picture of a company's operations, financials and future prospects. The company and the underwriter's counsel will draft a preliminary prospectus called an S-1 registration statement for US companies or an F-1 for non-US issuers, to be filed with the SEC, which can be filed on a public or confidential basis depending on the management's preferences. The Jump Start Your Business (JOBS) Act, which became effective in April 2012, provided companies that qualify as emerging growth companies (EGCs) with regulatory relief which allows for confidential filings as well as other benefits such as the ability to test the waters and go on non-deal roadshows. The law was designed to create more jobs by facilitating smaller, high-growth companies with easier access to capital markets.

SEC Review and Response The SEC typically takes approximately four to six weeks to perform their initial review of the filed S-1 or F-1. Once the registration statement is filed, there are usually two to three rounds of SEC comments and responses prior to launching the roadshow. The SEC's main objective during the review process is centered on company disclosure and fair representation to the public and not on whether the offering represents a "good investment". This phase is often also referred to as the "quiet period" (or "waiting period") as it is important that all company communications continue to be "normal course" and refrain from commenting publicly about the IPO whilst the SEC finishes its review process and declares the registration statement as effective. Any failure to comply with the federal communication limits during this period is referred to as "gun-jumping" and will have various consequences depending on the type of company in question. For example, if a quiet period violation occurs, the SEC may impose a "cooling-off" period, impose fines and rescission rights may be exercised. At the end of this process, prior to the roadshow launch, the S-1 or F-1 will have its final amendment, which will include the filing price range and the number of shares offered.

Marketing, Pricing and Aftermarket In the fourth and final stage of the process, the management and bookrunners will undertake a roadshow covering key geographic regions where potential investors are located. Bookrunners will receive investor feedback and consolidate indications of interest. The final pricing is dependent on overall investor demand and picking a price point that assures strong aftermarket trading performance. For shipping IPOs, an important factor in selecting an underwriter and bookrunners involves considerations revolving around their knowledge and experience in the shipping industry, experience in addressing shipowners' concerns about the process and fulfilling listing requirements, as well as established relationships with targeted shipping investors.

Aftermarket Trading of IPOs As illustrated in Fig. 7.5, MLPs and companies focusing on the LNG and LPG sector have performed the best in the aftermarket out of the shipping IPOs in the past few years. It is important that a company performs well in the aftermarket in order to facilitate any secondary offerings down the line. If aftermarket volume traded is poor, investors will likely be wary of investing in any follow-on offerings due to value depreciation and liquidity concerns. A fine balance should be targeted with a moderate IPO discount of approximately 10% of equity value to keep investors content with the result whilst securing an appropriate valuation for the company. Along the same lines, sufficient public float is also important to attract investors and reduce stock price volatility. "Public float" refers to the shares outstanding not held by insiders, directors or shareholders who control 10% or more of voting power. In a traditional IPO, the public float is typically 20–30% of the equity value.

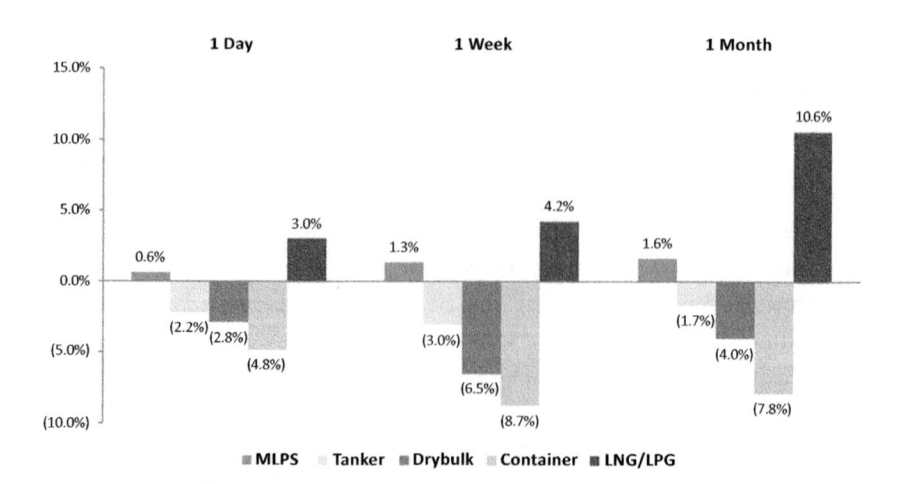

Fig. 7.5 Aftermarket trading: shipping IPOs 2008–14 (*Source*: Bloomberg)

What Makes a Good IPO? An ideal IPO couples a good IPO candidate company with an efficient, streamlined process resulting in a favorable outcome. Good IPO candidates typically have certain common traits. For example, a well-respected senior management team with a solid track record as well as experience in dealing with investor concern and media attention tends to add integrity to a company going through an IPO process. A company with sponsor backing also increases investor appetite as financial sponsors are considered to represent "smart money", which typically strengthens investor confidence in the company and its underlying operational capabilities and financial savviness. Secured newbuilding contracts and options and/or second-hand acquisition deals at beneficial contract prices are also advantageous characteristics as investors favor companies with a strong growth profile that can set the path to capital appreciation. Another good IPO candidate trait is related to the make-up of the company's counterparties. A diverse group of well-known counterparties ensures that investors have more protection against the adverse effect of one counterparty defaulting on its charter agreements. Additionally, investors generally prefer shipping companies with clear chartering strategies, a strong reputation as a counterparty and a willingness to be transparent.

Having an ideal IPO candidate alone doesn't guarantee a successful IPO. Various aspects of the IPO process and market dynamics are often instrumental in driving favorable outcomes. A window of opportunity for a shipping IPO to launch successfully is not something that is available at any time of the year or at every point of the economic cycle. There are certain market dynamics that need to be in place. Variables such as the number of comparable companies launching IPOs at the same time and general economic trends affect investors' appetite for investment. Appropriate pricing is also essential for an IPO to be deemed successful, which can be assessed by the stock's after-market trading. An issuer aims for positive after-market trading in order to drive interest in any future follow-on equity issuances while avoiding such trading from becoming too steep, which would indicate that the company has left money on the table. For MLPs in particular, whose growth is often dependent on future equity offerings to finance drop-downs to provide the growth investors are expecting, positive after-market trading is essential for their growth prospects.

The Shipping IPO Market As with any sector, a shipping IPO cannot launch without an open window of opportunity, which depends on various sector-specific trends, such as current freight rates and the freight rate projection trajectory as well as worldwide macro-fundamentals related to general economic cycles and international trade. The public equity markets will often experience shipping companies operating within a certain sector wanting to access the public equity market at the same time due to favorable market dynamics and sector-specific fundamental drivers. For example, roughly half of the shipping IPOs launched in the USA between July 2013 and July 2015 (including MLPs) were in the gas transport sector.

Investor appetite for shipping stocks has historically been limited due to a basic lack of investor understanding of the industry's fundamentals and its opaque traditions and business dynamics. Additionally, investor understanding of shipping companies has also been hampered by the sheer shortage of equity analyst coverage to enhance investor comprehension. In the past couple of years this trend has slowly been reversing as more equity analysts begin to cover the space, giving investors not only access to relevant research, but also providing a greater breadth of opinions and outlook on the sector. The JOBS act has also bolstered IPO activity by reducing regulatory requirements.

Pitfalls to Avoid When a company is evaluating its profile and the industry dynamics, in order to determine if it fits the profile of a good IPO candidate, there are pitfalls that the company should seek to avoid. Drawbacks such as having a mediocre industry position and high customer concentration make the company especially vulnerable to investor scrutiny. Pending material litigation, messy financials and auditor issues also make for a less than ideal IPO candidate.

7.2.4 Shipping Equity Valuation

While the scope of valuation metrics for publicly traded shipping companies is fairly limited, the key metrics primarily depend upon the company's legal formation, asset type and business model. Generally, limited liability companies and C-corporations that operate in shipping sub-sectors in which the assets owned/operated are highly liquid (e.g. dry bulk and crude oil) will be valued on an asset basis. Limited liability companies and C-corporations that operate in shipping sub-sectors in which the assets owned/operated are less liquid (e.g. containerships, LNG, LPG, drillships, platform supply vessels) will typically be valued on an earnings basis. MLPs, which often have business models that center around long-term charters to provide EBITDA visibility, are typically valued on their respective dividend yield.

Net Asset Value (Method 1)		Net Asset Value (Method 2)	
OTW Fleet Value	$ XXX,XXX,XXX	OTW Fleet Value	$ XXX,XXX,XXX
Newbuilding Fleet Value		Contruction-In-Progress	
Less: Remaining Capex		Contract Value	
Gross Asset Value	$ XXX,XXX,XXX	**Gross Asset Value**	$ XXX,XXX,XXX
Charter Adjustment		Charter Adjustment	
Adjusted Asset Value	$ XXX,XXX,XXX	**Adjusted Asset Value**	$ XXX,XXX,XXX
Less: Debt		Less: Debt	
Less: Minority interest		Less: Minority interest	
Plus: Cash		Plus: Cash	
Net Asset Value	$ XXX,XXX,XXX	**Net Asset Value**	$ XXX,XXX,XXX

Fig. 7.6 Net asset calculation (*Source*: Jefferies)

Net Asset Value (NAV) As previously mentioned, limited liability companies that own/operate vessels that are highly liquid, such as dry-bulk and crude oil vessels, tend to be valued on an asset basis or NAV for that matter. While the calculation to derive NAV varies depending on the inputs used, the definition remains the same: the liquidation value of the company.

As illustrated in Fig. 7.6, there are two generally equal methods to calculate the NAV of a shipping company. The first method consists of totaling the market value of the on-the-water fleet and newbuilding fleet, less the remaining capital expenditures for the newbuilding fleet, plus charter adjustment (the difference between the charter rate and the current market value of the charter, discounted by a rate commensurate with the charter party default risk), less debt, plus cash. The second method entails summing the market value of the on-the-water fleet, plus construction-in-progress payments made, plus change in contract value (the difference between the market value of the newbuilding fleet and the purchase price), plus charter adjustment, less debt, plus cash. Quite possibly, the most closely followed ratio in shipping equity valuation, price/NAV, shows whether the associated equity value trades at a premium or discount to its asset equity value. If a public shipping company is trading at a premium to NAV, it could have the ability to acquire ships or other shipping companies by using its shares as consideration instead of cash.

Forward Earnings: EBITDA Another valuation metric followed by investors in shipping equities is forward earnings, more specifically forward EBITDA. Investors will usually assess forward EBITDA on an enterprise value/forward EBITDA (EV/EBITDA) multiples basis. In order to assess whether a specific equity trades at a high or low EV/EBITDA multiple, investors must compare it to its respective comparable companies. Typically, higher multiples are a sign of companies that encompass higher growth, while lower multiples are a sign of little or no growth.

Dividend Yield The third key valuation metric for shipping companies that are incorporated as MLPs is dividend yield. In today's markets, MLPs have become attractive investment vehicles as long-term, fixed cash flows secured by companies are paid out to investors on a quarterly basis with management incentive programs incorporated so as to align company management and shareholders' interests. Dividend yield is assessed by investors on a forward basis and typically calculated as the most recent quarterly dividend annualized. Dividend yield is expressed as a percentage of the current stock price.

7.3 Private Equity

7.3.1 Private Equity Overview

Since the financial crisis of 2008 and the economic downturn, the shipping industry has experienced an unprecedented level of interest coming from financial sponsors; that is, hedge funds and private equity funds. Hedge funds are private investment funds that invest pools of capital in securities and other financial instruments. These funds typically engage in activities such as creative investment strategies based on active trading and combinations of long and short-term investments as well as borrowing money in an effort to increase investment gains. Investments in hedge funds tend to be fairly illiquid as restrictions ("gates") on redemptions that would adversely impact investors are often in place. Hedge funds are also typically only available as investment vehicles for individuals or entities with significant assets and are typically subscribed to by sophisticated investors.

A private equity (PE) firm is an investment management firm that makes investments in the PE of operating companies through a variety of investment strategies. PE firms usually raise pools of capital for a specific fund, which the firm then uses to fund the equity contributions for investment transactions that fit their given strategy. Typical investors include the PE firm's partners, ultra-high net worth individuals, institutions and sovereign wealth funds. PE funds tend to involve long-term investor commitments and even less liquidity than hedge funds. It may take a PE firm several years to invest all of a fund's assets and, with a PE investment horizon in any given company typically ranging from about three to five years, an investment may on occasions be locked up for as long as ten years.

7.3.2 Private Equity in Shipping

As opposed to public investors, financial sponsors make investments of various seniority levels across a company's capital structure, including investments in equity, junior equity, credit, convertible debt and mezzanine financing. The financial sponsors that have been most active within the shipping sector in the past couple of years are PE firms, or firms with specific funds that focus on distressed debt and/or special situations. The global downturn saw the shipping industry plummet from an unprecedented peak to a deep trough in the short space of a few months at the end of 2008. Many of the vessels were highly leveraged and with asset values falling, as illustrated in Fig. 7.7, much of the debt attached to these assets ended up under water and distressed. As a result, PE firms looking to gain eventually from the sector's anticipated bounce-back, as global trade levels recover and the vessel supply balance corrects itself, began buying up the debt and/or real assets. Additionally, the shipping industry has been appealing to PE firms and hedge funds with high volatility strategies. The industry is both highly cyclical and seasonal, allowing for ample opportunities for volatility plays.

Often, PE firms invest in the shipping industry by forming joint ventures (JVs) with existing shipping companies. This way, the PE firm has access to the commercial and technical shipping management abilities and resources of an experienced industry player. In other instances, PE firms will hire shipping professionals for the commercial business aspects, instead of partnering with an existing player. Shipping and PE JVs can generally be described as "bespoke" as each case is different. A key factor in determining the nature of the JV is how much capital is contributed by the shipping partner. Zero to minimal capital contribution makes a venture more difficult to create and, if

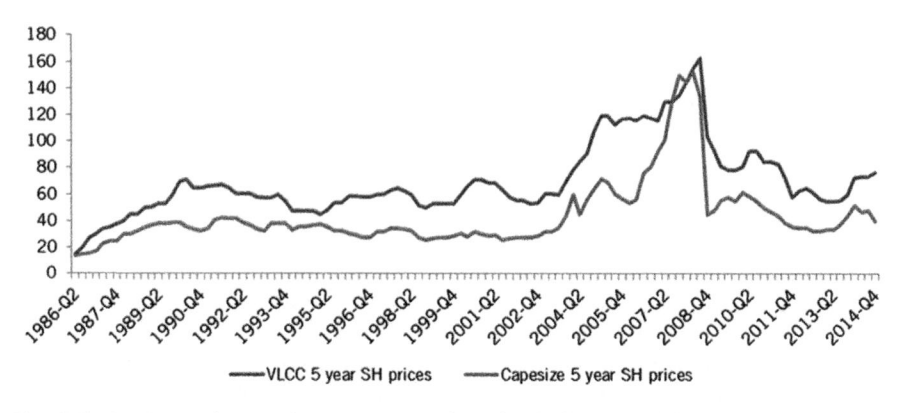

Fig. 7.7 VLCC and Capesize ~ 180,000 dwt dry-bulk second-hand prices (*Source: Clarksons*)

successful, the board and other control mechanisms will rest almost entirely with the PE partner. Another important factor is the robustness of the shipping partner's platform. If the partner is well-established and staffed with experienced individuals, creating a JV tends to be easier because of the enhanced industry know-how and reputation contributed to the venture by the partner.

The most common sticking points for JVs tend to surround the control of investment decisions, day-to-day management issues and the control of the ultimate exit decision. For the most part, the PE partner controls the board unless the shipping partner's investment in the JV is at, or very close to, 50%. A situation where the shipping partner makes about 50% of the investment in a JV is rare to unheard of. The management structure of the ships and related feeds can be a common sticking point as many JV operators will want to manage the assets with an existing external management company and charge fees to the JV. Additionally, conflicts may occur when the PE partner wants the shipping partner to refrain from being involved in other shipping activities and investments outside of the JV. JV economics start with a relative contribution and are in most cases augmented by a "promote", also called a "carried interest", in which the shipping partner can get a preferential return. These terms are highly negotiable; however, a typical provision might involve a preferred return to the shipping partner after a minimum hurdle to the PE partner is met.

Typical exit strategies include IPOs, M&A and spin-outs into listed equities. Figure 7.8 lays out the effects of an IPO versus a sale process as an exit option.

	IPO	Sale
Raise Profile	●	◐
Build Scale	●	●
Achieve Investor Liquidity	◐	●
Retain Upside	●	◐
Retain Control	●	○
Maintain Confidentiality	◐	●
Market Conditions	●	●
Drive Additional Growth	●	●

● Objective achievable through specific transaction   ○ Objective not achievable through specific transaction

Fig. 7.8 Monetizing investments (*Source*: Jefferies)

The decision to pursue one or the other is largely dependent on the expectations of the financial sponsor in what they are looking for, such as the level of liquidity desired, valuation and upside potential, as well as certainty and market risk exposure. In the past couple of years there have been several examples of PE-backed shipping companies going through various exit strategies.

Gordon and Amber Shipping[1] In 2010, Gordon, a PE firm focusing on the transportation industry, set up Amber Shipping, a ship owner and operator of fuel-efficient mid-range products and chemical tankers, in an attempt to take advantage of low asset values in the shipping industry. Amber was taken public in July 2013 with a USD140 million IPO and represented the first shipping IPO since March 2012 and the first growth shipping IPO since March 2010. Gordon selected a well-seasoned maritime management team lead by the former CFO of a well-known public maritime company, who has both extensive operational expertise as well as prior experience working for a public shipping company.

Watson's Investment in Noble Shipping[2] Deep-value investor Watson bought a majority stake in Noble Shipping in 2012, which was quoted on the pink sheet system and is the world's largest Handysize LPG carrier owner and operator. Watson took the company public on the NYSE in November 2013, in what was considered a highly successful IPO, at the high end of the pricing range and with the overallotment option exercised.

Oscar Private Equity/Opera Shipping/Sun Shipping[3] Oscar Private Equity, one of the most active PE investors in the world with more than USD40 billion of assets under management, has been particularly active within the shipping industry with interests stretching across several shipping sub-sectors that include dry bulk, tanker and offshore. However, Oscar's JV with industry veteran partners Opera Shipping represents one of the more interesting investments in the PE space due to Opera's ability to exchange the JV-owned assets for shares in Sun Shipping and receive a liquid currency, thereby allowing the JV to exit successfully its investment, provided they sell their Sun Shipping shares at a favorable price. Originally, Oscar and partners planned to take the company public in the first half of 2014. However, due to equity capital market conditions, which consisted of a strong backlog of IPOs on file and lackluster dry-bulk freight rates, Opera's opportunity to go public faded and forced the investors to consider other potential exits instead. In June 2014, Opera agreed to merge with Sun Shipping, a publicly traded dry-bulk company, of which one of the industry veteran partners was formerly the chairman of. The merger created the largest US-listed dry-bulk company with a fully delivered fleet of 69 vessels and one of the largest eco-fleets in the world. The merger consisted of Sun Shipping issuing 54.1 million shares of common stock to Oscar and partners at the transaction consideration. While an IPO would have been the preferred exit for Opera, the merger with Sun Shipping proved to be an optimal exit solution that provided Opera shareholders with a liquid currency and Sun Shipping shareholders with built-in growth, top-tier management additions (as the industry veteran partners stepped in as CEO and president) and an increased market capitalization.

7.3.3 Other

The Relationship Between PE Firms and Company Management PE investors are generally active investors, and as such the relationship between them and the company management is an important one to handle in order to ensure the success of an investment and potential exit strategy. Financial sponsors may seek to replace management team members or install operating partners in order to drive operational and strategic changes through which the PE firms look to provide the satisfactory return on their investment that they seek upon exit. The level of involvement in portfolio companies varies between PE firms and their preferred investment and operating methods. Additionally, a PE firm's funds have equity stakes in several different companies, which may do business with each other and that may result in a number of conflicts of interest. Fund operating agreements therefore tend to have specific terms related to how the sponsor is supposed to act if such a situation occurs and includes terms governing transactions related to affiliates.

7.4 Conclusion

The public equity capital markets and PE providers' roles in the maritime sector have strengthened over the past decade, but, as with so many things, timing is of the essence. Much of a shipping company's success in accessing public and private equity depends largely on the current point in the economic cycle and secular maritime fundamentals, the competitive market place and alternative investment opportunities, as well as investor confidence. In addition to handling the timing aspects, shipping companies must also carefully consider the implications and requirements that go along with being a public company and the involvement of outside investors before targeting either public or private equity as potential sources of funding.

Notes

1. "Gordon" and "Amber Shipping" are code names.
2. "Watson" and "Noble Shipping" are code names.
3. "Oscar Private Equity", "Opera Shipping" and "Sun Shipping" are code names.

References

Clarksons Research
Bloomberg L.P.
Jefferies LLC Materials
Latham & Watkins LLP "From Red Herring to Green Shoe: The Path to a Successful IPO", 2014.

8

Structured Finance in Shipping

Ioannis Alexopoulos and Nikos Stratis

8.1 The Changing Landscape of the Ship Financing Market

A key characteristic of the shipping industry is that it is highly capital intensive. The international shipowning community is at all times in need of significant amounts of capital in order to fund its fleet modernization and expansion strategy as well as to refinance its existing trading fleet. Traditionally, shipowners have satisfied their ship financing requirements through their own (or family and friends) equity resources as well as on bank debt finance, which represents the cheapest form of external capital when compared to other alternative sources. With China formally entering the World Trade Organization (WTO) in 2001, the international shipowning community was faced with an increased demand for its services, as it was called upon to assist fueling and facilitating the so-called BRICs' (Brazil, Russia, India and China) tremendous growth.

The period 2001–08 was a period of strong fundamentals and growth in the world economy, and trade and shipping was playing a key role in the

---

I. Alexopoulos (✉)
Eurofin S.A., 11 Neofytou Douka Str., 106 74 Athens, Greece

N. Stratis
Augustea Group, 57 Ullswater Crescent, London SW15 3RG, UK

© The Author(s) 2016
M.G. Kavussanos, I.D. Visvikis (eds.), *The International Handbook of Shipping Finance*, DOI 10.1057/978-1-137-46546-7_8

globalized environment. In order to meet the increased demand for shipping services, international shipowners embarked on an impressive fleet expansion and modernization process, placing a large number of newbuilding orders in Japan, China and Korea.

This tremendous fleet growth was primarily funded by bank debt and, more specifically, largely by European banking institutions. German, Scandinavian (Norwegian and Swedish), French, UK and Dutch banks dominated the ship finance industry during the period 2001–08, committing significant amounts of capital at very attractive (for the shipowner) leverage and pricing terms. During the peak of the dry-bulk shipping freight market (May 2008), competition within shipping banks had squeezed margins to levels below 100bp, whilst financings to the tune of 80–85% of the vessels fair market value was becoming the norm. The strength of the freight market, combined with readily available, cheaply priced debt finance, as well as the abundance of equity from the (US predominately) capital markets were fueling a continuous increase in asset values which had reached bubble levels.

That period of irrational exuberance had to somehow end and this happened very suddenly and violently on 15 September 2008 with the collapse of Lehman Brothers as a result of the mortgage subprime crisis in the USA. The Lehman collapse with its catastrophic effect on the global interbank market and the world trade and economy as well as the subsequent European sovereign debt crisis had a transformational impact on the ship financing industry. Traditional European shipping banks, which had been bailed out by their countries' respective governments, were no longer committed to the shipping industry. Since 2008, most global ship financing banks, the majority of which are European and which traditionally supported the international shipping industry, initiated a significant deleveraging, as most of them did not have adequate capital to support properly the capital-intensive shipping business.

During the period 2008–15, a number of traditional shipping banks either exited shipping altogether or started gradually running down their portfolio and reducing their overall shipping exposure. Regretfully, the ensuing gap has not been adequately covered by new shipping banks entering the market; there have been few newcomers, some of them from the USA and Australia. In view of the limited availability of "plain vanilla" senior debt finance during the post-Lehman collapse period, the international shipowning community intensified its efforts to diversify its capital structure, exploring and successfully tapping alternative financing structures.

Korean, Chinese and Japanese (to a lesser extent) government controlled financial institutions and export credit agencies (ECAs) represent an alternative capital source that was successfully tapped by the international shipping community. These institutions were quick to step in and support shipowners with their newbuilding programs in their respective countries. Furthermore, other alternative financing structures such as leasing and mezzanine finance have been largely explored during the last six years and have been employed in complementing shipping companies' capital formation. These forms of capital have always been available to shipowners but, during the pre-Lehman collapse period, they were largely ignored as the shipping community tended to favor cheaper, simpler and readily available bank finance.

Overall, in this unstable shipping and ship financing environment, where traditional debt finance sources have become scarce, shipowners have adapted and become more flexible and creative in order to ensure their companies' viability and growth. Structured finance instruments (i.e. complex financial transactions), and in particular ECA-backed ship finance, leasing and mezzanine ship finance, have assisted in this direction and are analyzed in this chapter.

8.2 ECAs

8.2.1 What Are ECAs?

ECAs are mostly government-controlled or quasi-governmental organizations whose role is to support their respective home country's export of goods and services by extending export finance structures. In view of the government's involvement, export finance is driven by the country's export policy and is fundamental for its economy, as it encourages manufacturing, industrial output and employment. Especially during periods of financial turmoil and slowing economic activity, necessary government support for the domestic industry is achieved through the involvement of ECAs as they may constitute the necessary catalyst to boost trade and stimulate exports.

Export credit finance has long been used as a source of capital in project finance as well as asset finance facilitating exports in a number of industries, such as telecommunications, technology, oil and gas, mining and metals, infrastructure, power and energy, and transportation (civil aviation, the offshore industry, cruise and maritime). ECAs of major shipbuilding countries have supported the international shipowning community for many years by funding their newbuilding programs in the ECAs' home countries. A list of the most important ECAs for the maritime, cruise and the offshore shipping sectors is provided in Table 8.1.

Table 8.1 The most important export credit agencies for the maritime, cruise and offshore shipping sectors

Area	Country	Export credit agencies
ASIA	Korea	Korea Trade Insurance Corporation (K-SURE)
		The Export–import Bank of Korea (KEXIM)
	China	China Export & Credit Insurance Corporation (SINOSURE)
		Export–import Bank of China (CEXIM)
	Japan	Nippon Export and Investment Insurance (NEXI)
		Japan Bank for International Cooperation (JBIC)
EU	Germany	Euler Hermes Kreditversicherungs-AG (HERMES)
	Norway	Norwegian Guarantee Institute for Export Credits (GIEK)
	France	Compagnie française d'Assurance pour le commerce extérieur (COFACE)
	Italy	SACE S.p.A. Servizi Assicurativi del Commercio Estero (SACE)
AUSTRALIA	Australia	Export Finance and Insurance Corporation (EFIC)

8.2.2 ECAs' Role in Ship Finance

Prior to the financial crisis and in particular during the period from 2000 to 2008, the role of ECAs in ship finance was rather limited. During that period traditional debt financing sources were readily available (on a large scale and attractively priced) from international as well as local shipping banks to fund shipowners' newbuilding projects. These banks were however adversely affected by the unprecedented events in the financial markets in 2008 as well as by the severe correction in freight rates and asset values in shipping.

As a result of the financial and shipping crisis, a number of shipping banks were faced with big problems in their shipping portfolios and increased regulatory (Basel III) constraints, which forced them to either scale down their lending or leave the industry altogether. The credit squeeze left a big funding gap for the shipping community, especially for shipping projects involving newbuilding vessels, which were still under construction. ECAs were quick to step in, providing a significant part of the necessary funding, either by extending direct funding to the shipowners or by issuing ECA guarantees/policies (assigned to the commercial banks) insuring commercial and/or political risks, managing, thus, to close that funding gap and supporting in that way their local shipbuilding activity.

Overall, during the last couple of years, as the availability of bank lending became tighter, the shipowning community has increased its interest in export credit finance. ECAs were there to meet this increased demand, and we have witnessed an important increase in lending volumes, particularly from ECAs of important shipbuilding nations such as Korea and China. The strong growth of ECA-backed financing is evident through figures published

Table 8.2 Examples of publicly reported export credit agency transactions concluded in the maritime, cruise and the offshore shipping sectors

Sector	Shipping company	Billion	Export credit agency	Newbuilding project
Cruise	Norwegian Cruise Line[3]	USD0.91	EULER HERMES	2 × Cruise vessels
Offshore	Ocean Rig[4]	USD1.35	GIEK & KEXIM	3 × Deepwater drillships
Cruise	Royal Caribbean[5]	EUR0.89	COFACE	1 × Mega-cruise vessel
Shipping	Scorpio Bulkers[6]	USD0.23	CEXIM	7 × Capesize vessels
LNG	Nigeria LNG Ltd[7]	USD0.72	KEXIM & KSURE	6 × LNG vessels
Cruise	Star Cruises[8]	EUR0.60	EULER HERMES	1 × Cruise vessel
LPG	Dorian LPG[9]	USD0.5	KEXIM & KSURE	18 × VLGC vessels

by *Seatrade Asia Week*,[1] which showed that the Chinese Export Import Bank (CEXIM) committed USD14 billion in loans to the shipping industry, up from USD12 billion in 2012 and USD11 billion in 2011.

Export credit finance is at present considered an important source of capital for the shipping industry, especially for expensive and capital intensive maritime projects. Under the present conditions, commercial banks would find it difficult to commit to such expensive projects, thus we are seeing ECAs playing an increasingly important role for such "high-value" projects in the cruise, offshore, LNG, LPG as well as in the traditional sectors. Some examples of publicly reported ECA transactions that have been concluded in the recent past are provided in Table 8.2.

8.2.3 ECA Ship Financing Structures

ECA involvement in maritime projects takes predominately two forms. The shipowner will either raise funding from international commercial banks, on the back of a guarantee or an insurance policy issued by an ECA, or he or she will raise the funding directly from the ECA. Under the first scheme, the "ECA-guaranteed" financing structure, the ECA promotes and facilitates the export of a maritime asset by issuing a guarantee/insurance product. Foreign commercial banks extend the necessary financing (a term loan facility) to the overseas buyer/importer of the maritime asset being constructed on the back of this ECA guarantee/insurance policy. Under this arrangement, the commercial bank is effectively assured that it will receive payment, by the ECA, in the event of a payment default by the shipowner (provided of course that the policy's conditions and requirements are met), whether connected to any insolvency event, any other commercial event or in connection with any political event. Since the guarantee/insurance cover is backed by the ECA's government, the commercial bank's guaranteed exposure is no longer considered and treated as a shipping risk but rather as a sovereign risk. K-SURE in Korea, SINOSURE in China and NEXI in Japan are common providers of such ECA-guaranteed financing schemes.

Figure 8.1 provides an outline of a basic ECA guaranteed/insured financing structure. It should be noted that an ECA guarantee involves costs related to its insurance policy, which must be borne by the shipowner; the most typical of these costs being the ECA cover fee (ECA premium). The amount of such a fee is calculated on the country risk of the importer. However, in shipping, due to the industry's international element and with a number of different jurisdictions coming into play, the ECA will first decide on the country to which it will allocate the risk of this financing; the ECA cover fee will be determined accordingly.

As an alternative to the ECA-guaranteed/insured financing structure, the export–import bank of the exporting (shipbuilding) country may extend a direct loan to the shipowner (importer/buyer of the maritime asset). Under this arrangement, it will either issue a term loan facility to the borrower or will participate in a banking consortium with other commercial lenders, which has been put together for the purposes of financing the specific asset (see Fig. 8.2). As an example, in Korea, China and Japan the respective

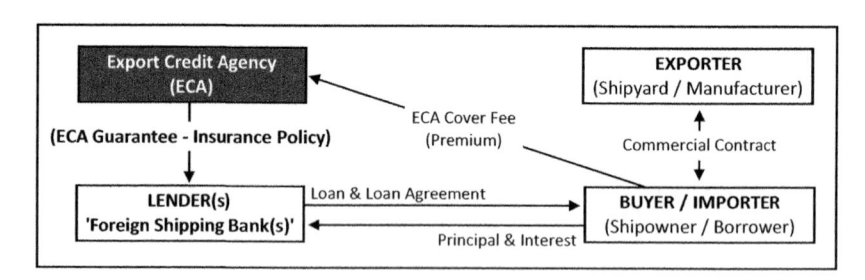

Fig. 8.1 Export Credit Agency guaranteed financing structure

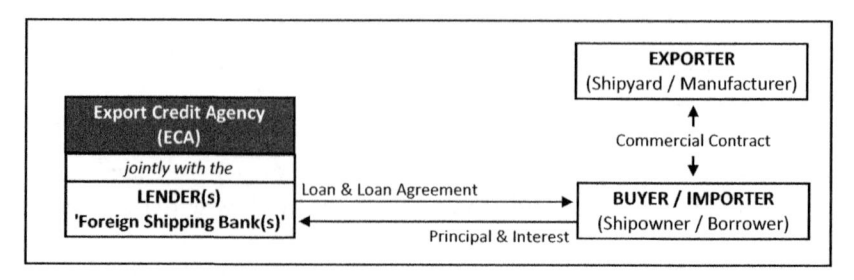

Fig. 8.2 Export Credit Agency direct loan to buyer/importer

export–import banks Korea Export Import Bank (KEXIM), CEXIM and Japan Bank for International Cooperation (JBIC) will be involved as direct lenders in such financing arrangements.

A financing may also be offered by an ECA in the form of an interest rate subsidy, whether with respect to a floating market rate (LIBOR plus a fixed margin) or, alternatively, to a fixed interest rate determined on the basis of the commercial interest reference rate (CIRR). Under the CIRR scheme, interest on the relevant facility accrues at a minimum interest rate, the CIRR rate, which is set monthly[2] by the OECD for government supported export credits.

8.2.4 ECA Requirements and OECD Guidelines

The role of ECAs is to promote exports and, as already mentioned, an ECA financing structure is usually government backed or funded. As a result, a key requirement that exists for these financings is for the transaction to have a strong element of local content. In shipping, this requirement is typically met in a transaction involving a newbuilding vessel constructed at a local shipyard. Another possibility would be for the asset to have a major equipment component that has been manufactured locally. In addition to the local content requirement, ECAs tend to be involved in large shipping transactions (involving either a large number of vessels or high-value shipping assets) as these have a larger impact on the local industry. Furthermore, ECAs tend to work and support big shipping clients who have a long track record and a critical mass in shipping as well as a transparent corporate holding structure and audited financials.

In their effort to support their local industries and economy, ECAs may enter into intense competition, which can have devastating effects on the international trade and shipbuilding. As a result, a number of countries have realized that some level of discipline is required and the OECD has formulated a set of principles and guidelines to be followed by all ECAs.

ECAs and shipping, in particular, is treated by the OECD guidelines in the "Sector Understanding on Export Credits for Ships (SSU)", which provides a set of non-binding guidelines for government-supported export credits for ships. This has been agreed with the participation of Australia, the European Community, Japan, Korea, New Zealand and Norway but, interestingly, Brazil and China are not members of the OECD. There have been recent talks about a more formal binding agreement, which would also involve Brazil and China, so the OECD guidelines may be revised in the near future. An overview of the OECD's SSU is provided in Table 8.3.

Table 8.3 OECD guidelines: export credits for ships

Ship	OECD guidelines apply for any new sea-going vessel of 100 GT and above
Repayment term	The repayment term for an export credit must be a maximum of 12 years after delivery
Cash payment	The importer (shipowner) who is buying the ship is required to make minimum cash payment of 20 % of the contract price by delivery
Repayment	The principal repayment of the export credit must be repaid in equal installments at regular intervals of normally 6 months and a maximum of 12 months
Interest	Interest must be paid every six months minimum and the first payment of interest shall be made no later than six months after the starting point of credit

Source: OECD Council Working Party on Shipbuilding (WP6), Sector Understanding on Export Credits for Ships (SSU)

8.2.5 Advantages and Disadvantages of ECA Ship Finance

ECAs play an increasingly important role for the shipowning community. These are institutions which have significant capacity and liquidity resources to support shipowners' fleet expansion, modernization and, in many cases, diversification strategy in high-value shipping sectors. Strategic objectives as such may not be possible to realize by the shipowners' traditional shipping banks, in view of the significant capital adequacy restrictions applied to them and their limited capability to provide funding of the magnitudes required, especially during periods of financial turmoil when shipping banks generally tend to cut back on lending. In addition to facilitating a shipping company's expansion, ECAs allow shipowners to diversify their finance. They represent a long-term, attractively priced, ship financing source for newbuilding projects, complementing shipping companies' capital structure and enhancing their value through the reduction of their overall weighted average cost of capital (WACC). ECA ship finance also allows shipowners to retain capacity of other capital sources (debt from their house banks as well as equity resources) for other shipping projects.

Export credit finance has a number of merits, but it also has some disadvantages. As discussed, the OECD guidelines introduce the requirement for the repayment of the export credit finance (down to zero) within a maximum period of 12 years. This can be considered a disadvantage of the overall financing arrangement when compared with commercial ship financing terms for newbuildings, which generally provide a repayment profile of 14–15 (and in some special cases even up to 18) years, depending on the type of the shipping asset and the financial strength of the shipowner. Moreover, the introduction of an ECA in a ship financing structure will invariably cause delays in the overall procedure. The agency will have to familiarize itself with the shipping client and the project under consideration, whilst there will be a number of internal processes that will have to be followed. Finally, from a documentation perspective, the loan agreement, the security documents as well as the guarantee/insurance issued by the ECA will necessitate the involvement of a number of experienced lawyers who, through their experience and use of new standardized terms, would enable the swift conclusion of a transaction. As a result, export credit finance often represents a more structured, complex and costly arrangement when compared with a traditional term loan shipping facility.

Overall, export credit finance has the attractiveness of being able to facilitate and promote exports, imports and international trade, and to finance assets by way of making available to borrowers products and terms which commercial lenders are simply not in a position to offer. This is particularly important during periods of slowing economic activity and financial instability. At present, their role in stimulating the global economy, manufacturing and employment is recognized globally by all governments. Thus, they are expected to continue being an important capital source for the maritime transportation industry in the near future.

8.3   Leasing Ship Finance

Despite the capital intensive nature of shipping, and contrary to all other capital intensive industries (e.g. aviation, rolling stock, telecoms, mining), shipping has historically lacked the benefits of organized alternative sources of capital, such as leasing and mezzanine finance, and has been dominated by plain vanilla debt and owners' equity. The reasons contributing to this can be summarized as follows:

(a) A high degree of fragmentation and non-transparency: there are thousands of unrated owners with different fleet sizes, fleet compositions in terms of age profile and vessel type, capital structures and operating standards.
(b) A non-standardization of assets classes, even when referring to the same asset type: a Panamax bulk carrier built in China could be significantly different to one built in Japan.
(c) A highly cyclical nature of the industry and unpredictability of earnings and asset values.

(d) The banks' dominant position in the ship finance space that has historically provided high advance ratios and low pricing, setting the pricing tone for all transactions (even if banks have, more often than not, mispriced the risk return profile of their loans).

The combination of the above has resulted in the reluctant participation of established alternative capital providers, such as leasing houses and mezzanine finance providers. Yet combinations of appropriate leasing and/or mezzanine finance structures can offer relevant benefits on companies' balance sheets to release capital for growth and prove accretive to equity returns; these benefits are discussed in detail below.

8.3.1 Ship Leasing

Leasing structures offer companies the opportunity to raise higher levels of financing compared with what they can traditionally access from the debt market. Leasing structures offer up to 100% asset financing, while it is also possible to support predefined working capital needs, resulting in 110–115% financings. As such, they can prove to be very useful tools in capital-intensive industries and allow companies to pursue growth opportunities (fleet renewal programs) with minimal upfront capital expenditure. Alternatively, they can be used as liquidity instruments during depressed freight markets and assist companies to raise liquidity by monetizing the equity value locked up in their assets (sale and lease back of assets).

However, and despite the potential attractiveness of 110% financing, lease structures can only be accessed by companies that are able to demonstrate an ability to service obligations of such instruments; in shipping, more often than not, this translates to a requirement for a strong balance sheet or a need for long-term employment backing for the financed assets.

When compared with senior, secured, plain vanilla debt finance, leasing structures effectively offer higher levels of leverage. As a result, leasing structures entail a higher level of default risk whilst their overall pricing is invariably higher compared with that of senior debt finance. Under normal circumstances, a leasing structure that offers 100% finance, at an overall pricing that is equal to or less than that of the shipping company's WACC, should be accretive to the company and should thus be pursued. Leasing structures rely on equity committed by the leasing company and senior debt sourced from banking institutions. As a result, the main two parameters that ultimately determine the overall cost (pricing) of a leasing structure are driven by the leasing company's return on equity requirements for undertaken risks and its ability to source adequate levels of debt at competitive pricing. This is why a wide variation on pricing exists between leasing companies.

As shown in Fig. 8.3, in a typical ship leasing structure, a leasing institution sets up a Special Purpose Company (SPC), which will own the vessel. The vessel is then acquired by a combination of equity capital, which is committed by the leasing institution and debt capital raised from a debt financier (shipping bank), which is secured by a first priority mortgage on the vessel. The raising of debt capital is also the responsibility of the leasing institution. The SPC then leases out the vessel to the shipowner, or, more specifically, to his or her leasing-in SPC. The leasing institution is referred to as the "lessor" (the asset legal owner) whilst the shipowner is referred to as the "lessee" (the asset disponent owner). At the inception of the lease arrangement, the shipowner provides to the leasing institution a performance guarantee for all obligations of his or her leasing-in SPC whilst, during the lease, he or she makes lease payments to the leasing company as per the terms stipulated in the lease contract.

Another significant factor that should be considered when evaluating a lease structure is the effect of the lease payment on the project's cash flow. As discussed above, lease finance structures involve equity committed by the leasing company and senior debt sourced from banking institutions. As a result, lease payments have to amortize and remunerate (a) the underlying debt component of the lease structure and (b) the leasing institution's equity component. Consequently, lease structures tend to have higher cash-flow servicing requirements than plain vanilla debt financings.

8.3.2 Types of Ship Leases

Leasing structures are classified in two categories: operating lease and finance lease. The first effectively results in off-balance sheet financing, and the latter is on-balance sheet, as per the current accounting rules, under which the distinction between on or off-balance sheet, and thus operating versus finance lease, depends on whether substantially all of the risks and rewards of ownership of the leased asset have been transferred from the lessor (the company leasing out equipment) to the lessee (the company leasing in equipment). Under an operating lease, the leased asset is recorded only on the balance sheet of the lessor and both lessee and lessor recognize rentals under their income statements for the duration of the lease. Under a finance lease also the lessee is obliged to record the leased asset on its balance sheet at the lower of the fair value of the asset or the present value of the minimum lease payments.

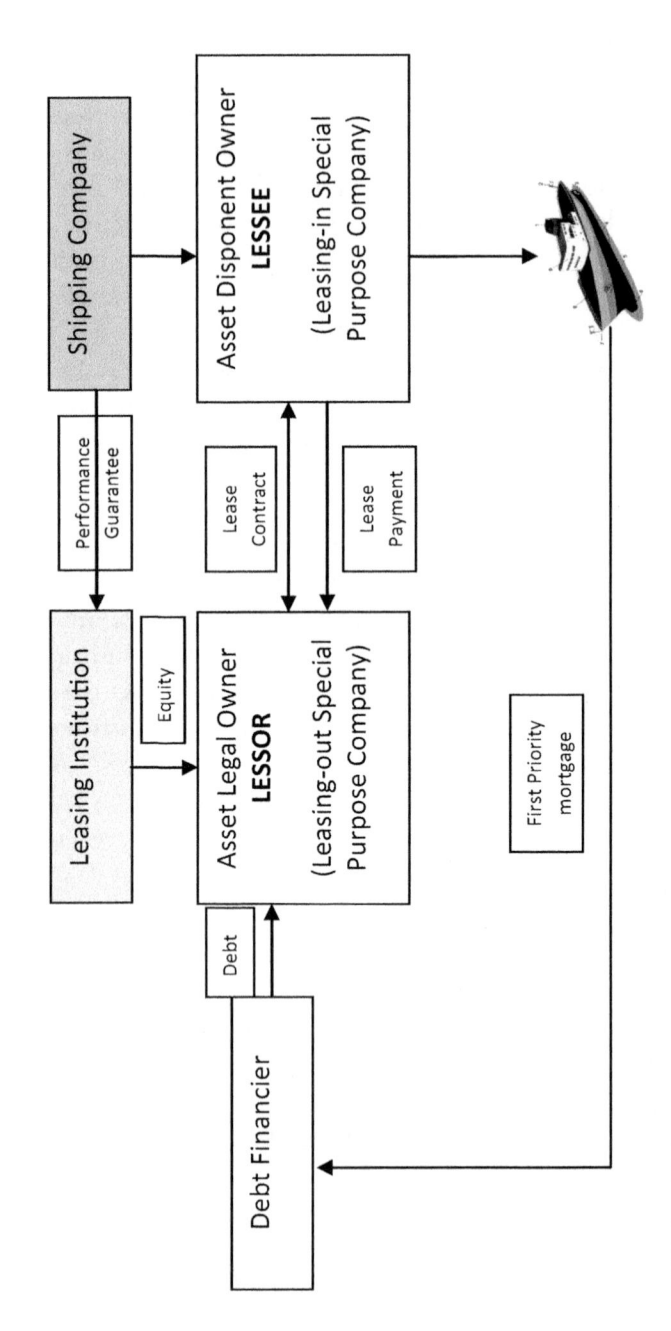

Fig. 8.3 Ship leasing structure

A lessee is classified as a finance lease if any of the following four criteria are met:

1. the lease contract specifies that ownership of the asset transfers to the lessee;
2. the agreement contains a bargain purchase option price, that is option price(s) that can be reasonably argued to be at a significant discount to a reasonably expected price level;
3. the fixed and non-cancelable lease term is equal to 75% or more of the expected economic life of the asset;
4. the present value of the minimum lease payments is equal to or greater than 90% of the fair value of the asset.

If none of these criteria is met, the lease can be classified as an operating lease.

8.3.3 Ship Leases: Benefits and Drawbacks

Both operating and finance leases offer lessees the ability to pursue growth opportunities with no, or reduced, upfront equity commitment from their side; both structures can be used as liquidity instruments for the conversion of the equity of assets into cash during low freight markets; and under both structures, asset ownership is held by the lessor.

Lessee Benefits of an Operating Lease There is no requirement to report the lease transaction on the lessee's balance sheet, meaning that operating leases result in "invisible" leverage, allowing the lessee to pursue growth opportunities without affecting its balance sheet's financial ratios (e.g. gearing) and improving return on assets. At the end of an operating lease, the lessee simply redelivers the leased asset(s) to the lessor; as such, it is the lessor who bears the full residual risk of the asset. In fact, sale and leaseback transactions can be pursued by lessees simply for the transferring of asset residual risk at later years while retaining use of the assets. In such operating lease arrangements, the shipowner charters in the vessel, operates it for a number of years and at the end of the charter period the vessel is delivered back to the leasing company, which, thus, assumes all asset residual risk, technical risk and operational risk. Dry-docking/special survey downtime is also borne by the lessor, who has the obligation to crew and maintain the asset.

Lessee Drawbacks of an Operating Lease As already discussed, lease structures generally tend to offer higher levels of finance than senior, secured, plain vanilla debt finance. The overall (high-leveraged) lease structure will, thus, have an increased pricing when compared against a (lower leveraged) traditional, senior, secured debt facility—this is one of the main drawbacks of operating leases in exchange for the benefits they offer. Furthermore, the increased leverage increases the financial and default risk, and before lease structures can be accessed, the lessee has to evidence to the leasing company a successful track record and creditworthiness. With operating lease rental payments expensed in full under the income statement, a deterioration of earnings before interest, taxes, depreciation and amortization (EBITDA) and reduced net profit is also experienced, adversely effecting possible company valuation when the EBITDA multiple method is used. Finally, the lessee has no control over asset quality and cannot modify it as its operating circumstances may require. Operating leases for the shipping industry typically manifest themselves as medium to long-term time chartering in of vessel(s), or sale and immediate time charter back of the same vessel(s). Such structures may grant the shipping company option(s) to terminate early the operating lease by acquiring the vessel(s) at pre-determined intervals and price levels. Care should be taken when structuring operating leases so as to avoid their possible reclassification into finance leases. A lease would be classified as a finance lease if any of the four criteria listed above are met.

Lessee Benefits of a Finance Lease Almost always, the lessee will retain control of asset quality and have responsibility for the crew and maintenance, at least according to predefined parameters. The direct results of such increased responsibilities for the lessee under a finance lease are typically expected to be translated into a more competitive cost of capital than in operating leases. Finance lease rental payments are split into an "interest" and "principal" portion based on the implicit cost of the capital of the lease, with only the interest element expensed via the income statement, resulting in a better EBIDTA and net profit (the "principal" portion is expensed under the cash-flow statement).

Lessee Drawbacks of a Finance Lease Finance leases are reported on the balance sheet of the lessee resulting in higher leverage and a reduced return on assets. Residual risk is typically borne by the lessee. Finance leases for the shipping industry usually manifest themselves as medium to long-term bareboat charter in of vessel(s) or as sale and immediate bareboat charter back of same vessel(s), and are accompanied with purchase obligations at the end of the lease. Careful structuring of bareboat-based transactions can result in these being classified as operating (off-balance sheet) leases as opposed to finance (on-balance sheet) leases.

8.3.4 Ship Lease Providers

Lease providers for the shipping industry can be classified into three broad categories:

1. Those with good understanding, active participation and long-term commitment to the industry (financing institutions engaging in ship finance).
2. Those who are incentivized to offer such products driven by specific accelerated depreciation rules on shipping offered by the legislation of certain countries (e.g. German limited partnerships, French leases, Japanese leases).
3. Occasional participants who enter and depart from the industry throughout its cycles (private equity firms, insurance companies, pension funds).

Under category 1, the drive for the finance institution is to lever on the existing client network, market coverage and industry understanding by offering a wider range of products to its clients, thus increasing the profitability per client. It is a model that a number of banks have adopted and offer. Lease structures under category 2 are driven by investors' interest in exploiting what effectively represent fiscal optimization techniques that exist within the tax legislation of a country. Within such legislation shipping assets afford accelerated depreciation during the first few years of their life that invariably result in net losses for those years. Owners of such assets (group of investors) are then able to offset tax liabilities they have from other businesses against such losses. Such schemes are usually further linked to specific requirements for the technical and commercial management of the vessels, flag and tonnage tax, all of which have to reside within the country schemes. The German KG is probably the most known and sizable scheme that has ever been developed in this field, but similar schemes exist in countries like France and Japan.

It has to be noted that, although administrators of such schemes may be experts about the risks and rewards of shipping, it does not necessarily mean that participating investors have a similar understanding; further, the incentives of such investors and scheme administrators can be significantly different and misaligned, which can result in irrational decisions. The collapse of the KG system and overcapacity of the container shipping segment post-2008 is such an example.

In relation to lease structures under category 3, it should be noted that post-2008 and in particular during the period 2010–13, significant influx of external capital has been attracted to the industry from the insurance, pension and PE sectors. Despite shipping not representing a typical industry for such capital providers due to high volatility and unpredictability of earnings and values, it has nevertheless attracted such capital. The interest of this capital in the industry has been fueled by the significant correction of earnings and values noted during the post-2008 financial crisis, and the evaporation of traditional ship finance sources following the banking crisis, while memories of extraordinary shipping super-cycle returns from 2004 to 2008 were still vivid.

Such capital providers tend to "acquire" knowledge by co-investing with shipping investment professionals under leasing structures or via the acquisition of companies, and they aim to create value by driving consolidation. Almost always, such investors have to follow specific horizons for their allocations and they tend to target returns that shipping does not always deliver within such tightly defined time frames.

8.4 Mezzanine Ship Finance

8.4.1 Forms of Mezzanine Finance in Shipping

Mezzanine finance is a form of capital which may have debt and/or equity characteristics and is applied between senior debt and common equity. It usually represents 15–25% additional leverage on top of senior debt that ordinarily provides 50–65% leverage, and carries an incremental risk profile, compared to senior debt, as mezzanine financiers' security position typically ranks below (is subordinated to) that of senior lenders (see Fig. 8.4).

Most commonly, in shipping, mezzanine finance takes the form of a debt instrument, a "mezzanine debt", which is also frequently referred to as "subordinated debt", since its security package is in every respect subordinated to that of senior debt. Senior debt always benefits from a first priority security package, including first priority mortgage and priority of payments, while mezzanine debt ranks second. The rights and obligations of these two debt instruments, which are usually provided by different lenders, are governed by

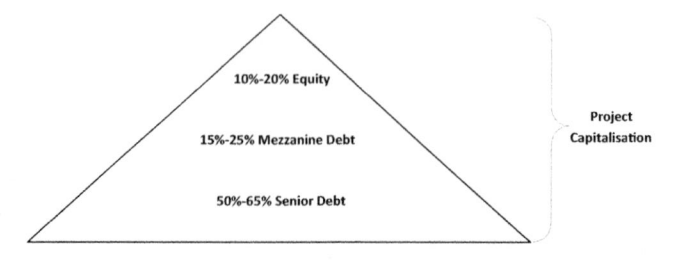

Fig. 8.4 Capital structure with mezzanine finance

what is commonly known as "an inter-creditor agreement" or "coordination deed". This document is negotiated between the senior and mezzanine lender and basically outlines that a mezzanine lender can enforce its securities only once the senior lender's obligations have been satisfied in full.

Mezzanine finance may also take other forms. It may be extended to a shipowner as a convertible bond, whereby the financier has the option to convert this debt instrument into a fixed number of shares of common (equity) stock in the shipping company. In view of their convertibility feature, convertible bonds offer to the financier an upside potential in case the company performs well and, as a result, they are issued with a relatively lower (coupon) pricing.

Mezzanine finance may also be extended to a shipowner in the form of preference shares, also known as "preferred equity". Under this form, mezzanine finance is not treated as a debt instrument. Preferred equity is not recorded on the liability side of a shipping company's balance sheet, but is instead recorded as equity, thus improving the company's gearing and leverage ratios. In their most common form, preference shares are issued with a fixed preferred coupon, usually as a percentage of the preferred equity portion par value (issue price). Preferred coupon payments take priority over common equity dividend payments; failure to pay the preferred coupon does not constitute a default of the shipping company's debt obligations.

8.4.2 Considerations in Mezzanine Finance

It needs to be highlighted that mezzanine financing not only is a riskier debt instrument, but that its "in-between" position in the capital structure also prevents it from exerting significant power or pressure on the borrower under stressed or workout situations. For example, in a scenario where the borrower is not performing his debt obligations as per the contract, a mezzanine financier may have difficulty enforcing his rights against his securities unless he fully aligns his interests with common equity, for example via a debt to equity conversion and surrendering all its securities, or taking out the senior lender in full (i.e. assuming full senior debt by pre-paying the senior debt amount in full). Therefore, mezzanine finance providers need to be flexible and always willing (and able) to accommodate such eventualities. Being a higher risk debt instrument, it always commands higher pricing and it is quite common to aim to enhance its pricing from equity linked performance parameters, such as an equity kicker or equity conversion rights.

Mezzanine facilities may follow an amortizing schedule, much like a senior debt loan, but may also offer what is known as a "bullet amortization", according to which no principal amortization occurs during the duration of the mezzanine facility and the full amount becomes due at the end. Bullet structures offer lower strain on project cash flows but assume higher risk on maturity as vessels are depreciating assets with high volatility. Mezzanine structures can also offer "pay in kind" (PIK) interest structures, meaning payment in kind for interest. Under PIK interest structures no interest is paid in cash during the duration of the mezzanine facility; the interest cost is capitalized in the outstanding mezzanine facility amount and is paid in full at maturity. A bullet PIK mezzanine facility would be a very aggressive financing structure by a mezzanine provider and highly sought by the project's common equity holders.

8.4.3 Applications of Mezzanine Finance

Mezzanine finance can be used by a shipowner during a shipping company's expansion phase so as to reduce the equity injection needed for a new project. In addition, a shipowner may opt to use it to complement his or her company's capital structure during low markets, as a liquidity instrument, so as to convert the assets' locked in equity into cash. Provided that the cash flow from operations is adequate to service mezzanine debt obligations, and as mezzanine pricing ought to be less than the cost of equity, it will almost always be accretive to equity returns; however, in a cyclical industry like shipping, care should be taken because if the cash flow from operations cannot support such incremental debt, even for short periods of time, mezzanine lenders (who also tend to be more aggressive and proactive than typical senior lenders) will inevitably seek to use the opportunity to take control of the project, usually at the expense of common equity.

Mezzanine finance may also be used by senior lenders as a restructuring tool during low markets. In this context, senior lenders who experience a breach of loan to value covenants, which may in turn trigger lender needs for provisions under that facility, may have the flexibility to convert part of their top level senior debt exposure into a mezzanine tranche, thus reinstating compliance of the now reduced senior debt piece and commanding incremental remuneration for such accommodation; all under the same level of total exposure that in any case the lender held.

8.4.4 Advantages and Disadvantages of Mezzanine Finance

Mezzanine finance is particularly attractive as it reduces the shipowner's own equity capital contribution requirement during expansion phases and is accretive to a project's cost of capital optimization. This form of finance is very flexible as it may be extended in different forms (the most typical of them being subordinated debt, convertible bond and preferred equity), its amortization and pricing can be structured according to the specific project's parameters, and it can be used creatively during stress situations. Last but not least, being a debt instrument, asset ownership and control continue to rest with the shipowner.

It should be noted that an important disadvantage of mezzanine finance (especially in its most typical form as subordinated debt) is that it can exert significant strain on cash flows during low shipping markets, increasing, thus, the risk and probability of default. Mezzanine finance is, therefore, best suited as a top-up leverage for vessels under long-term employment arrangements, as opposed to vessels trading spot. The incremental cost of mezzanine finance impacts on profitability, whilst equity performance-linked remuneration needs to be evaluated carefully so as to avoid mezzanine financiers from priming equity holders. Finally, mezzanine finance structures will generally increase complexity from a documentation perspective and will necessitate the involvement of experienced lawyers, representing an additional cost element for the shipowner.

8.5 Conclusion

Over the last couple of years and in particular since the credit crunch of 2008, structured finance has grown more popular in the shipping industry. As a consequence of the financial crisis and the ongoing problems in the traditional debt ship financing industry, structured ship financing methods are considered even more important than in the past. ECA-backed ship finance as well as leasing and mezzanine financing structures have been employed during the last couple of years by a number of shipping companies globally to support their capital-intensive projects. Invariably, leasing and mezzanine have also assisted shipowners in releasing equity that was tied up in their vessels, employing it for working capital purposes during the recent historically low freight rate environment.

During the last decade, the shipping as well as the ship financing landscape have dramatically changed. Almost all shipping sectors are characterized by significant overcapacity and, on the back of a slowing global economy, this is translated into a prolonged low freight rate environment and intense competition. At the same time, whilst the availability of traditional debt finance is significantly reduced, an increased amount of capital is being channeled into shipping from other sources (such as PE investors, government supported export financing schemes and bond investors); this has increased complexity and sophistication. To survive in this highly competitive shipping environment, companies have to grow in size. Through the development of a critical mass, companies can establish themselves in the global shipping arena as a reliable service provider and achieve economies of scale, both in the operation of their vessels (commercial and technical management) as well as in the funding of their shipping investments. Following the financial crisis and with the debt market being in disarray, shipping companies are becoming more transparent, more sophisticated and investor friendly, in order to diversify their capital structure and achieve growth by tapping new sources of finance; during that process, the role of structured ship-finance has become more relevant and important.

Acknowledgement We are indebted to Nils Christian Hanke, Associate Vice President of KfW IPEX-Bank and Christoforos Bisbikos, Partner, Watson Farley & Williams for their valuable comments and contribution in respect of this section of the chapter.

Notes

1. "China EximBank values entire ship financing loan agreements at $53bn", *Seatrade Asia Week*, Issue 202, 25 April 2014: http://seatradeasiaweek.com/202_SAW_25April2014.pdf.
2. Source: http://www.oecd.org/tad/xcred/rates.htm.
3. Norwegian Cruise Line, Form 8 k, Filed July 14, 2014: http://www.nclhltdinvestor.com/secfiling.cfm?filingID=1171843-14-3239&CIK=1513761
4. Capital Link announcement: Ocean Rig UDW INC. announces financing and contract developments, February 4, 2013: http://cdn.capitallink.com/files/docs/companies/ocean_rig/press/2013/oceanrig020413.pdf
5. Royal Carribean Blog, 13 July 2013: http://www.royalcaribbeanblog.com/2013/07/13/royal-caribbean-gets-financing-third-oasis-class-cruise-ship
6. Scorpio Bulkers, Press Releases, Dec 5, 2014, http://ir.scorpiobulkers.com/press-releases/scorpio-bulkers-inc-announces-a-memorandum-of-understanding-for-a-234-9-million-nyse-salt-1163245
7. Lloyds List, Thursday 21 March 2013: http://www.lloydslist.com/ll/sector/finance/article419441.ece

8. Maritime Trade Intelligence, June 06 2014: http://maritimeintel.com/star-cruises-obtains-us814m-financing-for-second-newbuild/
9. Lloyds List, Monday 29 December 2014: http://www.lloydslist.com/ll/sector/finance/article454702.ece

Bibliography

Harwood, S., (2006), Shipping Finance, 3rd Edition, Euromoney Institutional Investor Plc, London, UK.
Stopford, M., (2009), Maritime Economics, 3rd Edition, Routledge, Oxon, UK.
OECD, (July 2008), Council Working Party on Shipbuilding (WP6), Sector Understanding on Export Credits for Ships.
Brealy, R., Myers, S., Allen, F., (2011), Principles of Corporate Finance, 10th Edition, McGraw-Hill/Irwin, New York.
Maritime Briefing, (January 2013), Watson Farley Williams.
Seatrade Asia Week, (25 April 2014), Issue 202.
Davies, H., (May 2012), Export Credit Finance—A Solution to the Funding Gap?, Norton Rose Fulbright, UK.
Silbernagel, C. and Vaitkunas, D. (2012), Mezzanine Finance, Bond Capital.

9

Key Clauses of a Shipping Loan Agreement

Kyriakos Spoullos

9.1 Introduction

The aim of this chapter is to provide a general overview of certain key clauses commonly found in a shipping loan agreement. These are known as "commercial" terms and they purport to maintain throughout the loan period the business activities of the obligors under the loan agreement within a pre-agreed framework. This is frequently opposed by the obligors, who are seeking the least possible restrictions in running their business. This makes such provisions the subject of the toughest negotiation between the parties and therefore the most difficult to draft. The critical concern for the draftsperson, usually acting for the lender, is how to "tighten up" such clauses from a lender's perspective and, at the same time, ensure that they are well-adapted to reflect the secured nature of the transaction and the shipping background. This becomes even more challenging if, during the negotiations, certain borrower's comments are accepted by the lender. In that case, the draftsperson is required to amend such clauses, ensuring that the borrower's point is met, without unreasonably prejudicing the lender's position. Together with the financial terms of the relevant loan (e.g. the loan amount, the margin, the repayment profile, the interest periods, the last availability date), such clauses constitute

---

K. Spoullos (✉)
Norton Rose Fulbright, Palaia Leoforos Posidonos 1 & Moraitini 3, Palaio Faliro, Athens 17501, Greece

© The Author(s) 2016
M.G. Kavussanos, I.D. Visvikis (eds.), *The International Handbook of Shipping Finance*, DOI 10.1057/978-1-137-46546-7_9

the "heart" of most financing documents. We shall call such clauses "operative clauses" (a list and analysis of which can be found below).

In the review of the operative clauses, we shall make the following assumptions:

1. The loan agreement provides for a single currency, a floating interest rate and a term loan facility (i.e. a loan made for a given period, amortized by pre-agreed repayment installments over such a period and which, once repaid, may not be reborrowed) (the loan).
2. There is only one lender, which is a banking corporation (the bank), and a single borrower, which is a special purpose company (SPC) (the borrower). In other words, the loan agreement is bilateral.
3. The borrower is a wholly owned subsidiary of a shipping group; the ultimate holding company of that group (the parent) will guarantee the borrower's obligations under the loan agreement (and any corporate covenants will be given on a group-wide basis).
4. The loan will be drawn in a single advance and is provided for the purpose of financing the acquisition of a second-hand vessel or the delivery of a newbuilding (the ship) which will be the main asset securing the transaction.
5. The loan agreement is governed by English Law.

The ensuing analysis is not intended to be (nor can it be) exhaustive, and it will mainly focus on banking issues rather than on shipping concerns.

9.2 Operative Clauses

From the perspective of the bank, the loan agreement is, inter alia, an instrument for managing credit risk, which is the risk that the bank will not be able to recover its loan, interest and other cost incurred, at the time and in the manner described in the loan agreement. Although ship financing is categorized as an asset based transaction, it inevitably involves more than just an analysis of the value of the asset itself as collateral for the loan. The risks inherent in any such transaction include a full mixture of asset risk, project risk and corporate risk. The bank granting a shipping loan should not only assess if the asset value of the ship on which security is granted is enough to recoup the loan in case of enforcement, but also analyse the borrower's and the parent's financial strength as well as the income stream that the ship may generate throughout the period of the loan.

The operative clauses, as the most critical business provisions of the loan agreement, aim to protect the bank from the types of risk described above, at each different stage of a shipping loan transaction (i.e. before drawdown, after drawdown and on termination). Financiers, unlike shareholders, do not have, and do not want to have, any vote in the running and management of the borrower and the group to which it belongs. Nonetheless, they want to have some "say" in how the borrower runs its affairs. The loan agreement will seek to give some "voice" to the bank through the operative clauses.

The operative clauses consist of the following:

1. representations and warranties;
2. conditions precedent;
3. covenants;
4. mandatory prepayment events;
5. events of default;
6. assignment and transfer provisions.

Preferably, these provisions should not be drafted so tightly as to be unrealistic in terms of the borrower's/parent's performance, since this will lead to frequent breaches and consequential requests for waivers in order to avoid triggering events of default. The borrower will doubtless seek to negotiate the operative clauses to a position that works for it. At the same time, these provisions need to be sufficiently robust to provide the bank with adequate protection. Therefore, a balance needs to be found. The borrower will make an effort to limit or qualify the effect of the operative clauses. For example, it may seek to:

1. limit the lifespan of certain covenants, or qualify the scope of other covenants, by adopting limitations of liability (such as caps, baskets or other kinds of thresholds); and/or
2. ask for grace or remedial periods in the events of default; and/or
3. introduce into the representations and warranties the concepts of "materiality", "reasonableness" and other qualifications.

The borrower may also seek to narrow the scope of some of the covenants, representations and warranties, events of default and conditions precedent so that they capture only the borrower, the parent or a limited number of other obligors involved in the transaction. On the other hand, the bank may want to include a wider range of entities, as issues faced by other members of the borrower's group may alert the bank to credit issues that will ultimately affect the borrower's ability to pay. Even certain defined terms, such as the word "group", may in some cases be defined differently and more narrowly when used in respect of the information and financial covenants than when used in other operative clauses.

The extent to which the bank would accept the inclusion of thresholds and qualifications of the type described above will depend on factors such as the respective bargaining positions of the parties, the creditworthiness of the borrower, the group to which it belongs, the ship being financed, the economic climate when the loan agreement is negotiated and the bank's internal policies on such matters.

In an effort to avoid prolonged negotiations between the parties over such issues, lenders increasingly require documentation that meets market standards. Currently, the loan agreement form provided by the London Market Association is generally accepted as the basis for the "market standard". The requirement to follow established market standards is particularly important for a lender if it expects to sell down the loan shortly after signing, or indeed at any time in the future.

9.3 Representations and Warranties

The representations reflect the contractual basis upon which the bank is willing to enter a loan transaction. Depending on their nature, they can be either legal or factual. They can be made on the entering of the loan agreement as well as on a repeating basis throughout the life of the loan. When repeated, the representations are made by reference to facts and circumstances existing at the time of their repetition.

Legal representations cover matters such as the validity, binding nature and enforceability of the borrower's obligations under the loan documents, as well as the ranking and effectiveness of the security granted. The borrower will generally ask for the legal representations to be qualified by any legal reservations found in the legal opinions provided by the lawyers appointed to advise the bank in each jurisdiction relating to the transaction. Such legal reservations mainly relate to issues such as the time bar of claims, limitations on enforcement by laws relating to insolvency and limitations in relation to defenses and rights to set off or counterclaim. Factual representations, on the other hand, cover matters such as the borrower's financial condition, business and assets, and those of the parent.

The borrower needs to pay special attention to which representations are agreed to be repeating. For example, a representation that no withholding tax applies to any payment under the loan agreement, if repeated following drawdown, may become untrue due to a change of law at a future date. This would in turn lead to an event of default, as the statement would be a misrepresentation. As a consequence, a well-advised borrower will seek to ensure that such a representation is only given on the date of signing of the loan agreement. Similarly, a well-advised borrower will not want to repeat a "no default" representation, because a breach of this representation could turn a contractual breach, which has not and may never become an event of default (because the applicable grace period for that breach has not yet expired and because such a breach may be cured before it becomes an event of default), into an actual event of default for misrepresentation.

The bank may, instead of relying on representations, ask for important issues to be dealt with by negative or positive undertakings, or by an automatic event of default. For example, in the case of the withholding tax representation, a gross-up provision would be sufficient to protect the interests of the bank. In the event of a change of law resulting in the imposition of a withholding tax on payments under the loan agreement, an event of default would only be triggered if the borrower failed to make a payment on a grossed-up basis.

If a representation is incorrect or misleading, regardless of the borrower's innocence in making it, the bank will be able to refuse to advance further funds (if the loan has not yet been fully drawn). If a representation is proven untrue when repeated after the drawdown of the loan, it will trigger an event of default.

9.4 Conditions Precedent

The purpose of the conditions precedent is to assure the bank that all conditions required for the availability of the loan and the legality and enforceability of the borrower's obligations with respect to it are satisfied. The conditions precedent section of a loan agreement usually asks for:

1. the production of specified transaction documents (namely key charters, memoranda of agreement, shipbuilding contracts and management agreements), financial statements and legal opinions;
2. the execution and perfection of the security documents securing the borrower's obligations under the loan agreement;
3. all necessary assurances that certain factual conditions are fulfilled.

The borrower will try to limit the extent of the conditions precedent in an effort to simplify the steps required for the loan agreement to become effective and the funds to be drawn down. The bank may, however, require an extensive list of conditions precedent in order to comply with its internal credit sanctions for the transaction.

9.5 Covenants

The covenant's function in the loan agreement is to ensure that the borrower's financial condition, business, assets (including, without limitation, the ship) and any security on assets over which the bank will have recourse in the case of default remain within the parameters of the bank's initial credit approval of the loan. During the loan period, or any other specified period (e.g. any ship related covenants will only apply during the period the ship is mortgaged in favor of the bank), the bank may restrict action by the borrower (at least without the bank's prior consent) or, by contrast, require action to be taken by the borrower to address certain concerns. Positive undertakings often include issues such as the use of loan advances for agreed purposes, compliance with applicable laws, obtaining and complying with authorizations and providing financial statements and information as requested by the bank. Negative undertakings usually include restrictions on issues such as asset disposal, making loans, granting credit or giving guarantees, borrowing, allowing encumbrances and distribution of dividends.

A breach of a covenant (subject to expiry of any applicable grace period) will invariably trigger an event of default and the bank's right to accelerate repayment of the loan. Some breaches will result in immediate events of default, whilst others usually have attached a grace period which allows the borrower time to remedy the default. Assuming that the law of the place where the bank will take action provides such a remedy, the bank may take action to prevent the borrower from continuing to violate a covenant by applying for injunctive relief. Such action could include stopping the borrower from disposing of an asset. Although this rarely occurs, the bank may also ask for an order for specific performance, for example obliging the borrower to comply with environmental laws. The granting of such a relief or order is a matter for judicial discretion.

Breaches of certain covenants may also play the role of a "warning sign" for the bank, not necessarily leading to an event of default, at least not before any remedial action is, again, allowed to be taken. By having such "warning signs" incorporated in the loan agreement, the bank is likely to have more time and, in effect, more options when dealing with the relevant issues, either by taking measures early in the process to avoid a crisis or by exercising some influence on corrective action to prevent escalation. The most distinctive and effective warning signals in a loan agreement are that of the minimum-value clause (MVC) and the financial ratios (FRs).

9.5.1 Minimum-Value Clause (MVC) Test

The MVC seeks to foretell any deterioration in the market value of the ship below a minimum required level, usually expressed as a percentage of the outstanding principal amount of the loan. The MVC aims to ensure that, if the borrower defaults and the bank has to enforce its rights under the loan agreement, there will be sufficient value in the collateral to pay off the loan, interest accrued thereon and any other amounts outstanding under the loan agreement. If the MVC is breached, the borrower is required either to provide additional collateral to cure the breach or prepay part of the loan to achieve the same result.

The borrower may want to specify that any cash collateral, if it is offered, should be automatically acceptable as alternative collateral for the bank. If the borrower elects to provide cash collateral, it can recoup the cash back from the bank when the ship's value returns above the MVC.

It is interesting to note that, if cash is to be provided in rectification of the MVC (either by way of prepayment or the provision of cash collateral), the amount required may be calculated either by deducting X amount from the outstanding loan, or by adding Y amount to the existing security value. X is always going to be less than Y, so the borrower would require less immediate cash if it elected to provide cash collateral. That said, there might be other reasons why the borrower would prefer, in this scenario, to reduce its debt burden. If no remedial action is taken within any period specified to this effect, this will lead to an event of default.

9.5.2 Financial Ratios (FR) Test

The FRs, depending on the FR in question, seek to check the financial health (i.e. the financial condition by reference to historic and predicted financial results) of the company under examination (in our case, the parent) compared to the level assumed or predicted in the bank's credit approval. The purpose is to allow the bank to accelerate the loan and take enforcement action against the ship before any financial deterioration results in bankruptcy. The bank will usually require compliance with FRs at specified points of time, by reference to specified periods, but may, sometimes, require compliance on a continuing basis.

In order to monitor the parent's financial condition and performance and test whether it has complied with the relevant FRs, the bank will ask the borrower to provide financial information about the parent. The type of financial information (i.e. audited or unaudited accounts, consolidated or not and at what intervals) largely depends on which FRs are to be tested, and how often and what information will be used for this purpose. All audited accounts have to be prepared by applying agreed accounting standards.

Quite often, the borrower promises to provide the bank with a compliance certificate of the parent, together with each set of financial statements, whereby it is confirmed to the bank whether or not the parent has complied with the FRs for the period or at the time in question, and providing supporting details. The bank will prefer to rely on compliance certificates issued by the parent's auditors, which provide independent verification of the parent's self-certification of compliance. The auditors will ask to enter into an engagement letter with the bank, which will limit the scope of their work before reporting to the bank in respect of any compliance by financial covenants. Although such certificates are useful, in addition to them the bank will, most probably, make its own calculations to test compliance.

The FRs most often appearing in a shipping loan agreement would generally be selected from the following:

9.5.2.1 Balance Sheet Tests

Net worth A net worth covenant requires the parent to maintain a minimum book value of assets in the business after deducting the liabilities of the business (other than shareholders' funds, such as share capital and undistributed reserves). If it falls below the required level, the shareholders of the parent will be asked to inject further share capital. The test indicates what will be left to the shareholders if the assets are sold at book value and all liabilities have been paid in full. A more stringent variation of the covenant is the tangible net worth test, which excludes intangible items (like goodwill and trademarks), since they have little or no value in the case of liquidation, and provides for a more realistic measure of the true worth of the parent. In ship finance transactions, where the values of the ships are extremely volatile, the test goes one step further by taking into account the market value of the ships involved rather than their book value, which may be either higher or lower than their market value at any relevant time.

Gearing or leverage ratio or debt/equity ratio This is a measure of the risk attached to the capital structure of the parent. It shows the relation between external (commercial borrowings but not trade creditors' debt) and internal (equity and probably (subordinated) shareholders' loans) funding. The higher the ratio, the greater the risk for the bank.

Working capital and quick ratio The working capital ratio measures the ratio of current assets to current liabilities, indicating to what extent the current liabilities can be paid out of current assets. The quick ratio is more stringent in that it excludes from current assets those not easily liquidated, like work-in-progress.

9.5.2.2 Cash Flow Tests

Interest cover ratio This measures how easily the parent can pay interest out of the profit. It is the ratio of the cash inflow from the business less the cash used in running it, usually expressed as (consolidated) EBITDA, to the (consolidated) interest expense (namely, fees and interest payments).

Debt service ratio This measures the parent's ability to pay its debt ((consolidated) interest expense plus scheduled repayment installments under all consolidated borrowings, or only the borrowings under the relevant loan transaction) out of profit. It is the ratio of (consolidated) EBITDA to total debt service.

Liquidity The liquidity covenant provides that the parent should maintain minimum liquid assets in excess of a certain amount. Sometimes, it is linked to net debt (being the outstanding principal amount of all borrowings) expressed to be the higher of (i) some X amount, and (ii) some Y percentage of the net debt.

In certain situations, an "equity cure", by way of equity injection or subordinated debt, maybe allowed by the bank to be used by the parent to remedy an FR breach which, otherwise, would constitute an event of default.

The performance level of the FRs also may be used as a condition to determine:

1. the timing and amount of dividends paid by the parent to its shareholders;
2. the limitations on borrowings;
3. the limitations on capital expenditure;
4. the level of prepayments of the loan from excess cash;
5. the pricing of the loan because the interest margin will be adjusted by reference to performance.

Shipping loan agreements may also include business restrictions in the form of negative undertakings, especially when, as in our case, the bank bases its willingness to provide the loan on the parent's guarantee and the level and scale of its business activities.

One such undertaking is the negative pledge clause. In the context of a shipping loan where the borrower pledges all of its assets to the bank, the negative pledge is a contractual means to prohibit the creation by the borrower of any security on the relevant assets in favor of other creditors, or enter into commercially similar transactions with them.

The borrower will ask for a carve-out from the negative pledge clause, which is normally dealt with by introducing the concept of "permitted security", examples of which include:

1. liens arising by operation of the law or in the ordinary course of the business of the borrower (e.g. liens of ship repairers and outfitters, crew wages, salvage); and
2. security created by the bank's own security documents executed for the particular loan transaction.

Another common undertaking is a non-disposal covenant which prevents a member of the group, to which the borrower belongs, from transferring (either voluntarily or not) assets below their full market values, or outside of the ordinary course of business, to third parties. All shipping loans commonly include clauses restricting distributions and payments, which may include not only the declaration and payment of dividends but also the redemption of shares, the repayment and payment of interest on shareholders' loans and other similar payments. In the latter case, a well-advised borrower may ask for distributions to be allowed if certain financial performance criteria are met, and provided always that no default is continuing at the time, nor would result from any such distribution.

A shipping loan agreement is always secured by assets, where the main asset is the ship itself. The loan agreement will have ship related covenants to ensure that the ship's condition and operation is maintained throughout the loan period to an appropriate standard (as initially assessed by the bank).

The borrower undertakes that the ship will be kept in an efficient state of repair without modification of its type, structure and performance characteristics, with its class maintained and in compliance with its flag state's laws, the international safety management (ISM) code, the international ship and port facility (ISPS) code and any international environmental legislation. The borrower always pledges that the ship will not be employed in unlawful activities, will not enter into any war zones and that all debts, damages, liabilities and related outgoings (which may give rise to any kind of lien that may be enforced against it, its earnings or insurances) have been promptly paid and discharged. Financiers commonly require specific sanction clauses to be included in the loan agreements, seeking the compliance of the relevant obligors with sanction regimes imposed by the USA, the EU or individual countries (even when the relevant obligor's domestic law or the laws of the ship's flag state do not impose similar sanctions, or only impose less stringent ones). Obviously, the advantage of such clauses is that they give contractual options and remedies if sanctions ever become an issue. By introducing sanction provisions in the loan agreement, the lenders wish to ensure that they will neither be subject to civil or criminal penalties for failure to comply with applicable laws, nor will they damage their reputation by being involved in a transaction which gives rise to a breach of sanctions.

The borrower also undertakes to insure the ship and comply with all insurance requirements under the loan agreement throughout the loan period. The usual coverage required is for the ship to be insured against fire and the usual maritime risks, war risks, protection and indemnity (P&I) risks and (if specifically required by the bank) loss of earnings in an approved amount. In addition, the borrower undertakes promptly to reimburse the bank for the cost of taking out and keeping in force a mortgagee's interest insurance and an additional perils insurance, placed for the benefit of the bank for an amount up to the required minimum hull cover of the ship. The borrower may ask to make direct arrangements to place the mortgagee's insurances on behalf of the bank, and pay for them. This should be resisted by the bank since the borrower's brokers will face a conflict of interest, and any misrepresentation or non-disclosure by the borrower of issues known to it (but not to the bank) may entitle the insurers to avoid liability under the mortgagee's insurances.

Sometimes, the bank requires an additional covenant for the borrower to make regular transfers of funds to a retention account on which it maintains at all times a minimum account balance (with releases only if the balance on the account after such releases remains above a certain minimum level). The most common retention account is a debt-service one, which is a reserve for the next interest and scheduled loan repayments. Amounts are usually required to be paid into a debt service account (from the earnings on the ship) on a monthly basis, and the cash required will be calculated by dividing the amount of the next repayment installment and interest by the number of months between two consecutive repayment dates. If the borrower is unable to find the funds required to be transferred on each transfer date, this will result in an event of default. Other retention accounts may be designed to build up a working capital reserve, or a reserve for anticipated costs such as the likely cost of the next dry docking of the ship.

9.6 Events of Default

These are events set out in the loan agreement, which, should they occur, will entitle the bank to accelerate the loan (i.e. cancel any outstanding lending commitment and declare all amounts owed to the bank to be immediately due and payable or payable on demand) and enforce the security package. Events of default usually include non-payment, breach of a representation or covenant, insolvency and commencement of insolvency proceedings, cross-default, material adverse change (MAC) and ship related events.

Events of default are the "teeth" of the loan agreement. Even if the bank does not use them actually to accelerate the repayment of the loan, the threat they pose is always the best leverage for the bank during restructuring negotiations. Declaration of an event of default is at the discretion of the bank, though it needs to be certain of its "legal footing" before its declaration. The first concern for the bank is to make sure that an event of default has in fact occurred. This is not always crystal clear. There needs to be a high degree of certainty that any related event falls within the scope of the relevant event-of-default language.

A wrongful call of an event of default, and similarly a wrongful acceleration and enforcement, may render the bank liable for consequential damages to the business of the borrower and the group to which it belongs. In addition, an event of default declared under the loan agreement can result in events of default under other loan agreements containing cross-default provisions, which, in turn, may render the parent and the rest of its group insolvent.

Normally the borrower will try to limit the scope of such cross-default provisions through the use of at least one of the following qualifications:

1. limiting the provisions by reference to financial indebtedness as opposed to payments due in general; and/or
2. limiting the provisions by reference to a minimum threshold, so that they are only triggered on a cross-default over a certain amount; and/or
3. ensuring the provisions apply only to the borrower, or alternatively to the obligors under the transaction, and not other affiliated companies which are members of the group to which the borrower belongs but which are not obligors; and/or
4. crafting the provisions so that they are triggered by cross-acceleration instead of cross default (i.e. ensuring they are only triggered following the acceleration of a loan under another loan agreement, and not just due to a default or an event of default under that other loan agreement).

No matter how serious an event of default is, should the bank elect not to accelerate but rather first take a seat at the negotiation table, or adopt a "wait and see" approach, it is always advisable to issue a reservation of rights letter; otherwise, the borrower may successfully argue that the bank affirmed the contract and "waived" its right to terminate. A simple "no waiver" clause in the loan agreement, albeit set out to this effect, may not be sufficient to protect the bank without a reservation of rights letter.

Even if an event of default does occur and the bank has a legitimate right to accelerate, it will always ask itself whether enforcement is the most appropriate action for that particular financier at that time.

The bank will inevitably consider a range of factors including the following:

1. Where is the ship physically located?
2. How favorable is the relevant jurisdiction, where the ship is located, for arrest and enforcement procedures?
3. Is there an existing charter commitment which may be prejudiced by the arrest?
4. Are there any trade creditors with claims against the ship that may rank ahead of the mortgage in that jurisdiction?
5. Will the ship's trade creditors be cooperative?
6. Will the borrower cooperate?
7. Who is the manager of the ship and is there an ability to change the manager in the case of a lack of cooperation?
8. What is the cost of enforcement?
9. Are there prospective buyers for the ship?
10. Are there any foreign exchange rules in the jurisdiction where the ship is to be arrested, which could prevent or delay any remittance of sale proceeds?

The answers to these questions may assist the bank to determine whether it is preferable to accelerate and enforce or seek to negotiate a restructuring of the loan.

9.7 Mandatory Prepayments

We have already referred to the use of mandatory prepayment as a remedy in the case of a breach of the MVC test. Other events or circumstances may also lead to mandatory prepayment. The most common one in shipping loan agreements is the case of a ship sale or total loss. When only one ship is involved, its sale or total loss will result in full and final repayment of the relevant loan by making use of the sale or total loss proceeds. When the transaction is secured by more than one ship, the loan agreement will regulate how much is to be prepaid upon a sale or total loss of any one of the ships. This will always be (at a minimum) the outstanding amount of the part of the loan (plus accrued interest and breakage costs, if any) relating to the relevant ship that is sold or the subject of the total loss. However, in the case of any excess sale/total loss proceeds over and above this amount, the bank will want this excess to be applied to prepay any advances of the loan relating to other ships involved in the transaction. Conversely, the borrower will want the right to retain the excess money. This will be a point for negotiations between the parties.

Other mandatory prepayments may be triggered by a change of control due to the acquisition of a stake in the borrower and/or the parent by any third parties, whether via a public offering or a private placement. An intra-group change of shareholding may be allowed by the bank (and so, will not be a reason for a mandatory prepayment).

An excess cash-prepayment requirement may be found in the loan agreement when the bank seeks to capture a percentage of a better-than-expected performance by the borrower or the parent, so that the loan is repaid prior to its maturity. It is also quite common to come across such arrangements in cases where there is a deterioration in the financial covenants, so that the bank may either capture some cash before it is too late, or at least establish a right of expectation for future use if and when the borrower's financial condition improves. Excess cash flow mandatory prepayment mechanisms are heavily negotiated on issues such as whether they apply on net income or on EBITDA, what costs and expenses will be deducted, the period of application, and whether the full amount of excess cash or part thereof will be prepaid. As already noted in the section on covenants above, depending on whether the borrower continues to meet the requirements of the FRs, the percentage of excess cash prepayment may vary to the borrower's benefit or detriment. Obviously, an excess cash mandatory prepayment is an important feature of the transaction, which has to be agreed at the term sheet stage and cannot be left unaired until the loan agreement is negotiated. Finally, mandatory prepayment provisions may also apply where it becomes unlawful for the bank to make or maintain the loan after the signing of the loan agreement.

9.8 Assignment and Transfer

Usually there is a prohibition, or at least a restriction, on a transfer or assignment by the borrower of its rights and obligations under the loan agreement, and an express right of assignment or transfer for the bank (although this is sometimes subject to certain conditions). In the period since the global financial crisis, banks have generally sought greater freedom to dispose of loans and lay-off risk in a variety of circumstances, including to manage better regulatory capital, or because a change in lending policy at a bank in the future may require it to free up its balance sheet and reduce its exposure to certain industries. The bank may proceed with the "sale" of the loan by way of assignment, novation or sub-participation.

Under the assignment method the "seller" is transferring only the "benefit" of the loan to the "buyer". Since an "obligation" cannot be assigned under common law, the transfer by way of assignment is not practicable in the case of undrawn commitments under the loan agreement.

Under the novation method, the original parties (the bank and the borrower) are discharged from their rights and obligations under the loan agreement, and the buyer is substituted for the seller (being the lender of record) in respect of the latter's rights and obligations under the contract with the borrower. In the context of a bilateral loan, this can cause issues with security because the original contract is extinguished and replaced by a new contract, with the result that any security granted in respect of the original loan is also extinguished and needs to be re-created for the new loan (with attendant risks for the beneficiary of the security because new security can be vulnerable if the grantor is subject to insolvency proceedings during a "hardening period" following the provision of such security).

Under a sub-participation, the buyer agrees to put the seller in funds when a drawing is requested by the borrower, and so creates a back-to-back arrangement with the seller. The buyer takes the risk of the borrower's default without directly becoming party to the loan agreement or having any directly enforceable contractual rights against the borrower.

Potential assignees or transferees may be banks or other kinds of institution with different commercial objectives. Such market players could include:

1. banks, whether active in the shipping market or not;
2. other financial institutions, including, without limitation, specialist distressed-debt funds and hedge funds;
3. other corporate or individual investors engaged in purchasing or investing in loans, securities or other financial debt.

With any transfer there are various concerns for the borrower, such as confidentiality, the shifting of the decision-making process in the transaction to a third party with whom the borrower has no business ties (and which may have hostile plans and policies, especially towards companies in financial distress), and the risk of increased costs. Under a sub-participation in particular, such a third party may well influence the bank's voting behavior whilst being completely unknown to the borrower, as it is acting "behind the scenes".

Obviously, any transfer to a potential assignee or transferee is likely to result in a totally different business relationship developing between the borrower and the new lender. This relationship could seriously affect the day-to-day management of the loan relationship, especially in the context of a request for a waiver or amendment. The borrower may try to qualify the bank's complete freedom regarding the transfer by making it subject to:

1. the borrower's prior consent;
2. a specified minimum credit rating for the potential transferee;
3. no extra cost arising for the borrower following the transfer (additional costs could result from withholding taxes or other increased costs due to the fact that the new lender is in a different jurisdiction or has a different regulatory status as compared to the original lender); and
4. undertakings of confidentiality as to when and what information relating to the borrower, and the group to which it belongs, may be disclosed to any potential assignee or transferee.

9.9 Conclusion

There are shipowners who believe that, when a bank provides a loan, it is like giving an umbrella to someone to protect him or her in case it rains, but with the real intention of recovering this umbrella shortly after the rain begins. In reality the current trend seems to be quite the opposite. The bank often does leave the "umbrella" in the borrower's hands for quite some time after the "rain" begins. A well-drafted loan agreement (and in particular its operative clauses) has its role to play in ensuring that the bank has sufficient confidence in its contractual position to take this approach. The bank's rights should, of course, be fully protected by the loan agreement. Certainly this is the bank's prime concern. It should take enormous care to ensure that provisions are clear and unambiguous and that the rights created under those provisions are valid, binding and enforceable in the case of default. In addition, the terms of the loan agreement should not deviate too much from the market norms, so as to ensure that the loan is marketable should the bank decide to dispose of it. At the same time, however, the loan agreement needs to be reasonably balanced, so as to ensure that the arrangement is workable from the borrower's perspective and to avoid "hair trigger" defaults that will only serve to require waivers to be granted and amendments to be made on a periodic basis.

In addition, we should not forget that, in an English law document, the introduction of thresholds, carve-outs and grace periods is normal and justified by the fact that English law does not imply such terms in a commercial contract between sophisticated parties who have been independently advised. English law of contracts is a law of "strict liability" where recovery of damages operates without regard to fault. This can be contrasted to most other European legal systems. For example, sections 276 and 285 of the German Civil Code, section 1147 of the French Civil Code and Article 330 of Greek Civil Law base the concept of contractual liability on the existence of "fault" (either intentionally or negligently) if the other party to the contract is to support a claim for breach. The operative clauses aim to provide the mechanisms by which the bank may identify problems at an early stage, as well as the framework for strategies to deal with those problems. Their principal purpose should always be to reduce the risk of an irrecoverable loss and to provide the platform for a successful business relationship between the borrower and the bank.

Bibliography

Brown, M. (2014), Rough Waters Ahead: Non Performing Shipping Loans-Solutions Are Available, The Mayer Brown Practices.

Clifford Chance LLP, An Introduction to Loan Finance [2]

Dakin, J. (Nabarro Nathanson) (2008), Loan and Security Documents a Negotiating Handbook, 2nd Edition.

Slaughter and May. (2008), The ACT Borrower's Guide to the LMA Facilities Agreement for Leveraged Transactions, September.

Stevenson Harwood. (2006), Shipping Finance, Euromoney Books, 3rd Edition.

Wellis, C. and Doulai, A., Till Default Do Us Apart: Facility Agreement & Acceleration, Butterworths Journal of International Banking and Financial Law, Skadden, Arps, Slate, Meagher & Flom (UK) LLP.

Wright, S. (2013), The Handbook of International Loan Documentation, October.

10

Legal Aspects of Ship Mortgages

Simon D. Norton and Claudio Chiste

10.1 Mortgages: A Definition

In its basic form, a mortgage may be defined as a charge by way of lien over a vessel given to secure a loan. The lien is extinguished when the obligation has been discharged, and will usually "attach" to the asset, meaning that it can be seized and sold by the original lender, leaving the new owner with a separate claim against the vendor from whom it was bought. If the prior obligation is discharged, for example by full payment of the outstanding debt and any interest thereon, the lien will detach from the asset. However, if there is default in payment, then the creditor can initiate proceedings to seize and sell the asset to which the lien has attached. In such circumstance, the buyer in this later sale will obtain good title to the asset and will have no claim against the lienee who exercised the power to sell, unless the latter was acting in bad faith. The United Kingdom Merchant Shipping Act 1988, Schedule 1, Paragraph 21, provides as follows:

S.D. Norton (✉)
Cardiff Business School, Aberconway Building, Colum Drive, Cardiff CF10 3EU, UK

C. Chiste
Investec Bank Plc, 2 Gresham Street, London EC2V 7QP, UK

© The Author(s) 2016
M.G. Kavussanos, I.D. Visvikis (eds.), *The International Handbook of Shipping Finance*, DOI 10.1057/978-1-137-46546-7_10

A registered ship, or a share in any such ship, may be made a security for the repayment of a loan or the discharge of any other obligation; and on production of the instrument creating any such security (referred to in this Act as a mortgage), the registrar of the ship's port of registry shall record it in the register.

There are two competing theories regarding the legal nature of mortgages. First, there is the property transfer theory. According to this theory, title to the security interest, in this case the ship, rests with the mortgagee or lender; the value of the good exchanged depends, all things being equal, on the bundle of property rights conveyed in the transaction (Rose-Ackerman 1985). The alternative and currently prevailing legal theory relevant to mortgages is the statutory theory. This theory provides that the mortgage is a *sui generis* ("in a class by itself") statutory security, perfectible by registration. This latter approach results in the conclusive legal standing of registers of mortgages; even if a lender is unaware of the existence of a prior mortgage, if it has been properly registered, then it will gain priority over a later lender and any subsequent mortgage which he or she may take in respect of his or her loan (Meeson and Kimball 2011 at p. 17).

The earlier Merchant Shipping Act 1894 provided that only United Kingdom-registered ships are eligible for registration of statutory legal mortgages in the United Kingdom; any other type of mortgage can only constitute an equitable mortgage. Hill observes (1998, at p. 29):

> Any other mortgage relating to ships or shares must take effect as a purely equitable mortgage. Simply put, an equitable mortgage is that which a mortgagee has if he has merely received an equitable interest. It could be described as a mortgage created otherwise than by deed. If an equitable mortgage is effected on a registered ship, or shares therein, the big disadvantage is that it cannot be taken into account when deciding the priorities in relation to other legal (and properly registered) mortgages of that ship or shares(s).

As an alternative to a legal mortgage, Hill (1998, at p. 30) notes that an equitable mortgage may be affected by the deposit of the legal deeds required for a registered mortgage with another person in consideration of a loan. Circumstances giving rise to an equitable mortgage include a loan against an unregistered British ship, on foreign vessels and on unfinished vessels which are still in the dockyard. A disadvantage of an equitable mortgage is that the world is not deemed to have notice of it, as is the case with a properly registered legal mortgage. That said, the fact that such a mortgage is subject to the equitable jurisdiction of the court creates the possibility of the court looking at the "fairness" or otherwise of a remedy, as opposed to being restricted to the relatively mechanical nature of the common law and statute. Equitable maxims such as "he who comes to equity must come with clean hands", "delay defeats the right to an equitable remedy" or "equity will not act in vain" bring a sometimes welcome unpredictability to the law and court decision-making in the sense that fair as opposed to simply legalistic outcomes may emerge. However, for practical purposes, it is the statutory registered mortgage which is the common currency of bank security in ship finance today and which will form the basis of the discussion in this chapter.

In *Brown* v. *Tanner* (1868), it was held that a shipowner can bind the mortgagee in a charterparty, being to that extent in a different position from the mortgagor of real property who cannot bind his or her mortgagee by means of a lease. Commenting upon the case, Clarke J stated that this difference is justified by the particular characteristic of a ship, which carries goods from port to port, in the course of which its owners will enter into contracts of affreightment and carriage or hire, which will in turn generate subsidiary contracts. The parties to ships' mortgages may properly be taken to have intended different incidents to apply to such mortgages compared to those which apply to mortgages of land or shares (Panesar 2004). (However, this case reflects the property transfer theory of the legal status of mortgages and, given that it is now the statutory theory which prevails, is of historical interest regarding the evolution of law rather than present practice). The mortgage is the principal method by which a lender ensures it has priority over other creditors of the borrower who will invariably have unsecured status (Chambers 2000). The mortgage holder is subject to prior claims in the event of the borrower's insolvency, but is "higher up" in the ranking, or the application of assets, than would otherwise be the case if the loan had not been secured in this way. The law provides certain powers in favor of the mortgagee, subject to agreement between the parties in the deed of covenants. These powers include the following:

1. The right, in certain circumstances, to have the vessel arrested following default in servicing the loan to which the mortgage relates (Turner 1997). In some jurisdictions this may lead to the mortgagee's right to sell the vessel, to operate it or to apply to the court to have the vessel sold (some jurisdictions do not allow the mortgagee to sell the vessel without obtaining a court order first).
2. The right to operate the vessel following the taking of possession.
3. The right to auction the vessel in order to generate proceeds from which the outstanding loan can be repaid.

4. The right to impose terms upon the borrower, for example regarding value maintenance of the vessel, restrictions on where it might be traded, prohibition of sale or technical alteration without the lender's consent.

The powers of the mortgagee are provided for by law (owner-type rights on the mortgaged property, the ship); the law applicable to the mortgage is the *lex navis*, or "law of the flag" (e.g. laws relating to rights of enforcement of judgments differ in the contexts of Liberian and English law). As a general rule, the parties to the loan transaction cannot derogate from the rules as provided in these laws: they cannot negotiate between themselves for more extensive powers than those provided in statutory provision.

10.2 Limitations of Ship Mortgages as a Form of Security

Although mortgages are the traditional form of security for bank loans taken alongside other forms such as assignment of earnings, insurances and guarantees, they suffer from numerous weaknesses and risks. The first and probably most significant drawback is that the underlying asset to which a mortgage is attached can decline in value. In essence this can result in the all-too-familiar problem of "negative equity" as experienced in the collapse of the US property market bubble and the ensuing "credit crunch" of 2007–09: the value of the underlying asset declines below the total loan raised in respect of it and which is secured by the ship mortgage. Ship values are notoriously volatile (Kavussanos 1996; Kavussanos 1997), driven in part by the shipping cycle which itself lags behind the wider economic cycle (shipping service provision constituting a derived demand) (Stopford 2009). The mortgagee may experience a scenario in which to sell the asset would release funds, which would be insufficient to satisfy the outstanding debt. As an alternative to sale, the mortgagee may decide to trade the vessel or to continue with a charterparty entered into by the mortgagor with a third party, but as lenders such as banks are not in the business of operating ships, this is rarely an attractive proposition. Two main options may be available to lenders to avoid the consequences of this negative equity scenario. First, the lender may take out a ship mortgage indemnity policy, which provides insurance cover for the gap between the amount outstanding on the loan and the amount raised through asset disposal (Stephenson Harwood 2006; London Special Risks 2011). The policy indemnifies the lender in respect of the "net ascertained loss", defined as the outstanding balance due, inclusive of principal and interest and the lender's reasonable costs (such as litigation and vessel sale costs), after crediting the net proceeds of the disposal of the vessel covered by the mortgage, the realization of any additional collateral security, and any net income arising at the conclusion of any claim against the borrowers and guarantors if there are any. Insurance industry provision, and lender take-up of these policies, has however been patchy, and accordingly premiums can be high; the cost is usually passed on to the borrower. The specific future value of the vessel is of course difficult to quantify, and so to know in advance its insurable amount is problematic; only a range of possible values can be predicted, meaning that premiums payable in respect of the policy may be, unavoidably, either too high or too low. As an alternative, a lender may require inclusion of an asset protection clause (or value maintenance clause) in loan documentation entered into alongside the mortgage deed. This requires that the vessel's market value be re-estimated at regular intervals during the term of the loan: in the event of its aggregate value falling by a certain percentage relative to the size of the loan, the borrower provides additional security over the asset covered, or provides additional security (e.g. a partial guarantee), or prepays such part of the loan as will eliminate the shortfall. Failure to provide such additional security will amount to a default entitling the lender to call in the loan early.

The second drawback of this form of security is the problem which arises when a claim secured by a mortgage clashes with a claim secured by a maritime lien. In essence, the law chosen by the parties or even the forum previously agreed upon for dispute resolution cannot resolve the issue: according to English law, the existence of a maritime lien is to be judged according to the *lex fori* and not the *lex navis* ("law of the flag") or the *lex loci contractus* (the law applicable at the location where the contract was agreed). This dichotomy can result in so-called "forum shopping", where one party attempts to have a dispute adjudicated in a jurisdiction where the applicable law is more favorable to its claim than it is to that of the other party (Mukherjee 2003).

In *Bankers Trust International* v. *Todd Shipyards Corp* (*The Halcyon Isle*) [1981], a ship was arrested in Singapore in a mortgagee's action and was sold by court order. The proceeds of the sale were insufficient to satisfy all the creditors, and the mortgagees sought determination by the Singapore Court of the priority of payments. The respondents were American Ship Repairers who, under United States law, were entitled to a maritime lien over the ship for the price of repairs carried out in New York. The mortgagees succeeded. In proceedings *in rem* against a ship, the existence or otherwise of a maritime lien fell to be determined in accordance with the *lex fori* of the country whose court was distributing the proceeds of the sale; since, under Singapore law, the repairer's claim did not entitle them to a lien, they were not entitled to priority (Rares 2014). Similarly, in *Todd Shipyards Corp* v. *Altema Compania Maritima SA (The Ioannis Daskalelis)* [1974], it was held that, although in Canada a claim for necessary repairs did not give rise to a maritime lien, it did so in New York, and such lien was enforceable in Canada, and under Canadian law had priority over the mortgage (Tetley 1989).

The third drawback is that the vessel may itself be damaged at sea or sink, leaving the mortgagee with the possibility of costly litigation to determine rights on the wreck, assuming there is one and it is not an actual or constructive total loss, perhaps in a jurisdiction where rights of mortgagees under domestic legislation are not as favorable as in the jurisdiction of choice under the mortgage deed. The final drawback is that, although mortgage holders take priority over unsecured creditors, they are subordinate to others, for example those of registrants of earlier mortgages or maritime liens. Although some protection is better than none at all, this reality, derived from the doctrine of priorities, may result in the mortgagee receiving very little payment or none at all, following enforced sale of the vessel. Each of these issues will form the basis of discussion in the remaining part of this chapter.

10.3 Registration and the Priority of Mortgages

The order of priorities between registered mortgages in the United Kingdom is set out in paragraph 8, Schedule 1, of the Merchant Shipping Act 1995. Registration of a mortgage gives the mortgagee priority over the following security holders:

1. Earlier unregistered mortgages, irrespective of whether or not an affected party had notice of them. In this context, it should be borne in mind that registration is effective notice to "the world at large", notwithstanding that a subsequent lender did not have notice of its existence (because the relevant searches were not made against the vessel).
2. Later registered or unregistered mortgages. This reinforces the importance of registering the mortgage as soon as it is in place, and although this may be done by the mortgagor, a prudent mortgagee should take this step as soon as the loan is in place.
3. Additional advances subsequently made under a prior registered mortgage. This is so in the absence of stipulation in the loan agreement that the whole sum will be secured, despite the release of funds in tranches from time to time.

The mortgage itself will be subject to the following claims, which take priority upon the insolvency of the mortgagor/borrower:

1. Any earlier registered mortgage. According to Schedule 1 of the Merchant Shipping Act (MSA) 1995, section 8(1), where two or more mortgages are registered in respect of the same ship or share therein, the priority of the mortgagees between themselves shall be determined by the order in which the mortgages were registered, and not by reference to any other matter. Section 8(2) provides a short-term safeguard to an intending mortgagee. A priority notice can be registered 30 days in advance of the mortgage being agreed, ensuring that during the period between the notice and the final mortgage being granted, an intervening mortgage will not gain priority (since the notice will effectively have given notice to the world of the pending mortgage). This protects a mortgagee against the unscrupulous or "cash strapped" shipowner who negotiates simultaneously with several lenders, but without each having knowledge of the other, and grants mortgages in quick succession to each of them (Berlingieri 1988). It is the lender who files a notice, notwithstanding that a subsequent mortgage is registered earlier, which will gain priority.
2. Any unsecured claims ranking *pari passu* ("equal footing") in connection with which the vessel had already been arrested at the time when the mortgage was entered into, unless secured with a maritime lien. To a large extent, this may be a matter for which it is not possible for the mortgagee to ascertain, particularly if the vessel is already fully deployed and the financing negotiations are being dealt with elsewhere. The mortgagee may take a precautionary measure by requiring the mortgagor to covenant that the vessel is not subject to undisclosed encumbrances, and in some jurisdictions, for example the United Kingdom, this is an implied term under statutory rules. However, if these undisclosed claims result in an exhaustion of the proceeds realized from disposal of the vessel, then the mortgagee's only recourse is not against the third party claimant(s) but, instead, against the mortgagor. If the mortgagor is effectively a "straw man", without assets, then this legal redress may prove academic and the mortgagee's claim left unsatisfied.
3. Any possessory lien of a ship repairer. The possessory lien ranks before the maritime lien and before the mortgage unless the lienee releases the asset (the ship) from his or her possession.
4. Maritime liens, whether earlier or later (Allen 1998). These would include claims for the master's and the crew's wages, a claim in respect of salvage and a claim for damage done by a ship (e.g. a collision). Maritime liens give rights against a ship which survives a sale and which enjoys priority ahead of registered mortgages, even though they need not be registered themselves. According to *Bankers Trust International* v. *Todd Shipyards Corp* (*The Halcyon Isle*) [1980], under English law, whether a claim creates

a maritime lien is to be decided by the law of the place of arrest of a vessel, and not according to the local law of the claimant. In *The Turiddu* [1999], at the request of the owners of *The Turiddu*, Cuban national crew members were recruited by two agencies. Under the embarkation contracts, the wages of the crew were paid in part to them on board the vessel, and in part in Cuba. After a default on a loan agreement, the vessel was arrested. The crew claimed arrears of wages and were found to be entitled to a maritime lien. The bank argued against the finding at first instance that the crew's claim for that part of their wages paid through the agency had priority over its mortgage. It was held that the person to whom that part of the wages was ultimately paid would have a claim for any unpaid wages: the crew was entitled to rely on a maritime lien. The bank's charge could not take priority over the crews' unpaid wages merely because the crew had agreed to an allotment of part of their pay (Sabino and Susca 2001).

10.4 Powers of Mortgagees

In the United Kingdom, Schedule 1 of the Merchant Shipping Act 1995 specifies the statutory powers of mortgagees. The Schedule also provides significant protection to the mortgagee in stating that he or she shall not be treated as being the owner of the ship or share therein other than is necessary for making the ship or share available as a security for the mortgage debt. Accordingly, third parties who proceed against the shipowner but are disappointed, invariably because it lacks financial resources to meet their demands in full, have no alternative right of recourse against the mortgagee in respect of such claims. This "embedding" of rights and powers of mortgagees in specific legal provisions manifests the prevailing statutory theory of mortgages as opposed to the property transfer theory, as described at the beginning of this chapter. The practical question for the mortgagee is how to arrest physically or take possession of the vessel to which the mortgage is attached. The usual method would be through the actual taking of physical possession, although in some jurisdictions this may require a court order first, and failure to do so may constitute a criminal offence (Bowtle and Rymer 1998). If the vessel is seized, the mortgagee may then dismiss the master and replace him with his own, or continue with the same master, in which event he will become liable for his fees as an agent of the mortgagor. It should be noted that the master does not thereby lose his claim against the mortgagor for unpaid wages, which gives rise to a maritime lien. Full notification of the taking of possession should be given to the affected parties, particularly the insurers, to ensure that P&I cover is continued. Further, the mortgagee will continue to be affected by rights *in rem* against the vessel, which could have been brought by third parties against the mortgagor, but which can now be equally validly sustained against the new operator, the mortgagee.

Alternatively, the mortgagee may be obliged to settle for something short of actual possession, this being constructive possession. This may arise, for example, when the vessel is not within the mortgagee's jurisdiction; the mortgagee (e.g. the bank which has made a loan), has actual control over the vessel without having physical control at the same time. In this situation, the party with constructive possession has the same rights and remedies as a party with actual possession. To be effective, the mortgagee must give notice to all affected stakeholders, including insurers, underwriters, charterers and third-party claimants of which the mortgagee is aware, such as the crew for their unpaid wages. After taking possession, the mortgagee will be entitled to operate the vessel but must do so with due care for the mortgagor's interests; loss or damage due to negligence will fall to the mortgagee's account and risks, in some circumstances damaging the mortgagor's reputation. After taking possession, whether actual or constructive, the mortgagee is entitled to freight which is in the process of being earned under existing contracts, but not to freight already earned and fallen due but not yet paid. This must be credited to the mortgagor's account. In this context, in *Dry Bulk Handy Inc.* v. *Fayette International Holdings Ltd* (*The Bulk Chile*) [2013], it was decided that a shipowner was entitled to demand payment to himself of the freight under his bill of lading even though the charter provided for payment to another party, provided that he made the demand before the freight had been paid to that other party (Deering and Ward 2013; Moore 2013).

10.4.1 Power of Sale

By virtue of section 9 (1) of schedule 1 of the MSA 1995, every registered mortgagee shall have power, if the mortgage money or any part of it is due, to sell the ship or share in respect of which he or she is registered, and to give effectual receipts for the purchase money (Clarke 1997). Where two or more mortgagees are registered in respect of the same ship or share, a subsequent mortgagee shall not, except under an order of a court of a competent jurisdiction, sell the ship or share without the concurrence of every prior mortgagee. Where there are prior mortgages and a later mortgagee sells the vessel, he must account to prior mortgagees first, before satisfying his own debt. If the mortgagee is "first in the queue" and there are later mortgagees, then, after satisfying his own claim, he will hold any surplus on constructive trust for these later secured lenders. In *Den Norske Bank ASA* v. *Acemex Management Co. Ltd* (*The Tropical Reefer*) [2004], the issue arose as to whether a mortgagee owed a duty of care to a guarantor in deciding when to arrest a vessel. In the case, the bank had loaned USD6 million to borrowers for the purchase of vessels, secured by mortgages on the vessels and a guarantee provided by a third party. The loan agreement was subject to English law. The borrower defaulted on the loan and the lender, exercising its right under the mortgage, which was subject to the law of Cyprus, arrested one of the vessels. The vessel was carrying a cargo of bananas, which were to be discharged in Germany. However, to make a clean sale of the vessel in Panama, the bananas had to be discharged overboard at sea. The expense of doing so, USD204,140, was claimed as part of the costs of the arrest and formed a deduction from the proceeds of sale of the ship. The bank made a claim against the third party under the guarantee, but the party then claimed that the bank had impaired the value of the ship by being in breach of the duty to obtain the best reasonable price. The third party argued that the vessel should have been allowed to proceed to Germany to discharge the bananas and so, arrested there, avoid the costs of discharging the cargo. It was held that the bank, as mortgagee, was entitled to decide the timing of the sale, without regard to the interests of the borrower-mortgagor. It was appropriate to sell the vessel in Panama, but the mortgagees were also entitled to take the view that there was too great a risk in permitting the vessel to continue to Germany, given that insurance had already been withdrawn because of a default on premium payments. To allow the vessel to continue would have been to put at risk the principal source of security given in respect of the loan, the ship itself (Clarke 2002; Goddard 2006).

The mortgagee may indirectly be affected by the mortgagor entering into a charterparty with a third party. Three questions arise in this context. First, was the charter entered into before the mortgage was taken out, and if yes, did the mortgagee know of its existence? Second, was the charter taken out after the mortgage had been granted? Third, was the vessel in a fit state, or seaworthy, or equipped to discharge the charter at the time it was entered into? As a starting point, it was stated in *De Mattos* v. *Gibson* (1859) that where property, including a ship, is disposed of with notice of a prior contract entered into by the person disposing of it for its use in a particular manner, the person taking it with such notice (invariably the lender) may be restrained from using it otherwise. By virtue of this reasoning, a shipowner is free to trade a vessel in the same way as if there was not a mortgage in place, and the mortgagee cannot interfere with a charter once it is underway. In *De Mattos*, it was stated that a person who hires a vessel under a charterparty does so not merely from a wish to have his goods conveyed to a particular place, but upon a careful choice of the vessel itself as best adapted for his purposes; a vessel engaged under a charterparty ought to be regarded as a "chattel of a peculiar value" to the charterer and, accordingly, a court will restrain the employment of the vessel (by the mortgagee) in a different manner. The only exception to this would be if the vessel was put at risk or was unable to perform properly the charter, perhaps because of technical problems, or if insurance had lapsed. In such circumstances, the mortgagee's security could be at risk, and arrest of the vessel, or an action *in rem* against it, may be permissible. In *The Heather Bell* [1901], a mortgagee (the previous owner of the vessel sold) seized a vessel, a steam ship, for non-payment of an installment of the purchase money owed to him by the mortgagor. The vessel had been hired to the plaintiff to run on specified daily excursion trips for about six weeks, the plaintiff to have "a charge and lien on the boat ranking in the highest position the owners are able to fix the same, having regard to the existing circumstances". The mortgagee contended that the agreement between the plaintiff and the new owners (the mortgagors) was not binding upon him since it postponed his rights as mortgagee and depreciated the saleable value of the vessel. It was held that the seizure was wrongful; the charge and lien on the vessel given to the plaintiff by its owners were subordinated to the rights of the defendant as mortgagee so that his security was not impaired and the mode of employment was not unusual for a vessel of the description of the steamer in question, so that its saleable value was not reduced. The case illustrates that, should the mortgagor take out another loan ranking below the original mortgage, so that it does not gain priority, and provided the vessel continues to be operated in a usual way which does not undermine its value as security, the original mortgagee will not be justified in arresting the vessel. To make such an arrest could lead to an action in tort (an unintended harm caused by one party to another to whom a duty of care is owed) for damages by the affected third party (usually the charterer) for interference with the due performance of a contract.

The mortgagee must exercise the power of sale with due care (Berg 1993). In *The Calm C* [1975], mortgagees took possession in June 1969 of the mortgaged vessel, *The Calm C*, with a view to operating it and then selling it. In October 1970, they sold the vessel and then brought an action against the mortgagor for the deficiency in the sale price vis-à-vis the amount outstanding on the loan of USD59,883. The mortgagors argued that they were entitled to set off against this shortfall the losses caused by the lender's failure to operate the vessel wisely, and its later imprudent sale. It was held that the sale had indeed been imprudent and that the sale price should have been USD60,000. The mortgagee's conduct had been grossly unfair to the mortgagors who were accordingly entitled to set off an amount of USD27,382. The economics of the decision would appear to be that, if the mortgagee disposes of the vessel at a below-market price and at a loss to him or herself when an alternative sale option would have resulted in a lesser or no loss being suffered, any deficiency will fall to the mortgagee and cannot be recouped from the mortgagor. The burden of proof for establishing this alternative sale option will fall on the mortgagor.

Zeeland Navigation Co. Ltd v. *Banque Worms* [2002] is further authority for the nature of the duties owed to the mortgagor by the mortgagee when selling the vessel which has been the security for a loan. In the case, the claimant, Zeeland Navigation, sought damages or an account of profits arising out of the forced sale of the ship by the defendant bank, Banque Worms. The claimant had previously bought the vessel with a loan provided by the bank and secured by a mortgage. In 1994, the bank exercised its power of sale under the mortgage agreement and the vessel was sold for USD4 million to a company nominated by a shipowner who was an existing customer of the bank. The bank then entered into a project finance agreement with the client in which the bank acquired an interest in the vessel's profits. In 1997 the vessel was sold for USD33.75 million. Zeeland argued that Banque Worms had, in 1994, breached its obligation to take reasonable care to obtain a true market price for the sale, and had breached its duty to Zeeland to act in good faith and to use its power to sell the vessel for the sole purpose of securing repayment of the amount outstanding under the mortgage. The bank had instead acted improperly to derive a financial benefit for itself and enable its valued client to buy the vessel at a discount. It was held in the United Kingdom Queen's Bench Division (Commercial Court) that Zeeland had failed to establish that Banque Worms had been in breach of its obligation to take reasonable care to obtain a fair market price for the vessel. It was not for the bank to establish or prove its reasonableness: the burden of proving unreasonable behavior fell on the claimant. Further, Zeeland had itself failed to market the vessel within the contractual period of sale and had prevented the bank from doing so; this had resulted in there being no marketing of the vessel in any true commercial sense. The allegation of the bank's acting in bad faith was also not substantiated by the evidence adduced by Zeeland. In the course of the judgment it was stated that, whilst a mortgagee is obliged to take reasonable care to obtain a proper price, he was not obliged to delay the exercise of his power of sale and could accept the best price in a disadvantageous market provided that none of the adverse factors was due to any fault of his. A mortgagee could choose his moment for the exercise of his right, but had then to take proper and careful measures to secure the best price obtainable at the time of his choosing.

10.4.2 Power to Take Possession

The right to arrest a vessel as set out in section 21 of the Senior Courts Act 1981 is available either as a means to obtain possession of the vessel with the aim of operating it, or as a procedural step leading the vessel to a judicial sale such as an auction. If the mortgagor endangers the mortgagee's security, for example by trading the vessel in a danger zone or outside a geographically permitted zone as stipulated within its insurance policy (so that insurance cover no longer exists), then the mortgagee may arrest the vessel and take possession (Smith 2001). The question then arises as to what rights, if any, arise in favor of an affected third party, invariably a charterer. In *Anton Durbeck GmbH* v. *Den Norske Bank ASA* [2006], a ship had been arrested and lost cargo in Panama. The claimant, a charterer, claimed damages for financial loss suffered due to the defendant bank arresting and detaining a ship carrying the charterer's cargo—bananas being transported from Ecuador to Hamburg via Panama—with the result that it deteriorated and was lost. The bank had made a loan to the shipowners in return for a mortgage on the ship, but subsequent financial difficulties resulted in loan payments being missed and a default on the P&I premiums. The bank had the vessel arrested in Panama and it was accepted in the course of legal argument that the law governing the dispute was the law of the country in which the events constituting the tort had taken place, in this case Panama. The vessel was later sold at auction, enabling the bank to recoup some of the outstanding loan. As there was no market for the charterer's cargo in Panama and transhipment was impractical, the cargo deteriorated and was eventually disposed of, resulting in a loss to the charterers of EUR2.5 million. According to Panamanian law, a holder of a bill of lading whose cargo has been damaged or lost on account of a valid arrest of the carrying ship has the right to sue if the arrest, even if procedurally and legally correct as between the arrestor and the ship, was carried out in bad faith or with the intention of harming the holder of the bill of lading. An arrest that was likely to cause damage to cargo was not sufficient. In this case, there was no evidence that the mortgagee had intended harm to the charterer, and the former was entitled to look after its own interests and to take advantage of the security to which it was entitled, even if to do so would prejudice the charterer. Further, the bank would have damaged its own interests—its own security—if it had allowed the vessel to continue on its voyage to Hamburg without insurance. There was also the possibility that the vessel would have been arrested by another party for some other reason in another jurisdiction, potentially jeopardizing the bank's priority ranking vis-à-vis other claimants due to the unpredictability of local laws. The case illustrates the wider risks of arresting a vessel in general, and not only in the capacity of mortgagee.

The power to take possession also encompasses the ability to interfere with disadvantageous charterparties. In *The Myrto* [1977], it was decided that, where the mortgagor entered into a disadvantageous contract for deployment of the vessel with a third party (in this case the contract was held to be "speculative and impecunious" or unprofitable), and where maritime liens had arisen because of the conduct of the mortgagor (here, a claim for non-payment of wages to the crew) which would have priority over the mortgagee's claim, then arrest of the vessel by the mortgagee on the ground that it was a wasting asset would be legally justified and could not be opposed (and the vessel released) upon the application of an aggrieved charterer. In the context of endangering security, the following caveat regarding operating the vessel should be noted. In *Keith* v. *Burrows* (1877), it was stated that, subject to any agreement to the contrary between the owner and the lender-mortgagee, the owner is under no duty to operate the ship and may lay it up, provided that by doing so it does not deteriorate or its value decline because it is not kept in a suitable condition. The decision makes commercial sense: it must be for the owner to decide when to trade the vessel, bearing in mind fluctuations in the freight cycle. For example, it may be commercially sensible not to trade when rates have fallen to an unacceptable level in the spot market but, of course, in so doing the vessel will not then earn freight. If the mortgagee was then able to arrest the vessel because it had become an "idle asset", then it would take decision-making out of the hands of the shipowner who, in most circumstances, would have a greater awareness of market trends than the lender which is in all probability a financial institution.

In *The Manor* [1907], the borrower was in breach of a loan covenant to pay an insurance premium, and had also incurred debts which included canal dues and unpaid wages to the crew and master. The vessel's state of repair had also been neglected and would require a substantial sum to be expended in order to restore it. These combined liabilities were anticipated to exceed future freight earnings, which would be derived from a pending nine-month voyage charterparty. The date fixed for repayment of the mortgage amount was imminent and the mortgagee took possession of the ship. The issue for the court was whether the mortgagee's security would be materially impaired if left under the mortgagor's control; it was decided that there was sufficient impairing of the security to justify the mortgagee in taking possession.

10.4.3 Appointment of a Receiver

A mortgagee has the power to apply to the court for the appointment of a receiver to preserve disputed assets and obtain payment in respect of a debt or other liability. The application for appointment may be made without notice to the mortgagor but must be supported by written evidence. Upon proof of the default, a receiver is appointed to obtain payment but, importantly, not to put the mortgagor into liquidation, which is subject to a different procedure. An order appointing a receiver must be served by the party who applied for it on the person appointed as receiver and every other party to the proceedings, including other creditors. The principal purpose of the appointment is to preserve assets where there is a dispute pending a court decision on the matters in dispute. Where the application is disputed, the court will make a decision on a "balance of convenience" test, assessing the potential damage to each of the interested parties if a receiver were to be appointed. In practice, the court will assess the strength of the applicant's case and make the order if the assets in dispute are thought to be in jeopardy, for example at risk of being moved outside the court's jurisdiction.

Figure 10.1 places the enforcement options available to a mortgagee in a practical context. For example, the right of arrest cannot be considered in isolation: questions 1, 2 and 3 in the figure show that the mortgagee must first consider whether enforcement is financially worthwhile. Of practical relevance, it must also be ascertained whether or not the vessel is situated in a jurisdiction where a local enforcement procedure, principally arrest, is a viable, quick option. Furthermore, is the vessel already encumbered with pre-existing debts, which may rank in priority over a forced sale? Has the vessel already been arrested in respect of non-payment of an existing debt? It may also be the case that the mortgagee can resort to other security made available by the mortgagor at the time when the loan was entered into; for example, there may have been an assignment of insurances, guarantees from a parent or other companies within the group, or pledges. These other forms of security may be of greater practical significance and value than the vessel itself in which case arrest, and the cost and delay involved, may be avoided. Having considered the legal framework applicable to the mortgagee's rights, and the practicalities of enforcement, it is now appropriate to consider the rights of the borrower-mortgagor.

10.5 Rights of the Mortgagor

10.5.1 Right/Obligation to Insure the Vessel

The mortgagor has the right to operate the mortgaged vessel in his or her capacity as full owner of it, subject to not operating it in a way which prejudices the mortgagee's interest. The mortgagor also has the responsibility to

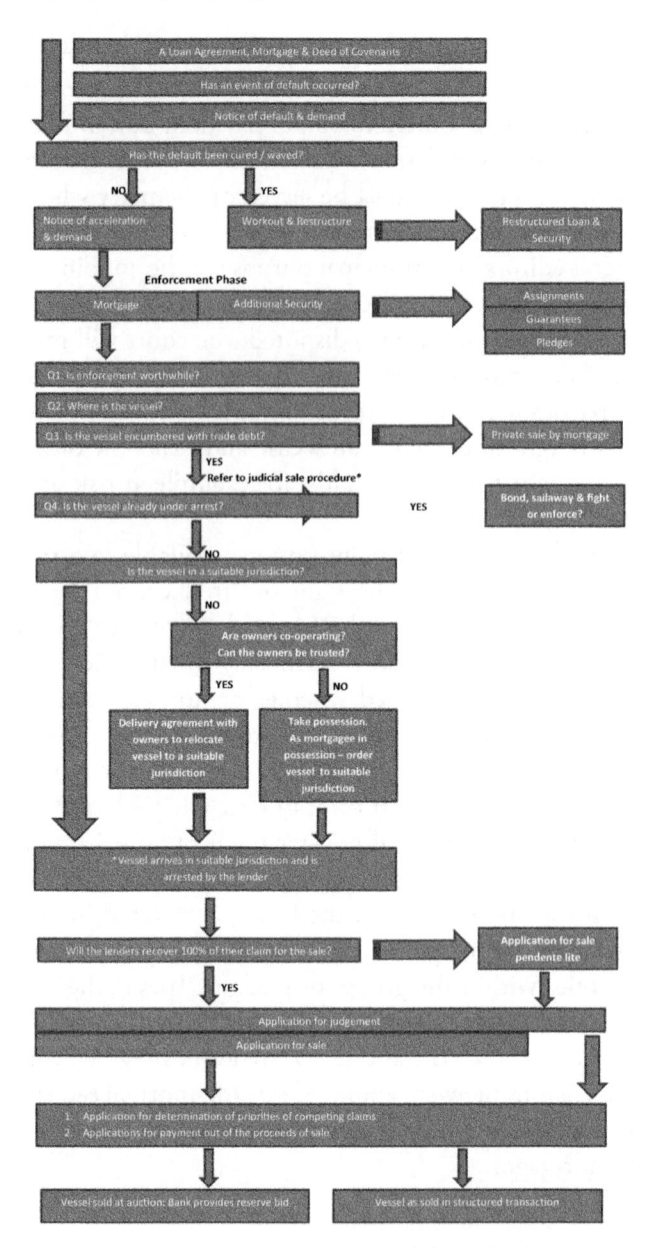

Fig. 10.1 Enforcement flow chart (*Source*: Watson Farley & Williams LLP)

take out insurance in respect of the vessel (Smith 1991). If this is not done, then the duty may be undertaken by the mortgagee and the cost added to the outstanding debt. If the mortgagee subsequently takes possession of the vessel, then the providers of the insurance must be notified of this; after possession, the mortgagee takes over all rights of the insured, and is subject to actions and counterclaims which would otherwise have been brought against the mortgagor by third parties, but for the event of subrogation.

10.5.2 Right to Sell the Vessel: Existence of Prior Encumbrances

The mortgagor, as legal owner of the vessel, has the power of sale. However, when the mortgage has been registered, this is effective notice of its existence to the world at large and, accordingly, the new owner will acquire the vessel subject to it. The mortgagee, after such a sale, would have the right to have his or her loan repaid, any surplus being paid into the new owner's account, such right being regulated by the deed of covenants. Invariably, there is a clause in the loan agreement preventing the mortgagor from selling the vessel without the mortgagee's prior consent, meaning that the registrar will refuse registration of the sale transfer unless and until evidence of such consent is furnished. If there is a shortfall, then the new owner would receive nothing, and the mortgagee would have to pursue the vendor—the mortgagor—for any balance. At this point any guarantee, for example one provided by a parent company, would become of paramount importance in meeting this shortfall. If the mortgagor is experiencing financial difficulties and needs to make a quick sale of the mortgaged vessel at a price below the market value, then this may be challenged by the mortgagee as prejudicing the security, particularly if the funds raised would be insufficient to satisfy the amount outstanding or would be exhausted in meeting those with prior claims, for example earlier creditors or holders of maritime liens.

10.5.3 Application for Sale by Court Order

Where the vessel is sold by order of the court, the mortgagee is prohibited from proceeding against the new owners in respect of any outstanding balance under the former loan. The effect of this is that the new owners gain unencumbered title to the vessel purchased: the mortgagee's action lies solely against the former owner, after first having made a claim against the sale proceeds. In *The Acrux* [1962], it was stated that it would be inequitable to permit the mortgagee to proceed against the new owners; their sole source of recourse was the balance produced by the sale, and if this proved insufficient, then they would have to proceed against the mortgagor in the usual way since an action *in rem*—against the vessel—would not be countenanced. If the mortgagee finds a buyer for the mortgaged vessel, and at a fair market price, then the Admiralty Marshal cannot circumvent the normal procedural requirement for an auction and simply sanction the sale to the new buyer.

10.5.4 Right to Redeem the Mortgage, and Foreclosure

The mortgagor has an equitable right to pay off the amount outstanding on the loan to which the mortgage relates, even if in default of payment of installments due. The practical implication of this rule is that, should the mortgagee take possession of the vessel following non-payment on the loan by the mortgagor, the latter may still demand return of ownership upon payment of the amount outstanding. This may have adverse consequences should the mortgagee wish to sell the vessel to a third party but is nevertheless compelled to return it to a possibly unreliable mortgagor who may default again in the near future. To counter this risk, the mortgagee may be able to bring an action for foreclosure in which the court grants an order that, unless the mortgagor pays the amount outstanding within a short period of time, the mortgagee will become the legal owner of the vessel with full power of sale. (It should be noted that this remedy of foreclosure is rarely applied for today). In *Fletcher and Campbell* v. *City Marine Finance* [1968], plaintiff (a) mortgaged a vessel to the defendant lender as security for a loan of GBP1,200 repayable in 24 equal installments. Plaintiff (b) was the beneficial owner of the vessel. The collateral deed setting out the terms of the financing stated that the bank could claim immediate payment of all sums due and sell the ship if default were made in payment. Following default in payment in the 11th month the bank wrote to plaintiff (a) saying that it would take possession of the vessel, which would only be released on payment of the full amount outstanding. Six days later, plaintiff (b) tendered the full amount, which the defendant bank refused to accept on the grounds that it could only accept the sum from plaintiff (a). Three days later, plaintiff (b) informed the bank that he was arranging for the amount to be paid by plaintiff (a). Four days later, the bank sold the vessel, and both plaintiffs sued. It was held that the bank had not taken possession before the sale and the purchaser had notice of plaintiff (b)'s beneficial ownership. The first tender of payment by plaintiff (b) was not conditional, and dispensed with the need for further tender; and the bank had been unreasonable in refusing this. The bank had notice before the sale that plaintiff (a) intended to pay and had a right to redeem. A mortgagor of a ship had a right to recover damages against his mortgagees if his right to redeem was prevented by the latter's wrongful act, and this had been the case here.

10.6 Future Directions in Ship Mortgages as a Form of Financing: Securitization

Securitization may be defined as the bundling together of future cash flows, their transference to a separate legal entity (a special purpose vehicle—SPV) and the issuance of tradable bonds by that entity to investors. The bonds are serviced from cash flows passed through to the entity from the lender or original owner of the cash flows, known as the originator. The bond issue is collateralized by the cash flows now legally assigned or transferred to the SPV by the originator, which now acts as a conduit or channel or collection agent of those cash flows. To be suitable for securitization, the cash flows must satisfy three financial (as opposed to legal) criteria. First, they must be stable and predictable. This would exclude, for example, vessel earnings in the spot market but would include earnings from a medium to long-term charterparty. Second, they must be homogeneous in the sense of being derived from one source or the same class of sources; charterparty receipts would satisfy this criterion. Third, they must be legally assignable: paragraphs 11–12, Schedule 1 of the Merchant Shipping Act 1995, provide that a registered mortgage may be transferred by an instrument made in the form prescribed by or approved under registration regulations, and where any such instrument is produced to the registrar, the latter registers the transferee in the prescribed manner. The ship mortgages would be transferred to the SPV since these are the assets collateralizing the bonds. Re-registration would be required since legal ownership of the loans originally accruing to the originator (the ship-financing bank) has now been transferred to the SPV. Investors' payments for the bonds issued by the SPV are used to purchase the cash flows, resulting in the originator receiving advance payment against those cash flows. In the event of default on the original loans securitized, the bringing of legal action will still fall to the originator as collecting agent. In 2014, Greece's Alpha Bank securitized EUR1 billion of shipping loans to raise about EUR500 million, the deal arranged by US bank Citigroup. Approximately 35 loans were bundled together as part of the deal, the legal rights being transferred to an SPV. The bonds issued had a maturity of five years and were privately placed rather than publicly issued. Details are limited but it may be assumed that, since the cash flows were assigned or sold to an SPV prior to the sale, the mortgages, if any, by which they were secured, were also similarly transferred. To do otherwise could result in the incongruous situation where ownership of the assets (the cash flows) by which the bonds were collateralized was transferred to the SPV, whilst the security or legal right to enforce those cash flows remained vested in another party, the bank or originator itself. The legal prerequisites for the transaction would be as follows. First, the SPV must have a genuine separate legal personality from the originator—the bank holding the mortgages and which originally granted ship loans. Second, the mortgages must be legally assigned from the originator to the SPV: any other outcome would result in those assets (future interest payments from borrowers) falling into the fund collected by receivers following any future insolvency of the originator. Third, the SPV proceeds to make a bond issue with the caveat that any potential future legal action by investors, for example in respect of a default in coupon payments, must be brought against the SPV itself and not against the originator. Securitization illustrates how mortgages can no longer be simply regarded as documentary aspects of bankers' security, but instead have become an integral part of financing in the wider capital markets as accessed by larger shipping companies.

10.7 Conclusion

This chapter has described the powers which mortgagees have in relation to vessels against which loans are secured. I have identified the statutory architecture within which mortgagor and mortgagee rights and duties are set out, and the rich case law in which these have been interpreted and delineated. Mortgages are just one of a range of different forms of security available to lenders but arguably the most traditional and effective, notwithstanding the limitations described at the beginning of the chapter. Although standard documentation exists, for example the Liberian, Bahamian and United Kingdom mortgage forms, parties invariably seek to add to these by means of a separate collateral deed, which takes priority in the event of a conflict between the two documents. Securitization illustrates how the law relating to mortgages, as well as their use as a central component in financial innovation, continues to evolve and adapt in a dynamic shipping finance environment.

Cases Cited

The Acrux [1962] 1 Lloyd's Rep. 405.
    Anton Durbeck GmbH v. Den Norske Bank ASA [2006] 1 Lloyd's Rep. 93.
    Bankers Trust International v. Todd Shipyards Corp (The Halcyon Isle), Privy Council (Singapore) [1981] A.C. 221.
    Brown v. Tanner (1868) LR 3 Ch App 597.

The Calm C [1975] 1 Lloyd's Rep. 188.
De Mattos v. Gibson, (1859 4 De G&J, 276.
Den Norske Bank ASA v. Acemex Management Co Ltd (The Tropical Reefer), [2004] 1 Lloyd's Rep. 1.
Dry Bulk Handy Inc v. Fayette International Holdings Ltd (The Bulk Chile), [2013] 2 Lloyd's Rep. 38.
Fletcher and Campbell v. City Marine Finance [1968] 2 Lloyd's Rep. 520.
The Halcyon Isle [1980] 1 Lloyd's Rep. 325.
The Heather Bell [1901] P 272, CA.
Keith v. Burrows (1877) 2 App. Cas. 636.
The Manor [1907] 2 Lloyd's Rep. 243.
The Myrto [1977] 2 Lloyd's Rep. 243.
Todd Shipyards Corp v. Altema Compania Maritima SA (The Ioannis Daskalelis), [1974] 1 Lloyd's Rep. 174
The Turiddu [1999] 2 Lloyd's Rep. 401.
Zeeland Navigation Co Ltd v. Banque Worms [2002] EWHC 1307.

Bibliography

Allen, J. 1998. Maritime lien for crew wages. International Journal of Shipping Law, 4 (Dec), 275–277.
Berg, A. 1993. Duties of a mortgagee and a receiver. Journal of Business Law, May, 213–241.
Berlingieri, F. 1988. Lien holders and mortgagees: who should prevail? Lloyd's Maritime and Commercial Law Quarterly, 2 (May), 157–176.
Bowtle, G. and Rymer, P. 1998. Caveat vendor. Lloyd's Maritime and Commercial Law Quarterly, 2 (May), 151–154.
Chambers, J. 2000. Maritime liens- priorities. International Maritime Law, 7 (2), 43–46.
Clarke, A. 1997. Mortgagees' powers of sale: contract or statute? Lloyd's Maritime and Commercial Law Quarterly, 3 (Aug), 329–337.
Clarke, A. 2002. Ship mortgagees' liability to charterers: mortgagees fight back. Lloyd's Maritime and Commercial Law Review, 4 (Nov), 462–466.
Deering, B., and Ward, C. 2013. Owners' right to intercept freight confirmed. Maritime Risk International, 27 (5), 18–19.
Goddard, K.S. 2006. "Yes, we have no bananas": reflections on ship mortgages and The Tropical Reefer. Lloyd's Maritime and Commercial Law Quarterly, 2 (May), 202–222.
Hill, C. 1998. Maritime Law. Fifth Edition. Lloyd's of London Press.
Kavussanos, M.G. 1996. Price risk modelling of different size vessels in the tanker industry using Autoregressive Conditional Heteroskedasticity (AECH) models. Logistics and Transportation Review, 32 (2), 161–176.

Kavussanos, M.G. 1997. The dynamics of time-varying volatilities in different size second-hand ship prices of the dry cargo sector. Applied Economics, 29 (4), 433–443.

London Special Risks, 2011. Ship Mortgage Indemnity: A Critical Assessment, at http://www.edge-gb.com/sites/default/files/pdfs/SMI-Critical.pdf

Meeson, N., and Kimball, J.A. 2011. Admiralty Jurisdiction and Practice. Informa.

Moore, L. 2013. Liening back and post-withdrawal syndrome: the Bulk Chile. Shipping and Transport International, 9 (4), 32–33.

Mukherjee, P.K. 2003. The law of maritime liens and conflict of laws. Journal of Maritime Law, 9 (6), 545–555.

Panesar, S. 2004. Is a ship mortgage inherently different from a mortgage over land? International Company and Commercial Law Review, 15 (8), 239–243.

Rares, S. 2014. Maritime liens, renvoi and conflicts of law: the far from Halcyon Isle. Lloyd's Maritime and Commercial Law Quarterly, 2 (May), 183–202.

Rose-Ackerman, S. 1985. Inalienability and the theory of property rights. Columbia Law Review 85 (5), 931–969.

Sabino, A.M., and Susca, N.E. 2001. An imperfect storm: Fifth Circuit denies seamen's liens against vessel sale proceeds. Lloyd's Maritime and Commercial Law Quarterly, 3 (Aug), 328–334.

Smith, C. 2001. Ship arrests: new developments. Shipping and Transport Lawyer International, 2 (3), 21–24.

Smith, D. 1991. Using insurance to protect lender's interest. Journal of International Banking Law, 6 (3), 107–115.

Stephenson Harwood, 2006. Shipping Finance. Euromoney.

Stopford, M. 2009. Maritime Economics. Routledge.

Tetley, W. 1989. In defence of the Ioannis Daskalelis. Lloyd's Maritime and Commercial Law Quarterly, 1 (Feb), 11–15.

Turner, J.M. 1997. Arrest-ship's mortgage- construction of deed of covenant. International Maritime Law, 4 (3), 67–68.

11

Mechanics of Handling Defaulted Shipping Loans and the Methods of Recovery

Dimitris C. Anagnostopoulos and Philippos E. Tsamanis

11.1 Introduction

Regulators worldwide try to ensure that banks and other financial institutions have sufficient capital to keep them strong to protect depositors, but also the rest of the economy, since the failure of a large bank could have negative repercussions on the financial stability of a country. Within today's globalized economy, this could create an increased systemic risk. In modern times, capital adequacy rules that have existed since the eighteenth century have been codified by the Switzerland based Bank of International Settlements (BIS). Through the years, the Basel Committee has defined the necessary financial ratios relating to the capital of banks versus their assets. It has also set a risk weight on each class of bank's assets (government bonds, unsecured loans, etc.), and defined the risk type of its capital (first tier, second tier).

The evolution of these basic "rules", that has taken place through modern times, is an ongoing process. It is characterized by the strong economic

---

D. Anagnostopoulos (✉)
Member of the Board of Directors, Aegean Baltic Bank S.A., 91 Megalou Alexandrou & 25th Martiou Street, Maroussi 15124, Greece

Ph. Tsamanis (✉)
Head of Shipping, Aegean Baltic Bank S.A., 91 Megalou Alexandrou & 25th Martiou Street, Maroussi 15124, Greece

© The Author(s) 2016
M.G. Kavussanos, I.D. Visvikis (eds.), *The International Handbook of Shipping Finance*, DOI 10.1057/978-1-137-46546-7_11

development and growth of the money markets and the world economy. Basel I rules have been "elevated" to Basel II, and are gradually building up to a stricter version of requirements (Basel III, due in 2018).

With the Lehman Brothers collapse and the financial crisis that followed it, the world banking system has more or less suffered with liquidity problems. Though capital adequacy has become a priority in the banking sector, the ability of a bank to build reserves against bad loans and absorb write-offs is still of limited capacity and sometimes impossible without central banks' assistance.

Although the technical principles of handling shipping problem loans remain virtually unchanged, banks' behavioral attitudes towards recording of reserves and write-offs have dramatically changed. This is a result of certain elements coming to the forefront in recent years, such as capital adequacy, liquidity, return on assets and return on capital, which may differ from bank to bank. In reality, lenders are "forced" to be more lenient, and hence more prepared to take a softer and longer term approach when negotiating with defaulted borrowers in order to find more peaceful solutions for minimizing losses for both sides.

11.2 The 1981–86 Shipping Crisis vs the Post-2008 Period

It is worth emphasizing the distinction of the treatment of defaulted shipping loans by lenders (banks) during the 1981–86 freight market crisis by comparison with a similar freight market depression post-2008, the year that Lehman Brothers collapsed. In the former, the freight market crisis only affected the shipping industry, thus diversified banks had a much easier task in enforcing collateral and absorbing immediate write-offs and rationalizing their books. Their balance sheets had sufficient reserves and liquidity in them. It is of interest to note that during the freight market crisis, a large number of vessels were auctioned while, after the collection by the banks of the auction proceeds, the respective unpaid loan balances were comfortably (for the banks) written off.

In contrast, the severe freight market correction that occurred after 2008 did not produce massive foreclosures and only very few auctions of shipping assets were witnessed. The majority of the banks' lending to the shipping industry have limited reserves to absorb losses as they struggle to maintain Basel II capital adequacy ratios that are closely monitored by the regulators. For every sum of provision or write-off taken, an injection of capital or reduction of assets is effectively mandated by the regulators. Finally, it is worth noting that the more lenient approach during the latter period was also encouraged by the prevailing low interest rates, that minimized the time-cost (and the actual monetary cost) of "kicking the can".

11.3 The Mechanics of Handling Problematic Bank Loans

This chapter refers to the standard technical method that is broadly applied, being a transcript of actions and procedures deriving from previous experiences. It should be noted that certain of our views regarding the procedural handling of problematic loans may differ substantially from what EU regulators and Central Banks have dictated since 2014. The reason is that bureaucratic and rather obstructive decision-making processes at the top management of large financial institutions prevent the customer who is dealing with bank officers from being quick, swift and realistic when taking actions that can maximize cash collection for loan recoveries.

Early detection is a key element in handling problematic loans; in particular, the earlier a problem is detected, the greater is the spectrum of options available to the bank. Immediate action is also important; that is, the prerequisite preparations that will pave the way to the development of a "game plan", which is either a work-out plan or a liquidation (voluntary, orderly, with owners' cooperation, or by force without cooperation).

11.4 Early Detection of Signs

The responsibility for the early detection of signs that an obligor, or a particular credit, may be entering into a period of challenge lies with the frontline officer (the "account officer") to whom the particular obligor or credit has been assigned. It is the latter who will trigger a downgrading of the rating assigned to the particular obligor/credit. There is a strong conviction that even the most generic rating system becomes thus a very useful tool, as it is almost impossible for an emerging problem to stay hidden within an organization that has a properly functioning loan grading system, be that judgmental or not.

Early detection is important; but how is this achieved? Which areas should be closely monitored? In order for the account officer to be in a position to detect problem shipping loans as early as possible, he or she should, first of all, follow shipping market movements and prospects.

As values tend to correct with a considerable time lag, downward freight rate spirals constitute an earlier indication of what challenges may lie ahead. Hence, the employment position (type of employment, rates, duration, redelivery parameters and counterparty/charterer) could either exacerbate concerns or provide short or medium-term relief. One has to be alert for any rate renegotiations or delays in the collection of hires, but also for any information concerning the wellbeing, financial solidity and underlying contract coverage of the charterers. This is better illustrated by the recent experiences in the offshore market, where, as a result of the abrupt and considerable drop in oil prices, projects are being temporized or canceled and in turn even the most solid of counterparties—in this highly oligopolistic market—approach owners demanding time-charter rate renegotiations.

Continuous pressure on liquidity (as a result of a less than lucrative earning generating capacity of a vessel or fleet) are in many cases reflected in bloated trade payables but also—further down the road—in poor maintenance. Although the former necessitates a well-established flow of information between the borrower and lender, the latter can be traced in findings of port state control inspections, which, since the turn of the century, are regularly reported on-line (such as by the US Coast Guard and Equasis). However, it takes a trained eye to weigh the significance of the reported detections or deficiencies.

When financial statements become available to the account officer, despite their being somewhat outdated (usually 90–180 days old), hidden "gems" may be found. In short, poor profitability in conjunction with increased trade payables and inadequate working capital should be more than enough to give rise to a downgrading exercise, regardless of the debt servicing record of the borrower. Other reasons for concern—not necessarily related to the fortunes of the freight market—are delays or overruns in newbuilding projects or on scheduled repair works.

Finally, thanks to the standard wording of the notices of assignment of insurances, brokers may be the ones to alert an account officer. However, in recent years, a reduced frequency of incidents has been witnessed concerning unpaid insurance premia; in the same way there have been fewer incidents of long overdue crew wages. More acute problems are more easily detectable as they may involve the failure to meet in a timely fashion the monthly retention payments (if applicable) and, of course, interest payments and principal installments. However, by no means can someone consider either of these as "early warning" signals: the problem is already there, and crucial time has already been lost.

11.5 Once the Problem Is Detected

A distinction should be made between an "early stage" and a more "progressed stage". As this is a very fine line, we do not attempt any definitions. It is worth noting that there are regulatory directives that recently have attempted to set out a framework for handling "arrears and non-performing loans" (ANPL), though we are not in complete agreement with this, especially as far as shipping finance is concerned. Therefore, what follows is our view on the subject, which may not necessarily be in-line with recent all-encompassing directives. The reason why our views may deviate from that of the regulators is that the latter allow very limited commercial and accounting flexibility on the part of Banks which may result in less efficient handling of troubled lending relationships. Greater room to maneuver could prevent defaulting loans from ending up at the stage of liquidation.

There are two "schools of thought" which must be distinguished here. The first school dictates that, at the emergence of a serious loan default (a missed payment of a principal installment and/or interest), the lending bank automatically switches the responsibility from the account officer into a "special credits department", which takes over and decides the strategic moves on this particular defaulted loan up until its solution (one way or the other). The second school dictates a less stringent involvement of the "special credits" division of the bank, basically allowing the account officer to continue handling the loan with minimum supervision and guidance from the specialists.

In the early stages (and assuming a "healthy operating environment"), the account officer should be primarily responsible. He or she has over the years invested in developing a level of rapport with the borrower and a level of trust with the borrower's officers that can be of immense assistance in formulating a clear picture of the borrower's predicament. The personal relationship will also amplify the chances of the information flow being uninterrupted.

It should be emphasized that the majority of shipping loans that go into default do so for reasons related to the status of the freight market. Table 11.1 summarizes the market characteristics in relation to the impact they have on both shipowning companies and banking institutions.

The aspects and the real-life ramifications of the handling of problem loans is a rather complicated exercise and one that is very often full of surprises. In our experience, no foreclosure or treatment of a problem shipping loan is identical to a previous one. Thus, the mobilization of the account officer, his or her manager, the bank's committees and external advisors, such as lawyers, engineers, marine insurance experts and other shipping professionals, is needed in order for a dedicated team to put a case together for each defaulted loan. It should be noted that, in our experience, the average time committed by bank employees to a problem shipping loan is commonly four times more than that committed to handling a performing (problem-free) shipping loan.

Table 11.1 Market characteristics in relation to the impact on shipowning and banking institutions

	Good market	Bad market
Vessels' values	Improving	Deteriorating/approaching scrap
Vessels' earnings	Adequate to cover operating expenses and debt service	Mostly adequate to cover operating expenses but inadequate to cover debt service
Trade debt	At low level; terms of payment shortening	Gradual increase of outstanding bills; Terms of payment lengthening
Company's cash	Liquidity high	Liquidity decreasing Evaporation of cash reserves
Owners' equity	Increased	Decreased
Balance sheet of single shipowning company and groups' financial position	Healthy All financial ratios in good shape	Poor Deterioration of financial ratios
Bank's balance sheet	Increase of loan portfolio, decrease of loan provisions and write-offs	Decrease of loan portfolio increase of reserves and appearance of write-offs
Bank's profit & loss	Profits from loan spreads and commissions	Usually profits tend to reduce or be absorbed by write-offs
Market information on shipowner's financial condition and behavior	Tends to be good for almost everybody	Tends to be poor for some
Shipping market general outlook	Euphoria	Pessimism

11.6 Preparation for Remedial Action

When a loan approaches default, the lender should be ready to take remedial action. Usually, breaches of certain financial covenants, such as the loan to value (LTV) ratio, constitute the so-called "technical defaults". Lenders will try to take mild remedial action to restore compliance with the terms and conditions of the loan agreement. However, if the borrower misses a principal or interest payment or both, the lender is then obliged to engage more forcibly with the borrower. In such cases, considerations of the lender should practically focus on a negotiation towards the restructuring of the debt facility with a simultaneous remedy of the breaches, which may include the conversion of hard collateral (vessels) into cash. The ultimate target of the lenders is either to maintain the loan in its current status or to get their money back—in an amicable or a forced way.

Before addressing the issue with the client, the account officer is expected to review carefully the credit file, to re-analyze the financial statements and overall position of the borrower thoroughly, and to review the loan documentation in order to identify clearly the rights of the mortgagee bank. At the same time, he or she should ensure that all securities are in place and valid, and embark on a "fact finding" mission regarding the following characteristics of the collateral vessel:

- Condition: if possible, and through the cooperation of the borrower, retain the services of a technical surveyor who will produce an updated condition survey report.
- Fair market value (FMV) and marketability: in cooperation with an independent S&P broker.
- Whereabouts: the trading area and employment commitments.

In addition, he or she should embark on a search for other assets, which could support a work-out plan. The above preparatory actions will have to be followed by a meeting with the borrower. In our opinion, it is advisable that, in such an initial meeting, the bank be represented by the account officer together with a more senior member of the bank. If the borrower wishes to retain the services of an external (financial restructuring) advisor, this should generally be welcomed, as the latter's presence, in most cases, has proven to be useful; such an advisor may bring expertise and be in a better position to convey or explain ideas from the borrower's perspective and produce the requested information in a meaningful (bank-friendly) format. If the borrower wishes to have an attorney present, it is advisable for the bank to also make provision for this.

The aim of the meeting will be to bring the issue/cause of concern to the attention of the borrower, which can be a first-class opportunity for the bank to obtain as much information as possible. Particular focus should be placed on the mortgaged vessel's trade debt, especially liens with priority over the bank's lien (such as maritime liens) as well as creditors in advantageous (not necessarily in legal terms) positions vis-à-vis the bank. The meeting will also give the borrower the chance to explain the situation and initiate a work-out discussion in which he or she can present his or her proposals/views on the issue.

On the basis of these actions, the account officer will be in a position to present his or her evaluation of the matter at hand to the internal bodies of the bank. A central point in this evaluation should be the determination of an estimate of the potential loss. This will form the mathematical "benchmark" for any further proposal or decision. In order to estimate the amount the bank would have to write off if the liquidation started on the same day, the following two core scenarios should be examined:

- liquidation with the client's cooperation (through orderly liquidation or through a court administered sale, such as a judicial auction);
- liquidation without the client's cooperation (through enforcement).

In addition, the account officer will have to identify clearly the primary and secondary sources of repayment. Primary sources are those associated with the cash-flow generating potential of the collateral, and secondary sources loosely refer to liquidation of the collateral and support by the guarantors, for example. A word of caution: while there may be a need to move swiftly, the account officer will have to take every precaution so that any action does not expose the bank to a lender liability suit.

11.7 Determinants of the Bank's Course of Action

There is a variety of factors and considerations which will determine the bank's course of action and strategy, in relation to a problematic shipping loan. These factors should not be viewed independently of one another, while the importance of each of them will vary on a case-by-case basis. All these elements constitute the facts that a credit committee of the lender will take into consideration on a cost–benefit basis in order to optimize its strategy and its actions, which will lead to the full or partial recovery of the loan.

The most important considerations are the following:

1. Financial considerations: size of the loan, financial environment, level of interest rates, bank's policy and ability to take reserves or write off losses, central bank's rules and regulations.
2. Ship-management considerations: management's competence to operate vessels, positive or negative contribution to the problems, payment record, attitude, ability to deal with problems, maturity, commitment to the industry.
3. Market considerations: current state of the shipping "cycle", future prospects and trends of the freight market. Has the collateral vessel another "life" to live?
4. Collateral/security considerations: creditors ranking higher than the mortgagee, collateral vessel's value, age, maintenance status, survey status, trade

debt attached, trading or port jurisdiction, terms of charter party, if the vessel is laden with cargo, ballast status, if it is laid up.
5. Bank's considerations: shipping policy and culture, top management understanding of shipping, cooperation with syndicate members (if the loan is syndicated), magnitude of losses vs bank's profitability, reaction of the market, bank's reputation as being supportive to its shipowners, accusation or bad publicity following disclosures.

After taking into account the above considerations and factors, a shipping bank will then be in a position to develop its strategy. One could argue that there are essentially four strategies a lender can follow in a problem shipping loan situation:

1. "Do nothing" scenario: "deferral" of the problem situation which will inevitably eventually "hit the fan" sometime later, unless the market picks up.
2. Stay-in and negotiate (S&N): this will give the bank the opportunity to correct any loan documentation deficiencies and attempt to improve its overall position. Simultaneously, it will give the parties the opportunity to buy time, usually through introduction of a soft repayment schedule (moratoria, principal holidays). Note that additional advances (for working capital purposes) should be ideally considered only in conjunction with additional collateral and guarantees. A possible outcome of an S&N strategy could be an agreement over the orderly liquidation of collateral, together with extension of working capital funding to safeguard the unobstructed progress of the liquidation process.
3. Forced refinancing: this is a hugely popular strategy in the post-Lehman period. This may be:

    - At par: the bank should seek the combination of measures that will put enough pressure on the borrower (and the other security parties, such us the guarantors) to cause the refinancing of the facility by another bank. In doing so, the bank should investigate whether other creditors, such as second priority mortgagees or other lenders to the same borrower (or group) with exposure in worse shape than that of the bank, exist, and if so whether they may be interested to "buy the bank out" by refinancing the loan in order to improve their overall position.
    - At a discount: the bank may need to consider the option of identifying a party that is interested in assuming the loan at a discount. The level of this discount should be determined by taking into account the difference

(gap) between the FMV of the collateral and the loan outstanding, as well as the employment status (if any). This option should be measured against the benchmark/estimate of potential loss.

4. Enforce collateral: this strategy is the least desirable of all and, in our opinion, should only be considered if everything else has failed to produce results. The collateral enforcement (auction) strategy is examined in detail later in this chapter; however, it should be pointed out that its most crucial factors are the location of enforcement and the overall parameters. The latter include the existence of maritime or other liens, trade creditors and employment. As can be seen, the relevant jurisdiction's legal framework should be reviewed by specialized shipping lawyers appointed for the specific task.

After the different strategies that a lender may consider in a problem shipping loan situation have been discussed, the S&N strategy is further analyzed; in most cases, this ends up being the bank's elected strategy. Experience suggests that, in order to maximize recovery, a lender may need to work closely with the borrower as much as is reasonably possible. His or her proposals should be thoroughly considered and may be rejected if there are prudent reasons to do so. It should be noted that, for a strategy to be successful and address a problem loan situation, the combination of ideas is a key factor. Under the S&N strategy, there should be an agreement on a realistic repayment or a liquidation schedule agreed by all parties. However, maturities and milestones should be kept as short as possible. In exchange for this forbearance, the bank should:

- Introduce additional covenants for closer monitoring of the situation.
- Seek additional collateral; if this is in the form of receivables, then an aggressive collection program should be established. Retaining the services of external advisors, such as legal counsel and/or insurance experts (depending on the nature of the receivable concerned), is strongly advised in such cases. In the event that there are other creditors with liens on this additional collateral, the bank may find it justifiable to buy them out in order to improve its security position.

If fresh bank funding is required for the work-out plan to be operational, this should be committed from the lender's side, in exchange for additional collateral, if available, and on the basis of a fully detailed schedule of pre-defined uses and upon production of tangible and acceptable supporting documents. In agreeing to the S&N strategy, the bank will have to keep in mind its regulatory framework concerning restructured credits, in order to weigh the magnitude of its impact on its balance sheet.

The following are areas where particular caution and attention should be paid, with respect to the S&N strategy:

- the bank and its officers should avoid becoming too deeply involved in the internal management of the borrower during a work-out, as there may be repercussions in the form of the lender's liability;
- if the guarantors are third parties and not the principals or the managers of the borrower, they need to be kept fully informed of the problem and the steps that are being taken to resolve it;
- any new agreement should be depicted in legally perfected documentation;
- if the S&N strategy is not working, it should be revised and a new strategy should be considered (whilst closely monitoring all of the milestones and the debt facility's new maturities).

11.8 Loan Recovery Through Auction of the Collateral Vessel

When all remedial measures and actions have been exhausted, and the lender is left with no other option but to foreclose on the loan and sell the collateral vessel either through an auction or by relying on the legal rights a mortgagee has, there are a number of rules of thumb that the mortgagee bank must have in mind and, most importantly, rigorously apply before initiating arrest and auction procedures. The decision to arrest should be seen as a last resort to gain control of vessels through the court, and not necessarily as a step towards the sale of the vessels at auction (or afterwards) to the highest bidder.

As part of the above fact-finding missions, the bank should have already retained the services of a shipping lawyer to investigate the legal framework of the intended jurisdiction of arrest and auction (e.g. priorities), as well as the local legal and procedural requirements. This investigation will enable the bank to obtain a clear view on the time element associated with the arrest and the auction at the intended jurisdiction, as well as the distribution of the auction proceeds to the creditors, including the mortgagees. Clearly, rights to appeal, delay and generally interfere with the process should be taken into consideration, while one may need to assess the likely impact of trade creditors and other claimants.

Another important element is that of the actual cost associated with an arrest and a subsequent auction. The account officer should prepare a budget—and, once this is approved, closely monitor the associated expenses. The main cost items can be loosely broken down as follows:

- Legal fees: the bank should strive to obtain capped fee quotations.
- Court and auction expenses.
- Ship maintenance and husbandry (agency fees) expenses.
- Crew sign-off, repatriation (in which case the crew's claim should be subrogated to the bank), and replacement by a minimum safety crew. The latter may greatly vary between jurisdictions and forms and areas of anchorage.
- Insurance costs: the bank will have to retain the services of insurance advisors to check what the insurance covers, and should try to obtain the best quotes possible for their services.

Finally, the bank should also have an idea of the attractiveness—from a marketing point of view—of the intended location of arrest and auction. Places where lots of prospective buyers can easily inspect, such as Piraeus, Gibraltar and Shanghai, may be more suitable from this "marketability of the vessel" aspect.

If either the legal framework, the time element or the cost element suggest that a specific legal jurisdiction is unfavorable to proceed with an arrest, the circumstances may justify the expense and the associated risk of relocating the vessel to a more favorable legal jurisdiction. This will be done by exercising as mortgagee-in-possession the pledge of shares, this being the legal right that the lender possesses to assume control of the vessel. Consequently, the bank should appoint a new, friendly shipmanager to undertake the task at hand. As these courses of action are generally less desirable, one should also investigate the possibility of trading the vessel or even enforcing the personal guarantee or other collateral (or even agreeing to certain concessions) in exchange for securing the cooperation of the owner in relocating the vessel to a favorable legal jurisdiction, arranging for the signing-off and repatriation of the crew (in which case the cost may be substantially lower than the cost the bank will incur), dealing with all initial logistic issues (e.g. handling cargo interests or dealing with certain creditors) and, most importantly, not interfering or obstructing the procedure. Uncooperative arrest actions meet with substantial owner opposition, resulting in delays, increased liquidation expenses and reduced ultimate sale proceeds, compared to those achieved with a cooperative shipowner.

Note the following areas of caution:

- Handling of cargo interests: a lot of preparatory work (in fields where banks have little knowledge) will need to be carried out before a bank decides to arrest a vessel, which is laden with any type of cargo.

- Handling of local unsecured creditors: it is up to the local lawyers to advise the bank of any preferred status that these may enjoy (as in the USA).
- Handling of opposing/uncooperative owner: concessions in exchange for their cooperation, however unpleasant, may be commercially justified.
- In extreme cases, where an asset has a very low FMV and is situated in an unfavorable trading or scrap location and/or in a jurisdiction unfavorable to the mortgagees, abandonment of the vessel and pursuit of other means towards loan recovery may be the most cost-effective decision for the bank.

Finally, once an auction date and reserve price have been set, the bank will have to decide on its strategy at the auction. The bank may elect to participate in the auction so as to acquire the vessel with a view to: (i) reselling it immediately; (ii) trading it (through a friendly party) in the short term, thus postponing the decision to sell; or (iii) laying it up (warehousing) so that it may be marketed at a later stage. As may be appreciated, the decision depends on the culture, expectations and risk appetite of the decision-making bodies of the bank as well as the vessel's prospects.

11.9 Situations a Bank May Face During a Vessel's Arrest

There is a great number of unexpected situations that may occur during the foreclosure process of a "precipitating" bank which aims to liquidate its collateral in order to eliminate or minimize its loss from a defaulted shipping loan. The moment a bank is engaged in a full blast action against a defaulted and uncooperative debtor, it should be prepared to encounter a number of unforeseen situations which may substantially increase the costs of its overall actions.

Situations that have contributed to increases in the liquidation costs of a bank are presented below. These may include: a change of flag during the vessel's trip which would result in invalid mortgages; continuous arrests by different creditors, the bank having no idea they existed (shipowners having misrepresented the level of their trade debt); the vessel lacking proper insurance cover; the vessel being declared as being "taken over" by pirates; a bank being unaware of the positioning of the vessel or the trade it is involved in; a secret agreement between the shipowner and the suppliers to arrest the vessel in a legally unfriendly jurisdiction to the mortgagee (thus blocking the bank's ability to arrest in a favorable jurisdiction); a bank finding illegal immigrants onboard the arrested vessel; a vessel found to be carrying drugs; unpaid crew starting to cannibalize the vessel; and selling parts of the vessel (this obviously reduces the value of the bank's security in the second-hand market). Other situations may involve the shipowning company and the captain of the arrested vessel taking advantage of the situation by: creating non-existent, crew-related expenses, as well as producing false, non-existent creditors and backdated invoices; repeated postponement of the auction by the courts; a vessel scrapped without the bank's consent, where the shipowner receives all the scrap proceeds (although this is rather rare); and alleged fraud by the bank's officers (protecting the borrower and not the interests of the bank).

11.10 Conclusion: The Other Side of the Coin

Loan work-outs may not only create losses for a bank; sometimes, they offer great commercial opportunities. If you don't panic when the freight market is in the doldrums, then you will see things getting better when the market improves, thus maximizing recovery and, in certain cases, making a profit at a later stage. Involvement in shipping requires commitment, consistency and continuity—a long-term approach irrespective of the market cycle is necessary for lenders to maximize returns from the shipping industry. It should not be forgotten that the best way to handle a problem loan is to, in so far as this is possible, avoid granting it in the first place.

References

Stephenson Harwood, *When Things Go Wrong*, Piraeus, Client Briefing, 1997.
Charles Buss, *Ship Mortgage Enforcement*, Oslo, Watson, Farley and Williams, 2004.
Anagnostopoulos, D., *Problem Loans*, Presentations at City University Cass Business School.
Rose, P.S., *Commercial Bank Management*, Irwin, 1991.
BIS, *Basel III: The Liquidity Coverage Ratio and Liquidity Risk Monitoring Tools*, January 2013.
Meyer Brown, *Non-Performing Shipping Loans*, 2014.
Stephenson Harwood, *Shipping Finance*, Euromoney Books, 2006.
Bank of International Settlements, *The Importance of Capital and Methods of Measuring its Adequacy*, Washington, D.C., 2004.

12

Marine Insurance

Marc A. Huybrechts and Theodora Nikaki

12.1 Overview

Building, financing and operating a vessel is a multi-million-dollar investment, which, given the nature of the risks involved, requires thoughtful planning from all parties involved (shipbuilders, financiers, owners/buyers). It is therefore very important that all parties make inter alia insurance arrangements which will cover the respective risks they are exposed to. This chapter will focus on the insurance coverage taken out by the shipyard, the vessel's financiers and the shipowners (as operators of the vessel). Due to spatial constraints, this chapter will only provide a concise discussion of the pertinent insurance policies and will not delve into a detailed analysis of their provisions.

The authors would like to thank Carl Moens of Marsh N.V., Captain Marc Nuytemans and Karel Stes of Exmar N.V., and Bart Mertens of Gard for their valuable input and critical comments.

M.A. Huybrechts (✉)
Law Faculties of Antwerp University & Catholic University of Leuven, Belgium

T. Nikaki
Institute of International Shipping and Trade Law (IISTL), College of Law and Criminology, Swansea University, Richard Price Building, Singleton Park, Swansea A2 8PP, UK

12.2 Builders' Risk Insurance

A shipyard is, by definition, a high risk environment for a number of reasons. First of all, the risk of loss of or damage to a new building vessel, which is normally of high value, rests with the shipbuilders until the exchange of the protocols of delivery and acceptance.[1] This is why shipbuilding contracts usually require that the shipyard obtains insurance that covers inter alia physical damage to or loss of the vessel while in construction.[2] In addition, other risks involved in building the vessel include the employment of third parties, such as sub-contractors, as well as the transit of the vessel between places during its construction to facilitate the completion of the project and its sea trials. In light of their exposure to such high risks, shipyards insure their risks through insurance contracts, which are a combination of basic marine insurance policies. Such insurance contracts cover physical damage to or loss of a vessel during the course of its construction, as well as the shipbuilders' liability (such as collision liability). The assured is commonly the shipyard but it may also include the buyers.[3] The insurance market has therefore developed a number of standard forms covering builders' risks, such as the Institute Clauses for Builders' Risks (ICBR) 1988 and the London Marine Construction All Risks Wording (MarCAR) 2007, governed by English law.[4]

Both the ICBR 1988 and MarCAR 2007 qualify as comprehensive policies. They take into account the complexity of the shipbuilding process and extend their coverage to the acts/omissions of both the shipyard itself and their sub-contractors. To that end, they cover the hull and machinery for the entire duration of the shipbuilding project; that is until the vessel is delivered to the buyers, irrespective of whether the construction takes place at the shipbuilders' yard or at the shipbuilders' sub-contractors premises, or the vessel is in transit between such locations whilst still in the construction stage.[5] It should be noted at this juncture that MarCAR 2007 sheds light on the ambiguity regarding the scope of such sub-contractors by defining them in clause 56.2, that is clarifying that they are covered only if the benefit of the builders' insurance has been provided for in their written contract with a contractor.[6]

The builders' risk cover under both ICBR 1988 and MarCAR 2007 insures against "all risks" for physical loss (including constructive total loss) or damage to the vessel.[7] In addition, they cover the shipbuilders' liability arising out of a collision (subject to the exclusions clearly enumerated in the policies) and their exposure to liability for their failure to launch, for general average and salvage, and for sue and labour.[8] They also include clauses on protection and indemnity (P&I).[9] Although the policy is an "all risks" one, the builders' risks coverage is made subject to a number of exclusions. On the one hand, both policies provide for a number of excluded risks. For example, ICBR 1988 excludes war, strikes, malicious acts and nuclear risks, as further defined in the pertinent clauses.[10] Nonetheless, the parties may extend the policy's coverage if they expressly agree to cover such risks by incorporating the standard additional clauses.[11] MarCAR 2007 also expressly excludes from its coverage: loss, damages, liabilities and expenses caused by wilful misconduct of the assured, insolvency, solely by ordinary wear and tear or by delay, as well as: certain types of war; strikes; terrorist, politically motivated and malicious acts; and nuclear risks.[12] On the other hand, both policies clarify that, unless agreed otherwise, their coverage does not extend to latent or design defects per se, but that it covers the cost of repairing physical loss or physical damage caused by such defects if discovered during the period of the insurance.[13]

12.3 Financiers' Insurance

Being a multi-million-dollar investment on the part of shipowners, building and/or purchasing a vessel requires the conclusion of complex financial agreements, which often take the form of ship mortgages. The financier, usually a bank, needs to protect its interests in the underlying asset (i.e. the hull). This is in fact reflected in section 14 (1) of the English Marine Insurance Act (MIA) 1906, which provides that the mortgagee has an insurable interest "in respect of any sum due or to become due under the mortgage". The mortgagee/bank therefore may agree with the mortgagor/owner that the mortgagee will be named as the co-assured under the hull and mutual insurance taken out by the owner or operator of the vessel. This is, however, far from ideal as the mortgagee/bank may, for instance, end up paying the premium if the owner/co-assured failed to effect such payment.

Another alternative is the legal assignment of the owner's/mortgagor's marine policies to the mortgagee/bank (unless it contains terms expressly prohibiting assignment).[14] By an assignment, a person will transfer a right to another person, the assignee. This enables the assignee to enforce the right assigned in its own name and without joining the assignor to the proceedings. Again, this solution is problematic as the mortgagee/assignee may sue the insurers in its own name but will not receive greater rights than the assignor. In other words, the insurer will be entitled to bring against the mortgagee all the defences he or she would have had against the mortgagor/assured,[15] including those arising out of the mortgagor/owners misconduct,[16] over which the bank has no control, which may result in the insurer being exonerated from its liability.[17]

The best solution by far is thus the conclusion of a separate marine insurance contract in the mortgagee's name to cover its interests. Such an insurance contract will cover the mortgagees' losses in the event that the owners' hull and machinery insurance, war risks insurance and/or P&I club insurance will not cover a claim, which would have otherwise been covered under the owners' insurance[18] but for the circumstances which have discharged the insurers from their liability.[19] The mortgagees interest insurance (MII) operates as a "back-up" policy for the mortgagee and is usually effected under the terms of the Institute Mortgagees' Interest Clauses (IMIC), Hulls (1/3/97),[20] also governed by English law. IMIC 1997 is designed to cover the interests of mortgagees holding a valid first mortgage on the vessel, as warranted by the mortgagee.[21] IMIC 1997, clause 2.1, provides an extensive list of insured perils outlining the circumstances which would lead to a loss of cover for the vessel owners under their insurance policy, that is breach of the owners' duty of good faith in respect of the claim at issue, misrepresentation or non-disclosure of any material circumstance by the owners, breach of the owners' duty to provide a seaworthy vessel, among others. Particularly in the field of marine insurance, the duty of good faith is a fundamental principle and forms the basis of the marine insurance contract; if the duty of the utmost good faith is not met by either of the parties, the aggrieved may avoid the contract as per article 17 of the MIA 1906. If the owners' loss of cover under their insurance policy falls within the scope of the insured perils, then the mortgagee/assured will be entitled to recover from the MII insurer its net loss, up to the amount insured on the mortgaged vessel.[22] Such net loss is further defined in clause 2.3 as encompassing the assured's loss under the loan agreement to the extent secured by the mortgage on the mortgaged vessel net of any amounts recovered or recoverable under all security arrangements contained in or collateral to the loan including, but not limited to, all mortgages, liens, any floating and fixed charges, security interests, guarantees, insurance policies and pledges. The mortgagee/assured will, however, lose its MII coverage if, for instance, the insured peril occurred or existed with the privity of the assured mortgagee ("privity", as a special meaning in the context of maritime law, means condoning in someone else's faulty behavior), or the assured's loss arose from the termination or the cancellation of the owners' policies and club entries for non-payment of premiums or calls, or the insolvency of any of the underwriters of the owners' policies and club entries.[23]

In addition to the MII cover,[24] the mortgagee/bank may take out a Mortgagee's Additional Perils (Pollution) Insurance (MAPP), usually on the terms of the Mortgagee's Additional Perils (Pollution) clauses LSW 489, also governed by English law. Specifically, the MAPP insurance is usually added to the MII. It provides coverage to a mortgagee holding a first mortgage on the vessel for the amount of its net loss under the loan, if the vessel is seized (that is expropriated, confiscated or its sale proceeds are sequestrated) to satisfy the pollution liabilities, which are in excess of the limits of liabilities under the owner's insurance policies and P&I coverage.[25] The mortgagee will, however, lose its coverage if the loss is caused by any of the excluded events enumerated in clause 3, such as the lack of proper documentation/authorizations to legitimize the entry of the mortgaged vessel into the jurisdiction the vessel is entering into or the default of the mortgagee to pursue any possible right or remedy against a third-party tortfeasor to mitigate the mortgagee's potential loss. Other exclusions encompass some types of war and nuclear risks.[26]

12.4 Owners' Insurance

Five items will be discussed in this chapter focusing on the owners' insurance. Any mortgagee or financial institution extending credit to a shipowner will require that the vessel be properly insured. Apart from that, every responsible prudent owner will want his valuable asset, his vessel, to be adequately insured. In the subsequent paragraphs, the following issues are addressed.

- Against which risks do the owners want insurance?
- Where is the relevant market to find proper insurance?
- By which insurers are these risks covered?
- At what price? What is the budgetary implication of marine insurance in the overall operational costs of vessel exploitation?
- What are the specifics of marine insurance, which an insured should always keep in mind?

12.4.1 What "Risks" Will a Shipowner Want to Be Covered?

As shipping is an industry full of unpredictable dangers and risks, a shipowner or a prospective shipowner will need insurance cover against an extensive number of these risks. Cover against some of them is considered as essential in the framework of a successful and safe operation; some of them are not that important and could be considered more of a luxury type. On the basis of the marine insurance broker's regular practice, the following risk covers are suggested for a shipowner in a safe insurance package.

12.4.1.1 Property

Hull and machinery (H&M) cover for named perils, particular average, general average, salvage and total loss, disbursements and increased values (excess H&M), and cover against war risks.[27] War perils are usually excluded under the standard H&M conditions, so it is necessary for an assured to buy cover against war risks separately.

A traditional war policy (which, for example, can be on the standard UK policy conditions or on the basis of the Nordic Marine Insurance Plan 2013) ought to cover against the risks of war, civil war, revolution, capture, seizure, derelict mines, torpedoes, strikes, terrorism and confiscation. An owner is also advised to seek cover against piracy incidents.

12.4.1.2 Liability

Liability arising out of war risks should also be covered by war risks insurance, but the traditional operational liabilities of a shipowner are to be covered by P&I insurance as per P&I rules. A shipowner is well advised to obtain cover for legal and contractual liabilities, indemnities such as the consequence of the running-down clause, or contact with fixed and floating objects, liabilities relating to wreck removal, crew liability, cargo liability, third-party liability regarding property, bodily injury and loss of life. These risks are not covered in a traditional H&M policy. The list of risks covered by P&I insurance is much longer but in the present paragraph only the most important risks have been mentioned. Evidently, pollution has to be covered as well, but, regarding oil pollution, it should be stressed that there is a maximum cover of USD1 billion. In addition to the cover against these risks, pre-delivery crew cover can also be provided as well as extended crew cover.

12.4.1.3 Legal

An owner is also well advised to seek cover for freight demurrage and defense as per club rules. By this cover, a shipowner is protected against the legal bills and expenses which he or she might incur, amongst others, in trying to claim outstanding freight and demurrage and general legal expenses caused by the operation of his or her vessel.

12.4.1.4 Lost Time

In a safe insurance package, an owner will also want cover against loss of hire. This cover provides a daily indemnity for loss of hire in the framework of H&M cover or in the framework of a warlike situation. With regard to insurance against "lost time", an owner may similarly prefer to obtain strike insurance which will provide a daily indemnity for loss (operational income) caused by strike, grounding and stranding, illness, injury or death, drugs, pollution, desertion from ship, action of authorities, stowaways on board, quarantine, machinery, damage, piracy and kidnap. In practice, it is important to distinguish between the "normal" loss-of-hire cover, which protects the shipowner from a daily loss of income arising from physical damage to the vessel, war loss of hire, and extended loss of hire which responds to the loss of income caused by delay/detention of a ship that has not been physically damaged. In the latter case, the loss of income may arise from P&I events, such as pollution spill resulting in third-party property damage, or cargo dispute leading to arrest of the vessel.

12.4.1.5 Varia

The market offers cover to an agreed limit for a number of non-traditional risks, such as kidnap and ransom insurance, payment of ransom, ransom lost in transit, response consultants' fees, additional expenses, legal liability and mortgagees' interest/additional perils and charters' default (which is basically a credit insurance providing cover against the financial insolvency of the charterer; it should be noted that, on account of the financial crisis of 2007–08, this cover has been significantly curtailed). The special cover should also be mentioned, which may include extended crew cover, crew managers' cover and, especially, shipowners' liability cover against risks excluded by the P&I clubs, known as the SOL, and further shipbuilders' risks like piracy loss-of-hire extension on the basis of a daily indemnity. In this category, one could also mention the insurance of bunkers; this is important because bunkers have become exceedingly expensive. Bunker insurance is in fact dealt with as a sort of cargo insurance. Most of the time, bunkers are bought by time charterers insured by them under their global cargo insurance policy.

12.4.1.6 Compulsory Insurance

The shipowner has to take into consideration the fact that, for certain type of risks, insurance has become compulsory on account of a number of international treaties.[28] Furthermore, if the shipowner wants to register the vessel within the European Union, or to trade within the European Union, he or she has to be aware of the compulsory insurance directive of 2009.[29] For all maritime claims for which there is a possibility to invoke the limitation of liability under the Convention on Limitation of Liability for Maritime Claims (LLMC), 1976 and its update, the European Union has imposed compulsory insurance for every vessel with a gross tonnage of 300 tons or higher; no trading of such a vessel will be allowed within Europe unless it is properly insured.

12.4.2 Purchase of Insurance Cover: Where Could a Shipowner or a Prospective Shipowner Go to Buy the Insurance Cover that He or She Will Need for a Successful and Safe Operation of His or Her Vessel?

The shipowner has to be aware that the market is fragmented and that various insurance products and policies are readily available; the assistance of an experienced and reliable marine insurance broker will be of the essence. The London insurance market plays a prominent role via Lloyd's of London and the traditional companies grouped together in the International Association of Underwriters. The leading P&I clubs (or mutuals) are based in London, Scandinavia (Norway and Sweden, Gard, Skuld and the Swedish Cub), Japan and the USA. For hull insurance, the market is shared mainly by Paris (4.1%), the Netherlands (4%), Italy (3.5%), Latin America (8.2%), Japan (8.3%), the UK market (Lloyd's) (16%) and the Nordic countries (Norway, Sweden, Finland, Denmark) (10.9%). The Norwegian Marine Insurance plan has been revised and updated and is now known as the Nordic Plan 2013. Zürich is well-known, but not exclusively, for reinsurance facilities.

12.4.3 By Whom Could These Various Risks Be Insured?

Lloyd's of London[30] is not an insurance company but an insurance marketplace where several marine insurers offer their business through various "syndicates" represented by an active underwriter. These syndicates are groups of individuals, known as "names", and will offer a consolidated facility/insurance against certain special risks. If one wants to insure a risk with Lloyd's of London, one needs also to rely on a Lloyd's marine insurance broker. The legal position of a marine insurance broker is dealt with in the English MIA 1906, articles 53 and 54. This broker will approach the proper syndicate, specialized in the particular risk, for instance H&M. Besides Lloyd's, one can also be insured by a traditional insurance company. If the risk is a large one, it will be insured by a number of these traditional insurance companies.[31] It is the duty of the marine insurance broker to place the risk with reliable and solvent insurers or insurance companies. The European authorities keep an eye on the financial health, or the solvency, of the various insurance companies doing business within the European Union, on the basis of the Solvency II directive,[32] which imposes the ratios which any insurance company has to comply with, in the same way as the Basel II directive imposes the ratios for banking institutions.

The operational liability of a shipowner is normally insured by a "mutual", or protection and indemnity club, abbreviated as P&I club.[33] These clubs constitute a special feature of the marine insurance industry. Although they claim that they are in the first place "indemnity" insurers, on the true construction of the facts, they insure the operational liability of a vessel owner against a number of operational risks to be agreed upon, on the basis of the rulebook or the "club rules" which each P&I club will offer to its members. Mutual insurance is indeed insurance and the basis of mutuality between the members of the club; that is, all the insured members (vessel owners) are all, at the same time, the insurers. This special feature is certainly not to be seen as a form of traditional marine insurance but it is a special approach for covering the many operational risks of an owner.

P&I insurance originated historically in the UK but now many maritime nations are home to some leading P&I clubs, such as the Scandinavian countries, the USA, Japan, China and Korea. Most of the leading P&I clubs are formally members of the International Group of P&I Clubs (IGA), with some noteworthy exceptions such as the China P&I Club and the Korean P&I Club.

No policy is issued; a certificate of entry and the insurance conditions are to be found in the "club rules". Also, no "premium" is to be paid but a "call", which in fact is an anticipated amount that the member will have to pay towards the various claims introduced by other P&I club members.

Twenty years ago, some of the traditional P&I clubs (non-members of IGA) also launched a novel product, which was in fact quite a deviation from the traditional principles of mutuality, offering P&I protection on the basis of a "fixed premium". The fixed premium clubs have not been that successful and are not so popular. It is said that these clubs are especially meant for small vessels or small fleet operators. Conversely, traditional P&I clubs offer a highly successful fixed premium insurance covering charterers' operational liabilities. An owner has to be fully aware that P&I clubs are not very happy with members who leave too rapidly, as they want to prevent "club hopping".

There are special rules for a member leaving a club: he or she will have to pay what is called a "release call" (or a release contribution); in addition the new club is required to charge at least the same "call" for the first year. One might wonder whether this practice is a serious limitation against free competition, since leaving the club is certainly not an easy and straightforward matter. Rule 45B of the club rules 2014 of the West of England contains nine subsections explaining the consequences for a member who leaves:

> If a Member ceases to be insured in respect of an insured vessel for any reason whatsoever, the Managers may at any time after termination of insurance of that vessel calculate and at the Member's request shall calculate, and notify such Member of the estimated amount of his liability for further Calls which the Association may levy in respect of such vessel, according to the Release formula determined from time to time by the Committee, together with the amount of all other sums due by such Member to the Association.

The release call may well amount to an additional year call; thus, leaving the club is certainly a step that should not be taken lightheartedly because it may cost the insured member a considerable amount of money.

The European Union is very mindful that the rules on free competition should be respected. This practice of P&I clubs or the IGA caught the attention of the European Union and the matter was seriously scrutinized at the time, followed by a number of protracted discussions between the European Commission and the IGA which resulted in a compromise,[34] though the Commission continues to keep a mindful eye on the practice of the P&I clubs as a recent examination illustrates.[35]

12.4.4 The Cost of Insurance: A Shipowner also Has to Address the Question "What Will the Insurance Cost?"

Marine insurance is, to a great extent, "market driven"; and there is great freedom of contract. As a consequence, what an owner will have to pay is, in many instances, the result of free negotiation and free competition. A new owner is advised to submit tenders to, at least, two or three P&I clubs before placing his or her marine insurance business.

An owner is also advised to budget for the amount for all the insurances he needs, drawing upon the advice of his marine insurance broker and also other specialist advisers in the marine insurance industry.

The proportion of marine insurance expenses to the total yearly operational expenses of an LPG tanker, for example, can amount to 8% of the overall expenses; for other vessels, a respective figure of 12% is considered normal. Statistical data with a detailed breakdown are provided by Drewry. These consultants also provide information of what a total safe insurance package will cost for various tonnages on a daily rate.

12.4.5 Specific Aspects of Marine Insurance

Assuming that the insurance policy is based on English law, the general principle of freedom of contract in English marine insurance should be noted: the insurer will compensate the insured for a loss in the matter and to the extent thereby agreed by the parties to the insurance contract, according to section 1 of the Marine Insurance Act.[36] As a consequence, proper cover is largely a question of contract.

With reference to hull insurance, the shipowner will have to seek protection against a number of "named" perils. It is the duty of a good broker to ensure that all these perils are properly listed and described. Traditional H&M insurance is not based on an "all risks" clause but on the approach that the risks have to be specifically named in order to be covered.

The shipowner has also to be very mindful of special insurance conditions qualified as "warranties", either expressed or implied.[37] These special conditions require strict compliance by the insured, otherwise the latter is in danger of losing automatically the benefit of insurance, as seen in *The Good Luck*[38] case.

In this regard, it is important to note that English law does not require the element of "causation" for a warranty to apply. If the insured does not strictly comply with the conditions of the warranty, even if the failure to do so is not in causal relation to the damage claimed for, he or she will nonetheless lose the benefit of the insurance.[39]

English law is peculiar with reference to the issue of causation; only the damage, which is "proximately" caused by a named peril, will be covered by the insurance. In other words, manifesting the legal maxim *causa proxima non remota spectatur*,[40] if the damage is not directly caused by an insured peril, the insured will not recover it even if the insured peril contributed to the damage but was not the direct cause of it. Finally, the special requirement of the utmost good faith in marine insurance must be considered.

The good faith requirement, according to section 17 of the MIA 1906, is also to be complied with; failure to do so will result in the insured losing the benefit of the insurance. In English law, the contract of marine insurance is said to be a contract of the "utmost good faith". Many cases have been decided and many books have been written on the subject. The main point, however, is that the good faith requirement has a double aspect: the insured is obliged to proceed to full disclosure of the risks or the interests he wants to be insured, and he should not misrepresent these risks.[41, 42]

But the changes introduced by the Insurance Act 2015 which will become applicable in August 2016, should not to be underestimated. The new Act makes a distinction between consumer and non-consumer insurance contracts.

This new statute changes the Marine Insurance Act 1906 to a large extent on some important issues such as duty to full disclosure, warranties and proportionate remedies for breach of fair presentation and fraudulent claims. Art 17 of the MIA 1906 is substantially altered in that the avoidance sanction attached to the duty of good faith is now abandoned and art 18 on the duty to provide full disclosure has been replaced by a duty to provide a fair presentation of the risk to insurer. Section 3 imposes upon the insured "a duty to make a fair presentation of the risk" to the insurer. Indeed the insured must disclose: "(a) every material circumstance which the insured knows or ought to know, or (b) failing that, a disclosure which gives the insurer sufficient information to put a prudent insurer on notice that it needs to make further enquiries …"

Section 4 defines what the insured knows or is supposed to know; and Section 5 defines the insurer's knowledge.

As a consequence the insurer has a more active role to play during the contract negotiations. As to warranties the changes are even more radical. Indeed Section 10 abolishes "any rule of law that a breach of warranty (express or implied) … results in the automatic discharge of the insurer's liability". So the automatic termination as held by "The Good Luck" comes to an end. See footnote 38. Section 11 provides that if the insured fails to comply with a term tending to reduce the risk, then the insurer may not rely on such breach if the non-compliance could not have increased the risk.

The Insurance Act 2015 also addresses the issue of "Fraudulent claims". And with reference to contract violations the Act provides is a phased regime of sanctions (proportionate remedies) according to the seriousness of the contract violation i.e. intentional or not.

12.5 Conclusion

Marine insurance is very special and can also be a tricky issue for a shipowner. A prospective new owner, before agreeing to a policy, should rely on experienced marine insurance, a maritime law consultancy and equally a very experienced maritime lawyer who can assist an owner on the exact meaning of the policy wording and the obligations of the insured in order to avoid disappointments. A shipowner should evidently also take into account the changes introduced by the new Insurance Act 2015, which comes into operation in August 2016.

Notes

1. See for example, BIMCO NEWBUILDCON, art. 31.
2. See for example, BIMCO NEWBUILDCON, art. 38(a)(ii).
3. Mar CAR 2007, cl.56.4.
4. In addition, in the United States, shipbuilders' risks are commonly underwritten under the American Institute Builders' Risks Clauses. For a comprehensive discussion of aspects of the builders' risk insurance, see Baris Soyer, "Evolving Nature of Builders' Risk Cover", published as Chapter 6 in B. Soyer and Andrew Tettenborn (eds), Ship Building, Sales and Finance (Informa 2015), p. 80.
5. ICBR 1988, sec. I and Mar CAR 2007, cls. 9.1 and 56.18.
6. See for example, *Hopewell Project Management v. Embank Preece Ltd* [1988] 1 Llloyd's Rep. 448.
7. ICBR 1988, cls.5.1 and 12 and MarCAR 2007, cls. 2.1 and 28.
8. ICBR 1988, cls.5.2 (failure to launch), 13 (general average and salvage), 17 (collision), 20 (sue and labour) and MarCAR 2007, cls. 33 (failure to launch), 4 (general average and salvage), 6 (collision), 25 (sue and labour).
9. ICBR 1988, cl. 19 and MarCAR 2007, cl. 7.
10. ICBR 1988, cls.21–24.
11. ICBR 1988, Institute War Clauses for Builders' Risks (1/6/88), Institute Strike Clauses for Builders' Risks (1/6/88). See also BIMCO NEWBUILDON, cl. 38(a) (ii) imposing on the builders the duty to effect and maintain at no cost to the buyer, Builders' Risk Insurance for the vessel and buyer's supplies on terms no less wide than Institute Clauses for Builders' Risk terms (1/6/88), including Institute War and Institute Strike Clauses.

12. War and strike risks are covered unless falling into the scope of the excluded risks. MarCAR 2007, cls.16–24.
13. ICBR 1988, cls. 5.1 and 8 and MarCAR 2007, cls. 3 and 57.
14. Marine Insurance Act 1906, s.50 (1).
15. Marine Insurance Act 1906, ss. 17–20, 33(3) and 55.
16. See for example the facts in *Continental Illinois National Bank* v *Alliance Assurance Co Ltd (The Captain Panagos DP)* [1986] 2 Lloyd's Rep 470.
17. Marine Insurance Act 1906, s.50(2). See also *Bovis International Inc. v. The Circle Ltd. Partnership* (1995) 49 Con. L.R. 12 at 22 (Staughton L.J.).
18. A duty to insure the vessel is normally imposed on the owner/mortgagor under the deed of covenant.
19. See for example the facts in *Schiffshypothekenbank Zu Luebeck A.G. v Norman Philip Compton (The "Alexion Hope")* [1988] 1 Lloyd's Rep 311 (CA).
20. The IMIC 1997 may be supplemented by the International Hull Mortgagees' Interest Clauses, 11/5/04.
21. IMIC 1997, Recital and cl.4.3.
22. IMIC 1997, cl.1.2.1.
23. IMIC 1997, cls. 1.1. and 3.1.
24. The mortgagee may also take separate insurance to cover the risk of the mortgagor's inability to repay their loan (mortgagee's financial loss cover). Such an insurance policy covers financial interest rather than a hull interest and therefore falls out of the scope of this chapter.
25. Mortgagee's Additional Perils (Pollution) clauses LSW 489, cls 1 and 2.
26. Mortgagee's Additional Perils (Pollution) clauses LSW 489, cls 4 and 5.
27. For definitions of these terms, see R.H. Brown, *Dictionary of Marine Insurance Terms* (4th Edition, Whiterby & C° Ltd, London) and the Lloyd's Glossary available at the Lloyd's of London website (http://www.lloyds.com/common/help/glossary).
28. A number of maritime and transport conventions provide compulsory insurance: the International Convention on Civil Liability for Oil Pollution Damage (CLC), 1969; the International Convention on Civil Liability for Bunker Oil Pollution Damage (BUNKER), 2001; the International Convention on Liability and Compensation for Damage in Connection with the Carriage of Hazardous and Noxious Substances by Sea, 2010 (2010 HNS Convention); the Athens Convention relating to the Carriage of Passengers and their Luggage by Sea (PAL Convention), 2002; and the Nairobi International Convention on the Removal of Wrecks, 2007.

29. Directive 2009/20/EC of the European Parliament and of the Council of 23 April 2009 on the Insurance of Shipowners for Maritime Claims ("Insurance Directive").
30. For further information on Lloyd's, please see http://www.lloyds.com/.
31. See further, http://www.iua.co.uk/.
32. Directive 2009/138/EC of the European Parliament and of the Council of 25 November 2009 on the taking-up and pursuit of the business of Insurance and Reinsurance (Solvency II), and the Commission Delegated Regulation (EU) of 10 October 2014 supplementing Directive 2009/138/EC of the European Parliament and of the Council on the taking-up and pursuit of the business of Insurance and Reinsurance (Solvency II) (to enter into force in 2016).
33. See for example, http://www.igpandi.org/.
34. Commission Decision of 12 April 1999 relating to a proceeding pursuant to Articles 85 and 86 of the EC Treaty and Articles 53 and 54 of the EEA Agreement (Cases No IV/D-1/30.373 P & I Clubs, IGA and No IV/D-1/37.143 P&I Clubs, Pooling Agreement), Official Journal of the European Communities L125/12 of 19. 05. 1999.
35. Press release Europe 26 August 2010; an investigation by the European commission concluded without further prosecution on 1 August 2012: "the market investigation was not sufficiently conclusive to confirm the Commissions' initial concerns". The full text of the press release is available at http://europa.eu/rapid/press-release_IP-12-873_en.htm?locale=FR.
36. MIA 1906, s. 1.
37. MIA 1906, ss. 33–41.
38. *Bank of Nova Scotia* v. *Hellenic Mutual War Risks Assn's (Bermuda) Ltd* (*The Good Luck*), [1991] 2 Lloyd's Rep. 191 (HL). Note however that the Insurance act 2015 has abolished this rule, see our comments below.
39. MIA 1906, s.33 (3).
40. MIA 1906, s. 55 (1).
41. MIA 1906, ss. 18–20.
42. The Insurance Act 2015 entered into force in August 2016. This new statute changed the MIA 1906 to a large extent on some important issues such as disclosure, warranties and proportionate remedies for breach of fair presentation and fraudulent claims. Art. 17 of the MIA 1906 is substantially altered in that the avoidance sanction attached to the duty of good faith is abandoned and art. 18 on the duty to provide full disclosure has been replaced by a duty to provide a fair presentation of the risk to the insurer. Also, the insurer has to play a much more active role during the contract negotiations.

References

Books

Bowtle, Gr. and McGuinness, K. (2001) The Law of Ship Mortgages, Informa, (particularly Chapter 5)
Brown, R. H. Dictionary of Marine Insurance Terms, 4th Edition, Whitherby & Co Ltd, London
Geoffrey Hudson, N., Madge, T. and Sturges, K. (2012) Marine Insurance Clauses, Informa.
Hazelwood, S. J. and Semark, D., P. &. I Clubs Law and Practice, 4th Edition, Informa.
Merkin, R. (2005) Marine Insurance Legislation, 3rd Edition, LLP.
Soyer, B. (2008) Reforming Marine and Commercial Insurance Law (eds), Informa.
Soyer, B. & Tettenborn, A. (2015), Ship *Building, Sales and Finance* (eds), Informa.
Soyer, B., Warranties in Marine Insurance, 2nd Edition, Routeledge.
Thomas, D. R. (2006), Marine Insurance: The Law in Transition, Informa.

Book Chapters/Articles

Blackwood, G. (2013), The Pre-contractual Duty of (Utmost) Good Faith: The Past and the Future, Lloyd's Maritime and Commercial Law Quarterly, 311.
Century Primer on the History, Structure and Future of the Backbone of Marine Insurance, Tulane Maritime Law Journal, 169.
Gold, E. Gard Handbook on P&I Insurance, 5th Edition.
Herschaft, J. A. (2005), Not Your Average Coffee Shop: Lloyd's of London—A Twenty-First Century Primer on the History, Structure and Future of the Backbone of Marine Insurance, Tulane Maritime Law Journal, 169.
Hertzell, D. and Burgoyne, L. (2013), The Law Commission and Insurance Contract Law, Reform: An Update, Journal of International Maritime Law 19.
Lemon II, R. T. (2007), Allocation of Marine Risks: An Overview of the Marine Insurance Package, Tulane Law Review, 1467.
MacDonald Eggers, P. (1998), Sue and Labour and Beyond: The Assured's Duty of Mitigation, Lloyd's Maritime and Commercial Law Quarterly, 228.
MacDonald Eggers, P. (2012), The Past and Future of English Insurance Law: Good faith and Warranties, UCL Journal of Law and Jurisprudence, 211.
Martin, S. (2003), Marine Protection and Indemnity Insurance Conduct, Intent, and Punitive Damages, Tulane Maritime Law Journal, 45.
Passman, M. H. (2009), Interpreting Sea Piracy Clauses in Marine Insurance Contracts, Journal of Maritime Law and Commerce, 59.
Pfeifer, R. M. (2004–5), Navigating Through the Shoals of the Marine Hull Policy: A Chart for Insurers, University of San Francisco Maritime Law Journal, 89.

Røsæg, E. (2000), Compulsory Maritime Insurance, Scandinavian Institute of Maritime Law Yearbook, 13.

Schoenbaum, T. J. (1998), The Duty of Utmost Good Faith in Marine Insurance Law: A Comparative Analysis of American and English Law, Journal of Maritime Law and Commerce, 1.

Soady, R. (2013), A Critical Analysis of Piracy, Hijacking, Ransom Payments and Whether Modern London Insurance Market Clauses Provide Sufficient Protection, Journal of Maritime Law and Commerce, 1.

Soyer, B. (2012), Defenses Available to a Marine Insurer, Lloyd's Maritime and Commercial Law Quarterly, 199.

Soyer, B. (2013), Beginning of a New Era for Insurance Warranties, Lloyd's Maritime and Commercial Law Quarterly, 384.

Soyer, B. (2015), Evolving Nature of Builders' Risk Cover, Published in B. Soyer & Andrew Tettenborn (eds), Ship Building, Sales and Finance, Informa.

13

Maritime Investment Appraisal and Budgeting

Stefan Albertijn, Wolfgang Drobetz, and Max Johns

13.1 Introduction

Shipping has always been a volatile business, one that is tightly linked to the business cycle. However, the recent global financial and economic crisis that started in 2008 is unprecedented. Industry revenues followed booming world trade fairly closely up until mid-2008, with the ClarkSea index of freight rates reaching its peak at the end of 2007. As the global financial crisis deepened in 2008, the index dropped almost 85% by April 2009. The market values of vessels followed freight rates down, with the Clarkson Second Hand Price Index falling roughly 40% during the same period. Since then,

---

S. Albertijn
Baltic Exchange Ltd., St. Mary Axe, London EC3A 8BH, United Kingdom

Ocean Finance and Consultancy BVBA (OFICON) and Hamant Beratungs- und Investitionsgesellschaft mbH, Zijwegel 11, 2920 Kalmthout, Belgium

W. Drobetz (✉)
Faculty of Business Administration, Hamburg University, Von-Melle-Park 5, 20146 Hamburg, Germany

M. Johns
German Shipowners' Association (Verband Deutscher Reeder, VDR), Burchardstraße 24, 20095 Hamburg, Germany

freight rates and vessel prices have remained low and are still far below the pre-crisis levels.

Boom-and-bust cycles in investment are widely studied phenomena in economics. Kydland and Prescott (1982) show that these cycles are more pronounced when there is a lag between investment plans and their realizations. The shipping industry is an ideal example. Supply is essentially fixed in the short run, and firms face long lags (12–36 months) between the order and delivery of a new vessel, while the uncertain demand for sea transport may change during this waiting period. Kalouptsidi's (2014) "time-to-build" model for dry-bulk shipping predicts that vessels' dynamic entry and exit combined with cyclical variation in the construction lag due to shipyard capacity constraints have a substantial impact on the level of investment. In a similar vein, Greenwood and Hanson (2015) study the link between boom-and-bust cycles and the return on capital in the dry-bulk sector. High vessel earnings just before the recent crisis were associated with high second-hand vessel prices and heavy investments in new vessels, but also with forecasted low future industry returns. Their theoretical model is based on behavioral biases and bounded rationality on behalf of market participants. In particular, shipping firms over-extrapolated exogenous demand shocks and partially neglected the investment response of competitors, that is they underestimated the investment response of their industry peers when reacting to demand shocks ("competition neglect"). Therefore, firms overpaid for vessels, overinvested in the boom because they did not foresee the endogenous supply response to the demand shocks, and have become disappointed by the low subsequent returns.

The experience from the recent financial and shipping crisis that started in 2008 indicates that maritime investment appraisal and capital budgeting can become a difficult task. In "normalized" and efficient markets (with many willing buyers and sellers and available credit), the price of a vessel is what a knowledgeable and independent buyer would pay to acquire the vessel from a seller who is equally well informed and trades voluntarily. Accordingly, in the past, the price of a vessel was routinely derived from the price of comparable transactions (the so-called "market approach" or "mark-to-market" approach). However, the question whether prices and fundamental or intrinsic values are the same—in particular, during crisis times with high volatility and high uncertainty as well as illiquid markets—follows a long-lasting debate in financial theory. The fundamental (or intrinsic) value of a vessel is based on the expected future financial benefits which both equity and debt investors can expect. The valuation approach that receives most academic credibility is the "income approach" or the discounted cash flow (DCF) valuation approach.

In the DCF approach, the fundamental value of a vessel is the present value of its expected cash flows, discounted at a rate that reflects their riskiness.

First, the approach requires a model for future cash-flow estimates. Second, the appropriate discount rate should be derived from standard asset pricing models. Therefore, the DCF approach is also commonly referred to as the "mark-to-model" approach. Arguably, fundamental values derived from the DCF approach are based on a long-term view, which offsets short-term market imperfections at least to some extent. The DCF approach is commonly used and widely accepted for the valuation of companies (e.g. in M&A transactions) and many long-lived assets (e.g. real estate, aircrafts and power plants). In the shipping industry, the market approach is still the dominant valuation method.[1] However, the recent crisis has generated discussions among shipowners and financial institutions, both expressing concerns of a divergence between market prices and fundamental values of commercial vessels. As a result, valuation approaches based on future earnings estimates have gained a lot of attention and are nowadays more widely used in the shipping industry.[2]

Understanding what determines the value of a vessel and how to estimate that value is a prerequisite for making value-enhancing decisions in the shipping industry. For example, shipowners depend on vessel valuations for accounting (e.g. an impairment test), financing (e.g. when issuing bonds or raising additional equity in the capital markets) and controlling purposes. Buyers and sellers of vessels make investment or divestment decisions based on valuations. Similarly, shipbrokers use valuations when advising their clients on purchase transactions. Shipping banks require value appraisals to accompany a loan application and to determine borrower compliance with existing loan covenants. Appraisals also determine bank compliance with capital adequacy standards and provisions for potential credit losses (Albertijn et al. 2011). Finally, vessel valuations are required as a reserve price in court sales, in a wide range of legal disputes and for insurance agents to determine coverage levels.

This chapter presents the basic principles of vessel valuation. We first introduce the market approach before illustrating the long term asset value (LTAV) method as an example of the DCF approach. We then discuss the necessary conditions for the equivalence of market prices and fundamental values of vessels before comparing the valuation levels and other commonly used financial ratios of listed shipping companies with a matched sample of manufacturing firms.

13.2 Market Approach

The market price of a vessel is determined by auction pricing, where the transaction price is accepted as the clearing price between willing and informed buyers and sellers. The market approach (or "relative valuation approach") is by far the most commonly used valuation method in the shipping industry and is based on how similar vessels are priced in the market. In particular, a prospective vessel buyer decides how much to pay for a comparable vessel by analyzing the prices paid in earlier transactions. This approach involves three steps. First, the buyer must identify a set of factors that determine comparability and value. Second, the buyer must search for a sufficient number of comparable (reference) transactions, that is a combination of the closest matches and the most recent transactions. Accordingly, the market approach is also referred to as the "mark-to-market" or "last-done" approach. Third, the estimated price for the vessel under investigation is computed as the mean or median price for the set of comparable transactions.

To identify a comparable vessel, the first matching criterion is the vessel type. For example, if the goal is to determine the price of a Capesize bulker vessel, comparable transactions should involve earlier sales of this type of vessel. Other vessel types, such as Panamax bulker vessels or even more so vessels from different segments of the market (e.g. tanker or container ships), are different in the routes they can serve, the cargo they can carry, their technology and their cost/revenue structure. Within a given vessel type, Adland and Koekebakker (2007) find that the second-hand price of a vessel can be well-described as a non-linear function of three factors: age, size (measured in deadweight tonnage—DWT) and the state of the freight market. As age determines the number of remaining years of use, it is negatively related to the vessel price. Newer vessels with more advanced technology may also be more fuel efficient and generate lower operating costs (e.g. lower repair and maintenance costs). In contrast, larger vessels can carry more cargo, thus there is a positive relationship with the price. Furthermore, as freight rates increase, vessel prices will go up; a strong positive relationship between the state of the freight market and the vessel price exists because freight rates are the cash flows a vessel can generate.[3]

Another important price determinant is the transaction date. Arguably, more recent transaction prices are more relevant than older ones. For example, a more recent purchase price might reflect a new use for a vessel or a new industry environment. Finally, some other factors that affect the value of a vessel are: the type of the main engine; confirmed time charter contracts with creditworthy counterparties; loading equipment (derricks and cranes); shipyard (original builder); and location (where the vessel was at the time of the sale).

To illustrate the identification of comparable transactions, assume that an investor wants to estimate the price of the *Blue Manaslu* in June 2014. The *Blue Manaslu* is a young, three-year-old Capesize bulk carrier with a capacity of 179,280 dwt. Table 13.1 summarizes a list of Capesize bulker sales

Table 13.1 Sales of Capesize ships

Sale date	Vessel name	Sale price (USD millions)	Year built	Age at sale (years)	Dwt (thousands)	Baltic Capesize Index[a]
June 2014	Blue Manaslu	52.00	2011	3	179.28	2,451
May 2014	Cape Oceania	10.40	1994	20	152.03	2,423
May 2014	F. D. Luigi d'Amato	40.00	2006	8	180.18	2,423
April 2014	Elegant Star	41.00	2005	9	177.22	2,364
April 2014	A Duckling	20.80	1999	15	171.20	2,364
April 2014	Lian Fu Star	18.50	1997	17	172.09	2,364
April 2014	Shagangfirst Era	54.50	2010	4	181.45	2,364
April 2014	Bulk China	55.00	2013	1	179.11	2,364
March 2014	Conches	53.50	2011	3	179.08	2,239
January 2014	Sanko Power	49.40	2010	4	181.20	2,142
December 2013	Pacific Challenger	12.00	1995	18	149.21	1,945
December 2013	Glory Advance	10.00	1996	17	171.04	1,945
December 2013	Houheng 3	50.00	2012	1	179.90	1,945
December 2013	Cape Provence	34.00	2005	8	177.02	1,945
November 2013	Pacific Crystal	16.00	1994	19	264.16	1,931
October 2013	Shiga	28.00	2006	7	176.99	1,809
October 2013	Grand Clipper	15.50	1996	17	168.15	1,809
October 2013	Atlantic Bridge	27.50	2005	8	177.11	1,809
October 2013	Su-oh	16.50	1997	16	171.08	1,809
October 2013	Cape Condor	24.00	2004	9	180.18	1,809
October 2013	Yangtze Marvel	17.00	1999	14	170.97	1,809
September 2013	Chrismir	13.50	1997	16	159,83	1,634
September 2013	Tai Fu Star	16.30	1998	15	178.63	1,634
August 2013	Bulk Canada	41.20	2012	1	179.40	1,559
August 2013	Lilac	36.00	2009	4	179.64	1,559
August 2013	CSK Enterprise	11.00	1997	16	168.40	1,559
August 2013	NSS Bonanza	12.30	1996	17	170.91	1,559

(continued)

Table 13.1 (continued)

Sale date	Vessel name	Sale price (USD millions)	Year built	Age at sale (years)	Dwt (thousands)	Baltic Capesize Index[a]
August 2013	Cape Shanghai	28.00	2007	6	174.11	1,559
June 2013	Mona River	16.30	2000	13	171.01	1,468
June 2013	Atlantic Princess	20.20	2003	10	180.20	1,468
June 2013	Mineral Sines	20.00	2002	11	172.32	1,468
June 2013	Star Fortune	15.30	1999	14	170.97	1,468
May 2013	F Elephant	16.16	1989	24	275.98	1,487
May 2013	Mona Century	16.00	2000	13	172.04	1,487
May 2013	Magnolia	34.00	2009	4	179.64	1,487
May 2013	Hai Shi	12.80	1997	16	172.09	1,487
April 2013	Seakoh	16.25	2000	13	172.25	1,511
April 2013	Pacific Tiara	25.25	2004	9	180.31	1,511
April 2013	Brilliant River	9.00	1994	19	154.25	1,511
April 2013	Tamou	27.00	2005	8	177.24	1,511
February 2013	Cape Awoba	12.00	1996	17	171.98	1,528
February 2013	Sri Prem Putli	44.40	1993	20	280.54	1,528
February 2013	Dong-A Saturn	7.50	1994	19	149.40	1,528
January 2013	Crystal Star	11.80	1998	15	178.63	1,571
December 2012	Vogebulker	10.15	1999	13	169.17	1,733
December 2012	Bulk Asia	19.00	2001	11	170.58	1,733
December 2012	Bulk Europe	19.00	2001	11	169.77	1,733
November 2012	Cape Australia	7.00	1990	22	149.51	1,796
November 2012	Cape Camellia	17.50	2000	12	172.50	1,796
November 2012	Aquabella	11.00	1995	17	161.01	1,796
November 2012	Great Pheasant	17.50	2000	12	178.82	1,796
November 2012	Amy N	25.00	1997	15	322.46	1,796
October 2012	Matilde	12.00	1997	15	160.01	1,908
October 2012	Rubin Ace	10.00	1996	16	151.28	1,908
October 2012	NSS Advance	10.00	1995	17	173.25	1,908

Table 13.1 (continued)

Sale date	Vessel name	Sale price (USD millions)	Year built	Age at sale (years)	Dwt (thousands)	Baltic Capesize Index[a]
September 2012	Azul Frontier	21.40	2003	9	177.25	2,051
September 2012	Gry Bulker	35.00	2009	3	174.79	2,051
September 2012	Hebei Winner	12.00	1993	19	258,08	2,051
September 2012	Rubin Hope	15.60	1999	13	170.41	2,051
September 2012	General	12.00	1992	20	238.82	2,051
September 2012	Orient Vega	36.70	2011	1	181.43	2,051
September 2012	Orchid River	12.90	1997	15	170.90	2,051
August 2012	Dong-A Ares	8.00	1994	18	151.44	2,123
August 2012	Chikuzen Maru	9.00	1993	19	150.84	2,123
August 2012	China Act	6.65	1995	17	151.69	2,123
July 2012	Baosteel Education	45.00	2009	3	228.53	2,175
July 2012	Christina Bulker	38.00	2011	1	179.43	2,175
June 2012	Road Runner	9.55	1993	19	147.05	2,227
May 2012	Cape America	9.00	1991	21	149.52	2,228
April 2012	Regena N	33.00	2006	6	180.28	2,237
March 2012	Vogesailor	11.60	1996	16	164.19	2,253

[a]Trailing one-year monthly average
Source: All data are taken from the Clarkson Shipping Intelligence Network (SIN) database

between March 2012 and May 2014, which can be used for relative valuation purposes.[4] The table provides information on the age and the size of vessels sold. In addition, it shows the state of the freight market at the time of a transaction. The trailing one-year average monthly Baltic Capesize Index (BCI) is used as a proxy for the market environment, reflecting the supply and demand forces in the dry-bulk shipping markets. Other factors, such as the vessel's overall condition, the type of main engine, fuel prices, steel prices (determining the scrap value) and the lending market environment (influencing how much of the purchase price banks are willing to lend) are omitted from the analysis.

There are several close matches for the *Blue Manaslu*. Most recently, the *Conches*, a vessel of the same age and size, was sold for USD53.5 million. As it was sold only three months earlier (in March 2014), it seems like a perfect comparison in our example. Another comparable transaction involves the *Shagangfirst Era*, which is a slightly larger vessel and was only one year older at sale; it changed ownership for USD54.5 million. Two other comparable vessels, the *Lilac* and the *Magnolia* (both of similar size and only one year older than the *Blue Manaslu* at the time of the sales) sold for only USD36.0 and USD34.0 million, respectively. These much lower transaction prices are attributable to the lower charter rates at the time of sale. In particular, while the trailing one-year average monthly BCI was 2,364 index points in April 2014, it was only 1,559 in August 2013 and even lower at 1,487 in May 2013, when the *Lilac* and the *Magnolia* were sold, respectively.

Apart from the *Conches*, there are only two other vessels in the sample with the same age at sale as the *Blue Manaslu*; however, both transactions (the sales of the *Gry Bulker* and the *Baosteel Education*) had occurred already in 2012, when freight rates were below the levels in June 2014, our evaluation date. Moreover, there were several transactions involving vessels with similar sizes as the *Blue Manaslu*, though these vessels were either younger or older when sold (such as the *Houheng 3*, the *Cape Condor* or the *Bulk Canada*, among the more recent transactions). While the *Conches* seems to be an almost perfect match for the *Blue Manaslu* in our example, an investor should clearly not rely on one single comparable transaction as the basis for an investment decision. However, no other match exists that is perfect in every dimension. Using the next best matches available in our sample, a comparable transaction analysis leads to a price range from as low as USD34.0 million (the *Magnolia*) to USD54.5 million (the *Shagangfirst Era*). This broad price range is only of limited use in practice. Based on all comparable transactions mentioned, the simple mean price is USD42.47 million.

13 Maritime Investment Appraisal and Budgeting

The main problem of the approach used so far is that it only allows controlling for differences in a single variable. Therefore, as shown in the example, a univariate comparison can lead to very wide price ranges. To account for the multivariate (and possibly even non-linear) relationship between vessel prices and price determinants and to narrow down the price range, ordinary least squares (OLS) regression analysis can be implemented to derive a predicted transaction price. As there is only one almost exact match for the *Blue Manaslu*, we now use all the information provided in Table 13.1 in a systematic way and estimate the following multivariate regression to determine the relationship between the vessel price and the pricing factors[5]:

$$TP_i = \alpha + \beta_1 \cdot Age_i + \beta_2 \cdot Size_i + \beta_3 \cdot Freight_i + \varepsilon_i \qquad (13.1)$$

where TP_i denotes the paid transaction price for vessel i (the running index i refers to each of the 70 transactions in Table 13.1), Age_i is the age of a vessel at the date of the transaction, $Size_i$ is the vessel size (measured in thousand dwt) and $Freight_i$ is the trailing one-year average monthly BCI at the date of the transaction (as a proxy for the state of the freight market).[6] α is a (constant) intercept term, β_1, β_2 and β_3 are sensitivity coefficients, and ε_i is an error term. Using OLS regression methodology to estimate the intercept term and the sensitivity coefficients, the linear relationship between the transaction price and the pricing factors is[7]:

$$TP_i = 5.8628 + (-1.7976) \cdot Age_i + 0.1280 \cdot Size_i + 0.0083 \cdot Freight_i \qquad (13.2)$$

Based on the adjusted R-squared (the standard measure of the goodness-of-fit), the right-hand side variables explain as much as 80% of the cross-sectional variability in the observed transaction prices (not reported). The signs of the estimated coefficients are as expected: size and state of the freight market have a positive influence on predicted transaction prices, while age has a negative impact. Given these coefficient estimates, the *Blue Manaslu*'s predicted price using its fundamental characteristics (and trailing one-year freight rates of 2,451 index points) is:

$$\begin{aligned} TP_{Blue\ Manaslu} &= 5.8628 + (-1.7976) \cdot 3 + 0.1280 \cdot 179.28 \\ &\quad + 0.0083 \cdot 2{,}451 \\ &= \$\,43.76 \text{ million} \end{aligned} \qquad (13.3)$$

This baseline regression framework can be refined in two ways. First, as Capesize freight rates are highest at the end of our sample period, more recent transactions will be more informative and possibly exhibit higher prices (all else being equal). To determine whether there is an additional price effect during the later months of the sample period, we extend the regression to include a dummy variable $I_{Recent,i}$, which takes the value of 1 if the transaction was one of the 35 most recent transactions, which occurred between May 2013 and May 2014, and 0 otherwise. Second, we add the interaction term $\left(I_{Recent,i} \cdot Age_i\right)$, which allows the age–price relationship to vary between the two subperiods. With the new dummy variable and the interaction term, the following extended regression mode can be estimated[8]:

$$TP_i = \alpha + \beta_1 \cdot Age_i + \beta_2 \cdot Size_i + \beta_3 \cdot Freight_i \\ + \beta_4 \cdot I_{Recent,i} + \beta_5 \cdot I_{Recent,i} \cdot Age_i + \varepsilon_i \quad (13.4)$$

Using OLS to estimate unbiased α and β coefficients, the relationship between the transaction price and the pricing factors is:

$$TP_i = -5.1174 + (-1.3412) \cdot Age_i + 0.1356 \cdot Size_i + 0.0090 \cdot Freight_i \\ + 13.2657 \cdot I_{Recent,i} + (-0.7137) \cdot I_{Recent,i} \cdot Age_i \quad (13.5)$$

The additional variables contain incremental information and add explanatory power (not reported), as indicated by the regression's goodness-of-fit; the adjusted R-squared increases to 86%, suggesting that the extended model captures the cross-sectional variation of observed transaction prices very well. Using the *Blue Manaslu*'s fundamental characteristics, the predicted transaction price is:

$$\begin{aligned} TP_{Blue\ Manaslu} &= -5.1174 + (-1.3412) \cdot 3 + 0.1356 \cdot 179.28 \\ &+ 0.0090 \cdot 2,451 + 13.2657 \cdot 1 + (-0.7137) \cdot 1 \cdot 3 \\ &= \$48.35\text{million} \end{aligned} \quad (13.6)$$

The coefficient estimates for the variables age, size and state of the freight market are similar to the baseline model, and their signs remain unchanged. The coefficient of the dummy variable $I_{Recent,i}$, indicating a recent sale, is positive; accordingly, there is a USD13.27 million premium in the price of transactions in the second half of the sample, even after controlling for all other factors. The coefficient of the interaction term with age, $\left(I_{Recent,i} \cdot Age_i\right)$, is negative, suggesting that the price discount for older vessels is larger in the more recent transactions during the second half of the sample. Because the *Blue Manaslu* is a young vessel, the estimated transaction price *TP* from the extended regression model is higher than that from the baseline model (USD48.35 million versus USD43.76 million).

The *Blue Manaslu* was sold for USD52.00 million in June 2014, thus the estimated price from the extended regression model is close to the actual transaction price. The relatively small pricing error is attributable to the model's high goodness-of-fit.[9] As a result, the regression approach seems particularly suited for the relative valuation of vessels, making sense of large and sometimes contradictory data about the relevant pricing factors.

While the market approach works accurately in our simple example, it nevertheless has some technical limitations. Most notably, the sample of comparable transactions is relatively small with only 70 observations. In small samples with asymmetric distributions of the model variables, a few large outliers could drive the results.[10] Furthermore, a standard OLS assumption is that the explanatory variables are independent of each other. For example, as size grows over time due to technological progress, age and size of vessels tends to be negatively correlated. High correlation across explanatory variables creates "multicollinearity" problems, which may negatively affect the precision of the estimated coefficients.

13.3 Discounted Cash-Flow Approach

13.3.1 LTAV: Theory

DCF valuation relates the value of an asset to the present value of expected future cash flows on that asset. Accordingly, under a DCF approach the value of an asset is not what someone perceives it to be worth, but it is a function of the expected cash flows occurring at some time in the future. The value of a vessel is obtained by discounting free cash flows (i.e. the amount of cash available for distribution among both equity and debt holders after taxes and reinvestment needs) at the weighted average cost of capital (WACC). Embedded in this approach are the tax benefits of debt (in the form of the after-tax cost of debt in the cost of capital) and the expected additional financial risk associated with debt (in the form of higher cost of equity and debt with increasing leverage). This so-called WACC approach is widely recognized in theory and valuation practice.[11] The LTAV method to evaluate vessels, which has been promoted by the Hamburg Shipbrokers' Association (Vereinigung Hamburger Schiffsmakler und Schiffsagenten e.V., VHSS) in cooperation with Pricewaterhouse Coopers, is based on the WACC approach.[12] The academic origin of this fundamental valuation approach in the shipping literature can be traced back to Kavussanos and Alizadeh (2002).

In particular, the LTAV of a vessel is obtained by discounting the free cash flows (FCF) to debt and equity holders at the WACC:

$$LTAV = \sum_{t=1}^{T} \frac{FCF_t}{(1+WACC)^t} = \sum_{t=1}^{T} \frac{(C_t - OPEX_t)}{(1+WACC)^t} + \frac{(RV_T)}{(1+WACC)^T} \quad (13.7)$$

where the free cash flows (FCF_t) in a future period t are obtained using the forecasted charter revenues (C_t) minus the expected operating costs ($OPEX_t$) for the vessel. In addition, at the end of the vessel's economic useful life (in period T), there is a residual (or scrap) value (RV_t). Implicit in this approach is the assumption that it captures both the tax benefits of borrowing and the expected bankruptcy costs.[13] The cash flows discounted are cash flows to the vessel, computed as if the vessel had no debt and no tax benefits from interest expenses. The effects associated with leverage and taxes are incorporated in the WACC, which is used as the discount rate.

As the WACC approach is based on the free cash flows available for distribution among equity and debt holders, the expected flows must be discounted using a weighted average of the required rates of return for the different sources of capital, both equity and debt. The standard expression for WACC is:

$$WACC = \frac{D}{V} \cdot r_D \cdot (1-\tau_C) + \frac{E}{V} \cdot r_E \quad (13.8)$$

where r_D is the cost of debt, r_E the cost of equity and τ_C the effective corporate tax rate. D is the market value of debt, E is the market value of equity and $V = D + E$. As interest is a tax-deductible expense (as opposed to dividend payouts to the shareholders), the WACC method uses the after-tax cost of debt, which is $r_D \cdot (1-\tau_C)$. As the debt ratio increases, the cost of equity increases due to the increasing financial risk (in particular, the increasing residual risk to equity holders), but the WACC nevertheless declines. Standard textbook theory shows that this decline is not caused by the use of "cheap" debt replacing "expensive" equity, though the WACC falls because of the "tax shields" on debt interest payments.

In applications related to shipping, it is normally not necessary to take into account the tax benefits of debt because many important shipping nations have implemented a tonnage tax regime, where taxation is independent of the earned profits. With $\tau_C = 0$, the WACC formula without corporate taxes is:

$$WACC = \frac{D}{V} \cdot r_D + \frac{E}{V} \cdot r_E \qquad (13.9)$$

The cost of debt and the cost of equity are weighted by the relative proportions of debt and equity, denoted as $\left(D/V\right)$ and $\left(E/V\right)$, respectively. The no-tax WACC formula still accounts for the effects of different degrees of financial leverage. The use of a constant WACC works for any patterns of cash flows as long as the degree of financial leverage, which a single project or firm can support, remains constant. Commercial vessels are typically financed with a 50–70% debt (while much higher gearing was common before the financial crisis), though leverage decreases over time as the loan is paid back.[14] However, assuming efficient capital markets (in the absence of taxes, information asymmetry or agency problems), Modigliani and Miller (1958) show that the WACC is constant and independent of a firm's capital structure. It follows that the cost of equity must increase with increasing financial leverage (i.e. with increasing residual risk of the equity holders). In the no-tax WACC formula, this increase in the cost of equity offsets any effects of changes in the weights, $\left(D/V\right)$ and $\left(E/V\right)$. As most shipowners have opted for the tonnage tax system (and not taking account of other possible market imperfections), the no-tax WACC formula depends only on business risk, and the value of a vessel is independent of its capital structure.

Ship financing is often based on the agreement of variable interest rates linked to interbank rates (e.g. the London Interbank Offered Rate, LIBOR, plus a credit risk premium or credit spread). Therefore, in practice, it is common to refer to the interest rate swap markets in determining the cost of debt r_D. A swap rate indicates the cost for hedging the risk of a change in the short-term interest rate by swapping to a fixed rate payment for the same maturity. The amount of the credit spread depends on many factors, such as the ability to realize the value of the vessel in the case of insolvency and the availability of long-term charters with high creditworthiness.[15]

The determination of the cost of equity r_E is more difficult and requires concepts from asset pricing theory. The most widely used model among financial practitioners is the capital asset pricing model (CAPM).[16] The cost of equity r_E according to the CAPM is the expected rate of return on equity:

$$r_E = r_f + \beta_E \cdot MRP \qquad (13.10)$$

where r_f is the risk-free rate, β_E is a firm's stock market beta (or equity beta) and MRP is the market-wide risk premium (i.e. the expected stock market return in excess of the risk-free rate). By definition, a risk-free asset has no default risk and no reinvestment risk. Therefore, the appropriate risk-free rate r_f depends on when the cash flows are expected to occur (term structure), which will vary across maturities. For vessel valuation purposes, the time horizon is generally long, thus a long-term (or duration matched) risk-free rate is preferable to a short-term rate (if the investor has to pick one). In contrast to government bond yields, the market risk premium MRP is not revealed in market prices. Therefore, most investors refer to historical premiums, i.e. the historical excess returns of stocks over riskless securities.

Another parameter in the CAPM is a firm's stock market beta, or equity beta β_E. The CAPM assumes that investors are well diversified, thus the only risk an investor perceives in an investment is the risk that cannot be diversified (i.e. market risk or systematic risk). The stock market beta is the model's measure of systematic risk contribution.[17] In particular, the CAPM asserts that investors care only about stock or project betas, because these measure the risk components which investors who hold a fully diversified portfolio (or the market portfolio) cannot diversify. Empirically, a firm's stock market beta can be estimated using OLS regression analysis, with the firm's stock return as the dependent variable and the market return (e.g. the S&P 500 index) as the explanatory variable.[18] The estimated beta coefficient indicates the percentage change in the firm's stock price in response to a 1% change in the market index, on average; a sensitivity coefficient above or below unity implies more or less risk in the sense of adding to or reducing the risk of the market portfolio, respectively. Therefore, projects contributing more risk (higher market beta) require a higher expected rate of return for equity investors who want them. Projects contributing less risk (lower market beta) require a lower expected rate of return.

The estimated equity beta is usually assumed to depend on three factors: (i) the cyclicality of a firm's operations (business risk); (ii) its operating leverage (i.e. the ratio of fixed costs to total costs); and (iii) its financial leverage. Given highly cyclical cash flows, high operating leverage and high financial leverage, one expects that firms in the shipping industry exhibit high stock market betas.[19] Drobetz *et al.* (2016b) find evidence for beta dynamics of shipping stocks that match the fundamental risk characteristics of the industry. In particular, the betas of listed shipping companies show pronounced industry-specific time-series variation compared to the average S&P 500 firm. As expected, changes in both economic conditions and industry-specific risk factors explain a large proportion of the beta variation in the cross-section of shipping firms and over time.

A final caveat is that a firm's beta (or asset beta, which is the leverage adjusted equity beta) only applies for valuing a single project (e.g. a vessel) with the same business risk characteristics as the firm. Single projects with different risk characteristics compared to the average project of a firm must be evaluated by using different asset betas. Failure to adjust the project cost of capital for differences in business risk, and instead to use a unique WACC within the firm, leads to hurdle rates that are either too high or too low for a given project, leading to value-destroying capital budgeting decisions.[20]

13.3.2 LTAV: An Example

The LTAV method is illustrated using a fictitious, charter-free, ten-year old, 1,700 TEU container vessel. The vessel has an expected total economic life of 25 years. All necessary assumptions and the computation of the vessel's LTAV are shown in Table 13.2.[21]

The first step in the WACC approach is to model the vessel's expected free cash flows over the remaining 15 years. We assume that the low current gross charter rate (to be earned in 2015) of USD7,500 per day adjusts linearly to the historical average within the next four years (by 2018).[22,23] After 2018, daily gross charter rates are assumed to grow only with the expected inflation rate of 2% per year. When the vessel reaches an age of 20 years (in 2025), an old ship reduction rate of 15% is applied.[24] The resulting net annual charter revenues depend on the number of available running days (depending on whether it is a year with or without service dry docking), the vessel's utilization rate and the amount of paid fees and commissions. Annual operating expenses include tonnage taxes and are also assumed to grow with the expected inflation rate of 2% per year. At the end of the economic life time (in 2030), the vessel's scrap value will be realized, which depends on the number of lightweight tons and the steel price (per lightweight ton). Based on net annual charter rates, annual operating expenses and the scrap value, the free cash flows can be computed in each calendar year for the vessel's remaining lifetime (as shown in column 12 in Table 13.2).[25]

Table 13.2 LTAV sample computation

Available running days	358 = maximum number of available running days (charter days) in a typical year
Utilization rate	343 = maximum number of available running days in years with dry docking (class renewal) 95% = booked days as a percentage of total available running days
Daily gross charter rate	USD7,500 = current charter rate for 2015
Historical charter rate	USD13,000 = 10-year historical average monthly charter rate
Old ship reduction rate	15% = reduction in the daily gross charter rate for ships with age ≥ 20 years
Fees and commissions	6.5% = ship management fee and freight commissions as a percentage of gross daily charter rate
Daily operating expenses	USD6,400[a]
Inflation rate	2.0%, affects the charter rate, operating expenses and scrap value
Tax rate	0%, assumes a non-tax paying owner
Cost of capital (WACC)	6.75% (see p. 302 for derivation)

Model year	Calendar year	Ship age (years)	Available running days[b]	Actual booked days[c]	Gross charter rate per day[d] (USD)	Net annual charter revenue[e] (USD)	Annual operating expense[a] (USD)	Taxes (USD)	EBIAT[f] (USD)	Scrap value[g] (USD)	Free cash flow[h] (USD)	Present value factor	Present value (USD)
(1)	(2)	(3)	(4)	(5)	(6)	(7)	(8)	(9)	(10)	(11)	(12)	(13)	(14)
1	2015	10	358	340	7,500	2,385	2,336	0	49		49	0.937	46
2	2016	11	343	326	9,599	2,924	2,383	0	542		542	0.878	475
3	2017	12	358	340	11,697	3,720	2,430	0	1,289		1,289	0.822	1,060
4	2018	13	358	340	13,796	4,387	2,479	0	1,908		1,908	0.770	1,469
5	2019	14	358	340	14,072	4,475	2,529	0	1,946		1,946	0.721	1,404

Table 13.2 (continued)

Model year	Calendar year	Ship age (years)	Available running days[b]	Actual booked days[c]	Gross charter rate per day[d] (USD)	Net annual charter revenue[e] (USD)	Annual operating expense[a] (USD)	Taxes (USD)	EBIAT[f] (USD)	Scrap value[g] (USD)	Free cash flow[h] (USD)	Present value factor	Present value (USD)
6	2020	15	358	340	14,353	4,564	2,579	0	1,985		1,985	0.676	1,341
7	2021	16	343	326	14,640	4,460	2,631	0	1,830		1,830	0.633	1,158
8	2022	17	358	340	14,933	4,749	2,683	0	2,065		2,065	0.593	1,225
9	2023	18	358	340	15,232	4,844	2,737	0	2,107		2,107	0.556	1,170
10	2024	19	358	340	15,536	4,940	2,792	0	$2,149		2,149	0.520	1,118
11	2025	20	358	340	13,470	4,283	2,848	0	1,436		1,436	0.487	700
12	2026	21	343	326	13,739	4,186	2,905	0	1,281		1,281	0.457	585
13	2027	22	358	340	14,014	4,456	2,963	0	1,494		1,494	0.428	639
14	2028	23	358	340	14,294	4,546	3,022	0	1,524		1,524	0.401	611
15	2029	24	358	340	14,580	4,636	3,082	0	1,554		1,554	0.375	583
16	2030	25	358	340	14,872	4,729	3,144	0	1,585	3,954	5,539	0.352	1,948
										Total			15,533

[a] Includes general and administrative costs, insurance, crew, operating expenses and dry-docking provisions (assumes the provisions are an annual expense)

[b] Ships require extensive maintenance, inspection and surveys every five years (dry-docking and class renewal), which reduces the number of available running days

[c] Number of booked days = total available days × utilization rate

[d] Gross daily charter rate starts at the current charter rate in year 1 (in 2015), adjusts linearly to the historical average by year 4, grows annually thereafter at the inflation rate of 2% to the end of the economic life of the vessel, in year 20 it is reduced by the old ship reduction rate of 15%, and continues to rise annually by the inflation rate thereafter (in years 21 to 25)

[e] Equals gross daily charter rate × number of booked days × (1 − fees and commissions rate)

[f] Earnings before interest and after taxes (EBIAT) calculation ignores depreciation, a non-cash charge, because there are no taxes. For taxpaying entities, depreciation is important

[g] Scrap value = number of lightweight tons × steel price = 8,000 tons × 360USD/ton × ((1 + inflation rate)^number of years); adjusted for taxable gains if a taxpaying entity

[h] Free cash flow = EBIAT + depreciation − increases in NWC − capital expenditures. Assumes minimal capital expenditures and investments in net working capital

In the second step, the annual expected free cash flows must be discounted to present values using the WACC. The 10-year swap rate at the beginning of 2015 was 2.3% (rates are for a fixed rate payer in USD in return for receiving three-month LIBOR), and the credit spread is assumed to be 400bp (or 4%). As a result, the cost of debt is 6.3% per year. To compute the cost of equity based on the CAPM, the risk-free rate, the equity beta and the stock market risk premium are needed. The current yield on 10-year US Treasury bonds of 2.2% per year is used as the risk-free rate.[26] Both Kavussanos et al. (2003) and Drobetz et al. (2016b) find that the average beta of listed container companies is, at least at standard levels of statistical significance, not different from 1. Without further information on the vessel's riskiness, but recognizing that equity betas increase during bad states of the shipping markets, we set $\beta_E = 1.2$. Based on long-run stock market data in Dimson et al. (2013), the geometric average global stock market return in excess of government bills (measured in USD) was 4.1% per year during the 1900–2012 period. We use this historical value as a proxy for the (future) equity risk premium.[27] The CAPM cost of equity r_E is:

$$r_E = r_f + \beta_E \cdot MRP = 2.2\% + 1.2 \cdot 4.1\% = 7.4\%. \quad (13.11)$$

Vessels are normally financed with a 50–70% debt. Assuming that the vessel is financed with a 60% debt, therefore $D/V = 0.6$, the WACC in our example is:

$$WACC = \frac{D}{V} \cdot r_D + \frac{E}{V} \cdot r_E = 0.6 \cdot 6.3\% + 0.4 \cdot 7.4\% = 6.75\%. \quad (13.12)$$

Using the WACC, the present value factor can be computed for each model year. For example, for model year 3 the present value factor is $1/(1+0.0675)^3 = 0.822$; the factors for all other model years are derived accordingly. Multiplying the expected free cash flows with the present value factors (see columns 13 and 14 in Table 13.2) and adding up all the present values delivers our valuation result. The vessel's fundamental value is USD15.5 million.

13.4 Comparing Value and Price

The two approaches to valuation—the market approach and the DCF approach—may yield different results for the same vessel. Differences come from different views on market efficiency.[28] In DCF valuation, it is assumed that markets make mistakes, that they correct the mistakes over time, and that the mistakes can occur in the entire shipping sector. In the market approach, the conjecture is that, while markets can make mistakes for a single vessel, they are correct on average. In particular, when we value a vessel relative to other recent vessels sold, two assumptions are made. First, the "law of one price" holds, implying that similar vessels will sell for the same price. Second, the market has priced these vessels correctly, on average, although it might have made mistakes in the pricing of each of the vessels individually.[29]

Implicit in these assumptions underlying the market approach are several other conditions that must hold. One condition is that there are many willing buyers and sellers (guaranteeing a steady deal flow), who should transact voluntarily (precluding "fire sales"). Another is that buyers and sellers are knowledgeable, i.e. market participants should be healthy industry insiders with lots of experience in and knowledge about the industry.[30] Moreover, transactions must take place between independent and unrelated parties acting in good faith ("arm's length" transaction). Additional criteria for a "functional" or "normalized" market include: credit is readily available to buyers; assets are homogeneous and in large supply; investor sentiment is not characterized by excessive optimism or pessimism; and search and transaction costs are low. Under these circumstances, the competitive pressure in a market with informed, rational and financially healthy investors is assumed to drive market prices to fundamental values. In short, market prices are characterized by fundamental efficiency.

Arguably, the market conditions that prevail since the outbreak of the financial and shipping crises in 2008 do not fulfill all requirements for fundamental efficiency, thus observed market prices and fundamental values may diverge.[31] However, it is also possible that fundamental values have crashed to such an extent that vessels are really not worth that much and may never earn more than their cost of capital.

A related question is why arbitrage does not necessarily drive market prices back to fundamental values. Empirical evidence illustrates that price deviations from fundamental values can be large and long-lasting, even in liquid financial markets. Therefore, one expects that deviations can be even larger and longer-lasting in markets for physical assets. Standard financial theory offers potential explanations. For example, few investors have the specialized knowledge to identify misvaluations, exploit them and then operate vessels efficiently. In addition, even large deviations from a vessel's fundamental value could last for a long time, longer that any arbitrageur can stay solvent ("noise trader" risk). In fact, deviations could even become larger before convergence starts (fundamental risk). Another obstacle is that arbitrageurs have to make large, undiversified bets on vessels. Shipping risks are highly cyclical and to a considerable degree systematic (e.g. freight rates are highly correlated with global economic activity), thus arbitrageurs may lack diversification opportunities. Finally, financial constraints due to restricted bank lending as well as high transaction costs may prevent arbitrage.

13.5 Financial Analysis of Shipping Companies

Shipping companies can be interpreted as portfolios of vessels. In principle, it is straightforward to extend the DCF approach to evaluate entire companies. To take a capital market perspective, it may be insightful to analyze how the stock market evaluates listed shipping companies and compares them to other listed companies. Panel A of Table 13.3 summarizes selected financial ratios and cash-flow variables for the sample used in Drobetz et al. (2016a), consisting of 255 listed shipping companies from 44 countries over the 1990–2012 period (3,038 firm-year observations).[32] All variables are denominated in USD. To compare shipping companies to other capital-intensive industries, a matching sample of manufacturing firms is constructed. The initial manufacturing sample is drawn from the countries contained in the shipping sample and comprises 186,878 firm-year observations. Out of this universe, a market-to-book and size matched sample that includes the two best fits for every shipping firm is constructed. This procedure results in a matched manufacturing sample (5,522 firm-year observations). Panel B of Table 13.3 shows financial ratios and cash-flow variables for this comparable sample.[33]

The ratio of a firm's market value of equity to its book value, or market-to-book ratio, is often used as a simple valuation measure. The market-to-book ratio is strongly connected with both a firm's return on equity and the expected growth rate. Most importantly, a higher market-to-book ratio implies that investors expect management to create more value from a given set of assets. As an asset-heavy industry, the shipping industry exhibits relatively low market-to-book ratios; panel A shows that the average during "normal" times was only 1.152 (i.e., the market value of the average firm's equity is higher than its accounting value). As a comparison, the average market-to-book ratio of all US (global) firms from all industrial sectors was 2.0 (1.5) at the beginning of 2012 (the last year of the shipping sample). All else being equal, the market seems to expect little future earnings growth for shipping companies.[34]

Panel A further shows that market-to-book and firm size exhibit high standard deviations, indicating a very heterogeneous sample containing both

Table 13.3 Financial analysis of listed shipping companies

Panel A: Shipping companies

	1990–2012/Full sample			1990–2012/Normal times			1990–2007/Pre-2008 crisis			2008–12/Recent crisis		
	N	Mean	SD	N	Mean	SD	N	Mean	SD	N	Mean	SD
Cash flow	3,038	0.069	0.114	1,600	0.081	0.110	389	0.073	0.109	1,049	0.048	0.119
Capital expenditures	3,038	0.100	0.158	1,600	0.114	0.192	389	0.062	0.086	1,049	0.094	0.111
Acquisitions	3,038	0.006	0.047	1,600	0.006	0.050	389	0.004	0.036	1,049	0.006	0.046
Asset sales	3,038	0.030	0.101	1,600	0.036	0.127	389	0.024	0.057	1,049	0.023	0.059
Share repurchases	3,038	0.023	0.101	1,600	0.030	0.128	389	0.007	0.028	1,049	0.017	0.065
Dividends	3,038	0.002	0.014	1,600	0.002	0.013	389	0.001	0.007	1,049	0.003	0.017
Equity issues	3,038	0.019	0.050	1,600	0.020	0.055	389	0.011	0.060	1,049	0.020	0.036
Market-to-book	3,038	1.152	0.414	1,600	1.241	0.435	389	1.140	0.410	1,049	1.021	0.343
Firm size	3,038	6.489	1.681	1,600	6.357	1.652	389	6.201	1.745	1,049	6.798	1.655
Cash holdings	3,038	0.120	0.103	1,600	0.127	0.121	389	0.105	0.084	1,049	0.123	0.113
Leverage	3,038	0.397	0.211	1,600	0.396	0.216	389	0.413	0.205	1,049	0.397	0.217
Net debt	3,038	0.277	0.260	1,600	0.269	0.275	389	0.308	0.234	1,049	0.274	0.282
Profitability	3,038	0.052	0.072	1,600	0.065	0.085	389	0.046	0.096	1,047	0.036	0.078
Tangibility	3,038	0.585	0.252	1,600	0.583	0.242	389	0.600	0.236	1,049	0.583	0.272

Panel B: Matched manufacturing companies

	1990–2012/Full sample			1990–2012/Normal times			1990–2007/Pre-2008 crisis			2008–12/Recent crisis		
	N	Mean	SD	N	Mean	SD	N	Mean	SD	N	Mean	SD
Cash flow	5,522	0.056	0.095	3,684	0.056	0.096	674	0.049	0.088	1,164	0.058	0.097
Capital expenditures	5,522	0.050	0.055	3,684	0.050	0.057	674	0.037	0.043	1,164	0.055	0.053
Acquisitions	5,522	0.005	0.031	3,684	0.005	0.032	674	0.002	0.019	1,164	0.006	0.030
Asset sales	5,522	0.005	0.021	3,684	0.005	0.018	674	0.005	0.020	1,164	0.006	0.028

(continued)

Table 13.3 (continued)

	N	Mean	SD	N	Mean	SD	N	Mean	SD
Share repurchases	5,522	0.015	0.064	3,684	0.017	0.070	674	0.007	0.035	1,164	0.014	0.059
Dividends	5,522	0.002	0.018	3,684	0.002	0.020	674	0.001	0.008	1,164	0.003	0.014
Equity issues	5,522	0.012	0.025	3,684	0.012	0.026	674	0.009	0.020	1,164	0.013	0.021
Market-to-book	5,522	1.188	0.484	3,684	1.203	0.482	674	1.192	0.502	1,164	1.141	0.475
Firm size	5,522	6.277	1.546	3,684	6.288	1.550	674	6.105	1.568	1,164	6.341	1.514
Cash holdings	5,522	0.131	0.124	3,684	0.131	0.126	674	0.129	0.126	1,164	0.139	0.141
Leverage	5,522	0.272	0.177	3,684	0.276	0.183	674	0.287	0.185	1,164	0.256	0.175
Net debt	5,522	0.141	0.249	3,684	0.145	0.256	674	0.158	0.258	1,164	0.117	0.263
Profitability	5,522	0.050	0.073	3,684	0.050	0.087	674	0.048	0.080	1,164	0.046	0.091
Tangibility	5,522	0.350	0.179	3,684	0.350	0.178	674	0.357	0.175	1,164	0.346	0.191

Notes: This table shows the number of firm-year observations (N), the mean, and the standard deviation (SD) of key financial figures for listed shipping companies (Panel A) and a matched sample of manufacturing companies (Panel B). The full sample in Panel A consists of 255 shipping firms (3,038 firm-years) from 44 countries during the 1990–2012 period. Firms are included in the sample if they own and/or operate commercial ships. The sample of manufacturing firms (Panel B) is matched according to country, market-to-book and size, as described in detail on p. 304. All figures, except for market-to-book and firm size, are expressed as fractions of firm total assets. All variables are winsorized at the 99% level. For detailed explanations of the variables see Drobetz et al. (2016b). Both panels show the descriptive statistics for the full sample (all years), the non-crisis years of 1990–2007, the crisis periods prior to 2008 and the recent crisis from 2008 to 2012 very young and mature firms. Moreover, cash flows and capital expenditures also exhibit large standard deviations, which is attributable to the strong cyclicality in the sources and uses of funds in the shipping industry. In fact, cash flows decline as the economic situation deteriorates. While average annual cash flows (scaled by total assets) are 8.1% during normal times, they decreased sharply to 4.8% during the recent financial crisis. As expected, the cyclicality in cash flows is also reflected in the market-to-book ratio, which varies strongly over the different economic states (from 1.24 during normal times to only 1.02 during the most recent crisis). Strong cyclicality is further observed in profitability, defined as the ratio of operating income before depreciation to book assets, ranging from 6.5% during normal times to only 3.6% during the most recent crisis. Similar to cash flows, average annual capital expenditures and short as well as long-term borrowings declined during the recent crisis compared to non-crisis periods.

Comparing shipping companies to the matched manufacturing companies (panel B), there are several important observations. First, ratios and variables generally tend to be less cyclical in the manufacturing sector. For example, while the level of profitability is similar during normal times in the two samples, there is much more variation over the economic states in the shipping sample. Moreover, as one expects, shipping companies are leveraged much higher than comparable manufacturing companies, indicating the higher residual risk that equity holders have to bear. Leverage is defined as the ratio of long and short-term debt to total book assets; during normal times, the ratios are 0.40 in the shipping industry and 0.28 in the matched sample. Finally, as shipping companies are portfolios of vessels, asset tangibility is notably high in the shipping sample; the ratio of fixed assets to book assets is 0.58 for shipping firms and 0.35 in the matched sample.

13.6 Conclusion

Since valuation is key to much of what modern finance is all about, it is not surprising that there are many different valuation approaches in use. In this chapter, we have examined two valuation approaches and shown how they can be used for maritime investment appraisal. The first and still most widely used approach in the shipping industry is the market approach, which evaluates a vessel in comparison to the recent sales of comparable vessels ("mark-to-market"). Regression analysis can be used if comparability depends on multiple criteria, such as age, size and the state of the freight market. The second approach is DCF valuation, which is forward-looking and determines the fundamental value of a vessel by its future expected cash flows, discounted using the cost of capital ("mark-to-model"). The choice between the two approaches is not always easy and mainly depends on one's view about market efficiency. Market prices and fundamental values will be close in "normalized" markets. If vessel markets are "dysfunctional" and market prices can diverge from fundamental values under certain conditions, a valuation model is needed that recognizes and explains this divergence.

The LTAV method was devised during bad times, when market prices arguably fell below fundamental values. However, if markets are efficient and market prices always reflect fundamental values, assuming that vessel values are worth more seems like a recipe for another shipping crisis. A final caveat is that market prices can fall below but also rise above fundamental values. In fact, when shipping markets are booming, market prices may exceed fundamental ship values. The LTAV method will thus constrain bank lending in good times. It may also prevent the possibility of prices running away by limiting collateral values.

Notes

1. In a survey, Cullinane and Panayides (2000) document that the valuation techniques used by many shipowners and operators are only rudimentary. They even conclude that a systematic approach to capital budgeting is absent among most shipowners and operators.
2. A third, and even less common, approach is the "replacement cost approach", in which the value of a vessel is equal to the cost of replacing it and its functionality. It is assumed that the value of the vessel is simply the cost of supplanting a replacement vessel in the present market environment. An obvious critique is that the cost of replacing the vessel is not necessarily the price that a third-party buyer would be willing to pay. This approach (not further analyzed in this chapter) is typically used to value vessels with unique functionality or customized features.
3. The underlying assumption is that the freight rate increase is due to scarcity rather than cost factors (e.g. rising fuel costs are passed through to customers and do not affect vessel prices).
4. All information is taken from the Clarkson Shipping Intelligence Network (SIN) database.
5. For a more detailed analysis of the use of statistical analysis in relative valuation, see Damodaran (2005).

6. Our model assumes a linear relationship between transaction prices and pricing factors. Non-linear relationships could be incorporated by adding quadratic (or even higher order) terms of the explanatory variables.
7. Using variables in levels (rather than ratios or percentages) could induce heteroskedasticity problems. The error terms are said to be heteroskedastic if they do not have constant variance but rather differ across observations. Regression analysis using heteroskedastic data still provides an unbiased estimate for the relationship between the transaction price and the pricing factors, but standard errors and thus inferences may be wrong. We thus do not report standard errors and significance levels of the coefficients, but use the estimates to generate unbiased predictions.
8. This model has also been used in Esty and Sheen (2010a).
9. R-squareds close to 90% are rare. In fact, Damodaran (2005) cautions that the goodness-of-fit in relative valuation regressions hardly reaches levels above 70%. When the R-squared decreases, the pricing accuracy decreases as well.
10. With regards to the minimum sample size that is necessary to derive reliable results, there are many rules-of-thumb available in the statistical literature. At an absolute minimum, five cases per explanatory variable are needed to provide reliable correlation estimates (which are required for the coefficient estimates).
11. In addition to the WACC approach, there are alternative DFC valuation approaches (most prominently, the adjusted present value or APV method). A comprehensive discussion of alternative DCF approaches is beyond the scope of this chapter. For a detailed review, see Damodaran (2005).
12. This section presents a simple example of how to use the LTAV approach. Mayr (2015) provides a detailed discussion of the method and the underlying assumptions. The VHSS also maintains a website with further information: http://www.long-term-asset-value.de/.
13. As cash flows earned by vessels are usually denominated in USD, the WACC discount rate should also be determined based on US capital market data. Harvey (2005) provides a review of different methods to compute the international cost of equity capital.
14. In a corporate context, with many vessels on the asset side of a company's balance sheet, it is assumed that a vessel's risks are the same as those of the company's other assets (business risk), and that they remain so for the life of the project. Moreover, the vessel supports the same degree of financial leverage as the company's overall capital structure, which remains constant for the life of the project. Drobetz et al. (2013) provide a detailed analysis of capital structure decisions in listed shipping companies.

15. See Grammenos's (2010) six Cs model for credit analysis in shipping.
16. See Graham and Harvey (2002) for a survey among US CFOs on the use of capital budgeting techniques and, in particular, on the methods used to estimate the cost of equity.
17. The cost of equity of an investment is lower when it offers diversification benefits for an investor holding the market portfolio, i.e. there is less reward required for less risk contribution. The contribution to overall portfolio risk is the market beta of a project—the measure of the project's "toxicity". A project that decreases in value when the market decreases in value, and increases when the market increases, has a positive beta—it is toxic and investors avoid it. In contrast, a project with a low (or even negative) beta helps an investor who holds the market portfolio that reduces the overall investment risk.
18. Fama and French (1997) provide a more detailed analysis of the computation of industry cost of equity using more advanced methods (e.g. a multifactor model that, in addition to market effects, also accounts for size and value effects). Drobetz et al. (2010) provide an empirical analysis of the multiple risk factors in the returns of shipping stocks.
19. See Drobetz et al. (2013) for an analysis of the financial characteristics of listed shipping companies.
20. This problem is known as the WACC fallacy. See Krüger et al. (2015) for empirical evidence on the severity of the problem.
21. The structure of Table 13.2 is based on Exhibit 8 in Esty and Sheen (2010b).
22. Note that the historical average daily charter rate is adjusted for inflation. Therefore, the charter rate increases to $13.796 (=$13.000×1,023) by year 2018 (see Exhibit 13.2).
23. A caveat is that the stage of the cycle when the asset is valued has a main effect on the calculated fundamental value. As the number of cycles extends, the average cash flow converges to the "normal" year, but the net present values (NPVs) do not, i.e. whether there are early high or low cash flows has a large impact on the valuation.
24. This penalty may only apply for container vessels. For example, for older bulk vessels it may ignore the benefits older tonnage has in dirty trades.
25. Depreciation is the most important non-cash expense which generally must be added to earnings before interest and after taxes (EBIAT) to derive the free cash flow. However, without taxes (and including the tonnage tax charges in the annual operating expenses), depreciation can be ignored. Capital expenditures and investments in working capital are also

assumed to be minimal and ignored in the computation of the free cash flow.
26. The US Federal Reserve provides both swap rates and bond yields: http://www.federalreserve.gov/releases/h15/data.htm.
27. See Fama and French (2002) and Dimson et al. (2003) for a detailed discussion of the problems with historical estimates of the equity risk premium.
28. An alternative explanation for the valuation differences between the two approaches could be that the static DFC approach fails to incorporate the real options character of vessel investments. For example, the shipowner has the flexibility to time the sale of the vessel, taking advantage of the benefits of a volatile and liquid market for secondhand ships ("option to abandon"). More generally, viewing vessels as complex options, the static DCF approach may understate the value of vessel investments. Even in the absence of managerial flexibility, the real option approach and the static DCF approach can lead to different results. While the static DCF approach discounts for risk at the aggregate net cash flow, the real option approach adjusts for risk within the cash flow components, thus allowing the differentiation of assets according to their unique risk characteristics. Samis et al. (2006) provide a more detailed discussion and examples for the mining industry.
29. Damodaran (2005) surveys empirical studies that compare the pricing accuracy of both approaches. He concludes that the relative valuation approach works well to explain cross-sectional differences across assets. However, when it comes to pricing differences that correct over time, the DCF approach is indeed more useful. For empirical tests of the validity of the efficient market hypothesis in the formation of dry bulk vessel prices (by examining the long-run or equilibrium relationship between vessel prices, operating profits and expected resale prices of vessels), see Kavussanos and Alizadeh (2002).
30. This condition ensures that the asset (vessel) is put into "best use." According to Shleifer and Vishny (1992), healthy industry participants will value an asset more than industry outsiders or financial buyers (who usually require a discount).
31. See Greenwood and Hanson (2015) and Drobetz et al. (2016a) for more detailed analyses. Using a large dataset of shipping sales during the period 1995–2011 and computing the fire sale discount as the difference between the transacted price of an arrested ship and the counterfactual price from a hedonic model, Franks et al. (2015) estimate an average fire sale discount of 26% compared with ships of similar age and use. However,

whereas roughly half of this fire sale discount is driven by market illiquidity, they also show that the other half is attributable to low maintenance of vessels and is largely concentrated in low valued vessels and corrupt ports.
32. The condition for firms to be included is that they own and/or operate commercial vessels. This selection implies that shipyards as well as passenger vessels, drilling vessels and inland vessels are excluded.
33. All information on data collection and data construction of both the shipping and the matched manufacturing sample are described in full detail in Drobetz et al. (2016a). They also provide the exact definition of "normal" years, the more moderate pre-2008 crisis years and the recent financial and shipping crisis from 2008 onward.
34. For US and global market-to-book data see the website of Aswhat Damodaran: http://pages.stern.nyu.edu/~adamodar/. Damodaran (2005) provides a more detailed discussion about the assumptions behind and interpretation of market-to-book ratios.

References

Adland, R., and S. Koekebakker, 2007, Ship Valuation Using Cross-Sectional Sales Data: A Multivariate Non-parametric Approach, *Maritime Economics & Logistics* 9, 105–118.

Albertijn, S., W. Bessler, and W. Drobetz, 2011, Financing Shipping Companies and Shipping Operations: A Risk-Management Perspective, *Journal of Applied Corporate Finance* 23, 70–82.

Cullinane, K., and P. Panayides, 2000, The Use of Capital Budgeting Techniques among UK-based Ship Operators, *International Journal of Maritime Economics* 2(4), 313–330.

Damodaran, A., 2005, Valuation Approaches and Metrics: A Survey of the Theory and Evidence, *Foundations and Trends in Finance* 1(8), 1567–2395.

Dimson, E., P. Marsh, and M. Staunton, 2003, Global Evidence on the Equity Risk Premium, *Journal of Applied Corporate Finance* 15(2), 8–19.

Dimson, E., P. Marsh, and M. Staunton, 2013, The Low-Return World, *Credit Suisse Global Investment Returns Yearbook 2013*, 5–15.

Drobetz, W., D. Gounopoulos, A.G. Merikas, and H. Schröder, 2013, Capital Structure Decisions of Globally-Listed Shipping Companies, *Transportation Research Part E* 52, 49–76.

Drobetz, W., R. Haller, and I. Meier, 2016a, Cash Flow Sensitivities During Normal and Crisis Times: Evidence from Shipping, *Transportation Research Part A* 90, 26–49.

Drobetz, W., C. Menzel, and H. Schröder, 2016b, Systematic Risk Behavior in Cyclical Industries: The Case of Shipping, *Transportation Research Part E* 88, 129–145.
Drobetz, W., L. Tegtmeier, and D. Schilling, 2010, Common Risk Factors in the Returns of Shipping Stocks, *Maritime Policy and Management* 37, 93–120.
Esty, B., and A. Sheen, 2010a, Compass Maritime Services, LLC: Valuing Ships, Case Study, Harvard Business School.
Esty, B., and A. Sheen, 2010b, Vereinigung Hamburger Schiffsmakler und Schiffsagenten e.V. (VHSS): Valuing Ships, Case Study, Harvard Business School.
Fama, E., and K. French, 1997, Industry Cost of Equity, *Journal of Financial Economics* 43, 153–193.
Fama, E., and K. French, 2002, The Equity Premium, *Journal of Finance* 57, 637–659.
Franks, J., O. Sussman, and V. Vig, 2015, Privatized Bankruptcy: A Case Study of Shipping Financial Distress, Working paper, London Business School.
Graham, J., and C. Harvey, 2002, How Do CFOs Make Capital Budgeting and Capital Structure Decisions?, *Journal of Applied Corporate Finance* 15(1), 8–23.
Greenwood, R., and S. Hanson, 2015, Waves in Ship Prices and Investment, *Quarterly Journal of Economics* 130, 55–109.
Grammenos, C., 2010, Revisiting Credit Risk, Analysis and Policy in Bank Shipping Finance, in: C. Grammenos (ed.): The Handbook of Maritime Economics and Business, Informa Law: London.
Harvey, C., 2005, 12 Ways to Calculate the International Cost of Capital, Working paper, Duke University.
Kalouptsidi, M., 2014, Time to Build and Fluctuations in Bulk Shipping, *American Economic Review* 104, 564–608.
Kavussanos, M., and A. Alizadeh, 2002, Efficient Pricing of Ships in the Dry Bulk Sector of the Shipping Industry, *Maritime Management and Policy* 29, 303–330.
Kavussanos, M.G., A. Juell-Skielse, and M. Forrest, 2003, International Comparison of Market Risks across Shipping Related Industries, *Maritime Policy and Management* 30, 107–122.
Krüger, P., A. Landier, and D. Thesmar, 2015, The WACC Fallacy: The Real Effect of Using a Unique Discount Rate, *Journal of Finance* 70, 1254–1285.
Kydland, F., and E. Prescott, 1982, Time to Build and Aggregate Fluctuations, *Econometrica* 50, 1345–1370.
Mayr, D., 2015, Valuing Vessel, in: Schinas, O., C. Grau and M. Johns (eds.), HSBA Handbook on Ship Finance, 141–163.
Modigliani, F., and M.H. Miller, 1958, The Cost of Capital, Corporation Finance and the Theory of Investment, *American Economic Review* 48, 261–297.
Samis, M., G.A. Davis, D. Laughton, and R. Poulin, 2006, Valuing Uncertain Asset Cash Flows when There Are No Options: A Real Options Approach, *Resources Policy* 30, 285–298.
Shleifer, A. and R.W. Vishny, 1992, Liquidation values and debt capacity: A market equilibrium approach, *Journal of Finance* 47, 1343–1366.

14

Financial Analysis and the Modeling of Ship Investment

Lars Patterson

14.1 Introduction

Financial modeling of ship investments can quantify downside risk and upside potential before a decision to invest is made, and also be used as a tool to monitor risks and performance during the investment period. A good financial model is also an excellent tool for communicating opportunities or potential problems to management, lenders and investors. This allows for opportunities or potential problems to be identified early and plans for alternative actions to be prepared in advance. Meaningful financial analysis and modelling of ship investments can, therefore, contribute to better management of risks and hence better risk-adjusted returns.

Some of the questions we may want answers to are:

1. How much capital is needed for the project?
2. What is the debt capacity of the project?
3. What is the timing of the purchase and sale, the chartering policy and the financing structure that maximizes the net present value (NPV) of equity invested?
4. What is the forecast cash impact of financing alternatives, chartering policies and market developments?

L. Patterson (✉)
Vetlejord, Eksingedalsvegen 356, 5728 Eidslandet, Norway

5. What is required to meet the target return on equity?
6. How long will current cash last under various scenarios?

A good financial model has the following characteristics:

1. key input parameters are clearly identified;
2. the model uses formulas to adjust automatically for changes in input parameters;
3. it has a user-friendly, interactive interface and clearly separates input (assumptions) and output (calculated results);
4. the model is dynamic, robust, covers multi-periods and produces all the important financial output metrics including NPV and internal rate of return (IRR).

14.2 An Example of a Financial Model

Table 14.1 shows an example of a very simple financial model for analyzing investment in a single ship. We estimate the cash flow and calculate the NPV and IRR based on certain assumptions (the Excel spreadsheet of Table 14.1 can be downloaded from the website: www.pacomarine.com).

Table 14.1 Example of a financial model of ship investment for a five-year-old Panamax (USD millions)

Ship investment cash-flow for			5 year old Panamax				
Year		0	1	2	3	4	5
Ship purchase price		−$27.0					
Charter income			4.6	4.4	4.6	4.6	4.6
Operating expense			−2.4	−2.4	−2.5	−2.6	−2.7
Dry docking/special survey			0.0	−0.3	0.0	0.0	0.0
Ship operating cash flow			2.2	1.7	2.0	2.0	1.9
Drawdown of debt		13.5					
Loan interest payments			−0.6	−0.6	−0.5	−0.5	−0.5
Loan repayments			−0.7	−0.7	−0.7	−0.7	−0.7
Repayment of debt on sale			0.0	0.0	0.0	0.0	−10.1
Residual value (ship sale)			0.0	0.0	0.0	0.0	37.0
Net cash-flow		−13.5	0.9	0.4	0.8	0.8	27.7
Discount factor	20.0%	1.00	1.20	1.44	1.73	2.07	2.49
PV of cash flows		−13.50	0.74	0.28	0.47	0.37	11.11
IRR		19.0%					
NPV		−0.53					

14 Financial Analysis and the Modeling of Ship Investment

Table 14.2 Assumptions for simple financial model

Ship type	Dry Bulk Panamax
Ship age at time of purchase	5 years
Ship purchase price	USD27.0 million
Timecharter rate	USD13,500 per day
Broker's commission on charter	5.00% of charter hire
Off hire days per year:	10 days
Operating expense	USD6,500 per day excluding DD/SS
Annual increase in OPEX	3.0% per annum
Dry-docking cost	USD0.3 million
Days in dry dock (off hire)	12
Ship residual value (sale price)	USD37.0 million, net of broker's commission
Year of dry docking	2 according to dry-docking schedule
Year of ship sale	5 years from time of purchase
Debt finance	50.0%, as percentage of ship purchase price
Loan profile	8 years with semi-annual installments
Loan balloon	USD8.0 million
Loan interest rate	4.5% p.a. payable semi-annually

Note: *DD* dry docking, *SS* special survey

Key assumptions are ship purchase price, charter income and operating expenses (OPEX) during the investment period and the ship sale price (residual value) at the time of exit. Assumptions are also made on the percentage of debt financing, the cost of debt and the debt repayment profile. This can be regarded as a conventional approach used to identify the right ship(s) to buy and the best possible charter fixture to take (in terms of length of period), together with a financing structure optimizing the return on equity (ROE). The standard decision rule is that a project that has a negative NPV does not generate a sufficient return to meet the required return, so as to justify the investment. All the assumptions used to calculate the cash flows in Table 14.1 are listed in Table 14.2.

Some of these assumptions are factual input at the time of making the investment decision. These include known market prices for ships, market rates for charters of different durations and available terms and conditions of debt financing. Other factors, like the future residual value, are not known, and to get a better understanding of the dynamics of future outcomes, sensitivity analysis is performed as summarized in Table 14.3. The table shows how the IRR for the equity invested varies in response to changes in the input assumption listed to the left of the IRR columns for each of the assumptions (OPEX per day, average time charter (TC) rate per day, ship residual value, ship purchase price and loan interest rate). This of course is in addition to detailed market analysis, which takes into account expected future demand and supply, as well as historical data.

Table 14.3 Sensitivity table I: sensitivity of equity IRR to changes in assumptions

	Ship OPEX (ex DD) (USD)	IRR (%)	Average TC rate per day (USD)	IRR (%)	Ship residual value (USD)	IRR (%)	Ship purchase price (USD)	IRR (%)	Loan interest rate (USD)	IRR (%)
	5,700	20.8	9,500	11.3	33.00	15.6	23.00	25.9	0.50	21.8
	5,900	20.3	10,500	13.2	34.00	16.5	24.00	24.0	1.50	21.1
	6,100	19.9	11,500	15.1	35.00	17.3	25.00	22.3	2.50	20.4
	6,300	19.4	12,500	17.0	36.00	18.2	26.00	20.6	3.50	19.7
Base case:	6,500	19.0	13,500	19.0	37.00	19.0	27.00	19.0	4.50	19.0
	6,500	19.0	14,500	20.9	38.00	19.8	28.00	17.4	5.50	18.3
	6,700	18.5	15,500	22.9	39.00	20.5	29.00	16.0	6.50	17.6
	6,900	17.6	16,500	24.9	40.00	21.3	30.00	14.5	7.50	16.8
	7,100	16.3	17,500	26.9	41.00	22.0	31.00	13.2	8.50	16.1

Table 14.4 Sensitivity table II: sensitivity of equity IRR to changes in ship residual value and average TC rate

		Average TC rate during project period					
		$11,500	$12,500	$13,500	$14,500	$15,500	$16,500
	$34.0	12.4%	14.4%	16.5%	18.5%	20.6%	22.6%
	$35.0	13.3%	15.3%	17.3%	19.3%	21.4%	23.4%
	$36.0	14.2%	16.2%	18.2%	20.1%	22.1%	24.2%
Ship residual value =>	$37.00	15.1%	17.0%	19.0%	20.9%	22.9%	24.9%
	$38.0	15.9%	17.8%	19.8%	21.7%	23.7%	25.6%
	$39.0	16.7%	18.6%	20.5%	22.4%	24.4%	26.3%
	$40.0	17.5%	19.4%	21.3%	23.2%	25.1%	27.0%
	$41.0	18.3%	20.2%	22.0%	23.9%	25.8%	27.7%
	$42.0	19.1%	20.9%	22.7%	24.6%	26.5%	28.4%

A two-way sensitivity analysis may also be performed to obtain an understanding of how the return (IRR) of the investment varies with the change of two variables, such as the ship sale price (residual value) and the average charter rate achieved during a given period, as shown in Table 14.4.

The table shows how the IRR for equity invested varies in response to changes in the assumptions for the combination of average TC rate and ship residual value. Key ratios and indicators are also calculated, as shown in Table 14.5. A discussion of these key ratios and indicators follows below.

Loan To Value (LTV) This is a ratio that shows the extent to which the balance of the outstanding loan is covered (secured) by the market value of

14 Financial Analysis and the Modeling of Ship Investment

Table 14.5 Key ratios and indicators

Year	0	1	2	3	4	5
LTV	120%	120%	120%	120%	120%	120%
Required minimum value (USD million)	16.2	15.4	14.6	13.7	12.9	12.1
Debt service ratio		1.7	1.3	1.7	1.6	1.6
Interest cover ratio		3.6	2.9	3.8	3.9	4.0
Debt service USD per day		3,626	3,663	3,452	3,365	3,278
Debt service break even USD per day		10,647	11,137	10,880	11,005	11,137

the ship. It is normally found as a covenant in term sheets and loan agreements. Traditionally, it used to be expressed as the ratio of the market value of the ship divided by the outstanding loan balance, in other words the "value to loan". It has, however, become more common to show the maximum outstanding loan balance allowed under this covenant as a percentage of the market value of the ship. For example, a covenant of maximum loan, being 50% of the market value of the ship, means that if the market value of the ship is USD20 million, then the maximum loan allowed is USD10 million. The reason banks traditionally used to express LTV the other way around is probably that the ratio of ship value to outstanding loan easily illustrates how much the ship can fall in value before the loan is not covered.

Required Minimum Value This figure shows the minimum market value the ship can have before a loan is in breach of its minimum value covenant. It is calculated by taking the outstanding loan balance and multiplying it by the LTV ratio. For example, if the loan balance is USD10 million and the LTV covenant is 130%, the required minimum value will be USD13 million. As the loan is amortized the required minimum value will be reduced, but the ship will also be older and subject to a fall in value, due to its having less remaining economic life. The repayment profile of most shipping loans is normally structured so that the loan balance is scheduled to reduce faster than the ship age, and an argument can be made that the LTV should be somewhat less onerous at the beginning of the loan.

Debt Service Ratio This ratio is calculated by taking the total cash flow available to service debt during a specified period and dividing it by the total amount of debt repayment plus interest payment for the same period. The period chosen is normally that from one debt repayment date to the next (typically, six months).

Interest Cover Ratio This ratio is calculated by dividing the total cash flow available to service debt during a specific period and dividing it by the amount of interest payments for the same period. Where interest is not being paid, the lending bank will have to account for the loan as being non-performing and make necessary loss provisions in its accounts. The bank may however agree to delay repayment of the principal loan balance without necessarily having to account for the loan as being non-performing. If a loan is classified as non-performing the bank has to make provisions for the potential loss and also increase its risk weighting for that loan. This again affects the cost of funding for the bank.

Debt Service Per Day This figure is calculated by taking the total debt service during a period and dividing it by the number of days in the period, but adjusted for off-hire. For example, if the debt service (scheduled loan repayments plus interest payments) for a period is USD1.2 million over 182 days and the expected off-hire in the same period is five days, then the debt service per day would be USD1.2 million divided by 177, which is USD6,780 per day.

Debt Service Break Even This is calculated by taking the debt service per day and adding the OPEX per day, including provisions for periodical dry docking (DD)/special survey (SS). If the debt service per day is USD6,780, the OPEX (excluding dry docking) is USD5,800 per day, and the estimated cost of the next dry docking is USD250,000 with 887 earnings days (30 months adjusted for ten days off-hire per year) to the next dry docking, then the debt service break even is USD12,862 per day, which is the required time-charter equivalent (TCE) earnings per day, net of any commissions payable.

14.3 Theory Behind the Ship Investment Criteria and Value Drivers

It is impossible to build or make meaningful use of a financial model without having an understanding of the financial theories upon which the model is based. In the following section some of the practical applications of financial theory, as they relate to ship investments, are discussed.

14 Financial Analysis and the Modeling of Ship Investment

The total return from a ship investment has two components: the return generated from a change in asset value (ship price), and the return generated from the cash flow provided by earnings: Total Return = Asset Return + Earnings Return. Risk is commonly expressed by the standard deviation of these returns. Figure 14.1 illustrates the historical risk/return trade-off for some generic ship types, where there is a large number of similar ships that are traded in active markets for sale and purchase (S&P), as well as chartering. The annual returns are calculated by using the income from one-year TCs minus the estimated operating expense for the same period (including age depreciation) divided by the ship price at the beginning of the period as a measure of earnings return. The asset return is calculated as the ship price at the end of the investment period minus the ship price at the beginning of the investment period divided by the ship price at the beginning of the investment period. The investment period used here is 12 months. As the earnings return has been calculated using the one-year TC rate, the earnings for tankers do not reflect the peaks and high volatility of spot earnings in the tanker market. Note also that when using the one-year TCE as a measure of earnings for containerships, we are measuring the earnings of ships on TC and not those of the container liner companies. The graph therefore has many limitations, but it illustrates that the ships with the highest volatility

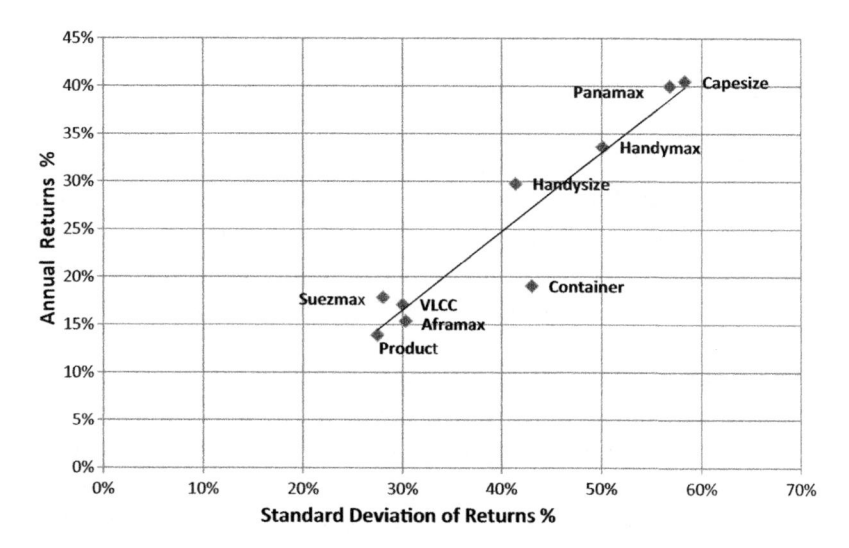

Fig. 14.1 Ship investment risk and returns (*Source*: Author's calculations based on data from Clarksons SIN)

in earnings and ship prices in general are compensated for the higher risk by a higher return.

The key value drivers of a ship investment are cash invested in purchasing the ship, cash generated during the time the ship is held as an investment, and the cash generated when the ship is sold. From a financial analysis point of view, the following investment criteria are used:

- NPV—which is calculated by discounting the future cash flows, using a discount rate reflecting the required return. A more risky investment requires a higher return than a less risky investment. When determining the level of risk the volatility of ship prices and charter rates are taken into account, as well as the market liquidity for the type of ship the analysis is performed.
- IRR—which is the discount rate that returns an NPV of zero.
- We also take into account the value of flexibility (the value of optionality) embedded in the ship investment.

Ships operate in a volatile trading environment. Freight rates, particularly in the spot market, can be extremely volatile, although term rates (that is, charters for fixed terms of months or years) may not reflect the degree of volatility seen in the spot market. The volatility of earnings is also reflected in ship prices. This volatility is, of course, a source of potential additional profit.

14.3.1 The Value of Flexibility (Optionality)

The timing of purchase of a ship, its sale, the type of charter chosen and the amount of debt financing provide the shipowner with many options. In the terminology of real options analysis (ROA), which often uses the terms "option to contract", "option to abandon", "option to expand" and "option to defer", some of the real options and how they apply to ship investments are:

1. Selling a ship is an example of an *option to abandon*.
2. Declaring an option on a newbuilding under a shipyard contract, or extending a charter, are examples of *options to expand*. Declaring a purchase option on a ship on charter with purchase options is also an *option to expand*.
3. Deciding to wait to buy a ship until market conditions are more favorable or financing is available on better terms are examples of *options to defer*.

4. Slow steaming (speed reduction) or the lay-up of ships are examples of *options to contract* for an individual ship or ships, but with the objective from the shipowner's perspective of improving market earnings by cutting supply (slow steaming reduces supply by voyages that take longer to perform, thereby more ships are needed to satisfy the same ton-mile demand).

Without taking into account the value of optionality, it is clear that the standard NPV analysis understates the value of a ship investment. Investors who are not aware of the value of the optionality may reject ship investments in favor of more traditional investments that in reality produce a lower return with a higher risk. Real options capture the value of flexibility and provide trigger points that inform as to when to take a decision.

The main factors determining the value of optionality, as the combined value of volatility and flexibility, are:

1. *Investment cost*
   The value of optionality depends on the cost of entry/cost of purchasing the ship. The lower the purchase cost, the higher the option value.
2. *Time to expire*
   A longer time to expiration increases the value of the option. For a ship investment, the time to expiry is the remaining economic life of a ship until scrapping. The decision on when to scrap a ship depends, amongst other things, on expected future charter rates and the (uncertain) costs of continued maintenance of an old ship. The remaining economic value (or "time to expiry") can therefore vary, and so we are dealing with a complex option.
3. *Uncertainty (volatility)*
   With managerial flexibility an increase in uncertainty (volatility) will increase the value of optionality.

Whilst it is useful to try to quantify the value of optionality using financial/mathematical models, there is in practice no substitute for understanding market dynamics based on market presence and experience. More important than arriving at any particular number is the structured process, which takes into account as many relevant factors and possible outcomes as possible. Financial models of ship investment making use of Monte Carlo simulation, sensitivity analysis and scenario analysis furnish the decision-maker with a range of possible outcomes and the probability with which they will occur.[1] Most importantly it also shows the consequences of what happens when the extreme possibilities occur.

14.4 A Few Comments on Ship Investment Practice

The following provides some useful hints on how a practitioner may approach some of the key ship investment issues in practice.

14.4.1 Ship Purchase and Timing of Exit

Figure 14.2 shows the historical monthly price of a five-year-old dry-bulk Panamax in the second-hand market for a ten-year period, from June 2005 to May 2015, together with the one-year TC rate (in USD per day) for the same period. The high correlation (0.98) between ship prices and one-year TC rates is noted. One explanation for this high correlation may be that there is no lead time to sell a second-hand ship in the market, as it can be sold more or less immediately, while it normally takes less than a year to build a new ship. Even with a backlog of orders for newbuildings, where the lead time from order to delivery is more than a year, shipowners are not willing to pay a lot for "hope value" or future expectations.

14.4.2 Newbuilding versus Second-hand Purchase

The difference of the NPV of an investment in a newbuilding and the NPV of an investment in a second-hand ship will depend on several factors, including:

- when delivery of the ship can be taken for use;

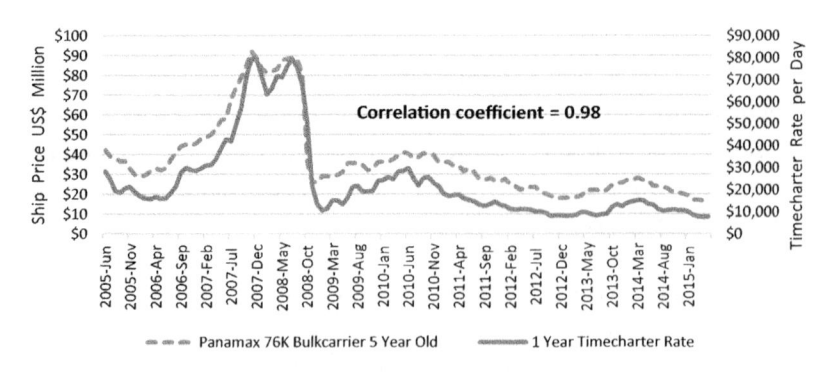

Fig. 14.2 Historical ship prices and one-year TC rates (*Source*: Author's calculations based on data from Clarksons SIN)

- the value of the income the second-hand ship can earn during the period before delivery of the newbuilding;
- the difference in numbers of years left before the secondhand ship will be scrapped compared to the number of years left before the newbuilt ship will be scrapped (difference in remaining economic life).

The status of the order book for shipyards may result in a growing lead time before work starts building a ship on order. The varying length of time from new order to delivery combined with the state of the freight market are the key factors in determining the spread between newbuilding prices and prices for ships in the second-hand market.

Ships have a limited economic life (typically 25–30 years from new), depending on, amongst other things, ship type, wear and tear in the trades where the ship has been employed, as well as maintenance policy and quality of maintenance. A ship can be bought and sold several times in the second-hand market before it is finally sold for scrap. If the investment strategy is "asset play", a ship is sold in the second-hand market when a considerable gain in the second-hand value over the original purchase price can be realized. For the purpose of quantifying potential upside when deciding to buy the ship, it is fairly normal practice to use the age-adjusted historical average second-hand price of the ship as a base case and then perform sensitivity analysis or scenario analysis using the historical maximum and minimum ship price to get a high and low case. Figure 14.3 shows the monthly historical ship price for a five-year-old and a ten-year-old dry-bulk Panamax ship over a period of 120 months, from June 2005 to May 2015. It is noted that the average ship

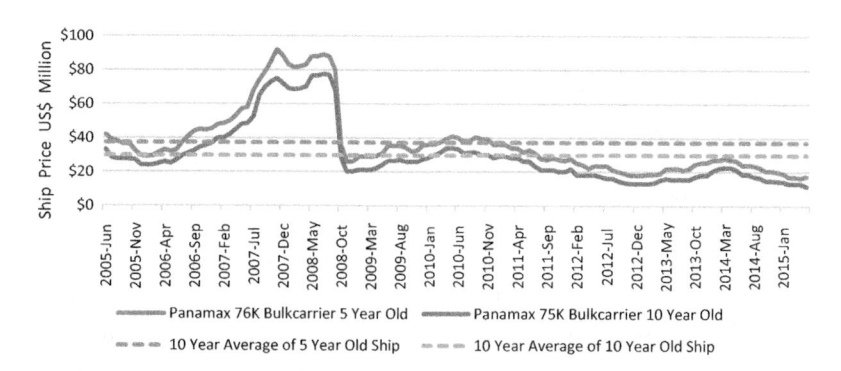

Fig. 14.3 Historical ship prices for five-year-old and ten-year-old dry-bulk Panamax (*Source*: Author's calculations based on data from Clarksons SIN
Note: The averages refer to those calculated over the entire period of the dataset displayed on the graph)

price for a five-year-old Panamax here is USD37.3 million and for a ten-year-old is USD29.7 million. However, whilst historical ship prices can give a fairly good idea about the range of possible outcomes and their probability distribution, we do not know *when* the prices will occur. It may also be advisable to exclude the extremely high values during a super cycle, as the one observed in 2007–08, when calculating historical averages as benchmarks for upside potential. Note that both the probability distribution and the average may change over time. There is no basis for suggesting mean reversion of either ship prices or charter rates. It can, however, be argued that the return expressed as cash yield (a function of both ship price and charter rate) is mean reverting.

14.4.3 Sale for Scrap

The financial evaluation of the decision to sell a ship for scrap can be made by comparing the present value of cash from scrapping the ship immediately, with the present value of the cash flow of future earnings from continuing to trade, followed by a delayed sale of the ship for scrap, minus the additional cost of docking the ship. Net receivable earnings from scrapping the ship is the net price paid for the scrap metal (steel, measured in scrap price per light weight ton or light displacement ton, minus the cost of sailing the ship to the scrapyard after delivery of its last cargo and the usual associated costs, such as repatriation of the crew and port and agency fees.

The main inputs for comparing the cash flows from scrapping with continued trading are:

1. future income from continued trading (which is likely to be uncertain);
2. cost of docking for an old ship (which is uncertain, although the owner will have a guesstimate);
3. the future scrap price;
4. opportunity value of cash (this is a given, but different owners will have different views on if/when/how to reinvest).

Amongst these, clearly the most important factors are the expectations (or hopes) for future earnings and the costs of maintaining the ship for the longer term, which include docking costs as well as anticipated daily running costs.

Figure 14.4 shows the historical scrap value and second-hand price for a ship similar to the dry-bulk Panamax used in our example. Note that in a high market the scrap value of the ship is a lower percentage of the charter free value of the ship than in a low market. For an old ship in a low market,

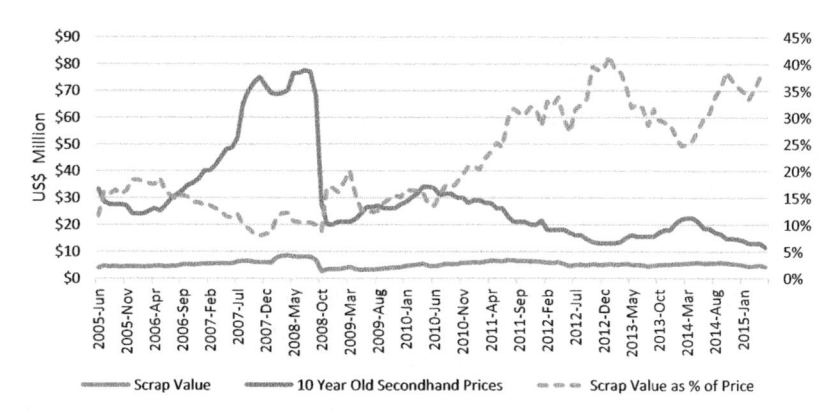

Fig. 14.4 Dry-bulk Panamax scrap value and ship price (*Source*: Author's calculations based on data from Clarksons SIN)

the scrap value will be a high percentage of the market value of the ship since the market value is related to the present value of the expected cash flow over the remaining economic life of the ship.

14.4.4 OPEX

The cost of operating a ship primarily consists of the following, where off-hire is not a cash expense, but a reduction in cash earnings:

- crew;
- spare parts;
- insurance;
- DD/SS, in accordance with DD/SS schedule.

Shipowners normally calculate and budget OPEX on the basis of 365 operating days per year, whether the ship is on-hire or not. When the ship is off-hire, the charterer does not pay charter hire, and off-hire is, therefore, an income reduction. In the model example, we have assumed ten days ordinary off-hire per year and a further 12 days off-hire for the period when the ship is being dry docked.

The regulatory regime requires a ship to pass through a "special" docking survey every five years and to undergo a cycle of regular maintenance in between, including, in most cases, an "intermediate" docking at 30-month intervals between the SSs. As the ship gets older, the wear and tear clearly shows, and the externally imposed upgrading/repair work becomes incrementally expensive. Whilst in many cases the shipowner may be able to anticipate roughly what the costs for a future docking will be, the actual cost will only be ascertained once the independent assessment (by a representative of the vessel's classification society) has been carried out with the ship already in dock to the SS requirements. Once the SS has been successfully undertaken, the ship is allowed to trade for another 30 months, before a further (the intermediate) docking is required. The decision to pay for the dry docking can be looked upon as buying an option with 30 months to expiry, with the pay-out on the option being dependent on the realized charter income and future scrap price.

When shipowners or shipmanagers quote a figure for OPEX per day, it is important to check if that is a figure which includes a daily provision for the future cost of DD/SS or not. A provision is an accrued cost. For the purpose of calculating NPV and IRR the cash expense of DD/SS is timed when it takes place in accordance with DD schedule. It is, however, crucially important to make sure that sufficient cash is available to pay for DD either from accumulated cash flow or, if necessary, from extra cash injected by the owner. Financial modeling will show how much cash will be generated under various scenarios and under what circumstances it may be necessary for the owner to inject further cash. Great attention is paid to the OPEX number, sometimes at the expense of what really matters, which is to keep the ship operating to ensure its safe and uninterrupted performance as an earnings-generating asset and to preserve its quality in a cost efficient way, with a view to maximizing its value when sold. As can be seen from the sensitivity table in Table 14.3, OPEX is not the most critical number in terms of investment performance. The IRR of a ship investment is not highly sensitive to higher/lower OPEX within a small margin. The overall cash flow is what matters, and in this context it is important to keep OPEX under tight control without impairing the value of the ship.

14.4.5 Employment: "The Decision to Fix"

The type of employment chosen for the ship affects the volatility of earnings, the percentage of debt that can be used (debt capacity) and the expected average earnings. Short-term charters generally have higher expected earnings but more volatility. Longer-term charters to good credits normally make it possible to use more debt. In practice, there is a trade-off between market risk and credit risk. Credit risk is in principle a function of to whom the ship is chartered and for how long. This is the ability of the charterer to perform his or her contractual obligations, which may vary depending on the tenor. The level of exposure at future dates can be calculated by taking the difference between the agreed rate in the charter committed to perform and the current market rate for a charter of similar tenor to the balance still outstanding. This is "marking-to-market" the charter contract exposure. If, for example, we have committed to perform a two-year TC at a rate of USD25,000 per day and there is one year left of the charter, and the current market rate is USD12,000 per day, then our credit exposure on the remaining charter is USD25,000 minus USD12,000 multiplied by 365 days minus relevant off-hire days. With seven off-hire days, the exposure is USD4.7 million, which we then subject to a credit risk weighting based on the financial solidity and reputation of the charterer.

If we do not fix the ship on a long-term charter, we are fully exposed to market risk (the short-term continuous fluctuations in charter rates and availability of cargoes) and can expect to be able to obtain less debt financing. As Fig. 14.5 illustrates, in this case the average TCE from long-term charters are significantly less than the average TCE for shorter charters or TCE from spot operations. We should, therefore, take into account in the financial analysis of the ship investment that less debt on the project (whilst requiring a larger equity investment) may well produce a higher return due to higher average earnings in the spot market. It should also be noted that it does not make sense to lock into a long-term charter in a low market, where the result may be that we do not benefit from an upturn in charter rates when the market improves.

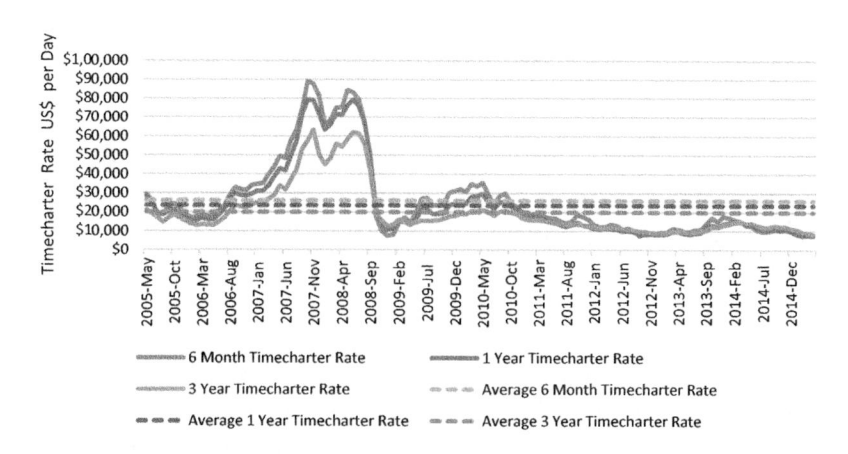

Fig. 14.5 Comparison of six-month, one-year and three-year TC rates (*Source*: Author's calculations based on data from Clarksons SIN
Note: The averages refer to those calculated over the entire period of the dataset displayed on the graph)

It should be noted that in a low market environment older ships will have more days when they are not earning money (off-hire) due to an inability to find immediate employment. Charterers, particularly in softer market environments, can afford to pick and choose between ships, and will tend to ignore older ones if younger ones are available. As the ship gets older, and uncertainty related to possible technical breakdown and off-hire increases, term charter may not be an option for the owner—i.e. he cannot find a charterer willing to take his ship on a term charter even if that is his preference. He will, therefore, have to make assumptions about possible spot earnings.

14.4.6 Financing

One of the benefits of a good financial model for analysis of a ship investment is the ability to identify what financing arrangement adds most value to the deal. Once the deal cash flow (and its uncertainties) is established, financing is structured to match it. The following should be noted:

1. there is normally a trade-off between the benefit of a higher percentage of debt and the lenders' requirement for long-term charter employment to support higher debt;
2. a higher percentage of equity provides flexibility in terms of employment and possible dividend payments;
3. banks typically have restrictions on age, in terms of not lending on ships older than 12–15 years and those free of any debt by a certain age (e.g. 20 years).

The example in Table 14.6 shows how the maximum debt capacity is calculated for a ship investment based on the cash flow estimated in the earlier example; when applying it to the loan criteria used by the bank we are asking to provide debt financing (normally a first priority ship mortgage loan).

When evaluating a debt financing of a ship, it is also useful to calculate what we may call the "trade out rate" of a loan. This is helpful to both the lender and the borrower as it gives an indication of the ability of a ship to generate enough cash to make interest payments and pay off the loan in full over the remaining economic life of the ship to scrap. Calculation of the trade out rate is shown in Table 14.7.

The calculation of the bareboat rate per day required to pay off the outstanding loan balance over the number of years when the ship still is young

14 Financial Analysis and the Modeling of Ship Investment   331

Table 14.6 Individual bank lending criteria (illustrative assumptions)

Maximum age at final repayment	20 years
Loan profile	15 years
Bank loan tenure	8 years
Loan residual value (as % of historical average ship price)	20%
Calculation of debt capacity	
Ship operating cash flow per year	USD4.0 million
Required debt service ratio	1.4
Debt service capacity	USD2.9 million
Tenure of loan	8 years
Debt service during loan term	USD22.9 million
Minus sum interest payments	USD5.3 million
Equals sum total instalments	USD17.6 million
Plus maximum balloon	USD6.0 million
= Maximum loan	**USD23.6 million**

Table 14.7 Calculation of loan trade out rate

Ship age at end of current employment (TC)	10 years
Remaining economic life of ship	15 years
Loan required to be repaid by ship age	20 years
Remaining time for loan to be repaid	10 years
Loan balance when coming off TC	USD13.6 million
Cost of future debt	4.5% p.a.
Required loan trade out rate to zero	USD1,894 per day bareboat
Estimated scrap value	USD1.2 million
Required loan trade out rate to scrap	USD1,792 per day bareboat

enough to meet the banks loan criteria is simply the annuity (PMT function in Excel) of the specified number of years, using the cost of debt and dividing by 365 days. To make this into a TC or TCE rate, we simply add the estimate for OPEX per day going forward and adjust for estimated off-hire days.

When comparing the calculated rate (expressed as either bareboat or TCE, in USD per day) with not only the historical average but also with the historical minimum rate, we see that even if the market continues to be weak, the ship providing security for the loan will be able to pay all interest and the principal. If the bank agrees to restructure the loan to allow repayment over the remaining economic life of the ship, the loan will be repaid in full even if we do not take into account any residual value. If we allow for some contribution from the scrap value of the ship, the rate required to pay off all the debt is even lower. It must of course be added that as soon as the market picks up again, the original debt repayment schedule can be resumed, possibly with an acceleration of repayment to get back on track.

14.5 Ships as an Investment

Ships as investments have many features similar to marketable financial instruments like shares, bonds or traded options:

1. The market price of a ship can be interpreted as the present value of the expected cash flow from the ship during its remaining economic life, discounted at a rate of return that reflects the market's perception (pricing) of downside risks and upside potential.
2. The cash flow generated by operation of the ship over a period of time can be expressed as a percentage of the ship price. This is similar to the yield from the dividends on a listed share or the yield from the coupon on a bond.
3. Charters have different durations and rates may vary with the tenor (period) of the charter.
4. There are yield curves for charters, which reflect forward expectations (a rising market or a falling market). Clarkson's SIN database normally reports six-month, one-year, three-year and five-year charter periods. The forward curve can also be read out of the various market reports for forward freight agreements (FFA).
5. Ships are traded in liquid, transparent and well-reported global markets continuously throughout the day.
6. The cash flow is subject to credit risk (counterparty risk on charters).
7. The cash flow is subject to market risk (changes in ship prices and charter rates).
8. The age of the ship determines the remaining economic life to demolition, which can be seen as similar to the remaining life to maturity for bonds and options.

Since ship prices and income are determined in active liquid markets subject to volatility (risk), it is also relevant to consider the following issues when analyzing a ship investment.

14.5.1 Are Ships Priced in Efficient Markets?

Without making any bold statements about market efficiency, it is taken for granted that an investment in a ship with a higher level of risk requires a higher level of (expected) return than a less risky investment. For the purpose of the analysis, it is assumed that ship prices and charter rates reflect all relevant information at any time, and that new information will be reflected quickly in changing ship prices and charter rates. An efficient market prices risk so that a more risky investment will require a higher expected return than a less risky investment. In real life, markets may not always be 100% efficient and assets may be overpriced or underpriced.

When evaluating a ship investment, the fundamental questions are:

- When will ship prices and charter rates increase or fall?
- How long will ship prices and charter rates remain at various levels?

Much effort is put into forecasting supply and demand in shipping markets. What is often overlooked is the dynamics of how supply adjusts in response to ever changing demand. For the purpose of investment analysis it is therefore helpful to look at the formation of ship prices as a stochastic process. This means that ship prices are a random variable, but each of the possible values of the variable ship price does not have equal probability. The rate of change of the ship price ("speed of change") and the amount of change in ship price ("step change") are also subject to change and vary over time. Add to that the relationship between ship prices and charter rates, and the picture becomes quite complex. The rate at which the change takes place ("acceleration") is also relevant. The ship price or charter rate today does not predict the ship price or charter rate tomorrow. In that sense, it is stochastic. A stochastic variable has a probability distribution where some outcomes may be more likely than others.

14.5.2 Are Ship Prices, Charter Rates and Investment Returns Mean Reverting?

There are different opinions on this. In practice, it is useful to use historical averages of ship prices and charter rates as a benchmark for the long-term equilibrium of ship prices and charter rates, but this should be done with caution. As mentioned earlier, it may be advisable to exclude extreme values we may observe during a "super-cycle". However, extremely high values are indeed possible. Also bear in mind that the averages will change over time due to factors such as cost increases of the necessary input factors when building a new ship (steel, labor, machinery and equipment), as well as the costs of operating it (crew, supplies, insurance). It is also useful to look at the historical maximum and minimum values of ship prices and charter rates to form a view of potential upsides and downsides. Extremely high and extremely low prices do not last for very long; that is, the market is "self-correcting".

14.6 Conclusion

Financial modeling of ship investments helps the analyst to get a better understanding of the deal. It makes him or her mindful of the deal and helps to identify what makes it work. Some seasoned shipowners can do this perhaps intuitively on the back of an envelope. For the rest of us, financial modeling is a necessary tool, not least so as to be able to document the thought process to third-party investors.

Note

1. Monte Carlo simulation is a computerized mathematical technique used to analyze risk. Monte Carlo simulation performs risk analysis by building computer models of possible results by substituting a range of values—a probability distribution—for any factor that has uncertainty. It then calculates results over and over, each time using a different set of random values from the specified probability function for each factor. It furnishes the decision-maker with a range of possible outcomes and the probability they will occur for any action—it shows how variations in important factors interact. It also shows the extreme possibilities. Results show not only what could happen, but how likely each outcome is. Probability distributions are a much more realistic way of describing uncertainty in variables than deterministic or "single-point estimate" analysis.

References and Links

Market Data

Clarksons Shipping Intelligence Network contains the full range of information collected by Clarkson Research including its periodicals, extensive lists and analysis of the fleet, order book and time-series of key commercial shipping data: https://sin.clarksons.net.

OPEX Data

Moore Stephens provide online data as a benchmarking tool for all major vessels' operating costs, currently covering 24 vessel types: www.moorestephens.co.uk/Shippingopcost.aspx.

Software for Financial Modeling of Ship Investments

Microsoft Excel® is most widely used for financial modeling and users can either employ Excel to build their own models from scratch, or make use of some of the Excel based ship investment applications like ShipInvest (www.scscom.demon.co.uk), Invest in Ships (www.seaxl.com) or Pacoship (www.pacomarine.com).

Bibliography

Benninga, S. (2014), Financial Modeling, John Wiley & Sons, Inc., Hoboken, New Jersey.

Benninga, S. (2010), Principles of Finance with Excel, John Wiley & Sons, Inc., Hoboken, New Jersey.

Copeland, T. and Antikarov, V. (2003) Real Options: A Practitioners Guide, Thomson-Texere, New York.

Fabozzi, F.J., Focardi, S.M., and Kolm, P.N. (2006), Financial Modeling of the Equity Market. From CAPM to Cointegration, John Wiley & Sons, Inc., Hoboken, New Jersey.

Merton H.M. and Modigliani, F. (1958), The Cost of Capital, Corporation Finance and the Theory of Investment, The American Economic Review.

Pires, F.C.M., Assis, L.F. and Fiho, M.R. (2012), A Real Options Approach to Ship Investment Appraisal, African Journal of Business Management, vol. 6(25), 7397–7402.

Razgaitis, R. (2003), Dealmaking Using Real Options and Monte Carlo Analysis, John Wiley & Sons, Inc., Hoboken, New Jersey.

Rees, M. (2008), Financial Modelling in Practice: A Concise Guide for Intermediate and Advanced Level, The Wiley Finance Series.

15

Maritime Business Freight Risk Management

Manolis G. Kavussanos and Ilias D. Visvikis

15.1 Introduction

Due to the volatile nature of the shipping industry in rates and prices, market practitioners attempt to minimize the impact of adverse price movements of freight rates, bunker fuel prices, interest rates and foreign exchange rates, among others, through the use of financial derivatives products.[1] This risk management process has enabled companies operating in the industry to stabilize cash flows (revenues and costs), have more effective budgets, secure their shipping loans, and protect their corporate firm values. This chapter presents an overview of the various derivatives products and markets available to hedge the most important source of risk in the industry—namely, the freight rate risk—and to provide the trade specifics, uses and changes in regulations of freight rate derivatives.[2]

We first provide an overview of the freight derivatives market, then present the underlying assets of shipping freight derivatives, before analyzing the various markets and products. We then discuss the Baltic Forward Assessments

---

M.G. Kavussanos (✉)
Athens University of Economics and Business, Patission 76 Street, 10434 Athens, Greece

I.D. Visvikis (✉)
World Maritime University, Fiskehamnsgatan 1, SE-211 18 Malmö, Sweden

© The Author(s) 2016
M.G. Kavussanos, I.D. Visvikis (eds.), *The International Handbook of Shipping Finance,* DOI 10.1057/978-1-137-46546-7_15

(BFAs) and present the available trading screens. We conclude with the regulatory changes in derivatives trading.

15.2 Freight Derivatives Market

Forward freight agreements (FFAs) were introduced in 1992 as over-the-counter (OTC) derivatives contracts. They are private, principal-to-principal contracts-for-difference (CFDs) between a seller and a buyer to settle a freight rate, for a specified quantity of cargo or type of vessel, for usually one, or a combination, of the major trade routes of the dry-bulk, tanker or container sectors of the shipping industry. For a detailed description of the freight derivatives market, with applications and exercises, see Kavussanos and Visvikis (2006a, 2007, 2011, 2014) and Kavussanos et al. (2014a).

Voyage freight derivatives contracts on a particular route of the Baltic Exchange dry-bulk indices are settled on the difference between a fixed forward price (in USD/ton) and the average spot price of the route over the last seven working days of the settlement month.[3] Time-charter contracts on either individual routes or baskets of routes are settled on the difference between the contracted price (in USD/day) and the average price over the calendar settlement month. Tanker freight derivatives contracts are agreements between two participants on a future value of the freight rate, measured in Worldscale (WS) or as a time-charter equivalent (TCE) rate, on an individual tanker route of the Baltic Exchange tanker indices. Settlement, at the end of each month, is made on the difference between the agreed forward price and the monthly average of the spot price of the tanker route. Container forward swap agreements (CFSAs) are cash-settled contracts between two participants to transport a specific number of containers on a particular trade route of the Shanghai Containerized Freight Index (SCFI) or on a route of the World Container Index (WCI) at a specified future date, at a box-rate agreed today. These are measured in USD/FEU (forty-foot equivalent units) for the US routes and USD/TEU (twenty-foot equivalent units) for all other routes. The settlement price at the maturity of a CFSA contract is estimated as the average index-measured box rate over the contract period.

Shipowners, selling the freight service and wanting to protect their income from freight rate decreases, take a short (sell) position on FFA/CFSA contracts, while charterers, buying the freight service and wanting to protect their costs from freight rate increases, take a long (buy) position. If freight rates end up falling below the agreed (FFA/CFSA) rate, the buyer of FFAs pays the difference, between the agreed FFA/CFSA price and the settlement price, to the

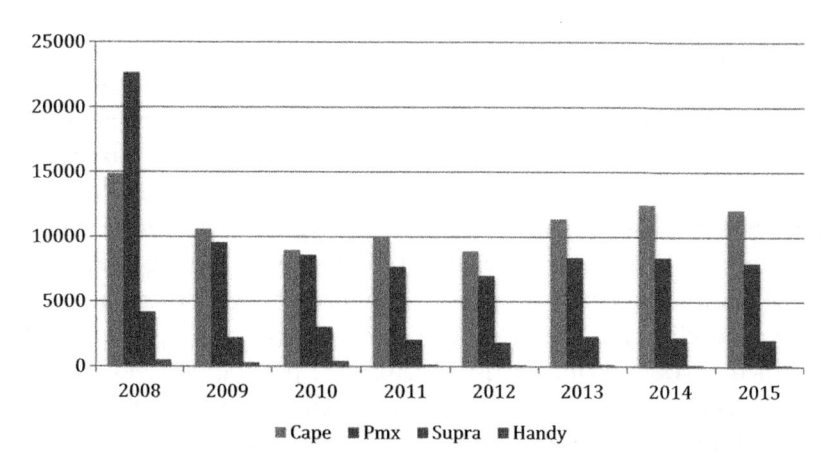

Fig. 15.1 Weekly average of total trade FFA dry-bulk volumes (in lots) (*Source*: Authors' calculations based on data from the Baltic Exchange)

seller of the FFAs/CFSAs. The opposite is true if freight rates increase above the agreed (FFA/CFSA) price.

Figure 15.1 presents the annual trade volumes (in lots) for different segments of the dry-bulk sector. As can be observed, apart from 2008, Capesize volume trades are the highest, followed by Panamax trades. Supramax trades are quite low, while Handysize trades are almost non-existent, mainly due to the increase in vessel sizes over the years.

To demonstrate how hedging works, assume that a shipowner or a charterer believes that freight rates in a specific freight route, with a specific vessel/cargo size, might move against his or her physical position in the near future. The shipowner (charterer) can sell (buy) FFA contracts, via a broker, written on the specific freight route. The shipowner's (charterer's) broker will search to find a counterparty with opposite expectations to his or her client, thereby wanting to buy (sell) FFAs. If an agreement is reached, then the FFA contract is written between the counterparties. At settlement, if freight rates fall below the agreed rate, the buyer of the freight derivative contract (i.e. the charterer) pays the difference between the agreed freight derivatives price and the settlement spot price; if rates increase, then the buyer of the freight derivatives contract receives the difference. The opposite is true for the seller of the freight derivatives contract, that is, for the shipowner.

FFAs can be used by various market participants and for a number of reasons. More specifically, for hedging purposes, shipowners can use FFAs to protect their income from falling freight rates and to trade on market views.

Charterers can also use FFAs to hedge—to protect their costs from rising freight rates but also to trade on their views regarding the freight market. Operators can reduce risks coming from cargo or vessel commitments depending on their position in the market; thus, if they have already fixed a vessel they would be looking to protect themselves against freight rate decreases by selling FFAs, while if they are looking to fix a vessel in the future, they look to protect themselves against freight rate increases by buying FFAs. Finally, financial institutions, such as banks and funds, amongst others, use FFAs to support their clients in areas such as risk management, proprietary trading[4] and to hedge vessel financing risks against the possibility of adverse future cash flows and earnings of clients or even the clients' inability to satisfy their ship-loan terms. In addition, the use of FFAs allow banks to increase the number of products they offer to clients in the sense that they can provide them with clearing accounts, valuation and pricing of derivatives products, margin (credit line) financing, quotation of prices, as well as advisory and consultancy services, among others.

15.3 Freight Rate Indices: The Underlying Assets of Freight Derivatives

The underlying assets of freight derivatives contracts are freight rates for various trade cargoes, such as coal, iron ore, crude oil and container boxes, transported in various maritime trade routes around the world by dry-bulk, tanker or container ships. The underlying assets of freight derivatives contracts are individual dry-bulk and tanker routes or baskets of routes of the Baltic Exchange Freight Indices, which are published on a daily basis. In the container sector, the underlying assets of the freight derivatives contracts are routes of the SCFI or of the WCI.

The Baltic Exchange appoints independent shipbrokers (the so-called panelists) around the world to "give their professional judgment as to the prevailing level of the open market within the parameters of the route they have been asked to assess". According to the Exchange, the factors taken into consideration by panelists in providing their assessment are: (1) known and recently concluded fixtures, (2) current negotiations, (3) vessels available, (4) laycan,[5] (5) prompt delivery of the vessel and (6) age factors, among others.[6] Once the freight assessments are received by the Exchange, their average for each individual route is calculated and sectoral freight indices are created, for instance for Capesize, Panamax and Supramax vessels, which are then reported to the market. Over the years, several sectoral indices have been created to meet the needs of market participants trading in these sectors. These are discussed next, but see also Kavussanos and Visvikis (2006a) for a detailed description of earlier periods.

In the dry-bulk sector, the Baltic Exchange Dry Bulk Index (BDI) was launched back in 1985; the Baltic Panamax Index (BPI) in 1998; the Baltic Capesize Index (BCI) in 1999, which was revised in May 2014 (BCI 2014) substituting routes C8_03, C9_03, C10_03 and C11_03; the Baltic Supramax Index (BSI) in 2005; the Baltic Handysize Index (BHSI) in 2006; the Baltic Exchange Panamax Asia (BEP Asia) and the Baltic Exchange Supramax Asia (BES Asia) in 2013; and the new Supramax index (BSI 58) and the Baltic Exchange Supramax 58 Asia (BES 58 Asia) in 2015. Panels A to H, of Table 15.1, present the compositions of the BCI 2014, BPI, BEP Asia, BSI, BES Asia, BES 58 Asia, BSI 58 and BHSI indices, respectively, as they stand in January 2016. The table, for each index, presents: the vessel size, in metric tons; the constituent route descriptions; the cargo carried in each route; and the weights of each route, representing the relative importance of each route

Table 15.1 The Baltic Exchange Dry-Bulk Freight Indices, January 2016

Routes	Vessel size (metric tons)	Route description	Cargo	Weights (%)
Panel A: Baltic Capesize Index (BCI)				
C2	160,000	Tubarao (Brazil)–Rotterdam (Netherlands)	Iron Ore	5
C3	160,000–170,000	Turabao–Qingdao (China)	Iron Ore	15
C4	150,000	Richards Bay (S. Africa)–Rotterdam	Coal	5
C5	160,000–170,000	W. Australia–Qingdao	Iron Ore	15
C7	150,000	Bolivar (Colombia)–Rotterdam	Coal	5
C8_14	180,000	Transatlantic round voyage, redelivery Gibraltar–Hamburg range	TC	5
C9_14	180,000	ARA (Amsterdam–Rotterdam–Antwerp) or passing Passero (Mediterranean), redelivery China–Japan	TC	7.5
C10_14	180,000	Pacific round voyage, delivery and redelivery China–Japan range	TC	15
C14_14	180,000	Qingdao–Brazil round voyage, redelivery China–Japan range	TC	15
C15	160,000	Richards Bay–Fangcheng (China)	Coal	5

(*continued*)

Table 15.1 (continued)

Routes	Vessel size (metric tons)	Route description	Cargo	Weights (%)
C16	180,000	North China–South Japan range, trip via Australia or Indonesia or US West Coast (USWC) or South Africa or Brazil, redelivery UK/Continent/Mediterranean within Skaw–Passero (North West Europe–Mediterranean)	TC	7.5
C17	170,000	Saldanha Bay (South Africa)–Qingdao	Iron Ore	0
Panel B: Baltic Panamax Index (BPI)				
P1A_03	74,000	Transatlantic round voyage	TC	25
P2A_03	74,000	Skaw–Gibraltar range to Far East, redelivery Taiwan–Japan range	TC	25
P3A_03	74,000	Japan–South Korea range to Pacific round voyage, redelivery Japan–South Korea range	TC	25
P4_03	74,000	Japan–South Korea range, redelivery Skaw–Passero range	TC	25
Panel C: Baltic Panamax Asia (BEP Asia)				
P5	74,000	South China Fuzhou–Hong Kong range or passing Taipei southbound for a trip to Indonesia, redelivery South China	TC	100
Panel D: Baltic Supramax Index (BSI)				
S1A	52,454	Antwerp (Belgium)/Skaw trip Far East, redelivery Singapore–Japan	TC	12.5
S1B	52,454	Canakkale (Turkey) trip Far East, redelivery Singapore–Japan	TC	12.5
S2	52,454	South Korea–Japan transpacific round voyage, redelivery South Korea–Japan	TC	25
S3	52,454	Japan–South Korea trip, redelivery Gibraltar–Skaw range	TC	25
S4A	52,454	US Gulf, redelivery Skaw–Passero range	TC	12.5
S4B	52,454	Skaw–Passero range, redelivery US Gulf	TC	12.5
S5	52,454	Delivery West Africa (Dakar–Douala range), trip via east coast South America, redelivery North China (Shanghai–Dalian range)	TC	0

(continued)

Table 15.1 (continued)

Routes	Vessel size (metric tons)	Route description	Cargo	Weights (%)
S9	52,454	Delivery West Africa (Dakar–Douala range), trip via east coast South America, redelivery Skaw–Passero range	TC	0
Panel E: Baltic Supramax Asia (BES Asia)				
S8	52,454	South China trip via Indonesia to east coast India	TC	33.33
S10	52,454	South China via Indonesia to South China	TC	33.33
S11	52,454	Mid-China (Changjiangkou–Ningde range)–Australia or transpacific round voyage	TC	33.33
Panel F: Baltic Supramax 58 Asia (BES 58 Asia)				
S8_58	58,328	South China trip via Indonesia to east coast India	TC	33.33
S10_58	58,328	South China trip via Indonesia to South China	TC	33.33
S11_58	58,328	Mid-China (Changjiangkou–Ningde range)–Australia or transpacific round voyage	TC	33.33
Panel G: Baltic Supramax 58 (BSI 58)				
S1B_58	58,328	Canakkale trip via Mediterranean or Black Sea to China South Korea	TC	5
S1C_58	58,328	US Gulf trip to China–South Japan	TC	5
S2_58	58,328	North China–Australia or Pacific round voyage	TC	20
S3_58	58,328	North China trip to West Africa	TC	15
S4A_58	58,328	US Gulf Trip to Skaw–Passero	TC	7.5
S4B_58	58,328	Skaw–Passero trip to US Gulf	TC	10
S5_58	58,328	West Africa trip via east coast South America to North China	TC	5
S8_58	58,328	South China trip via Indonesia to east coast India	TC	15
S9_58	58,328	West Africa trip via east coast South America to Skaw–Passero	TC	7.5
S10_58	58,328	South China trip via Indonesia to South China	TC	10
Panel H: Baltic Handysize Index (BHSI)				
HS1	28,000	Skaw–Passero trip, redelivery Recalada (Argentina)–Rio de Janeiro (Brazil) range	TC	12.5
HS2	28,000	Skaw–Passero trip, redelivery Boston–Galveston (USA) range	TC	12.5

(continued)

Table 15.1 (continued)

Routes	Vessel size (metric tons)	Route description	Cargo	Weights (%)
HS3	28,000	Recalada–Rio de Janeiro range, redelivery Skaw–Passero range	TC	12.5
HS4	28,000	US Gulf trip via US Gulf or North Coast South America, redelivery Skaw–Passero	TC	12.5
HS5	28,000	Southeast Asia trip via Australia, redelivery Singapore–Japan range	TC	25
HS6	28,000	South Korea–Japan via North Pacific, redelivery Singapore–Japan	TC	25

Notes: The 180,000 dwt five-time-charter route basket (5TC) of the BCI has the following weighting: C8_14: 25%; C9_14: 12.5%; C10_14: 25%; C14_14: 25%; and C16_14: 12.5%. For the Panamax, Supramax and Handysize time-charter baskets the weightings are the same as in Panels B, D and H. The new BCI 2014 index substituted the following routes, which were serving as the time-charter average basket (4TC) of 172,000 dwt vessels: C8_03: delivery Gibraltar–Hamburg range, redelivery Gibraltar–Hamburg range; C9_03: delivery ARA or passing Passero (Sicily), redelivery China–Japan range; C10_03: delivery China–Japan range round voyage, redelivery China–Japan range; and C11_03: delivery China–Japan range, redelivery ARA or passing Passero. In the BPI routes the following cargoes are transported: grains, petroleum, coke, coal or similar. In Supramax S8 and S10 routes coal is transported, while in the S11 route coal, grain or similar are transported. In the BEP Asia P5 route coal is transported
Source: Baltic Exchange

in the construction of the index. The Baltic Exchange then reports, on each business day, freight rate values for each route in the indices, each index, and "baskets" of time-charter routes for each sectoral index. For instance, the BCI5 is reported for the Capesize sector, which consists of the time-charter routes C8, C9, C10, C14 and C16. In some cases, such as for Panamax, the "basket" coincides with the index.

Figure 15.2 shows historical data for the BCI, BPI, BSI and BHSI indices from January 2000 to December 2015.

In the tanker sector, the Baltic Exchange launched the Baltic International Tanker Route (BITR) and the BITR Asia indices in January 1998 to cover the markets for the transportation of dirty (crude oil) and clean (crude oil products). In October 2001, it split the BITR into the Baltic Dirty Tanker Index (BDTI) to represent the dirty oil cargoes/markets and the Baltic Clean Tanker Index (BCTI) to cover the oil product markets. This was done in recognition of the fact that the dirty and clean tanker markets are separate

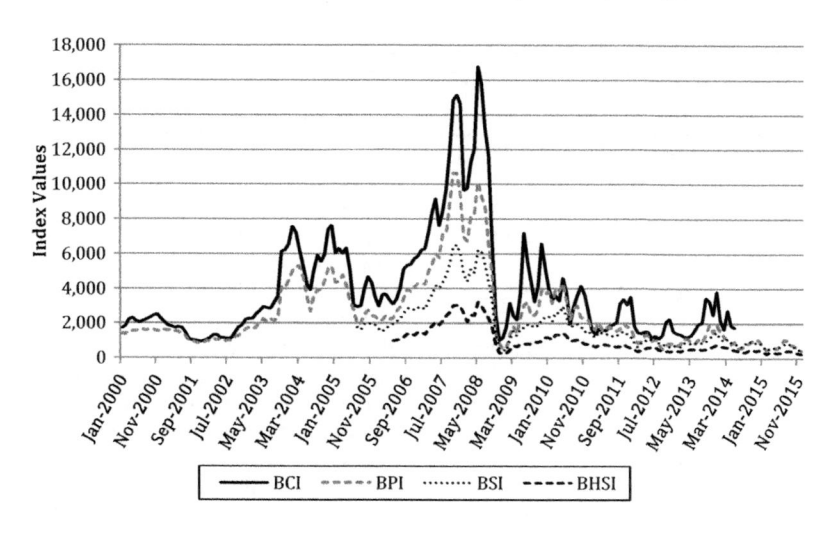

Fig. 15.2 Baltic Capesize, Panamax, Supramax and Handysize Indices (January 2000–December 2015) (*Source*: Clarksons Shipping Intelligence Network)

sectors, driven by distinct market conditions, and as such should be represented by separate freight indices. Panels A, B and C of Table 15.2 present the BDTI, BCTI and BITR Asia indices and their constituent freight routes, respectively, as they stand in January 2016. Just as with the dry-bulk freight indices, the Baltic Exchange collects, on each business day, freight information from tanker panelists on each individual route of the indices, calculates the average for each route over the panelists' values, and then reports these to the market, on a Worldscale measurement basis. In addition, the TCE freight rates, in USD/day, are also calculated as averages of individual freight routes; thus, the average of TD1 and TD3 is reported as the VLCC-TCE rate to represent the VLCC sector, the average of TD6 and TD20 is reported as the Suezmax-TCE rate, while the average of TD7, TD8, TD9, TD14, TD17 and TD19 is reported as the Aframax-TCE rate. Finally, the values of the BDTI, BDTI Asia and BCTI are reported in the market by the Exchange.

Figure 15.3 shows historical price fluctuations of the BDTI and BCTI from January 2000 to December 2015.

For the container sector, there are two freight rate indices, where the rates of their individual routes are utilized as the underlying assets of container freight derivatives. Their values are reported on a weekly basis, every Friday. The first is the Shanghai Containerized Freight Index (SCFI), constructed and published by the Shanghai Shipping Exchange (SSE). Its freight rates are quoted in USD/TEU for all routes, except for the US west and east coast

Table 15.2 The Baltic Tanker Freight Indices, January 2016

Routes	Vessel size (metric tons)	Type of vessel	Route description
Panel A: Baltic Dirty Tanker Index (BDTI)			
TD1	280,000	VLCC	Middle East Gulf to US Gulf. Ras Tanura (Saudi Arabia) to LOOP (USA)
TD2	270,000	VLCC	Middle East Gulf to Singapore. Ras Tanura to Singapore
TD3	265,000	VLCC	Middle East Gulf to Japan. Ras Tanura to Chiba (Japan)
TD6	135,000	Suezmax	Black Sea to Mediterranean. Novorossiysk (Russia) to Augusta (USA)
TD7	80,000	Aframax	North Sea to Continent. Sullom Voe (UK) to Wilhelmshaven (Germany)
TD8	80,000	Aframax	Kuwait to Singapore. Mena al Ahmadi (Kuwait) to Singapore
TD9	70,000	Panamax	Caribbean to US Gulf. Puerto La Cruz (Venezuela) to Corpus Christi (USA)
TD12	55,000	Panamax	ARA to US Gulf. Antwerp (Belgium) to Houston (USA)
TD14	80,000	Aframax	Southeast Asia to East Coast Australia. Syria to Sydney
TD15	260,000	VLCC	West Africa to China. Serpentina floating production storage and offloading (FPSO) and Bonny (Nigeria) Offshore to Ningbo (China)
TD17	100,000	Aframax	Baltic to UK Continent. Primorsk (Russia) to Wilhelmshaven (Germany)
TD18	30,000	Handysize	Baltic to UK Continent. Tallinn (Estonia) to Amsterdam (the Netherlands)
TD19	80,000	Aframax	Cross-Mediterranean. Ceyhan (Turkey) to Lavera (France)
TD20	130,000	Suezmax	West Africa to UK Continent to Rotterdam
TD21	50,000	Panamax	Caribbean to US Gulf. Mamonal (Colombia) to Houston (USA) (not contributing to BDTI)
VLCC-TCE	300,000	VLCC	TCE average of the rates derived from TD1 and TD3
Suezmax-TCE	160,000	Suezmax	TCE average of the rates derived from TD6 and TD20
Aframax-TCE	105,000	Aframax	TCE average of the rates derived from TD7, TD8, TD9, TD14, TD17 and TD19
TD3C	270,000	VLCC	Trial Middle East Gulf to China. Ras Tanura to Ningbo
Panel B: Baltic Clean Tanker Index (BCTI)			
TC1	75,000	Aframax	Middle East Gulf to Japan. Ras Tanura to Yokohama (Japan)
TC2_37	37,000	Handysize	Continent to US Atlantic Coast. Rotterdam to New York
TC5	55,000	Panamax	Middle East to Japan. Ras Tanura (Saudi Arabia) to Yokohama

(continued)

Table 15.2 (continued)

Routes	Vessel size (metric tons)	Type of vessel	Route description
TC6	30,000	Handysize	Algeria/Euromed. Skikda (Syria) to Lavera (France)
TC8	65,000	Panamax	Middle East Gulf to UK Continent. Jubail (Saudi Arabia) to Rotterdam
TC9	22,000	Handysize	Baltic to UK Continent. Primorsk to Le Havre (France)
TC14	38,000	Handysize	US Gulf to Continent. Houston to Amsterdam
TC15	80,000	Aframax	Trial Mediterranean/Far East (Naphtha)
TC16	60,000	Panamax	Trial Amsterdam to offshore Lome (Togo)
Panel C: Baltic Exchange Tanker Routes (BITR) Asia			
TC4	30,000	Handysize	Singapore to Japan. Singapore to Chiba (Japan)
TC7	30,000	Handysize	Singapore to EC. Australia. Singapore to Sydney
TC10	40,000	Handysize	South Korea to West Coast North Pacific. South Korea to Vancouver (Canada) to Rosarito (Mexico) range
TC11	40,000	Handysize	South Korea to Singapore
TC12	35,000	Handysize	West Coast India to Japan. Sikka (India) to Chiba

Notes: TD4, TD7, TD10, TD11 and TD12 dirty routes are excluded from BCTI and reported as stand-alone routes (BITR Asia), with a publishing time of 1600 Singapore time. TC12 route: product carrier carrying naphtha condensate.
Source: Baltic Exchange

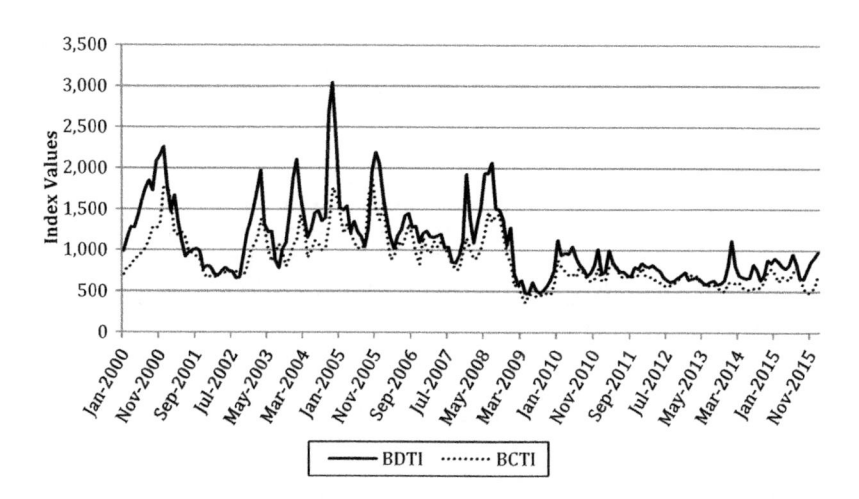

Fig. 15.3 Baltic Dirty and Clean Tanker Index (January 2000–December 2015) (*Source*: Clarksons Shipping Intelligence Network)

Table 15.3 Shanghai Containerized Freight Index (SCFI), January 2016

Line service	Route description	Unit	Weights (%)
1	Europe (base port)	USD/TEU	20
2	Mediterranean (base port)	USD/TEU	10
3	USWC (base port)	USD/FEU	20
4	USEC (base port)	USD/FEU	7.5
5	Persian Gulf and Red Sea (Dubai)	USD/TEU	7.5
6	Australian/New Zealand (Melbourne)	USD/TEU	5.0
7	East/West Africa (Lagos, Nigeria)	USD/TEU	2.5
8	South Africa (Durban)	USD/TEU	2.5
9	South America (Santos, Brazil)	USD/TEU	2.5
10	West Japan (base port)	USD/TEU	5.0
11	East Japan (base port)	USD/TEU	5.0
12	Southeast Asia (Singapore)	USD/TEU	5.0
13	South Korea (Pusan)	USD/TEU	2.5
14	Taiwan (Kaohsiung)	USD/TEU	2.5
15	Hong Kong (Hong Kong)	USD/TEU	2.5

Notes: The freight rate includes ocean freight and surcharges; all routes have as origin the port of Shanghai. Base port: Mediterranean Sea: Barcelona/Valencia/Genoa/Naples; Europe: Hamburg/Antwerp/Felixstowe/Le Havre; USWC: Los Angeles/Long Beach/Oakland; USEC: New York/Savannah/Norfolk/Charleston; West Japan: Osaka/Kobe East Japan–Tokyo/Yokohama.
Source: Shanghai Shipping Exchange

Table 15.4 World Container Index (WCI), January 2016

Line service	Route	Representative trade	Weights (%)
1	Shanghai–Rotterdam	Far East to North Europe	23.5
2	Rotterdam–Shanghai	North Europe to Far East	10.7
3	Shanghai–Genoa	Far East to Mediterranean	13.0
4	Genoa–Shanghai	Mediterranean to Far East	4.4
5	Shanghai–Los Angeles	Far East to US west coast	22.7
6	Los Angeles–Shanghai	US west coast to Far East	11.0
7	Shanghai–New York	Far East to US east coast	8.3
8	Los Angeles–Rotterdam	US west coast to North Europe	0.30
9	Rotterdam–Los Angeles	North Europe to US west coast	0.50
10	New York–Rotterdam	US east coast to North Europe	2.5
11	Rotterdam–New York	North Europe to US east coast	3.0

Source: Cleartrade Exchange

routes for which the rates are quoted in USD/FEU. The second index is the World Container Index (WCI), which is a joint venture between Drewry Shipping Consultants and Cleartrade Exchange. Its routes are quoted in USD/FEU. Tables 15.3 and 15.4, respectively, present the SCFI and WCI indices and their composition.[7]

15.4 Freight Derivatives Markets and Products

Freight derivative contracts can be traded as exchange-based futures or options products in organized derivatives exchanges. Alternatively, they can be found as OTC forward (swap) or option products, with or without clearing.

15.4.1 Forward Freight Agreements (FFAs)

FFAs are OTC private contracts between two counterparties to trade a freight route or a basket of freight routes on one of the freight indices described in the previous section. Being private contracts, they incorporate counterparty risk, which may or may not be eliminated by the parties involved in the contract in one of the clearing houses offering the service. In the case where one counterparty to an FFA contract wishes to sell the credit risk, that is, when clearing is required for OTC products, then these "hybrid" FFA contracts (or block futures[8]) are mark-to-market cleared in a clearing house. This allows FFAs to retain their flexible OTC nature, while eliminating the credit risk they bare. Hybrid FFAs can be cleared at the London Clearing House Clearnet (LCH. Clearnet) or at Singapore Exchange AsiaClear (SGX AsiaClear).

Since 2007, due to the financial crisis and the ensuing 2008 shipping crisis that amplified credit risk, but also due to new regulatory reforms on OTC derivatives markets (see later in the chapter), almost 99% of OTC FFA trades are cleared. Figure 15.4 presents the annual trade volumes of cleared versus

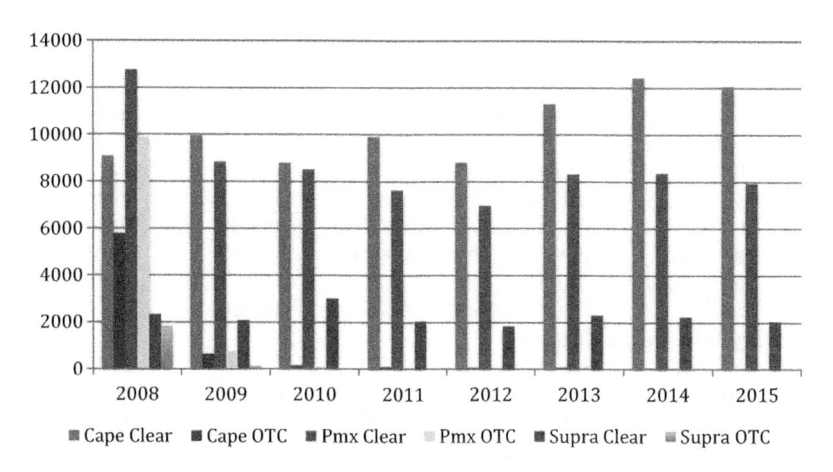

Fig. 15.4 Weekly average trade volumes cleared vs OTC by sector (in lots) (*Source*: Authors' calculations based on data from the Baltic Exchange)

OTC FFA trades in the dry-bulk sector. As can be seen, since 2009, in all sectors, OTC trades are almost non-existent.

In terms of liquidity of FFA contracts, the Capesize time-charter average "basket" is the most liquid contract. The Pananax and Supramax time-charter average "basket" contracts follow, in terms of liquidity. For Capesize, the individual routes are not so liquid, with few market participants trading them. However, some trading takes place on the C3/C5 spread. For Panamax, routes P2A and P3A are traded for nearby positions, say up to six months out.

15.4.2 Freight Futures Contracts

Freight (block) futures contracts trade at the Chicago Mercantile Exchange (CME Group, formerly New York Mercantile Exchange, NYMEX) and are cleared in ClearPort, its associated clearing house. Tanker freight derivatives were launched in May 2005 at NYMEX, followed by dry-bulk freight derivatives, launched in 2010. The underlying assets of these are freight routes of the Baltic Exchange, and in some cases the tanker routes of Platts. Table 15.5 presents the specifications of the available freight derivatives contracts at CME group. Panel A shows the *dirty* tanker futures contracts, namely TD3 and TD7; panel B presents the available *clean* tanker futures, that is TC2,

Table 15.5 CME group freight futures, January 2016

Routes	Sector	Route description	Vessel size (metric tons)	Settlement index
Panel A: Dirty tanker freight futures				
TD3	VLCC	Middle Eastern Gulf to Japan	260,000	Baltic
TD7	Aframax	North Sea to Continent	80,000	Baltic
Panel B: Clean tanker freight futures				
TC2	MR	Europe to USAC	37,000	Baltic
TC5	LR1	Ras Tanura to Yokohama	55,000	Platts
TC6	MR	Algeria to Euromed	30,000	Baltic
TC12	Handysize	Sikka (west coast India) to Chiba	35,000	Baltic
TC14	Handysize	US Gulf to Continent	38,000	Baltic
Panel C: Dry-bulk freight futures				
–	Capesize	Time-charter average (4TC)	TC	Baltic
–	Capesize	Time-charter average (5TC)	TC	Baltic
–	Panamax	Time-charter average (4TC)	TC	Baltic
–	Supramax	Time-charter average (6TC)	TC	Baltic
–	Handysize	Time-charter average (6TC)	TC	Baltic

Notes: *LR* long range, *MR* medium range
Source: CME Group

TC5, TC6, TC12 and TC14; while panel C lists the available time-charter "basket" average futures.

According to CME Group, these contracts are listed in both full (1 day) and quarter-day (0.25 day) sizes to allow for more flexibility for "trade splitting and shaping across months". The settlement price for each contract month equals the arithmetic average of the time-charter average for the specific vessel type, as published by the Baltic Exchange, starting from the first business day of the month through to the last trading day, inclusive.

Since March 2011, ICE Futures Europe offers a range of products for trading, designed to cover the needs of customers in areas such as agriculture, foreign exchange, energy, ferrous metals, freight, indices and environment products. Table 15.6 presents the dry-bulk and tanker freight (block) futures contracts available. These are cleared by ICE Clear Europe. For balance-of-month (BALMO) contracts, the settlement price for each contract month is a price in USD which is based on the arithmetic average of the assessments for the specific vessel type as quoted by the Baltic Exchange (TC2 BALMO, TC6 BALMO, TC7 BALMO, TC14 BALMO) or Platts TankerWire (TC4 BALMO, TC5 BALMO), starting two business days forward of the "trade day" and continuing through to the end of the contract month (up to two consecutive months).

The International Maritime Exchange (IMAREX) in Oslo has traded freight futures since 2001 and options since 2005, while clearing took place at the Norwegian Options and Futures (NOS) clearing house. In May 2011, Marex Group, a broker of wholesale energy and other commodity products, acquired (from IMAREX) Spectron Group Ltd to become Marex-Spectron. This is a UK based broker of commodity and energy financial products, providing voice and electronic trading and clearing services. In July 2012, NASDAQ OMX Stockholm AB, which is a part of NASDAQ OMX Group Inc., acquired (from IMAREX) the NOS clearing house and became fully integrated in NASDAQ OMX Clearing in April 2014. Table 15.7 presents the NASDAQ OMX clean and dirty tanker futures in panel A, the Capesize and Panamax single route futures in panel B, and the dry-bulk time-charter average "baskets" in panel C.

15.4.3 Cleared Forward Derivatives

Since in OTC markets each counterparty accepts credit risk from the other party, clearing houses provide the mechanism through which credit risk can be sold to them for a fee. Thus, in the case of default, the party that made a

Table 15.6 ICE futures Europe, January 2016

Routes	Sector	Route description	Vessel size (metric tons)	Settlement index
Panel A: Dirty tanker futures				
TD3	VLCC	Arabian Gulf to Japan	265,000	Baltic
TD7	Aframax	North Sea to Continent	80,000	Baltic
TD20	Suezmax	West Africa to UK Continent	130,000	Baltic
Panel B: Clean tanker futures				
TC2	MR	North-west Europe to USAC	37,000	Baltic
TC2 BALMO	MR	North-west Europe to USAC	37,000	Baltic
TC4	MR	Singapore to Japan	30,000	Platts
TC4 BALMO	MR	Singapore to Japan	30,000	Platts
TC5	LR 1	Arabian Gulf to Japan	55,000	Platts
TC5 BALMO	LR 1	Arabian Gulf to Japan	55,000	Platts
TC6	MR	Skikda to Lavera (Cross-Med)	30,000	Baltic
TC6 BALMO	MR	Skikda to Lavera (Cross-Med)	30,000	Baltic
TC7	MR	Singapore to EC Australia	30,000	Baltic
TC7 BALMO	MR	Singapore to EC Australia	30,000	Baltic
TC14	Handysize	US Gulf to Continent	38,000	Baltic
TC14 BALMO	Handysize	US Gulf to Continent	38,000	Baltic
Panel C: Dry-bulk freight futures				
–	Capesize	Time-charter average	TC	Baltic
–	Panamax	Time-charter average	TC	Baltic
–	Supramax	Time-charter average	TC	Baltic
–	Handymax	Mini-time-charter average	TC	Baltic

Note: BALMO balance-of-month
Source: ICE futures Europe

profit will still be paid by the clearing house through its daily mark-to-market mechanism. Following the 2008 financial crisis, almost all freight derivatives transactions are cleared.

In December 2003, London Clearing House (LCH) Limited merged with Clearnet S.A. to form LCH.Clearnet Group. During September 2005, LCH.Clearnet launched a clearing and settlement system for freight derivatives. Table 15.8 presents the available freight derivatives contracts cleared on LCH.Clearnet. Panel A presents the four cleared dry-bulk voyage FFAs, written on Capesize voyage routes C3E, C4E, C5E and C7E, traded as months, quarters and calendars, where their settlement is the average of all prices in the settlement month (indicated by the symbol "E"). C3E and C4E are traded out to three whole calendar years (a maximum of 47 months—for example, in

Table 15.7 NASDAQ OMX futures, January 2016

Routes	Sector	Route description	Vessel size (metric tons)	Settlement index
Panel A: Tanker futures				
TC2USD	MR	Continent–USAC	37,000	Baltic
TC6USD	MR	Algeria–Euromed	30,000	Baltic
TC7USD	MR	Singapore–EC Australia	30,000	Baltic
TC12USD	MR	West Coast India–Japan	35,000	Baltic
TC14USD	MR	US Gulf–Continent	38,000	Baltic
TD3USD	VLCC	Arabian Gulf–East	265,000	Baltic
TD7USD	Aframax	North Sea–Continent	80,000	Baltic
TD8USD	Aframax	Kuwait–Singapore	80,000	Baltic
TD20USD	Suezmax	West Africa–Continent	130,000	Baltic
MRA	MR	Atlantic Basket (TC)	47,000	Baltic
Panel B: Dry-bulk singe route futures				
C4 AVG	Capesize	Richards Bay–Rotterdam	150,000	Baltic
C5 AVG	Capesize	W. Australia–Qingdao	160,000	Baltic
C7 AVG	Capesize	Bolivar–Rotterdam	150,000	Baltic
P1A/P1A AVG	Panamax	Transatlantic RV	TC	Baltic
P2A/P2A AVG	Panamax	Skaw Gibraltar–Far East	TC	Baltic
P3A/P3A AVG	Panamax	S. Korea–Japan Pacific RV	TC	Baltic
Panel C: Dry-bulk TC basket futures				
CST4TC	Capesize	Time-charter average	–	Baltic
CS5TC	Capesize	Time-charter average (2014)	–	Baltic
PM4TC	Panamax	Time-charter average	–	Baltic
SM6TC	Supramax	Time-charter average	–	Baltic
HS6TC	Handymax	Mini-time-charter average	–	Baltic

Source: NASDAQ OMX clearing

January 2016 someone can trade up to December 2019, that is, 11 months plus 36 months ahead); C7E is traded out to five whole calendar years (a maximum of 71 months—for example, in January 2016 someone can trade up to December 2021; that is, 11 months plus 60 months ahead); and C5E is traded out to one whole calendar year (a maximum of 23 months—for example, in January 2016 someone can trade up to December 2017, that is, 11 months plus 12 months ahead). Their final settlement is the floating price, which is calculated as the mean of the daily Baltic Exchange spot price assessments for every trading day in the expiry month.

Panel B presents the five time-charter average "baskets" on Capesize (CTC), the new Capesize 2014 (CPT), Panamax (PTC), Supramax (STC) and Handysize (HTC) vessels. CTC, CPT and PTC are traded as months, quarters and calendars, out to seven whole calendar years (a maximum of 95 months), while STC and HTC are traded out to five whole calendar years (a maximum of 71 months). Their final settlement is the floating price, calculated similarly.

Table 15.8 Freight derivatives cleared at LCH.Clearnet, January 2016

Routes	Sector	Route description	Cargo size (metric tons)
Panel A: Dry voyage routes			
C3E	Capesize	Tubarao–Qingdao	160,000–170,000
C4E	Capesize	Richard Bay–Rotterdam	150,000
C5E	Capesize	West Australia–Qingdao	160,000–170,000
C7E	Capesize	Bolivar–Rotterdam	150,000
Panel B: Dry time-charter "Basket" routes			
CTC	Capesize	Capesize 4TC routes average	TC
CPT	Capesize	Capesize 5TC routes average (2014)	TC
PTC	Panamax	Panamax 4TC routes average	TC
STC	Supramax	Supramax 6TC routes average	TC
HTC	Handymax	Handymax 6TC routes average	TC
Panel C: Dry trip time-charter routes			
P1A (P1E)	Panamax	Transatlantic round voyage	TC
P2A (P2E)	Panamax	Continent trip Ffar East	TC
P3A (P3E)	Panamax	Transpacific round voyage	TC
Panel D: Container routes			
CNW	Container	Shanghai–North West Europe	TEU
CSW	Container	Shanghai–US west coast	FEU

Source: LCH.Clearnet

Panel C presents the three dry trip time-charter FFAs on Panamax time-charter P1A (P1E), P2A (P2E) and P3A (P3E) routes. The Panamax contracts are also traded as months, quarters and calendars, out to three whole calendar years (a maximum of 47 months). In respect of the final settlement for P1A, P2A and P3A, the floating price is the mean of the last seven Baltic Exchange spot price assessments in the expiry month, while the final settlement for P1E, P2E and P3E is the mean of the daily Baltic Exchange spot price assessments for every trading day in the expiry month. Finally, panel D shows the two container CFSAs on CNW (North West Europe) and CSW (US west coast) cleared at LCH.Clearnet. They are traded as front three months, front quarter plus the following three quarters, and a calendar year.

In May 2006, Singapore Exchange Limited (SGX) launched SGX AsiaClear, an OTC clearing facility for energy and freight derivatives. Singapore Exchange Derivatives Clearing Ltd supports clearing for the SGX AsiaClear facility. SGX offers a trade platform of freight products comprising freight futures, FFAs and freight options, whereas clearing takes place at SGX AsiaClear. Freight futures are in most aspects similar to their corresponding contract specifications for swaps. Both share the same daily and final settlement prices and expiry dates. Once these contracts are submitted for clearing, the risk management treatment and pay-offs for the two contracts are identical.

Table 15.9 Freight derivatives cleared at SGX AsiaClear, January 2016

Routes	Sector	Route description	Cargo size (metric tons)
Panel A: Dry bulk voyage forwards			
C5	Capesize	West Australia/Beilun–Baoshan	160,000–170,000
Panel B: Dry bulk time-charter "basket" forwards			
CTC	Capesize	Capesize 4TC routes average	TC
CTC 2014	Capesize	Capesize 5TC routes average	TC
PTC	Panamax	Panamax 4TC routes average	TC
STC	Supramax	Supramax 6TC routes average	TC
HTC	Handysize	Handysize 6TC routes average	TC
Half-Day CTC	Capesize	Capesize 4TC routes average	TC
Half-Day PTC	Panamax	Panamax 4TC routes average	TC
Half-Day STC	Supramax	Supramax 6TC routes average	TC
Half-Day HTC	Handysize	Handysize 6TC routes average	TC
Panel C: Dry bulk trip time-charter forwards			
P2A	Panamax	Skaw–Gibraltar/Far East	TC
P3A	Panamax	Transpacific Round–Japan	TC

Note: Half-day contracts refer to ½ day = 1 lot. The rest are full-day contracts
Source: SGX AsiaClear

Table 15.9 presents the FFA contracts cleared at SGX AsiaClear. They include: one dry-bulk voyage FFA written on Capesize voyage route C5, as shown in panel A; since November 2007 four full-day and four half-day dry-bulk time-charter "baskets" on Capesize, Panamax and Supramax vessels and since June 2009 on Handysize vessels, and one full-day time-charter basket on the new Capesize 2014, all presented in panel B; and finally, two dry trip-time-charter FFAs, written on Panamax time-charter P2A and P3A routes, shown in panel C. These *hybrid* FFAs seem to combine the best of futures and forwards into one contract type; that is, counterparty risk is removed and yet they retain their flexibility by adjusting their terms according to the needs of the counterparties.

CME Clearing Europe was launched in May 2011 in London as a subsidiary of CME Group. The clearing house handles OTC contracts including energy, agriculture, freight and precious metals, as well as OTC financial derivatives. In August 2014, CME Group announced that CME Clearing Europe had received authorization as a central counterparty clearing house (CCP). The authorization covers all OTC derivatives and futures products currently cleared by CME Clearing Europe. Table 15.10 presents the available dirty (TD3, TD5, TD7) and clean (TC2, TC5) tanker derivatives offered for clearing by CME Clearing Europe.

From December 2012, freight derivatives that trade OTC through brokers registered with the Shanghai Clearing House (SHCH) can be settled

Table 15.10 Freight derivatives cleared at CME Clearing Europe, January 2016

Baltic routes	Sector	Route description	Cargo size (metric tons)	Settlement index
Panel A: Dirty tanker swaps				
TD3	VLCC	Middle East Gulf to Japan	260,000	Baltic
TD5	Suezmax	West Africa to USAC	130,000	Baltic
TD7	Aframax	North Sea to Europe	80,000	Baltic
Panel B: Clean tanker swaps				
TC2	MR	Europe to USAC	37,000	Baltic
TC5	LR 1	Ras Tanura to Yokohama	55,000	Platts

Source: CME Clearing Europe

in Chinese RMB, with the Baltic Exchange indices as the underlying assets. The Shanghai Pudong Development Bank acts as a general clearing member (GCM) of the SHCH, and provides central counterparty clearing. Several brokers, such as Freight Investor Services, Simpson, Spence & Young, Windely, JoinOcean Shipbroker, Shanghai Seamaster Shipbroking and Barry Rogliano Salles are registered as RMB-FFA brokers. Shipping companies, which meet the registration requirements in China, are now permitted to trade RMB freight derivatives for hedging and trading purposes. This development creates an "on-shore market" in China to satisfy the demand of local participants.

15.4.4 Freight Options

Freight options were introduced in the early 2000s, either in OTC markets or in organized derivatives exchanges. The underlying "commodities" are individual dry-bulk and tanker routes, and baskets of time-charter routes. Freight options are Asian type puts (floors) or calls (caps), as they settle on the difference between the average freight rate over a defined period of time and an agreed strike price. Similar to European style options, they are exercised only on their settlement date.

For hedging purposes, shipowners can protect themselves against a fall in freight rates by buying a put freight option; that is, they pay the (option) premium in order to buy and have the option (but not the obligation) to sell the freight service at a specified date in the future at a freight price—the strike price—agreed on at the time of the transaction. The option is exercised, to sell at the agreed price, if the market freight rate falls below the agreed (strike) price. In the case where the freight rate is higher than the strike price, the option expires worthlessly as it is not worth exercising. The option premium is received by the issuer (the writer/seller) of the put option, who has the obligation to pay the buyer if the latter decides to exercise the option. The opposite is true for the charterers, as, in order to protect themselves against an increase in freight rates, they will buy a call option; that is, they pay the call (option) premium in order to have the option (but not the obligation) to buy the freight service at a specified date in the future at a freight price they agree on at the time of the transaction. If the freight rate rises above the strike price, they will exercise the option to buy at the lower price agreed. If at expiry the freight rate is below the strike price then it is not worth exercising the option, as the charterer can simply buy the freight service in the market at a lower price than that agreed— in that case, the option buyer is losing the option premium paid.

The Baltic Exchange publishes the Baltic Options' Assessments (BOA) as the average of daily assessments of implied volatility for at-the-money freight options provided by brokers trading these options. These daily assessments are submitted by brokers (panelists) to the Baltic Exchange and are announced by the latter to the market at 1730 London time. Implied volatilities are reported for Capesize 2014, Capesize, Panamax, Supramax and Handysize baskets of time-charter routes.

The CME Group offers one dirty tanker freight option on route TD3 and two clean tanker freight options on routes TC2 and TC5, as shown in Table 15.11. Tanker freight options are settled against the Baltic Exchange quotes, with the exception of route TC5, where the Platts assessment is used for settlement.

NASDAQ OMX Clearing has also been clearing freight options since 2012. Table 15.12 presents the clean and dirty tanker options that can be cleared in panel A, the Capesize and Panamax single route options in panel B, and the dry-bulk TC average "baskets" in panel C.

In 2008, LCH.Clearnet launched a clearing service for dry-bulk freight options for Capesize, Panamax, Supramax and Handysize time-charter "basket" contracts. Table 15.13 presents the freight option contracts cleared at LCH.Clearnet. They are European style, cash settled and denominated in USD/day, where 1 Lot = 1 Day.

In April 2013 ICE Futures Europe launched trading and clearing freight options on dirty and clean tanker routes, as can be seen in Table 15.14.

Table 15.11 CME group tanker freight options, January 2016

Baltic routes	Product symbol	Sector	Route description	Cargo size (metric tons)	Type of contract	Settlement index
TD3	TL	VLCC	Middle Eastern Gulf to Japan	260,000	Options	Baltic
TC2	TM	MR	Europe to USAC	37,000	Options	Baltic
TC5	TH	LR 1	Ras Tanura to Yokohama	55,000	Options	Platts

Source: CME Group

Table 15.12 NASDAQ OMX options, January 2016

Routes	Sector	Route description	Vessel size (metric tons)	Settlement index
Panel A: Tanker freight options				
TC2USD	MR	Continent—USAC	37,000	Baltic
TC5USD	LR1	AG—Japan	55,000	Platts
TC6USD	MR	Algeria—Euromed	30,000	Baltic
TC7USD	MR	Singapore—EC Australia	30,000	Baltic
TC12USD	MR	West coast India—Japan	35,000	Baltic
TC14USD	MR	US Gulf—Continent	38,000	Baltic
MRA	MR	Atlantic basket	47,000	Baltic
TD3USD	VLCC	AG—East	265,000	Baltic
TD3_TCE	VLCC	AG—East	265,000	Baltic
TD5USD	Suezmax	West Africa—USAC	130,000	Baltic
TD7USD	Aframax	North Sea—Continent	80,000	Baltic
TD20USD	Suezmax	West Africa—Continent	130,000	Baltic
Panel B: Dry bulk single route freight options				
C4 AVG	Capesize	Richards Bay—Rotterdam	150,000	Baltic
C5 AVG	Capesize	W. Australia—Qingdao	160,000	Baltic
C7 AVG	Capesize	Bolivar—Rotterdam	150,000	Baltic
P1A/P1A AVG	Panamax	Transatlantic RV	TC	Baltic
P2A/P2A AVG	Panamax	Skaw Gibraltar—Far East	TC	Baltic
P3A/P3A AVG	Panamax	S. Korea—Japan Pacific RV (round voyage)	TC	Baltic
Panel C: Dry-bulk TC freight options "basket"				
CST4TC	Capesize	Time-charter average	TC	Baltic
CS5TC	Capesize	Time-charter average (2014)	TC	Baltic
PM4TC	Panamax	Time-charter average	TC	Baltic
SM6TC	Supramax	Time-charter average	TC	Baltic
HS6TC	Handymax	Mini-time-charter average	TC	Baltic

Source: NASDAQ OMX Clearing

Table 15.13 LCH.Clearnet dry-bulk freight options, January 2016

Sector	Route baskets
Capesize	4TC Average
Capesize	5TC Average
Panamax	4TC Average
Supramax	6TC Average
Handysize	6TC Average

Source: LCH.Clearnet

15.5 The Baltic Forward Assessments

Since September 2003, the Baltic Exchange constructs and reports to the market BFAs. These are based on mid-bid–ask FFA prices, as provided by a panel of FFA brokers appointed by the Baltic Exchange. The panelists report to the Exchange, by 1630 London time, their professional judgment of mid-FFA

Table 15.14 ICE Futures Europe freight options, January 2016

Routes	Sector	Route description	Cargo size (metric tons)	Settlement index
Panel A: Dirty tanker futures				
TD3	VLCC	Arabian Gulf to Japan	260,000	Baltic
TD7	Aframax	North Sea to Continent	80,000	Baltic
Panel B: Clean tanker futures				
TC2	MR	North-west Europe to USAC	37,000	Baltic
TC4	MR	Singapore to Japan	30,000	Platts
TC5	LR 1	Arabian Gulf to Japan	55,000	Platts
TC6	MR	Skikda to Lavera (Cross-Med)	30,000	Baltic
TC14	Handysize	US Gulf to Continent	38,000	Baltic

Source: ICE futures Europe

market prices on each Baltic index publication day, for the routes defined by the Exchange. The Exchange calculates an average of the panelists' figures for each route and then reports these BFA prices to the market by 1730 London time. If no actual FFA trade has been conducted on a specific day for a specified maturity, the panelists take into account all market information available before quoting the BFA price.

The panelists are FFA brokers, must be members of the Baltic Exchange and of the FFA Brokers Association (FFABA). They must follow the rules and regulations for the production of the BFAs in the *Manual for Forward Panellists* and in the *Guide to Market Benchmarks*, both drafted by the Baltic Exchange. BFAs are regarded as the most representative FFA data, as they include information from the most active FFA brokers.[9]

BFAs are used by clearing houses and market participants (traders) to mark-to-market the open FFA positions, in order to determine the relevant margin calls, and for internal risk management reasons. Moreover, forward curves can be derived from BFAs, which can be used as indicators of the future direction of the physical freight market. BFAs have been reported since September 2003 for various trading routes (and baskets) of the dry-bulk sector and since February 2006 for the trading routes of the tanker sector.

BFAs are quoted for the dry-bulk Capesize single routes C3, C4, C5 and C7, for the Panamax single routes P1A, P2A and P3A, and for the time-charter "baskets" of the Capesize (BCI 5TC average), Panamax (BPI 4TC average), Supramax (BSI 6TC average) and Handysize (BHSI 6TC average) sectors. Tanker BFAs are quoted for six clean routes, that is for TC2_37, TC5, TC6, TC7, TC12 and TC14; and for six dirty routes, that is for TD3, TD7, TD8, TD17, TD19 and TD20. They are quoted both in WS and in USD/metric ton. Finally, route TD3 and the MR (Medium Range) Atlantic Basket, being a combination of TC2 and TC14, are quoted in USD/day.

For the single dry-bulk routes, the reported maturities are the current month, the next nearest month, the first month of the next nearest quarter, and the next five calendar years. For the time-charter baskets, the reported maturities are similar to those of the dry-bulk routes but here the reporting concentrates on quarters (three consecutive FFA monthly contracts) and calendar years (12 single-month contracts from January to December of the same year) rather than on individual months. Each maturity contract is reported until one working day before the maturity of the current contract and the rollover to the next nearest maturity contract on the settlement of the current contract.[10] For the single tanker routes, the reported maturities are the current month, the nearest five months, the current quarter, the nearest five quarters and the next two calendar years.

15.6 Trading Screens

Trading screens have also been developed for freight derivatives markets. The need for transparency, efficiency, decrease of transactions costs, liquidity, price discovery, faster trade execution and compliance with recent regulations (see below), among other reasons, were all accelerated by the world financial and economic crisis of 2007–08 and the ensuing credit and systemic risk problems. The Baltic Exchange trading screen (Baltex) in London, the Cleartrade Exchange (CLTX) screen in Singapore and the Shanghai Shipping Freight Exchange Co. (SSEFC) screen in Shanghai are such examples, all launched in June 2011.

Baltex is a Financial Conduct Authorities (FCA) approved multilateral trading facility (MTF) for dry-bulk freight derivatives, operated by Baltic Exchange Derivatives Trading (BEDT) Limited. According to the Baltic Exchange, Baltex promotes price transparency, counterparty anonymity, increased liquidity, flexible ways of working with a broker, straight-through processing to clearing (STC) and a clearing house choice (LCH.Clearnet or NOS Clearing). The Baltex market is open from 0700 to 1800, London time.

Table 15.15 presents the freight derivatives contracts that trade on the Baltex screen. They include the following single routes and time-charter baskets: Capesize routes C3, C4, C5 and C7 are shown in panel A; Panamax time-charter trip forward routes P1A, P2A and P3A are shown in panel B; and Capesize 4TC, Capesize 2014 5TC, Panamax 4TC, Supramax 6TC and Handysize 6TC time-charter average "baskets" are shown in panel C.

The CLTX provides a screen for OTC freight derivatives trading. It is a recognized market operator (RMO), regulated by the Monetary Authority of

Table 15.15 Baltex trading screen products, January 2016

Routes	Sector	Route description
Panel A: Dry-bulk voyage routes		
C3	Capesize	Tubarao—Qingdao
C4	Capesize	Richards Bay—Rotterdam
C5	Capesize	West Australia—Qingdao
C7	Capesize	Bolivar Roads—Rotterdam
Panel B: Dry-bulk trip time-charter routes		
P1A	Panamax	Transatlantic round voyage
P2A	Panamax	Skaw–Gibraltar/Far East
P3A	Panamax	Japan–SK/Pacific round voyage
Panel C: Dry-bulk time-charter average "baskets"		
–	Capesize	4TC Time-charter
–	Capesize	5TC Time-charter (2014)
–	Panamax	4TC Time-charter
–	Supramax	6TC Time-charter
–	Handysize	6TC Time-charter

Source: Baltic Exchange

Singapore (MAS), with offices in London. It offers an electronic order book with a suite of over 40 different derivatives contracts, covering the ferrous metal, agricultural, energy and freight markets. The CLTX screen also offers a block trade facility, trade processing and reporting services, and STP[11] to multiple clearing houses. CLTX works on a membership basis and is open to participation from inter-dealer brokers, traders/principals and general clearers. Table 15.16 presents the available dry-bulk derivative contracts that trade on CLTX (panels A to C) and cleared on LCH.Clearnet, SGX and NOS Clearing. Panel D of the table shows the container derivative contracts (written on SCFI) that trade on CLTX and cleared on LCH.Clearnet and SGX Asia Clear. The time-charter baskets CTC, PTC, STC and HTC are traded in months, quarters and calendar years out to a maximum of 72 months. The dry voyage and trip time-charter routes are traded in months, quarters and calendar years out to a maximum of 36 months. Finally, the container routes (CSW, CNW) are traded in months, quarters and calendar years out to a maximum of 24 months.

The SSEFC is a freight third party centralized trading platform founded by the SSE and the Shanghai Hongkou District State-owned Assets Operation Co., Ltd. It is controlled by SSE and supervised by the Municipal Government of Shanghai and the Ministry of Transport of the People's Republic of China. SSEFC offers the possibility to trade the shipping capacity of container freight derivatives on two of SSE's SCFI routes. These are cleared at LCH.Clearnet and settled against the monthly average price of the settlement month. SSEFC also offers two dry-bulk time-charter products and one China coastal bulk (coal) freight derivatives product (Qinhuangdao to Shanghai). These are

Table 15.16 CLTX trading screen products, January 2016

Routes	Sector	Route description
Panel A: Dry-bulk voyage		
C3E	Capesize	Tubarao—Qingdao
C4E	Capesize	Richards Bay—Rotterdam
C5E	Capesize	West Australia—Qingdao
C7E	Capesize	Bolivar Roads—Rotterdam
Panel B: Dry-bulk trip time-charter		
P1A (P1E)	Panamax	Transatlantic round voyage
P2A (P2E)	Panamax	Skaw–Gibraltar/Far East
P3A (P3E)	Panamax	Japan–SK/Pacific round voyage
Panel C: Dry-bulk time-charter average baskets		
CTC	Capesize	TC
PTC	Panamax	TC
STC	Supramax	TC
HTC	Handysize	TC
Panel D: SCFI container routes		
CNW (USD/TEU)	–	Shanghai—North West Europe
CSW (USD/FEU)	–	Shanghai—US west coast

Notes:
The settlement price of P1A, P2A and P3A is the mean of the last seven Baltic Exchange spot price assessments of the expiry month
The settlement price of C3E, C4E, C5E, C7E, P1E, P2E and P3E is the mean of the daily Baltic Exchange spot price assessments for every trading day in the expiry month
Source: Cleartrade Exchange

Table 15.17 SSEFC trading screen products, January 2016

Underlying index	Sector	Route description
SCFI (USD/FEU)	Container	Shanghai–US west coast
SCFI (USD/TEU)	Container	Shanghai–Europe
Supramax (USD/day)	Supramax	Time-charter
Panamax (USD/day)	Panamax	Time-charter
China Coastal Bulk (Coal) Freight Index (CNY)	Coal	Qinhuangdao–Shanghai

Source: SSEFC

summarized in Table 15.17. Six consecutive months, starting with the current month, can be traded. The trading hours are 0855–1130 and 1330–1500, Beijing time. In 2014, transactions exceeded RMB500 billion, with trade volume around 27 million lots.

15.7 Regulations in Derivatives Markets

Since 2010, there have been several attempts both in the USA and in Europe to regulate further the OTC derivatives markets, with mandates for compulsory exchange trading and clearing requirements.

In the USA, the Dodd-Frank Wall Street Reform and Consumer Protection Act (DFA), passed in July 2010, forces all swaps to be cleared through a derivatives clearing organization (DCO) and executed (in most cases) in an exchange or swap execution facility (SEF). A registered SEF or designated contract market (DCM)[12] must submit swap transaction and pricing data to a registered swap data repository (SDR) immediately after a public swap transaction has been executed. Furthermore, for every swap executed on an SEF or DCM that entity must report to the market all relevant data. The aim of the DFA is to reduce systemic risk and increase transparency by further regulating the OTC derivatives markets. The counterparties with substantial swap positions or who are highly leveraged are required to be registered with the US Commodity Futures Trading Commission (CFTC) or the US Securities and Exchange Commission (SEC) as either swap dealers (SDs)[13] or major swap participants (MSPs). Companies that fall under the SD and MSP categories face new capital and margin requirements, additional reporting requirements over the life of the transaction (e.g. to report daily trading records, financial terms of the transaction, confirmation data of the transaction), aggregate position limits, increased technological investments and increased clearing costs, as they have to clear their products through one of the established markets.

The European Markets Infrastructure Regulation (EMIR) was first drafted in September 2010, and adopted in August 2012, in order to regulate the OTC derivatives markets. It follows the technical standards published by the European Securities and Markets Authority (ESMA). It aims to achieve three interlinked goals: (i) to increase transparency (trades are reported to a trade repository, e.g. the CME European Trade Repository); (ii) to reduce counterparty risk (by requiring all trades to be cleared via a CCP); and (iii) to reduce operational risk (trades are managed electronically). ESMA adopts three criteria for the central clearing of OTC contracts originating from financial counterparties: (i) reduction of systemic risk in the financial system; (ii) availability of fair, reliable and generally accepted pricing information; and (iii) liquidity and standardization of contracts. Non-financial counterparties are obliged to clear their contracts when a specified *clearing threshold* has been exceeded, as set by ESMA in conjunction with the European Systemic Risk Board (ERSB). Counterparties and CCPs must report all derivatives contracts to a registered trade repository (TR). Financial and non-financial counterparties, whose highly tailor-made and illiquid derivatives contracts are not suitable for CCP clearing, must implement monitoring systems and credit and operational risk-reducing processes. EMIR requires all counterparties and clearing houses to report the details of any derivative contracts to a registered trade repository within one working day.

The Markets in Financial Instruments Directive (MiFID) came into force on 1 November 2007 and was the building block of the EU's regulation of financial markets. MiFID aimed at increasing competitiveness, harmonizing EU financial markets and decreasing transactions costs. On 20 October 2011, MiFID was reformed into proposals for an updated MiFID II and a companion regulation, the Markets in Financial Instruments Regulation (MiFIR). The EU approved MiFID II in April 2014 to deal with changes in market structure and technology and to improve transparency. MiFID II broadens the scope of the original MiFID to include uncovered financial products, services and entities, but also covers authorization and organization of trading venues, and the definition of legislative and ruling power. It dictates that all forms of trades must take place via a regulated market (RM),[14] an MTF[15] or an organized trading facility (OTF),[16] while they are obliged to make data available to regulators; that is, aggregate trade data (e.g. investment strategies and risks, costs and associated charges) and classification of their clients (e.g. regional governments, public sector entities, local public authorities and municipalities), among others. MiFIR covers the disclosure of transactions to regulators, the public disclosure of trading data and the clearing of derivatives contracts on trading venues. EMIR's definition of derivatives relates to MiFID; that is, a product that is a MiFID instrument is within the scope of EMIR and thus liable to the latter regulation.

The BEDT received authorization from the FCA to operate as an MTF, which is regarded as a highly regulated exchange platform. Also, Baltex, in December 2014, launched a block trade facility that allows brokers and members to continue using LCH.Clearnet's clearing services, as FFAs have been reclassified as futures contracts. This increases post-trade transparency, as Baltex members can track their own trades throughout the trading day and view and export a complete list of all trades reported to Baltex at the end of the day. Finally, it has to be noted that the January 2015 *Guide to Market Benchmarks* ensures compliance with the "Principles for Financial Benchmarks", issued by the International Organization of Securities Commissions (IOSCO).

Since November 2014, LCH.Clearnet has reclassified its OTC EnClear contracts (contracts traded via brokers) as block futures. These contracts are subject to the rules of an exchange (regulated trading venue) and cleared by a CCP. The two exchanges are the Baltex with dry-bulk freight contracts and CLTX with all the EnClear "futurized" products (dry-bulk freight, containers, iron ore, steel and fertilizers). Baltex (and CLTX) provide a block futures facility to allow bilaterally negotiated agreements in its contracts (in EnClear contracts) entered into by Baltex (CLTX), respectively, as off-exchange freight futures. Trades from all the venues are cleared by LCH.Clearnet as block futures.

15.8 Conclusion

Risk management is an extremely important issue in the highly volatile shipping industry. Freight derivatives, since 1985, have provided the necessary means to do that. This chapter has provided an overview of them, including a description of all markets and available products, as well as the current trends and developments. More specifically, the various dry-bulk, tanker and containership routes and indices which are used as underlying assets of freight derivatives have been presented; the OTC and cleared freight forward contracts, freight futures and freight options have been discussed; and the various exchanges and clearing-houses that incorporate freight derivatives in their list of products have been analyzed. Finally, the institutional and regulatory changes that have occurred since the global financial crisis of 2007–08 have had an impact on the freight derivatives markets as well. These have also been discussed and they provide an up-to-date overview of the existing working environment, including the introduction of freight derivatives in exchange trading screens and their clearing. More detailed information about risk management and derivatives in shipping, including trading examples, can be found in Kavussanos and Visvikis (2006a, 2011). Finally, a comprehensive bibliography in the area of freight derivatives and risk management in shipping is provided for the interested reader.

Notes

1. For a complete discussion of the alternative sources of business risks present in the shipping industry, and traditional (without the use of derivatives) ways of managing them, see Kavussanos (2010).
2. For the management of freight and other sources of business risks in the shipping industry, see Kavussanos and Visvikis (2006a).
3. However, it should be noted that more and more routes are traded on the average of all index days in a month instead of the last seven days.
4. Proprietary trading refers to banks taking trading positions on FFAs for their own account.
5. Laycan indicates the earliest date at which the laydays can start and the date after which the charter can be canceled if the vessel has not arrived by then.
6. A detailed description of the Baltic indices' creation and panelists' reporting can be found in the Baltic Exchange's *Guide to Market Benchmarks* (January 2016).

7. On 23 October 2015, the Baltic Exchange and the Ningbo Shipping Exchange (NBSE) announced that the NBSE container freight rates from Ningbo to Europe and the Middle East would be available on the Baltic Exchange's website. The weekly Ningbo Containerized Freight Index (NCFI) compiled by NBSE reflects the rates of 20-foott, 40-foot and High-Cube containers (which are the same in structure as standard containers but taller at 9'6") and covers Ningbo to the East Mediterranean (Piraeus and Istanbul), the West Mediterranean (Barcelona, Valencia, Genoa), Europe (Hamburg and Rotterdam) and the Middle East (Dammam and Dubai). The routes are based on transactional data submitted by a panel of 11 Ningbo based freight forwarders, including various surcharges. The NCFI is reported every Friday at 1600 (Beijing time).
8. According to Chicago Mercantile Exchange (CME) Group, a block trade is a "privately negotiated futures, options or combination transaction that is permitted to be executed apart from the public auction market … Block trades are permitted in specified products and are subject to minimum transaction size requirements which vary according to the product, the type of transaction and the time of execution".

    According to Intercontinental Exchange (ICE) Futures, a block trade "allows Members to bilaterally negotiate ICE Futures Contracts without the normal requirement to first reveal the order to the Market, so long as the order meets or exceeds a minimum volume threshold".
9. The dry-bulk BFA panelists are Barry Rogliano Salles, Clarkson Securities Ltd, Freight Investor Services, GFI Brokers, Simpson, Spence Young, and Pasternak Baum & Company Inc. The tanker BFA panellists are ACM-GFI, ICAP and Marex Spectron (as of January 2015).
10. More details about the rules of the reporting maturities can be found in the *Guide to Market Benchmarks* (Baltic Exchange).
11. STP enables the entire trade process for derivatives transactions to be conducted electronically without the need for rekeying or manual intervention, subject to legal and regulatory restrictions.
12. DCMs are exchanges that may list for trading purposes all types of commodity futures or option contracts and allow access to their facilities by all types of traders.
13. A company is defined as an MSP if "it has a substantial position in interest rate, currency exchange, credit default, equity and commodity swaps". A company is defined as an SD if "it deals swaps with a gross notional amount of US$100 million or more, deals swaps to more than 15 counterparties or enters into more than 20 swaps transactions annually".

14. An RM is a multilateral system operated by and/or managed by a market operator, which brings together or facilitates the bringing together of multiple buyers and sellers' interests in financial instruments in a way that results in a contract.
15. An MTF is a multilateral system (a non-exchange financial trading venue), operated by an investment company or a market operator, which brings together multiple buyers and sellers in financial products.
16. An OTF is any facility or system that is not an RM or MTF which is designed to bring together multiple buyers and sellers or orders related to financial instruments (bonds, structured finance products, emission allowances and derivatives).

Acknowledgment We would like to thank Satya Ranjan Sahoo for his research support.

Bibliography and References

Alizadeh, A. H. (2013): Trading Volume and Volatility in the Shipping Forward Freight Market, Transportation Research—Part E, Logistics and Transportation Review, 49: 250–265.

Alizadeh, A. H., Adland, R. and Koekebakker, S. (2007): Predictive Power and Unbiasedness of Implied Forward Charter Rates, Journal of Forecasting, 26: 385–403.

Alizadeh, A. H., Kappou, N., Tsouknidis, D. and Visvikis, I. D. (2015): Liquidity Effects and FFA Returns in the International Shipping Derivatives Market, Transportation Research—Part E, Logistics and Transportation Review, Forthcoming 2015.

Angelidis, T. and Skiadopoulos, G. (2008): Measuring the Market Risk of Freight Rates: A Value-at-Risk Approach, International Journal of Theoretical and Empirical Finance, 11: 447–469.

Batchelor, R., Alizadeh, A. H. and Visvikis, I. D. (2005): The Relation between Bid-Ask Spreads and Price Volatility in Forward Markets, Journal of Derivatives & Hedge Funds, 11: 105–125.

Batchelor, R., Alizadeh, A. H. and Visvikis, I. D. (2007): Forecasting Spot and Forward Prices in the International Freight Market, International Journal of Forecasting, 23: 101–114.

Chang, Y. and Chang, H. (1996): Predictability of the Dry-Bulk Shipping Market by BIFFEX, Maritime Policy and Management, 23: 103–114.

Cullinane, K. P. B. (1991): Who's Using BIFFEX? Results from a Survey of Shipowners, Maritime Policy and Management, 18: 79–91.

Dinwoodie, J. and Morris, J. (2003): Tanker Forward Freight Agreements: The Future for Freight Futures, Maritime Policy and Management, 30: 45–58.

Goulas, L. and Skiadopoulos, G. (2012): Are Freight Futures Markets Efficient? Evidence from IMAREX, International Journal of Forecasting, 28: 644–659.

Haigh, M. S. (2000): Cointegration, Unbiased Expectations and Forecasting in the BIFFEX Freight Futures Market, Journal of Futures Markets, 20: 545–571.

Haigh, M. S. and Holt, M. T. (2002): Hedging Foreign Currency, Freight and Commodity Futures Portfolios, Journal of Futures Markets, 22: 1205–1221.

Kavussanos, M. G. (1996): Comparisons of Volatility in the Dry-cargo Ship Sector. Spot versus Time-charters, and Smaller versus Larger Vessels, Journal of Transport Economics and Policy, XXX: 67–82.

Kavussanos, M. G. (1996): Price Risk Modelling of Different Size Vessels in the Tanker Industry using Autoregressive Conditional Heteroskedasticity (ARCH) Models, Logistics and Transportation Review, 32: 161–176.

Kavussanos, M. G. (1997): The Dynamics of Time-varying Volatilities in Different Size Second-Hand Ship Prices of the Dry-cargo Sector, Applied Economics, 29: 433–443.

Kavussanos, M. G. (2003): Time Varying Risks Among Segments of the Tanker Freight Markets, Maritime Economics and Logistics, V: 227–250.

Kavussanos, M. G. (2010): Business Risk Measurement and Management in the Cargo Carrying Sector of the Shipping Industry—An Update, Chapter 25, pp. 709–743 in 'The Handbook of Maritime Economics and Business, Lloyds of London Press, London.

Kavussanos, M. G. and Dimitrakopoulos, D. N. (2011): Market Risk Model Selection and Medium-term Risk with Limited Data: Application to Ocean Tanker Freight Markets, International Review of Financial Analysis, 20: 258–268.

Kavussanos, M. G. and Nomikos, N. (1999): The Forward Pricing Function of the Shipping Freight Futures market, Journal of Futures Markets, 19: 353–376.

Kavussanos, M. G. and Nomikos, N. (2000a): Hedging in the Freight Futures Market, Journal of Derivatives, Fall: 41–58.

Kavussanos, M. G. and Nomikos, N. (2000b): Futures Hedging when the Structure of the Underlying Asset Changes: The Case of the BIFFEX Contract, Journal of Futures Markets, 20: 775–801.

Kavussanos, M. G. and Nomikos, N. (2000c): Constant vs. Time-varying Hedge Ratios and Hedging Efficiency in the BIFFEX Market, Transportation Research Part E: Logistics and Transportation Review, 36: 229–248.

Kavussanos, M. G. and Nomikos, N. (2003): Price Discovery, Causality and Forecasting in the Freight Futures Market, Review of Derivatives Research, 6: 203–230.

Kavussanos, M. G. and Visvikis, I. D. (2004): Market Interactions in Returns and Volatilities between Spot and Forward Shipping Markets, Journal of Banking and Finance, 28: 2015–2049.

Kavussanos, M. G. and Visvikis, I. D. (2006a): Derivatives and Risk Management in Shipping, Witherbys Publishing Limited & Seamanship International, UK.

Kavussanos, M. G. and Visvikis, I. D. (2006b): Shipping Freight Derivatives: A Survey of Recent Evidence, Maritime Policy and Management, 33: 233–255.

Kavussanos, M. G. and Visvikis, I. D. (2007): Derivatives in Freight Markets, Special Report Commissioned by Lloyd's Shipping Economist, A Lloyd's MIU Publication, Informa Business, London.

Kavussanos, M. G. and Visvikis, I. D. (2008): Freight Derivatives and Risk Management: A Review, (In Eds.) Geman, H., Risk Management in Commodity Markets: From Shipping to Agriculturals and Energy, John Wiley & Sons Ltd.

Kavussanos, M. G. and Visvikis, I. D. (2010): The Hedging Performance of the Capesize Forward Freight Market, (In Eds.) Cullinane, K., The International Handbook of Maritime Economics and Business, Edward Elgar Publishing.

Kavussanos, M. G. and Visvikis, I. D. (2011): Theory and Practice of Shipping Freight Derivatives, Risk Books and Journals, Incisive Media Publishers.

Kavussanos, M. G. and Visvikis, I. D. (2014): Shipping Freight Derivatives: Practical Examples and Applications, (In Eds.) Xu, J., Contemporary Marine and Maritime Policy, Nova Science Publishers.

Kavussanos, M. G., Visvikis, I. D. and Batchelor, R. (2004): Over-The-Counter Forward Contracts and Spot Price Volatility in Shipping, Transportation Research—Part E, Logistics and Transportation Review, 40: 273–296.

Kavussanos, M. G., Visvikis, I. D. and Dimitrakopoulos, D. (2014a): Risk Management in the Shipping Industry, (In Eds.) Roncoroni, A., Fusai, G. and Cummins, M., The Handbook of Multi-Commodity Markets and Products: Structuring, Trading and Risk Management, John Wiley & Sons Inc.

Kavussanos, M. G., Visvikis, I. D. and Dimitrakopoulos, D. N. (2014b): Economic Spillovers between Related Derivatives Markets: The Case of Commodity and Freight Markets, Transportation Research Part E: Logistics and Transportation Review, 68: 79–102.

Kavussanos, M. G., Visvikis, I. D. and Dimitrakopoulos, D. N. (2010): Information Linkages between Panamax Freight Derivatives and Commodity Derivatives Markets, Maritime Economics and Logistics, 12: 91–110.

Kavussanos, M. G., Visvikis, I. D. and Goulielmou, M. A. (2007): An Investigation of the Use of Risk Management and Shipping Derivatives: The Case of Greece, International Journal of Transport Economics, XXXIV: 49–68.

Kavussanos, M. G., Visvikis, I. D. and Menachof, D. A. (2004): The Unbiasedness Hypothesis in the Freight Forward Market: Evidence from Cointegration Tests, Review of Derivatives Research, 7: 241–266.

Kleindorfer, P. and Visvikis, I. D. (2009): Integration of Financial and Physical Networks in Global Logistics, (In Eds.) Kleindorfer, P., Wind, Y. and Gunther, R.E., The Network Challenge: Strategy, Profit, and Risk in an Interlinked World, Pearson Education Inc., Publishing as Wharton School Publishing, Upper Saddle River, NJ.

Koekebakker, S. and Adland, R. (2004): Modelling Forward Freight Rate Dynamics—Empirical Evidence from Time Charter Rates, Maritime Policy and Management, 31: 319–336.

Koekebakker, S., Adland, R. and Sodal, S. (2007): Pricing Freight Rate Options, Transportation Research—Part E, Logistics and Transportation Review, 43: 535–548.

Lyridis, D., Zacharioudakis, P., Ioardanis, S. and Daleziou, S. (2013): Freight-Forward Agreement Time series Modelling Based on Artificial Neural Network Models, Journal of Mechanical Engineering 59: 511–516.

Prokopczuk, M. (2011): Pricing and Hedging in the Freight Futures Market, Journal of Futures Markets, 31: 440–464.

Samitas, A. and Tsakalos, I. (2010): Hedging Effectiveness in the Shipping Industry during Financial Crises, International Journal of Financial Markets and Derivatives, 1: 196–212.

Sclavounos, P. (2010): Modelling, Valuation and Risk Management of Assets and Derivatives in Energy and Shipping, Chapter in Encyclopaedia of Financial Models. Edited by Frank Fabozzi. Wiley & Sons Inc.

Spreckelsen, C., Mettenheim, H-J. and Breitner, M. H. (2014): Spot and Freight Rate Futures in the Tanker Shipping Market: Short-Term Forecasting with Linear and Non-liner Methods, Operations Research Proceedings 2012, Springer International Publishing Switzerland.

Tezuka, K., Ishii, M. and Ishizaka, M. (2012): An Equilibrium Price Model of Spot and Forward Shipping Freight Markets, Transportation Research Part E, 48: 730–742.

Thuong, L. T. and Vischer, S. L. (1990): The Hedging Effectiveness of Dry-Bulk Freight Rate Futures, Transportation Journal, 29: 58–65.

Tsai, M., Saphores, J-D. and Regan, A. (2011): Valuation of Freight Transportation Contracts Under Uncertainty, Transportation Research Part E: Logistics and Transportation Review, 47: 920–932.

Zhang, J., Zeng, Q. and Zhao, X. (2014): Forecasting Spot Freight Rates based on Forward Freight Agreement and Time Charter Contract, Applied Economics, 46: 3639–3648.

16

Mergers and Acquisitions in Shipping

George Alexandridis and Manish Singh

16.1 Introduction

Mergers and acquisitions (M&A) have played a vital role in shaping various global industries, and the shipping industry has had a fairly active track record for a range of M&A transactions. In a sector affected by sharp and significant peaks and troughs in freight rates as well as asset values, the ability to effectively originate, cultivate and integrate acquisitions, mergers or strategic alliances offers a valuable competitive advantage. Over the past few years in particular, consolidation within the shipping industry has picked up significantly, especially among shipping services such as ship management companies, ship agencies and broking firms that are coming together to realize synergistic gains from their combined scale. In the ship-owning spectrum, although traditional, synergy-driven deals are not as frequent, structural shifts in market conditions are likely to result in M&A activity gathering more pace. The recent trend towards more capital intensive strategies, aiming to capture economies of scale and reduce costs and financial risks, as well as the constant evolution and growing diversity of the shipping finance market highlighted

---

G. Alexandridis (✉)
ICMA Centre, Henley Business School, University of Reading, Whiteknights, RG6 6BA, Reading, UK

M. Singh
V.Group Limited, 1st Floor, 63, Queen Victoria Street, London EC4N 4UA, UK

© The Author(s) 2016
M.G. Kavussanos, I.D. Visvikis (eds.), *The International Handbook of Shipping Finance*, DOI 10.1057/978-1-137-46546-7_16

in this handbook, are likely to trigger further consolidation across an industry that has traditionally resisted it, calling for a contemporary, in-depth analysis of this rather under-explored area within the maritime spectrum.

16.2 The Shipping M&A Market

Shipping M&A activity largely arises from businesses seeking to complement organic growth, to access specific tonnage types and regional markets, and to diversify and enhance their market share. M&As may also provide access to specific know-how, assets and capabilities. The amalgamation of two or more businesses with complementary resource bases is likely to create operating and financial synergies and efficiency gains, with potential benefits for the involved parties as well as their combined client base.

Shipping is crucial for servicing the demands of growing global trade and facilitates the creation of reliable and cost-effective supply chains. As part of this process, related businesses seek to acquire skills and expertise in handling certain cargoes, providing specialist tonnage types and enduring periods of market volatility and acute cost pressures. It is therefore not surprising that leading industry players, from tonnage providers (e.g. AP Moeller Maersk, CMA-CGM, Fredriksen Group, Kirby Corporation, Teekay, Tidewater, Star Bulk Carriers) to service providers (e.g. Clarksons, DNV GL, ISS, James Fisher, Kuehne + Nagel, V.Group) and port operators (e.g. APM, DP World, Hutchison, PSA), have all sought to enhance their growth through carrying out a number of transformational business deals.

The market for corporate control in shipping is a multifaceted one in terms of the different types of participants and transactions being carried out. Figure 16.1 depicts the key players and M&A activity flows between companies in different maritime segments. Arrows highlight typical acquisitiveness flows (i.e. acquirers buying targets) among these sub-segments.[1] While intra-segmental, purely horizontal integration is a key component of acquisition activity in the shipping industry, more congeneric or vertical combinations across the value chain among ship-owning companies, service providers and port operators are also prevalent. Moreover, the involvement of private equity in shipping and associated sectors is also a catalyst for increasing M&A activity, since private equity funds invested heavily in shipping businesses and assets, seeking efficiency gains and taking advantage of the tight credit markets and low valuations that emerged following the 2008 market downturn. Finally, acquisitions of assets and fleets are prevalent in the shipping industry, particularly among ship-owning companies and investors, because the synergies sought for by buyers can often be realized by simply purchasing the

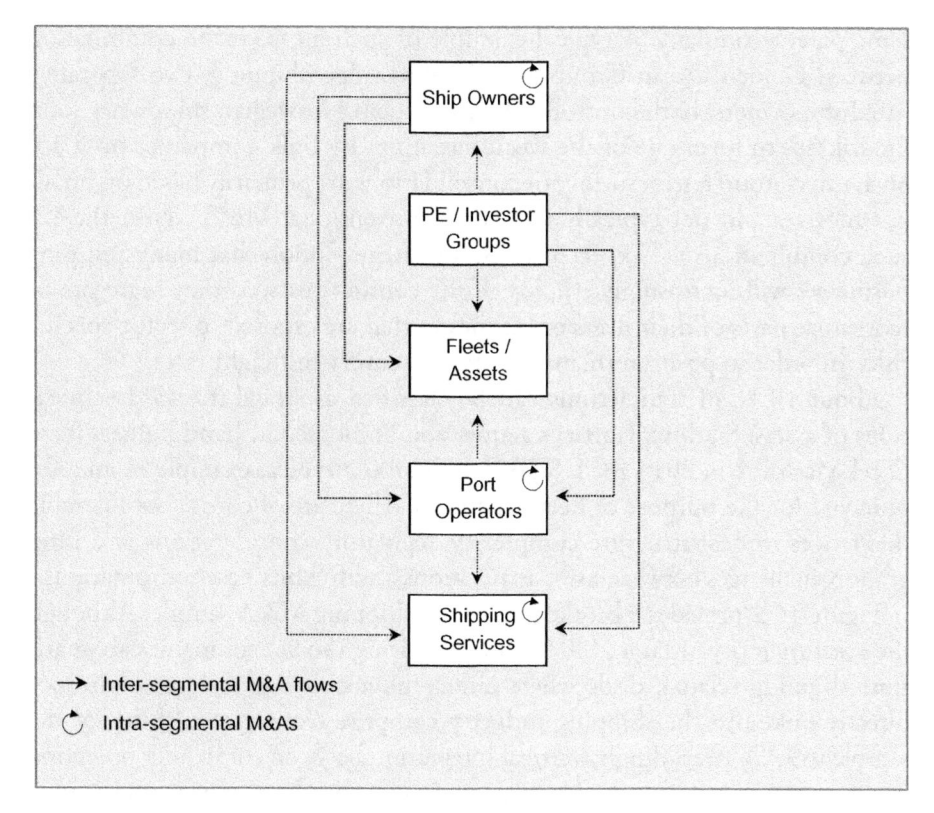

Fig. 16.1 Shipping M&A key participants and flows

target business's assets without the need to carry out more complex deals that involve full-scale integration of operations.

In order to provide valuable insights on the structure and historical trends of the shipping M&A market, we have utilized an exhaustive sample of deals from 1990 to 2014 from Thomson Reuters SDC Mergers and Acquisitions Database, the premier source of information on individual M&A transactions. The sample includes all completed M&A deals where the acquiring or target company's primary industry classification is associated with sea freight transportation, deep sea passenger transportation, and port related and other sea transport services.[2] We have retained and analyzed only mergers, acquisitions of majority interest, acquisitions of assets and acquisitions of partial and remaining interest (spin-offs, recapitalizations, self-tenders, exchange offers and repurchases were excluded as they are beyond the scope of this analysis).

This sample comprises of 6,296 M&A deals, valued at USD371 billion (although transaction value is disclosed for about half the cases).[3] About 11 % of sample transactions (687 deals) are classified as intra-corporate consolidation or financial restructuring, as the acquirer and target are controlled by the same parent company. A typical example of such a case is the combination between Golden Ocean Group and Knightsbridge Shipping, two separately listed shipowners, both controlled by prominent Norwegian shipowner John Fredriksen, to form one of the world's leading dry bulk companies in 2015. Such inter-group restructurings or consolidations are primarily based on financial motives and not typically viewed as conventional M&As. Nonetheless, such combinations are expected to be a strategic option that many shipping businesses will increasingly employ in the coming years, as they segregate or reorganize parts of their fleets or businesses that are exposed to sector-specific risks, in order to position themselves for a recovery in freight rates.

About 10 % of transactions can be classified as straightforward acquisitions of assets. Starbulk Carrier's acquisition of 34 second-hand bulkers from Excel Maritime in 2014 for USD634 million is a typical example of an asset purchase for the purpose of fleet expansion. There are of course considerable differences in deal-structure complexity, regulatory considerations and integration challenges between asset acquisitions and full business combinations.[4]

Figure 16.2 provides a breakdown of the shipping M&A sample. Although the great majority of target (80 %) and acquiring (56 %) companies are maritime shipping related, deals where either the acquirer or the target are not directly linked to the shipping industry comprise close to two-thirds of the sample (69 %). Accordingly, vertical integration between companies operating in the water, land, rail and air transportation supply chain appears to be common as are deals that involve energy and materials related acquirers or targets.

A large number of the inter-industry transactions are investor led. This is consistent with the recent surge of private equity activity in the shipping industry, discussed more extensively in Chap. 7. Private equity provides opportunities to grow swiftly, thus sidelining individual egos who have hindered consolidation for many years, particularly among ship-owning companies. Private equity companies such as Apollo Global Management, Blackstone Group and Oaktree Capital invested heavily in bulk carriers, tankers and containerships, acquired shipping companies and ports, and purchased shipping loan books from banks. The USD5 billion takeover of Associated British Ports by a Goldman Sachs, Borealis, GIC and Prudential led consortium, as well as V.Group's acquisition by OMERS private equity for USD520 million, are two recent examples. Oaktree Capital became the leading private equity investor in shipping in 2014 and controlled the largest (based on dwt) dry bulk ship-owning company in the world, Starbulk Carriers. Overall, private equity pumped more than USD50 billion into shipping between 2012 and 2014, oiling the wheels of a new wave of shipping M&As.

Figure 16.2 offers further insights into shipping M&A activity. As far as horizontal deals are concerned (where both the acquirer and the target are shipping

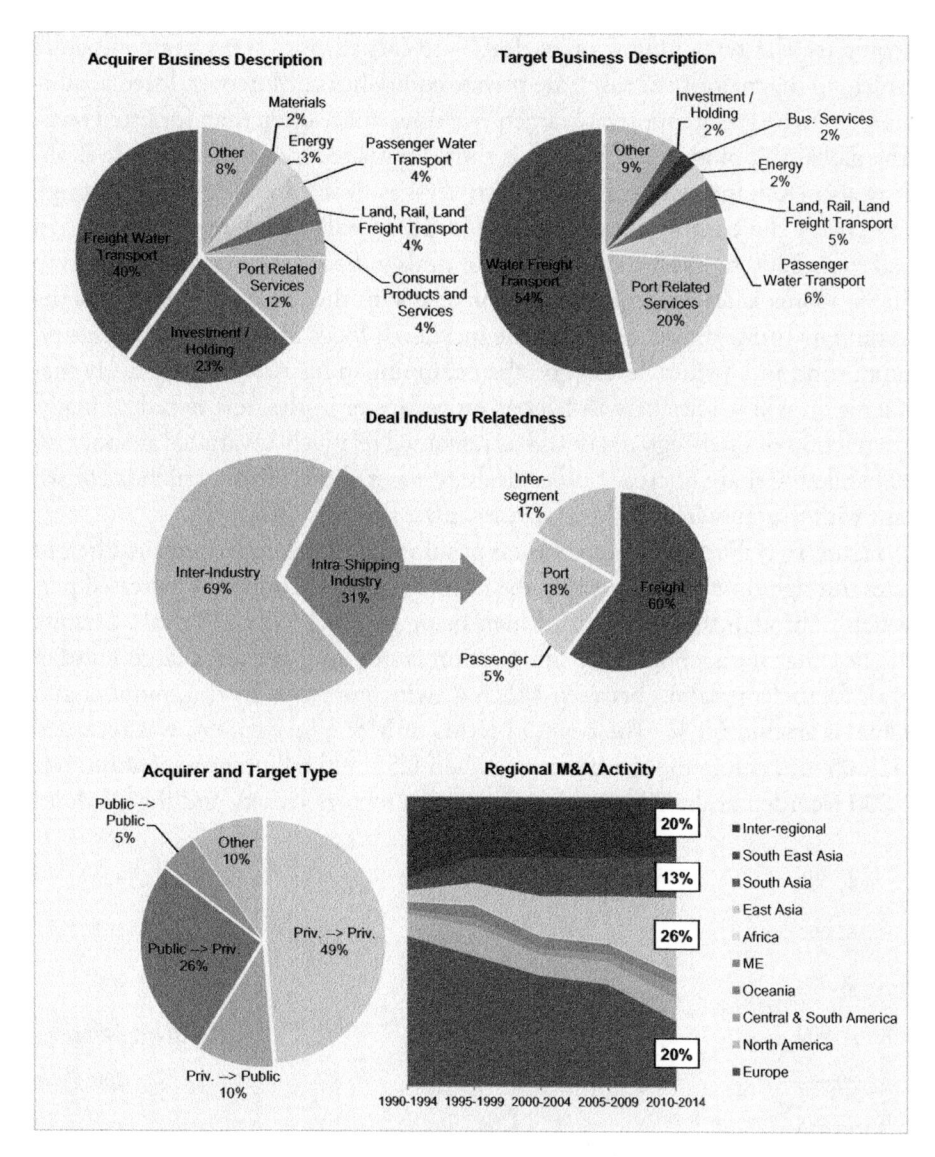

Fig. 16.2 Breakdown of shipping M&As, 1990–2014 (*Source*: Thomson Reuters SDC, 1990–2014)

oriented), around 60 % are between maritime shipping companies, 18 % are port related, less than 6 % are linked to passenger shipping and the remaining 17 % are "congeneric" deals between companies that operate in different sub-segments of the shipping spectrum. Statistics on the listing status of the companies involved convey further interesting information. For around half of all shipping M&As, both the acquiring and the target company are private, while 15 % are linked to publicly listed targets, a third of which are initiated by listed acquirers. The remaining "public deals" are carried out by private companies which, in the majority of cases, are private equity firms. Moreover, listed acquirers seem to be going for private targets five times more often than for listed ones. The global shipping M&A market is thus dominated by smaller, private deals. It is also clear that regional M&A activity has evolved considerably through time, with the contribution of intra-European deals shrinking by more than half from 2000 to 2015, and the share of deals in East Asia increasing sixfold to 26 % (China is driving much of this surge). With the emergence of Asia as the leading maritime center, and with the increasing focus of local governments on supporting and further developing their shipping industries, it seems likely that the region will see its share in M&As grow further in the next decade. Finally, the fraction of inter-regional deals has remained relatively invariable at about 20 %, while the share of cross-border deals averages about 37 %, which is consistent with the truly international nature of the shipping industry.

Figure 16.3 illustrates the evolution of shipping M&A activity against freight rates through time. It appears that the number of transactions has increased persistently through time, the record high being in 2012 with 378 deals. Despite the fact that transaction value information is not available for a large number of deals, the correlation between M&A activity, measured by deal number and value, is around 60 %. The peak, in terms of M&A investment, was recorded in 2005–08, before the market crash, when USD106 billion was spent on over 1,200 recorded deals. The association between merger activity and the ClarkSea

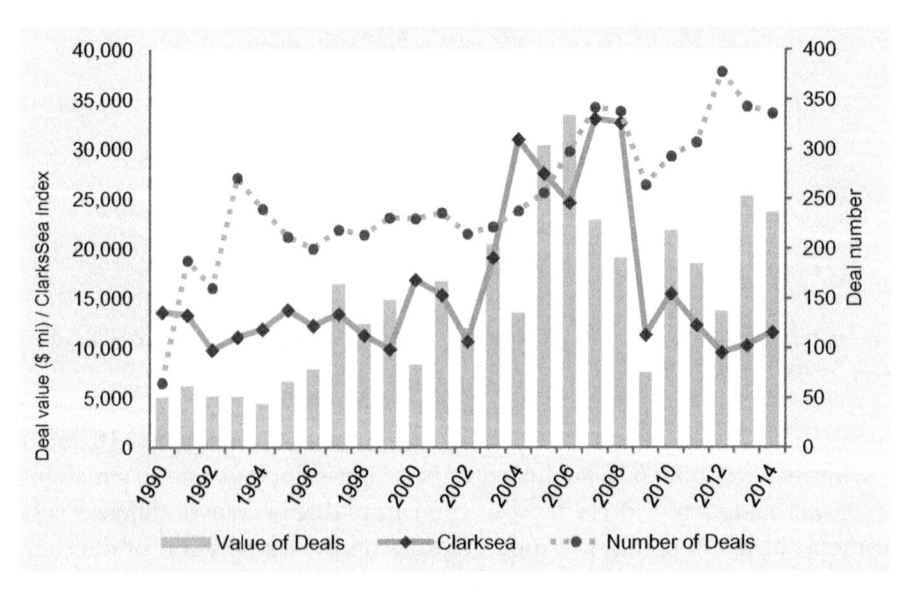

Fig. 16.3 Shipping M&A activity vs freight rates (*Source*: Based on data from Thomson Reuters SDC and Clarksons Research)

index (an index of earnings for the main vessel types published by Clarksons Research) is particularly compelling. With a 50 % correlation between the index and the value of deals, it appears that years of high freight rates tend to be linked to surges in acquisition activity. This is consistent with both neoclassical and behavioral explanations of merger waves (see Alexandridis et al. 2013), which predict respectively that the availability of abundant liquidity and high market valuations can trigger M&A deals.[5] However, as the global financial crisis started to grip the markets, M&A activity in shipping experienced considerable contraction (mainly in terms of the value of deals closed). The gradual rebound in deal activity in more recent years can be explained by the low asset values and the more pronounced financial distress, which can also foster or urge consolidation. The emergence of private equity investments in shipping during this period corroborates this conjecture. In the case where market conditions remain poor beyond 2015 for an extensive period of time, it is likely that further acceleration of acquisition activity will be observed, even among ship-owning companies.

The rest of the chapter focuses on some key aspects of M&As in shipping. The motives for different types of transactions are discussed, as well as the fundamentals of the M&A process and the participants involved. An overview of the valuation approaches and the financing techniques commonly employed in shipping M&As is also provided. Finally, the distinct features that lead to successful and value-creating deals are considered, the key methods used to assess value creation are reviewed, and brief insights are offered into the regulatory considerations pertaining to M&As in shipping.

16.3 Motives for M&As in Shipping

In this section, some general motives that drive consolidation in the shipping industry are considered. Heaver et al. (2010) and Brooks and Ritchie (2006) argue that shipping players carry out M&As to maximize profits, to enhance their market share, to gain control over a broader scope of activities in the logistics chain or to diversify their operations. Revenue synergies, cost reductions and efficiency gains make the value of a combined entity greater than the sum of the values of the companies being consolidated. They tend to be among the most frequently quoted reasons why M&As are undertaken, although drivers can vary significantly among different segments (e.g. ship-owning, port operators and other services) and transaction forms (e.g. M&As among operating companies, acquisitions of assets/fleets and investor-led deals).

Figure 16.4 provides a summary of the key M&A motives that apply to the shipping industry: growth and market share enhancements, and diversification

M&A Motive	Reasoning	Relevance to Shipping M&A
Complement organic growth in existing business	Since corporate executives are increasingly expected to generate growth, this is one of the fundamental motives for M&As. Internal growth can be slow and uncertain while growth through acquisition is a more rapid process (although it is also associated with risks).	• The acquisition of entire fleets is a typical example of pursuing fast-track growth, which, if market timing is right, can produce significant benefits. • Growth through acquisitions can be particularly valuable in mature sectors/companies faced with increased competition and slowing growth opportunities (e.g. liner sector). • The international nature of the shipping industry induces growth through cross-border acquisitions which enables acquirers to rapidly utilize local specialization and distribution networks (e.g. liner and shipping services) as well as gain access to new geographical markets (e.g. acquisition of Safmarine by Maersk in 1999, various international acquisitions by Australian port services company Adstream and Crowly's acquisition of Accord ship management in 2014). • For services companies, entering new service areas may facilitate additional growth, give access to new customer segments and strengthen their core offerings to their clients.
Operating synergies in the form of cost reduction and revenue enhancement opportunities	Economies of scale, scope and vertical integration can increase operational efficiency and reduce unit-costs, resulting in significant savings. Gaining access to new markets, distribution networks and expertise or technology can also generate new opportunities for revenue growth. Revenue enhancing synergies are often more uncertain and challenging to achieve than cost-related ones.	• Operating synergies are vital in shipping M&A. For ship-owning companies, a larger (and more modern) fleet and better combination and coordination of chartering services can result in significant cost savings though improvements in vessel movements and positioning, reduction of ballast voyages and associated running costs, most notably bunkers, creating a competitive advantage. • Bringing together complementary specialization can lead to sizeable efficiency gains (e.g. the 2015 merger between Genmar and Navig8 Tankers brought together market leading skills on capital markets, technical management, operational/chartering and trading). • Vertical integration in the liner sector is another example whereby cost reduction can be facilitated through taking control of the supply chain. • Operating synergies in shipping services often involve gaining access to complementary areas and/or geographies of expertise (e.g. Clarksons-RS Platou deal in 2014) and/or adding scale/capabilities to further strengthen the core business (e.g. DNV-GL merger).
Financial Synergies	A larger entity can gain better access to capital markets and lower its cost of capital.	• Liquidity is a key factor for investors, with ship-owning companies pursuing larger market capitalizations to gain access to cheaper and larger-scale financing (e.g. the merger of Star Bulk Carriers with Ocean Bulk and Excel Maritime's fleet made the combined company more attractive to investors). • Financial synergy is a key motive behind several recent private equity backed/driven shipping deals as well as intra-corporate restructurings.
Market-share enhancement and reduction of competition	Horizontal integration can result in market-share and market-power increases in sectors where a deal can have some impact on competition and market prices.	• Aggregating fleet capacity can enhance market share in niche target segments. For instance, strategic alliances and M&As in liner shipping (see Figure 16.5) tend to result in competition and market-power related gains. The resulting benefits from cost synergies and combined capabilities can often lead to more competitive pricing. • Similarly, a key motive behind PE investment in prominent shipping services companies has been market-share consolidation through follow-on acquisitions.
Diversification of asset base	Diversification can provide tangible benefits, mainly deriving from risk reduction (although it may also end up destroying value if it dilutes specialization).	• Diversifying across different ship-owning segments (with low earnings correlation) can reduce business risks and serve as a vehicle to enter more profitable industries (e.g. the acquisition of Ocean Rig allowed DryShips to venture into Offshore shipping and benefit from diversification when dry bulk rates tumbled).

Fig. 16.4 Main motives in shipping M&As

> Liner shipping involves the operation of specialized vessels along defined trade routes. Consolidation in this market is particularly effective in creating economies of scale and improved utilization by combination of the fleets and associated shore-based supply chains of the partnering businesses. Liner carriers have traditionally shown preference for consolidation of operations by means of strategic alliances. Some of the reasons behind such alliances are in line with the primary motives for M&As discussed in this section. They include improved utilization of fleets of the partnering operators, servicing a wider selection of routes, benefit from scale advantages in marketing and commercial operations, reduction in competition and improvement in pricing power, gaining access to new regional markets and leveraging off the combined know-how and technologies.
>
> Following from the hangover of frenzied ship-building as well as the weak demand post global financial crisis, shipping companies were faced with considerable cost pressures, sub-optimal capacity utilization and unstable market conditions, making long-term strategy formulation ever more challenging. In 2014, Liner shipping leaders with the largest market share i.e. Maersk (15%), Mediterranean Shipping Company (14%) and CMA-CGM (9%) decided to pool their resources and create what got coined as the ill-fated 'P3 alliance'. Together, this alliance would see the 3 partners create a joint network of over 250 vessels, aggregating in excess of 2.5m TEU capacity, operating in almost 30 routes. Maersk would have been the biggest fleet contributor with circa 42% of the P3 fleet, with CMA-CGM being the smaller partner with about 24% share and MSC with about 34% of the combined fleet. The alliance was expected to create global economies of scale as well as operating efficiencies through a combined operational and commercial hub, termed JVOC or Joint Vessel Operating Centre.
>
> The P3 alliance failed to secure the approvals of the Chinese competition authorities as it was viewed as generating considerable competitive barriers for smaller players in the main East-West liner trades. Maersk and MSC however re-cast their co-operation under the 2M Partnership, though this did not realize the full extent of the benefits envisaged from the joint fleet ownership, JVOC and pricing mechanisms. However, the 2M partnership trigged further consolidation in the liner shipping market with other players promptly mobilizing to maintain footholds through combinations such as the Ocean Three (CMA CGM, UASC and China Shipping) which joined the already operating CKYHE alliance (Cosco, K Line, Yang Ming, Hanjin Shipping, Evergreen) and G6 alliance (APL, Hapag-Lloyd, HMM, MOL, OOCL, NYK).
>
> The financial crisis of 2008 had a profound impact on the structure of the market. The newly formed alliances highlight the trend towards capacity consolidation in the sector and might be a step towards further consolidation as shipping lines attempt to further control their network costs by increasing their operations' scale. The alliances are expected to gradually push smaller competitors out of the benchmark Asia-Europe route, stabilizing freight rates through more effectively regulating tonnage supply.
>
> Although M&As in liner shipping are less common, 2014 did see the first merger in many years among top liner companies, with Chilean carrier CSAV's container business activities merging into Germany's Hapag-Lloyd. Synergistic gains were quoted as the main motives and, specifically, network optimisations, improvements to productivity and cost reductions. Closing the gap to main competitors was of course the primary motive behind this deal. Since the industry is likely to continue to face significant headwinds in terms of supply-and-demand imbalances, one should expect more selected consolidation moves among liner companies as well as moves towards focusing on more core container shipping operations. Further consolidation of overlapping businesses to reduce competition, enhance economy of scale and efficiency are also likely among state-owned enterprises in China, as part of a wider plan to revitalise economic growth. The rumoured mega-deal between Cosco and China Shipping at the time of writing this section provides a good example. The potential for such deals could signal further scope for full-scale consolidation ahead in the liner sector and beyond.

Fig. 16.5 Consolidation in liner shipping (*Source*: Compiled by authors based on various sources, including Lloyds List and TradeWinds)

and efficiency gains through operating and financial synergies. These drivers relate mainly to buyers in acquisition deals (the buy-side perspective) or to both buyers and sellers in mergers. It should be noted that, although the motives appear segregated in the figure, some may exhibit a degree of interrelation. Figure 16.5 provides a discussion of the motives behind consolidation in liner shipping as a special case study.

There are also other potential buy-side drivers for shipping M&As not reported in Fig. 16.4. For instance, companies led by poorly performing executives are sometimes acquired with the view to reaping the benefits from managing them more efficiently, in line with Dietrich and Sorensen's (1984) poor management hypothesis. Cash-rich companies are also more likely to carry out acquisitions, according to Harford's (1999) free-cash-flow takeover theory, while over-confident CEOs exhibit a tendency to overestimate the returns on their investment projects and hence make more deals (Doukas and Petmezas 2007). Moreover, defensive bidding (to prevent being taken over) or "positioning" deals (to become a more attractive merger candidate) are also among the reasons why M&As occur (Gorton et al. 2009). In some other cases, an acquirer may be merely buying undervalued assets/fleets, without much further justification, in order to position the company for an improvement in market conditions. This was a key driver during the shipping market crisis following 2008, where all-time-low freight rates impaired valuations. The risk inherent in this strategy is that, absent of a market turnaround to justify it, further growth may actually hinder rather than improve a company's prospects.

Although the above comprise the bulk of motivations behind acquisitions in the maritime sector, the shipping M&A market is a multifaceted one, with different types of transactions and participants. Thus, the reasons behind consolidation may vary or be more synthetic, subject to the deal or buyer type in each case. Private equity investors, for instance, that provide an increasingly important alternative source of capital, tend to acquire target assets and businesses offering attractive growth opportunities and potential for improvement in performance/returns. Therefore, the key motives in this case are the opportunity for asset play and attractive exit valuations, follow-on acquisitions offering further cost and revenue synergies, as well as other efficiency gains realized through more effective financing structures and improved business models.

Sell-side motives can differ significantly from buy-side motives. As globalization has shaped and reshaped supply chains with increasing speed and complexity, several businesses have faced the prospect of business model stagnation and have sought parents (acquisitions) or partners (mergers) to maintain competiveness of their business and longer-term survival of their installed base.

Some of the key motivations for sellers of shipping businesses include:

1. specific parts of their business becoming non-core to their longer term strategy;
2. weak organic growth due to limitations in the seller's business model or a protracted downturn in the seller's core markets;

3. projected change pointing to unfavorable market conditions or a poor market for an extensive period of time;
4. inability to sustain organic growth due to cash-flow or liquidity issues (e.g. inadequate access to capital);
5. failure to take new products/services to market;
6. consolidation within the business's core market, driven by the need for scale economies;
7. a new generation in a family owned business, wishing to dispose and walk out.

16.4 M&A Process

This section explores how shipping businesses successfully develop and manage individual M&A transactions and, in some cases, a pipeline of targets as part of a longer term structured M&A program. As discussed later, a high proportion of M&A transactions fail to deliver the envisaged result. Often, this failure can be linked to the M&A process not being robust enough to ensure that the strategic and investment rationale of an acquisition or merger have been thoroughly considered and plans for managing the value drivers as well as the inherent risks are clearly laid out and endorsed by the acquisition and integration team. M&A processes can be highly varied, depending on the sizes, nature or the objectives of the transaction. As illustrated in Fig. 16.6, the M&A process is broadly described as a function of M&A strategy formulation, origination and analysis of targets, cultivation of M&A prospects, typical due diligence process and post-acquisition integration.

16.4.1 M&A Strategy Formulation

Before formulating their M&A strategy, acquiring or merging businesses give consideration to the growth opportunities and challenges associated with their organic business model. Such reviews will help to identify any limitations or gaps in the business model, barriers to new market entry and specific areas

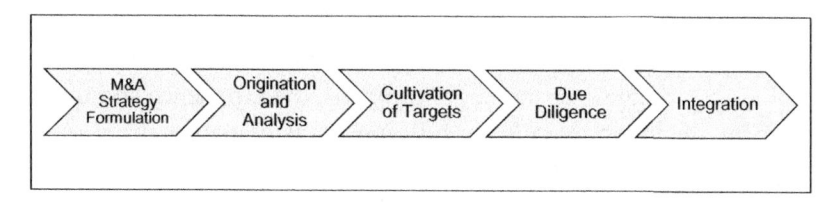

Fig. 16.6 The M&A process

where organic growth could be complemented by way of acquisitions, mergers or strategic alliances. In addition to evaluating possibilities for core business growth through M&A, businesses consider attractive adjacent markets that they could enter by way of an M&A. In shipping, this could mean owners or operators acquiring a target with the required assets and expertise to enable entry into a desired tonnage sector or a shipping-service business, acquiring a capability that brings new cross-selling capabilities or customer base.

When maritime businesses undertake M&As in areas that are at the core of their current business model, they tend to focus on enhancing market share, economies of scale, cost reduction and access to new customer segments or geographies, amongst some of their key objectives. Alternatively, they may also use M&As as a diversification strategy to enter markets that are adjacent to their core business or customer segments. In such cases, the rationale is focused on adding new expertise or capabilities, gaining access to clients beyond the acquirer's organic base and accessing unique assets. M&As outside the acquirer's core business involve new customers, suppliers, skill sets, geographies and therefore potentially involve greater execution risks and require more robust strategic consideration and integration planning.

Effective M&A strategies specify objectives or criteria against which potential M&A targets can be assessed for strategic fit and investment attractiveness. In shipping businesses, this could include the nature of assets, specific capabilities or expertise involved, the organizational culture, size and composition of market share and the geographies in which target companies operate. In addition to identifying acquisition or merger opportunities, business model reviews and M&A strategy formulation may also prompt the disposal of certain business units or assets that are considered non-core, thereby freeing up capital for further investment in priority areas.

16.4.2 Identification and Analysis of M&A Targets

Once the acquirer has specified the segment(s) within which an M&A is sought, it will typically draw up a detailed list of all prospective targets in its areas of interest. The process of analyzing and filtering the overall population to a shortlist of targets is performed by applying the selection criteria established in the M&A strategy formulation. Such criteria may include quality and strategic fit of assets belonging to the target company, the experience and quality of management, alignment of culture, customer overlap, market share, resources and capabilities, level of profitability and recent financial performance, cash conversion, CAPEX requirements, client concentration and level of synergies achievable. Further considerations are the size of the target company, the geography in which it operates, and the level of operational and integration risk. Taking into account the strategic rationale and investment attractions for each of the shortlists of targets, the acquirer will then engage with the highest priority targets to establish their availability, their expectations on valuation as well as the associated risks. Sellers planning for the disposal of certain business assets or business segments follow a similar approach, by starting with a list of all potential buyers for the business on sale and refining this to a shortlist of preferred acquirers.

16.4.3 Cultivation of M&A Targets

Having established a list of priority M&A targets, a structured engagement process will be undertaken between the buying, selling or merging businesses. Both the buy side and the sell side may appoint industry experts or M&A advisors to assist with the transaction support, or may have introduced such advisors at an early stage of target identification. In preparation to engaging prospective acquirers, sellers may undertake a vendor due diligence (VDD) through their advisors, thereby delivering comprehensive information memorandums (IMs) allowing prospective buyers to consider the investment attractions and submit indicative bids. As argued below, synergies play a central role in M&A transactions and provide the basis for any valuation premium that acquiring businesses are prepared to pay as part of their investment rationale. The cultivation process may therefore require access to relevant operational, commercial, personnel, among a range of other information, in order to establish the synergy case. Revenue synergies will include incremental revenue opportunities arising as a result of the proposed combination of businesses. This may be driven by a combination of capabilities, channels to market and customer bases, among other factors. Cost synergies will include opportunities to rationalize the combined cost base through efficiency gains, economies of scale, amalgamation of installed base and resources.

Merging or acquiring businesses will carry out comprehensive risk analysis to record both the likelihood and impact of all foreseeable personnel, legal, commercial, financial, technical or other risks faced by the combined entity post-merger or acquisition. Acquiring companies will consider the valuation of the target (see pp. 384–394) and assess returns on investment, factoring the above risks against the investment and the synergy case for the proposed merger or acquisition. The funding mechanism for M&A transactions (see pp. 394–398) will also have a significant impact on the returns' analysis as well as the scoping of the due diligence process, depending on the structure and stakeholders involved in the financing of the transaction.

When M&A activity is undertaken as part of a structured on-going and often long-term program, the process of identification and analysis of possible targets will help shortlist the highest priority prospects. The process of cultivation involves the active engagement between buy and sell sides, often starting with the signing of non-disclosure agreements (NDA) to establish intent and exchange all relevant information necessary for considering a possible transaction. Before detailed negotiations or diligence commences between the two sides, there will typically be an indicative offer, articulating the strategic rationale for an acquisition or merger, and the key terms of a potential offer. The structure of the proposed deal is outlined and the financing method is clarified. Before issuing the indicative offer, the merging partners or buyer will consider the investment rationale for the transaction and seek board approval. As M&A proposals tend to receive significant investor/market interest, all parties will carefully anticipate market response to a proposed deal before the exchange of any indicative proposal or commencement of negotiations.

16.4.4 Due Diligence

As outlined above, the offer for acquiring or merging businesses is underpinned by certain assumptions that inform the strategic and investment rationale. These will be the drivers of incremental value generated from the M&A transaction that will be tested through a comprehensive diligence process. Depending on the way a transaction is structured, whether assets or business entities are being acquired, and factors such as the nature of the business, size, variability, organizational structure and complexity, jurisdictions, regulatory requirements and other factors, the degree and scope of due diligence process will vary considerably. Within the scope of this chapter, it is only possible to outline broadly a typical due diligence process and the key areas of financial, commercial, tax, legal, operational/technical, HR and intellectual property diligence. In addition to the acquisition of businesses, M&A transactions have also been discussed that involve fleets of vessels or vessel operating entities as a key area of M&A activity in shipping. The diligence in such cases will focus on the suitability, quality and performance of the vessels/fleets as well as the charters/commercial arrangements associated with the operating vessels and/or operating entities. Regulatory considerations in M&A include, but are not limited to, approvals required from statutory bodies, anti-trust/competition, anti-bribery and employment unions.

16.4.5 Post-acquisition Integration Process

A high proportion of M&A transactions that fail to generate the envisaged value and synergies suffer from poor planning or ineffective post M&A management of the integration of the businesses involved. The design of the integration process itself starts to take shape as early as the target selection. This is because the integration process may vary from target to target, and will take into account the envisaged benefits of the transaction, the degree of amalgamation of the businesses involved, as well as the key challenges arising from the combination. So, a merger, acquisition or a strategic alliance in liner shipping may involve an integration process which requires a comprehensive amalgamation, not only of the fleets or assets associated with the transaction, but also of the composition of the leadership team and alignment of personnel, the operational installed base, the marketing and commercial support and other elements of the supply chain so as to derive synergies from the transaction. Integration programs often require considerable resources and multifunctional teams led by a designated integration manager and planning or steering groups.

16.5 Shipping M&A Valuation

The price agreed between acquiring and target companies for the closing of an M&A deal is unambiguously the ultimate result of the negotiation process. Since, theoretically, a mutually acceptable price should cater for the interests of both the acquiring and target company shareholders, agreeing on a net worth that delicately balances the interests of the two sides often proves quite challenging. The process utilized in order to arrive at a final offer price involves thorough business valuation, often driven by the respective parties' financial advisors employed for the purpose of valuing, structuring the deal and arranging the required financing. Alternative valuation methods tend to offer quite different price estimates as a result of the diverse principles and assumptions they are based on. While it is beyond the scope of this chapter to provide an in-depth analysis of all the different business valuation principles and methods, we do offer an overview of the main income, market and asset based approaches used in the context of M&As within different segments of the shipping industry.

The main purpose of the M&A valuation process is to determine a fair purchase price. The deal pricing principles will depend greatly on the type of deal in question. In a typical strategic business combination (merger or acquisition of a controlling stake of shares) that involves a synergy gain, the value of the

```
┌─────────────────────────────────────────────────────────────────┐
│                    Value of the Combined Company                │
│                              V_C                                │
├──────────────────────┬──────────────────────┬───────────────────┤
│ Intrinsic Value of   │ Intrinsic Value of   │ Total Synergy Gain│
│      Acquirer        │       Target         │        V_S        │
│        V_A           │         V_T          │                   │
│                      ├──────────────────────┼───────────────────┤
│                      │     Deal Value       │   Value to        │
│                      │        V_D           │   Acquirer        │
│                      │                      │     NPV           │
│                      │                ┌─────┴───────┐           │
│                      │                │   Offer     │           │
│                      │                │  Premium    │           │
│                      │                │    O_P      │           │
└──────────────────────┴────────────────┴─────────────┴───────────┘
```

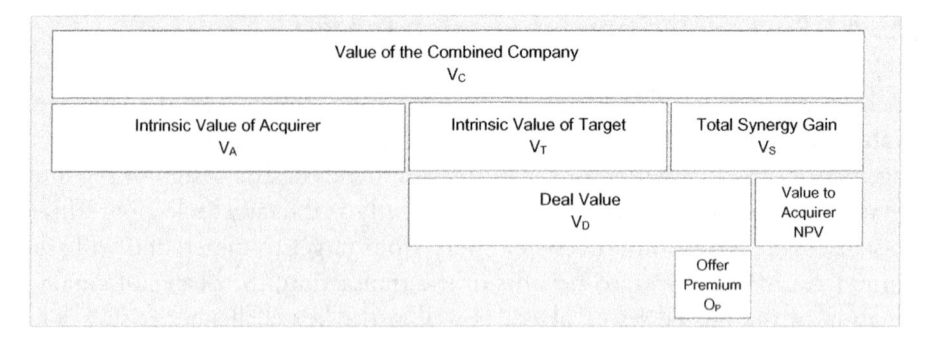

Fig. 16.7 M&A pricing framework

combined entity is expected to be higher than the standalone value of the two companies involved. The distribution of the synergy gains between the acquiring and target shareholders is determined by the offer price. Figure 16.7 illustrates a basic M&A pricing framework. The sum of the standalone values of the acquirer (V_A), the target (V_T) and the synergy gain from the combination (V_S) yields the total value of the combined company (V_C). The purchase price or deal value (V_D) tends to be higher than the standalone value of the target by an amount equal to the offer premium (O_P).[6] This is the share of the synergy gain allocated to target shareholders. Any residual value generated from the combination over and above the price paid by the acquiring company (and any acquisition process expenses incurred) is the net present value (NPV) accruing to acquiring shareholders.[7]

It becomes obvious that estimating a standalone intrinsic value for the target company as well as the synergies from the combination is central to M&A valuation. The ultimate value of the target to the acquiring company is given by:

$$V_{T_{max}} = V_T + V_S \qquad (16.1)$$

If V_{Tmax} is paid by the acquirer, then the entire value of synergies (V_s) is allocated to target shareholders, and the NPV of the deal for the acquiring company is zero. This is a key threshold in M&A valuation and, if exceeded, the deal will destroy value for acquiring shareholders (see pp. 398–406). Thus, the final offer price will typically be between V_T ("floor value") and V_{Tmax}, when acquiring and target shareholders share the synergistic gains from the combination.

The main valuation methods commonly employed in the shipping industry are discounted cash flow (DCF), market and transaction multiples, and asset-based valuation. Since one size does not fit all in shipping, there are certain valuation methods that are more appropriate when pricing M&A deals in specific segments. Nevertheless, the reliability of the estimates tends to improve when employing multiple approaches and taking into account the sensitivity of the final estimates to the assumptions applied. Below, the processes and associated inputs of the main valuation methods employed within the maritime context are reviewed.

16.5.1 Cash Flow Valuation

In DCF valuation, the value of the combined company (V_C) is typically estimated by taking the sum of the present value of all forecasted future cash flows generated by the acquiring and target companies as standalone entities and the present value of the synergistic cash flows from the combination. To obtain the total net worth of a deal, the projected cash flows, net of investment needs, or free cash flows (FCFs) available to the company's claim holders are discounted by the appropriate cost of capital. Since the primary component of the FCF is the company's earnings (adjusted for non-cash expenses and capital expenditures), this approach may produce largely ambiguous estimates in sectors where it is difficult to forecast earnings. Ship-owning companies, for instance, offer a largely homogeneous service, in a sector with low entry barriers and for rates that are determined by global demand and supply (price takers). The high variability in rates causes future earnings and, in turn, FCFs to be uncertain/unstable, rendering their estimation extremely challenging. Consequently, DCF valuation may, in this case, result in ambiguous estimates when valuing business combinations. Along these lines, a landmark decision by the bankruptcy court examining the case of Genco Shipping and Trading in 2014 established a clear precedent, casting doubt over the validity of the DCF method in estimating a realistic enterprise value for a dry bulk ship-owning company. While the DCF approach is not commonly used to value ship-owning companies, it can be employed, among other methods, within segments where cash flows are more stable, such as shipping services or port operators. Moreover, DCF valuation may still be used for ship-owning companies not widely exposed to spot-rate volatility (i.e. those that tend to utilize long-term charter contracts) such as, for instance, LNG shipping companies. Figure 16.8 illustrates the DCF valuation process, along with the key inputs required.

A young company can be valued using a two-stage DCF model. During the first stage it experiences a high growth rate in sales (g_t) which is expected to

$$EV_T = \boxed{\text{Short-term valuation component}} + \boxed{\text{Terminal value}}$$

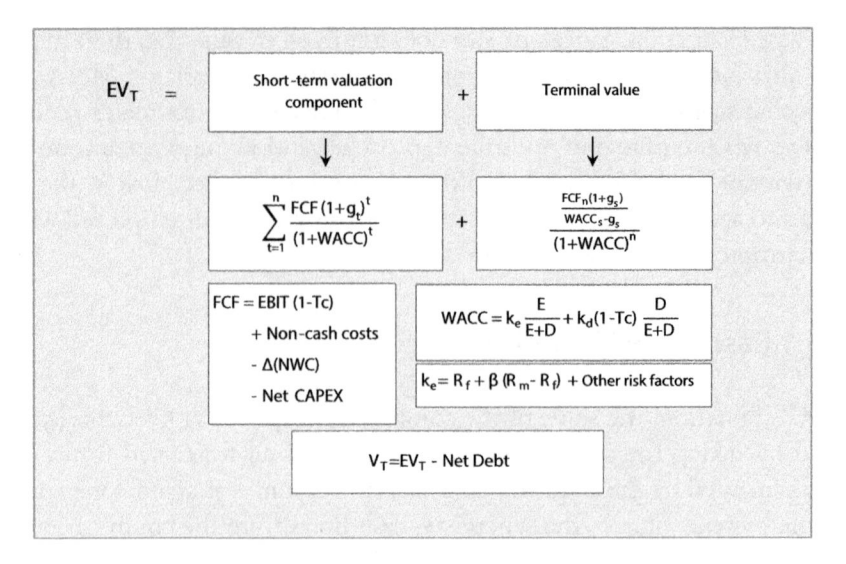

$$\sum_{t=1}^{n} \frac{FCF(1+g_t)^t}{(1+WACC)^t} \quad + \quad \frac{\frac{FCF_n(1+g_s)}{WACC_s - g_s}}{(1+WACC)^n}$$

FCF = EBIT (1-Tc)
+ Non-cash costs
− Δ(NWC)
− Net CAPEX

$$WACC = k_e \frac{E}{E+D} + k_d(1-Tc)\frac{D}{E+D}$$

$$k_e = R_f + \beta(R_m - R_f) + \text{Other risk factors}$$

$V_T = EV_T -$ Net Debt

Fig. 16.8 Overview of DCF valuation approach

converge to a rate more in line with the overall growth of the economy in the second stage (steady state growth, g_s). The standalone value of a target in this case would be equal to the sum of the present value of the FCFs from the high growth period (i.e. the *short-term valuation component*)—typically five to ten years—and the present value of the FCFs from the steady state (i.e. the *terminal value*). For more mature companies in the shipping industry that experience more stable growth in line with the general economy, a multi-stage approach is unlikely to provide better valuation estimates. After all, a multi-stage model requires more assumptions and inputs that may not improve the accuracy of the final estimate. In this case a constant growth valuation model used in the estimation of the terminal value in Fig. 16.8 can be sufficient. The steady-state growth rate (g_s) is generally assumed to be equal to the long-term growth forecast of the segment (or economy) within which the company operates. Since shipping is an international business, g_s can be estimated as a weighted average of the economic or demand growth in the relevant regions. A long-term risk-free rate (which comprises an economic growth component and an inflation component) is typically used by analysts to proxy for the long-term growth rate (g_s).[8]

When the DCF valuation method is employed to provide an estimate of the company's enterprise value (i.e. what the acquirer would have to pay for the target's equity including the cost of assuming responsibility for its debt), FCF denotes the cash flow available to all investors holding claims (equity and debt holders) on the company's resources.[9] This enterprise cash flow is a before-interest cash flow estimated by adding back non-cash charges (such as depreciation and amortization) to earnings before interest after tax (EBIAT) and deducting net reinvestment needs (net CAPEX) and the increase in net working capital (ΔNWC).[10] For a maritime company, capital expenditures can be sizable and include vessel repair and replacement costs and dry docking fees.

Enterprise cash flows are discounted by the company's weighted average cost of capital (WACC), the minimum required return for investors. This is a weighted average of the company's cost of equity (K_e) and after-tax cost of debt, $k_d(1-Tc)$.[11] The cost of equity can be estimated using an equity pricing model (the capital asset pricing model—CAPM or a multi-factor model).[12] Estimating k_e based on the CAPM assumes that the required rate of return for buying equity in a certain company is higher than the risk-free rate of return (r_f) by an amount that depends on the company's beta (i.e. its sensitivity to market movements) and the equity risk premium (R_m–R_f). The yield of a long-term government bond (e.g. ten year) can be used as the risk-free rate from the point of view of a strategic acquirer. The company's beta is estimated using past stock returns or, in the case of a private company, using the beta of comparable listed companies with similar operations and capital structure. The equity risk premium is the difference between the expected return on the home equity market index (or an international index for a company with multinational exposure) and R_f. Typically, historical market risk premia going back several decades are used as proxies of expected risk premia.[13] The cost of debt (k_d) can be calculated as a weighted average yield-to-maturity (YTM) of the company's outstanding bond issues and/or the interest charged for recent bank loans. The equity and debt weights in WACC reflect the company's target capital structure. Note that current financing mix may differ from the target capital structure significantly. Since the DCF approach involves valuing future cash flows, it is important that all inputs reflect the future rather than the past or present. The market value of long-term debt is not straightforward to estimate, since only few companies in the shipping industry have all their debt in the form of traded corporate bonds. One way to approximate the market value of all debt is to treat its book value as a coupon bond, in which the coupon is the annual interest payment on all debt and the maturity is a weighted average of the maturity of all debt outstanding on the valuation date, and value this bond as an annuity, using the company's cost of debt (k_d).

The value of the standalone target's equity (V_T) is then given by subtracting the market value of the company's debt from the enterprise value of the target EV_T and adding any excess cash that can be used for the purpose of debt repayment (i.e. net debt).[14] Comprehensive sensitivity analysis of the final estimate to the varying values for key inputs/assumptions is also essential, and a range of estimates is typically considered. To estimate V_{Tmax} in Eq. (16.1), the standalone valuation inputs discussed above need to be adjusted to reflect the scenario where the target company operates as the acquiring company's fully owned subsidiary or is fully integrated within the acquirer. In this case, the EBIT in the estimation of the FCF would be modified to include any operating synergies arising from the combination. In addition, the cost of capital utilized should reflect the capital components of the combined company. This will normally involve adjusting the market values of debt and equity, as well as the beta, to reflect the post-deal capital structure. The effects of any additional leverage used for financing the deal should also be taken into account.[15]

16.5.2 Relative Valuation

Relative valuation involves valuing businesses or assets relative to how the market values similar businesses or assets. The approach involves the estimation of an indicative (or implied) value by utilizing valuation multiples of comparable companies. Multiples are financial ratios that express market value (MV) relative to a key accounting indicator that is assumed to relate to value, such as earnings, sales, operating cash flow or book value. Such ratios can be estimated for comparable ("peer") companies (typically within the industry of the company being valued) or comparable transactions (transaction multiples). The key advantage of relative valuation is that it is less complex and involves fewer assumptions than DCF valuation. The implied value of a target company can be approximated as follows:

$$V_T = \left(\frac{V}{I}\right)_{COMP} \times I_T \qquad (16.2)$$

where

V_T is the implied value of the target company,[16]
I_T is the indicator of value for the target company and
$(V/I)_{COMP}$ is the value multiple of a comparable company, group of companies or transaction.

The *comparable company approach* involves estimating the equity or enterprise value of a target (V_T) as a function of a measure of its own earnings—for instance EBITDA—and the corresponding multiple of a single or a group of comparable companies with similar business/product, growth, profitability/cash flow, financial and operational risk profiles. Since variations in such characteristics may lead to significantly different valuation multiples, the process of selecting appropriate peers is critical. When valuing a liner company, for instance, one should select other liner companies of similar size, fleet profile and operations, which tend to compete among common routes. Deriving the value of a diversified liner company using multiples of container "charter owners", for instance, may result in distorted estimates. It is thus important to establish first why a certain peer's multiple is higher or lower than that of the company being valued before reaching conclusions on its relative under or over-valuation. Typically, analysts derive a range of implied valuations from different types of multiples and a number of comparable companies or the median company in the industry segment.

The most common valuation multiples used in the shipping industry are the EV/EBITDA (or EBITDA multiple), the MV/net income (the P/E multiple) and the MV/book value (or P/B multiple).[17] Sales and cash flow can also be used as value indicators. Trailing valuation multiples (where the denominator is derived from past value indicators) do not reflect the future expectations about investment and growth that are embedded in the numerator. Hence, projected or forward looking ratios where the denominator is derived from consensus analyst forecasts can be more intuitive. Moreover, one should interpret results from relative valuation cautiously in shipping industry segments characterized by excessive earnings and cash flow variability. Figure 16.9 reports projected valuation multiples for a number of container/liner companies.

Company	P/E	P/B	P/CF	EV/Sales	EV/EBITDA
AP Moller Maersk	10.7x	1.0x	5.3x	1.2x	5.1x
China Shipping Container Lines	35.7x	2.0x	16.2x	1.4x	21.9x
COSCO Shipping	21.8x	1.6x	7.8x	2.0x	13.3x
Costamare	12.4x	1.7x	7.6x	6.3x	9.3x
DANAOS	5.9x	0.8x	2.7x	6.6x	9.1x
Evergreen	16.3x	1.2x	6.4x	0.9x	9.6x
Mitsui O.S.K Lines	13.5x	0.7x	4.1x	0.9x	13.6x
Neptune Orient Lines	22.7x	0.9x	3.7x	0.7x	10.1x

Fig. 16.9 Forward valuation multiples for selected container/liner companies (*Source*: Data from Bloomberg)
Note: Forward ratios are estimated using 2015 fiscal year end consensus analyst estimates from 2014

Most multiples exhibit large variation among different companies. Their average EBITDA multiple is 11.5. Accordingly, a potential acquisition target with USD100 million EBITDA would be priced at USD1.15 billion (including debt liabilities), based on how this group of peers are currently valued. Note, however, that the profile of the potential target being valued would determine the most appropriate comparables. For instance, when valuing a container tonnage provider (instead of a liner company), Costamare and DANAOS from Fig. 16.9 would constitute better reference peers than the rest.

Comparable deal multiples are also commonly used to derive an implied value for a target relative to how other targets have been valued in similar recent transactions. In this approach, $(V/I)_{COMP}$ in Eq. (16.2) would reflect a transaction multiple (e.g. deal value/target's EBITDA). A main difference with comparable company multiples is that the resulting valuation estimate includes an offer premium over and above the target's intrinsic value. Thus, this type of valuation method can be seen as a way to derive an indicative estimate of the value of a target company, including the synergies from the combination. As with valuation multiples, it is vital to identify transactions that are genuinely comparable. Figure 16.10 reports deal EBITDA multiples and other information for a number of noteworthy M&A deals in the wider shipping industry.[18] Given the large variation in multiples, it becomes obvious that the matching process is of crucial importance. While the focus in this process is normally on

Acquirer	Target	Year Announced	Deal Value (2014$)*	4-week premium[†]	DV/EBITDA
Neptune Orient Lines	American President Lines	1997	$1.30bil	43%	4.1x
OSG	Stelmar Shipping	2004	$1.06bil	38%	6.7x
AP Moller-Maersk	Koninklijke P&O Nedlloyd	2005	$3.66bil	27%	5.4x
Investor Group	Associated British Ports	2006	$6.05bil	47%	14.1x
DryShips Inc.	Ocean Rig	2008	$849.5mil	17%	13.3x
Excel Maritime	Quintana Maritime	2008	$1.83bil	14%	9.4x
Maersk Tankers	Broström	2008	$635.9mil	24%	6.0x
BW Offshore	Prosafe Production	2010	$496.1mil	21%	2.4x
Dry Ships	Ocean Freight	2011	$127.0mil	150%	3.5x
Kirby Corp	K-Sea Transportation Partners	2011	$613.6mil	53%	10.4x
Clarksons	RS Platou	2014	$441.5mil	-	10.6x

Fig. 16.10 Selected M&A transaction multiples (*Sources*: Data from Thomson Reuters SDC and company reports)
*Deal value includes debt liabilities
[†]The four-week premium is reported for listed targets

the business and risk profile of the target, taking into account the nature of the acquiring company, the state of the market and the degree of success of the past comparable transactions can increase the reliability of the estimates.

16.5.3 Asset-Based Valuation

Asset-based valuation estimates the value of a business as the fair market value of its assets less the value of its liabilities. It is often referred to as a "cost-based approach" since the value assigned to a company is equal to the cost of acquiring its physical assets. It is frequently used to value companies with a large asset base and assets that are critical to their earnings' capacity. Due to the highly volatile and capital-intensive nature of the shipping industry, asset-based valuation methods tend to be used extensively within the ship-owning segment, particularly for tanker and dry-bulk companies. Since book value is based on historical asset values, which tend to ignore the current market value of the company's fleet, the NAV approach tends to be preferred.[19] Moreover, as the market has become increasingly conservative in valuing shipping players over the years, NAV has also been extensively used to estimate a "floor" purchase price (or disposal value) in M&A transactions. NAV is based on the current market value of a company's vessels and any newbuilding contracts, and is adjusted for non-operating items. A drawback of NAV is that it does not take into account aspects such as the management quality and may, for instance, understate value in a rising market. Hence, attaching certain premia to the NAV in M&A valuation can result in more realistic estimates.

While analysts use different variations of NAV, in its simplest form it can be estimated as follows:

$$NAV_T = V_{VESSELS} + NLA - V_{DEBT} \qquad (16.3)$$

where:

$V_{VESSELS}$ is the MV of vessels using current newbuilding, resale and second-hand prices obtained from a vessel valuation company or shipbrokers' databases.[20]
This needs to be adjusted for any remaining payments to the seller/shipyard.
NLA is net liquid assets.
V_{DEBT} is the MV of debt outstanding.

One may also apply a premium to the above (depending on the spot charter rates) for any long-term charterparty agreements, and add the market value of any minority stakes the company holds in other businesses. While NAV_T can form the basis of analyzing the value of a ship-owning target company in an M&A deal, it may only be utilized as a "floor value" in cases where the combination is expected to generate additional operational synergies.

Although the above comprise the bulk of the valuation methods employed in the context of shipping M&As, different variations of these methods or entirely different complementary approaches may be employed depending on the special features of a deal. Some shipping M&As, for instance, encompass strategic real options that are associated with potential opportunities for further investment. This can further accelerate growth contingent on the successful integration of the deal in question (the option to expand to a new market or business segment). Alternatively, the option to divest an acquired business (or certain assets) in case a deal does not work (the option to abandon) also has value.[21] Thus, under certain circumstances, the optionality inherent in M&A transactions may be viewed as an integral part of M&A valuation.[22] Since a large part of the value of real options is derived from the volatility in the value of the underlying asset, taking such options into account is particularly meaningful in shipping, considering the significant volatility in freight rates and vessel prices.

16.6 Financing of Shipping M&As

The structuring of the terms of a deal is central to the M&A acquisition process and is closely related to how the risk involved and attained gains are shared among the counter-parties. Assuming that the form of the deal (acquisition of stock, assets or statutory merger) and the post-acquisition structure of the combined entity (full integration, partial integration, owned subsidiary, etc.) have been agreed, the financing method and terms are key to the deal structuring process. Understanding acquisition financing options is vital from both the buy-side and sell-side perspective. For acquiring companies, the payment method has a pertinent impact on their ownership structure, financing cost and, as a result, post-acquisition cash flow and return-on-investment. For target companies, the final offer price and share in the upside are also, to a large extent, associated with the financing terms. When an offer is put together, the acquiring company should typically take into consideration its capital structure, debt capacity and access to debt financing, profitability and availability of internal funds, the two companies' market valuations, the target's preferences and ownership structure, as well as tax implications and legal ramifications, among other factors. The financing mix is also contingent on elements such as the business type (e.g. ship-owning vs services) and the

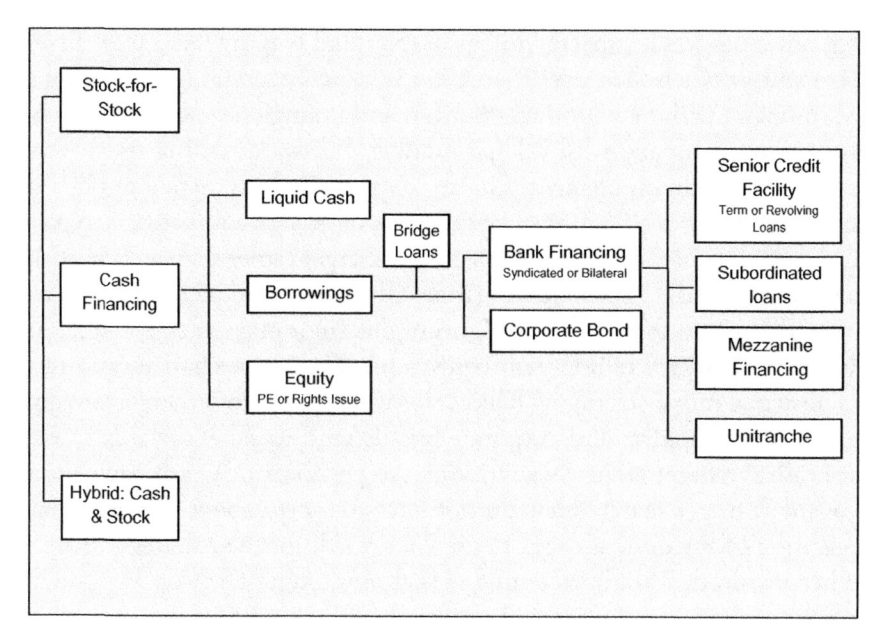

Fig. 16.11 Shipping M&A financing methods

associated risks and assets involved. Moreover, leveraged buyouts carried out by private equity companies typically involve more complex financing structures. Figure 16.11 provides a summary of the main financing methods used in M&As in the shipping industry.

A *stock-for-stock* exchange involves a swap of shares between acquiring and target shareholders. The acquirer issues new stock directly to the seller's shareholders who, in exchange, tender their shares based on a pre-agreed exchange ratio.[23] In a stock deal, the target shareholders share the risk that the benefits of the acquisition will not be realized since, in this case, the market will end up penalizing the acquiring company's stock. In a way, a stock-for-stock exchange requires that the two companies' shareholders know and trust each other.

From a tax perspective, target shareholders do not recognize taxable gains in the short term but pay tax on their capital gain later, when they choose to sell the acquiring company's shares. However, from a liquidity point of view, stock deals are not typically preferred by target shareholders. An acquirer is more inclined to use stock as a currency when it believes its stock is highly valued relative to the target's as, in this case, it can offer fewer shares to pay for an acquisition (Travlos 1987). Moreover, buying companies tend to have a preference for paying with stock when they have limited borrowing capacity and/or excess cash (Faccio and Masulis 2005), when the deal is large and the integration process is expected to be complex and lengthy (Alexandridis et al. 2013) and/or when the target's valuation is more uncertain (e.g. a young service company with new product offerings and intangible assets, or a dry bulk ship-owning company with a large number of vessels trading spot). Stock-for-stock as a form of payment is more common in deals carried out by listed acquirers (Faccio et al. 2006) since the stock of private companies is typically illiquid. An all-shares deal tends to signify a merger rather than an acquisition. Accordingly, in 2015, General Maritime Corp. acquired all shares of Navig8 Crude Tankers to form Gener8 Maritime Inc. in a pure stock-for-stock deal valued at a USD1.4 billion cash equivalent. With an exchange ratio of 0.9 and no actual money changing hands, this was technically a merger-of-equals.

Selling shareholders and corporate boards tend to skew towards *cash bids* since cash is a highly liquid way for them to get an exit. A cash payment also means that target shareholders do not have to worry about the potential or integration of the deal, as they obtain a net worth for their shares and are not further involved. The shortcoming is that any longer-term upside potential for the acquirer's share price will not be shared with target shareholders. Of course, a cash payment also involves a tax payment in the short run. Acquiring companies tend to use cash when they have substantial borrowing capacity or cash reserves, when their shares are less highly valued and/or when they are reluctant to dilute their shareholders' stakes by creating outside block holders.

Although in a cash bid the target shareholders receive cash in exchange for their shares, the source of the cash in not always the acquirer's internal cash reserves (*liquid cash*). The acquirer may either raise debt to pay in cash or include debt in the structure of the deal. It is important to note that securing debt financing can be quite challenging, particularly during years where credit markets are "locked". *Bank financing* tends to be the most flexible and affordable source of funding for shipping M&As and normally comes in the form of a *syndicated credit facility.* Syndicated loans are typically used in deals that require significant funding and involve a group of lenders and arrangers that form the syndicate. While both first and second lien senior loans are common sources of senior debt M&A financing, second lien loans are common in leveraged buyouts (LBOs) when the borrower's financing needs exceed the maximum threshold of senior secured lenders.[24] *Mezzanine financing* may take the form of *subordinated* high yield debt, convertible debt or private mezzanine securities (debt with warrants or preferred equity). *Unitranche loans* are hybrids of senior and mezzanine/subordinated debt in one instrument, and are primarily offered by specialty finance companies such as credit funds for LBOs sponsored by private equity companies.

Bridge loan financing serves to fill the gap between the deal announcement and the arrangement of formal long-term financing. It involves a short-term commitment, provided by an investment bank, that financing will be available until the closing date of an acquisition deal. The investment bank providing the bridge loan commitment is not typically involved directly in the long-term financing of the deal but acts as a financing arranger and financial advisor in the underlying acquisition.

Tapping the capital markets provides additional sources of funds in order to finance an M&A deal. An underwritten *rights issue*, whereby an acquirer issues additional shares to existing shareholders and uses the proceeds to pay in cash, is utilized relatively infrequently. A bond issue is another potential option, but the issuance process makes it more costly than traditional debt financing, although bonds can be issued with much longer maturities than bank loans.

Figure 16.12 provides financing mix information for a sample of 1,408 deals with complete method of payment data from our shipping M&A sample

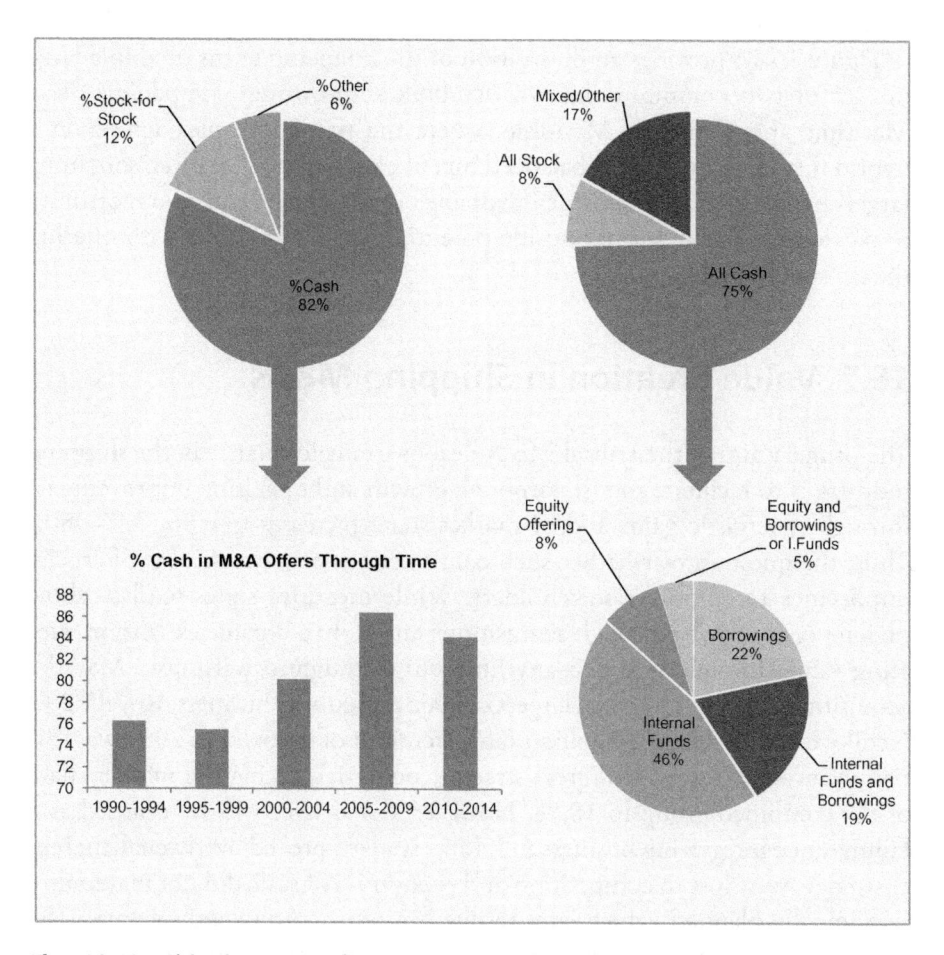

Fig. 16.12 Shipping M&A financing: 1990–2014 (*Source*: Data from Thomson Reuters SDC, 1990–2014)

discussed earlier, covering the period 1990–2014. Cash is, unambiguously, the dominant form of M&A financing in the shipping industry, with the average offer comprising of 82 % cash and only 12 % stock. In fact, three-quarters of all deals are paid entirely with cash. The fact that only a third of the deals are carried out by listed targets and that a large number of the rest are carried out by investor groups/PE justifies this pattern. The sub-classification of the cash segment is based on one-fifth of the sample where additional details on the financing source are available. About half of the cash deals are financed entirely through internal funds, 22 % through debt and 24 % involving a combination of liquid cash (or equity offerings) and debt. Notably, the share of cash in M&A offers increased considerably in 2000–04, and even further in 2005–09, due to the liquidity abundance in the shipping industry. Despite retreating marginally as the credit markets tightened during the shipping cycle trough of 2010–14, it still remained the prevailing financing form for M&As.

Figure 16.13 provides an illustration of the financing terms used in a large merger of two commonly known dry bulk ship-owning companies, Excel Maritime and Quintana Maritime, where the two companies agreed on a hybrid financing method. A balanced mix of cash and stock is often sought by target shareholders, as it provides favorable tax advantages and an opportunity to participate in any further upside potential at the same time with offering the certainty of cash.

16.7 Value Creation in Shipping M&As

The primary aim of the typical M&A deal or strategic alliance in the shipping industry is to facilitate robust corporate growth and operating improvements through synergistic gains and/or market share increases (see pp. 377–380). Thus, the question of whether such combinations are successful is of crucial importance to corporate stakeholders. While executive suites tend to show preference to growth through acquisitions rather than organic expansion, creating value through M&As is anything but a straightforward task. Maersk's acquisition of the then fourth largest container shipping business, Royal P&O Nedlloyd NV, for EUR2.3 billion (at a premium of 40.6 %) in 2005 was initially viewed as a deal with great strategic potential, taking the market share of the combined group to 18 %. However, it was later widely regarded as a failure since integrating business units and systems proved overly challenging, customers were lost to competition and economies of scale did not materialize as originally planned, which later resulted in restructuring and job cuts. The costs of carrying out large mergers involving duplicate operations can often

Deal Details
- **Date Announced:** 29/01/2008
- **Effective Date:** 15/04/2008
- **Acquirer:** Excel Maritime Carriers Ltd (NYSE: EXM)
- **Acquirer's business:** dry bulk freight transportation
- **Acquirer's Fleet:** 18 vessels (1.1 million dwt)
- **Target:** Quintana Maritime Limited (NASDAQ: QMAR)
- **Target's business:** dry bulk freight transportation
- **Target's Fleet:** 37 vessels (4.1million dwt) including new-buildings on order
- **Deal Type:** Merger agreement whereby Quintana would become a wholly owned subsidiary of Excel. Involved full Integration of Quintana's fleet, systems and management capability.
- **Target's Shares Acquired:** 100%
- **Overall Transaction Value:** $2.45 billion including assumed net debt and other costs.
- **Equity Transaction Value:** $1.63 billion or $26.48 per Quintana share (based on Excel's closing price of $33.00 on Jan 28)
- **Offer Premium:** 57% to Quintana's Jan 28 price and 35% to Quintana's 30-day average price.
- **Deal Value-to-EBITDA:** 9
- **Financial Advisors:** Deutsche Bank (Excel) and Citi (Quintana)

Deal Financing Terms
- **Payment Method:** Combination of Cash and Stock. Each Quintana share to receive $13 in cash and 0.408 shares of Class A Excel stock
- **Cash consideration (44.54%):** $13.00 per share of Quintana common stock
- **Cash source:** $1.4 billion from a syndicate of international banks led by Nordea (also acted as an administrative and syndication agent). The other lead arrangers for the credit facility were Deutsche Bank, DVB Bank AG, General Electric Capital Corporation and HSH Nordbank AG. National Bank of Greece, Credit Suisse and Fortis Bank acted as co-arrangers.
- **Loan type:** $1bil term loan and $400 million revolving loan (at LIBOR + 1.25% per annum)
- **Guarantees:** Credit facilities are guaranteed by direct and indirect subsidiaries of Excel, and the security for the credit facility included, among other assets, mortgages and assignments of earnings with respect to certain vessels owned and/or operated by Excel or Quintana.
- **Stock consideration (55.46%):** $13.48 per share of Quintana common stock based on Excel's and Quintana's closing price on Jan 28 ($33.00 and $16.89 respectively).
- **Exchange ratio:** 0.408 shares of Excel class A common stock per share of Quintana common stock (eventually reduced to 0.398 at effective day of the deal to reflect dividends paid by Quintana).
- **Upside clause:** In the event the average closing price of Excel's Class A common stock during the 15-day trading day period ending before the effective date of the merger would exceed $45 per share, the exchange ratio would be adjusted so that the total value delivery per Quintana share including cash to be $31.38, unadjusted for any dividend payments.

Additional closing terms
The transaction is subject to customary closing conditions, including receipt of financing, approval of Quintana's shareholders and receipt of regulatory approvals.

Fig. 16.13 Financing terms of a shipping mega-deal (*Sources*: Company press releases, Bloomberg, Marketwatch, Thomson Reuters SDC)

outweigh the gains. On the dry-bulk ship-owning spectrum, Excel Maritime acquired Quintana Maritime in 2008 for USD2.45 billion, almost tripling its fleet size and becoming one of the largest dry-bulk shipping companies in the world, right at the brink of a major shipping downturn. Although Quintana shareholders gained significantly from the deal (the premium offered was 57 %), it proved disastrous for Excel, which ultimately went bankrupt in 2013. Bad market timing was blamed among other factors. Along these lines, Eagle Bulk and Genco shipping both filed for bankruptcy not long following large and ambitious acquisitions.

The complexities in creating value through M&As are not confined to the shipping industry. The topic of value creation through business combinations has received great attention in the finance literature. The consensus of existing research is that target-company shareholders enjoy significant gains from M&A deals, and that the combined benefit to acquirers and targets (i.e. the synergy gain) is also positive. This outcome is quite reasonable given the hefty premia paid by acquiring companies to secure a positive response from the target's shareholders. But since the great majority of deals are technically acquisitions, they should offer tangible NPV benefits to the acquiring shareholders. Nonetheless, existing empirical evidence suggests that, in more than half of the cases, M&As in the USA, Europe and Asia destroy rather than create value for acquiring company shareholders (Eccles et al. 1999). This is also consistent with more recent evidence provided by Alexandridis et al. (2012) on the sixth merger wave that occurred during the last decade. Bruner (2002) provides a comprehensive review of the research findings on value creation through M&As.

Market experience contradicts the consensus that M&As tend to destroy value and suggests that this is less than half the story. M&A professionals often argue that the success of a consolidation is very much case specific and largely dependent on a plethora of different factors. Along these lines, recent research has identified several deal, company, management and market wide characteristics that seem to determine the gains to business combinations. These factors include the offer premium, the size of the deal and the companies involved (Alexandridis et al. 2013; Moeller et al. 2004), the listing status of the target company (Faccio et al. 2004; Chang 1998), the method used to finance the transaction (Travlos 1987), the relative valuation of the acquirer and target company (Dong et al. 2006, and Fu et al. 2013), the skills (Jaffe et al. 2013) and attitudes of the management team (Malmendier and Tate 2005), the quality of the financial advisors employed (Golubov et al. 2012), the corporate governance of the two companies (Masulis et al. 2007 and Wang and Xie 2009) and their ownership structure (Bauguess et al. 2009), the competition in the market for corporate control (Alexandridis et al. 2010) and the market cycle (Bouwman et al. 2009), among other factors. This section provides an overview of the most commonly employed measures to assess value creation in M&As, reviews some of the research findings on the success of business combinations in shipping, and provides a summary of the most significant value creation drivers.

16.7.1 Measuring Value Creation

There are several different approaches to measuring value creation in M&As. A quantifiable measure would reflect the economic effects of a consolidation to the owners of the business. While in practice a deal has an impact on other stakeholders such as employees or society, these effects are not easily measurable and are normally evaluated on an anecdotal basis. Since the actual results of a consolidation are not fully apparent before full integration of the joining businesses is achieved, long-term performance measures would capture the effects of a deal in the value of the companies involved more effectively. However, such long-run measures can be subject to the confounding effects of other events occurring during the period under examination. Hence, a surge or deterioration in the share price or operating performance of the acquiring company during a one to five year window from the completion of an M&A deal might be attributed to other events that have occurred during this period rather than the deal itself. An improvement in market conditions, an unrelated fundamental change in strategy, policy or governance, and even another M&A deal itself are some of the factors that can affect company performance.

The empirical literature on M&As has therefore focused more on the market reaction around the announcement of a deal captured in short-run share price movements. Undeniably, this approach assumes full-market efficiency in that all the information associated with the value creation potential of a proposed deal is available to market participants at the acquisition announcement, which they all interpret rationally and efficiently. In other words, this approach entails that the long-term potential of the deal is reflected fully and accurately in the involved company's stock prices at the acquisition proposal. This might seem to be a rather strong assumption because a measure on value creation based on the immediate share price reaction to a deal announcement might not provide enough time for the market to assess the valuation effects and implications of a deal. However, research has shown that, in fact, abnormal share price changes around M&A announcements provide, in most cases, a good indication of the value creation potential of a combination. It is also important to mention that the market reaction around the deal announcement comprises information not only about the potential synergies arising from the combination but also the value split between the acquirer and the target, as well as their standalone valuations.

While short-term measures of value creation in M&As tend to be more commonly used, it can be argued that the question of which type of measure is more appropriate is contingent on the trade-off of the pros and cons of each approach. From a methodological perspective, short-term approaches offer "cleaner" measures of value creation. In fact, there is strong evidence that abnormal returns around M&A announcements are taken seriously by the acquiring company's executive suite in the decision of whether to complete eventually or withdraw a deal (Luo 2005). This indicates that managers believe that the market is, in fact, quite efficient in pricing M&A valuation effects and take this feedback seriously.

Although short-term approaches are more straightforward to use, a comprehensive assessment of the value implications of an M&A should involve alternative measures and windows. Figure 16.14 offers a summary of the main methods used to assess the value creation of M&As in the shipping industry. The typical approach to examining market expectations about the valuation implications of the involved parties' shareholders is to use a measure of cumulative abnormal (risk adjusted) stock return (CAR) around the deal announcement (event window). This approach involves obtaining the necessary parameters used in the estimation of abnormal returns from a pre-event window market model regression, as illustrated in Fig. 16.14.[25] The long-term valuation implications of a deal can be assessed based on the impact of the deal on the acquiring company's stock or operating performance over a 12-month to 5-year window, following the deal announcement/completion.

16.7.2 Do Shipping M&As Create Value?

Empirical research on the valuation effects of M&As in the shipping industry is relatively scarce. All of this evidence is based on CARs acquiring target companies around the acquisition announcement. Figure 16.15 provides a summary of some recent findings.

Panayides and Gong (2002) examined the effect of two large deals in the liner segment that took place in the late 1990s: the UK's P&O Containers acquisition of Netherland's Royal Nedlloyd and the merger between Singapore's Neptune Orient Lines and US based American President Lines, both in 1997. These "game changing", cross-border transactions were among the very first consolidation moves in the container industry and represented major strategic moves that offered very tangible synergy benefits for the companies involved. As a result, they were associated with hefty increases in P&O's and NOL's share prices (83 % on average). Although it is not reported by the authors, P&O's stock price rose sixfold in two years, which corroborates the particularly favorable market reaction at the deal announcement and suggests that some shipping M&A deals have indeed created significant value for shareholders.

Syriopoulos and Theotokas (2007) focused on the tanker segment and specifically on the case of the acquisition of Stelmar Shipping by OSG in 2004, following two alternative bids by OMI and Fortress Investment Group. The first was rejected by the target's board and the second was eventually withdrawn

Estimation Window

$$R_{i,t} = a_i + \beta_i \times R_{m,t} + \varepsilon_{i,t} \quad (3)$$

Conventional methods for event studies rely on excess returns estimated using an asset pricing model (Brown and Warner 1985). Research studies use a simple market model approach to estimate daily abnormal returns for the sample firms. This method requires share price data for a long estimation period prior to the event window, to ensure that the estimated risk parameters are independent of the effect of the event itself. Estimating the model's parameters involves running a market model regression for each of the sample firms/events over a 200 to 250-day period preceding the acquisition announcement. Schwert (2000), for example, uses a window of (-301,-64) relative to the announcement day, to estimate the market model parameters. Alternatively, one may use a (-255,-6) window assuming that the estimation and return window do not overlap.

Event Window

$$CAR_{i,(t_1,t_2)} = \sum_{t=t_1}^{t_2} AR_{i,t} \quad (1)$$

In this approach, $CAR_{i,(t_1,t_2)}$ is the aggregate abnormal return for firm i over a window t_1,t_2 around the announcement day of the deal: t. Three or five-day windows are the most commonly employed, but more extensive windows can more effectively account for any pre-announcement information leakage and/or any initial over or under-reaction to merger announcement information.

$$AR_{i,t} = R_{i,t} - E(R_{i,t}) \quad (2)$$

AR is given by the difference between $R_{i,t}$, the stock return of firm i at day t, and $E(R_{i,t})$, a measure of the expected return.

$$E(R_{i,t}) = \hat{a}_i + \hat{\beta}_i \times R_{m,t} \quad (4)$$

$R_{m,t}$ is the realised market return for day t, and $\hat{a}_i$ and $\hat{\beta}_i$ are the parameter estimates of the market model obtained in (3). This approach assumes that the expected return of firm i over day t is a function of the market return on the same date, the past sensitivity of the stock to market movements (i.e. systematic risk) and a_i, a measure of the firm's past abnormal stock performance relative to the market index.

$$SCAR_{D,(t_1,t_2)} = w_A CAR_{A,(t_1,t_2)} + w_T CAR_{T,(t_1,t_2)} \quad (5)$$

The deal synergy gain ($SCAR_D$) can then be estimated as the market value weighted sum of the acquirer and target firm CARs.

Post-Event Window

$$BHAR_i = \prod_{t=1}^{T}(1+R_{i,t}) - \prod_{t=1}^{T}(1+R_{Benchmark,t}) \quad (6)$$

In the buy-and-hold abnormal return (BHAR) approach, the $R_{i,t}$ is the return of acquirer i at month t, $R_{Benchmark,t}$ is the return of the corresponding benchmark, and T is the number of months in the post-acquisition window. Alexandridis, Doukas and Mavis (2015) use different benchmarks in BHAR estimation (25 size and book-to-market portfolios, control firms, control deal and a simulation approach).

$$CTAR_{i,t} = R_{i,t} - R_{Benchmark,t} \quad (7)$$

An alternative is the calendar-time approach (CTR) as in Mitchell and Stafford (2000). In CTR, acquirers enter the portfolio on the month following the announcement month and remain for 12 to 60 months. Monthly calendar time abnormal returns (CTARs) are then estimated by subtracting the return of a benchmark at month t, $R_{benchmark,t}$ from the return of acquirer i at month t, $R_{i,t}$.

$$AOP_{i,t} = ROA_{i,t} - ROA_{Benchmark,t} \quad (8)$$

An alternative long-term assessment of value creation from M&As is based on the acquiring firm's operating performance. Prior studies match acquiring firms' Return-On-Assets (ROA) with a control group on the basis of industry, size, and pre-event performance (Barber and Lyon, 1996; Lie, 2001), and then compare their post-event operating performance. The difference between the average ROA of an acquiring firm for a specific post-acquisition window (usually 1-3 years) and the corresponding ROA of the benchmark provides an estimate of a deal's abnormal impact on the operating results of the acquiring company.

Fig. 16.14 Measuring M&A value creation

Study	Segment	Sub-Sectors / Companies	Deal Sample	Sample Period	Countries Examined	Type of Study	Value Creation Measure	Bidder CAR	Target CAR	Synergy Gain
Panayides and Gong (2002)	Liner Shipping	P&O Containers Acquisition of RNL and NOL merger with APL	2	1995-1999	UK, US, The Netherlands, Singapore	Case Study	CAR [-5+5]	83%	136%	-
Samitas and Kenourios (2007)	Tramp Shipping	Tanker, LNG, Dry-Bulk, Chemicals, Offshore	15	2000-2007	US listed	Quantitative	CAR [various windows]	-0.3% to +0.8%	-	-
Syriopoulos and Theotokas (2007)	Tanker Shipping	Acquisition of Stelmar Shipping	2	2004	US listed (NYSE)	Case Study	CAR [-30,+28] CAR [-10,+10] CAR [-5,+5] CAR [-1,+1]	-22.4% to 1.6%	5.1 to 22.1%	-15.8% to 6.1%
Andreou, Louca and Panayides (2012)	Freight Transportation	Railroad Haul Operating, Freight Motor Trucking and Storage, Water Transport, Freight and Services, Freight Transportation Arrangements	285	1980-2009	US listed (NYSE, NASDAQ, AMEX)	Quantitative	CAR [-10,+1]	2.3%	24.5%	3.3%
Alexandrou, Gounopoulos and Thomas (2014)	Water Transportation and Related Services	Water Freight Transportation, Passenger Water Transportation, Port related services, Water Transportation services	1,266	1984-2011	Global (67 equity markets)	Quantitative	CAR [-3,+1]	1.2%	3.3%	-

Fig. 16.15 Recent research of value creation through shipping M&As

by the private equity bidder in a chain of disputes between the Stelmar's executive suite and its major shareholder. All three bids resulted in a considerable increase in Stelmar's share price around the acquisition proposals. Nonetheless, the market, at best, did not anticipate any gains for any of the acquiring company's shareholders. In fact, OSG's market capitalization reduced by around 22 % during a 21-day window surrounding its bid announcement. This is not surprising since, effectively, OSG offered a premium of almost 100 % relative to Stelmar's market value prior to the three separate bids. Accordingly, the general evidence in the M&A literature suggests that the gains to acquiring companies are often hampered by the hefty premiums paid to secure a positive response from the target shareholders, which tend to neutralize any combined gains from the deal. While the study focuses on the short-term valuation effects of the bids for Stelmar, looking at OSG's share price over a one-year horizon, does not alter the main conclusion that acquiring companies in the shipping industry often fails to create value for their shareholders. Along the same lines, Samitas and Kenourios (2007) provide evidence that among 15 M&A deals in the tanker, dry-bulk, chemicals, LNG and offshore segments that took place between 2000 and 2007, acquiring companies failed to create value for their shareholders around the bid announcement.

The most significant drawback with the studies discussed above is their sample size, which is quite restrictive and does not allow for a generalization of their conclusions. Two more recent studies have used more extensive samples to examine short-term valuation effects in shipping M&As. Andreou et al. (2012) use a US sample that spans across the entire freight transportation industry, including water, rail and trucking, between 1980 and 2009. The study finds that business combinations create value for both acquirers and targets and, as a result, offer significant synergistic gains. Shareholders of target companies appear to capture most of the synergy gain (24.5 % CAR) relative to bidding companies (2.3 % CAR). Their result that M&As in freight transportation are subject to positive abnormal returns for acquirers may be driven by the group of deals where the target company is not listed. An important finding of this study is that vertical integration (across different supply chain segments) yields additional value relative to horizontal integration, although the bulk of this gain is captured by the target's shareholders.

Alexandrou et al. (2014) focus entirely on M&As within the water freight and passenger transport segment, including port related services. They examine a global sample of 1,266 deals that took place between 1984 and 2011, and find significant gains to acquiring (CAR of 1.2 %) and target (CAR of 3.3 %) shareholders. Notably, gains to acquiring companies are higher in passenger transport, marinas and services, compared to the freight transport or cargo handling segments. Moreover, Asian and North American deals create more value for acquirers than business combinations in the rest of the world. Most importantly, and contrary to the general M&A literature, this study finds that acquisitions of private targets create more value relative to deals involving listed targets. This is a particularly interesting result since there is unanimous evidence that acquisitions of unlisted targets create more value for acquirers. Among the reasons cited in the literature are the heftier premia offered to attract shareholders of listed companies (i.e. private companies are associated with liquidity discounts), the more concentrated ownership of private companies (which, in the case of a stock-for-stock deal, for instance, creates large outside block holders in the acquiring company that act as efficient monitors) as well as the lower integration complexity associated with deals of smaller target-to-bidder relative size. The fact that "public deals" yield higher acquirer gains in the freight transport segment suggests that some sort of structural sector-specific peculiarity invalidates the above effects. Alternatively, the bulk of the gains to M&As of listed targets may be emanating from countries where the market for corporate control is less competitive, resulting in significantly lower offer premia (see Alexandridis et al. 2010 for more general evidence on M&As).

Value creation drivers in an M&A transaction

- All stakeholders buy into the acquisition rationale
- Motivation of combined leadership and workforce
- Effective integration of the combined installed base / assets
- Combined asset-base and service offering to be more compelling
- Improved market positioning due to consolidation
- Realistic and time-bound plan to achieve synergy gains

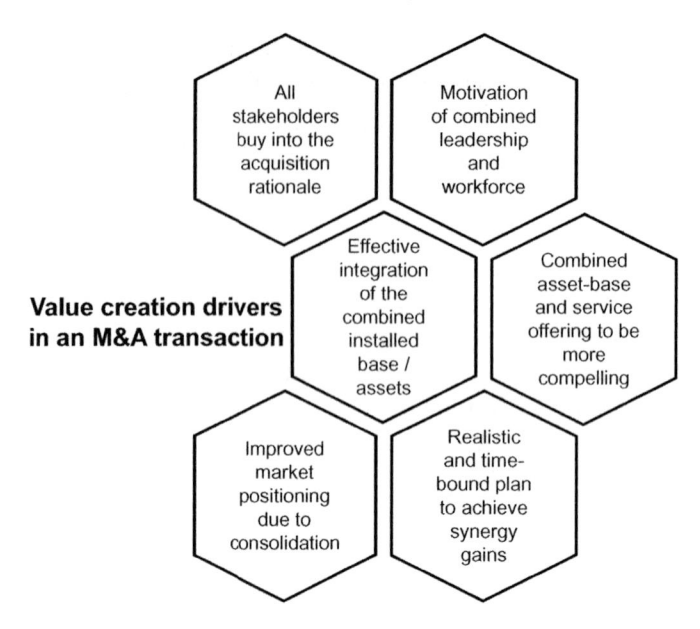

Fig. 16.16 Some key ingredients of shipping M&A success

It becomes obvious that examining large samples of shipping M&As comes with merits and drawbacks. The success potential of a certain deal is often case-specific and depends on a plethora of factors, which might be difficult to account for in large-scale empirical studies. In addition to the value creation drivers discussed above, Fig. 16.16 illustrates some additional key ingredients (indicators) of M&A success, commonly quoted by shipping M&A practitioners. For a business combination to create value, the strategic rationale for the deal needs to be sensible, the cost, revenue and other synergy and efficiency gains articulated and accurately projected, and the size of the offer premium should allow for a significant part of the total gain to be captured by acquiring shareholders. Whilst this comprises a deliberately simplistic summation of value enhancement through M&As, longer term value from the M&A transaction is delivered by the enhancement of the combined business model when amalgamating the acquirer and target's market share, scale of operations, human capital, unique assets, technology and resources, intellectual property and other value items. A committed integration team is vital to delivering improvement in the combined business financial performance, through achieving the synergy and efficiency gains envisaged in the acquisition plan. The aggregation of businesses (or fleets in the ship-owning context) leads to consolidation of market share and more comprehensive and compelling offerings to the clients of the combined business. The more cross-selling is the nature of the combined customer base and the routes to market for the combined business, the higher tends to be the value enhancement from the M&A transaction.

16.8 Conclusion

This chapter has reviewed the key aspects of M&As in the shipping industry. The volatile and capital intensive nature of the maritime sector, the trend to reduce costs and financial risks, as well as the shift in the shipping finance landscape have all driven the developments in consolidation within the industry. Globalization and the continued expansion of seaborne trade have resulted in an increasingly multi-dimensional M&A market in terms of types of transactions and participants involved, setting off a climb to record highs for merger activity in the last few years. Acquisition activity has accelerated among shipping service providers, port operators as well as ship-owning firms, whereas the 2009 market downturn and the resulting drop in maritime asset values has also caught the attention of private investment groups that have emerged as major players. The effects of the persistent supply-and-demand imbalance have brought M&A motives, such as cost cutting and efficiency improvements, at the core of corporate strategy in a sector seeking to complement organic growth amid a stagnating global economic landscape. With corporate liquidity and public equity market appetite having dried up relative to the previous decade, traditional bank and other financing means will need to continue providing funding for consolidation in the sector if it is to continue to thrive until the next market upturn. As of 2016, a number of indicators point to a further acceleration of consolidation across the industry for the next decade. Most importantly, the persistent conditions of financial distress in the ship-owning segment induced by a prolonged shipping cycle trough are likely to re-shape the industry's landscape leading to more business failures and strategic combinations.

Along with the primary drivers and trends in shipping M&A and their financing, the importance of developing a comprehensive M&A function within the modern maritime corporation has also been highlighted, as well as the fact that the success of certain deals in delivering the estimated gains can be attributed, to a large extent, to the efficacy of such M&A process. The valuation approaches utilized are a key part of this process and can vary greatly depending on the shipping segment in question. The accuracy of the assumptions employed are instrumental in deriving accurate estimates for the synergistic benefits and thus for the potential success of a deal. Finally, although there has been considerable research on the value creation drivers of maritime

M&As, it becomes obvious that important aspects, such as the valuation effect differentials within different ship-owning segments and the success of private equity investment in the industry, warrant further investigation.

Notes

1. The aim here is to highlight the business combinations that tend to occur most frequently. However, it should be noted that there are additional combinations not highlighted in Fig. 16.1 (for instance, port operators and shipping services firms acquiring various assets).
2. The sample also includes transactions announced in 2013–14 that were still pending in 2015.
3. Transaction values are in 2014 USD.
4. Although a certain deal may involve two operating companies, this may still essentially constitute an acquisition of assets. Setting such deals apart from business consolidations would involve a detailed examination of press articles and announcements associated with each deal, which goes beyond our scope. However, it should be noted that a deal between two operating companies may still actually be an asset purchase and that this is particularly the case among ship-owning companies. So in practice, acquisitions of assets are more frequent than typically appears in the data.
5. According to neoclassical theories, M&As are driven by value-maximization incentives (see Jovanovic and Rousseau (2002) and Harford (2005)). On the contrary, behavioural explanations are based on market psychology and suggest that market valuations drive merger waves (see Rhodes-Kropf and Viswanathan (2004) and Shleifer and Vishny (2003)).
6. For the purpose of this illustration, V_T, V_A, V_D and O_P are associated with the equity values, and assumed liabilities are ignored.
7. The building blocks described here may vary in other types of transactions such as acquisitions of assets, distressed deals or leveraged buyouts (LBOs).
8. This assumes that the company's long-term cash flows grow with the overall economy.
9. Instead, equity cash flows may be used when one is interested in directly estimating the company's equity value. In this case, net income is used instead of operating profit after tax (EBIAT) and an additional adjustment is introduced for net debt issuance (new debt–debt repayment) in addition to accounting for non-cash charges, for the change in working capital and for reinvestment needs. When discounting equity cash flows the cost of equity k_e is used instead of WACC. The same is the case when

discounting the company's DCFs instead of its FCFs in dividend valuation.
10. The appropriate tax rate to use in EBIAT is the company's marginal tax rate.
11. After-tax cost of debt is used since the interest expense reduces taxable income and hence the actual cost of borrowing.
12. To improve the accuracy of the CAPM one may use a multi-factor asset pricing model to estimate k_e. The Fama and French (1993) model, for instance, includes, in addition to the market risk premium (R_m–R_f), two factors that account for the company size and market-to-book risk premia.
13. See Fernandez et al. (2014) and Dimson et al. (2011) for equity risk premia estimated for different markets/countries.
14. In practice, the final equity value may also need to be adjusted for the effect of operating leases, non-controlling interests and employee stock options, among other things.
15. For instance LBOs are financed primarily with debt secured against the target company's assets (or cash flows). Therefore, its valuation needs to be based on the resulting capital structure and the debt weights, and the cost of capital and beta should be adjusted to reflect this as well as the debt repayment schedule.
16. Note that, in this context (i.e. relative valuation), V_T may refer to either equity or enterprise value, for simplicity.
17. EV/EBITDA is estimated as the sum of the market values of equity and interest bearing debt (adjusted for excess cash), divided by the company's EBITDA. EBITDA's advantage is that it is less susceptible to manipulation as it excludes non-cash items such as depreciation. Moreover, EBITDA is negative less often than net income or FCF, and its "before-interest" nature in combination with the enterprise value based numerator ensures that it can be used to compare companies with different capital structures. EBITDAL can be used instead of EBITDA when comparing companies in the shipping industry with different asset structures (it adds back operating leases and makes vessel operators comparable to ship-owning companies). P/B is typically employed within the ship-owning segment. While book value is considered as a rather inefficient indicator of true value, as it is based on historical prices, it can provide an indication of the value of a company where it comprises mainly of liquid assets such as freight or passenger vessels.
18. Although, in practice, the last 12 months' (LTM) EBITDA is used when deriving transaction multiples, the EBITDA used in the multiples of Fig. 16.10 is a previous fiscal year-end EBITDA.

19. When vessels are not marked to market on the balance sheet (despite the fact that the sale and purchase market for vessels is very liquid and fluctuates constantly on pure supply and demand factors), there can be a large divergence between depreciated book asset values and true market values.
20. For instance, the online system VesselsValue.com provides instant values for bulkers, containerships, LNG, LPG, tankers and offshore vessels, using sophisticated algorithms. The Shipping Intelligence Network (by Clarksons Research) and the Baltic Sale and Purchase Assessments (BSPA) are also frequently used as sources of S&P values.
21. Entering into deal negotiations itself may also involve an option to walk away in case the deal is rejected but return under more favorable circumstances for a better deal later (the option to delay).
22. Damodaran (2005) provides a good summary of real options valuation.
23. For example, a 0.5 exchange ratio would imply that the acquiring company offers 0.5 of its shares for 1 share of the target. The exchange ratio can be fixed (i.e. remains unchanged until the closing of the deal) or variable to account for any appreciation/depreciation in the acquirer's shares or other adjustments.
24. Most LBOs are backed by private equity companies and are funded primarily (typically up to 75 %) by borrowed funds secured by the target company's assets and some equity raised by the fund's investors. The debt financing structures used in this case are often more complex than in deals carried out by operating companies, and may involve a combination of leveraged loans, high yield bonds, mezzanine finance and/or seller notes.
25. Under certain circumstances, the pre-event window market model estimation may be eliminated completely, as the resulting parameters may be biased (see Fuller et al. 2002). Effectively, the coefficients in this case would be set equal to zero and one respectively, and the abnormal return model would become R_i-R_m. It is important to note that, for short-run windows, it is unlikely that weighting the market return by the company's beta improves estimation significantly. Moreover, there is no evidence that using a Jensen's alpha type measure of abnormal return in a single (CAPM) or multifactor (Fama and French three-factor model) asset pricing framework, instead of the market model approach discussed here, can largely improve estimation accuracy.

References

Alexandridis, G., Petmezas, D. and Travlos, N.G., 2010, 'Gains from M&As Around the World: New Evidence', *Financial Management* 39, 1671–1695.

Alexandridis, G., Mavrovitis, C.F and Travlos, N.G., 2012, How Have M&As Changed? Evidence from the 6th Merger Wave, *European Journal of Finance* 18, 663–688.

Alexandridis, G., Fuller, K., Terhaar, L. and Travlos, N.G., 2013, Target Size, Acquisition Premiums and Shareholder Gains, *Journal of Corporate Finance* 20, 1–13.

Alexandridis, G., Doukas, J.D, and Mavis, C.P., 2015, Does Firing a CEO Payoff? Working Paper.

Alexandrou, G., Gounopoulos, D. and Thomas, G.M., 2014, Mergers and Acquisitions in Shipping, *Transportation Research Part E: Logistics and Transportation Review* 61, 212–234.

Andreou, P.C., Louca, C. and Panayides, P.M., 2012, Valuation Effects of Mergers and Acquisitions in Freight Transportation, *Transportation Research Part E: Logistics and Transportation Review* 48, 1221–1234.

Bauguess, S.W., Moeller, S.B., Schlingemann, F.P., and Zutter, C.J., 2009, Ownership Structure and Target Returns, *Journal of Corporate Finance* 15, 48–65.

Brooks, M.R. and Ritchie, P., 2006, Mergers and Acquisitions in the Maritime Transport Industry 1996–2000, *Transportation Journal* 45, 7–22.

Brown, S.J. and Warner, J.B., 1985, Using Daily Stock Returns—The Case of Event Studies, *Journal of Financial Economics* 14, 3–31.

Bruner, R., 2002, Does M&A Pay? A Survey of the Evidence for the Decision Maker, *Journal of Applied Finance* 12, 48–68.

Chang, S., 1998, Takeovers of Privately Held Targets, Methods of Payment and Bidder Returns, *Journal of Finance* 53, 773–784.

Damodaran, A., 2005, The Promise and Peril of Real Options, NYU Working Paper

Dietrich, J. and Sorensen, E., 1984, An Application of Logit Analysis to Predicition of Merger Targets, *Journal of Business Research* 12, 393–402.

Dimson, E., Marsh, P. and Staunton, M., 2011, Equity Premia Around the World, Working Paper.

Dong, M., Hirshleifer, D., Richardson, S., and Teoh, S-H., 2006, Does Investor Misevaluation Drive the Takeover Market?, *Journal of Finance* 61, 725–762.

Doukas, J.A. and Petmezas, D., 2007, Acquisitions, Overconfident Managers and Self-Attribution Bias, *European Financial Management* 13, 531–577.

Eccles, R.G., Kersten, L.L., and Wilson, C.W., 1999, Are You Paying Too Much for That Acquisition? *Harvard Business Review* July/August, 136–146.

Faccio, M. and Masulis, R.W., 2005, The Choice of Payment Method in European Mergers and Acquisitions, *Journal of Finance* 60, 1345–1388.

Faccio, M., McConnell J.J., and Stolin, D., 2006, Returns to Acquirers of Listed and Unlisted Targets, *Journal of Financial and Quantitative Analysis* 41, 197–220.

Fama, E.F. and French, K., 1993, Common Risk-Factors in the Returns on Stocks and Bonds, *Journal of Financial Economics* 33, 3–56.

Fernandez, P., Linares, P. and Acin, I.F., 2014, Market Risk Premium Used in 88 Countries in 2014: A Survey with 8,228 Answers, Working Paper.

Fu, F., Lin, L., and Officer, M.S., 2013, Acquisitions Driven by Stock Overvaluation: Are They Good Deals?, *Journal of Financial Economics* 109, 24–39.

Fuller, K.P., Netter, J. and Stegemoller, M., 2002, What Do Returns to Acquiring Firms Tell Us? Evidence from Firms That Make Many Acquisitions, *Journal of Finance* 57, 1763–1793.

Gorton, G., Kahl, M. and Rosen, R., 2009, Eat or Be Eaten: A Theory of Mergers and Firm Size, *Journal of Finance* 64, 1291–1344.

Jaffe, J.F., Pedersen, D.J. and Voetman, T., 2013, Skill Differences in Corporate Acquisitions, *Journal of Corporate Finance* 23, 166–181.

Jovanovic, B. and Rousseau, P.L., 2002, The Q-Theory of Mergers, *American Economic Review* 92, 198–204.

Harford, J., 1999, Corporate Cash Reserves and Acquisitions, *Journal of Finance* 54, 1969–1997.

Harford, J., 2005, What Drives Merger Waves?, *Journal of Financial Economics* 77, 529–560.

Heaver, T., Meersman, H., Mogiia, F. and Van de Voorde, E., 2010, Do Mergers and Alliances Influence European Shipping and Port Competition, *Maritime Policy and Management* 27, 363–373.

Lyon, J.D., Barber, B.M. and Tsai, C-L., 1999, Improved Methods for Tests of Long-Run Abnormal Stock Returns, *Journal of Finance* 54, 165–201.

Luo, Y., 2005, Do Insiders Learn from Outsiders? Evidence from Mergers and Acquisitions, *Journal of Finance* 60, 1951–1982.

Malmendier, U. and Tate, G., 2005, CEO Overconfidence and Corporate Investment, *Journal of Finance* 60, 2661–2700.

Masulis, R.W., Wang, C. and Xie, F., 2007, Corporate Governance and Acquirer Returns, *Journal of Finance* 62, 1851–1889.

Mitchell, M. and Stafford, E., 2000, Managerial Decisions and Long Term Stock Price Performance, *Journal of Business* 73, 287–329.

Moeller, S.B., Schlingemann, F.P. and Stulz, R.M., 2004, Firm Size and the Gains from Acquisitions, *Journal of Financial Economics* 73, 201–228.

Panayides, P.M. and Gong, X., 2002, The Stock Market Reaction to Merger and Acquisition Announcements in Liner Shipping, *Maritime Economics and Logistics* 4, 55–80.

Rhodes-Kropf, M. and Viswanathan, S., 2004, Market Valuation and Merger Waves, *Journal of Finance* 59, 2685–2718.

Samitas, A.G. and Kenourgios, D.F., 2007, Impact of Mergers and Acquisitions on Stock Returns of Tramp Shipping Firms, *International Journal of Financial Services Management* 2:4, 327–343.

Shipping Intelligence Network, Clarksons Research Limited.

Shleifer, A. and Vishny, R.W., 2003, Stock Market Driven Acquisitions, *Journal of Financial Economics* 70, 295–311.

Syriopoulos, T. and Theotokas, I., 2007, Value Creation Through Corporate Destruction? Corporate Governance in Shipping Takeovers, *Maritime Policy and Management* 34, 225–242.

Thomson Reuters SDC, Mergers and Acquisitions Database, Thomson Reuters.

Travlos, N.G., 1987, Corporate Takeover Bids, Method of Payment, and Bidding Firms' Stock Returns, *Journal of Finance* 42, 943–963.

Wang, C. and Xie, F., 2009, Corporate Governance Transfer and Synergistic Gains From Mergers and Acquisitions, *Review of Financial Studies* 22, 829–852.

Index

A
accounting value, 304
acquiring company, 385, 390, 393–5, 400–2, 404, 405, 409n23
Adjusted Present Value (APV), 309n11
affirmative covenant, 162
Aframax vessel, 24
AHTS. *See* anchor handling tugs
all-shares deal, 396
amortization schedule, 14, 131, 156
anchor handling tugs (AHTS), 36
angel investing, 120
ANPL. *See* arrears and non-performing loans
anti-trust/competition, 384
appointment of receiver, 244–5
APV. *See* Adjusted Present Value
Arctic route, 12
arrears and non-performing loans (ANPL), 257
ASEAN. *See* Association of South-East Asia Nations
Asian options, 356
asset-backed bonds, 155, 161, 162, 167

asset-backed finance, 41–69
asset disponent owner, 201
asset play, 14, 325, 380
asset return, 321
asset risk, 42, 67, 214
asset risk assessment, 41–69
assignment of charter hire, 104
assignment of insurance, 104, 111, 112, 245, 256
assignment transfer, 226–8
Association of South-East Asia Nations (ASEAN), 10

B
balance of convenience, 245
Balance-of-Month (BALMO), 351
ballast water treatment, 12
balloon payment, 78, 117, 156, 164
BALMO. *See* Balance-of-Month
Baltex. *See* Baltic Exchange trading screen
Baltic Capesize Index (BCI), 292, 293, 341, 344

Note: Page numbers followed by 'n' refer to foot notes.

© The Author(s) 2016
M.G. Kavussanos, I.D. Visvikis (eds.), *The International Handbook of Shipping Finance*, DOI 10.1057/978-1-137-46546-7

Index

Baltic Clean Tanker Index (BCTI), 344, 345
Baltic Dirty Tanker Index (BDTI), 344, 345
Baltic Dry Index (BDI), 7, 18, 151, 156, 341
Baltic Exchange, 338, 340, 341, 344, 345, 350, 351, 353, 354, 356–60, 365n6, 365n7, 366n10
Baltic Exchange Derivatives Trading (BEDT), 360, 364
Baltic Exchange Panamax Asia (BEP Asia), 341
Baltic Exchange Supramax 58 Asia (BES 58 Asia), 341
Baltic Exchange Supramax Asia (BES Asia), 341
Baltic Exchange trading screen (Baltex), 360, 361, 364
Baltic Forward Assessments (BFAs), 337–8, 358–60
Baltic Handysize Index (BHSI), 341, 344, 359
Baltic International Tanker Route (BITR), 344, 345
Baltic Options' Assessments (BOA), 357
Baltic Panamax Index (BPI), 341, 344
Baltic Sale and Purchase Assessments (BSPA), 409n20
Baltic Supramax Index (BSI), 341, 344
bank debt financing, 72, 76, 84, 94
bank guarantee, 122
Bank of International Settlements (BIS), 253
bankruptcy, 81, 111, 122, 135, 160, 166, 219, 296, 387, 399
bareboat charter, 7, 136, 205
barter trade, 102, 115
Basel Committee, 253
Basel I, 253
Basel II, 253, 254, 275
Basel III, 194, 253

basis points (bp), 75, 155
BCI. *See* Baltic Capesize Index
BCTI. *See* Baltic Clean Tanker Index
BDI. *See* Baltic Dry Index
BDTI. *See* Baltic Dirty Tanker Index
BEDT. *See* Baltic Exchange Derivatives Trading
BEP Asia. *See* Baltic Exchange Panamax Asia
BES Asia. *See* Baltic Exchange Supramax Asia
BES 58 Asia. *See* Baltic Exchange Supramax 58 Asia
best-effort, 80, 106
BFAs. *See* Baltic Forward Assessments
BHSI. *See* Baltic Handysize Index
bilateral loan, 227
BIMCO NEWBUILDCON form, 122, 279n1, 279n2
BIS. *See* Bank of International Settlements
BITR. *See* Baltic International Tanker Route
blank check company, 91, 92, 171
blocked currency schemes, 102, 104, 115
block futures, 350, 351, 364
block trade, 361, 364, 366n8
BOA. *See* Baltic Options' Assessments
bondholder, 138, 165
bond indenture, 138, 148
bond issuing, 149, 150, 156, 157, 159, 160, 162
bond yield, 85, 107, 149, 152, 154–6, 302, 389, 409n24
book building, 87
borrowing arrangement, 196, 227, 228
BPI. *See* Baltic Panamax Index
branding event, 174
breach of covenant, 135, 218, 244, 319
breakage costs, 226
bridge (loan) financing, 396, 397
budgeting, 285–312

builders' risk insurance, 268–9, 279n4, 279n11
bulk shipping, 3, 15–20, 59–63, 92, 192, 286, 292, 399
bullet amortization, 208
BUNKER. *See* Civil Liability for Bunker Oil Pollution Damage
bunker charge, 8, 12, 27, 56
business plan, 100, 104, 120, 171
Buy-and-Hold Abnormal Return (BHAR),
buyer's credit, 107

C

Calendar Time Abnormal Returns (CTARs),
Calendar-Time Approach (CTR),
call option, 107, 357
Capesize 2014 time-charter basket (CPT), 353
Capesize time-charter basket (CTC), 350
Capesize vessel, 16, 18, 288, 289, 340, 353, 355
CAPEX. *See* capital expenses
capital adequacy, 126, 198, 253, 254, 287
capital asset pricing model (CAPM), 298, 389
capital expenditures, 183, 307, 310n24, 387, 389
capital expenses (CAPEX), 2, 8, 9, 13, 14, 33, 382, 389
CAPM. *See* capital asset pricing model
CAR. *See* cumulative abnormal return
Carriage of Passengers and their Luggage by Sea (PAL), 280n28
cash-prepayment, 226
causa proxima non remota spectatur, 277
CCFI. *See* China Containerized Freight Index

C-corporation, 170, 171
CCP. *See* central counterparty clearing house
central counterparty clearing house (CCP), 355, 363, 364
CEXIM. *See* Chinese Export Import Bank
CFSAs. *See* Container Forward Swap Agreements
CFTC. *See* Commodity Futures Trading Commission
CGT. *See* compensated gross tonnage
Charter-in, 7, 83, 329
Charter-out, 5, 8, 26
charterparty, 78, 233, 234, 240, 241, 244, 249
chemical tanker, 48, 49, 187
Chicago Mercantile Exchange (CME) Group, 350, 351, 355, 357, 363, 366n8
China Containerized Freight Index (CCFI), 30
Chinese Export Import Bank (CEXIM), 47, 108, 194–5, 197
CIRR. *See* commercial interest reference rate
Civil Liability for Bunker Oil Pollution Damage (BUNKER), 280n28
Civil Liability for Oil Pollution Damage (CLC), 280n28
ClarkSea index, 14, 15, 72, 285, 377
Clarkson Shipping Intelligence Network (SIN), 308n4, 332
classification society, 129, 134, 328
CLC. *See* Civil Liability for Oil Pollution Damage
clearing house, 349–52, 355, 360
Cleartrade Exchange (CLTX), 348, 360, 361, 364
CLO. *See* collateralized loan obligations
club deal syndicate, 80
CMAC Shanghai form, 121

CME. *See* Chicago Mercantile
    Exchange Group
COA. *See* contract of affreightment
collar, 110
collateral, 41, 72, 76–81, 100, 104,
    107, 117, 126, 160–2, 214,
    219, 248, 250, 254, 260–2,
    264, 265, 270, 308
collateralized loan obligations (CLO),
    162
commercial bank credit, 104
commercial interest reference rate
    (CIRR), 197
commercial lenders, 141, 196, 199
commercial risk, 3, 115
commercial ship management, 2
commitment fee, 79, 132, 136
Commodity Futures Trading
    Commission (CFTC), 363
common equity, 82, 84, 86, 91, 170,
    206–8
comparative advantage, 11
compensated gross tonnage (CGT), 45,
    52
competition neglect, 286
competitor plan, 100
compound annual growth rate
    (CAGR), 15, 17, 23, 28, 34,
    46, 56, 57
compulsory insurance, 274, 280n28
conditions precedent, 130–1, 215,
    217–18
consolidation, 47, 48, 206, 371–4,
    377, 379, 380, 400, 401, 403,
    406, 407n4
consultancy services, 340
Container Forward Swap Agreements
    (CFSAs), 338, 339, 354
container liner, 3, 87, 322, 391
containership, 9, 26, 48, 49, 72, 83,
    91, 182, 322, 365, 374,
    409n20
container shipping, 3, 7, 9, 13, 27, 30,
    38, 176, 205, 398

Container Ship Time Assessment Index
    (ConTex), 31
contract of affreightment (COA), 6
contract of employment, 137
contracts-for-difference (CFDs), 338
contractual liability, 229
conversion rights, 106, 208
convertible bond, 164, 165, 207, 209
coordination deed, 207
corporate backed funding, 41, 42
corporate bond, 84–6, 160, 161, 167,
    389
corporate guarantee, 78, 79, 81, 107,
    112
corporate loan, 82
correlation estimates, 309n10
cost-based approach, 393
cost of capital, 74, 77, 148, 154, 173,
    204, 209, 299, 303, 308, 387,
    390, 408n15
cost of debt, 295–7, 302, 317, 331,
    389, 408n11
cost of equity, 82, 208, 295–8, 302,
    309n13, 310n16–n18, 389,
    408n9
cost structure, 1, 8–9, 37
counter-cyclicality, 43–53
coupon bond, 149, 164, 389
coupon payment, 85, 139, 148–50,
    156, 160, 162, 164, 166, 207,
    250
covenant, 79, 82, 85, 106, 107, 111,
    112, 134–5, 138, 142, 148,
    151, 156, 162, 208, 214–16,
    218–24, 226, 233, 237, 244,
    247, 258, 262, 280n18, 287,
    319
CPT. *See* Capesize 2014 time-charter
    basket
credit committee, 157, 260
credit facility, 77, 144, 396
credit line, 82, 340
credit rating, 102, 105, 151–2, 156,
    160, 228

Index

credit risk premium, 297
creditworthiness, 78, 102, 104, 157, 160, 204, 216, 297
C's of Credit, 162
CTC. *See* Capesize time-charter basket
cumulative abnormal return (CAR), 402, 404
current ratio, 104
cyclicality, 9, 13, 14, 37, 42–53, 56, 62, 63, 65–7, 156, 298, 307

D

DCF. *See* discounted cash flow
DCM. *See* designated contract market
DCO. *See* derivatives clearing organization
deadweight (DWT), 15, 16, 20, 22, 101, 121, 288
debt service break even, 320
debt service per day, 320
debt service ratio, 221, 320
debt to equity ratio, 104
default risk, 141, 183, 200, 204, 298
deleveraging, 48, 52, 66, 192
demolition market, 4, 6, 37
derivatives clearing organization (DCO), 363
derived demand, 234
designated contract market (DCM), 363
DFA. *See* Dodd-Frank Wall Street Reform and Consumer Protection Act
discounted cash flow (DCF), 287, 295–304, 387
diversified portfolio, 298
dividend yield, 171, 182, 184
Dodd-Frank Wall Street Reform and Consumer Protection Act (DFA), 363
Drewry Shipping Consultants, 348
drillship, 50
dry-docking (DD), 204

dry lease, 108
due diligence, 109, 133, 179, 381–4
DWT. *See* deadweight

E

earnings before interest and after taxes (EBIAT), 310n24, 389, 408n9, 408n10
earnings before interest, taxes, depreciation, and amortization (EBITDA), 182, 183, 204, 391, 392, 408n17, 409n18
earnings return, 321
EBIAT. *See* earnings before interest and after taxes
EBITDA. *See* earnings before interest, taxes, depreciation, and amortization
EBITDA multiple, 183, 204, 391
ECA. *See* export credit agency
ECA-backed financing, 141, 194
ECA-guaranteed, 196
ECA-insured, 141
economies of scale, 11, 27, 57, 59, 66, 210, 371, 381, 383, 398
emerging growth company (EGC), 179
EMIR. *See* European Markets Infrastructure Regulation
Emission Control Area (ECA), 113–14, 141, 193–9, 209
energy efficiency, 6, 12, 68n24
Energy Efficiency Design Index (EEDI), 63, 68n24
enforce collateral, 262
English law, 125, 128, 135, 142, 143, 214, 229, 234, 235, 237, 240, 268, 270, 271, 277, 278
enterprise value (EV), 183, 387, 388, 390, 391, 408n16, 409n17
entry barriers, 13, 37, 99, 387
equitable jurisdiction, 232
equitable maxims, 233
equity beta, 298, 299, 302

Index

equity risk premium, 302, 311n26, 389
ERSB. *See* European Systemic Risk Board
Euribor. *See* Euro Interbank Offered Rate
Euro Interbank Offered Rate (Euribor), 110, 132–3
European Central Bank, 133
European Markets Infrastructure Regulation (EMIR), 363, 364
European option, 356
European Securities and Markets Authority (ESMA), 363
European Systemic Risk Board (ERSB), 363
EV. *See* enterprise value
EV/EBITDA, 183, 391, 408n17
event of default, 81, 85, 105, 111, 112, 130, 134, 135, 159–61, 166, 217–19, 221, 223–5, 249
exchange rate derivative, 75, 131
exchange rates, 11, 337
exploration & production (E&P), 32, 33
export credit agency (ECA), 113–14, 140–1, 193, 195–8, 209
export credit finance, 193–5, 198–9
export-import bank, 113, 196

F

face (par) value, 148–50, 166
fair market value (FMV), 65, 192, 259, 262, 265, 393
FATCA. *See* Foreign Account Tax Compliance Act
FCA. *See* Financial Conduct Authorities
FCF. *See* free cash flows
FDI. *See* foreign direct investment
feeder vessel, 26
FEU. *See* forty-foot equivalent unit
FFA. *See* forward freight agreements
FFABA. *See* FFA Brokers Association
FFA Brokers Association (FFABA), 359

F-1 form, 179
finance lease, 74, 108, 109, 201, 203, 204
financial analysis, 98, 304–7, 315–35, 329
Financial Conduct Authorities (FCA), 360, 364
financial covenant, 79, 134, 216, 220, 226, 258
financial crisis, 13, 18, 37, 42, 43, 54, 60, 75, 80, 107, 119, 155, 166, 184, 194, 206, 209, 210
financial indebtedness, 134, 224
financial leverage, 147, 297, 298, 309n14
financial modelling, 100, 315–20, 321, 323, 328, 334, 335
financial planning, 98
financial ratio (FR), 165, 203, 219–23
financial restructuring, 259, 373
financial risk, 295, 296, 371, 406
financial statements, 113, 134, 161, 217, 218, 220, 256, 259
financiers' Insurance, 269–71
financing amount, 78
financing plan, 100
fire sales, 303, 311n30
first mortgage, 79, 104, 106, 111, 270, 271
fixed-rate bond, 302
floating production storage and offloading (FPSO), 22, 346
floating rate bond, 165
floating storage and regasification unit (FSRU), 22
flooding effect, 48–50
floor (value) price, 385, 393, 394
FMV. *See* fair market value
follow-on offering, 74, 87, 169, 177, 180
forecasting, 41–69
foreclosure, 248, 254, 265
Foreign Account Tax Compliance Act (FATCA), 135

foreign direct investment (FDI), 53, 67n8
forty-foot equivalent unit (FEU), 338, 348
forward freight agreements (FFA), 7, 33, 332, 338–40, 349–50, 352, 354–6, 358–9, 360, 364, 365n4
FPSO. *See* floating production storage and offloading
FR. *See* financial ratio
free cash flows (FCF), 91, 159, 295–6, 299, 302, 310n24, 378, 387–90, 408n9, 409n17
freight derivative, 7, 75, 337–58, 360–1, 365
freight forwarder, 1, 3, 37, 366n7
freight forwarding, 3
freight futures, 350–251, 354, 364, 365
freight markets, 7, 9, 156, 200, 203, 361
freight options, 354, 356–9, 365
freight rate indices, 340-8
freight risk management, 337–67
freight swaps, 354
FSRU. *See* floating storage and regasification unit
fundamental efficiency, 303
fundamental value, 286–7, 302, 303, 308, 310n22

G

GAAP. *See* generally accepted accounting principles
GCM. *See* general clearing member
GDP. *See* gross domestic product
gearing ratio, 203, 207, 220–1
general clearing member (GCM), 356
generally accepted accounting principles (GAAP), 109
good faith, 148, 242, 270, 278, 281n42, 303

goodness-of-fit (R-squareds), 294, 295, 309n9
gross domestic product (GDP), 10–11, 15, 27, 37, 53–6, 71
gross tonnage (GT), 4, 9, 12, 15, 20, 26, 31, 45, 274

H

Hamburg Shipbrokers' Association, 296
Handymax vessel, 15, 19, 58
Handysize time-charter basket (HTC), 357
Handysize vessel, 355
hardening period, 227
heads-of-agreement, 97
heavy fuel oil (HFO), 8
hedge fund, 42, 82, 84, 184, 185, 227
hedging, 164, 297, 339, 356
HFO. *See* heavy fuel oil
high yield bond, 74, 107, 152, 154–6, 409n24
high yield debt, 73, 396
H&M. *See* Hull and Machinery
Hong Kong Convention, 6
horizontal integration, 372, 404
HTC. *See* Handysize time-charter basket
Hull and Machinery (H&M), 268, 270, 272, 273, 275, 277
human resources plan, 100, 174
hunting license, 132
hybrid contract, 349, 355
hybrid financing schemes, 104, 114–15

I

ICBR. *See* Institute Clauses for Builders' Risks
ICE. *See* intercontinental exchange
ICS. *See* International Chamber of Shipping

Index

IDR. *See* incentive distribution rights
IGP&I. *See* International Group of P&I Clubs
IM. *See* information memorandums
IMAREX. *See* International Maritime Exchange
IMF. *See* International Monetary Fund
IMIC. *See* Institute Mortgagees' Interest Clauses
incentive distribution rights (IDR), 90
income approach, 286
inflation-linked bond, 165
information memorandums (IM), 383
initial public offering (IPO), 42, 86, 87, 91–3, 102, 119–20, 169, 174–82, 186–8
in rem, 235, 239, 241, 247
Institute Clauses for Builders' Risks (ICBR), 268–9
Institute Mortgagees' Interest Clauses (IMIC), 270
institutional investor, 41–2, 105, 119, 151, 152, 158–60
interaction term, 294, 295
intercontinental exchange (ICE), 110, 351, 352, 357, 359, 366n8
inter-creditor agreement, 207
inter-dealer broker, 361
interest cover ratio, 221, 319, 320
interest rate derivative, 75
interest rate swap, 110, 116, 297
inter-industry transaction, 374
internal rate of return (IRR), 140, 149, 316–18, 322, 328
International Chamber of Shipping (ICS), 71
International Group of P&I Clubs (IGP&I), 275, 276
International Maritime Exchange (IMAREX), 351
International Monetary Fund (IMF), 11
International Organization of Securities Commissions (IOSCO), 364

international ship and port facility (ISPS) code, 222
investment appraisal, 285–312
investment fund, 2, 184
investment grade, 85, 102, 107, 151, 152, 154
investment insurance agency, 113
investment yield, 150
IOSCO. *See* International Organization of Securities Commissions
IPO. *See* initial public offering
IRR. *See* internal rate of return
Islamic finance, 110, 115–17
ISPS code. *See* international ship and port facility code

J

joint ventures (JV), 92, 185–7
Jumpstart Our Business Startups (JOBS), 179, 182
junior (subordinated) loan, 79, 139
junk bond, 102, 106–7, 152, 155
jurisdiction, 76, 79, 91, 103, 128, 135, 142, 151, 159, 171, 196, 216, 225, 228, 232, 233, 235–9, 243, 245, 261–5, 271
JV. *See* joint ventures

K

K-1 form,
KG scheme, 41
K-1 schedule, 90, 171
K/S limited partnership, 83, 102

L

last twelve months (LTM), 409n18
law of one price, 303
Laycan, 340, 365n5
lay-up, 12, 323
LBO. *See* leveraged buyouts

LCH. *See* London Clearing House
LCH.Clearnet. *See* London Clearing House Clearnet
LDT. *See* light displacement ton
leasing finance, 82–4
leasing house, 200
leasing structure, 144, 200–2, 206
legal representations, 216
lessee, 83, 108, 109, 116, 136–7, 201, 203, 204
lessor, 83, 108, 109, 136, 137, 201, 203, 204
letter of intent, 97
leveraged buyouts (LBO), 395, 396, 408n7, 408n15, 409n24
leveraged lease, 109
lex fori, 235
lex loci contractus, 235
lex navis, 234, 235
LIBOR. *See* London Interbank Offered Rate
light displacement ton (LDT), 326
lightweight tonnage (LWT), 6
limited partnership (LP), 114, 115, 170–1
liner shipping, 71, 379, 384
liner traffic, 53
liquefied natural gas (LNG), 10, 13, 20, 22, 38, 48–9, 91, 139, 155, 176, 180, 195, 387, 404
liquefied petroleum gas (LPG), 20, 22, 38, 48, 49, 176, 180, 182, 187, 195, 277, 409n20
liquidity, 9, 10, 32, 41, 42, 47, 49, 52, 66, 75, 78, 79, 82, 83, 85, 116, 120, 125, 154, 156, 158, 171–4, 180, 184, 187, 198, 200, 203, 208, 221, 254, 256, 350, 360, 363, 377, 380, 395, 398, 405, 406
Lloyd's marine insurance broker, 275
LNG. *See* liquefied natural gas
loan amortization, 78

loan interest rate, 114, 317, 318
loan to value (LTV), 65, 104, 112, 208, 258, 318–20
London Clearing House (LCH), 349, 352, 354, 357, 358, 360–1, 364
London Clearing House Clearnet (LCH.Clearnet), 349, 352, 354, 357, 358, 360, 361, 364
London Interbank Offered Rate (LIBOR), 75, 78, 80, 85, 110, 132, 133, 156, 157, 162, 165, 197, 297, 302
London Market Association, 216
London Stock Exchange (LSE), 176
long position, 338
long range (LR), 21, 352, 356, 357, 359
long term asset value (LTAV), 287, 295–302
loss-of-hire cover, 273
lost time, 273
LP. *See* limited partnership
LPG. *See* liquefied petroleum gas
LR. *See* long range
LSE. *See* London Stock Exchange
LTAV. *See* long term asset value
LTM. *See* Last Twelve Months'
LTV. *See* loan to value
LWT. *See* lightweight tonnage

M

M&A. *See* mergers & acquisitions
M&A activity flows, 372–7
MAC. *See* material adverse clause
major swap participants (MSP), 363, 366n13
mandatory prepayment, 132, 225–6
Manufacturing Sourcing Cost Index, 54–5
MAPP. *See* Mortgagee's Additional Perils (Pollution) Insurance
MarCAR. *See* Marine Construction All Risks

Marex-Spectron, 351
margin (credit line) financing, 75, 340
Marine Construction All Risks (MarCAR), 268–9
marine insurance, 257, 267–81
Marine Insurance Act, 269, 270, 275, 277, 278, 281n42
maritime lien, 112, 235–8, 244, 247, 259
maritime value chain, 1–4, 37
market approach, 256, 286–95
market beta, 298, 299, 310n17
marketing plan, 5, 100
market (systematic) risk, 161, 187, 298–9, 302, 328–9, 332, 389, 408n12
market risk premium (MRP), 298, 302, 408n12
Markets in Financial Instruments Directive (MiFID), 364
Markets in Financial Instruments Regulation (MiFIR), 364
market-to-book ratio, 304, 307, 312n33
market value (MV), 79, 83, 88, 91, 130, 131, 149, 172, 183, 192, 219, 220, 222, 235, 247, 285, 296, 304, 318–19, 326–7, 389–90, 393, 394, 404, 408n17, 409
mark-to-market approach, 286, 288, 307, 349, 352
MAS. See Monetary Authority of Singapore
master limited partnership (MLP), 73, 84, 87–91, 104, 120, 170–2, 180–2, 184
M&A strategy, 381–2
material adverse clause (MAC), 224
material impact, 150
M&A valuation, 384–94, 402

medium range (MR) vessel, 359
Merchant Shipping Act (MSA), 231, 232, 236, 237n1, 238, 239, 249
merchant vessel, 6, 9, 12, 14, 96
mergers & acquisitions (M&A), 186, 187, 371–410
mezzanine finance, 139–40, 193, 199, 200, 206–9, 409n24
mezzanine lenders, 107, 139, 140, 208
MiFID. See Markets in Financial Instruments Directive
MiFIR. See Markets in Financial Instruments Regulation
MII. See mortgagees interest insurance
minimum quarterly distribution (MQD), 90
mission statement, 95, 97, 100–1
MLP. See master limited partnership
mobile offshore unit (MOU), 32, 34
Monetary Authority of Singapore (MAS), 360–1
monetary policy, 149
monetizing investment, 186
mortgage-backed loan, 73, 76, 77, 79
mortgagee-in-possession, 143, 264
Mortgagee's Additional Perils (Pollution) Insurance (MAPP), 270–1
mortgagees interest insurance (MII), 270–1
MOU. See mobile offshore unit
MQD. See minimum quarterly distribution
MRP. See market risk premium
MR vessel. See medium range vessel
MSA. See Merchant Shipping Act
MSP. See major swap participants
MTF. See multilateral trading facility
multi-currency option, 131
multilateral trading facility (MTF), 360, 364, 367n15, 367n16

N

MV. *See* market value
MV/book value (P/B multiple), 391
MV/net income (P/E multiple), 391

NAFTA. *See* North America Free Trade Agreement
NASDAQ OMX Stockholm AB, 351
NAV. *See* net asset value
NBSE. *See* Ningbo Shipping Exchange
NDA. *See* non-disclosure agreements
negative covenant, 162
negative equity, 234
net asset value (NAV), 183, 393
net present value (NPV), 19–20, 310n22, 315–17, 322–4, 328, 385, 400
newbuilding, 2, 4–6, 9, 12, 16, 19–20, 25–6, 31–2, 35, 45, 48, 52, 57, 66, 71, 72, 80–1, 128–32, 137, 140–1, 176, 181, 183, 192–5, 197–9, 214, 256, 322, 324–6, 393
newbuilding market, 4, 5, 37
new Panamax vessel, 26, 28
New York Mercantile Exchange (NYMEX), 350
New York Stock Exchange (NYSE), 87, 119, 176, 177, 187
Nicaragua Canal, 12
Ningbo Containerized Freight Index (NCFI), 366n7
Ningbo Shipping Exchange (NBSE), 366n7
noise trader risk, 303
non-disclosure agreements (NDA), 383
non-financial covenant, 79
non-investment grade, 152
normalized market, 303, 308
North America Free Trade Agreement (NAFTA), 10

Norwegian OTC (NOTC), 177
NOTC. *See* Norwegian OTC
novation transfer, 227
NPV. *See* net present value
NYMEX. *See* New York Mercantile Exchange
NYSE. *See* New York Stock Exchange

O

OB. *See* Oslo Børs
OECD. *See* Organization for Economic Cooperation and Development
off-balance sheet, 109, 201
offshore market, 31–7
offshore support vessel (OSV), 32, 34–8
OPEC. *See* Organization of Petroleum Exporting Countries
operating expenses (OPEX), 2, 4, 8, 9, 13–14, 78, 139, 156, 159, 258, 296, 299, 310n24, 316, 317, 320, 327–8, 331, 334
operating lease, 108–9, 201, 203–5, 409n17
operating ratio, 104
operational income, 273
operational risk, 203, 275, 363, 391
operations plan, 100
operative clauses, 214–126
OPEX. *See* operating expenses
options issuer, 85, 107, 152, 154, 165–6, 356
options premium, 356–7
options writer, 356
option to abandon, 311n27, 322, 394
option to contract, 323
option to defer, 322
option to expand, 322, 394
order book, 24, 28, 47–9, 56–9, 62, 66, 325, 334, 361
ordinary share, 118

Organization for Economic Cooperation and Development (OECD), 10, 11, 26–7, 108, 140–1, 197–8
Organization of Petroleum Exporting Countries (OPEC), 22
organization plan, 100
organized trading facility (OTF), 364, 367n16
Oslo Børs (OB), 153, 176, 177
OSV. *See* offshore support vessel
OTC. *See* over-the-counter
OTF. *See* organized trading facility
overcapacity, 27, 47, 51, 57, 205, 210
over-the-counter (OTC), 7, 176, 177, 338, 349–51, 354–6, 360, 362–5
owners' insurance, 270–8

P

Panama Canal, 12, 27, 61
Panamax time-charter basket (PTC), 353, 355, 360, 361
Panamax vessel, 8, 28, 56, 57, 288, 339–41, 353
panellists, 359, 366n9
parcel sizes, 7, 26, 38
pari passu, 81, 237
par value, 118, 148, 207
passage and port charges, 2, 8, 9
pay in kind (PIK), 208
pension funds, 41, 84, 103–5, 119, 205
performance bond(s), 121, 122
permitted security, 222
perpetual bonds, 164
PIPE. *See* private investment in public equity (PIPE)
plain vanilla swap, 110
platform supply vessel (PSV), 32, 36, 50, 182
pledge of shares, 264

pooling, 96, 99, 281n34
portfolio risk, 41, 310n17
port operators, 372, 377, 387, 406, 407n1
post-delivery loan(s), 81
Post-Panamax vessel, 26
powers of mortgagees, 238–45
predatory pricing, 99
pre-delivery loan, 81
preferred equity, 84, 87, 170, 207, 209, 396
preferred mortgages, 142
principal amount(s), 111, 138, 148, 149, 158–60, 164, 165, 219, 221
principal rights, 142–3
principal-to-principal, 7, 338
private equity (PE), 13, 42, 73, 76, 82, 84, 92–3, 119, 120, 126, 155, 169–89, 205, 206, 210, 372, 374, 376, 377, 379, 395, 396, 398, 403, 407, 409n24
private investment in public equity (PIPE), 169
private placement(s), 84, 104, 119–20, 150, 151, 169, 226
problematic bank loans, 255
project management, 95–8
proprietary trading, 340, 365n4
prospectus, 87, 91, 119, 150–1, 159, 161, 179
protection & indemnity (P&I), 111, 112, 223, 238, 243, 268, 270–7, 281n34
protocols of acceptance, 268
protocols of delivery, 103, 268
PSV. *See* platform supply vessel (PSV)
PTC. *See* Panamax time-charter basket (PTC)
public deals, 376, 405
public debt markets, 147–67
public equity offerings, 86–7
purchasing power, 10, 85
put option, 356

Q

qualified (accredited) investor, 150, 151
quasi-equity, 139, 164
quick ratio, 221
quiet period, 179

R

real options analysis (ROA), 322
rebating, 99
recognized market operator (RMO), 360
refund guarantee(s), 81, 121–3, 129, 144
registration, 142, 179, 232, 236–8, 247, 249, 356
regulated market (RM), 364, 367n14, 367n16
regulatory capital, 227
relative valuation approach, 287, 311n28
remedy, 218, 221, 225, 233, 248, 258, 271
repayment(s), 2, 8, 41, 77, 78, 82, 83, 85, 102, 104–6, 108, 110, 111, 117, 126, 127, 130–2, 138, 139, 141, 148–50, 159, 161, 164–5, 199, 213–15, 218, 219, 221–6, 232, 242, 244, 260–2, 317, 319, 320, 331, 390, 408n9, 408n15
repayment of loan facility, 131–2
replacement cost approach, 308n2
representations, 133–5, 215–17
required minimum value, 319–20
residual value (RV), 97, 108, 109, 137, 316–18, 331, 385
return-on-assets (ROA), 203, 204, 254
return on equity (ROE), 201, 298, 304, 316, 317
rights issue, 397
rights of enforcement, 234
rights of mortgagor, 245–8

risk-adjusted returns, 315
risk-free rate, 110, 155, 298, 302, 388, 389
risk management, 94, 337–67
RMO. *See* recognized market operator (RMO)
ROA. *See* real options analysis (ROA)
R-squareds. *See* goodness-of-fit

S

sale & leaseback, 73, 83, 154, 203
sale & purchase (S&P), 4–6, 9, 37, 102, 116, 151, 259, 298, 299, 315, 321, 409n19, 409n20
sanction provision, 223
SCFI. *See* Shanghai Containerized Freight Index (SCFI)
S-corporation(s), 178
scrapping, 2, 6, 12, 17, 24, 28, 29, 33, 35, 37, 38, 45, 56, 58, 63, 117, 323, 326
seasonality, 13, 25, 53, 62, 63
SEC. *See* Securities and Exchange Committee (SEC)
secondary public market, 148
second-hand market, 2, 5, 266, 324, 325
second-hand price(s), 6, 19, 20, 25, 26, 31, 52, 185, 288, 325, 326, 393
second-hand vessel purchase, 96
second mortgage, 79, 104, 106, 111
second-tier owners, 156
Sector Understanding on Export Credits for Ships (SSU), 197, 198
secured loan, 48
Securities and Exchange Committee (SEC), 87, 150, 176, 178, 179, 363
securitization, 249–50

428 Index

security, 41, 47, 79, 80, 105, 111–13, 117, 126, 127, 129–31, 134–7, 139–44, 154, 158, 161, 169, 199, 206, 207, 214, 216–19, 222, 224, 227, 232–6, 238, 240–5, 247–50, 260–2, 266, 270, 331, 339
SEHK. *See* Stock Exchange of Hong Kong (SEHK)
seller's credit, 74
senior loan(s), 79, 138, 139, 396
senior unsecured bonds, 155, 163, 166
sensitivity analysis, 317, 323, 325, 390
settlement price, 338, 351, 354, 362
S-1 form, 179
SGX. *See* Singapore Exchange Limited (SGX)
SGX AsiaClear. *See* Singapore Exchange AsiaClear (SGX AsiaClear)
Shanghai Clearing House (SHCH), 355, 356
Shanghai Containerized Freight Index (SCFI), 7, 13, 30, 338, 340, 345, 348, 361, 362
Shanghai Shipping Exchange (SSE), 345, 348, 361
Shanghai Shipping Freight Exchange Co. (SSEFC), 360–2
shares charge (pledge), 144
SHCH. *See* Shanghai Clearing House (SHCH)
shipbuilders' liability, 268
ship conversion, 96
ship investment, 119, 315–35
ship-management, 260
ship manager(s), 1–4, 8, 37
shipping finance, 1, 2, 71–94, 250, 255, 257, 371, 406
shipping investment(s), 13, 14, 126, 153, 206, 210
shipping operation(s), 7, 105, 379
ship purchase price, 316, 317
ship residual value, 317, 318
ship valuation(s), 112, 113
shipyard(s), 2, 43, 45–52, 56, 63, 65–7, 69n25, 76, 81, 97, 101–4, 107, 108, 122, 123, 197, 235, 236, 237n4, 267, 268, 286, 288, 312n31, 322, 325, 393
shipyard utilization, 47, 63
short position, 48, 116, 228, 262, 338
short-term valuation component, 388
SIN. *See* Clarkson Shipping Intelligence Network
Singapore Exchange AsiaClear (SGX AsiaClear), 349, 354, 355
Singapore Exchange Limited (SGX), 354, 361
single purpose company (SPC), 1, 76, 77, 128, 137, 201, 214
slot chartering, 96
SPAC. *See* special purpose acquisition company (SPAC)
spare parts, 327
SPC. *See* single purpose company (SPC)
special purpose acquisition company (SPAC), 73, 91, 92, 171, 172
special survey (SS), 204, 316, 317, 320, 327, 328
spin-offs, 73, 373
spot (voyage) market, 5, 7, 83, 152, 244, 249, 322, 329
SSE. *See* Shanghai Shipping Exchange (SSE)
SSEFC. *See* Shanghai Shipping Freight Exchange Co. (SSEFC)
SSU. *See* Sector Understanding on Export Credits for Ships (SSU)
Standardized Cumulative Abnormal Return (SCAR),
standard loan facility, 126
statutory mortgages, 142
statutory theory, 232, 233, 238

stay-in and negotiate (S&N), 261–3
STC. *See* straight-through processing to clearing (STC)
Stock Exchange of Hong Kong (SEHK), 176
stock-for-stock exchange, 395
straight-through Processing (STP), 360, 366n11
straight-through processing to clearing (STC), 353–5, 360–2
strategic plan, 95, 98, 100, 101
strike price, 356, 357
subordinated bond, 166
Sub-Panamax vessel, 56, 58
sub-participation transfer, 227
Suez Canal, 12
Suezmax vessel, 91
sui generis, 232
super cycle, 43–53, 206, 326, 333
Super Post Panamax (SPPx) vessel, 57
supplier's credit, 108
Supramax index (BSI 58), 341
Supramax time-charter basket (STC), 350
Supramax vessels, 340, 355
swap data repository (SDR), 363
swap dealers (SD), 363, 366n13
swap execution facility (SEF), 363
sweeteners, 165
syndicated loan facility, 127
syndication, 80, 102, 105–6, 127–8, 136, 137, 399
systemic risk, 253, 360, 363

T

tax benefits, 83, 88, 105, 108, 109, 115, 120, 171, 295–7
tax-deductible expense, 296
tax legislation, 205
tax shield, 297
technical default, 258
technical risk, 203

technical ship management, 2
technology plan, 100
tenor, 78, 127, 130–4, 328, 329, 332
terminal charges, 8
term loan facility, 132, 196, 214
TEU. *See* twenty-foot equivalent unit (TEU)
Thomson Reuters SDC Mergers and Acquisitions Database, 373
time-charter(s), 58, 64, 78, 83, 156, 256, 320, 338, 344, 350–62
time-charter average basket, 344, 362
time-charter equivalent (TCE), 320, 322, 329, 331, 338, 345, 346
time to delivery, 50, 51
timing of exit, 324
Tokyo Stock Exchange (TSE), 176
tonnage, 4–6, 9, 12, 15, 20, 21, 24, 26, 28, 31, 43, 45, 53, 56, 58, 60–4, 126, 129, 205, 274, 277, 288, 297, 299, 310n24, 372, 379, 381, 391
total debt coverage, 104
total return, 321
trade agreement(s), 10, 55
trademarks, 220
trade out rate, 330, 331
trade patterns, 43, 55, 58, 61, 66
trade repository (TR), 363
trading screen(s), 338, 360–2, 365
trailing valuation multiples, 391
tramp shipping, 7
TSE. *See* Tokyo Stock Exchange (TSE)
twenty-foot equivalent unit (TEU), 12, 27–30, 53–7, 299, 338, 345, 379

U

ULCC. *See See* ultra large crude carrier (ULCC)
ultra large container vessel (ULCV), 26

ultra large crude carrier (ULCC), 20, 56
ultramax vessel, 64
UNCTAD. *See* United Nations Conference on Trade and Development (UNCTAD)
underlying assets, 337, 340–8, 350, 356, 365
underwriter(s), 87–9, 104, 119, 123, 148, 150, 152–4, 179, 180, 239, 270, 274
United Nations Conference on Trade and Development (UNCTAD), 71
unitranche loans, 396
unsecured loans, 104, 106, 253
US-Treasury bill, 156
utilization rate, 33, 34, 50–2, 57–9, 62, 65, 299, 301

V

value maintenance clause (VMC), 79, 235
value of flexibility (optionality), 322–3
vendor due diligence (VDD), 382
vertical integration, 374, 378, 404
very large container ship (VLCS), 56–8
very large crude carrier (VLCC), 8, 9, 22, 24, 25, 155, 185, 345
very large ore carrier (VLOC), 15, 16
vessel design, 65, 101

VLCC. *See* very large crude carrier (VLCC)
VMC. *See* value maintenance clause (VMC)
voyage charter(s), 4, 6–8, 15

W

WACC. *See* weighted average cost of capital (WACC)
warranties, 133–4, 135, 215–17, 277, 278, 281n42
war risks, 223, 270, 272
weighted average cost of capital (WACC), 198, 201, 295–7, 299, 302, 309n11, 309n13, 310n20, 389, 408n9
wet lease, 108
working capital, 117, 131, 200, 209, 221, 223, 256, 261, 301, 310n24, 389, 408n9
World Container Index (WCI), 338, 340, 348
Worldscale rate (WS), 338, 345, 359
World Trade Organization (WTO), 10, 68, 84, 108, 155, 191
write offs, 254, 258
WTO. *See* World Trade Organization (WTO)

Y

yield-to-maturity (YTM), 389